INTEGRATING THE AMERICAS:
FTAA AND BEYOND

Edited by
Antoni Estevadeordal
Dani Rodrik
Alan M. Taylor
Andrés Velasco

Published by Harvard University
David Rockefeller Center for Latin American Studies

Distributed by Harvard University Press
Cambridge, Massachusetts
London, England
2004

Printed in the United States of America

Library of Congress Cataloging-in-Publication Data

Integrating the Americas : FTAA and beyond / edited by Antoni Estevadeordal . . . [et. al].
p. cm.
Includes bibliographical references and index.
ISBN 0–674–01484–7 (pbk. : alk. paper)
1. America—Economic integration. 2. Free trade—America.
3. Commercial treaties—America. I. Estevadeordal, Antoni.

HC94.I576 2004
382′.917—dc22
2003026724

To my father,

A.E.

Contents

Tables

Figures

Preface

In the next few years, a series of difficult and complex negotiations will determine the pace and pattern of economic integration in the Americas for decades to come. The main event is the process leading to an agreement to create a Free Trade Area of the Americas (FTAA). The FTAA talks are coinciding with a proliferation of bilateral and subregional trade agreements as well as a new round of global trade negotiations under the aegis of the World Trade Organization. The economic future of the countries in the hemisphere, as well as their politics and culture, will be shaped by the outcome of these crucial efforts.

When economists, historians, and policy makers look back on the first decade of the twenty-first century, they may do so to learn from and perhaps even to marvel at the statesmanship embodied in regional and global free trade agreements that laid the foundation for an era of rapid, equitable, environmentally sustainable economic growth. This future may not yet be considered a probability by many, but it can be realized if the key actors and their many constituencies can find a way to align their interests and get through the rough spots.

Free trade cannot guarantee a bright economic future, but it can facilitate many of the other economic and institutional changes that are needed both to underpin growth and to ensure that productivity gains are reflected in sustained improvements in equity. Virtuous circles can do wonders, especially for those who need it most.

But free trade can also be costly for people in the industries that lose protection. And rapid economic growth, whether export led or not, can accelerate environmental damage, overwhelm weak regulatory systems, facilitate corruption, and intensify regional and social inequalities. Thus, as efforts to reduce barriers to trade intensify, so do the anxieties of certain groups of society about the forces of "globalization."

Most of the fears generated by the prospect of free trade in the hemisphere and the world are not irrational or even implausible. They can only be assuaged by force of vision and intellect. Political vision is needed to link free trade to progress in combating poverty, arresting the scourge of preventable disease, improving and extending education, and protecting the environment.

The substance of such a vision and the policy to support it can benefit from discourse among scholars and researchers. In this spirit, this volume is the product of collaboration between the Institute for the

Integration of Latin America and the Caribbean (INTAL), Integration and Regional Department (INT), of the Inter-American Development Bank (IDB) and the David Rockefeller Center for Latin American Studies (DRCLAS) at Harvard University, together with economists and other social scientists from many other institutions.

As readers will quickly learn, the diversity of viewpoints, approaches, and subjects collected in this volume makes it a unique contribution to serious and thoughtful debate on the FTAA as well as broader trends toward globalization. We thank the editors and contributors for producing a major work on a topic so crucial to the future of our hemisphere.

Enrique V. Iglesias
President
Inter-American Development Bank

John H. Coatsworth
Monroe Gutman Professor of Latin American Affairs
Director, David Rockefeller Center for Latin American Studies
Harvard University

Acknowledgments

The editors of so large a volume naturally owe grateful thanks to many people and institutions—all the more so since our supporters not only patiently and indulgently helped such an outrageously oversized project to reach fruition, they even allowed it to get started in the first place.

The initial idea for a conference project and volume on FTAA was presented to the Integration and Regional Programs Department of the Inter-American Development Bank in Washington, D.C. through its Institute for the Integration of Latin America and the Caribbean (INTAL), based in Buenos Aires, and to two centers at Harvard University, the David Rockefeller Center for Latin American Studies (DRCLAS) and the Center for International Development (CID). The enthusiastic support given from the start by all three sponsors has greatly helped the editors and participants in the completion of this project, and the financial backing we received has been truly generous.

This volume comprises an introduction and twenty-two chapters based on papers delivered at two conferences. A preconference meeting was held at Harvard's Rockefeller Center in May/June 2002 and was sponsored by CID and DRCLAS. A second conference was held in Punta del Este, Uruguay, in December 2002, and was sponsored by INTAL. The editors are also indebted to the following individuals for their special efforts in making this project possible: John Coatsworth, Robert Devlin, Enrique Iglesias, Nohra Rey de Marulanda, Steve Reifenberg, Jeffrey Sachs, and Juan José Taccone. Also, special thanks are due to Susana Filippa, Zoe McLaren, Anni Pirinen-Valme, Martha Skinner, and Ernesto Talvi for their support in the organization of the two conferences. For their critical contribution to the final conference and their immeasurable impact on the quality of the papers in this volume, we should also like to thank the distinguished team of discussants in attendance: Jorge Chami Batista, Guillermo Calvo, Gerardo della Paolera, Renato Flores, Caroline Freund, Guillermo Perry, José Manuel Salazar, Pablo Sanguinetti, Jeffrey Schott, Diana Tussie, and Marcel Vaillant.

Lastly, the process of turning a set of papers into a book is by no means straightforward, and the editors are deeply grateful for the skilled work of all involved: for making it all work, with more stamina and patience than is reasonable, June Carolyn Erlick at DRCLAS; for the smooth publication process, Susan Seymour at Harvard University Press; for resolute and rigorous copyediting, Jennifer Robin Collier; for emergency proofreading at the very last minute, Sidney Hall, Jr.; for handling all that text, Puritan Press; for the graceful cover, Kelly McMurray of kellydesign; and for permission to invoke Diego Rivera's homage to Pan American Unity, the keepers of the mural at City College of San Francisco.

A. E.
D. R.
A. M. T.
A. V.

About the Contributors

Mark Barenberg

Mark Barenberg is Professor of Law at Columbia University in New York City. He specializes in labor law, constitutional law, and international law, and has taught labor relations, comparative economic history, and international labor law at Harvard, Yale, and Peking University. His publications include "The Political Economy of the Wagner Act" (1993), "Democracy and Domination in Labor Law" (1994), "Coordinated Decentralization in Supranational Labor Regimes" (2001), "Workers: The Past and Future of Labor Law Scholarship" (2003), and many other articles and book chapters.

Mario Berrios

Mario Berrios is a trade specialist at the Inter-American Development Bank (Washington, D.C.) where he has worked on FTAA negotiations, trade-related capacity building programs, and research on trade issues. Prior to joining the IDB he served as a trade official in Canada's trade and agriculture ministries. His current research interests focus on agriculture trade policy issues.

Bernardo S. Blum

Bernardo S. Blum is Assistant Professor of International Economics at the Rotman School of Management in the University of Toronto. He graduated in 2002 from UCLA with a Ph.D. in economics. His research investigates the underlying factors that explain changes in U.S. wage inequality.

Matías Braun

Matías Braun is an Assistant Professor of Economics and Finance at the Anderson School at UCLA. His research interests are in the areas of financial markets, corporate finance, international finance, and development economics. Between 1995 and 1999 he worked at a Chilean business conglomerate and taught economics at Universidad Católica de Chile. He received his Ph.D. in economics from Harvard University.

Inés Bustillo

Inés Bustillo is Director of the Washington Office of the United Nations Economic Commission for Latin America and the Caribbean (ECLAC). She has been involved as coordinator of ECLAC' s provision of technical support to the ongoing negotiations for a free trade area in the Western Hemisphere. Prior to joining ECLAC, she was Professor of Economics at Universidad Anáhuac in Mexico and Visiting Faculty at The American University in Washington D.C. She is the author of several articles and is a frequent lecturer on Latin American issues. She holds a doctorate in economics from The American University.

Julian L. Clarke

Julian L. Clarke is a Research Fellow at the World Trade Institute in Switzerland. He received his Masters in International Law and Economics (*summa cum laude*) from the World Trade Institute. Clarke spent several years working in the private sector of various countries including Singapore, Thailand, Australia and France. He has worked for the Trade Directorate of the OECD in Paris and as a consultant for several international organizations. He has published several articles and book chapters on the subject of multilateral competition policy and is writing his doctoral dissertation on the same subject.

John H. Coatsworth

John H. Coatsworth is the Monroe Gutman Professor of Latin American Affairs at Harvard University, where he also serves as Director of the David Rockefeller Center for Latin American Studies. He was elected president of the American Historical Association in 1995. His recent books include *The United States and Central America: The Clients and the Colossus* (Twayne Publishers, 1994) and *Latin America and the World Economy since 1800* (edited with Alan M. Taylor, David Rockefeller Center for Latin American Studies, Harvard University, 1998).

Christian Daude

Christian Daude is currently a Ph.D. student at the University of Maryland at College Park. He has been an assistant researcher at the Research Department of the Inter-American Development Bank, as well as an associated researcher of CINVE-Uruguay. His areas of research are international finance and macroeconomics.

I. M. Destler

I. M. (Mac) Destler is Professor at the School of Public Affairs, University of Maryland, and Visiting Fellow at the Institute for International Economics. His recent books include *Misreading the Public: The*

Myth of a New Isolationism (co-authored with Steven Kull, Brookings Institution Press, 1999) and *Protecting the American Homeland* (multiple authors, Brookings Institution Press, 2003). He is currently working on the fourth edition of his prize-winning work, *American Trade Politics*, last published by IIE in 1995.

Robert Devlin

Robert Devlin is Deputy Manager of the Integration and Regional Programs Department of the Inter-American Development Bank. Formerly, he had worked since 1975 with the United Nations Economic Commission for Latin America and the Caribbean, in Santiago, Chile where his last position was Deputy Director of the Division of International Trade, Finance and Transport. He has published four books and numerous articles in the area of international economics and economic development. He has recently edited (with Antoni Estevadeordal) *Bridges for Development: Policies and Institutions for Trade and Integration* (IDB, 2003). He holds a Ph.D. in economics from American University.

Barry Eichengreen

Barry Eichengreen is the George C. Pardee and Helen N. Pardee Professor of Economics and Professor of Political Science at the University of California, Berkeley. He is also Research Associate of the National Bureau of Economic Research and Research Fellow of the Centre for Economic Policy Research. He has published widely on the history and current operation of the international monetary and financial system. His books include *Capital Flows and Crises* (MIT Press, 2003), *Financial Crises and What to Do About Them* (Oxford University Press, 2002), and *Golden Fetters: The Gold Standard and the Great Depression, 1919–1939* (Oxford University Press, 1992).

Kimberly Ann Elliott

Kimberly Ann Elliott is a joint research fellow at the Institute for International Economics and the Center for Global Development, both in Washington, D.C. Recent and forthcoming publications include *Can Labor Standards Improve Under Globalization* (with Richard B. Freeman, Institute for International Economics) and *Economic Sanctions Reconsidered*, third edition (with Gary Clyde Hufbauer and Jeffrey J. Schott, Institute for International Economics, forthcoming 2004).

Antoni Estevadeordal

Antoni Estevadeordal is a principal trade economist and research coordinator at the Integration, Trade and Hemispheric Issues Division of the Inter-American Development Bank (IDB). His most recent research has been published in *American Economic Review*, *Quarterly Journal of Economics*, *Journal of Economic Integration* and *Journal of World Trade*. He has recently edited *Beyond Borders: The New Regionalism in the Americas* (with R. Devlin and E. Stein, IDB, 2002) and *Bridges for Development: Policies and Institutions for Trade and Integration* (with R. Devlin, IDB, 2003). He holds a Ph.D. in economics from Harvard University.

Daniel C. Esty

Daniel C. Esty is Professor of Environmental Law and Policy at Yale University and Director of the Yale Center for Environmental Law and Policy. He is the author or editor of eight books and numerous articles on environmental policy issues and the relationships between the environment and trade, globalization, security, competitiveness, international institutions, and development. From 1989 to 1993, he served in a variety of positions at the U.S. Environmental Protection Agency, including deputy chief of staff and deputy assistant administrator for policy. He was the EPA's lead NAFTA negotiator.

Peter Evans

Peter Evans is Professor of Sociology, Department Chair, and Marjorie Meyer Eliaser Chair of International Studies at the University of California, Berkeley. His research has focused on the role of the state in industrial development, as reflected in his book *Embedded Autonomy: States and Industrial Transformation* (Princeton University Press, 1995). His current research examines strategies aimed at increasing labor's global bargaining power being jointly explored by labor movements of the United States, Europe, and the global South.

Simon J. Evenett

Simon J. Evenett is Lecturer in International Business at the Said Business School, Oxford University; Fellow of Corpus Christi College, Oxford; and a non-resident Senior Fellow at the Brookings Institution in Washington, D.C. He obtained his Ph.D. in economics from Yale University and he conducts research on national and international competition policy as well as on international trade.

Paolo Giordano

Paolo Giordano is an Economist with the Integration and Regional Programs Department of the Inter-American Development Bank. He has previously been appointed at the Mercosur Chair of Sciences Po, where he lectured on International Economics and Trade Policy and served as the Coordinator of the Working Group on EU-Mercosur Negotiations. Having published in international journals on topics related to regional integration in Latin America, his latest edited publication is "An Integrated Approach to the EU-Mercosur Association" (2002). He holds a Ph.D. in economics from the Institut d'Etudes Politiques de Paris (Sciences Po).

Jaime Granados

Jaime Granados is a trade specialist and coordinator of the technical support of the Inter-American Development Bank to the FTAA negotiations. He was Director of International Trade Negotiations at the Ministry of Foreign Trade of Costa Rica. His recent publications include articles in specialized journals and collective publications on U.S.–Central America free trade area negotiations, export processing zones, integration and trade negotiations in Central America, and FTAA-WTO interactions.

Gordon H. Hanson

Gordon H. Hanson is Professor of Economics in the Graduate School of International Relations and Pacific Studies and in the Department of Economics at the University of California San Diego. He is also Co-Director of the Center for U.S.-Mexican Studies at UCSD and a research associate at the National Bureau of Economic Research. His current research examines multinational enterprises, U.S.-Mexico trade and immigration, and the globalization of production. His most recent book is *Immigration Policy and the Welfare System* (Oxford University Press, 2002).

Ricardo Hausmann

Ricardo Hausmann is Professor of the Practice of Economic Development at the John F. Kennedy School of Government at Harvard University. Previously, he served as Chief Economist of the Inter-American Development Bank, Minister of Planning of Venezuela, member of the board of the Central Bank of Venezuela, Chair of the IMF-World Bank Development Committee and Professor of Economics at the Instituto de Estudios Superiores de Administracion (IESA) in Caracas. His research interests include issues of growth, macroeconomic stability, international finance, and the social dimensions of development. He holds a Ph.D. in economics from Cornell University.

David Hummels

David Hummels is Associate Professor of Economics at Purdue University and Faculty Research Fellow at the National Bureau of Economic Research. He has written extensively on barriers to international integration and the effect of transportation costs on trade.

Marcos S. Jank

Marcos S. Jank is Associate Professor at the School of Economics and Business, University of São Paulo and President of the Institute for International Trade Negotiations. In 2002 he served as special trade expert at the Inter-American Development Bank. The former Special Counselor to the Brazilian Minister of Trade in 1999, he was also the first holder of the Canada Chair in Brazilian Studies and Visiting Scholar at Georgetown University and the University of Missouri. He is author or coauthor of over 160 publications. He holds a Ph.D. from the School of Economics and Business at the University of São Paulo.

Edward Leamer

Edward Leamer is the Chauncey J. Medberry Professor of Management, Professor of Economics, Professor of Statistics, and Director of the UCLA/Anderson Business Forecast Project, and Research Associate of the National Bureau of Economic Research. He is a Fellow of the Econometrics Society and a Fellow of the American Academy of Arts and Sciences. Recent research interests include the effect of globalization on wages and the nature of the U.S. business cycle.

Eduardo Levy-Yeyati

Eduardo Levy-Yeyati is Professor at the Business School of Universidad Torcuato Di Tella, where he also has served as Director of the Center for Financial Studies. He is a former chief economist of the Central Bank of Argentina. His recent work has been published in *American Economic Review*, *Journal of International Economics*, *Journal of Financial Intermediation*, and *European Economic Review*, among other professional journals. He is also editor of *Dollarization: Debates and Policy Alternatives* (with Federico Sturzenegger, MIT Press, 2003).

Luis F. López-Calva

Luis F. López-Calva is Associate Professor of Economics at Universidad de las Américas, Puebla (México), where he is also the Director of the Institute of Public Policy and Development Studies. He obtained his Ph.D. in economics at Cornell University and served as Professor and Researcher at El Colegio de Mexico for two years.

Ernesto López-Córdova

Ernesto López-Córdova is an economist with the Inter-American Development Bank in Washington, D.C. His research focuses on the implications of economic integration, in particular on the Mexican economy. He is a former member of Mexico's trade negotiations team at the Ministry of Trade and Industry. He holds a Ph.D. in economics from the University of California Berkeley.

Nora Lustig

Nora Lustig is President of the Universidad de las Américas, Puebla, and Professor of the Department of Economics in the same university. She was Senior Advisor and Chief of the Poverty and Inequality Unit at the Inter-American Development Bank; Senior Fellow of the Foreign Policy Studies Program at the Brookings Institution (currently, she is a nonresident Senior Fellow); professor of economics at El Colegio de México; Visiting Fellow at MIT, and Visiting Professor at the University of California, Berkeley. She co-directed the World Bank's World Development Report 2000/2001 "Attacking Poverty." She has published extensively in the fields of economic development and determinants of poverty and inequality in Latin America. Lustig holds a Ph.D. in economics from the University of California, Berkeley.

Aaditya Mattoo

Aaditya Mattoo is Lead Economist in the Development Research Group of the World Bank. His recent publications include *Development, Trade and the WTO: A Handbook* (edited with Bernard Hoekman and Philip English), *Domestic Regulation and Services Trade Liberalization* (edited with Pierre Sauvé), *India and the WTO: A Strategy for Development* (edited with Robert M. Stern) and *Moving People to Deliver Services* (edited with Antonia Carzaniga).

Mauricio Mesquita Moreira

Mauricio Mesquita Moreira is a trade economist at the Department of Integration of the Inter-American Development Bank. He has also worked at the Research Department of Brazil's Development Bank and as a lecturer at the Federal University of Rio de Janeiro. His recent publications include the chapter "Exports and Trade Finance: Brazil's Recent Experience" and article "Trade Liberalization in Brazil: Creating or Exporting Jobs" (*Journal of Development Studies*, 2000).

Josefina Monteagudo

Josefina Monteagudo has been an economist at the Inter-American Development Bank since 1998. Previously, she was Visiting Professor of Economics at the Universidad Autónoma de Barcelona. Her areas of expertise include trade and integration issues and cooperation and coordination policies. Her publications have appeared in *Journal of Monetary Economics*, *Économie Internationale*, and *Integration and Trade Journal*. She holds a Ph.D. in economics from the University of California, San Diego.

José Antonio Ocampo

José Antonio Ocampo is Under-Secretary General for Economic and Social Affairs and former Executive Secretary of the United Nations Economic Commission for Latin America and the Caribbean. He has also held a number of posts in the government of Colombia, including Minister of Finance, Planning and Agriculture. His most recent books include *A Decade of Light and Shadow: Latin America and the Caribbean in the 1990s* (with Juan Martin, ECLAC, 2003) and *Globalization and Development: A Latin American and Caribbean Perspective* (with Juan Martin, Stanford University Press and World Bank, 2003).

Marcelo de Paiva Abreu

Marcelo de Paiva Abreu is Professor of Economics at the Department of Economics, Pontifical Catholic University of Rio de Janeiro. His publications include "Import substitution and growth in Brazil, 1890s–1970s," with A. Bevilaqua and D.M. Pinho (in E. Cardenas, J. A. Ocampo, and R. Thorp, *An Economic History of Twentieth-Century Latin America*, vol. 3, Palgrave and St. Antony's College, Oxford, 2000); "O Brasil e a economia mundial, 1930–1945" (Civilização Brasileira, Rio de Janeiro, 1999); and *A ordem do progresso. Cem anos de política econômica republicana, 1889–1989* (edited, Rio de Janeiro, Campus, 1990).

Andrew Powell

Andrew Powell is Professor and Director of the Masters of Finance in the Business School of the Universidad Torcuato Di Tella. Previously he was the Chief Economist of the Central Bank of Argentina, and Lecturer at the University of Warwick and Queen Mary and Westfield College, University of London, and Prize Research Fellow at Nuffield College, Oxford. His recent research has focused on the role of the international institutions (*Journal of International Money and Finance*, *Economic Journal*), credit markets (*Journal of International Money and Finance*), fiscal policy (*Journal of Development Economics*) and Argentina's crisis (*Brookings Trade Conference Journal*). He is currently working on the role of foreign banks in Latin America, inflation targeting, and dollarization.

Lant Pritchett

Lant Pritchett is a Lecturer in Public Policy at the Kennedy School of Government, Harvard University, where he also serves as the faculty chair of the MPA/International Development program. His forthcoming book is *The Future of Migration: Irresistible Forces Meet Immovable Ideas*.

Raymond Robertson

Raymond Robertson is Associate Professor of Economics at Macalester College. Specializing in the effects of trade liberalization on labor markets in Latin America, he has published in *Journal of International Economics*, *Review of Economics and Statistics*, and *American Economic Review*. He also has served as a consultant to the World Bank and the Inter-American Development Bank.

Dani Rodrik

Dani Rodrik is Professor of International Political Economy at the John F. Kennedy School of Government, Harvard University. He has published widely in the areas of international economics, economic development, and political economy. His recent books include *The New Global Economy and Developing Countries: Making Openness Work* (1999) and he is editor of *In Search of Prosperity: Analytic Narratives on Economic Growth* (2003).

Pierre Sauvé

Pierre Sauvé is Director of Studies at the Groupe d'Economie Mondiale, Institut d'Etudes Politiques de Paris (Sciences Po) in Paris. His most recent books are *Trade Rules Behind Borders: Essays on Services, Investment and the New Trade Agenda* (Cameron-May Publishers, 2003) and *Domestic Regulation and Service Trade Liberalization* (edited with Aaditya Mattoo, Oxford University Press/World Bank, 2003).

Alexandre Skiba

Alexandre Skiba is a graduate student in economics at Purdue University.

Ernesto Stein

Ernesto Stein is Principal Research Economist at the Inter-American Development Bank. He holds a Ph.D. in economics from the University of California, Berkeley. His interests include regional integration, foreign direct investment, and monetary unions. He has published articles in journals such as the *American Economic Review, Journal of International Economics*, *Journal of Development Economics*, and *Economic Policy*. He has edited (with J. Frieden) *The Currency Game: Exchange Rate Politics in Latin America* (Johns Hopkins University Press, 2001), and has coordinated (with R. Devlin and A. Estevadeordal) *Beyond Borders: The New Regionalism in Latin America* (IADB, 2002).

Federico Sturzenegger

Federico Sturzenegger is Dean of the Business School of the Universidad Torcuato Di Tella since 1998. He was Secretary of Economic Policy in Argentina, Chief Economist of YPF S.A. and Assistant Professor of economics at the University of California at Los Angeles. He has written many articles for international journals, and he is consultant for different corporations and international organizations. He is author of four books: *La Economía de los Argentinos* (Planeta, 2003); *Dollarization* (MIT Press, 2003); *Coordinación de Políticas Macroeconómicas en el MERCOSUR* (Fondo de Cultura Económica, 2000) and *The Political Economy of Reform* (MIT Press, 1998). He holds a Ph.D. in economics from the Massachusetts Institute of Technology.

Alan M. Taylor

Alan M. Taylor is Professor of Economics and Chancellor's Fellow at the University of California, Davis; a Research Associate of the National Bureau of Economic Research; and a Research Fellow of the Centre for Economic Policy Research. His recent books include *Glob-*

alization in Historical Perspective (edited with Michael D. Bordo and Jeffrey G. Williamson, University of Chicago Press, 2003), *A New Economic History of Argentina* (edited with Gerardo della Paolera, Cambridge University Press, 2003), and *Global Capital Markets: Integration, Crisis, and Growth* (with Maurice Obstfeld, Cambridge University Press, 2004).

Andrés Velasco

Andrés Velasco is Sumitomo Professor of International Finance and Development at Harvard University and a Research Associate of the National Bureau of Economic Research. He is the editor of *Economia*, the journal of the Latin American and Caribbean Economic Association. He is the author of over sixty articles on international economics, development, and political economy.

Anthony J. Venables

Anthony J. Venables is Professor of International Economics at the London School of Economics and directs the international trade research programs at the Centre for Economic Performance. He was previously research manager of the trade group in the research division of the World Bank. He has published extensively on international trade issues, including work on trade and imperfect competition, and economic integration. His recent work on trade and economic geography is published in *The Spatial Economy: Cities, Regions and International Trade* (with M. Fujita and P. Krugman, MIT Press, 1999).

Masakazu Watanuki

Masakazu Watanuki is a consultant at the Integration and Regional Programs Department of the Inter-American Development Bank. He has expertise in applied general equilibrium modeling, and his research focuses on the effects of regional integration and trade liberalization in the Western Hemisphere. His recent publications are "The Economic Effects of An EC-MERCOSUR Free Trade Agreement" (*Integration and Trade*, 2002) and "Regional Trade Agreements for MERCOSUR: The FTAA and the FTA with the European Union" (*Economie Internationale*, 2003).

Jeffrey G. Williamson

Jeffrey G. Williamson is the Laird Bell Professor of Economics at Harvard University. He has been Chairman of the Economics Department (1997–2000) and President of the Economic History Association (1994–95). His recent books include *Globalization and History* (with K. O'Rourke, MIT Press, 1999) and *Globalization in Historical Perspective* (with M. Bordo and A. Taylor, University of Chicago Press, 2003). He is currently finishing *Global Migration: Two Centuries of Policy and Performance*, with T. Hatton.

L. Alan Winters

L. Alan Winters is Professor of economics at the University of Sussex, Research Fellow of the Centre for Economic Policy Research (CEPR, London), and Senior Visiting Fellow of the Centre for Economic Performance, London School of Economics. He is editor of the *World Bank Economic Review*, and his recent books include *Regional Integration and Development* (with Maurice Schiff, Oxford University Press, 2003) and *Trade Liberalisation and Poverty: A Handbook* (with Neil McCulloch and Xavier Cirera, CEPR, 2001).

Abbreviations

AEII: agriculture export intensity index

ALADI: see LAIA

ANZCER: Australia–New Zealand Closer Economic Relationship

ASEAN: Association of South East Asian Nations

AVE: ad valorem equivalent

CACM: Central American Common Market

CAFTA: Central American Free Trade Agreement

CAP: Common Agricultural Policy (of the European Union)

CARICOM: Caribbean Community

CEFTA: Central European Free Trade Area

CET: common external tariffs

CGE: Computable General Equilibrium Model

EC: Economic Commission

ECB: European Central Bank

ECLAC: Economic Commission for Latin American and the Caribbean

EEC: European Economic Community

EFTA: European Free Trade Agreement

EMS: European Monetary System

EPZ: export processing zones

EU: European Union

FDI: foreign direct investment

FTA: free trade agreement *or* free trade area

FTAA: Free Trade Area of the Americas

GATS: General Agreement on Trade in Services

GATT: General Agreement on Tariffs and Trade

GDP: Gross Domestic Product

GSP: Generalized System of Preferences

HS: Harmonized System

IDB: Inter-American Development Bank

ISI: import-substitution industrialization

LAC: Latin American and Caribbean

LAFTA: Latin American Free Trade Agreement

LAIA (ALADI): Latin American Integration Association (Asociación Latinoamericana de Integración)

MERCOSUR: (Common Market of the South (Mercado Común del Sur)

MFN: most favored nation

NAFTA: North American Free Trade Agreement

NTM: nontariff measure

OECD: Organization for Economic Cooperation and Development

PSE: producer support estimate (OECD measure)

REST: regional export sensitive tariff index

RIA: regional integration agreement

RTA: regional trade agreement

TFP: total-factor productivity

TRQ: tariff rate quota

UNCTAD: United Nations Conference on Trade and Development

URAA: Uruguay Round Agreement on Agriculture (WTO)

USTR: United States Trade Representative

WH: Western Hemisphere

WTO: World Trade Organization

PART I

Introduction

1

Introduction

Antoni Estevadeordal, Dani Rodrik, Alan M. Taylor, and Andrés Velasco

At a 1994 summit in Miami leaders from throughout the Western Hemisphere laid out a plan for economic integration in the region more ambitious than anything previously envisaged—a free trade zone stretching from Alaska to Tierra del Fuego, the Free Trade Area of the Americas (FTAA). At the time it must have seemed futuristic, and for a while it received little attention. Many observers saw it as an acronymic gesture that would fade away like so many other well-intentioned plans for Pan-American cooperation.

A decade later, *everyone* is paying close attention. Concerned opponents range from the increasingly vocal antiglobalization activists to the political and business constituencies endorsing protectionism, and avid proponents include statesmen and economists keen to pursue an internationalist agenda through deep integration. Developed countries (notably the United States) are seeking new export markets for their own products, while developing countries (such as the G21 members) hope to pry open the tightly closed markets for their products in the North. Scholars, journalists, students of current affairs—all citizens throughout the hemisphere now ponder the implications of an FTAA.

The simple reason for all of this attention is that the FTAA process, far from derailing, has remained on track. Talks are far advanced and completion is now within sight. One cannot prejudge the outcome—indeed, the recent faltering of the WTO process provides ample grounds for caution. Yet as multilateral talks stutter, the scope for bilateral and regional agreements may expand.

Major progress to this point also highlights the need for careful analyses of potential outcomes. What would an FTAA mean? How is it taking shape? What has gone right, or wrong? What challenges remain? To understand all the details and implications of this complex and historic agenda is a mammoth task, as the weight of this tome attests. The expert contributors could not cover all the possible ground, but their work represents a breathtaking *tour d'horizon.*

The Americas are certainly not the first continent to launch an ambitious integration scheme, nor is this the first such scheme in the history of the Americas. What do historical and (more recent) international experiences suggest about the prospects for a successful FTAA? One observation is that protectionism has a long history in Latin America (and of course in the United States and Canada as well), stretching back to the mid-nineteenth century. Even during the supposedly free trade period prior to 1914, Latin America had some of the world's highest tariffs. This suggests that doing away with protection may turn out to be a harder task than many optimists currently predict, especially if sustained and deep liberalization requires a fundamental political commitment, as the European experience strongly suggests. Without the grand vision of a politically integrated Western Hemisphere, will negotiators have the mandate to push forward when costs become clear and political pressures arise? The broad nature of the negotiations may help in this regard. Under the "old regionalism," agreements were confined to trade in goods. In the "new regionalism," which an FTAA is meant to embody, negotiations will take place over a much wider range of issues. This might help in structuring deals that contain something for everyone. But it will also require countries to make concessions in politically sensitive areas, including labor, investment, agriculture, and services. Which of these two countervailing forces will prevail remains very much to be seen.

The actual negotiations for an FTAA agreement comprise an important dimension in any analysis of the overall process. It is sometimes forgotten that the negotiations were launched in the context of a broader hemispheric agenda at the 1994 summit. That meeting brought together the leaders of an overwhelmingly democratic region that was implementing wide-ranging market reforms and displaying a renewed interest in economic integration. Moreover, NAFTA's inception at the start of that year had signaled a new phase in north-south trade and economic relations. From the outset, the FTAA negotiations have been a fascinating exercise in political economy and have offered fertile ground for researchers interested in trade bargaining issues. The negotiating process has not always been smooth, and at the time of writing the possible outcomes of the final stage remain unclear.

The idea of making a hemispheric free trade area a centerpiece of the Miami Declaration originated in the South, not in the United States. Washington initially favored a southern extension of NAFTA one country at a time. How has the FTAA process influenced (and in turn been affected by) simultaneous initiatives on other fronts, such as MERCOSUR's efforts to negotiate a South American Free Trade Agreement, the European Union's sudden interest in concluding FTAs with Latin American partners, or the United States' more recent aggressive bilateral trade strategy, to name just a few? What is the relationship between the regional FTAA negotiations and the simultaneous commitment to a multilateral agenda in the WTO? How can countries in the region assess the optimal tradeoffs among a complex set of issues in a far-reaching trade agenda being negotiated according to the principle of a "single undertaking"? From a political-economy perspective, what are the main determinants of the defensive and aggressive postures that countries adopt in the negotiations?

A comprehensive analysis of complex negotiations in the FTAA could fill several volumes. The pertinent chapters in this book focus on some key traditional and nontraditional areas of the talks—such as agriculture, services, and competition policy—to illustrate more general problems, while others examine the north-south aspects of the political-economy determinants of the FTAA.

What would be the likely economic impact of an FTAA? While a traditional approach to trade analysis might be purely economic in focus, as the breadth of this volume indicates, we believe the answers are tied up with many other issues, including history, politics, macroeconomics, social policies, and the environment. Moreover, how an FTAA is perceived in terms of its effects on these related issues, and how those issues play out in the political-economy arena, will of necessity depend on what prospective changes actors believe will be seen in areas such as welfare, trade flows, investment, and so forth. A large section of this volume addresses these topics.

In assessing FTAA prospects we find that there is no simple bottom line—as our textbook theory teaches us, trade liberalization can create winners and losers, and this is no less true for an FTAA. The good news is that in many areas large prospective benefits are in sight in the forms of technology transfer, FDI creation, scale economies in shipping, and potentially large increases in trade volumes. If realized, these aggregate benefits could far outweigh the costs. The challenge is to harness these benefits and guard against uneven outcomes that will undermine welfare gains in particular sectors, occupations, and regions—inequalities that could undermine an FTAA's economic promises and political legitimacy.

Although the FTAA process is primarily about trade, discussion of the future of economic integration in the Americas inevitably has to address the question of how much macroeconomic coordination is both feasible and desirable. Economic volatility—especially where capital flows and exchange rates are concerned—may present a serious obstacle to growing trade integration, as the members of MERCOSUR know well. The example of the European Union is also pertinent: there, the drive toward a single currency was a central component of the integration strategy. Can it also be in the Americas? Should it be?

Macroeconomic coordination (whether of the "soft" kind, such as harmonized information and jointly agreed-upon targets for some variables, or of the "hard" kind, exemplified by a common currency) is devilishly hard to achieve. Some of the difficulty is political: witness, for instance, the almost complete inability of European countries to enforce the fiscal requirements of the Maastricht Treaty. Much of it is also technical: highly unstable capital flows, for example, can easily wreck the best-laid plans for managed currencies. Another word of caution is that it is by no means obvious that more coordinated macro policies necessarily improve welfare in Latin America. The credibility gains of a common currency (or dollarization) would have to be large in order to offset the costs of foregoing exchange-rate flexibility in a world of large and highly asymmetric shocks.

Free trade agreements are no longer solely about trade and the policies that directly affect trade. They have become embroiled in a much larger set of issues and a broader range of institutional considerations. Ask Latin American government leaders what they hope to get out of an FTAA, and in the same breath they discuss not only market access but also their ambitions to solidify their economic reforms, improve governance, energize their private sectors, and enhance market confidence. The links between any of these and the specific details of an FTAA agreement may be tenuous, but the expectations are very real. Indeed, it is not too much of an exaggeration to say that many governments in the region see an FTAA as the next beacon of hope in the long and arduous road of economic reform along which they have been traveling. The payoffs to the strategy of liberalization, privatization, and openness have been meager and disappointing to date. Will an FTAA be able to reverse this, and finally allow Latin America to reap the potential benefits of globalization?

Historical and Global Perspectives

If successful, the free trade agreement will dismantle most kinds of protectionism in the Americas. That is a tall order indeed. As John Coatsworth, Jeffrey Williamson, Robert Devlin, and Paolo Giordano show in Part II, protectionism has a long and distinguished history in the hemisphere, and particularly in Latin America.

The standard account of Latin American commercial policy offers the following narrative. The region was mostly open and enjoyed export-led growth during a *belle époque* that lasted from approximately 1870 until 1914. First World War I and then the Great Depression (in addition to significant protectionism in the advanced countries) forced Latin America to erect trade barriers and focus on expanding the domestic market. That import-substituting phase lasted until the 1960s, when a slow and often painful process of opening up resumed.

The first part of this account, argue Coatsworth and Williamson, is quite simply wrong. Latin America had the world's highest tariffs from the 1860s until 1914. Moreover, those tariffs were rising until the last decade of the nineteenth century, just as the world went through its first round of globalization. Only during the Great Depression did the rich countries of the North raise their own tariffs to something approaching Latin American levels. The evidence presented in their chapter is not only of historical interest but also relevant to a debate that has surrounded the FTAA negotiations. The United States wants the developing countries of the hemisphere to open up, critics charge, yet that is not how the United States itself grew rich; it did so behind tariff barriers. True enough, confirm Coatsworth and Williamson. They find that high tariffs in the industrial core nations were associated with higher per capita growth in the late-nineteenth century and again in the 1930s. But the same was not true of the peripheral countries in America or Europe. For Latin America, the net effect of tariffs on growth was negative in the period 1875–1908. Arguably, the Latin countries tried to follow the U.S. recipe back then—but it did not work. The refrain "do not as the United States says, but as the United States did," may be incorrect after all.

More recent history also offers relevant lessons for the integration effort underway today in the Americas. What does the FTAA want to resemble when it grows up? "The European Union" is a common response. The European case is indeed inspiring: the story of how a war-torn and divided continent pulled itself together and achieved deep economic and political integration in less than half a century offers many examples from which Latin Americans could learn. But the dissimilarities are great, and they should be kept in mind if the right lessons are to be heeded.

One key difference, argue Anthony Venables and Alan Winters in Chapter 3, has to do with the political motivation for cutting tariffs and expanding trade: "Perhaps the most important factor in understanding the history of postwar European integration is to see that it was essentially a political-ideological phenomenon. It was not driven by the careful calculation of economic costs and benefits, and still less by trade negotiators, but by a grand vision that had fortunate economic side effects." Rhetoric about a trade block stretching from Alaska to Patagonia aside, that grand vision is mostly absent in the Americas.

That should not come as a surprise. Europe's was a gradual union of equals, anchored by the Franco-German alliance. With over 78 percent of the hemisphere's GDP, the United States would have no equal within an FTAA. Relative symmetry, argue Venables and Winters, made it easier for the European nations to build a number of institutions, some of them political, on the economic foundation of the initial European Coal and Steel Community. Those institutions, in turn, have helped push integration further. In its first stage an FTAA is likely to have a small technical secretariat and little else. Yet such an agreement will doubtless need perfecting (and perhaps also deepening) at a later stage. One has to wonder from where the political-bureaucratic impetus to do that will come.

On the purely economic front, Venables and Winters argue that European integration has caused a good deal of trade creation, both internally and externally with imports from outside the block replacing members' domestic production. But there is also some evidence of trade diversion, especially since 1980, when internal liberalization was not accompanied by major external tariff cuts. The authors are optimistic that trade diversion will be limited in an FTAA, since—in a north-south agreement—countries' comparative advantages within the bloc are likely to coincide with their worldwide comparative advantages.

Venables and Winters find a "rather modest" increase in manufacturing specialization in Europe. But the Single Market Initiative completed in 1992 fostered a great deal of intraindustry reorganization as more efficient firms expanded beyond their local markets. This brought efficiency gains in that it permitted firms to be larger *at the same time as* markets became more competitive. Venables and Winters see great potential for such scale and competitive gains to occur in Latin America, but warn that achieving them can be quite difficult. Even markets that seem to be integrated can remain segmented because of small differences in regulation, product standards, transportation systems, and the like. Europe overcame such barriers through *deep integration*; for instance, by adopting the "mutual-recognition principle" in which goods allowed for sale in one member state are acceptable in all. This is bad news for an FTAA. In the Americas, differences in size and development make it more difficult that a harmonization of norms and mutual recognition will be achieved in the foreseeable future.

One can learn about integration by studying disintegration. That is the premise of Chapter 4 by Matías Braun, Ricardo Hausmann, and Lant Pritchett. The number of sovereign states has tripled over the last fifty years. New states have been created in three waves: immediately after WWII, through decolonization in the 1960s and 1970s, and most recently after the demise of the Soviet Union. This results in more borders, more currencies, higher transaction costs, and arguably higher obstacles to trade. What are the economic consequences of this experience? What is the impact of disintegration on trade and growth?

The following conceptual framework helps in pondering these questions. Suppose efficiency and specialization (and perhaps, therefore, growth) depend on two factors: market size and government policies. Political disintegration and the proliferation of sovereigns almost surely mean lower market size. But smaller countries may choose better policies, either because they are now free to follow them or because, being smaller, they are more homogeneous and less hindered by political conflict. This means that in principle the net effect of disintegration is ambiguous.

The empirical results presented by Braun, Hausmann, and Pritchett do suggest that market size matters for postindependence growth. The typical country in the sample lost 78 percent of its secured market. Given the estimated coefficient, this would imply a growth rate that is 2 to 3 percent slower. A one-standard-deviation change in market size would explain a 0.6 percent growth difference. These results hold after controlling for the quality of policies, an endogenous variable that also turns out to be an important determinant of growth rates. Evidence from case studies also points to the costs of independence. In the Caribbean, for instance, it is striking that the old independent nations are the poorest while the still-dependent ones are the richest.

But such conclusions must be qualified in several ways. On average, newly independent countries saw their growth rates decline relative to the OECD, but not relative to other developing countries that were already independent. This suggests that there may be factors at work other than independence and market size. The other caveat is that independence brings great dispersion in economic outcomes. Some countries do quite well (e.g., the Baltics and some Caribbean Islands) while others do terribly (e.g., much of sub-Saharan Africa and portions of the former Soviet Union).

Trade integration may be the fashion today in Latin America, but this is not the first time the fad has hit the continent. The 1960s and 1970s also witnessed a wave of integration agreements, albeit of a very different kind. In Chapter 5 Robert Devlin and Paolo Giordano compare the old regionalism and the new regionalism, and argue that the more recent variation is also better. They argue that the old regionalism was part of an import-substituting strategy, not a free trade strategy. External tariffs remained high and uneven, with stratospheric rates of effective protection. Policies such as industrial planning and the negotiated assignment of given sectors to specific countries were common, and smaller countries were given differential treatment. All of this was done outside of GATT.

The new regionalism claims to be different. Beyond the rhetoric, is it? Devlin and Giordano are optimistic. One reason is that an FTAA would be a north-south agreement. The United States, "a relatively open, world-class economy," would presumably prevent an FTAA from lapsing back into protectionism. More to the point, current regional negotiations were preceded by substantial unilateral liberalization by most Latin American countries. And, as argued by Venables and Winters, in a north-south agreement regional and worldwide comparative advantages tend to coincide. These two factors should limit the potential for trade diversion.

Regionalism, whether old or new, still relies on discriminatory preferences. How does this square with the multilateral opening to which all countries in the Western Hemisphere presumably are committed? An FTAA is supposed to be compatible with the WTO, and probably will be, because the political and precedent-setting costs of doing otherwise would be too high. Devlin and Giordano go further, arguing that a "WTO-plus" agreement could be used by the United States (perhaps in alliance with Latin America) as a negotiating tool to push forward a liberalizing agenda in the Doha Round and beyond—just as was done with NAFTA in the Uruguay Round.

Another benefit of an FTAA is that it would help clean up the "spaghetti bowl" of bilateral and plurilateral agreements among Latin American countries. Some of those agreements date back to the old regionalism, while others are of a more recent vintage. An FTAA is supposed to absorb agreements of lesser scope and depth, but Devlin and Giordano recognize that not all subregional agreements would be erased or subsumed. MERCOSUR, for one, is too politically important to simply fade away. The authors claim that such parallel arrangements could be "pursued simultaneously and coexist"—but the details of how to achieve that kind of compromise remain unclear.

Macroeconomics of the Free Trade Agreement

One dimension along which an FTAA may come to differ from earlier integration attempts in Latin America is macroeconomics, a topic that is taken up in Part III. Because the old regionalism took place at a time of capital controls and fixed exchange rates, there was little need or incentive to coordinate macro policies. The context is very different today. Capital flows are many times larger than trade flows. Sharp exchange-rate fluctuations can derail a trade liberalization plan, as Argentina and Brazil learned recently. Thus any attempt to enhance integration will eventually face the question of how monetary and exchange-rate arrangements have to be adapted to render that integration feasible.

Enthusiasts may argue that the experience of the EU points in a clear direction, since increasing intra-European trade eventually paved the way for monetary union. This is not to say, of course, that a common currency for the Americas is on the horizon. In Chapter 6 Barry Eichengreen and Alan Taylor ask how free trade will affect monetary and exchange-rate arrangements in the Americas, and their answer is cautious. They argue that the analogy to Europe may be of limited relevance. Again, the main difference is political. In Europe, the common currency is part of the grand vision of European integration. Since there is no such grand design in the Americas, politicians are not eager to move in the direction of monetary unification. Even within NAFTA "there has been surprisingly little pressure (surprising, at least, when seen from a European perspective) to stabilize exchange rates, coordinate monetary policies, and discuss monetary unification."

When trying to imagine possible monetary and exchange-rate scenarios for Latin America after an FTAA, a key question is whether increased trade affects exchange-rate outcomes—and, in particular, whether it tends to reduce real bilateral exchange-rate volatility. If so, then an FTAA might build in a tendency for de facto macro synchronization, with markets—not government policy—doing the synchronizing. The evidence on this point, argue Eichengreen and Taylor, is mixed. In the relevant regressions, more bilateral trade is associated with less bilateral exchange-rate volatility, *ceteris paribus.* But this effect is swamped by other financial and political factors, which in the case of Latin America—and in particular for the MERCOSUR countries—tend to increase volatility.

Eichengreen and Taylor interpret this to mean that even if an FTAA increases trade substantially, managed exchange rates have dim prospects in Latin America. If that is the case, can governments prevent excessive exchange-rate volatility from impairing efforts to liberalize trade? Eichengreen and Taylor's prescription, in line with much current thinking on the issue, turns to inflation targeting. "The argument, in a nutshell, is that a credible policy of inflation targeting provides a nominal anchor for expectations and that, with an anchor for expectations, exchange rates will settle down."

The jury is still very much out on whether the last part of this statement will turn out to be true. At the turn of the century the currencies of Latin America's (currently) successful inflation targeters—Brazil, Chile, and Mexico—have turned out to be quite volatile indeed. But the larger point stands. It is not so much high-frequency volatility as it is long-delayed, and therefore massive, exchange-rate realignments (consider Brazil in 1999 or Argentina in 2001) that can derail regional trade arrangements. The combination of flexible rates plus inflation targeting almost by definition should avoid this latter and destructive phenomenon.

This can be taken as an encouraging conclusion, or it can be read as damning with faint praise. After all, what is the optimal exchange-rate regime for Latin American countries? Is that regime the same for all countries, or does the choice depend heavily on specific country characteristics? And, most intriguingly, does the optimal policy for one country depend on what other countries are already doing? These are the questions Andrew Powell and Federico Sturzenegger tackle in Chapter 7.

Powell and Sturzenegger consider a model with monetary and real shocks. When a country is viewed in isolation, as is standard, flexible exchange rates seem to help stabilize output if shocks are primarily real, but can be destabilizing if shocks are mostly monetary. However, if this model economy is placed into a multicountry world, shocks (again real and monetary) can be systemic as well as country specific. A key issue is whether shocks are symmetric across borders or not. Asymmetric real shocks make flexible exchange rates more desirable; asymmetric monetary shocks make them less so. As in Mundell's theory of optimal currency areas, the desirability of floating, fixing, dollarization, or creating a monetary union depends on the relative variance of shocks and on their international covariance.

Powell and Sturzenegger apply vector autoregressions to obtain a measure of shocks for several Latin American countries. They then use the estimated values to simulate the model. The results highlight two facts: the optimal regime varies widely with country characteristics, and there is plenty of room for exchange-rate disagreements. Brazil, which has large monetary shocks of its own, would like to dollarize. Mexico is in the opposite situation, and would like to have a common currency with Chile and Uruguay, which also have low monetary volatility. Chile, however, would prefer to invite Colombia and Uruguay into such an arrangement, but to exclude Mexico. History can also matter: Chile's eagerness to join up with Colombia and Uruguay would vanish if these two countries already had a currency union with Brazil. Preferred policy for one country can depend on the choices others have already made.

What about the role of trade in affecting the desirability of alternative exchange-rate arrangements? Powell and Sturzenegger equate greater trade with greater correlation of real shocks, and ask whether this makes a difference. The answer is that conceptually it does, but quantitatively it does not. Real convergence causes virtually no change in predicted optimal policies and does little to reduce output variability. However, they do find a large potential gain in the reduction of individual monetary shocks. In this sense their conclusion is quite similar to that of Eichengreen and Taylor: an inflation-targeting regime, or any other arrangement that succeeded in reducing nominal volatility, would make a great contribution to the welfare of Latin America independently of the success of an FTAA.

Negotiating an FTAA Agreement

An analysis of the FTAA negotiating process is central to capturing the dynamics of the economic interests and the political economy that underlie this hemispheric initiative. The FTAA negotiating mandate is broad, and covers areas that go beyond topics on the multilateral agenda. The current process includes negotiating groups in nine policy areas: market access; agriculture; investment; services; intellectual property rights; government procurement; dispute settlement; subsidies, antidumping, and countervailing duties; and competition. In addition, three committees address horizontal issues related to the negotiations: the consultative group on smaller economies, the committee of government representatives on the participation of civil society, and the joint government–private sector committee of experts on electronic commerce.

While a comprehensive examination of this agenda is not possible in this volume, Part IV provides critical frameworks within which such analysis should emerge. Three chapters highlight some traditional and nontraditional issues in the conceptual and policy debates on FTAA: negotiations in agriculture, services, and competition policy. However, in order to have an integral understanding of this process one should not forget the domestic political factors that drive it. Two additional chapters address this aspect and examine the political economy of an FTAA, one from the perspective of the United States, the larger and most industrialized country, and the other from a Latin American perspective.

Since GATT went into effect, agricultural trade liberalization has been one of the most difficult and controversial issues on any traditional trade negotiating agenda. Currently, agriculture is seen as the deal breaker for the FTAA as well as for the Doha negotiations, as the crisis at Cancún clearly demonstrated. In a unique way, the agricultural sector embodies the complexities of any trade-liberalization process of this nature, including the multiplicity of trade policy instruments used for protectionist purposes, and therefore the difficulties of assessing the effective levels of protection; the economic and strategic importance of this sector for growth, development, and poverty reduction; the strong political-economy components underpinning the negotiating process caused by sensitivities attached to specific products; the growing importance of nontrade considerations in the discussions for further liberalization; and, finally, the intertwined nature of the negotiations at regional and multilateral levels.

An additional element in this complex FTAA mosaic is the asymmetric nature of this sector. This is particularly true in a deal between northern and southern participants, since the "offensive" interests of some countries are likely to clash with the "defensive" concerns of others. Five experts at the Inter-American Development Bank—Mario Berrios, Jaime Granados, Marcos Jank, Josefina Monteagudo, and Masakazu Watanuki—take on the task of assessing this complex negotiating scenario in Chapter 8.

The authors' first task is to sketch a detailed picture of the sector and provide new estimates on protection levels. They accomplish this by carefully computing ad valorem equivalents of the numerous specific tariffs and tariff rate quotas that still affect a significant number of agricultural products, as well as by quantifying levels of export subsidies and domestic support (particularly in the United States). Then, using only information on tariffs, the authors construct an index of the relative negotiating position of each country in the regional context. They compare each country's "faced" tariffs (from its partners) with its "imposed" tariffs, all appropriately weighted. It is an elegant indicator to assess the value of the concessions that each country would have to make relative to those received, assuming full elimination of tariffs. The indicator clearly shows that Chile, Central America, and MERCOSUR would achieve net gains under full tariff liberalization in the hemisphere. No wonder, then, that Chile was the first to secure an agreement with the United States, and that Central America has just followed suit with the CAFTA Agreement.

In order to go beyond this partial-equilibrium analysis the authors set up a state-of-the-art, computable general-equilibrium model with a novel feature. They have simulated explicitly the impact of eliminating the three-key distortionary policies that affect agricultural trade: tariffs, domestic support, and export subsidies. They have done this individually for each distortionary policy and simultaneously. The results show that, despite the weight given to export subsidies and domestic support in policy debates, their potential impact appears quite limited. Tariffs are still the foremost trade barrier. The discriminatory nature of tariffs makes this instrument a relevant issue in a regional negotiation such as the FTAA, while the nondiscriminatory nature of other policies will probably have to await multilateral talks. Thus, agriculture is still a central issue in these negotiations despite opinions that, to the contrary, agricultural talks should be excluded from the FTAA table.

At the opposite extreme of the economic production spectrum, one might consider the growing importance of services in international trade. Too often economic theory lags behind reality and our understanding of service-trade liberalization does not accord with the relative importance of the service economy today. To what degree do services differ from other traded products? And, as a result, how much do we need to modify our economic insights with respect to the impact of preferential liberalization? What happens when countries liberalize service trades faster in a regional agreement than at the multilateral level? And, assuming we can answer those questions, what are the conditions and principles that should govern a regional negotiation such as the FTAA?

In Chapter 9, Aaditya Mattoo and Pierre Sauvé navigate through those difficult conceptual waters by carefully examining different regional experiences of services liberalization within and outside the region. They utilize the benchmark of the multilateral disciplines agreed upon in GATS, and then ask a fundamental question: In the area of services liberalization, what is the policy space left for an FTAA that can ensure that it adds value to existing and future WTO agreements? There is no straightforward answer, and several dimensions need to be taken into account. Based on the achievement record of previous regional agreements, the authors conclude that expectations that an FTAA will produce path-breaking results should probably be tempered. Due to the extraordinary diversity of sectors and regulations involved, experience shows that service-trade liberalization comes in small increments and often consists more in policy consolidation than in market opening. Moreover, the sheer size of a "super-regional" agreement such as the FTAA may well be an obstacle to policy innovation, as is the case with bilateral agreements (in particular north-south).

In spite of those constraints, there is some space for FTAA negotiators. One of the most controversial issues refers to the type of architectural links between services and investment in a free trade agreement, and an FTAA agreement in particular. This is rooted in a more profound economic debate over the conceptual equivalence between the movement of capital and labor under a trade agreement. The authors tend to favor a NAFTA-type architecture (as opposed to GATS) consisting of a set of disciplines on cross-border trade in services, together with separate chapters with disciplines on the movement of capital and investment. In this regard we should note the recent, controversial innovation introduced by the United States in its bilateral agreement with Chile on the use of capital controls.

Innovations in an FTAA are likely to come through the signing of these bilateral deals. The authors emphasize the possibilities open to an FTAA in terms of strengthening regulatory transparency, addressing domestic regulatory impediments to trade and investment, and liberalizing government procurement practices. But by far the most novel recommendation regards an issue for which there is no dedicated negotiating group—labor mobility. Recent studies have suggested that the gains from allowing temporary access to workers from developing countries can be much greater than gains from the abolition of all traditional merchandise barriers. Therefore, labor mobility provisions should be incorporated in the same way as investment provisions.

Chapter 10 by Julian Clarke and Simon Evenett on competition policy offers a powerful example of the demands imposed by trade agreements on domestic policies, legal frameworks, and institutional architectures. A comprehensive chapter in the FTAA on competition policy would establish a set of disciplines requiring state companies, public monopolies, state-designated monopolies, and private monopolies to refrain from engaging in anticompetitive practices that could undermine the anticipated effects of a free trade agreement. It would also ask signatory countries to enact and enforce laws against anticompetitive corporate practices. Clarke and Evenett ask whether such a binding obligation in a treaty would benefit most countries in the region, and suggest that they should pass two tests: feasibility and economic desirability.

First, the authors establish a feasibility test by reviewing and comparing the existing national legislation in place in the three FTAA countries of Chile, Brazil, and Peru (although Colombia and Venezuela also have pertinent legislation). According to the authors, the fact that some countries have marshaled the expertise and resources necessary to deal with cartels suggests that countries are prepared to take on this kind of internal commitment. However, it is not clear that an FTAA on its own would play the same role in promoting this type of domestic policy and institutional reform in all countries.

Clarke and Evenett then approach the economic desirability test with an innovative empirical case study. The study quantifies the overcharges paid by Latin American countries on vitamin imports during the ten-year long international conspiracy to cartelize the market in those goods. The study found that nations without active cartel enforcement paid vitamin import bills at least eight percentage points higher than nations with such regimes. Given the importance of vitamin imports in the region, the econometric estimates imply that active anticartel enforcement saved some countries millions of U.S. dollars. For instance, in the case of Brazil, for this hardcore cartel alone, the reduction in overcharges equaled just under half of state outlays for enforcement of all competition laws.

Based on this case study, the authors conclude that countries would benefit by adopting provisions to enact and enforce anticartel laws, and that an FTAA could contribute to this effort. However, important caveats should be taken into account. The impact of an FTAA would depend on the specific provisions of the agreement, in particular the sectoral exemptions as well as the economic costs and institutional challenges that some countries may face. This is particularly true for small economies that would have to set up such a regime from scratch.

Trade policy is deeply rooted in domestic political factors, and the final outcome of the FTAA negotiations cannot be understood without paying attention to them. The theoretical and empirical literature has dwelt on two types of considerations. The first is the distribution of individual preferences, which describes the choice set available to policy makers. The second is the institutional structure of the political regime, which constrains this choice set by defining the revealed and aggregate preferences. These conceptual considerations find their application in the FTAA context in Chapter 11 by I. M. Destler, which focuses on the political economy of the United States, and Chapter 12 by Marcelo de Paiva Abreu, on Latin America.

Destler offers a fascinating account of the political-economy constraints facing the negotiators for the U.S. Trade Representative in the FTAA, drawing the boundaries that probably act as constraints on the hemispheric initiative. First, Destler argues, the United States feels that it has limited stakes in an FTAA. Although U.S. trade with other Western Hemisphere countries accounts for roughly one-third of its total global trade, the preponderance of this trade is with its NAFTA partners. The same is true for investment. Destler acknowledges that the potential benefits of further liberalization can be very large for the U.S.; the problem is that potential benefits seldom translate into active political support from potential beneficiaries. In this sense, the FTAA lacks a robust political base in the United States. This lack of interest from the business sector makes the FTAA vulnerable to those pushing other trade agendas, in particular the WTO Doha Round.

The second constraint on U.S. negotiators in the FTAA process comes from the difficulties of removing residual protection in the United States after a remarkable process of liberalization over the past half-century. The areas that need to be liberalized are all of great interest to Latin America, and will all be hard to crack. They consist of a limited but highly protected number of products in agriculture and textiles, as well as the thorny issue of trade remedy laws, most notably antidumping. The Trade Promotion Authority legislation, approved by a narrow congressional margin in December 2002, now contains language regarding the ability of the USTR to seek further liberalization in those areas in future trade agreements. Although none of these entrenched interests represents a major economic force, their leverage has been enhanced by the lack of a broad, bipartisan consensus to support trade liberalization in the U.S. Congress.

According to Destler, "unlike on prior major trade legislation, the process of enacting the TPA has not created a bipartisan support consensus in the House. And as long as that is absent, with approval hanging on a handful of votes, entrenched protectionist interests will have enhanced power." This narrow, partisan base on trade has its roots in the traditional opposition of organized labor to trade liberalization. A new ingredient also came into play during the 1990s—the demand to include trade and environmental provisions in trade agreements. How this will play out in the FTAA context is still an unknown.

Last but not least, Destler's third observation regarding the limits on U.S. representatives to the FTAA negotiations is that support for an FTAA has been heavily undercut by the fading of the vision, strong in the early 1990s, of increasingly prosperous and fully democratic economies are emerging in the hemisphere. Recent economic and political turmoil throughout the region have tarnished this vision. Given these three major U.S. constraints, Destler projects that the road to an FTAA will not be easy, but he does not believe it is hopeless. An FTAA can only be realized if there is a desire to rediscover (or reinvent) the original broad macropolitical vision of the initiative, and at the same time deal with the micropolitics of specific issues. The United States will succeed in moving the FTAA process forward only if the economic case can be folded into a larger political argument emphasizing the importance of building a democratic and congenial neighborhood. But this "vision thing" needs to be accompanied by an urgent effort to reach across the political divide in the U.S. Congress and find ways to broaden the political base for trade liberalization. The mobilization of the potential trade winners in the U.S. business sector is essential to this effort. We must not forget that the United States' trading partners throughout the hemisphere can increase the number of such winners with some strategic bargaining with U.S. interests. This should be done with an eye to creating and strengthening political allies within the U.S. political system.

In the final chapter of this section, Marcelo de Paiva Abreu examines the political economy of protection and trade liberalization in the rest of the hemisphere. His account is based on the premise that the equilibrium of the domestic political-economy forces at a given moment in time emerges from the distributive impact of the costs and benefits entailed by protection. The key challenge facing FTAA negotiators is to find ways to disturb the present perverse equilibrium—which allows protectionism to thrive in practically every economy of the hemisphere, including the United States—and move toward a new zero-protection equilibrium to be reached after a transition period.

The reciprocal dismantlement of protection in FTAA economies depends crucially on whether countries can successfully mobilize political support among groups likely to benefit from hemispheric integration. This mobilization is needed to counter the political weight of groups favored by protection that stand to be hurt by trade liberalization. All countries would favor a strategy that minimizes offers of improved access to their own market up front, and assures prompt access to export markets of other members. During the transition period, the political economy of the FTAA for each member boils down to finding an acceptable balance between benefits for exporters and dislocation of domestic producers whose output is displaced by imports. However, how is this accomplished in practice with the limited number of instruments available to a trade negotiator?

De Paiva Abreu acknowledges the complexity of such a task, reviewing the pros and cons of alternative policy instruments. Special emphasis is placed on the temptation of postponing real concessions to the end of the period of implementation and even of excluding some products, making use of the "substantially all trade" clause under the 1994 Article XXIV of GATT. Moreover, the interaction in terms of substance and timing between the FTAA negotiations and other negotiations, especially in the WTO, has to be taken into account when evaluating the exchange of concessions.

These are very difficult calculations to process. In the end the author favors a very pragmatic approach, asking: "What can the United States offer to Latin America that may clinch the deal?" This question counters the present reluctance of some future FTAA partners. The answer seems straightforward: "to a large extent what can be offered by the United States and could ease the political pain of concessions by Latin America is concentrated in its list of sensitive imports." Thus, the ability and willingness of the United States to open its markets to such products is crucial to the FTAA's success.

Economic Impact of a Free Trade Agreement

Part V of this book assesses the economics of an FTAA. The direct impacts of such an agreement on areas traditionally viewed as trade-related—such as production, patterns of trade, wages, and FDI—demand our attention if we are to understand the likely costs and benefits, the winners and losers, and the short- and long-run implications of the shift to a more liberal trading order in the hemisphere. These chapters take up the challenge of envisioning what those changes might be.

Chapter 13 by Antoni Estevadeordal and Raymond Robertson poses the seemingly innocuous question, "Do preferential trade agreements matter for trade?" Whilst on the face of it the answer once seemed obvious, whether for past FTAs or the putative FTAA, economists are now not so sure. In addition to the traditional concern that "trade diverting" aspects of FTAs might counterbalance their "trade creating" force, recent research has questioned whether, on net, trade agreements (including the WTO) have made any difference whatsoever to participating countries' trade. Such findings may be counterintuitive, but they also may be very plausible in a world where the deep structure of multiple FTA deals is so complex. In a "spaghetti bowl" of regional and bilateral deals, the impact of any marginal new agreement is hard to discern. This is precisely the problem in the Americas, where a myriad of trade agreements have spawned a truly impressive array of acronyms, especially in the last decade or two. Theory can offer no unambiguous prediction about shifts in trade patterns here—it is an empirical problem.

Estevadeordal and Robertson tackle the empirical problem by moving beyond the usual constraints of previous studies. A typical econometric approach has been to code an FTA relationship between countries as a dichotomous variable, but this does not capture the rich variety of FTAs and their variegated tariff structures. This mismeasurement could seriously understate the effect of tariffs on trade. Thus the authors laboriously examine the detailed evolution of FTA regimes in the Americas and construct measures of protection so that preferential tariffs (within the bloc) can be compared to the external MFN tariffs vis-à-vis the rest of the world.

Using the workhorse gravity model of trade, this setup embeds the theoretical finding that an important determinant of trading patterns should be the relative size of barriers to trade with different partners ("multilateral resistance"). Finding that this more sophisticated model performs well and reveals strong effects of tariffs on trade, the authors are able to simulate counterfactual bilateral trade patterns that might emerge after an FTAA agreement. Most Latin American countries might expect a change in trade flows of between 20 and 60 percent, with a larger impact on import shares. The largest impacts are predicted in Mexico, Peru, Bolivia, and Venezuela. The United States (15 to 20 percent) and Canada (under 5 percent) would be expected to have smaller increases in trade, with a larger increase in export shares. This asymmetry could reflect the fact that the Latin American countries are starting from a much more protected position.

If the effects of tariff liberalization on trade in the Americas promise to be large, then much else in the trade structure could require reconsideration too. As David Hummels and Alexandre Skiba show in Chapter 14, arbitrage costs could be dramatically affected by increasing returns as the density and frequency of traffic increases on intrahemispheric routes. Should this occur, as seems likely, a "virtuous circle" could result in which transaction costs are lowered first by tariffs and then, endogenously, still further by changes in shipping technology.

To demonstrate this claim, the authors explicitly model the aspects of arbitrage normally taken for granted: costs of shipping, warehousing, and distribution. Such costly activities may be strongly affected by fixed costs, but once a large volume of trade is established, those fixed costs might become much smaller as a part of average costs. Such savings could include the costs of inputs as well as time costs if shipping frequency changes and goods spend less time sitting in transit. Denser routes also allow new technologies, such as feeder routes or specialized ship designs (for example, bulk cargoes, refrigeration, or automobiles). Heavier demand could also induce pro-competitive effects via the entry of new firms into the shipping business. And, because of the geographical nature of the shipping problem, spillovers are likely: more ships plying the route from, for example, Buenos Aires to New Orleans are also available to pick up and drop off goods at intermediate ports.

An elegantly simple model captures these effects and allows for the endogenous choice of technologies outlined above. A number of econometric exercises suggest the likely magnitudes of such effects in actual settings. Since the 1970s the spread of containerization (perhaps the most dramatic new transport technology of the twentieth century) has been strongest on those routes with the most rapid growth of trade volumes. Since vessel scales are limited, frequency of visits also matters, and the authors show that the elasticity of shipping times with respect to trade volume is –0.1. Such time effects can be costly, as time costs may amount to 1 percent of the value of the good for each day spent in transit. Lastly, the authors are able to demonstrate empirically the spillover effects from route traffic to individual freight rates for location pairs along a route. The effect on transaction costs is potentially large, and the spillover might be almost as large as the direct effect of tariff reduction.

The authors conclude with some important perspectives on an FTAA. Economically, the effects on trade could be much larger than imagined once shipping technology adjusts to the increase in market opportunities. Politically, the spillover effects could encourage a more cooperative approach to liberalization once policy makers understand that a denser transport network has benefits for all. In this setting, regionalism could deliver large gains, and not necessarily smaller than those under multilateralism.

Moving beyond the impacts on trade itself, Gordon Hanson in Chapter 15 looks at the likely impact of an FTAA on wages, using evidence from the NAFTA episode as an example. The analysis is based on an analysis of Mexican wage data that is disaggregated by skill and region, with comparisons to the U.S. wage data. This permits us to see how an FTA can create winners and losers via trade and investment channels. The Mexican case is illustrative because liberalization there has been so aggressive, first unilaterally in the 1980s (the trade share of Mexico has tripled in the last twenty years) and then more so through the 1994 NAFTA agreement with respect to its close neighbor and major trading partner to the north (now almost 90 percent of Mexican exports go to the United States).

Hanson finds that these policy shifts have wrought enormous changes on Mexican wage distribution. The wages of skilled workers have risen relative to those of unskilled workers, and wages have risen generally in the northern border regions relative to the rest of the country. Overall this has created greater wage dispersion in the country as a whole, but is perhaps consistent with theoretical predictions: in the United States also there has been a rising skill premium, and in this sense the two countries' wage distributions have converged. Moreover, the effects have been strongest in the *maquiladora* zones near the frontier, where transaction costs are smallest and the impacts of trade and FDI are strongest. The outsourcing of certain low-skill activities from the United States to Mexico may have amplified these effects by raising the skill premia in *both* countries.

Whilst Hanson cautions that Mexico's unique position created effects that other FTAA countries will not experience (e.g., fluid emigration to the United States that affects the local economy's wage equilibrium and heavy ex ante protection of low-skill industries), the case is still illustrative. Since the United States would be the largest trading partner in an FTAA, countrics need to assess what convergence to something more like the U.S. (relative) wage distribution would imply for their domestic economies (and polities). Further, the boom in northern Mexico suggests that an FTAA would affect not just national economic prospects, but regional economic fortunes too. Areas with the best access to the international economy have the most to gain; more remote regions could get left behind. Low-skill workers in isolated areas might fare very poorly. An example would be Chiapas in southern Mexico—a cautionary tale.

Bernardo Blum and Edward Leamer give further attention to living standards, inequality, and growth over the longer run in Chapter 16, which asks, "Can FTAA Suspend the Law of Gravity and Give the Americas Higher Growth and Better Income Distribution?" They see trading patterns as revealing three sources of comparative advantage: resources, remoteness, and climate. In turn, these patterns are strongly associated with wealth and income distribution. In that sense, "you are what you export."

An intensive cross-country econometric study shows that an export mix dominated by manufactures leads to growth and equality (but is most likely in temperate, high skill, integrated economies, such as Europe and North America), whereas exports of crops and raw materials go hand in hand with poverty and inequality (usually in tropical, low-skill, economically isolated regions). For the Latin American countries, then, the questions is: Are these patterns simply destiny? Or, by design, institutional or otherwise, can the region shape its future? And is an FTAA one such design?

The optimistic scenario posits that, despite presumably immutable characteristics of climate and physical geography, the boost in integration provided by an FTAA (the direct elimination of protection as well as the endogenous scale economies in transport and communication) might well bring the region "closer" to global GDP, as well as to other economies in the region. If so, an FTAA might allow a shift in the production mix toward the manufacturing mix that is strongly correlated with wealth and equality. This might, in turn, generate more investment in human capital in the region, enhancing the structural shift still further.

However, a pessimistic interpretation is also possible. Unless an FTAA has very strong impacts, the authors caution that such a wholesale change might be too much to hope for and should not be taken for granted. Policy makers may think they have more control over economic outcomes than they actually do, since the region's remote and tropical characteristics might be too powerful to be overturned easily. Countries in Latin America do not have trade volumes and trade patterns significantly different from those with similar resources and remoteness in the rest of the world. Admittedly, the other poor, remote, tropical regions are often populated by highly protected economies too, so the prospects for change depend on how much an FTAA can truly promote trade while holding other factors constant and, over a longer horizon, how trade expansion can induce skill accumulation. The good news is that remoteness from the rich core economies did not consign Japan and the newly industrialized countries, nor Australia and New Zealand, to poverty and inequality. Natural-resource abundance did not hold back Canada and Sweden. If the region can imitate the success of these nations by intensifying human capital and diminishing economic, legal, and cultural "distance" from the core, the future may be brighter.

A complementary theme appears in the next chapter by Ernesto López-Córdova and Mauricio Mesquita Moreira. They examine the experiences of Brazil and Mexico to assess whether there is evidence that regional integration can deliver on its promise to enhance productivity growth. The two countries have engaged in major FTA policy experiments—MERCOSUR and NAFTA, respectively—so they represent useful objects of study. The authors allow that integration can enhance productivity via the trade channel (better inputs, technology acquisition, import discipline, and turnover) or via the FDI channel (entry, competition, knowledge spillovers, and "linkage" effects). Integration at the regional level may mute or enhance some of these effects.

The authors set out to search for these effects, and the case studies seem to offer prima facie evidence. The more aggressively reformist Mexico enjoyed substantially faster productivity growth than Brazil, and within each country the more heavily traded industries enjoyed faster productivity growth. The latter gains were largely driven by turnover or reallocation of resources from low- to high-productivity firms. Naturally, more refined econometric analysis is necessary to move from correlation toward causation or, at least, some better understanding of the mechanisms at work. Using firm-level data, the authors find that, for the trade channel, import discipline appears to have been strong; evidence of scale effects, learning, or input quality is more mixed. For the FDI channel, the presence of foreign firms does seem to lead to spillovers to domestic productivity.

The authors conclude that an FTAA offers some promise of increased productivity growth in the region—hopefully, at least at the level of the Brazilian performance under the feeble integration allowed by MERCOSUR, or even at the pace seen in Mexico under the more aggressive reforms undertaken before and after NAFTA.

Finally, focusing on the implications of an FTAA for foreign direct investment, Eduardo Levy Yeyati, Ernesto Stein, and Christian Daude in Chapter 18 seek to understand the role that regional FTAs play in determining the location of FDI. Care is needed to disentangle the impacts on host and source countries and on the different flavors of FDI, such as "horizontal" and "vertical," whilst controlling for other economic fundamentals such as factor endowments and, of course, the trade regime.

On these questions, theory is silent as to the size or even direction of the net effects, so an empirical tack is taken, using bilateral data on OECD FDI outflows and FTA participation from 1982 to 1999, and applying a gravity-type model. Several variables are constructed to detect the effects of being an FTA partner (ambiguous, since "horizontal" FDI may be discouraged but "vertical" FDI may be encouraged), enjoying an extended market in an FTA as a host (presumed to encourage FDI), or enjoying an extended market in an FTA as a source (presumed to "dilute" FDI flows in the FTA as the number of rival hosts increases).

The authors find that these intuitive impacts are backed up by the data, and robustly so. Being partners in an FTA increases FDI flows by 27 percent ("vertical" FDI growth plus investment provisions more than offset "horizontal" FDI losses). FDI flows with respect to host extended market size have an elasticity of 0.10, and with respect to source extended market size have an elasticity of –0.05.

To grasp the intuition better, the authors run an interesting simulation to see how FDI from the United States to Mexico and Argentina might be affected by the onset of an FTAA. Argentina would gain from the partner effect 27 percent, would gain from the host extended market (all of the FTAA region and not just MERCOSUR) another 27 percent, and would lose 0.7 percent due to source extended market "dilution" effects, since the United States would gain little market size from an FTAA versus NAFTA. For Mexico the results are understandably quite different: since Mexico is already in NAFTA it has nothing to gain as a partner, its extended market effect would be small (just 1.25 percent), and source "dilution" effects would again be an offset (–0.7 percent). There is a large FDI gain to Argentina, but very little for Mexico, and this illustrates the political-economy tensions that could arise during FTAA negotiations for an "insider" such as Mexico versus an "outsider" such as Argentina.

Applying this simulation method to the whole of the FTAA recipient area and all sources, the authors estimate that an FTAA would boost overall stocks of FDI in ten large Latin American countries by large amounts—in MERCOSUR by about 90 percent and in the Andean Community by over 120 percent. For small countries—such as Chile, Panama, and Costa Rica—the impacts are even bigger, so large are the extended market effects.

The authors conclude with a cautionary note, however. Gains in FDI do not automatically translate into gains in economic welfare, and much may depend on the market environment, distortions and subsidies, human capital, institutions, potential for spillovers, and other fundamentals that attracted the FDI. If competition for FDI becomes too intense, the possibility arises that the bidding will allow most of the gains to be extracted by the FDI sources in the North, with little benefit to the South.

Beyond Free Trade

The lesson from economic history is that convergence in living standards requires more than just free trade. It requires some combination of resource and technology transfers across national boundaries (as in the European Union), mobility of labor (as with Puerto Rico), and significant improvement in the quality of domestic institutions. In an FTAA, the first two avenues are pretty much closed off politically. Global capital markets supply some investment to Latin America, but the flows are limited and volatile. Under an FTAA, however, the United States is unlikely to acquiesce in the establishment of regional or structural funds that might spur or smooth development, at least not on a scale comparable to the EU's initiative. Global labor markets are somewhat fluid (informally), easing labor surplus in poorer regions; but under an FTAA a significant relaxation in U.S. immigration rules (e.g., those governing temporary worker visas), desirable as it would be, is off the agenda. Institutional change, therefore, is our best hope. A lot hangs on the nature of the deeper institutional changes that may accompany an FTAA. Part VI of this book takes a close look at some of the key issues involved.

An important difficulty here is that institutional convergence and harmonization do not yield a reliable path to higher-quality domestic institutions when underlying national circumstances are different. A standard theorem in economics states that price arbitrage is efficiency enhancing. There is no parallel theorem for institutional arbitrage. One cannot simply assume that U.S. rules and practices are a good fit for Latin American countries. Nowhere is this clearer than in the areas of labor and environmental standards.

As Kimberly Elliott emphasizes in Chapter 19 on labor standards, the usual core list of standards consists essentially of human rights—freedom from forced labor and from discrimination, the right to associate and bargain collectively, and the abolition of child labor (this last being the only really controversial item on this list)—from which no country can or should exempt itself on account of poverty or a low level of development. The questions are whether these issues ought to be linked to trade negotiations, and if so, what form their implementation should take. The first of these questions is by now moot. It has become politically and intellectually impossible to leave labor out of the negotiations when intellectual property, investment rules, and so many other issues have been loaded on the agenda. The debate is no longer about whether, but about how.

Elliott makes the case that freedom of association and collective bargaining are a useful complement to the more directly economic aspects of free trade agreements. A society with vibrant, broad-based trade unions is more likely to produce the trust and social dialogue needed to maintain economic dynamism. Mechanisms of voice are generally helpful to good economic performance.

Universality does not imply uniformity, however. Unlike the WTO's agreement on trade-related intellectual property (TRIPs), for example, which imposed minimum patent-length requirements, Elliott favors an approach that focuses on the universal elements of labor rights, leaving specific application to national legislation. Paradoxically, the greatest obstacle to requiring adherence to the ILO's core labor standards is that the United States itself has ratified so few of them (only two out of eight). She argues that the way forward involves putting labor issues on a parallel track with trade issues, while ensuring that the trains run on similar speeds on each track. This requires that all governments take the labor track seriously, put money on the table for technical assistance, and be prepared to undertake systematic national assessments of the adjustments needed (along the lines of environmental assessments).

In Chapter 20 on the environment, Daniel Esty makes an argument that runs parallel to Elliot's argument for labor standards. The logics of economics and politics have irrevocably created a linkage between trade and the environment, and Esty lays out the case for managing this nexus overtly and forcefully. How do we reconcile environmentalists' worry that trade rules create a systematic bias against environmental values with exporters' concern that environmental standards are protectionism by another name?

Interestingly, at the launch of the FTAA process in 1994, a decision was made *not* to establish an environmental negotiating group. As Esty notes, this represents a significant departure form the precedent set in NAFTA negotiations, during which the environment played an important role. This "step back" apparently reflects the disappointment felt by the Mexicans regarding the environmental outcomes of NAFTA and the broader suspicion in the region regarding U.S. motives. Esty argues that this "just say no" attitude is unlikely to go anywhere. When the WTO's Doha Round itself includes negotiations on environment, it is doubtful that the FTAA can keep the item off the agenda. Moreover, Esty judges the NAFTA experience in managing the trade-environment nexus to have been generally positive.

According to Esty, FTAA negotiators have the opportunity to advance the agenda of international cooperation in this area. Procedurally, he calls for more transparency in the negotiations of the rules, a commitment to environmental assessments of the proposed agreement, and a commitment to bring into the negotiations those environmental issues that are clearly linked to trade. Substantively, he calls for a modernized dispute-settlement procedure that is more quasi-judicial in nature, language clarifying that trade rules not trump multilateral environmental agreements, incentives (and disciplines) for eco-labeling, a rejection of the traditional distinction between products and production processes, and a phasing out of subsidies that both distort trade and harm the environment.

In Chapter 21 Luis Felipe López-Calva and Nora Lustig focus directly on economic convergence, taking the experience of the European Union as a guide. They document the general, if nonuniform, trend toward convergence within the EU, and link this process to the policies followed at the national and regional level. Empirical studies have reached no clear consensus on the effectiveness of the EU's "cohesion funds." The authors summarize these studies and argue that the role of cohesion funds in fostering convergence has not been negligible, particularly where these funds were complemented with strong regional development policies. Effectiveness is also enhanced when funds are allocated progressively, for example, to the poorer rather than richer regions (which has not always been the case in the EU).

The authors then apply these findings to Mexico and the Central American region, using the Puebla-Panama Plan as an example. The plan was launched in 2001, on the suggestion of Mexican president Vicente Fox, as an initiative aimed at improving the basic attractiveness of the region for investment. At its center is a Meso-American network of highways aimed at reducing transport costs and enhancing regional integration. López-Calva and Lustig argue that one could view the Puebla-Panama Plan as an experiment along the lines of EU cohesion funds and as a potential model to emulate within an FTAA.

The southern part of Mexico has tended to lag behind the rest of the country, exhibiting more Central American than North American tendencies. Further, Central America's convergence to the North has slowed significantly since 1980. López-Calva and Lustig find that differences in investments in education and infrastructure (measured by telephone density) explain a large part of the convergence performance of the region affected by the plan (or, more accurately, the lack thereof). The implication is that additional resources in these two areas would help close the economic gap between Central and North America. However, the open question is whether an FTAA can mobilize the resources needed. The EU's structural/cohesion funds have disbursed quite large sums: Portugal, Greece, and Ireland have each received more than €300 per capita per year during the period 1994–99, and Spain has received around €200. There is little reason to think that resource transfers of such a scale can be reached in the context of an FTAA.

Chapter 22 by Inés Bustillo and José Antonio Ocampo addresses regional asymmetries in a broader fashion. Beyond cohesion/integration funds, this chapter calls for "margins of flexibility in FTAA disciplines" to allow governments to follow more activist, production-oriented developmental policies and to manage the capital account of the balance of payments. It also calls for increased labor mobility.

As Bustillo and Ocampo emphasize, the hope of creating a "level playing field" through an FTAA—by formulating a single undertaking with a reciprocal set of obligations—may backfire when the underlying economic conditions facing the richer and poorer countries in the region are different. For example, the greater vulnerability of Latin American countries to macroeconomic shocks makes it desirable to assign a larger role for managing capital-account volatility, including the use of prudential capital-account restrictions. An investment agreement that eliminates—or narrows—the scope for such management would create, in the words of Bustillo and Ocampo, a "false equality." Similarly, restrictions on the ability of governments to carry out policies that promote productive restructuring, innovation, and nontraditional exports potentially reduce the eventual gains from regional integration. Stringent intellectual property rules may hamper domestic technological capabilities. Common rules may aggravate rather than reduce economic disparities.

The context in which Bustillo and Ocampo draw these conclusions is the experience of Latin America in the 1990s. As the authors emphasize, the region exhibited significant export dynamism in this period, with the average annual rate of increase in the volume of exports reaching 8.4 percent. Meanwhile, overall output grew at a third of this rate—2.6 percent—low not only in absolute terms, but also in relation to Latin America's pre-1980 performance. Bustillo and Ocampo attribute this disappointing outcome to specialization in relatively nondynamic sectors and to the absence of a policy framework that strengthened the links between exports and other sectors of the economy. Hence they caution that greater openness on its own cannot be relied upon to generate productive dynamism. While activist sectoral policies do not guarantee success either, "success without [them] seems to be the exception rather than the rule." The authors discuss the experience of Puerto Rico, where much more than free trade has been at play in generating rapid convergence with the U.S. economy. Puerto Rico benefited from a regime of generous tax incentives for inward investment (under both Puerto Rican and U.S. laws), unrestricted labor mobility with the mainland, and strongly countercyclical federal transfers.

Finally, Chapter 23 by Mark Barenberg and Peter Evans focuses broadly on the implications of an FTAA for democratic governance in the region. The authors define governance as the rules and practices "that enable societies to deliberate about what goals are desirable, make choices about the set of norms and administrative apparatuses that will best realize these goals, implement those choices, adjudicate disputes regarding their implementation, and engage in reflexive evaluation, experimentation, and transformation of these institutions." They argue that, whether intended or not, an FTAA will create the "beginnings of 'constitutive ground rules' for hemispheric governance." What form will these rules take, and will their effects be salutary?

On the basis of its negotiating history, Barenberg and Evans find that NAFTA-type institutions, particularly those relating to investor rights in Chapter 11, are likely to be at the core of an FTAA. They argue that Chapter 11 institutions are defective from the perspective of both democratic governance and administrative effectiveness. Insofar as Chapter 11 tribunals have sought to impose a pre–New Deal conception of the regulatory state, the results have been in tension with prevailing democratic norms. Under Chapter 11, foreign investors are entitled to compensation in a wide range of circumstances: if they are treated less favorably than domestic investors or investors from other countries, if they do not receive full protection and security as defined by international law, if they face performance requirements, or if they are subject to any measure that is "tantamount to expropriation." In a key departure from international legal practice, Chapter 11 creates an investor-state dispute mechanism instead of a state-state mechanism. While there have been comparatively few complaints filed under Chapter 11, Barenberg and Evans argue that its effects have been significant.

Some of the NAFTA tribunal rulings can be interpreted as providing far-reaching authority to challenge and override domestic regulations where they affect the interests of foreign companies. For example, the use of the "necessity" and "least restrictive of international trade" rules to judge the appropriateness of regulations—as opposed to the "rationality" test that is common in domestic jurisprudence—can result in very stringent interpretations of what governments are allowed to do. Moreover, Chapter 11 rules require that investors be compensated for "excessive" discretion even when government behavior is not found to be arbitrary and is carried out pursuant to sovereign authorization. This too is a step backward, Barenberg and Evans argue, because it can conflict with the modern notion of delegation under which administrative agencies are provided with broad, as opposed to narrow, discretion in implementing regulatory rules.

Chapter 11 was designed in part to provide stronger rule-of-law protection to foreign investors than exists currently under Mexico's judiciary. But Barenberg and Evans argue that the Chapter 11 dispute mechanism is, ironically, in tension with all prevailing conceptions of the rule of law. It is not transparent, lacks due process, does not have to follow precedent, is presided over by arbitrators selected on an ad hoc basis, cannot provide for continuity and competence in subject matter, and is not politically accountable. Therefore, it does not necessarily generate a predictable and uniform application of the rules. The Barenberg-Evans critique suggests several avenues for fixing these flaws. The authors themselves favor a "democratizing" approach, which they illustrate using the labor side agreement in NAFTA.

It may be naïve to expect that the many diverse perspectives and solutions on offer in these chapters will find reflection in the final FTAA agreement. But these analyses collectively reveal a key and probably enduring insight: international trade agreements have become too important to leave to trade negotiators. The FTAA will intersect with and shape domestic economic, social, and legal arrangements throughout an entire continent. We had better walk into it with our eyes open—and focused on not only the potential benefits, but also the potential risks.

PART II

The FTAA: Historical and Global Perspectives

2

The Roots of Latin American Protectionism: Looking before the Great Depression

John H. Coatsworth and Jeffrey G. Williamson

Introduction

This chapter uncovers a fact that has not been well appreciated: Tariffs in Latin America were far higher than anywhere else in the world from the 1860s to World War I, long before the Great Depression. Indeed, they were even *rising* in the decades before the 1890s, a period that was part of what has been called the first global century (O'Rourke and Williamson 1999). This fact is surprising for three reasons: first, because this region has been said to have exploited globalization forces better than most during the pre-1914 *belle époque;* second, because standard economic histories say so little about it; and third, because most of us have been taught to view the Great Depression as *the* critical turning point when the region is said to have turned toward protection and de-linked itself from the world economy for the first time.

After establishing this fact, this chapter shows that its explanation cannot lie with some perceived GDP per capita gains from protection, since, while such gains were certainly present in industrial Europe and its non-Latin offshoots (Clemens and Williamson 2001), they most definitely were *not* present in Latin America. On the contrary, those countries with the highest tariff rates in Latin America grew slowest, and those who had the lowest tariff rates grew fastest. The chapter then explores Latin American tariffs as a revenue source, as a reaction to deindustrialization fears, as a strategic response to trading partners tariffs, as a redistributive device for special interests, and as a consequence of other political economy struggles. While the exploration is mostly qualitative for the first half-century of independence, it is quite quantitative for the period 1870–1950, using annual data for a sample of eight Latin American countries treated both as a panel and with fixed effects.

Belle Époque Latin America Was the World's Most Protectionist Region!

There is a well-developed literature that debates the measurement of economic openness (e.g., Anderson and Neary 1994; Sachs and Warner 1995; Anderson 1998). That literature makes it clear that trade shares are poor measures of openness since they are endogenous. Among the explicit policy measures of openness available, the average tariff rate is by far the most homogenous protection measure and the easiest to collect across countries and over time,[1] and it is most effective prior to the 1930s before the introduction of widespread non-tariff barriers. This chapter uses the computed average tariff rate to explore the policy experience of eight Latin American countries compared with twenty-seven others around the world between 1865 and World War II: the United States; three members of the European industrial core (France, Germany, United Kingdom); three non-Latin European offshoots (Australia, Canada, New Zealand); ten from the European periphery (Austria-Hungary, Denmark, Greece, Italy, Norway, Portugal, Russia, Serbia, Spain, Sweden); ten from Asia and the Mideast (Burma, Ceylon, China, Egypt, India, Indonesia, Japan, the Philippines, Siam, Turkey), and eight from Latin America (Argentina, Brazil, Chile, Cuba, Colombia, Mexico, Peru, Uruguay).[2]

Figure 2.1 plots average world tariffs before World War II (unweighted and weighted by export shares in world markets), and Figure 2.2 plots them for some regional clubs.[3] Figure 2.2 plots six regions—the United States, the European core, the European periphery, European non-Latin offshoots, Asia, and Latin America—the country members of which were identified above. Four important observations can be drawn from these figures.

First, Figure 2.1 documents a steady climb in tariff rates worldwide between 1870 and the 1890s, although qualitative evidence surveyed elsewhere (Coatsworth and Williamson forthcoming) suggests that the climb started much earlier. Was this a globalization backlash or was it driven by other forces? In any case, the climb marked a slow but steady retreat from the liberal and pro–global trade positions in the mid-century (Williamson 1998). The interwar surge to world protection is, of course, better known.

Figure 2.1 Average World Tariffs before World War II

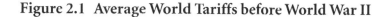

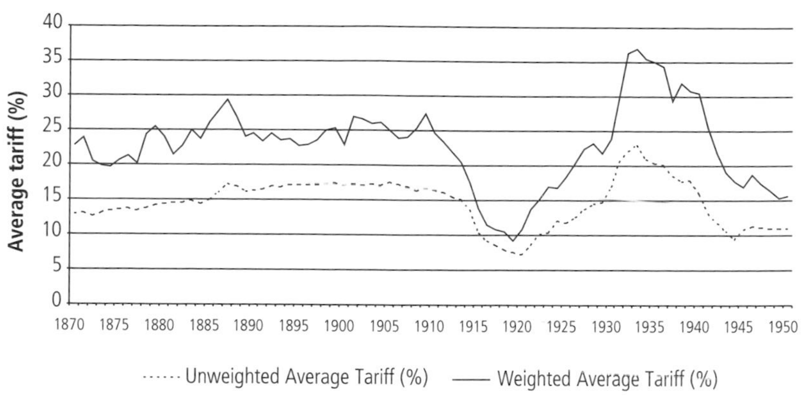

Figure 2.2 Unweighted Average of Regional Tariffs before World War II

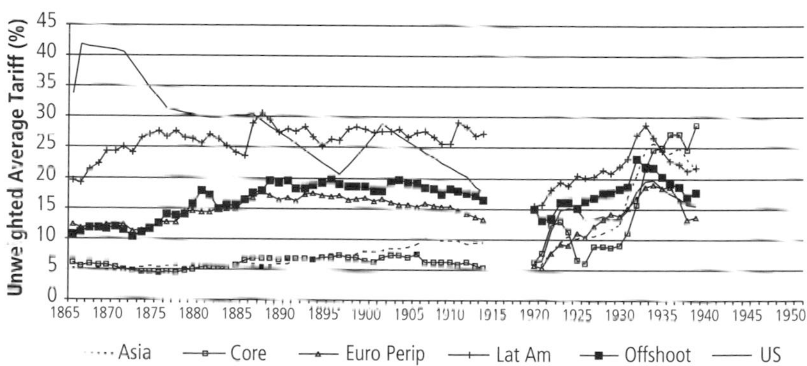

Second, note the enormous variance in levels of protection between the regional club averages. The richer new-world European offshoots had levels of protection more than twice that of the European core around the turn of the last century. When the United States is shifted to the rich European offshoot club, the ratio of tariffs between European offshoot and core jumps to more than three times. To take additional examples, in 1925 the European periphery had tariffs 2.4 times higher than those in the European part of the industrial core. And in 1885 the poor but independent parts of Latin America (Brazil, Colombia, Mexico, and Peru) had tariffs 4.6 times higher than those in the poor and dependent parts of Asia (Burma, Ceylon, China, Egypt, India, Indonesia, and the Philippines).

Third, there was also great variance *within* these regional clubs. In 1905, tariffs in Uruguay (the most protectionist land-abundant and labor-scarce country; see Figure 2.4) were about 2.5 times those in Canada (the least protectionist land-abundant and labor-scarce country). In the same year, tariffs in Brazil and Colombia (the most protectionist of Latin American countries) were almost ten times those in China and India (the least protectionist in Asia). The same high-low range appeared among the industrial core countries (the United States five times the United Kingdom) and the European periphery (Russia six times Austria-Hungary). Thus, explaining differences between countries before 1940 is at least as challenging as explaining changes in tariff policy over the eight decades after 1865—perhaps more so. This observation applies with special force to Latin America, where the range just prior to World War I was about 17 percent in Chile to about 48 percent in Columbia (Figure 2.4).

Finally, note the most critical fact that motivates this chapter. With notable exceptions, historical accounts argue that the reluctance of Latin American countries to open in the late-twentieth century was the product of the Great Depression and the de-linking import-substitution strategies that arose to deal with it (Diaz-Alejandro 1984; Corbo 1992; Taylor 1998). Yet, nineteenth-century Latin America—whether our poor four (Brazil, Colombia, Mexico, Peru), our rich three in the southern cone (Argentina, Chile, Uruguay), or even Cuba—already had *by far* the highest tariffs in the world (Figure 2.4). With the exception of the United States, Latin American tariffs were the highest in the world by 1865. At the crescendo of the *belle époque*, Latin American tariffs were at their peak, and still soaring above the rest of the world. Furthermore, the rise in Latin America's tariffs from

Figure 2.3 Gap Between Latin American Tariffs and World Average

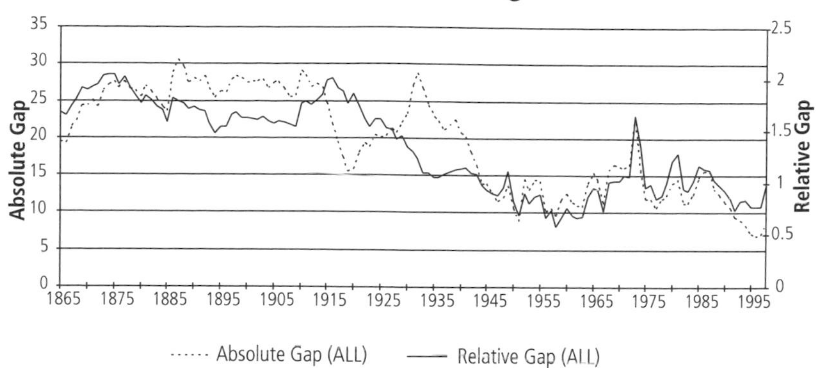

the late 1860s to the turn of the century was much steeper than in Europe, including France and Germany about which so much tariff history has been written.

Apparently, the famous export-led growth spurt in Latin America was consistent with extremely high tariffs (even though the region might have done even better without them). Latin American tariffs were still the world's highest in the 1920s, although the gap between Latin America and the rest of the world had shrunk considerably (Figure 2.3). Oddly enough, it was in the 1930s that the rest of the world (the European Core and Asia) finally surpassed Latin America in securing the dubious distinction of being the most protectionist. By the 1950s, and when import-substitution industrialization (ISI) policies were flourishing, Latin American tariffs were actually *lower* than those in Asia and the European periphery.[4] Thus, whatever explanations are offered for the Latin American commitment to protection, we must search for its origin well before the Great Depression.

There are some surprises in these tariff data that have not been noticed by those who have concentrated on one epoch, one region, or even just one country. This chapter stresses the first big Latin American surprise: Latin America had the highest tariffs in the world as early as 1865, a position it held until the 1930s. The second big Latin America surprise is this: The traditional literature written by European economic historians has made much of the tariff backlash on the continent after the 1870s (Kindleberger 1951; Bairoch 1989; O'Rourke and Williamson 1999). Yet, this heavily researched continental move to protection is relatively minor when compared with the rise in tariff rates over the same period in our four poor Latin American countries (up 6.9 percentage points to 34 percent), and this for a region that has been said to have exploited the pre-1914 globalization boom so well.

In the interwar decades, tariffs worldwide took two big leaps upward. The first leap was in the 1920s, which might be interpreted as a policy effort to return to 1914 levels. It might also have been due to postwar deflation. Inflations and deflations seem to have influenced tariff rates in the 1910s, the 1920s, and at some other times, a phenomenon labeled "specific-duty-inflation effect," to which we will return later in this chapter. The second interwar leap in tariff rates was, of course, in the 1930s, with aggressive beggar-my-neighbor policies reinforced by the specific-duty-inflation effect. Except for the two countries with the highest prewar tariffs, Colombia and Uruguay, tariffs rose everywhere in Latin America. But note that for most Latin American countries, tariff rates rose to levels in the late 1930s that were no higher than they had been in the *belle époque* (Figure 2.4).[5]

So, what was the political economy that determined Latin American protection in the century before the end of the Great Depression?

Protection Did *Not* Foster Economic Growth in Latin America

Does protection help or hinder growth? We need to answer this question first to see whether anything in the experience of the Latin Amer-

Figure 2.4 Own Tariffs in Latin America before World War II

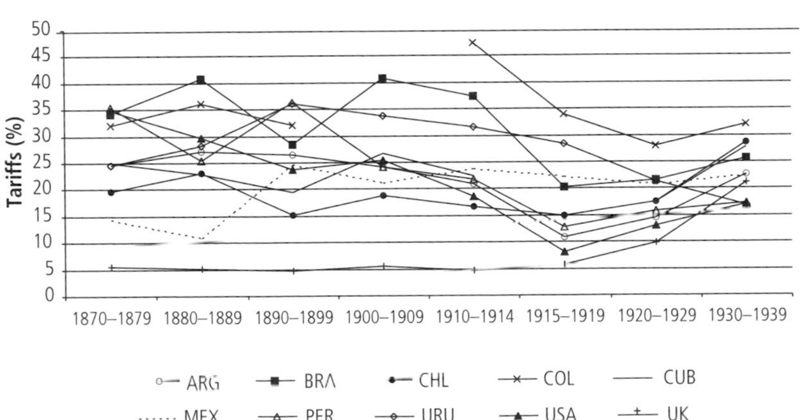

ican countries could have persuaded policy makers in the ninteenth century to adopt or persist in maintaining high levels of protection.[6] Let us start with the familiar late-twentieth century evidence. It is unambiguous on the issue, and can be found in four kinds of studies.[7]

First, the authors of a large National Bureau of Economic Research project assessed trade and exchange-control regimes in the 1960s and 1970s by calculating deadweight losses (Bhagwati and Krueger 1973–76). They concluded that the barriers imposed significant costs in all but one case. However, these standard welfare calculations have been criticized by those who have pointed out that such studies fail to allow protection a chance to lower long-run cost curves, as in the traditional infant-industry case, or to foster industrialization and thus growth, as in those modern growth theories in which industry is the carrier of technological change and capital deepening. Thus, economists have had to look for more late-twentieth-century proof to support the openness-fosters-growth hypothesis.

Second, analysts have contrasted the growth performance of relatively open economies with that of relatively closed economies. The World Bank has conducted such studies for forty-one countries going back before the first oil shock. The correlation between trade openness and growth is abundantly clear in these studies (Lindert and Williamson 2001: Table 3), but the analysis is vulnerable to the criticism that the effect of trade policies alone cannot be isolated since other policies usually change at the same time. Thus, countries that liberalized their trade also liberalized their domestic factor markets, liberalized their domestic commodity markets, and set up better property-rights enforcement. The appearance of these domestic policies may deserve more credit for raising income, while the simultaneous appearance of more liberal trade policies may deserve less.

Third, there are country event studies in which the focus is on periods when trade policy regimes change dramatically enough to see their effect on growth. Growth improved where there was a move toward liberalization in the 1960s (Krueger 1983, 1984). More recently, David Dollar and Aart Kraay (2000) examined the trade liberalizations in the 1980s and 1990s, finding, once again, the positive correlation between freer trade and faster growth. Of course, these reform episodes may have changed more than just global participation, so that an independent trade effect may not have been isolated.

Fourth, macroeconometric analysis has been used in an attempt to resolve the doubts left by the simpler historical correlations revealed by the other three kinds of studies. This macroeconometric literature shows that free trade policies have been associated with fast growth in the late-twentieth century, especially with many other relevant influences held constant. The most famous study is by Jeffrey Sachs and Andrew Warner (1995), but many others have also confirmed the openness-fosters-growth hypothesis for the late-twentieth century (e.g., Dollar 1992; Edwards 1993; Bloom and Williamson 1998; Dollar and Kraay 2000). While this recent macroeconometric literature is not without its critics (Rodriguez and Rodrik 2001), it is certainly consistent with forty years of previous research.

If free trade has been associated with fast growth since World War II, why was it associated with slow growth before then? About thirty years ago, Paul Bairoch (1972) argued that protectionist countries grew *faster* in the nineteenth century, not slower as every economist has found for the late-twentieth century. Bairoch's sample was mainly from the European industrial core, it looked at pre-1914 experience only, and controlled for no other factors. Like the second group of modern studies listed above, it simply compared growth rates of major European countries in protectionist and free trade episodes. More recently, Kevin O'Rourke (2000) got the Bairoch finding again, this time using macroeconometric conditional analysis on a ten-country sample drawn from the pre-1914 Atlantic economy. In short, these two scholars were not able to find *any* evidence before World War I supporting the openness-fosters-growth hypothesis.

These pioneering historical studies suggest that a tariff-growth paradox took the form of a regime switch somewhere between the start of World War I and the end of World War II: before the switch, protection was associated with growth; after the switch, free trade was associated with growth. Was Latin America part of this paradox, or was it only an attribute of the industrial core? Recent work by Clemens and Williamson (2001) has shown that protection *was* associated with fast growth in the industrial core before World War II, but that it was *not* associated with fast growth in most of the periphery. Table 2.1 offers a revised version of the Clemens-Williamson result, where the model estimated is of the convergence variety, but is conditioned only by the country's own tariff rate and regional club dummies. The tariff rate and GDP per capita level are both measured at year *t*, while the subsequent GDP per capita growth rate is measured over the half decade following. The two world wars are ignored (but they are not ignored in the rest of the chapter).

Table 2.1 Tariff Impact on GDP per Capita Growth by Region

	5-Year Overlapping Average Growth Rate			
Dependent Variable	(1)	(2)	(3)	(4)
Included countries	ALL	ALL	ALL	ALL
Years per period	1	1	1	1
Time interval	1875–1908	1875–1908	1924–1934	1924–1934
ln GDP/capita	0.18	0.12	−1.01	−0.86
	1.88	*1.23*	*−3.52*	*−3.03*
ln own tariff	0.09	0.36	−0.04	1.45
	1.06	*2.28*	*−0.13*	*2.93*
(European periphery dummy) × (ln tariff rate)		−0.53		−2.23
		−2.48		*−3.38*
(Latin America dummy) × (ln tariff rate)		−1.04		0.37
		−3.22		*0.33*
(Asia dummy) × (ln tariff rate)		0.20		−2.41
		0.79		*−3.56*
European periphery dummy	−0.18	1.12	−0.37	5.63
	−1.36	*2.05*	*−0.93*	*3.14*
Latin America dummy	0.25	3.36	−0.91	−2.51
	1.54	*3.39*	*−2.12*	*−0.74*
Asia dummy	−0.31	−0.50	−2.32	4.18
	−1.77	*−0.95*	*−4.27*	*2.25*
Constant	−0.24	−0.43	9.50	4.21
	−0.32	*−0.54*	*3.47*	*1.41*
Country dummies?	No	No	No	No
Time dummies?	No	No	No	No
N	1,180	1,180	372	372
R^2	0.0359	0.0516	0.0618	0.1091
Adjusted R^2	0.0318	0.0451	0.0490	0.0894

Note: t-statistics are in italics.

The tariff-growth paradox is stunningly clear in Table 2.1. In columns 2 and 4, the estimated coefficient on log of the tariff rate is 0.36 for 1875–1908 and 1.45 for 1924–34, and both are highly significant. Thus, and in contrast with late-twentieth century evidence, tariffs were associated with fast growth before 1939. But was this true the world around, or was there instead an asymmetry between industrial economies in the core and primary producers in the periphery? Presumably, the protecting country has to have a big domestic market, and has to be ready for industrialization, accumulation, and human capital deepening if the long-run, tariff-induced dynamic effects are to offset the short-run gains from trade given up. Table 2.1 tests for asymmetry in columns 2 and 4, and the asymmetry hypothesis wins—in the Latin American case especially if we focus on the pre-World War I decades. That is, protection was associated with faster growth in the European core and their English-speaking offshoots (again, the coefficient on own tariff 1875–1908 is 0.36 and highly significant), but it was *not* associated with fast growth in the European or Latin American periphery (the negative coefficient on the interaction term exceeds the positive coefficient on the tariff rate alone), nor was it associated with fast growth in interwar Asia. Most important, note that before World War I protection in Latin America was associated significantly and powerfully with *slow* growth (0.36 + (–)1.04 = –0.68).

The moral of the story is that while Latin American policy makers may have been aware of the pro-protectionist infant-industry argument[8] offered for *Zollverein* Germany by Frederich List and for federalist United States by Alexander Hamilton, there is absolutely no evidence after the 1860s that would have supported those arguments for Latin America. We must look elsewhere for plausible explanations for the exceptionally high tariffs in Latin America long before the Great Depression. As a signal of things to come, one place to look for alternative explanations is to note that the causation in Table 2.1 could have gone the other way round in Latin America. That is, countries achieving rapid GDP per capita growth would also have undergone faster growth in imports and in other parts of the tax base, thus reducing the need for high tariff *rates*. And countries suffering slow growth would have had to keep high tariff rates to ensure adequate revenues.

The Political Economy of Latin American Tariffs: War, Insurrection, and Revenue

The "Protectionist" Stage Is Set: The First Half-Century of Independence

In young, recently independent economies with low or even declining capacity to tax, few bureaucratic resources to implement efficient collection, and limited access to foreign capital markets, customs duties are an easy-to-collect revenue source essential to support central government expenditures on infrastructure and defense.[9] This was certainly true of the newly independent United States. It was even more true for a Latin America beset in the first half of the nineteenth century with the end "of the de facto customs union, capital flight, ... the collapse of the colonial fiscal system," civil wars, and violent border disputes (Prados de la Escosura 2002: 2). Nor did Latin America gain access to European capital markets until later in the century, an event which would have eased the need for tax revenues in the short run. The average share of customs duties in total revenues across eleven Latin American republics was 57.8 percent between 1820 and 1890 (Centeno 1997: Table 1).[10] Customs revenues were even more important for federal governments (65.6 percent), since local and state governments who form a union typically are reluctant to give up their limited tax weapons. Furthermore, customs revenues are especially important for land-abundant countries with federal governments since they do not have the population and tax-payer density to make other forms of tax collection efficient. Now add to these conditions the huge revenue needed to fight wars and we get the high U.S. Civil War tariffs in the early 1860s and the high (and rising) tariffs in a newly independent Latin America that experienced almost continuous war and civil strife between the 1820s and the 1870s.

Mares (2001) reports ten major Latin American wars between 1825 and 1879, but limits his data to conflicts that produced at least one thousand battlefield deaths. Centeno (1997) has counted thirty-three major international and civil wars between 1819 and 1880, but his data exclude Cuba altogether as well as numerous small- and medium-scale internal conflicts and a number of costly international wars. Of the eight countries for which we have data on levels of protection, all fought at least two major wars between independence and 1880. Only Brazil and Chile (after 1830) avoided violent military coups. All eight experienced episodes of massive and prolonged civil strife. In six countries, internal civil wars raged more or less continuously for decades after independence.

The universal preoccupation with national defense and internal security pushed the newly independent Latin American countries toward higher revenue-maximizing tariffs. Military expenditures quickly rose to consume over 70 and often more than 90 percent of all revenues (Centeno 1997). Weak governments, under attack from within and without, abandoned internal taxes that required an extensive and loyal bureaucracy, and concentrated tax collection efforts instead on a few ports and mines. The ratio of tariff revenues to imports, and thus levels of protection, rose in every country for which there are data, as did customs revenues as a percentage of national government revenues. Policymakers were not seeking to protect local producers but rather to keep troops in the field against foreign and domestic enemies. The fiscal imperative of the region's endemic military conflicts swamped all other preoccupations.

Revenue Targets and Optimal Tariffs for Revenue Maximization

Were the newly independent Latin American nations searching for some optimal tariff? Maybe or maybe not, but as Douglas Irwin (1997: 8–12) has pointed out for the United States and Victor Bulmer-Thomas (1994: 141) for Latin America, the revenue-maximizing tariff hinges crucially on the price elasticity of import demand. Tariff revenue can be expressed as

$$R = tpM \qquad (1)$$

where R is revenue, t is the average ad valorem tariff rate, p is the average price of imports and M is the volume of imports. Totally differentiating (1) with respect to the tariff, and assuming that the typical nineteenth-century Latin American country was a price taker for manufacturing imports, yields

$$dR/dt = pM + (tp)dM/dt. \qquad (2)$$

The revenue-maximizing tariff rate, t^*, is found by setting $dR/dt = 0$, in which case

$$t^* = -1/(1 + \eta) \qquad (3)$$

where η is the price elasticity of demand for imports. Irwin (1997: 14) estimates the price elasticity to have been about –2.6 for the United States between 1869 and 1913. Since the import mix was similar for the United States and Latin America, suppose the price elasticity for the latter was about –3. Under those conditions, the average tariff in Latin America would have been very high indeed, 50 percent.[11]

Suppose instead that some Latin America government during the *belle époque*—riding on an export boom between the 1870s and World War I—had in mind some target revenue share in GDP ($R/Y = r$) and could not rely on foreign capital inflows to balance the current account (so $pM = X$). Then

$$r = tpM/Y = tX/Y. \qquad (4)$$

Clearly, if foreign-exchange earnings from exports (spent on imports) were booming (an event which could even be caused by a terms-of-trade boom, denoted here by a fall in p, the relative price of imports), the target revenue share, r, could have been achieved at lower tariff rates, t. The bigger the export boom and the higher the resulting export share (X/Y), the lower the tariff rate.

So, did Latin American governments act as if they were meeting revenue targets? Ceteris paribus, did they lower tariff rates during world primary product booms when export shares were high and rising, and did they raise them during world primary product slumps?

The Political Economy of Latin American Tariffs: What Else Might Have Mattered?

The Specific-Duty-Inflation Effect

It has been argued that inflations and deflations have had a powerful influence on average tariff rates in the past. Import duties were typically *specific* until modern times, quoted as pesos per bale, yen per yard, or dollars per bag.[12] Under specific duties abrupt changes in price levels would change import values in the denominator, but not the legislated duty in the numerator, thus producing big equivalent ad valorem or percentage rate changes. Ad valorem rates are more common today, so that equivalent tariff rates are less affected by inflation and deflation. The impact of inflations during the two world wars was quite spectacular, and had nothing to do with policy. Thus, actual tariff *rates* fell sharply in all regions between 1914 and 1919, and again between 1939 and 1947 (Figure 2.1). Similarly, part of the rise in tariff rates immediately after World War I was due to postwar deflation. Price deflation after 1929 was even more spectacular, and it too served to raise tariff rates at least on imports still subject to specific duties. The process was repeated during the World War II inflation, but, in contrast, there was no return to the very high prewar rates of the 1930s.

This argument assumes, of course, that changing the legislated tariff structure is politically expensive, and thus is only infrequently changed by new legislation. We are certainly not the first to notice this specific-duty-inflation effect. Douglas Irwin has made the same point in accounting for the U.S. tariff experience between the Civil War and the Great Depression (Irwin 1998: 1017), and Graciela Márquez Colin has made it for prerevolutionary Mexico (Márquez 2002: 307), but, as far as we know, it has not been explored for a larger sample.

Strategic Trade Policy, the Terms of Trade and Tariffs

A well-developed theoretical literature on strategic trade policy predicts that nations have an incentive to inflate their own terms of trade

Figure 2.5 Unweighted Regional Average of Principal Trading Partners' Tariffs

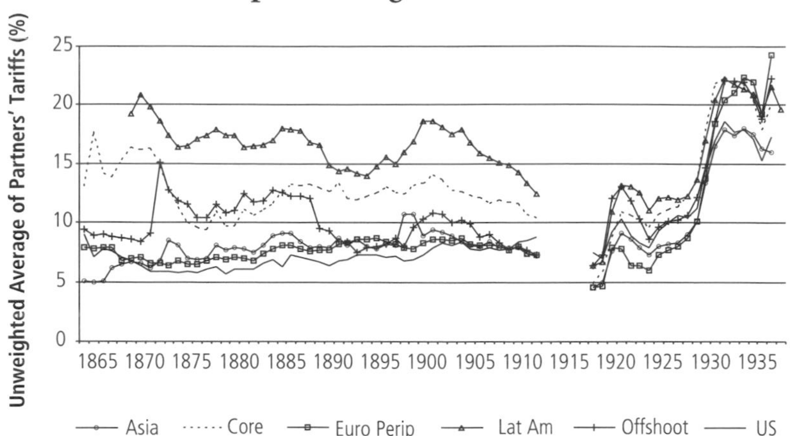

with high tariffs, thereby lowering global welfare.[13] In as much as favorable terms of trade translate into better economic performance, we might expect a country's own tariffs to depend at least in part upon the country's external tariff environment. Thus, Figure 2.5 plots a principal-trading-partners-tariff index for the same regional clubs. It is calculated in this way: first, we identify the major trading partners for each country (up to five); second, we calculate exports going to each major trading partner as a share of total country exports going to all major trading partners; third, we use these shares as weights by which to construct the average tariff faced by each country; finally, we construct an unweighted average for each region.

Figures 2.2 and 2.5 tell us that in the two decades before World War I, every region except the industrial core faced lower tariff rates in their main export markets than they themselves erected against competitors in their own markets. The explanation, of course, is that the main export markets were located in the core, where tariffs were much lower. Thus, the periphery faced lower tariffs than did the core (for the European periphery this was true throughout, but for the rest of the periphery it was true only up to just before 1900, when the United States replaced Britain as a major export market for them). During the interwar, every club faced very similar and high tariff rates in export markets, but those rates were rising very steeply outside the core as the core itself made the biggest policy switch—compared with the other clubs—from free trade to protection.

Figure 2.5 also tells us that Latin America faced *far* higher tariffs than anyone else since they traded with heavily protected countries such as the United States and each other. So, did this "hostile" policy environment abroad trigger a like response at home?

Deindustrialization Fears

If Latin Americans feared that globalization might inhibit industrialization or even induce local deindustrialization, they would have paid close attention to the competitive position of manufacturing at home relative to that abroad. The best indicator of foreign manufacturing's competitiveness would be its ability to drive down the relative price of manufactures in world markets through productivity advance. Thus, deindustrialization fears ought to have been manifested by a rise in Latin American tariff rates when the relative price of manufactures fell in world markets. Figure 2.6 suggests that there was, in fact, little to fear since, relative to the price of Latin America's key primary-product exports, the price of manufactures *rose* in world markets. Another way of saying the same thing is that the price of Latin American primary products fell in world markets relative to manufactures.[14] Of course, booms and busts may have mattered more to policy formation than long-run trends (which, after all, may simply have reflected long-run relative quality improvements in manufactured goods). In any case, if

Figure 2.6 Trend in Latin America's Relative Price of Export Products 1870–1950

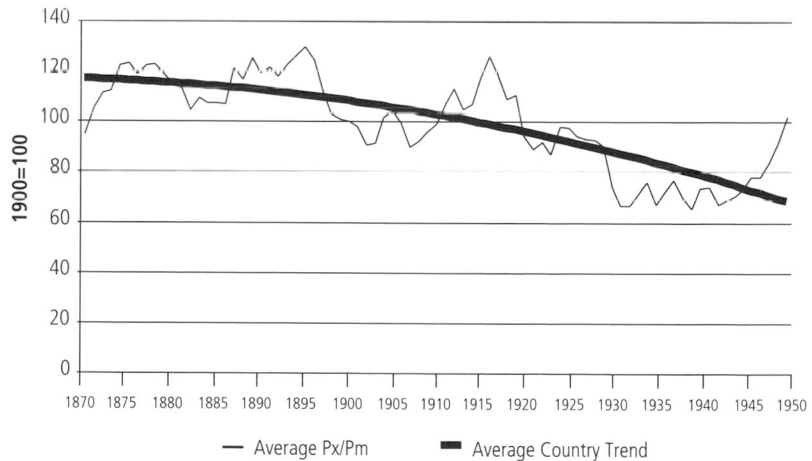

the qualitative literature is correct in identifying a switch in the motivation behind *belle époque* tariffs from revenue to industrial-protection goals late in the century, then we should see evidence of the switch in the terms-of-trade effect as well.

The Tariff-Transport Cost Trade Off

Whatever the arguments for protection of manufacturing, high transport costs on imports from one's trading partner are just as effective as high tariffs. And when transport costs fall dramatically, the winds of competition thus created give powerful incentive to import-competing industries to lobby for more protection. Since there certainly *was* a nineteenth-century transport revolution (O'Rourke and Williamson 1999: Ch. 3), manufacturing interests in the periphery must have been given plenty of incentive to lobby for protection as the natural barriers afforded by transport costs melted away. This connection was confirmed long ago for "the invasion of grains" into Europe from Russia and the New World (O'Rourke and Williamson 1999: Ch. 6). But what about Latin America and the "invasion of European manufactures"? There are two reasons to doubt that the tariff-transport cost trade-off, at least along sea lanes, prevailed with the same power in Latin America as in Europe. First, while overseas freight rates along the northward routes to Europe from the coasts of Latin America followed world trends by collapsing after the 1840s, they fell much less along the southward leg (Stemmer 1989: 24). The northward leg was for bulky Latin American staple exports such as beef, wheat, and guano, the high-volume, low-value primary products whose trade gained so much by the transport revolution along sea lanes. The southward leg was for Latin American imports such as textiles and machines, the high-value, low-volume manufactures whose trade gained much less from the transport revolution. Second, overseas freight costs were a much smaller share of the CIF price (cost, insurance, and freight) of traded manufacturers than was true of traded primary products in the 1860s (Stemmer 1989: 25). However, transport costs into the Latin American interior were much more important protective barriers for local manufacturers—except for Buenos Aires, Montevideo, and Rio de Janeiro—than were overseas transport costs. In 1842, the cost of moving a ton of goods from England to Latin American capital cities was (in pounds sterling): Buenos Aires and Montevideo 2, Lima 5.12, Santiago 6.58, Caracas 7.76, Mexico City 17.9, Quito 21.3, Sucre or Chuquisca 25.56, and Bogotá 52.9 (Brading 1969: 243–4).

Thus, transport revolutions along the sea lanes connecting Latin America to Europe probably had far less to do with tariff responses than did investment in railroads at home. Where railroads integrated the Latin American interior with the world economy, we should see a protectionist response to the extent that import-competing industries were successful in lobbying for protection from these new winds of competition.

The Stolper-Samuelson Theorem and Latin American Capitalists

Even if the motivation for Latin American tariffs lay with revenues or some other source, they were still protective. After all, tariffs served to twist relative prices in favor of import-competing sectors, thus suppressing growth in the export sector and stimulating urban-based manufacturing. But was protection of manufacturing a *central* motivation for high tariffs in Latin America, especially after the export-led boom filled treasuries with new revenues that reduced debt service to manageable dimensions?

Ronald Rogowski (1989) has used the Stolper-Samuelson theorem to search for a political economy explanation for those extraordinarily high tariffs during the *belle époque*. Though their economies certainly varied in labor scarcity, every Latin American country faced relative capital scarcity and relative natural resource abundance. Thus, according to Stolper-Samuelson thinking, Latin American capitalists should have been looking to form protectionist coalitions as soon as *belle époque* peace and growth began to threaten them with freer trade. In most cases, they did not have to look far, either because they managed to dominate oligarchic regimes that excluded other interests, or because they readily found coalition partners willing to help, or both.

Peace, political stability, and economic growth after the 1870s did not produce democratic inclusion. Most Latin American countries limited the franchise to a small minority of adult men until well into the twentieth century. Literacy and wealth requirements excluded most potential voters in virtually every country (Engerman and Sokoloff 2001). Of course, nonvoters found other (more violent) ways to express their political interests, but except for Argentina (after 1912), independent Cuba, postrevolutionary Mexico (after 1917), and Uruguay, restrictions on the adult male franchise did not fall until after 1930 when the votes of scarce labor began to count.

Throughout Latin America, potentially pro–free trade agrarian interests were politically underrepresented. Large landowners certainly dominated local politics in rural areas, but at the national level urban capitalists—linked to external trade and finance—played a dominant role.

Rogowski has argued to the contrary that unlike the United States, Canada, New Zealand, and other frontier regions, free-trading landowners seized control in nineteenth-century Latin America (Rogowski 1989: 47). Rogowski appears to have gotten both the politics and tariff policy outcome wrong. Four of the five Latin American agricultural exporters examined here (Argentina, Brazil, Colombia, and Uruguay) expanded export production in the late-nineteenth century by putting new lands to the plough or modernizing and extending pastoral production (cattle and wool) for export. In backward economies with high land-labor ratios, Rogowski argued that expanding trade should produce assertive free-trading landed interests pitted against defensive populist alliances of capitalists and workers. In all four of these frontier nations, however, tariff rates were substantially higher than in other world regions. Either export producing landowners had less political clout or had weaker free trade preferences than this account suggests—or both.

Free-trading mineral export interests usually had less direct leverage in governmental decision making, despite the size and significance of their investments. This is because modern mining enterprises tended to be foreign owned and concerned more with controlling labor agitation and keeping taxes low. In the case of the three mineral exporters (Mexico, Chile, and Peru), mining interests could have allied themselves with powerful regional agricultural interests to lobby against protection. Yet, this did not happen, nor were agricultural exporters very effective in forging free trade coalitions with other interests. Perhaps one reason it did not happen is that they feared even more likely alternatives to tariff revenues, such as higher taxes on mineral production or new taxes on land (Bulmer-Thomas 1994: 140).

In short, urban capitalists secured explicitly protectionist tariffs for existing and new industries beginning in the 1890s. They did so against weak opposition and in close collaboration with modernizing political elites. They did not yet need the populist coalitions that emerged in the interwar decades.

Policy Packages and Real Exchange Rate Trade-Offs

Few policies are decided in isolation from others. Indeed, there were other ways that Latin American governments could have improved the competitive position of import-competing industries if such protection was their goal, and they explored many of these alternatives in the 1930s and in the ISI years that followed. One powerful tool was manipulating the real exchange rate. If governments chose to go on the gold standard or to peg to a core currency, they got more stable real exchange rates in return. However, protection via real exchange rate manipulation was forgone, or so the argument goes. Was this true for Latin America even before the 1930s?

The Political Economy of Latin American Tariffs 1870s–1950s: Looking at All Factors in Conjunction

Empirical Strategy

Of course, the potential explanations for Latin American protectionism discussed above are not necessarily competing: each may have played a role between independence and the Great Depression. But even if we can show this to be true, we would still like to know which played the biggest roles in accounting for the fact that Latin America was so protectionist for the century before the 1930s. We would also like to know whether things were different before and after World War I.

Table 2.2 is an econometric attack on the problem in four ways: first, it treats the Latin American eight-country historical experience as a pooled OLS panel, 1870–1950; second, it treats the experience as comparative Latin American economic history by using country-fixed effects (TS), third, it explores the cross-section variance across these Latin American countries by using time-fixed effects (CS); and finally, it uses fixed effects for both (FE). Although Table 2.2 presents all four of these regression estimates, we prefer the comparative history (TS) in the second column and the fixed effects (FE) in the last column, primarily because we think the random effects (RE) and OLS results are suspect for three reasons. First, RE is best used when we think the estimated effects are based on a randomly drawn sample from a large population. Our Latin American sample is small, so randomness is doubtful. Second, RE is typically more efficient and unbiased when the unobserved explanatory variables are uncorrelated with the observed explanatory variables. In our case, we think it is likely that the unob-

Table 2.2 Comparative Regressions of Endogenous Tariff Determinants, 1870–1950

	ln (Own Tariff)			
	(1)	(2)	(3)	(4)
Dependent Variable	OLS	TS	CS	FE
ln(lagged exports/GDP)	–0.13	–0.07	–0.04	–0.10
	–3.34	*–1.42*	*–1.12*	*–1.90*
	–0.21	**–0.12**	**–0.08**	**–0.17**
ln(GDP/capita)	–0.21	–0.07	0.01	0.06
	–3.36	*–1.02*	*0.14*	*0.76*
	–0.26	**–0.09**	**0.01**	**0.08**
ln(population)	–0.12	–0.76	0.26	–0.66
	–2.99	*–10.23*	*4.79*	*–5.27*
	–0.31	**–1.91**	**0.67**	**–1.66**
ln(lagged partner tariffs)	0.24	0.22	0.19	–0.02
	5.55	*5.31*	*3.49*	*–0.37*
	0.25	**0.23**	**0.20**	**–0.03**
ln(effective distance)	0.07	–0.01	0.07	–0.12
	2.56	*–0.52*	*1.93*	*–1.71*
	0.12	**–0.03**	**0.13**	**–0.21**
ln(km railways)	0.05	0.37	–0.18	0.17
	1.58	*10.03*	*–5.28*	*2.70*
	0.15	**1.22**	**–0.60**	**0.57**
ln(primary school enrollment)	–0.29	0.07	–0.14	–0.01
	–5.02	*1.22*	*–2.09*	*–0.17*
	–0.43	**0.10**	**–0.20**	**–0.02**
Inflation	–0.006	–0.005	–0.004	–0.004
	–3.79	*–3.94*	*–2.40*	*–3.01*
	–0.17	**–0.15**	**–0.11**	**–0.12**
Inflation^2	0.00011	0.00014	0.00013	0.00015
	2.02	*3.08*	*2.47*	*3.26*
	0.09	**0.12**	**0.11**	**0.13**
Federal system	–0.03	–0.20	–0.16	–0.19
	–0.87	*–4.62*	*–3.60*	*–4.17*
	–0.04	**–0.23**	**–0.18**	**–0.22**
ln(% population urban)	0.15	–0.61	0.27	–0.39
	2.45	*–7.41*	*4.31*	*–3.99*
	0.22	**–0.92**	**0.40**	**–0.59**
ln(lagged *Px*/*Pm*)	–0.16	–0.33	–0.45	–0.26
	–2.39	*–5.35*	*–5.30*	*–3.28*
	–0.10	**–0.21**	**–0.29**	**–0.17**
Gold standard	0.30	0.15	0.22	0.12
	8.68	*4.94*	*5.40*	*3.04*
	0.36	**0.18**	**0.26**	**0.14**

Continued on next page

Table 2.2 Comparative Regressions of Endogenous Tariff Determinants, 1870–1950, continued

	ln (Own Tariff)			
	(1)	(2)	(3)	(4)
Dependent Variable	OLS	TS	CS	FE
Constant	5.86	10.91	2.49	11.05
	8.60	*15.82*	*3.03*	*8.82*
Country ($N = 8$) dummies?	No	Yes	No	Yes
Year ($T = 81$) dummies	No	No	Yes	Yes
R^2	0.3487	0.5801	0.5413	0.6546
Adjusted R^2	0.3323	0.5636	0.4497	0.5789
Number of observations	530	530	530	530
Fixed effects comments				n/t
F-stat, H_0: all coeff's = 0	21.25	35.15	5.91	8.66
F-stat, H_0: all dummies = 0	40.06	2.47	20.33/1.25	
Number of groups		8	76	8/76
Average obs. per group		66.3	7	66.3/7.0
Hausman test statistic		404	185	156/31

Notes: t-statistics are in italics. Beta values are in bold.

served time and country-fixed effects are correlated with the observed right-hand side variables in Table 2.2. Third, econometric tests indicate that the FE results appear to be more efficient and unbiased than the RE results. This is confirmed by the Hausman test, which essentially compares the RE and FE results to see if they are significantly different. The high test statistic reported in Table 2.2 indicates that they *are* substantially different, and that the RE results should be discarded.

Having revealed our bias in favor of FE, we must confess that it contains eighty-seven dummy variables, a big number that makes us nervous about the efficiency of the FE estimates. Our expositional strategy will be to focus on the TS results in column 2 and the FE results in column 4 of Table 2.2, but we shall note (the infrequent cases) where the time series (TS) and cross sections (CS) sharply differ.

The right-hand side variables used throughout are the following (all but dummies in logs):

Lagged Exports/GDP, a measure of export boom. We expect booms in the previous year to diminish the need for high tariff rates in the current year—if government revenues are the goal as the qualitative literature suggests—thus yielding negative coefficients in the regression;

GDP/capita and Primary School Enrollment, the latter a rate. We take both of these variables as proxies for skill endowments, with the expectation that the more abundant the skills, the more competitive the industrial sector, and the less the need for protection, thus yielding a negative coefficient in the regression;

Population. Large countries have bigger domestic markets in which it is easier for local firms to find a spatial niche. Alternatively, bigger populations imply higher density, and higher density implies more efficient internal tax administration and less need for revenue tariffs. Thus, the demand for high tariffs should be lower in larger countries, and the regression should produce a negative coefficient;

Lagged Partner Tariffs, measured as a weighted average of the tariff rates in the trading countries' markets, the weight being trade volumes, lagged. Strategic tariff policy suggests that Latin American countries should have imposed higher tariffs in the current year if they faced high tariffs in their main markets abroad in the prior year;

Effective Distance, the distance from each Latin American country to either the United States or the United Kingdom (depending on trade volume), that distance adjusted by seaborne freight rates specific to that route. If protection was the goal, effective distance should have been viewed as a substitute for tariffs, so the regression should yield a negative coefficient;

km Railways, railway mileage added in kilometers. Poor overland transport connections to interior markets serves as a protective device. Railroads reduce that protection, requiring higher tariffs to offset the effect. Thus, the regression should yield a positive coefficient;

Inflation and Inflation Squared, the rates in home markets. To the extent that Latin America used specific duties, we expect inflation to lower tariff rates, thus yielding a negative coefficient. However, very rapid inflation might well have triggered a speedier legislative reaction with increases in specific duties, thus yielding a positive and offsetting coefficient on the squared term in the regression;

Federal System, a dummy variable; if a federal system = 1, if centralized = 0. Federal governments had a stronger need for customs duties, while centralized governments could better exploit internal revenue sources. Thus, the regression should report a positive coefficient;

Percent Population Urban, taken as share of population in cities and towns greater than 20,000. We take this urbanization statistic to be a proxy for the lobbying power of urban capitalists and artisans, thus yielding a positive coefficient in the regression;

Lagged Px/Pm. This terms of trade variable measures the price of each *j*th Latin American country's primary product exports (Px_j) relative to the price of import products (*Pm*) in world markets. There are two possible results here, and they will help discriminate between two hypotheses: While the export-share variable includes the combined effect of both price and quantity booms, the terms-of-trade variable here could also have a separate influence if the revenue motivation was dominant. This implies a negative coefficient since a boom in *Px* implies a boom in imports and in tariff revenues, thus diminishing the need for high tariff rates. Alternatively, if deindustrialization fears were dominant, a positive coefficient should appear. That is, as productivity growth achieved by industrial trading partners lowered the relative cost of manufactures in the long run (thus raising *Px*/*Pm*), a greater threat to import-competing industries in Latin America would be generated (e.g., inviting deindustrialization), encouraging a protective tariff response. In short, price shocks in world markets that were good for Latin American export sectors were bad for import-competing sectors. Thus, the sign on ln(lagged *Px*/*Pm*) should tell us whether revenue motivations dominated deindustrialization fears;

Capital inflows. This variable measures annual British capital exports to the Latin American country in question. It is expected that countries favored by British lending would have less need for tariff revenues and thus would have lower tariffs.

Gold Standard. A dummy variable that takes on a value of one when the country is on the gold standard or pegged to a core currency. It is expected that countries that give up some control over the real exchange rate will raise tariffs to help protect the now more exposed import-competing industries.

The Determinants of Latin American Tariffs, 1870–1950

Table 2.2 suggests that the regression model does quite well in accounting for almost a century of Latin American tariff policy. Furthermore, the *t*-statistics on all these variables are typically high enough to pass conventional significance tests. Most importantly, almost everything seems to be of right sign (taken from the TS column in Table 2.2). The results are organized around nine issues:

1. Revenue Goals

Consistent with government revenue motivation, the coefficient on ln(lagged exports/GDP) is negative (–0.07). While the estimate does not pass conventional significance tests for TS (*t*-statistic –1.42), it does for FE (–1.90). Thus, export booms were correlated with lower tariff rates (but perhaps even higher tariff revenues). Symmetrically, export slumps were correlated with higher tariff rates (to extract higher tariff revenues). Furthermore, this revenue effect was fairly big, as measured by the beta coefficient (–0.12 in TS and –0.17 in FE) entered in bold in the row under the *t*-statistic.[15] Furthermore, we shall see in a moment that revenue motivation is also confirmed by the coefficient on the terms of trade variable. In combination, these two variables tell us that revenue goals were one of the more important motivations driving Latin American tariffs to such lofty heights over the eighty years before 1950. Note, however, that the Federal System dummy has the wrong sign in both the TS and FE results, and the result is highly significant. Our expectation was that federalist governments, prior to the interwar rise in the welfare state, would have had more difficulty securing local taxes, and thus would have had to rely more heavily on customs duties. While this may have been the case during the first half-century of independence, it was not the case after 1870. The coefficient on Federal System is negative in TS (–0.20), not positive, and significant. It is negative everywhere in Table 2.2 and significant everywhere but in the OLS version. This result suggests to us that in a Latin America with a turbulent past, member states wanted to keep their federal governments weak.

2. Relative Price of Manufactures in World Markets

If there were deindustrialization fears in Latin America, they should have been reflected by changes in the relative price of manufactures. Table 2.2 explores the inverse of the relative price of manufactures (*Px*/*Pm*), namely the price of Latin American primary-product exports divided by the price of manufactures, both quoted in British or U.S. markets. *Pm* is a weighted average of the commodities imported by each Latin American country, and *Px* is a weighted average of the prices of the main primary products exported by each Latin American country. When the relative price of manufactures (*Pm*) fell in world markets—reflecting relatively fast productivity advance in European or North American industry, the threat of an invasion of manufactures should, according to the deindustrialization-fears prediction, have triggered a powerful protectionist response in Latin America, but it did not. Indeed, the coefficient on ln(lagged *Px/Pm*) is *negative* and highly significant (–0.33 in the TS). We interpret this result to mean that revenue goals dominated protectionist goals. When the relative price of manufactures fell in world markets, the relative price of Latin American export goods rose, increasing foreign exchange earnings, generating an import boom, and creating a tariff revenue glut. With a revenue glut, high tariff rates could be reduced. Symmetrically, a decline in the relative price of Latin American exports put upward pressure on tariff rates, helping account for the observed "globalization backlash" during the Latin America *belle époque* as well as during the interwar years. But the backlash in Latin America was not driven by fear that the penetration of lower-priced foreign imports would destroy domestic industry, but rather by a fall of export prices eroding government revenue.[16] These results are consistent with those on ln(lagged exports/GDP). Revenue goals were central in driving Latin American tariff rates.

3. Protectionist Policy

While revenue motivations may have dominated tariff policy, that fact does not necessarily mean that protectionist forces were absent. After controlling for everything else, were these Latin American countries acting as if they had the protection of local manufacturing in mind when they set tariffs? The answer is yes. Consider the coefficients on two variables. The variable ln(effective distance) has the predicted negative coefficient (–0.01), but it does not pass conventional significance tests: countries that were protected by higher transport costs along the sea lanes connecting European and local Latin American ports, had lower tariffs, but the effect was weak. However, the variable ln(km Railways) has a positive and highly significant coefficient (0.37): countries that developed better internal railroad networks also raised tariffs, presumably to protect domestic producers from foreign penetration of their internal domestic markets. We also note that the beta coefficient on ln(km railways) is *much* bigger than that on ln(effective distance), and the second biggest in Table 2.2, fully consistent with our predictions that overcoming the hostile geography of Latin America was a much more important contributor to globalization forces than were productivity changes along the sea lanes. The combined effect of these two variables suggests that high Latin American tariffs were in part driven by protectionist goals. This does not mean, of course, that protectionist goals dominated revenue goals. Indeed, we have already seen that the response of tariff policy to terms-of-trade movements in world markets was dominated by revenue needs, not deindustrialization fears. They may have had those fears, but they did not dominate. Finally, note that the positive and significant coefficient on the Gold Standard dummy is also consistent with an explicit protectionist policy favoring import-competing industries. When Latin American countries pegged their exchange rates by going on the gold standard (or pegging to a core currency), they gave up much of their ability to manipulate the real exchange rate in favor of those industries. It appears that they increased tariffs as an offset.

4. Market Size and Density

Big countries, as measured by population size, had lower tariff rates (–0.76), a result consistent with the view that big domestic markets were more friendly to foreign imports since local firms would have found it easier to carve out regional and product niches, or since internal tax revenues would have been easier to collect in more densely populated countries, or both. Producers in countries with relatively small markets—such as Chile, Cuba, and Uruguay in our sample—would have found it harder to hide in spatial niches, thus lobbying for higher tariffs, and the low efficiency in internal tax collection may have favored their efforts. The beta coefficient (–1.91) is the biggest in Table 2.2.

5. Strategic Tariff Policy

These eight Latin American economies also seem to reveal strategic tariff policy behavior to the extent that the coefficient on ln(lagged partner tariffs) is positive (0.22) and significant: countries trading with high tariff partners (mainly the United States) adopted high tariffs themselves; countries trading with low tariff partners (mainly the United Kingdom) adopted low tariffs themselves. Still, the beta coefficient in TS (0.23) suggests that it was not a central determinant of Latin American tariff policy, at least prior to World War I, and the absence of any the effect in FE is consistent with that conclusion.

6. Education, Skills, and Industrial Competitiveness

The ln (Primary School Enrollment) variable is a proxy for skilled labor endowment, and thus for capacity to compete with imported foreign manufactures. The coefficients estimated here do not offer powerful support for the hypothesis: in the CS and OLS, higher skill endowment was associated with lower tariffs (on manufactured goods, of course); however, it was associated with higher tariffs in TS (0.07), and insignificant in FE. The negative coefficient on ln(GDP/capita) in CS is consistent with the result that richer countries—who get that way by being more productive and investing more in human and physical capital per capita—had lower tariff rates (–0.21), but none of the other coefficients are significant.

7. Stolper-Samuelson Political Economy
It appears that classic Stolper-Samuelson forces receive only mixed support from Latin American history, at least when we control for other factors. Urban interests should have favored protection in Latin America. The negative coefficient on ln(% population urban) does not support this assertion in TS (–0.61), but we note that it is *strongly* supported in the CS results (0.27) and highly significant. What was true in the cross section was not true in the time series, and we need to learn more about why.

8. Inflation and Specific Duties
Inflation had exactly the predicted effect during an epoch when specific duties were so much more common than ad valorem duties, although, as predicted, very rapid inflation rates apparently triggered faster adjustment. Thus, tariff rates were lower during inflationary episodes, as long as the inflations weren't too spectacular. However, judging by the beta coefficients, this inflation effect had a pretty modest influence on tariffs compared to other forces at work.

9. External Finance
Latin American countries that were successful in getting external finance would have had less reason to use high tariffs to augment revenues for short-run expenditure needs. Elsewhere, we have explored this idea using data on British capital exports before World War I (Coatsworth and Williamson forthcoming). While these data do not cover all sources of capital nor all years, we found a negative coefficient on the variable, in other words more foreign capital was associated with lower tariffs, a result consistent with revenue motivation.

Were the Determinants of Tariffs Different after the Belle Époque?

One would think that the determinants of tariffs might change over time. For example, Márquez (2002: Ch. 3) documents that after 1887 the increase in internal tax collections and better access to international credit markets made it possible to redirect Mexican tariff policy toward the goals of industrial growth. Were these forces ubiquitous across Latin America?

Table 2.3 reports an attempt to test the null hypothesis that the years after *belle époque* were the same as those before, at least in the way that tariffs were determined. The third column under each of the four estimation procedures, "All," covers the full 1870–1950 period, and it repeats Table 2.2. The other two columns report the estimation for the period up to 1913 (the *belle époque*) and after 1914 (the post–*belle époque* interwar dark ages). The comparison is not without problems, since the data base for the earlier period is probably not as good; indeed, the *belle époque* is missing many country-year observations. Nonetheless, we predict the tariff levels for both periods, and then perform a *t*-test to see if the means are the same in the two periods. The *t*-test is performed three times each for both the OLS and the time series: 1870–1913 versus 1870–1950 (was the *belle époque* the same as the full period?); 1914–50 versus 1870–1950 (was the post–*belle époque* the same as the full period?); and 1870–1913 versus 1914–50 (were the *belle époque* and the post–*belle époque* the same?). In all cases, we can reject the null hypothesis that the predicted levels are the same.

So, not only were tariffs very high in the *belle époque*, but the determinants of tariff policy were different then too. How were they different? Consider the time series results in Table 2.3 (where country dummies = country fixed effects). Some of the tariff determinants remain unchanged on either side of 1913, such as population size, railways, effective distance, and urbanization (our Stolper-Samuelson proxy). Two remain unchanged in sign, but change in magnitude: the impact of inflation on tariff rates was much more powerful after 1913 than before, and being on the gold standard served to raise tariffs much more (and more significantly) after 1913 than before. Another underwent no change in sign or magnitude when we might reasonably have expected the opposite: the impact of ln(lagged *Px*/*Pm*) was pretty much the same before and after World War I, implying that revenue needs dominated deindustrialization fears even after the *belle époque*. The remaining five explanatory variables *did* undergo change. Consider three. First, strategic tariff policy as reflected by ln(Lagged Partner Tariffs) was not only more powerful after 1913, but was not present at all in the *belle époque*. The rise of strategic tariff policy in Latin

Table 2.3 Were Tariff Policy Determinants Different after the *Belle Époque*?

	ln(Own Tariff)					
	(1)	(2)	(3)	(4)	(5)	(6)
	Pooled OLS			Time Series		
Dependent Variable	1870–1913	1914–1950	All	1870–1913	1914–1950	All
ln(lagged exports /GDP)	0.13	–0.55	–0.13	0.01	–0.36	–0.07
	2.47	*–9.46*	*–3.34*	*0.13*	*–4.66*	*–1.42*
	0.29	**–0.78**	**–0.21**	**0.02**	**–0.52**	**–0.12**
ln(GDP/capita)	0.27	–0.83	–0.21	0.09	–0.51	–0.07
	3.19	*–8.75*	*–3.36*	*0.84*	*–3.05*	*–1.02*
	0.38	**–1.01**	**–0.26**	**0.13**	**–0.62**	**–0.09**
ln(population)	0.36	–0.71	–0.12	–0.35	–1.12	–0.76
	6.05	*–9.09*	*–2.99*	*–2.36*	*–5.47*	*–10.23*
	1.07	**–1.52**	**–0.31**	**–1.06**	**–2.40**	**–1.91**
ln(lagged partner tariffs)	0.44	0.22	0.24	–0.01	0.24	0.22
	7.00	*3.68*	*5.55*	*–0.14*	*3.77*	*5.31*
	0.59	**0.21**	**0.25**	**–0.01**	**0.23**	**0.23**
ln(effective distance)	0.30	0.06	0.07	0.02	0.01	–0.01
	6.58	*1.83*	*2.56*	*0.03*	*0.88*	*–0.52*
	0.54	**0.12**	**0.12**	**0.03**	**0.01**	**–0.03**
ln(km railways)	–0.20	0.32	0.05	0.20	0.49	0.37
	–5.67	*6.04*	*1.58*	*4.40*	*3.38*	*10.03*
	–0.80	**0.83**	**0.15**	**0.82**	**1.27**	**1.22**
ln(primary school enrollment)	–0.08	–0.22	–0.29	–0.20	0.06	0.07
	–0.87	*–2.41*	*–5.02*	*–2.61*	*0.58*	*1.22*
	–0.12	**–0.25**	**–0.43**	**0.31**	**0.07**	**0.10**
Inflation	–0.0022	–0.0084	–0.006	–0.0019	–0.0064	–0.005
	–1.29	*–3.61*	*–3.79*	*–2.61*	*–2.83*	*–3.94*
	–0.07	**–0.24**	**–0.17**	**–0.06**	**–0.10**	**–0.15**
Inflation^2	0.00008	0.00012	0.00011	0.00009	0.00013	0.00014
	1.33	*1.74*	*2.02*	*1.96*	*1.83*	*3.08*
	0.08	**0.11**	**0.09**	**0.08**	**0.12**	**0.12**
Federal system	–0.15	0.17	–0.03	–0.15	0.02	–0.20
	–3.07	*2.17*	*–0.87*	*–2.75*	*0.27*	*–4.62*
	–0.22	**0.17**	**–0.04**	**–0.23**	**0.02**	**–0.23**
ln(% population urban)	0.03	0.34	0.15	–0.01	–0.28	–0.61
	0.38	*4.17*	*2.45*	*–0.01*	*–1.42*	*–7.41*
	0.06	**0.46**	**0.22**	**0.00**	**–0.38**	**–0.92**
ln(lagged *Px/Pm*)	–0.39	–0.23	–0.16	–0.38	–0.42	–0.33
	–4.01	*–2.37*	*–2.39*	*–5.03*	*–3.91*	*–5.35*
	–0.24	**–0.14**	**–0.10**	**–0.23**	**–0.26**	**–0.21**

Continued on next page

Table 2.3 Were Tariff Policy Determinants Different after the *Belle Époque*?, continued

	ln(Own Tariff)					
	(1)	(2)	(3)	(4)	(5)	(6)
	Pooled OLS			Time Series		
Dependent Variable	1870–1913	1914–1950	All	1870–1913	1914–1950	All
Gold standard	0.28	0.28	0.30	0.04	0.18	0.15
	6.96	*5.16*	*8.68*	*1.07*	*3.22*	*4.94*
	0.41	**0.31**	**0.36**	**0.06**	**0.20**	**0.18**
Constant	–1.43	11.39	5.86	6.91	14.16	10.91
	–1.43	*10.85*	*8.60*	*5.89*	*7.99*	*15.82*
Country dummies?	No	No	No	Yes	Yes	Yes
Year dummies	No	No	No	No	No	No
R^2	0.3796	0.4709	0.3487	0.6917	0.5945	0.5801
Adjusted R^2	0.3501	0.4420	0.3323	0.6687	0.5578	0.5636
Number of observations	288	242	530	288	242	530
t-Tests on ln (predicted tariffs):						
1870–1913 = 1870–1950			–14.8133			–10.1379
1914–1950 = 1870–1950			–3.615			–3.6715
1870–1913 = 1914–1950			6.6729			5.198

Notes: t-statistics are in italics. Beta values are in bold.

America during the years when the global economy was disintegrating is certainly consistent with the traditional literature and with other recent quantitative work (Clemens and Williamson 2001). Second, and much to our surprise, the revenue effects as measured by ln(lagged exports/GDP)—export booms being associated with lower tariffs and export slumps with higher tariffs—was entirely a *post*-1913 phenomenon: when we control for everything else, the effect of Exports/GDP was absent from the *belle époque*, a result completely at odds with the "unconditional" qualitative literature. Third, the negative association between tariff height and Federal System was entirely a pre-1913 phenomenon, a result consistent with the view that after the nation-building chaos between the 1820s and the 1870s members were suspicious of federal authority and kept them weak, but that this suspicion had evaporated by World War I.

Concluding Remarks and an Agenda on Historical Persistence

This chapter started by uncovering a fact that has not been well appreciated. Tariffs in Latin America were far higher than anywhere else from the 1860s to World War I, long before the Great Depression. Indeed, tariff rates in Latin America were even on the rise in the decades before 1914, a period that has been called the first globalization boom for the world economy and the *belle époque* for Latin America. To repeat our introductory remarks, this fact is surprising because: this region has been said to have exploited globalization forces better than most during the pre-1914 *belle époque*; standard economic histories say so little about it; most of us have always been taught to view the Great Depression as *the* critical turning point when the region is said to have turned toward protection and de-linked from the world economy for the first time.

High tariffs should have favored the domestic import-competing industry, and that was manufacturing in Latin America. It also should have taken some of the steam out of the export-led boom during the *belle époque*. But was it protection and deindustrialization-from-globalization fears that motivated those high tariffs?

This chapter showed that the explanation for high tariffs in Latin America since independence almost two centuries ago cannot lie with some perceived GDP per capita gains from protection, since such gains were never present in Latin America. On the contrary, those countries with the highest tariff rates in Latin America grew the slowest, and those with the lowest tariff rates grew fastest. The chapter then explored the motivation for Latin American tariffs as a revenue source, as a response to deindustrialization fears, as a strategic policy response to trading partners tariffs, as a redistributive device for special interests, and as a consequence of other political economy struggles.

The bottom line is that tariff formation in Latin America was complex and that *all* the forces suggested by the new literature on the political economy of tariffs were present. But revenue needs were always the key to those exceptionally high tariffs, and this motivation had its roots in the exceptional levels of military conflict in the region for a half-century or more when the rest of the world was enjoying Pax Britannica.

While the chapter concludes by showing exactly how *belle époque* tariff determination differed from the period after 1913, it does not report whether the same pro-protection conditions that existed more than a century ago also exist today. Surely, that should be the next item on any agenda that intends to explore the political economy of protection in Latin America. Even if generated by conditions and motivations long since erased by time, high tariffs in the distant past can remain high in the present as a result of institutional and political habit.

References

Anderson, James E. 1998. "Trade Restrictiveness Benchmarks." *Economic Journal* 108 (July): 1111–25.

Anderson, James E., and J. Peter Neary. 1994. "Measuring the Restrictiveness of Trade Policy." *The World Bank Economic Review* 8 (May): 151–69.

Bagwell, Kyle W., and Robert W. Staiger. 2000. "GATT-Think." National Bureau of Economic Research Working Paper 8005, Cambridge, MA.

Bairoch, Paul. 1972. "Free Trade and European Economic Development in the Nineteenth Century." *European Economic Review* 3 (November): 211–45.

Bairoch, Paul. 1989. "European Trade Policy, 1815–1914." In *The Cambridge Economic History of Europe,* vol. III, edited by P. Mathias and S. Pollard. Cambridge: Cambridge University Press.

Beatty, E. 2001. *Institutions and Investment: The Political Basis of Industrialization Before 1911.* Stanford: Stanford University Press.

Bhagwati, Jagdish, and Anne O. Krueger, eds. 1973–1976. *Foreign Trade Regimes and Economic Development.* 9 vols. New York: Columbia University Press.

Blattman, Christopher, Michael A. Clemens, and Jeffrey G. Williamson. 2002. "Who Protected and Why?: Tariffs the World Around 1870–1937." Paper presented to the Conference on the Political Economy of Globalization, Trinity College, Dublin, August 29–31.

Bloom, David E., and Jeffrey G. Williamson. 1998. "Demographic Transitions and Economic Miracles in Emerging Asia." *World Bank Economic Review* 12 (September): 419–55.

Brading, C. W. 1969. "Un analisis comparativo del costo de la vida en diversas capitales de hispanoamerica." *Boletin Historico de la Fundacion John Boulton* 20 (March): 229–63.

Bulmer-Thomas, Victor. 1994. *The Economic History of Latin America Since Independence.* Cambridge: Cambridge University Press.

Centeno, M. A. 1997. "Blood and Debt: War and Taxation in Nineteenth-Century Latin America." *American Journal of Sociology* 102 (May): 1565–605.

Cleary, D. 1998. "'Lost Altogether to the Civilized World': Race and the Cabanagem in Northern Brazil, 1750–1850." *Comparative Studies in Society and History* 401 (January): 109–35.

Clemens, Michael A., and Jeffrey G. Williamson. 2001. "A Tariff-Growth Paradox? Protection's Impact the World Around 1875–1997." National Bureau of Economic Research Working Paper 8459 (September), Cambridge, MA.

Clemens, Michael A., and Jeffrey G. Williamson. 2002. "Closed Jaguar, Open Dragon: Comparing Tariffs in Latin America and Asia before World War II." Paper presented to the Latin American and Caribbean Economic Association Meetings, Madrid, October 11–13.

Coatsworth, John H. 1988. "Patterns of Rural Rebellion in Latin America: Mexico in Comparative Perspective." In *Riot, Rebellion, and Revolution: Rural Social Conflict in Mexico,* edited by F. Katz. Princeton: Princeton University Press.

Coatsworth, John H., and Jeffrey G. Williamson. 2002a. "The Roots of Latin American Protectionism: Looking Before the Great Depression." National Bureau of Economic Research Working Paper no. 8999 (June), Cambridge, MA.

Coatsworth, John H., and Jeffrey G. Williamson. Forthcoming. "Always Protectionist? Latin American Tariffs from Independence to Great Depression." *Journal of Latin American Studies.*

Corbo, Vittorio. 1992. "Development Strategies and Policies in Latin America: A Historical Perspective." International Center for Economic Growth Occasional Paper No. 22 (April): 16–48. San Francisco.

Diaz-Alejandro, Carlos. 1984. "Latin America in the 1930s." In *Latin America in the 1930s,* edited by R. Thorpe. New York: Macmillan.

Dixit, Avinash K. 1987. "Strategic Aspects of Trade Policy." In *Advances in Economic Theory: Fifth World Congress,* edited by T. F. Bewley. New York: Cambridge University Press.

Dollar, David. 1992. "Outward-Oriented Developing Economies Really Do Grow More Rapidly: Evidence from 95 LDCs, 1976–1985." *Economic Development and Cultural Change* 40 (April): 523–44.

Dollar, David, and Aart Kraay. 2000. "Trade, Growth, and Poverty." World Bank, Washington, DC (October). Photocopy.

Drake, Paul W. 1989. *The Money Doctor in the Andes: The Kemmerer Missions 1923–1933.* Durham, NC: Duke University Press.

Edwards, Sebastian. 1993. "Openness, Trade Liberalization, and Growth in Developing Countries." *Journal of Economic Literature* 31 (September): 1358–94.

Engerman, Stanley L., and Kenneth L. Sokoloff. 2001. "The Evolution of Suffrage in the New World: A Preliminary Examination." Paper presented to the 2001 Cliometrics Conference, Tuscon, AZ, May 18–20.

Irwin, Douglas A. 1997. "Higher Tariffs, Lower Revenues? Analyzing the Fiscal Aspects of the Great Tariff Debate of 1888." National Bureau of Economic Research Working Paper no. 6239 (October), Cambridge, MA.

Irwin, Douglas A. 1998. "Changes in U.S. Tariffs: The Role of Import Prices and Commercial Policies?" *American Economic Review* 88 (September): 1015–26.

Irwin, Douglas A. 2001. "The Optimal Tax on Antebellum U.S. Cotton Exports." National Bureau of Economic Research Working Paper no. 8689 (December), Cambridge, MA.

Kindleberger, Charles P. 1951. "Group Behavior and International Trade." *Journal of Political Economy* 59 (February): 30–46.

Krueger, Anne O. 1983. "The Effects of Trade Strategies on Growth." *Finance and Development* 20 (June): 6–8.

———. 1984. "Trade Policies in Developing Countries." In *Handbook of International Economics*, vol. 1, edited by R. Jones and P. Kenan. Amsterdam: North-Holland.

Leff, Nathaniel H. 1982. *Underdevelopment and Development in Brazil.* Vol. 1, *Economic Structure and Change, 1822–1947* and vol. 2, *Reassessing the Obstacles to Economic Underdevelopment.* London: Allen & Unwin.

Lindert, Peter H., and Jeffrey G. Williamson. 2001. "Does Globalization Make the World More Unequal?" National Bureau of Economic Research Working Paper 8228 (April), Cambridge, MA.

Mares, D. 2001. *Violent Peace: Militarized Interstate Bargaining in Latin America.* New York. Columbia University Press.

Márquez Colin, Graciela. 1998. "Tariff Protection in México, 1892–1909: *Ad Valorem* Tariff Rates and Sources of Variation." In *Latin America and the World Economy Since 1800*, edited by J. H. Coatsworth and A. M. Taylor. Cambridge, MA: Harvard University Press.

———. 2002. "The Political Economy of Mexican Protectionism, 1868–1911." Ph.D. dissertation, Harvard University (March).

McGreevey, W. P. 1971. *An Economic History of Colombia, 1845–1930.* Cambridge: Cambridge University Press.

O'Rourke, Kevin H. 2000. "Tariffs and Growth in the Late Nineteenth Century." *Economic Journal* 110 (April): 456–83.

O'Rourke, Kevin H., and Jeffrey G. Williamson. 1999. *Globalization and History.* Cambridge, MA: MIT Press.

Prados de la Escosura, Leandro. 2002. "The Economic Consequences of Independence in Latin America." Universidad Carlos III, Madrid. Photocopy.

Prebisch, Raúl. 1950. "The Economic Development of Latin America and Its Principal Problems." Reprinted in *Economic Bulletin for Latin America* 7 (1962): 1–22.

Pritchett, Lant. 1997. "Divergence, Big Time." *Journal of Economic Perspectives* 11 (Summer): 3–18.

Rodriguez, Francisco, and Dani Rodrik. 2001. "Trade Policy and Economic Growth: A Skeptic's Guide to the Cross-National Evidence." In *NBER Macroeconomics Annual 2000*, vol. 15, edited by B. S. Bernake and K. Rogoff. Cambridge, MA: MIT Press.

Rogowski, Ronald. 1989. *Commerce and Coalitions: How Trade Affects Domestic Political Alignments.* Princeton, NJ: Princeton University Press.

Sachs, Jeffrey D., and Andrew Warner. 1995. "Economic Reform and the Process of Global Integration." Brookings Institution Papers on Economic Activity no. 1, Washington, DC.

Singer, Hans W. 1950. "The Distribution of Gains between Investing and Borrowing Countries." *American Economic Review* 40: 473–85.

Stemmer, Juan E. Oribe. 1989. "Freight Rates in the Trade between Europe and South America." *Journal of Latin American Studies* 21, (1) (February): 22–59.

Taylor, Alan M. 1998. "On the Costs of Inward-Looking Development: Price Distortions, Growth, and Divergence in Latin America." *Journal of Economic History* 58 (March): 1–28.

Williamson, Jeffrey G. 1998. "Globalization, Labor Markets and Policy Backlash in the Past." *Journal of Economic Perspectives* 12 (Fall): 51–72.

Notes

A data appendix for this chapter is available upon request from Williamson. The tariff data have been taken from collaboration between Jeffrey Williamson and Michael Clemens (2001), and we are grateful to the latter for allowing us to use that data here too. We have also received superb research assistance from Chris Blattman, David Clingingsmith, and István Zöllei. In addition, we have benefited from conversations with Graciela Márquez, Richard Cooper, Alan Dye, Toni Estevadeordal, Ron Findlay, Jeff Frieden, Steve Haber, Elhanan Helpman, Doug Irwin, Leandro Prados, Dani Rodrik, Dick Salvucci, Ken Sokoloff, Alan Taylor, and participants at joint development, international, and history workshops at Copenhagen, Harvard, and Yale, the Harvard Workshop on Political Economy, the Conference on the Political Economy of Globalization (Dublin, August 29–31, 2002), and the FTAA and Beyond conference meetings at Cambridge (May 31–June 1, 2002) and Punta del Este

(December 15–16, 2002). Williamson acknowledges with pleasure financial support from the National Science Foundation SES-0001362.

1 The average tariff rate is measured here as customs revenues (import duties only) as a share of total import values.

2 This chapter is part of an ongoing series of papers. In another, the present authors explore the qualitative evidence and the pre-1870 period in Latin America much more extensively (Coatsworth and Williamson forthcoming). In addition, Clemens and Williamson (2002) have explored the differences between Asia and Latin America. Finally, Blattman, Clemens, and Williamson (2002) have recently used the full tariff sample to explore many of the same issues raised in this paper.

3 As in Figure 2.1, we have calculated (but do not report) weighted tariff averages for the regional clubs in Figure 2.2, where weights are the country's total export share in regional exports or its GDP share. However, we prefer to treat countries as independent policy units regardless of size.

4 This finding—higher levels of protection in Asia than in Latin America before the 1970s—is confirmed by Alan Taylor (1998: Table 2, p. 7) even when more comprehensive measures of protection and openness are employed that include nontariff barriers.

5 Of course, quotas, exchange-rate management, and other non-tariff policy instruments served to augment the protectionist impact of tariff barriers far more in the 1930s than in the *belle époque*, when nontariff barriers were far less common.

6 Policy makers of that time didn't have the models, methods, and evidence that we exploit in Table 2.1, but they certainly had the intuition.

7 This section draws on a recent survey paper by Peter Lindert and Jeffrey Williamson (2001) and some new work on the impact of tariffs on growth before 1950 (Clemens and Williamson 2001).

8 And *late*-nineteenth century Latin American policy makers were certainly aware (Bulmer-Thomas 1994: 140). However, it is important to stress *late* since the use of protection specifically and consciously to foster industry does not appear to occur until well after the 1860s, e.g., Argentina with the 1876 tariff, Mexico by the early 1890s, Chile with its new tariff in 1897, Brazil in the 1890s, and Colombia in early 1900s (influenced by Mexican experience). True, Mexico saw some precocious efforts in the late 1830s and 1840s to promote modern industry, but these lapsed with renewed local and international warfare. So, the qualitative evidence suggests that domestic industry protection becomes a motivation for Latin American tariffs only in the late-nineteenth century.

9 A century later, things had changed, at least with the appearance of the

"money doctor," Princeton Professor Edwin Kemmerer, and his team of young economists (including Kossuth M. Williamson; see Drake 1989).

10 In the words of Bulmer-Thomas (1994: 140), the tariff "was the main source of government income in all [Latin] countries and virtually the only source in a few republics." It was still true of the late-nineteenth century, at least in Mexico where import duties between 1884–85 and 1890–91 were on average 46.1 percent of total revenue (Márquez 2002: 160). The big change in that share took place in the 1880s (Márquez 2002: 203).

11 We should note that for the *antebellum* United States Irwin (2001) also reports that the optimal export tax would have been about 50 percent at a time when U.S. cotton was King in world markets. In simple trade models, an export tax and an import tariff can be equivalent.

12 They were also specific in nineteenth-century Latin America (Bulmer-Thomas 1994: 141).

13 Exemplified by Dixit (1987) and recently surveyed in Bagwell and Staiger (2000).

14 Figure 2.6 is consistent, of course, with the initial findings of the great terms of trade debate launched by Prebisch and Singer a half century ago. Furthermore, and although we do not show it in Figure 2.6, all of that average downward trend is for six Latin American countries—Brazil, Chile, Columbia, Cuba, Mexico, and Peru—and none of it is for Argentina and Uruguay. In addition, the downward slide appears to start in the mid 1890s.

15 The beta coefficient is defined as the estimate of the coefficient on the explanatory variable in question multiplied by the ratio of the standard deviation of the underlying explanatory variable to that of the dependent variable. The beta coefficient is one indicator of the relative importance of different regressors; it is the number of standard deviations of the regressand explained by one standard deviation of the regressor.

16 This result appears whether the *Px/Pm* variable is measured as deviation from trend (e.g., Table 2.2) or as the actual *Px/Pm*, or even as trend and deviation component together. The result also appears to have been equally strong on either side of 1913.

3

Economic Integration in the Americas: European Perspectives

Anthony J. Venables and L. Alan Winters

Introduction

Europe's integration project has now been running for half a century, a period spanning the postwar birth of economic cooperation and the more recent enlargements and deepening of the union. The project has been enormously successful in both political and economic terms, although there have been frequent tensions and undoubted failures.

This chapter draws out some of the main messages from the European experience of integration. We look at both the political and the institutional development of the European Union, and at its economic development. What have been the driving forces behind the integration process? What institutions have developed to manage integration? What has been the impact of integration on trade flows and income levels across European countries?

We then endeavor to draw out the parallels between Europe and the Americas and the lessons from European experience for the FTAA. Evidently, the two continents are very different in both political and economic terms. On the economic side, integration has had a large impact on European trade and incomes, but one might argue that the Americas offer an even greater potential for trade creation and for using integration as a competitive force to drive economic development. Relatedly, however, the Americas may well suffer greater economic divergence as a result of integration than has Europe, its initial differences in size and income levels being so much larger.

On the political level, European experience suggests that achieving economic gains requires continuing and far reaching policy measures. These, in turn, require a deep political commitment to integration and the existence of institutions to promote integration and protect it from the inevitable inter-member frictions and preoccupations with national goals. In Europe progress has been driven largely by the Franco-German partnership and by the Brussels institutions. It is hard to see what their equivalents in the Americas might be.

The remainder of the chapter comprises five sections. The second explores the political economy of European integration, considering the history of and commitment to integration among its members, the roles of the institutions that it has created, and the particular nature of its inter-member relations. In each case it explores the parallels with and lessons for the FTAA, frequently arguing that these are rather weak. The third section assesses trade and production, arguing that Europe has seen both trade creation and trade diversion, that integration generally has been a force for increasing competition, and that specialization in member countries has tended to increase slowly. It discusses the importance of foreign direct investment and of (the relatively weak constraints on) national policies. It concludes that, on the whole, the evolution of the European economies has been in line with comparative advantage and efficiency. With its greater diversity between members, the FTAA may generate greater trade creation, investment flows, and competitive pressures than did European integration, but possibly at the expense of greater divergence between members. Reaping such benefits, however, will require ongoing integration, gradually rolling back the various barriers and frictions on interregional trade.

The fourth section contrasts labor markets and migratory flows between Europe and America: despite the former's greater commitment to labor mobility de jure, it is the latter that will have the more mobility de facto. The final section considers the experience of income convergence in Europe and again argues that America cannot be entirely confident that it will achieve similarly benign outcomes. This is especially so if the FTAA does not pursue a deeply integrationist agenda including a degree of redistribution.

Political Economy

This section reviews the histories of European integration and institutions to see what lessons they contain for the FTAA. It will become plain that the European and American processes are fundamentally different and that the casual drawing of parallels could be very misleading.

The EU as an Institution

A Grand Vision

European integration is an ancient aspiration, although its current manifestation arises from the geopolitics of the mid-twentieth century—the desperate need, following World War II, to find a way of preventing future Franco-German conflict, coupled with a strong sense of internationalism that saw the future in terms of institutionalized cooperation between countries.[1] Perhaps the most important factor in understanding the history of post-war European integration is to see that it was essentially a political-ideological phenomenon. It was not driven by the careful calculation of economic costs and benefits, and still less by trade negotiators, but by a grand vision that had fortunate economic side effects.

This fact has had fundamental effects on Europe's evolution, for the grand vision helps to move internal debates beyond mercantilism and the calculation of benefits issue by issue. It induces a generalized reciprocity whereby every party gains in the end, but everyone recognizes the value of the system as a whole and is prepared to accept losses on some deals. The day-to-day compromises necessary to achieve cooperative outcomes become easier to make, including easier to sell at home.

Grand vision is not completely absent from the FTAA, but at least for the major partners, it is not a primary motivation. Thus, great political will power will be required to prevent the FTAA process from being held to ransom by powerful interests in powerful countries. Moreover, that will power should not be created by too exclusive a focus on hemispheric issues, which would be bad for both the Americas and the rest of the world.

Political Institutions

The first major step in modern European integration was the European Coal and Steel Community (ECSC), whose origins illustrate the political motivation for integration. Its purpose was to stimulate the recovery of heavy industries in (West) Germany while making it impossible for their output ever to be used to wage war again. The proposal—championed by Jean Monnet and Robert Schuman—was that, by establishing a truly common European market in coal, iron, and steel, countries would become so interdependent that war would be not only "unthinkable, but materially impossible" (The Schuman Declaration, May 9, 1950). The customs union was supplemented by the

High Authority, which had the power to dictate national output quotas, establish maximum and minimum prices, and enforce competition. The High Authority was an administrative body, controlled in policy but not day-to-day matters by the Council of the Community on which the separate governments were represented and also by a European Parliament. The Court of Justice was established to oversee the legal aspects of the Community.

Following the ECSC, attempts were made to establish both a defense community and a political community. Both failed, so the "integrationists" were thrown back onto economic integration in the form of the European Economic Community (EEC), and the atomic energy community (Euratom), which were created in the Treaties of Rome in 1957. At first, the EEC and Euratom existed separately from, but parallel to, the ECSC, but in 1967 the three bodies were merged to form the European Communities (EC) with one commission (successor to the High Authority), one council, one parliament, and one court.

These institutions of integration have evolved and expanded, but the basic structures remain as they always were. Thus, although the EU now has a common currency and (limited) powers to make common political and foreign policies, it is in essence just a continuation of the old EEC, with institutions designed primarily for deep microeconomic integration. Its governance is shared between a commission, a council, a parliament, and a court.

The Commission comprises twenty commissioners appointed by member states for four-year terms, two from each of the larger members and one from the others. It initiates Union policy and executes it, but it cannot actually make policy—that authority falls to the Council. The Commission is explicitly supranational and is charged with preserving and promoting the European ideal.

The Council formally comprises the foreign ministers of all member states, although much business is conducted by other ministers concerned with specific issues (e.g., agriculture ministers discuss the Common Agricultural Policy [CAP]).[2] The Council shares executive power with the Commission. It may adopt the latter's policy proposals, in which case they become law, but it may not generally amend them. Decisions theoretically are taken by qualified majority vote, requiring sixty-two out of eighty-seven votes, in which votes are allocated to member states according to size. Until the 1990s, however, all countries informally had a right of veto on issues of alleged fundamental national interest (under the so-called Luxembourg Compromise). As a result, decisions had to be reached by trading compromises (often on unrelated issues) to obtain a unanimously acceptable package. Recently, strong efforts have been made to re-establish majority voting in most spheres (but not, for example, fiscal policy and various "pet areas" such as audio-visual policy) and there is hope that this will reduce the horse trading. Nonetheless, the tradition of consensus remains strong within the EU.

As a direct consequence of its relatively consensual nature, policy making in the EU is patchy, inconsistent, and ragged. Compromise and pragmatism have been the watch words, rather than efficiency and elegance, with particular members being granted official derogations from some measures, while the enforcement of others relies heavily on the Commission turning a blind eye. One might regret this, but it is notable that, despite a number of shocks, European integration has avoided serious setbacks for half a century.

The FTAA's goals are less ambitious than those of the EU, but nonetheless they will engage the fundamental beliefs and values of some member countries. Without the institutional depth or the political motivations of the EU there is a serious danger of stalemates. The issue will be particularly pressing in the United States, which has least to gain from the FTAA and probably the most confrontational attitude toward trade negotiation.

The Court of Justice interprets EU law. Its findings are binding even on member governments. The judges are appointed by member states, but they are required to be quite independent of national interests and cannot be removed by member governments. The dispute settlement procedure for the FTAA is not settled yet, but, following traditions in American regional blocs to date, it will presumably be intergovernmental and without direct effect in national law (i.e., rulings require domestic legislation to become effective).

The European Parliament has a small but growing role in the Union. It must be consulted by the Commission and the Council before deciding many issues, and it has some power over the EU budget. Its greatest power is to dismiss the Commission en masse, although this is such an unwieldy weapon that it is of little practical use. The FTAA proposes no popular legislature at all.

These institutions form a constitutional structure just as complex and delicately balanced as the U.S. Constitution, but without, of course, its democratic legitimacy. Like the latter, they have to balance "states' rights" against the center and rely on powerful legal bodies for enforcement. Arguably such balances are necessary to create the confidence that allows member governments to proceed with deeper aspects of integration that impinge directly on issues of sovereignty and internal distributions of income.

Although it is fashionable, and to some measure warranted, to decry Brussels' bureaucracy and interventionism, one should not lose sight either of its origins or of its role in the integration process. The institutions stem from a period when there was much greater faith in governments than exists now, when governments were much more heavily involved in economic management, and when the essential task was political. Arguably, the subsequent difficulties were not due to the original structures per se, but their inability to evolve as circumstances changed. The danger of such inflexibility is another lesson for today's would-be integrators.

Inflexibility is similarly the problem with agriculture. The CAP stems from a period when agriculture provided a substantial part of employment in all six original member countries and was strongly protected. The error should be seen less in the original policies, which were thought to make sense at the time, but in the danger of giving particular sectors special constitutional standing (agriculture is singled out in the Treaty of Rome) and/or their own bureaucracies. Each makes reform very difficult when circumstances change. As the FTAA is put together, it is important to avoid institutionalizing the special cases that are bound to arise, and instead to recognize them as explicit failures and exceptions so that they can be addressed later.

Redistribution

The original six EEC members were fairly homogenous in terms of income levels, but later expansions of the membership began to introduce a wider spread, especially the southern enlargement to Greece (1981) and Spain and Portugal (1986). Their accession raised serious issues of intra-EEC distribution, not only in terms of helping the new poorer members to catch up, but also within existing members. The so-called structural funds for poorer regions were greatly strengthened with the southern enlargement as a way of assuaging fears, especially in Britain, that poorer, nonagricultural regions would suffer. In fact, distribution is a major factor in much EU decision making, and the existence of institutions to address it helps to prevent it from becoming a barrier to progress and an impediment to efficiency-enhancing decisions. The transfer mechanism—small as it is compared with those in federal and unitary states—has been essential to the running of the EU since the southern accession.

Guardians of the Vision

European integration has always been a rather "on and off" affair with periods of enthusiasm and rapid advance followed by periods of doubt and retrenchment. Understandably, the former are associated with economic booms and the latter with recessions. Thus the early 1980s found the EU very much down in the dumps. After the severe anti-inflationary policies at the beginning of the decade, the United States and Japanese economies began to recover, but those of the EU seemed firmly stuck in the mire. Moreover, the rapid increase in intra-EU trade that had characterized the early stages of integration seemed to have halted or even gone into reverse. The cry was frequently heard that "the steam had gone out of integration" and doubts were expressed about the viability of the EU as an institution, let alone about any further progress.

During such depressions, the Commission's role as the guardian and champion of the European ideal has been vital to the goal of integration. While member governments, and thus the Council of Ministers, are focusing on their local problems, the Commission is constitutionally required to take a broader, longer, and more European view. In the mid-1980s its response to the lethargy of the European economy was dramatic and imaginative. It had long been recognized that the actual integration of the EU economies fell short of the aspirations of the Treaty of Rome. Recalling the stimulus that the initial creation of the EEC had induced, and following the prevailing intellectual trend toward economic liberalism, the Commission proposed a bold step toward complete economic integration with the launch in 1986 of the Single Market Initiative.

Similarly, the Commission was the driving force behind the Maastricht Treaty of 1992, which formally created the EU and extended the competence of the Union to foreign affairs and justice. This move was far from popular, being rejected by a referendum in Denmark and very nearly so in France. It illustrates a further cycle in the dynamics between the Commission and the states: flushed with one success (in this case the single market), the Commission attempts to follow it with further integration and centralization, only to find it rejected by governments and electorates. These rejections, however, do not threaten the basic fabric of the common market—a tribute to its deep foundation in European perceptions and to its pragmatic and non-confrontational mode of progress.

Intrabloc Relations

As noted already, the EU and the FTAA have different objectives for the degree and style of their integration. Behind them lie fundamental differences in their structures and intrabloc relationships, which further complicate the drawing of parallels between the two groups.

The Balance of Power

The preceding section showed the importance of political will to EU development, and following from that, its institutional depth. A key driver of both has been, and continues to be, the Franco-German relationship.

It is at this fundamental level that the FTAA looks most different from the EU. Not only is the postwar political imperative absent, but so too is the balance of power that obtains within the EU. Table 3.1 gives income shares of countries in the Americas and in the EU. The motive force in Europe has been the imperative for two roughly equal-sized powers to cooperate and create something new that is different from either of them. The third power, the United Kingdom, is large enough to be taken seriously but not to derail the whole enterprise. As Table 3.1 shows, France, Germany, and the United Kingdom accounted for 19.7 percent, 26.6 percent, and 14.1 percent of EEC output in 1973. The American predicament, on the other hand, is that, while without the United States the FTAA would be stillborn, the United States has only relatively mild incentives to cooperate. Thus with 78.8 percent of total American output in 2000, the United States clearly has a veto over the current conception of the FTAA—and probably over any other, for it is difficult to see it blessing (or even tolerating) a regional market of which it is not part. Overall, the different size distributions of members in the FTAA and the EEC make it difficult to perceive strong parallels in the two groups' political dynamics.

Alternative Visions

A recurrent theme of European integration has been the United Kingdom's reluctance to commit to the integrationist goal while simultaneously attempting to give market economics a central role in the European edifice. Indeed, more or less throughout the postwar

Table 3.1 GDP Shares, the Americas and Europe

	2000	1958	1973	1998
Americas				
U.S.	78.8			
Canada	5.7			
Mexico	4.8			
Brazil	4.7			
Other South America	5.2			
Central America and Caribbean	0.8			
Europe				
EU15				
Germany		20.1	26.6	25.1
France		21.2	19.7	17
United Kingdom		23.2	14.1	16.7
Italy		11	12.9	14
Other EU		7.3	11.7	27.2
Other non-EU		17.2	15	0

Source: World Development Indicators, World Bank.

period Britain has sought open markets but no, or very limited, political integration.

The attitude of the United States toward the FTAA is similarly market based, anti-bureaucratic, and Anglo-Saxon pragmatic, but its position is utterly different. The challenge in the FTAA is not to accommodate a significant player's doubts, but to try to bring the critical player far enough on board to make the game worthwhile. One might see stronger parallels between the United Kingdom's position and those of Mexico (4.8 percent of output) and Brazil (4.7 percent), but even here the circumstances are different. Mexico may wish the FTAA would go away—in order to keep its preferred status with the United States—but would not wish to exacerbate the latter's dilution by remaining outside if the FTAA goes ahead (similar to Canada's attitude to NAFTA). Brazil also has clear reservations about the FTAA, including that it would constrain interventionary policies too much. Brazil would almost certainly be prepared to stay outside if it could build its own minor trading arrangement with certain neighbors. This would look a little like the divide between the EEC and the European Free Trade Association (EFTA) of the 1960s, and may similarly see the dominant economy in the minor grouping experiencing irresistible pressure to defect.

Numbers

Numerically, and in terms of size distribution, the creation of the FTAA (thirty-five countries) parallels the enlargement of the EU from a "core" of fifteen members to twenty-five, but that is as far as the parallel goes. The FTAA and the EU are, as we have seen, fundamentally different and whereas the former is constructing its institutions de novo, the EU is absorbing new (and relatively small) members into its existing structures. In addition, EU enlargement is more concerned with transfers than is the FTAA and is less reversible. (It is virtually impossible to leave the EU, let alone be ejected from it. The FTAA can contemplate exit and entry purely because it is not so "deep".)

Trade and Production

Since the FTAA is primarily a trade agreement, as opposed to an attempt at deeper political integration, we now turn to the economics of integration. The EU is far from a perfect parallel, being more compact geographically, more homogenous in income levels, more intent on deeper integration, and formed in an earlier era than the FTAA, but it provides our best view of the long-run effects of regionalism on trade patterns. The European trade regimes of the late 1950s were about as restrictive as are current regimes in Latin America, thus the internal trade liberalisation foreseen in the FTAA is probably about the same size as that of the EEC's original members, with many countries having initial tariffs of around 15 percent (see Table 3.2).

As well as experiencing internal integration, the EU also adopted a common external trade policy and liberalized its external trade significantly, and we have yet to see if FTAA members will do similarly.[3] Nonetheless, EU experience probably provides an upper bound on the

Table 3.2 Tariff Rates, the Americas and Europe

Americas	2001	Europe	1957
U.S.	4.1	Germany	8.3
Canada	4.1	France	17.2
Mexico	15.9	BeNeLux	11
Brazil	13.2	Italy	17.5
Other South America*	11.7		
Central America and Caribbean*	11.5		

Sources: Political and Economic Planning (1962), Ocampo and Bustillo (2003).
* Simple average

prospects for trade reorientation following the FTAA. For example, its greater compactness and homogeneity will have allowed greater growth in intraindustry trade than the FTAA will see; it has certainly been more hostile to internal barriers to trade than the FTAA will be—for example, it eliminated contingent protection internally and made little use of rules of origin.

European integration had a dramatic effect on the geographical patterns of members' trade. Every member has seen a strong reorientation of its trade toward other members following accession or the formation of the EEC. Moreover, this is as true of manufacturing (and probably services) as of the grotesquely distorted agricultural trade. Figure 3.1 plots the shares of three EU members' imports coming from the original EC-6. As an original member, Germany experienced increasing integration with the remaining five from 1957, with duty-free and quota-free access from 1968. The United Kingdom acceded on January 1, 1973 and Spain on January 1, 1986. The pattern is very clear: starting slightly before the formal date of the integration, the trade share starts to rise. It rises for ten to twelve years and then stabilizes. For Spain the growth is still continuing at the end of the period. Freund and McLaren (1999) have explored the dynamics of regionalism more formally using both trade shares and trade intensity indices.[4] For the latter—the more appropriate measure analytically—they find some evidence of anticipation effects, starting on average 2 years before formal integration, followed by 9 years of higher growth before achieving a new steady

Figure 3.1 Share of Imports from EC-6

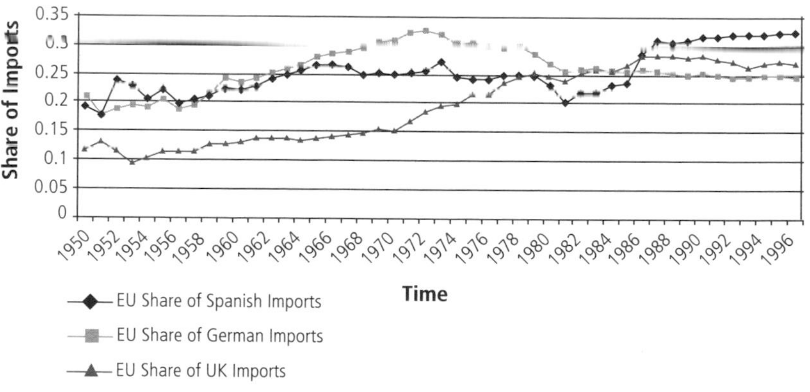

Source: European Commission

state.[5] On average EU countries increased their intrabloc trade intensity by 53 percentage points over this process.

Much of the growth in trade in Europe has been intra- rather than inter-industry trade. Table 3.3 reports levels of intraindustry trade for various EU member countries' intra-EU trade. They are high and growing, and far in excess of anything observed among American countries.

The economic effects of these changes in trade flows can be divided into two main types. First, trade permits industrial specialization, although the real income effects of this depend on whether or not countries are specializing according to their comparative advantage—the issue of trade-creation versus trade-diversion. Second, within industries, trade promotes competition and enables more efficient firms to expand and benefit from economies of scale. We look at the European experience with respect to these two types of effects.

Industrial Specialization, Trade Creation, and Trade Diversion

The benefits of changing interindustry trade flows arise as each country's production structure reorganizes to exploit comparative advantage and possible benefits from spatial clustering of sectors.

Table 3.3 Share of Intra-Industry Trade in Intra-EC Trade (as percentage of total intra-EC trade)

Country	1958*	1963*	1970*	1970**	1980**	1987**
Belgium-Luxembourg	0.54	0.60	0.66	0.69	0.70	0.77
Denmark	—	—	—	0.41	0.52	0.57
France	0.61	0.68	0.73	0.76	0.83	0.83
Germany	0.47	0.57	0.67	0.74	0.78	0.76
Greece	—	—	—	0.22	0.24	0.31
Ireland	—	—	—	0.36	0.61	0.62
Italy	0.42	0.48	0.59	0.63	0.55	0.57
Netherlands	0.50	0.57	0.64	0.67	0.73	0.76
Portugal	—	—	—	0.23	0.32	0.37
Spain	—	—	—	0.35	0.57	0.64
United Kingdom	—	—	—	0.74	0.81	0.77

Source: Sapir (1992).
* Computed with EC-6 trade data.
**Computed with EC-12 trade data.

Sectoral Specialization

There is evidence that EU integration has been associated with a rather modest increase in manufacturing specialization. Measures of the difference between the industrial structures of EU countries have been computed (at the level of thirty-six industrial sectors, Midelfart-Knarvik et al. 1999). All EU countries except the Netherlands have, since the late 1970s, seen their industrial structures become more dissimilar from that of other EU countries. Figure 3.2 reports these measures averaged over groups of countries according to the date of their accession to the EU. The different heights of the curves essentially reflect different country sizes (large countries tend to have similar industrial structures, so EC1 is relatively low because of the predominance of Germany, France, and Italy). More interesting are the different patterns of change. For the initial entrants there is a more or less

Figure 3.2 Krugman Specialization Indices

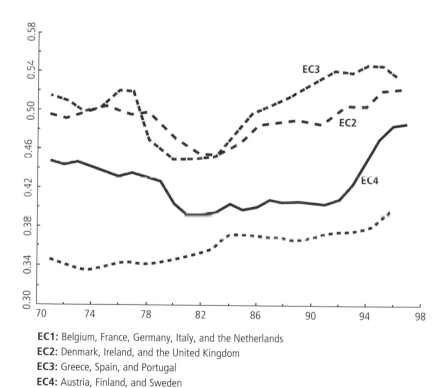

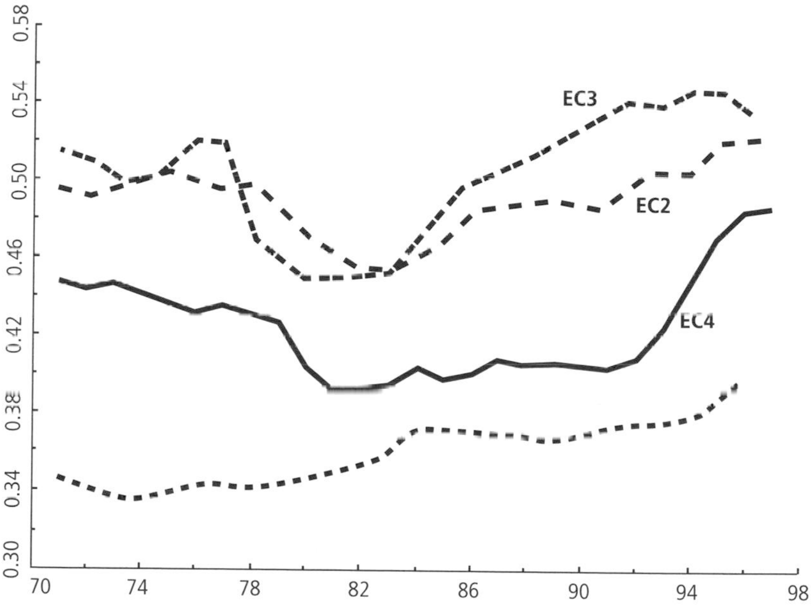

EC1: Belgium, France, Germany, Italy, and the Netherlands
EC2: Denmark, Ireland, and the United Kingdom
EC3: Greece, Spain, and Portugal
EC4: Austria, Finland, and Sweden

Source: Midelfart-Knarvik et al. (1999).

steady increase throughout the period, indicating industrial structures becoming more dissimilar. The 1973 and 1980s entrants (EC2 and EC3) exhibit an increase from the early 1980s. The last wave (EC4) shows increasing specialization from around 1992 onwards.

Econometric analysis of these changing patterns of specialization indicates that it is largely in line with intra-EU comparative advantage. For example, skilled-labor-intensive activities have tended to relocate toward skilled-labor-abundant countries, and research-and-development-intensive activities have relocated toward scientist-abundant countries (Midelfart-Knarvik and Overman 2002). However, reallocations in line with intra-EU comparative advantage are not necessarily welfare increasing, as they could be accompanied by trade diversion.

Analysis at the level of countries and thirty-six industrial sectors likely understates the degree of specialization that is occurring. At the level of quite narrow sectors there is evidence of increasing clustering of activity, and specialization is increasing at the subnational as well as the national level. However, despite this, EU countries and regions remain very much less specialized than comparable size geographical units in the United States. So far at least, integration has not caused specialization and clustering of activity to go as far as the U.S. experience suggests would be expected in a single country.

Trade Creation and Trade Diversion

It is frequently assumed that increased intrabloc trade is indicative of successful economic integration, especially in popular debate; but, of course, it shows no such thing. The traditional economic question hinges around whether the share increases as a result of trade creation or trade diversion. There is no doubt that European integration has been accompanied by a good deal of trade creation—both internal as well as so-called external trade creation—in which imports from outside the bloc displace members' domestic production and/or expand consumption. Thus, Truman's (1975) decomposition of apparent consumption of manufactures into shares attributable to imports from partners, imports from nonpartners, and domestic supplies shows both sources of imports growing strongly at the expense of the domestic share. Truman finds that out of fifty-three country-sector combinations observed from 1960 to1968, thiry-one display such "double trade creation," while a further thirteen display internal creation and external diversion. From 1975 to 1982 Jacquemin and Sapir (1989) find roughly similar proportions of double trade creation and less evidence of trade diversion, while Sapir (1992) finds double creation for aggregate EC-9 trade from 1980 to 1991.

The predominant pattern of double trade creation does not imply absence of trade diversion, as external trade should be compared with what it would have been in the absence of integration. There is an unavoidable need to specify the *anti-monde* when estimating integration effects. The simple before and after comparisons implicit above and in Figure 3.1 implicitly assume that in the absence of integration the shares would not have changed. That is manifestly flawed when different parts of the world economy have been growing at such different rates, and general levels of protection have been falling. Two approaches exist to modeling the *anti-monde* more explicitly. First, one can model trade flows in terms of prices and incomes and explicitly allow for the different tariffs faced by different suppliers. This requires considerable information and some effort to model the determinants of trade flows through time in a theoretically coherent fashion. Winters (1983) takes this approach to UK manufacturing trade following its accession to the EEC in 1973. He finds relatively little trade diversion, but certainly some evidence of it.

The second approach is to use a gravity model, which essentially uses trade between other (unrelated) countries to identify the *anti-monde* for partners' trade. Gravity models typically (and correctly) refer to total trade rather than just manufactures. Hence for Europe, they would be expected to display greater diversion, and this is, indeed, evident from the more careful gravity-model studies extant.

The gravity model explains trade between two countries in terms of their incomes, populations, location, and geographical characteristics, plus at least two sets of dummy variables to capture the effects of each regional arrangement: one on intrabloc trade and one on trade between partners and nonpartners. The coefficients on such dummy variables reflect a huge variety of effects and can be significantly different from zero at any point in time. Hence to measure integration effects one needs to observe not their levels but their changes over periods when regional integration has occurred.

Within Europe, Bayoumi and Eichengreen (1997) find strong signs of EEC/EFTA trade falling below expected values as the EEC was formed, and some evidence of the acceding countries' trade with nonmembers similarly falling below par as they joined.[6] Sapir (1998) similarly finds EU/EFTA trade penalized by EEC formation and enlargement. Soloaga and Winters (2001) use a much wider range of countries than just Europe to define their *anti-monde*, but at the expense of considering only the period 1980–96. They use three dummies to capture trade effects, breaking the extrabloc trade effect into an export and an import effect. Figure 3.3 reports Soloaga and Winters' results for the EU. In 1980 the EU shows unusually strong trade with nonpartners and lower than expected trade within the bloc. (This is a common result in gravity models based on large samples of countries.) As integration deepens and Iberia enters the EU, however, these effects decline absolutely—that is, intra-EU trade grows relative to expectations and extra-EU trade falls. Moreover, Soloaga and Winters show that these changes are statistically significant, suggesting the presence of trade diversion.

The 1980s and 1990s are an interesting period for observing the effects of union integration, for deepening and enlargement were not accompanied by major external liberalizations—only the Tokyo Round. Thus these results are perhaps a good indicator of the effects of the FTAA if members do not adjust their current levels of trade barriers against the outside world. Under these circumstances, trade diversion *is* a significant threat.

Figure 3.3 1986 Single European Act: Spain and Portugal Joined EC

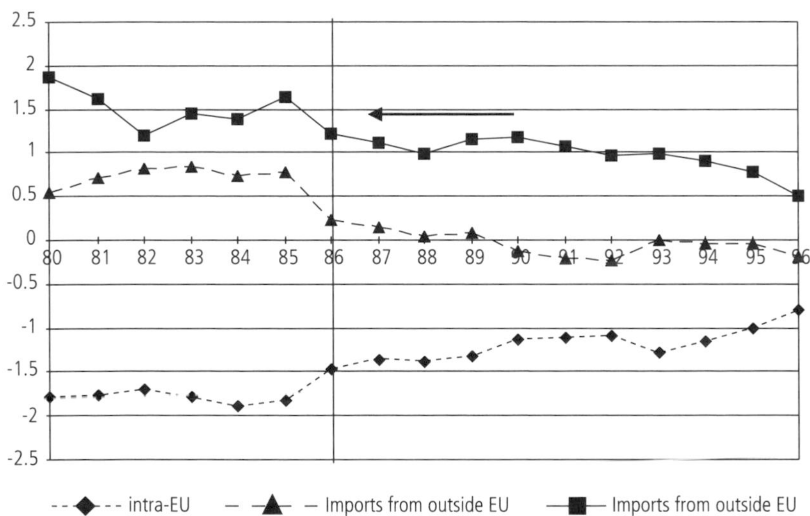

Source: Soloaga and Winters (1999).

Specialization, Trade Creation, and Trade Diversion in the Americas

Does the European experience hold any messages for the possible effects of integration in the Americas? The European experience indicates that trade diversion can and does occur. There are, however, reasons for thinking that it does so to a lesser extent in the Americas than in the EU. In a north-north regional integration scheme all member countries' comparative advantages are "on the same side" of the world average. These are precisely the circumstances in which trade diversion is likely, as trade is diverted in line with intra-EU comparative advantage rather than world comparative advantage. For example, labor intensive imports may be diverted from low-income nonmember countries to middle-income members. Integration in the Americas includes countries with a wider range of comparative advantage, so countries' intra-FTAA comparative advantage is more likely to coincide with their full world comparative advantage. There is then less likelihood of trade diversion occurring (Venables 2003).

Gains from specialization according to comparative advantage are increasingly achieved through the development of production networks and trade in parts and components, as well as through trade in final products. However, such trade crosses borders multiple times, and is vulnerable to disruption and small trade frictions. Simply eliminating tariffs may be necessary, but is probably not sufficient for the promotion of such trade, suggesting the need for deep integration. Furthermore, comparative advantage is determined by factor prices and factor productivity. Technology transfer—for example by multinational firms—is necessary if factor-endowment-based comparative advantage is to be fully exploited.

Competition, Scale, and Market Integration

Gains from trade liberalization derive not just from specialization and clustering of activity, but also from intra industry reorganization. Small, national, segmented markets are liable to be dominated by a few national producers, possibly operating at the subnational scale and exploiting considerable monopoly power. Market integration should remove this segmentation, allowing firms to compete more effectively in other national markets and permitting expansion of relatively efficient firms. It permits firms to be larger *and* markets to be more competitive. EU experience has indicated that, in some sectors at least, achieving these gains can be quite difficult. Even when tariffs have been eliminated, markets appear to remain segmented, with substantial price differentials between countries, and borders continuing to have a strongly negative effect on trade flows. These observations were among the motivations for the Single Market Initiative (SMI).

The Single Market Initiative was launched in 1986 for completion in 1992 with the objective of eliminating market segmentation and "completing the internal market." The economic policy measures introduced fall into four main categories: the simplification or removal of frontier formalities, facilitating and speeding the flow of goods across borders; the simplification of product standards, in particular the adoption of the "mutual recognition principle," whereby goods approved for sale in any member state are deemed acceptable in all; the deregulation of transport sectors, allowing for improved efficiency in the internal distribution of goods; and the opening up of public procurement to supply from all member states.

Although individually small, these measures were estimated collectively to reduce the costs of trade across borders by an amount equal to several percent of the value of goods traded. More importantly, their indirect effects were predicted to lead to gains equivalent to several percent of EU GDP, as markets became more competitive *and* firms reorganized, increasing their scale to that of the larger integrated market. Evidence on actual gains is patchy. The SMI was accompanied by a burst of merger activity, and there is some evidence of further trade creation (Pelkmans 2001). Griffith (2001), in a study of UK manufacturing, finds a significant increase in both labor productivity and total factor productivity in establishments in sectors that were particularly affected by the SMI. Increased scales of operation have been attributed to the SMI—particularly in sectors where liberalization of public procurement was important—although the size of firms in the EU remains generally smaller than their U.S. counterparts.

What messages come from this experience for FTAA? First, the potential gains from scale and competition effects will depend heavily on country characteristics. The industrial sectors of many developing and middle-income countries are characterized by low levels of competition, so the pro-competitive effects of trade might be particularly large. However, countries at different stages of development have relatively low levels of intraindustry trade. In sectors where there is no comparative advantage and local firms are weak, the response to opening is likely to be loss of firms, rather than reorganization into larger and more efficient firms able to export to northern markets.

Second, to realize the gains, the European experience points to the importance of "deep integration." The pro-competitive and scale-economy gains of market integration can be impeded by frontier frictions that individually appear quite minor, but collectively allow firms to retain dominant positions in their home markets. The list of such frictions is long. A free trade area, as opposed to a customs union, is bound to retain border formalities as well as rules of origin. Contingent protection has been widely used both by the United States and within MERCOSUR, and its "trade chilling" effects are well known. Meeting national product standards is costly, and harmonization of standards almost impossible. Europe took the mutual recognition route, but this involves a level of acceptance of foreign standards and a willingness to delegate product approval to foreign institutions that is inconceivable in the FTAA.

Finally, intraindustry trade can occur for quite distinct reasons. Implicit in the discussion so far is the idea that this trade is primarily horizontal (cross hauling goods at the same stage of production). However, some intraindustry trade is vertical (trading inputs or parts and components within a sector).[7] It is possible to envisage strong growth in vertical trade (for example, along the lines suggested by Ethier [1998] in his celebration of regionalism), as has already occurred between the United States and Mexico. But in this context too, small border frictions present significant trade barriers. Timely delivery is extremely important, and parts and components may cross borders many times, embodied in different stages of production. Deep integration is equally important in promoting this trade.

Foreign Direct Investment

Accompanying the rapid growth of trade in the EU has been an expansion of foreign direct investment (FDI). World FDI stocks have grown faster than both income and trade in recent decades, and the EU-fifteen holds around one-third of the stock of inward FDI. This share surged to over 40 percent at the time of the Single Market Initiative driven by a cross-border merger wave. The importance of FDI for EU economies is illustrated by the fact that 47 percent of Irish manufacturing employment is in foreign-owned firms, and even for large countries the numbers are substantial (France 26 percent and the United Kingdom 16 percent; OECD 1999).

Much of the growth of FDI within the EU has been from intra-EU investments, which account for a majority of the total. Investments from outside the region have also been important as economic integration has allowed outside firms to supply the entire European market from a single plant. Indeed, for many suppliers FDI is a much more important means of reaching the European market than is foreign trade. For manufacturing as a whole, sales of goods by U.S. subsidiaries in the EU were, in 1998, 3.75 times larger than EU manufacturing imports from the United States. There is also considerable evidence that some of the inward Japanese investments of the 1980s was driven largely by EU tariff and nontariff barriers.

These investments are perceived to have important positive effects. Productivity is generally higher in firms that are multinational than in firms that supply only the domestic market (Martin and Criscuolo 2001). Particular importance attaches to FDI in services, as this may be the only means through which foreign competition can enter the domestic market. Consequently, both the entrenched interests of incumbent firms and the potential economic gains from liberalization are large. Opening up of service sectors to competition was one of the objectives of the SMI, imposing on member states the obligation to abolish restrictions on the free movement of services and extend mutual recognition to professional qualifications. However, progress remains slow, with differing legal standards and regulatory regimes still impeding cross-border investments and competition.

What lessons does the EU FDI experience hold for the Americas? It is useful to distinguish between horizontal and vertical investments. The former are made mainly in order to serve the local market, and involve making investments that duplicate investments in the home country, as when an assembly plant is built in each market. The latter are made to minimize production costs, and involve moving stages of the production process to lowest-cost locations, such as the relocation of unskilled, labor-intensive stages of production to low-wage economies. Theory predicts that horizontal, inward investments will tend to be greater the larger the market and the higher the trade barriers to reaching the market. Vertical investments are driven by factor price differentials and by low trade barriers, as output from the project is exported for further processing in other locations.

Although it is not always possible empirically to identify one type of investment from the other, the evidence suggests that inward investment in the EU is overwhelmingly horizontal rather than vertical. Almost all sales of U.S. affiliates in the EU are to the EU market, and only 4 percent re-exported to the U.S. This contrasts with reexport rates of 40 percent for Mexico (see Shatz and Venables 2001).

There is scope for expansion of both types of investment within the Americas. Easier intra-regional trade means that market-serving investments can serve a wider area, thereby raising their profitability. This may attract inward investment from outside the region as well as within the region. The far greater range of wages across the FTAA region creates the scope for much more extensive vertical FDI.

The EU experience also suggests that inward investments are extremely prone to cluster in a few selected locations—for the EU, in Ireland. In part this may be due to underlying characteristics of the location (such as the English language), but also this trend becomes self-reinforcing, both because of demonstration effects and because of the development of pools of suitably skilled labor and interfirm linkages.

National Policy Incentives

Economic integration changes the policy environment within which national governments operate. Activity may become more "footloose" within an integrating region, changing governments' incentives to use alternative policy instruments. The effects of this can cut in different directions for different policies.

Once free market access is assured, it becomes much more difficult and expensive for governments to pursue a number of distortionary policies because they can be undermined by international trade. Thus, for example, if imports can move into the domestic market, a government finds it much harder to justify shackling its own firms by excessive regulation.

This is perhaps encouraging for the FTAA, which is, after all, mainly concerned with market access. However, implicit in this policy environment is the tendency for greater market access to increase pressures for other harmonization. If they cannot be addressed one may find progress on market access slowing or even reversing. Think, for example, of the calls to link market access to labor standards. An FTAA with no institutional foundation will face serious challenges in addressing these problems. The simplest solution is the hegemonic one whereby the dominant power decides and the others follow, as, for example, in SACU (South Africa) or the Closer Economic Relations agreement between Australia and New Zealand. This seems more or less impossible for the FTAA for political reasons and because of the region's very wide range of incomes.

While increased mobility of firms can reduce the incentives to use burdensome regulation, it can also increase incentives to use distortionary subsidy policies, and this has been an issue in the EU. National interventions can take many different forms. At one extreme are direct state aids to industry, which amounted to some 4 percent of EU manufacturing value added from 1986 to 1988, a figure that had declined to below 3 percent by the late 1990s. The bulk of this goes to research and development support and to meet regional policy objectives. Of the part that goes to specific industries, aid is highly concentrated on a few sectors, particularly shipbuilding and steel. Other national policies include general infrastructure and training schemes and use of corporate taxation; low corporate taxes in Ireland have been viewed as highly effective in attracting mobile FDI projects to Ireland from other potential locations in the EU.

Aware of the possible distortions to competition that would arise if countries were free to subsidize industry, Articles 92 and 93 of the Treaty of Rome explicitly prohibit such subsidies. These articles are policed by active monitoring and intervention. For example, between 1998 and 2000 more than 1500 cases were reviewed by the Commission and in 7 percent of these cases negative decisions were reached requiring recovery of aid (European Commission 2001). As for corporate taxation, Ireland has had several instances of conflict with the EU. Negotiations with the Commission led to termination of a complete corporate tax holiday on profits related to export sales and to an increase of the basic rate of corporate income tax from 10 percent to 12.5 percent. The weakness of these policies lies in the number of loopholes. For example, state aids are allowed in order to reduce regional disparities, and can take the form of regional incentives to enterprises in selected (but large) regions. Total expenditures to an enterprise are capped, and aids to new investments are preferred to ongoing subsidies.

While policy in these areas is still developing, the broad conclusion of the research literature is that these policies have done little to distort the location of industry. Midelfart-Knarvik and Overman (2002) show that specialization is taking place according to comparative advantage, despite the use of state aids. Braunerhjelm et al. (2000) conclude that competition for activity generally takes the form of measures that count as good economic management, rather than wasteful tax or subsidy competition. Perhaps this is an area in which the FTAA need not regret its lack of institutional depth. Yet, if subsidies are the precursor to stiff countervailing duties or if they swamp the dispute settlement procedures with intractable cases, they could undermine the FTAA's market access momentum. The real need is the need for internal disciplines on subsidies among FTAA members. It seems very unlikely that the FTAA could impose discipline where governments seriously wished otherwise.

Labor Markets

One of the starkest differences between Europe and the FTAA is that the former legally has almost unlimited labor mobility between members, whereas the latter intends to do nothing to enhance mobility at all. In fact the difference is probably much less extreme, for Europe has seen rather little intrabloc mobility while the members of the FTAA have seen, de facto, quite a lot.

Table 3.4 shows the number of foreign workers in the EC6 in the early years as internal mobility was gradually introduced; it suggests that flows were indeed quite significant. However, fewer than half the migrants were from other EC members. The table also shows the peak in 1973: after that date, at least until very recently, immigration to Europe became much more difficult for workers from outside the member states. But at around the same time, internal migration also appeared to decline in the EU, the stock of migrants from other EC states falling from 3.2 percent of the workforce in 1973 to 1.9 percent in 1985 (Molle 1994).

Braunerhjelm et al. (2000) also document the decline in European migration over the period since 1960, even from the traditionally poorer sending countries. Thus, for Greece, emigration rates per

Table 3.4 Estimates of the Number of Foreign Workers in EC Member States, 1960–1980

	Thousands				As % of Host Labor Force			
	1960*	1970*	1973**	1980**	1960*	1970*	1973**	1980**
Germany	461	1,727	2,519	2,072	2	6	11	9
France	1,294	1,584	1,900	1,643	6	8	11	9
Netherlands	47	134	121	194	1	3	3	4
Belgium	170	257	211	333	5	7	7	11
Luxembourg	20	27	43	51	16	21	35	37
Italy	20	30	55	57	—	—	—	—
EC6	2,012	3,759	4,849	4,350	3	5	7	6

Source: Molle (1990).
*Labor force
**Dependent workers

thousand of population peaked at about ten in 1964 and 1970 but have been below five since 1973. Those for Portugal reached twenty in 1970 but have never exceeded five since 1975, while for Spain the peak was about four in 1970, but has remained less than one since 1975. Moreover, even internal migration within the EU member states has been low by world standards, and is falling.

Braunerhjelm et al. attribute the low propensity of Europeans to migrate to distortions in labor and housing markets, inappropriate industrial and regional policies, high levels of unemployment in Europe since 1973, and "home bias" in location decisions. In other words, despite large continuing differences in real wages around Europe, migration is far from inevitable. Moreover, the entirely permissive legal regime for internal migration has done virtually nothing to boost migration flows. Despite the oft-expressed fears that new poorer members will swamp northern European labor markets, nothing of the kind has happened.

The contrast with the new world is striking. Here migratory flows are large and buoyant, especially if one includes illegal migration. Much is from outside the FTAA area (especially from Asia into the United States and Canada), but much is also from within. The FTAA will not formally inhibit migration, and so as we contemplate the future of the FTAA, the likelihood appears to be one of more buoyant migratory flows than Europe has ever experienced since 1970. This is particularly true in the light of research that shows that in relatively poor countries increasing incomes boost emigration by relaxing liquidity constraints. The FTAA may not seek to encourage mobility, but de facto, it may do so by increasing contact between member states and boosting incomes.

Income Convergence

The most important economic questions concern the effects of regional integration on growth. Is regional integration likely to be good for growth in the region as a whole, and for poorer countries in particular?

The EU has experienced significant, although by no means steady, convergence of per capita income across member states. The outstanding features are the rapid catch up of Ireland, Spain, and Portugal, and at the same time the continuing poor performance of Greece. The overall experience of convergence has been analyzed by many authors and can be summarised in many different ways. Summary measures of the cross-country dispersion of per capita income in the EU indicate significant convergence through the 1960s and 1970s, although no further aggregate change during the 1980s. There was some resumption of convergence across countries from the late 1980s, although this was accompanied by divergence at the subnational level (Puga 2002).

Standard neoclassical trade theory presumes that integration should lead to convergence of factor prices and incomes—with the limit being factor price equalization. However, a number of qualifications need to be made to this benchmark case. Even if integration brings convergence of per capita income, it need not bring steady convergence of all factor prices. Feenstra and Hanson (1997) show how the relocation of production activities to low-wage countries can reduce wages of unskilled labor in these countries. The argument is that the activity that relocates may be unskilled-labor intensive relative to other activities in the high-wage country, but skilled-labor intensive relative to activities in the low-wage host country. In a more general model in which comparative advantage stems both from endowments and from location (with remote regions having a comparative disadvantage in high transport costs goods), reducing trade barriers brings peripheral countries into the trading system and raises their real incomes. However, changes in the prices of individual factors can go either way, depending on both the location and the endowments of individual countries (Venables and Limao 2002).

Some analyses of wage differences across Europe have focused less on factor endowment differences across countries, and more on the relationship between locations with good market access (the "center") relative to those with worse access (the "periphery"). Empirically, European cross-country wage differentials follow a strong center-periphery wage gradient, and there has been concern about the possibility that integration might draw activity out of peripheral regions and into the center. Theory suggests that this gives rise to a U-shaped relationship between the ratio of wages in the periphery to those in the center as the degree of integration changes (Krugman and Venables 1990). When trade barriers are high, local manufacturing is protected, allowing higher wages to be maintained; at the other extreme, perfectly free trade brings factor price equalization. It is at intermediate levels of trade barriers that firms are drawn into central regions, which offer large markets and from which they can supply the periphery. Peripheral regions are poor locations for manufacturing, and as a consequence have lower wages in equilibrium.

In the European context it generally has been argued that barriers are low enough that countries are on the upward slope of the U. Further reductions in trade barriers cause firms to relocate to lower wage peripheral regions, thus flattening wage gradients. Empirically, the evidence on convergence suggests that this has—to a limited extent—happened.

However, the effect is much less obvious in the FTAA context. As trade barriers are reduced, firms with the benefits of large domestic markets (the United States) may benefit more than those with smaller markets. The models then predict that peripheral firms survive only if there is a widening of wage gaps between center and periphery. These wage gaps can be amplified if there are clustering forces (Fujita, Krugman, and Venables 1999). A productive area for future research may be the application of these modeling frameworks, developed largely in the European context, to the Americas.

The persistence of regional disparities within the EU has motivated an active policy of regional transfers. Table 3.5 gives the net budgetary position of EU member states (contributions to the EU budget minus receipts) as a percentage of national GDP. It indicates that these transfers are substantial, amounting to more than 4 percent of Irish and Greek GDP. The common agricultural policy is the largest element

Table 3.5 Net Contributions to the EU Budget (% GNP)

	1992	1993	1994	1995	1996	1997
Austria	—	—	—	–0.49	–0.12	–0.41
Belgium	–0.16	–0.25	–0.47	–0.18	–0.30	–0.52
Denmark	0.27	0.30	0.18	0.25	0.16	0.03
Finland	—	—	—	–0.15	0.08	0.04
France	–0.14	–0.11	–0.23	–0.14	–0.03	–0.08
Germany	–0.62	–0.72	–0.78	–0.72	–0.58	–0.60
Greece	4.65	5.16	4.61	3.98	4.19	4.12
Ireland	5.84	6.54	4.42	4.45	4.84	4.82
Italy	–0.03	–0.14	–0.29	–0.09	–0.13	–0.02
Luxembourg	–0.59	–0.74	–0.52	–0.43	–0.26	–0.35
Netherlands	–0.34	–0.49	–0.63	–0.65	–0.76	–0.73
Portugal	2.91	3.42	2.48	3.06	3.40	3.11
Spain	0.60	0.73	0.78	1.69	1.34	1.27
Sweden	—	—	—	–0.53	–0.35	–0.59
United Kingdom	–0.29	–0.38	–0.13	–0.56	–0.24	–0.17

Source: European Commission.

underlying these transfers, but the second largest element of the EU budget is regional policy. The main instruments of regional policy are the structural funds of around €30 billion per annum, articulated around three "objectives." Seventy percent goes to objective one—"to promote the development and structural adjustment of regions whose development is lagging behind"—eligible regions being those with per capita income below 75 percent of the EU average. In addition, Greece, Ireland, Portugal, and Spain are eligible for cohesion funds of a further €3 billion per annum.

The bulk of expenditure from the structural funds and cohesion funds go to infrastructure projects and training and education, with some direct grants going to firms. The value of these expenditures can be assessed in both economic and political terms. Economically, the direct transfers have been very substantial. The extent to which they have promoted regional growth over and above their direct effect remains moot. Alogoskoufis (1995) argues that transfers to Greece have been antigrowth—they permitted the continuation of poor macroeconomic policies longer than would otherwise have been possible.

Conclusions

The refrain throughout this chapter is that European integration has been successful because it has been a continuing process of steps to achieve deeper integration, going far beyond the removal of tariffs. In comparison, the size and heterogeneity of the Americas offers large potential gains from integration, but there will be undoubted stresses arising from tensions over particular policies and perceived unevenness in the distribution of the benefits. The EU experience shows how these stresses can be handled and points to the importance of deep integration in achieving the full potential of a regional agreement. However, the EU performance is grounded in the deep political commitment of its members and in the creation of a political and institutional framework that can pursue integration and regional reform independently of national governments. It is in these dimensions that the Americas are most fundamentally different from the European Union, and the possibility of following the European model is most limited.

References

Alogoskoufis, George. 1995. "The Two Faces of Janus: Institutions, Policy Regimes and Macroeconomic Performance in Greece." *Economic Policy: A European Forum* 20 (April): 147–84.

Baldwin, Richard. E., and Anthony J. Venables. 1997. "International Economic Integration." In *Handbook of International Economics*, vol. 3, edited by G. Grossman and K. Rogoff. Amsterdam: North Holland.

Bayoumi, Tamim, and Barry Eichengreen. 1997. "Is Regionalism Simply a Diversion: Evidence from the Evolution of the EC and EFTA." In *Regionalism versus Multilateral Trade Arrangements*, National Bureau of Economic Research East Asia Seminar on Economics vol. 6, edited by T. Ito and A. O. Krueger. Chicago: University of Chicago Press.

Braunerhjelm, Pontus et al. 2000. "Integration and the Regions of Europe: How the Right Policies can Prevent Polarization." Monitoring European Integration Series no. 10. London: Centre for Economic Policy Research.

Ethier, Wilfred J. 1998. "Regionalism in a Multilateral World." *Journal of Political Economy* 106 (6): 1214–45.

European Commission. 2001. *State Aid Scorecard*. Brussels. http://europa.eu.int/eur-lex/en/com/rpt/2001/com2001_0403en01.pdf.

Feenstra, Robert C., and Gordon Hanson. 1997. "Foreign Direct Investment and Relative Wages: Evidence from Mexico's Maquiladoras." *Journal of International Economics* 42: 371–93.

Fontagne, Lionel, Michael Freudenberg, and Nicholas Peridy. 1997. "Intra-Industry Trade and the Single Market: Quality Matters." Centre for Economic Policy Research Discussion Paper 1959, London.

Freund, Caroline, and John McLaren. 1999. "On the Dynamics of Trade Diversion: Evidence from Four Trade Blocks." International Finance Discussion Paper no. 637, Board of Governors of the Federal Reserve System, Washington, DC.

Fujita, Masahisa, Paul Krugman, and Anthony J. Venables. 1999. *The Spatial Economy: Cities, Regions, and International Trade*. Cambridge, MA: MIT Press.

Griffith, Rachel. 2001. "Product Market Competition, Efficiency and Agency Costs: An Empirical Analysis." Institute for Fiscal Studies Working Paper 01/12, London.

Jacquemin, Alexis, and André Sapir. 1989. "International Trade and Integration of the European Community: An Econometric Analysis." In *European Internal Market: Trade and Competition, Selected Readings*, pp. 202–12. Oxford: Oxford University Press.

Krugman, Paul, and Anthony J. Venables. 1990. "Integration and the Competitiveness of Peripheral Industry." In *Unity with Diversity in the European Community*, edited by C. Bliss and J. de Macedo. Cambridge: Cambridge University Press.

Martin, Ralf, and Chiara Criscuolo. 2001. "A Note on Ownership and Productivity in UK Businesses." Centre for Economic Performance, London School of Economics. Photocopy.

Midelfart-Knarvik, Karen Helene, and Henry G. Overman. 2002. "Delocation and European Integration: Is Structural Spending Justified?" *Economic Policy* 35: 321–59.

Midelfart-Knarvik, Karen Helene, Henry G. Overman, Stephen Redding, and Anthony J. Venables. 2000. "The Location of Industry in Europe." Economic Papers no. 142, European Commission Directorate General for Economic and Financial Affairs, Brussels.

Molle, Willem. 1994. *The Economics of European Integration: Theory, Practice and Policy*. 2d ed. Brookfield, VT: Dartmouth Publishing.

Organization for Economic Cooperation and Development (OECD). 1999. *Measuring Globalization*. Paris.

Pelkmans, Jacques. 2001. *European Integration: Methods and Economic Analysis*. London: Pearson.

Political and Economic Planning. 1962. *Atlantic Tariffs and Trade*. London: Allen & Unwin.

Puga, Diego. 2002. "European Regional Policy in the Light of Recent Location Theories. *Journal of Economic Geography* 2 (4): 372–406.

Sapir, André. 1992. 'Regional Integration in Europe." *Economic Journal* 102: 1491–506.

———. 1998. "The Political Economy of EC Regionalism." *European Economic Review* 42: 717–32.

Shatz, Howard J., and Anthony J. Venables. 2001. "The Geography of International Investment." In *The Oxford Handbook of Economic Geography*, edited by G. L. Clark, M. P. Feldman, and M. S. Gertler. Oxford: Oxford University Press.

Soloaga, Isidro, and L. Alan Winters. 2001. "Regionalism in the Nineties: What Effect on Trade?" Centre for Economic Policy Research Discussion Paper Series no. 2183, London.

Truman, Edwin M. 1975. "The Effects of European Economic Integration on the Production and Trade of Manufactured Products." In *European Economic Integration*, edited by B. Balassa. Amsterdam: North-Holland.

Venables, Anthony J. 2003. "Gainers and Losers from Regional Integration Agreements." *Economic Journal* 113: 747–61.

Venables, Anthony J., and Nuno Limao. 2002. "Geographical Disadvantage: A Heckscher-Ohlin-von Thunen Model of International Specialization." *Journal of International Economics* 58: 239–63.

Winters, L. Alan. 1983. "British Imports of Manufactures and the Common Market." *Oxford Economic Papers* 36: 103–18.

Notes

1 The same internationalism that produced the United Nations, the International Monetary Fund, the World Bank, and the General Agreement on Tariffs and Trade (GATT).

2 The meeting of heads of government is known as the European Council. It has regular biannual meetings.

3 Tariffs converged to an EEC average common external tariff (CET) of 10.4 percent in 1968 and 6.6 percent following the Kennedy Round.

4 The trade intensity index for *i*'s trade with *j* is $(T_{ij}/T_{iw})/[(T_{wj}-T_{ij})/T_{ww}]$, where *T* represents trade in both directions and where subscript *w* represents the world.

5 Anticipation effects have been noted previously—e.g., in Winters (1983) for the United Kingdom.

6 Just as with the apparent consumption exercise, these exercises are colored by the reduction in the accedants' tariffs on other countries as they adopted the common external tariff. In this case, however, the external trade changes may reasonably be attributed to integration.

7 Fontagne, Freudenberg, and Peridy (1997) show that there is a strong degree of vertical IIT within Europe, although the definition they use—an absolute difference of over 15 percent in the unit value—is very generous towards finding vertical IIT.

4

The Proliferation of Sovereigns: Are There Lessons for Integration?

Matías Braun, Ricardo Hausmann, and Lant Pritchett

Introduction

Economic integration has been a stated goal of many polities throughout the years. From the time of the *Zollverein* among German-speaking states in the nineteenth century to the current plans for a Free Trade Area of the Americas, and in many other initiatives such as the European Union, the Latin American Free Trade Area (known by its Spanish acronym ALALC), the North American Free Trade Area, MERCOSUR, the Andean Pact, the Central American Common Market, and the Asian-Pacific Economic Cooperation, significant efforts have been made to achieve greater economic integration. The typical content of these arrangements involves inter alia the reduction in tariff and nontariff barriers to trade, the liberalization of migratory flows, the harmonization of market regulations and macroeconomic policies, the adoption of common currencies, and the commitment to a process of conflict resolution in the process of cross-border investments and contract enforcement. While these efforts to integrate sovereign states have been taking place at differing speeds in different regions, a much more dramatic change has taken place in the opposite direction: the number of sovereign states has tripled over the last fifty years, multiplying the constraints that sovereignty imposes on economic integration.

Integration efforts exist to compensate for the often-unintended obstacles to trade created by the existence of sovereign states—which is often the result of political *dis*integration. It is sovereign states that, through their trade policy, impose barriers to the movement of goods across borders. It is sovereign states that restrict migratory flows across borders. It is sovereign states that insist on having a national currency, an autonomous macro policy and an adequately suited regulatory framework. Economic integration agreements are there to lower some of the negative consequences for economic integration that sovereign states create. The typical agreement involves a multilateral renunciation of the sovereign exercise of discretion in exchange for other members also letting go of that discretion. The subtext of these agreements is: we will give up our sovereign right to discriminate against your goods and factors provided that you give up your right to do the same to ours.

The purpose of this chapter is to shed light on the potential growth implications of greater economic integration by studying the impact that political *dis*integration has had on the growth experience of the newly independent countries. The first section describes the process of formation of newly independent states. The second presents a brief theoretical framework that relates sovereignty to income and growth. It highlights the importance of market size and policies in determining the net effect of independence. The third section proposes a difference of differences analysis of the historical record and finds that in general, countries that became independent saw a growth reduction relative to the OECD countries, although they grew at rates similar to those of old independent countries. The fourth section studies the case of the Caribbean and finds that the still dependent countries are ten times richer than the old independent countries and about two times richer than the newly independent states.

The fifth section studies the variance in growth performance within a state and between states. To do this analysis we use data on growth for regions of India and compare it to growth performance among newly independent states. We find that the variance of growth performance is an order of magnitude larger in independent states. This suggests that independence increases significantly the variance of results, with some countries doing significantly better and others doing worse.

The final section tries to account for the variance of growth performance among fifty-one newly independent states as a function of the loss of secured market access and domestic policies. It finds evidence that both have important effects on growth. In particular, controlling for the quality of policies, the loss of market access has a large impact on growth.

The Proliferation of Independence

In 1940 there were only 65 independent countries; as of 2000 there are (roughly) 190 independent countries. One hundred and twenty five new countries have been created in the last sixty years, more than double the number that existed in 1940.[1] This proliferation of states has come about in three waves (of differing size and intensity). Figure 4.1 presents the raw numbers of new nations in each year by former controlling country, while Figure 4.2 shows the distribution by region.

First, far and away the largest in terms of population, many Asian states became independent in the immediate aftermath of World War II—including India and Pakistan in 1947 and Indonesia, the Philippines, and Korea in 1945. The second big wave was the process of decolonization of British, French, Belgian, and Portuguese colonies. These were numerically concentrated in sub-Saharan Africa, but also included possessions in the Caribbean and in the Indian Ocean. The bulk of this process took place between 1956 and 1968, but the pattern was somewhat drawn out over time. Most French and Belgian colonies became independent in 1960, and British colonies largely became independent between 1956 and 1963 (with the exception of what was

Figure 4.1 Number of Newly Independent Countries in Each Year, by Former Controlling Country

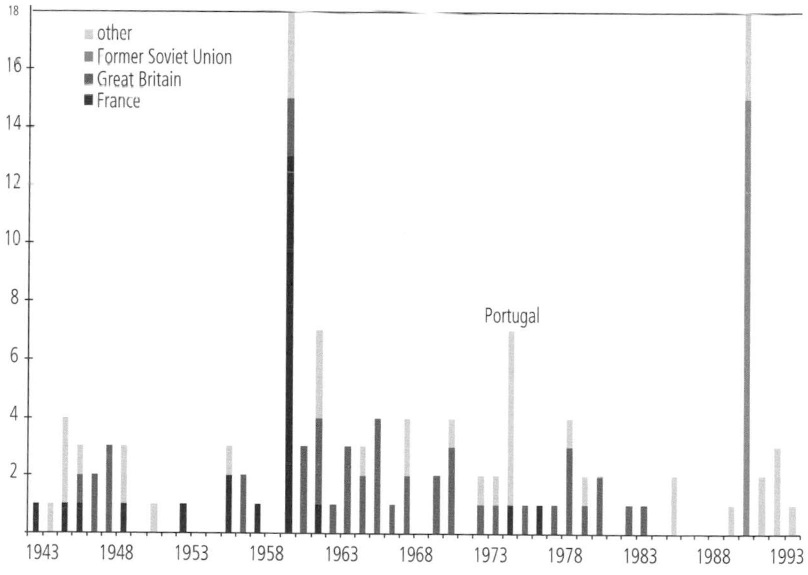

then Rhodesia). Within this group, large countries typically became independent first, while smaller countries followed suit later, often in a steady trickle during the 1970s and 1980s and especially in the Caribbean and the Pacific. Thus the larger countries in the Caribbean—Trinidad and Tobago and Jamaica—became independent in the early 1960s while the Bahamas and Belize did so only around 1980. By contrast, Portugal granted independence to its colonies late and suddenly after it underwent its own political revolution in 1975.

The third big wave of independence was the disintegration of the Soviet Union (and its Eastern European satellites), which has occasioned the creation of new countries both out of the USSR and from the division of other Eastern European countries such as Czechoslovakia and Yugoslavia.

There are today a number of "still dependent" entities, which are neither fully integrated parts of states nor fully independent. The United States maintains arrangements with Puerto Rico, Guam, American Samoa, and the U.S. Virgin Islands. France possesses overseas jurisdictions such as Guadeloupe, Martinique, and French Guiana, and the Netherlands claims sovereignty over Aruba, Curacao, and Bonaire. Dependent countries are typically very small.

Figure 4.2 Number of Newly Independent Countries in Each Year, by Region

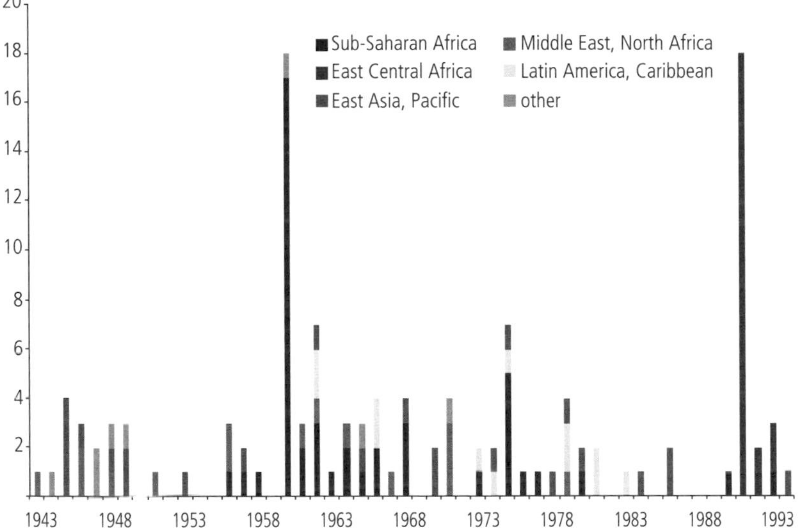

Since independence events are driven by internal and external facts there is very little relationship between timing of independence and country characteristics such as size, openness, income level, ethnic fractionalization, and so on. That is, while the large Asian countries became independent first, followed by the generally smaller states in Africa, the newly independent states from the USSR are larger than the African states and richer than either. However, for each colonizer, and especially for Britain, it is the case that larger, more distant entities became independent first, while smaller jurisdictions did so at a later stage.

What Is the Expected Growth Impact of Independence?

Before examining the data on the economic performance of countries before and after independence we want to specify what we might expect. State sovereignty in the modern world systems implies control of at least five economic features: first, the control of the movement of *labor* across national boundaries; second, the control of the movement of *goods* across national boundaries; third, the choice (not always exercised) to maintain a national *currency* (which implies at least the potential for control of capital flows), and which in turn implies a macroeconomic policy of some sort; fourth, the control of the *enforcement of contracts* within the nation (since contract enforcement in the limit implies compulsion); and fifth, the ability to set a wide range of legal and regulatory conditions, which include policies to subsidize and promote certain activities that affect economic activities within national boundaries.

Said differently, when a border is set up in a previously undivided economic entity, people on one side of the border will:

- lose the right to work on the other side;
- lose the right to trade with the other side unless they obtain a special dispensation, which may be taxed or restricted in the present or in some future scenario;
- expect to be paid in a currency different from that used on the other side;
- have problems having their contracts signed on this side of the border enforced by the authorities on the other side of the border;
- and need to adapt products and practices to the rules of the other jurisdiction.

Notice that many of these consequences of borders are exactly the issues that integration agreements are meant to alleviate.

Independence will have two, potentially offsetting impacts. One is that independence almost certainly will reduce market size—in spite of the most open trade policies. The other is that independence allows the new sovereign more freedom in choosing national policies. On the one hand, if the new policies are superior, growth could accelerate; on the other hand, the risk exists of worsening policies.

Market Size

Market size will be affected by sovereignty in several ways. We define "market size" as the scale of economic activity over which agents can contract. This definition is built around the notion of the benefits of specialization. Increasingly, larger markets allow agents to become more and more specialized. But, to the extent specialization requires specific investments (in physical capital, in human capital, in marketing channels), the desired degree of specialization is informed not just by current, but also future, anticipated probabilistic distribution of market size.

The geographic scope of markets both is probabilistic and depends on the particular market. That is, if I am a producer in California, the odds that I will not be able to sell goods into Oregon now and in the future are infinitesimally small; the odds that I will not be able to sell in Canada are small, but non-zero; and the odds that I will not in the future be able to sell my goods in Mexico are still small, but a larger non-zero. The odds that I will not be able to sell my goods in Nigeria are reasonably high. These same odds are different for movements of labor, capital, and ideas. *Certain market size* is much smaller than *expected market size,* which in turn could be larger or smaller than *current market size.*

Some might argue that if trade policies are sufficiently open, borders become irrelevant, as market size is defined by the entire world only. This appears not to be the case, as borders matter for trade, price equalization, and capital flows even in countries with very open policies. The impact of borders on economic integration has attracted a lot of attention since McCallum (1995) found that trade between Canadian provinces was twenty times larger than between those provinces and equidistant American states.[2] This result was particularly surprising as the U.S.-Canadian border is among the least problematic to cross: after all, both countries share a language and a legal tradition, have similar levels of development, and enjoy a history of peaceful coexistence. If the effects of a border can be so large between these two countries, what can we expect among others? Helliwell (1998) estimated border effects for several Latin American countries with estimated coefficients between thirty-five and sixty.

With a different strategy, Engel and Rogers (1996) explored the implications of borders for the equalization of prices across different cities. They found that crossing a border is the economic equivalent of adding thousands of miles to the distance between two cities. In particular, Parsley and Wei (2000) estimate that crossing the U.S.-Japanese border adds 43,000 trillion miles to the process of price convergence between cities. Bradford and Lawrence (2003) still find that both quantity and price evidence suggest that the presence of a border per se has an enormous impact on the quantity of trade and price convergence.[3] Their new results, based on detailed examinations of prices across markets, suggest that "international fragmentation among industrial countries remains considerable, even among countries with low or no tariff barriers," as the typical price differential was 20 percent in adjacent countries in North America and Europe and 30 to 50 percent across countries in different continents.

Helliwell and McKitrick (1998) find that the U.S.–Canadian border also distorts the flow of capital between provinces and states: at the national level, savings and investment seem to be correlated, but this is not true at the provincial level: the Feldstein-Horioka puzzle is a national phenomenon, not one that can be observed within Canadian provinces.

Finally, in a sequence of papers, Rose and various coauthors have studied the impact of currency unions on trade.[4] They typically find that a currency union increases trade between its members by a large extent, with measures going from increases of 80 to 200 percent. This means that the exercise of monetary sovereignty has implications for the volume of trade. This effect is separate from that of belonging to a political union. Frankel and Rose (2000) estimate that both a currency union and a political union triple trade. This means that two regions that belong to the same sovereign and share a currency are estimated to trade nine times more than if they had separate sovereignties.

In addition to the spatial dimension, the market size relevant for investment decisions also has an important temporal dimension, since profits are forward looking. In dealing with sovereign states, contract enforcement to prevent predation may be impossible, so that it is impossible to reliably contract into the future over anything. That is, the authorities in the sovereign country may decide to favor the domestic entrepreneur or the government in adjudicating a complaint or in carrying out the orders of a foreign court. Alternatively the sovereign could carry out a "taking" by a direct seizure of assets, prevent future transactions through regulatory action, or otherwise limit the scope of competitive economic activity (for instance through providing subsidies to some firms and not others). It is important not to confuse this risk with the risk of repudiation of government debt (as might be proxied by sovereign bond premia) but rather the risk that, if a producer makes a specialized investment in a fixed asset (property in downtown Lima, a CAT scan machine in Buenos Aires, an accounting degree in Rio), the government will undertake some action (zoning, price control, regulation) that would affect the returns to this asset. Generally, these risks are perceived to be higher than the pure sovereign-country risk, explaining the common practice by credit-rating agencies of setting a sovereign ceiling on private corporate bonds. In fact, these risks need not involve other countries: if the protection of property rights is poor, the effective domestic market size will be limited.

These distinctions can make a large difference in thinking about the relevant market size, which is often simply considered as ratios of GDPs (or exports). But, as Table 4.1 shows, if the market is considered to be the net present value of the current flow discounted at a rate that reflects the uncertainty of being able to realize gains in the future, markets are even smaller relative to developed country markets than is commonly measured. In dollar terms, the Brazilian market is 10 percent of the U.S. market. However, suppose that there is sufficient certainty about contracting that the discount rate that reflects the risk to a specific asset is 3 percent in the United States and 10 percent in Brazil. Then the market over which a producer would make decisions about investment and specialization is only 3 percent as large in Brazil as in the United States—the whole net present value of Brazilian market is barely equal to the current U.S. flow.

Does market size really matter? In a related literature, Alesina, Spolaore, and Wacziarg (2000) study the endogenous formation of countries. They posit that a larger entity has a larger internal market, but also more diversity in preferences, which complicates the choice of common policies. The optimal size of a country will depend on a balance between these two forces. They show that more open economic policies should imply smaller countries. We take from this literature

Table 4.1 Role of Uncertainty in Market Size

	GDP 1997 (US$Billions)	NPV (flow/r) of Market Size at Various Discount Rates (US$Billions) 3%	5%	10%	20%
United States	8,110	270,333	162,200	81,100	40,550
Germany	2,103	70,090	42,054	21,027	10,514
Brazil	804	26,804	16,082	8,041	4,021
NPV(r) relative to U.S. NPV(3%)	9.9%	9.9%	5.9%	3.0%	1.5%
NPV(r) relative to U.S. flow		331%	198%	99%	50%
India	431	14,352	8,611	4,306	2,153
NPV(r) relative to U.S. NPV(3%)	5.3%	5.3%	3.2%	1.6%	0.8%
NPV(r) relative to U.S. flow		177%	106%	53%	27%
Indonesia	215	7,167	4,300	2,150	1,075
NPV(r) relative to U.S. NPV(3%)	2.7%	2.7%	1.6%	0.8%	0.4%
NPV(r) relative to U.S. flow		88%	53%	27%	13%
Nigeria	57	1,884	1,131	565	283
NPV(r) relative to U.S. NPV(3%)	0.7%	0.7%	0.4%	0.2%	0.1%
NPV(r) relative to U.S. flow		23%	14%	7%	3%

the idea that countries that become independent have an incentive to adopt more open policies in order to limit the consequences of the reduction in market size. Singapore, Taiwan, Slovenia, and the Baltic states are an example of this, as may be some of the islands in the Caribbean. By contrast, as we shall see later, many newly independent countries ended up with very large black market exchange rate premia, suggesting that domestic policy imbalances limited their degree of openness.

While borders seem to have quite negative effects on trade, does this affect output levels (and growth as a transition to the new, higher level)? There is an ample debate on this matter. In a recent paper, Frankel and Romer (1999) argue that trade has a significant and large effect on income.[5] They argue that an increase trade by 1 percent raises income by one-third of 1 percent over twenty years. If this is the case, then borders, by restricting trade, lower expected income in a significant manner. Countries that become independent increase the number of transactions that need to cross borders, thus lowering expected income.

There have been numerous studies that have tried to estimate the benefits of economic integration. Many of these studies have been prospective: efforts have been made to calculate the potential impact of the single market policy in Europe (European Commission 1988) or of NAFTA. The point of all these studies is to assess the potential effects of a move toward more integration. In this chapter we move in the opposite direction: we will try to learn about the potential benefits from integration by looking at the effects of political disintegration.

Policies

In addition to market size (which is itself a function of institutions and policies), production and investment decisions are determined by *effective policies and institutional performance.* The phrase *effective policies* is intended to emphasize two things. First, a *policy* is a (possibly unconditional) rule that maps states of the world to policy actions. The literature often confuses *policy actions*—such as a budget deficit, or a given pattern of tariffs—with a *policy.*[6] The second point is that a policy is not an *effective* policy without the specification of the means by which the policy will be implemented. That is, a protectionist policy to "place high tariffs on goods whose production has high backward linkages" is not an *effective* policy without a specification of how the determination of the "state of the world" will be undertaken. The same *stated* policy of protecting goods with "high backward linkages" can lead to very different outcomes depending on the incentives of those making the policy. The same policy can mean very different *effective policies* if the determination of which goods those are is left to executive discretion, an expert commission (with what incentives?), a trade ministry with a given administrative decision process, legislative discretion, or any other authority.

Similarly, we wish to emphasize *institutional performance*, to distinguish between institutions and institutional performance, as empirically there may be very little link between the formal structure and design of institutions and their institutional performance. Take for example an institutional characteristic such as "rule of law." The legal systems may by formally identical in two countries (e.g., Britain and Kenya), and yet their outcomes completely different. Similarly, the legal systems may have completely different institutional foundations and yet produce roughly equivalent outcomes (e.g., the laws of the U.S. state of Louisiana are based on the French civil code, and yet rule of law does not vary significantly between Louisiana and its neighboring states). Effective policies and institutional performance are constrained by (though not completely determined by) the *institutional framework.*

Within any given geographic territory effective policies in each of the five dimensions of sovereignty (trade, labor, monetary control, contract enforcement, regulatory environment) and institutional performance can be determined in one of three stylized fashions: *no sovereignty, full sovereignty,* or *limited sovereignty.* No sovereignty is the condition of completely colonial or dependent jurisdictions in which decisions are made—not necessarily in the interests of the residents—by some other sovereign authority. In a classic colonial situation the colony did not have rights to control key policies, and even if those rights were granted they were revocable by the colonial power. This dependency should not be overstated: a recent study by Clemens and Williamson (2002) of tariffs in the pre-WWI era suggests that even colonies did have some tariff autonomy. So, while to some extent colonies followed the tariff policies of their colonial power, there was scope for difference.

Under the condition of *full sovereignty*, not only does the state control the policies, but also the state has not undertaken any obligations that limit its sovereignty over policy choices by binding commitments to other sovereign states or supranational bodies. It may be useful to distinguish the creation of two separate sovereignties from a situation in which all the population had equal citizenship rights and policies are decided democratically from the emancipation of a colony in which the laws were decided by a government of which they were not citizens. For example, the separation of Quebec from Canada is different from the independence of the Belgian Congo. Quebecois are citizens of Canada, arguably with equal rights, while the Congolese had policies determined by Belgium, a country that did not grant them citizenship rights. Thus, the Belgian government could create policies for the Congo that it did not have to impose on its citizens. In other words, more exploitative policies were feasible in the Congo relative to Quebec. Consequently, the impact of sovereignty on growth should be greater in the Congo than in Quebec, as the distance between actual policies under colonialism and policies desired under sovereignty is that much larger.

An interesting case is *limited sovereignty*, in which a state chooses to make binding agreements with other states or supranational bodies. Obviously trade agreements are a classic example in which countries agree to forswear certain policies (e.g., quantitative restrictions, export subsidies) in connection with a reciprocal agreement from other states. This limits the range of policies the state can adopt and still be consistent with the agreement. Of course the state can always exit from the agreement, but this usually involves some cost, at the very least freeing other sovereign states from their reciprocal obligations.

The range of limited sovereignty agreements can extend from the very specific (e.g., the recent debate about ceding legal jurisdiction over actions involving "crimes against humanity" to a supranational court) to the very deep and broad. The progressive stages of the EU from free trade area to more and more common policies—including common currency and free labor flows—illustrates the range of limits to members' national sovereignty.

Given the conditions of no, full, or limited sovereignty in any given policy dimension, an effective policy outcome depends on supranational commitment and a range of political, institutional, and organizational factors (e.g., implementation capacity and corruption in administration). Therefore the effective polices (which are not "real numbers" or even vectors of real numbers but are mappings from states of the world to policy actions) in any policy area, such as trade, can be expressed as a function of sovereignty commitments (S), which in our stylized system can be No, Full, or Limited, and other factors (Z):

$$EP^{Trade} = EP^{Trade}(S^{Trade}, Z), EP^{Macro} = EP^{Macro}(S^{Macro}, Z), etc.$$

The economic policy climate is the set of all policy areas:

$$\mathrm{EP} = \begin{bmatrix} EP^{Trade} \\ EP^{Macro} \\ \vdots \end{bmatrix}$$

Model of Economic Growth

Before moving to an empirical investigation of the impact of independence we want to establish a reasonably complete but general model that allows us to discuss the expected impacts. This model will move from the proximate determinants of output, to the determinants of the desired and supportable level of proximate determinants, to the dynamics of those determinants.

The direct proximate determinants of national income at any point in time are the level of accumulated factors—capitals of various kinds (physical, human, social)—called K, natural resources R, and raw labor and the efficiency with which those factors are used A. We write this as an income determination function $Y()$:

$$Y = Y[A(), K(), R(), L()].$$

Market size is determined by effective policies and institutional performance as well as by other natural factors we call geography G.

$$MS = MS(EP, IP, G).$$

Each of the components of income determination—accumulated factors, productivity, and even resources and raw labor—has some maximal *supportable* level that is determined by market size and independently by effective policies and institutional performance. We use the term *supportable* to mean equilibrium subject to constraints, where the constraints may include feasible and sustainable levels of state compulsion. For instance, Singapore may require contributions to a provident fund that are much larger than individuals would choose in the absence of those compulsions. In this situation one could talk about the equilibrium level of the capital stock, conditional on this compulsion, but we prefer to talk about the supportable level of the capital stock to make it clear that the equilibrium in these systems involves producers and consumers choosing over options that are constrained by state action in a myriad of ways. In this model the long-run level of income is determined by the levels of policies and institutional performance.

The exception is that the supportable level of productivity A is determined in part by the world technological frontier T, which progresses at some rate. This creates the constant *possibility* of convergence, since countries below the world achievable productivity frontier may make rapid progress toward that frontier through imitation:

$$K^* = K(MS, EP, IP, A^*)$$
$$A^* = A(MS, EP, IP, T^W)$$
$$R^* = R(MS, EP, IP, A^*)$$
$$L^* = L(MS, EP, IP, A^*).$$

If actual or anticipated effective policies or institutional performance change, the effect is change in the level of supportable proximate determinants of income. We assume a dynamic adjustment function so that proximate determinants adjust toward their supportable level. This adjustment is not instantaneous, and not all elements adjust at the same rate. There is another set of country specific factors (W) that may independently determine the speed of adjustment (e.g., the efficacy and flexibility of the financial system):

$$\frac{dK}{dt} = g^K(K_t - K^*, W)$$
$$\frac{dA}{dt} = g^A(A_t - A^*, W)$$
$$\frac{dR}{dt} = g^R(R_t - R^*, W)$$
$$\frac{dL}{dt} = g^L(L_t - L^*, W)$$

This means that economic growth is determined by (1) the relationship between current and supportable levels of the proximate determinants of the level of income, which are themselves functions of policies and institutions, market size, and the productivity frontier, and (2) the adjustment dynamics of those proximate determinants:

$$\frac{dY() = g^Y(\Delta EP, \Delta IP, W, T^W)}{dt}$$

Countries could undertake policy reforms that raise the supportable level of income substantially (which intrinsically involves expectations), which then occasions an episode of rather rapid growth as agents act to move toward the supportable level. Conversely, governments can act in ways that reduce supportable income—to levels even below current income—in which case agents act in ways that lead to negative growth.

We now return to our two fundamental questions: Would deeper integration lead to more or less rapid economic growth? And, did countries that have moved from no sovereignty to full sovereignty experience higher or lower income growth? As countries become independent from colonialists (or other sovereigns), *EP* and *IP* moved from their values under no sovereignty to values under full sovereignty (which nevertheless may have involved some commitments to limited sovereignty in some policy dimensions). Before moving to the empirical evidence let us ask: What would we expect the impact to be? There are three possible movements (Figure 4.3).

a. The independence episode may correspond to a reduction in market size because of inevitable border effects, which in turn would lead to a decrease in supportable levels of income and hence an adjustment of lower growth relative to the no-independence counterfactual.

b. The independence episode allows the newly sovereign state to choose policies that are superior to the policies that were formerly imposed on the entity. In this case supportable income could increase (possibly dramatically), which then should produce economic growth more rapid than in the counterfactual condition. In fact, as Alesina, Spolare, and Wacziarg (2000) have argued, the choice of becoming independent may go hand in hand with the choice of adopting more open policies.

c. If the underlying political and social determinants of effective economic policies and institutional performance (Z) are unfavorable, the independence episode may unleash a dynamic in which policies even *worse* for supportable income than those imposed by the colonialist are adopted. This case could result in growth that is slower than the counterfactual—perhaps even negative.

One implication is that the *average* growth rate might not shift in any particular direction comparing pre- and post-independence, as there might be a mix of countries some of which adopt better policies and some worse policies. However, controlling for policies, one should observe that the larger the secured market lost, the greater the reduction in growth. In any case the variance of growth rates should be high whether or not the mean increases.

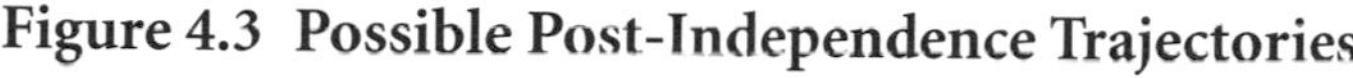

Figure 4.3 Possible Post-Independence Trajectories

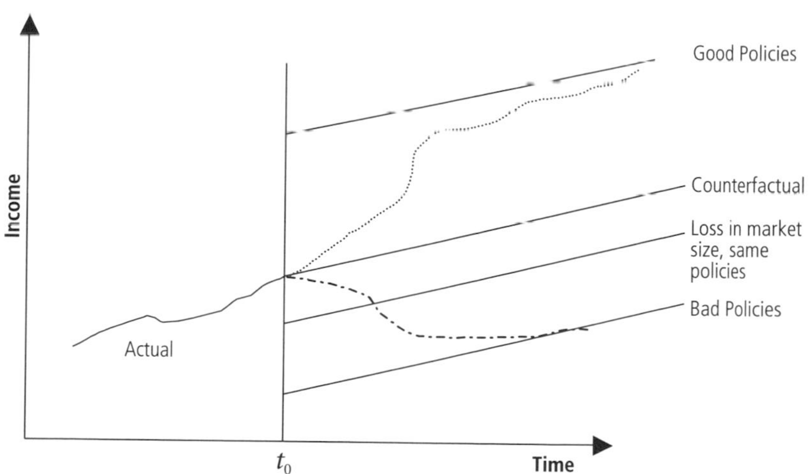

Episodic Evidence on the Impact of Independence on Per Capita Income

The episodic method has been used to examine a wide variety of phenomena from exchange rate devaluation to inflation stabilization. Empirically using the episodic method to examine the impact of independence is quite simple. For the *i*th country with date of independence t_0^i we calculate the growth rate of GDP per capita for periods of various length before and after t_0^i (ten, twenty, and thirty years, and the "maximum available sample," which is, at most, from 1900 to t_0^i and from t_0^i to 1992). This gives a simple *before-and-after* estimate.

$$\textit{Before and after } (n): g^i_{t_0^i, t_0^i+n} - g^i_{t_0^i, t_0^i-n}\,.$$

But the before-and-after approach ignores other factors that may have caused growth rates to be higher or lower for all countries (or, more particularly, for the country of interest). Another possible estimate is to compare the *difference* in growth rates over the postindependence period of a newly independent country versus a comparator set of countries over the same period:

$$\textit{Difference } (C,n): g^i_{t_0^i, t_0^i+n} - \overline{g}^C_{t_0^i, t_0^i-n}\,.$$

Since what we really want to determine is how much faster or slower a country would have grown had it not experienced an independence episode, we need to take into account the possibility that the country grew slower (or faster) than comparator countries because of persistent country-specific factors. Hence, when we have both before and after data for a set of countries that did and did not experience independence in a given time period we can calculate the estimate of the *difference of differences*, which is the growth acceleration (before and after independence) of a newly independent country less the before and after of the comparator countries over that same period:

$$\textit{Differences of differences } (C,n): (g^i_{t_0^i, t_0^i+n} - g^i_{t_0^i, t_0^i-n}) - (\overline{g}^C_{t_0^i, t_0^i+n} - \overline{g}^C_{t_0^i, t_0^i-n})\,.$$

Historical Evidence

Table 4.2 presents these three estimates for six countries that have long historical times series and that experienced independence in the post-WWII period (countries and comparator countries are determined by data availability). One comparator is the growth rate of average GDP per capita in seventeen developed countries.[7] The other is the growth

Table 4.2 Episodic Analysis of Countries with Long Historical Times Series
(Growth Rate, %, Since Independence)

	Year of Independence	Years Since Independence 10	20	30	Maximum[a]
Before and After					
India	1947	1.50	1.70	1.40	1.70
Indonesia	1945	1.00	1.30	2.20	2.20
South Korea	1945	2.20	5.20	5.60	4.50
Taiwan	1949	−1.80	3.20	6.00	5.40
Ghana	1957	1.3			−2.30
Philippines	1946	2.30			0.50
Average		1.08			2.00
Difference of Differences with Developed Countries					
India	1947	−2.70	−2.80	−3.30	0.00
Indonesia	1945	−4.20	−3.30	−2.50	0.50
South Korea	1945	−3.00	0.60	0.90	2.90
Taiwan	1949	−5.70	−1.50	1.40	3.80
Ghana	1957	0.90			−3.30
Philippines	1946	0.00			−1.00
Average		−2.45			0.48
Difference of Differences with Six Latin American Countries					
India	1947	−3.10	−2.00	−2.50	2.00
Indonesia	1945	−3.10	−2.30	−1.70	2.40
South Korea	1945	−1.90	1.60	1.70	4.90
Taiwan	1949	−7.60	−1.10	1.90	5.90
Ghana	1957	2.70			−1.20
Philippines	1946	0.40			1.00
Average		−2.10			2.50

Source: Calculations based on Maddison (1995) on real GDP per capita.
[a]For all countries except Ghana and the Philippines the "maximum" data is from 1900 to 1992, for Ghana the data begins in 1913. The interwar data (1938–46) is missing for the Philippines, so the comparison is 1929–38 versus 1950–60. The "maximum" comparison is 1900–38 versus 1950–92.

rate of six Latin American countries—which are developing countries but which had experienced independence much earlier (in the early-nineteenth century), so presumably any transitional independence effects had played out.

Several points should be highlighted. First, these countries growth rates did accelerate in the postindependence period in the short run and long run by 1 and 2 percentage points per annum respectively. Second, the data reveal the importance of comparison with developed countries. The years after independence were good years for growth for nearly all countries compared to the previous twenty years (depression followed by war). This means that, although countries' growth accelerated postindependence, so did that of the developed countries. Compared to the acceleration of the developed countries over this same period the acceleration of the newly independent countries was much lower—2.45 percentage points less. This same relative growth deficit persisted on average through twenty years—three of the four countries have postindependence growth accelerations smaller than the developed countries. Only in the very long run, comparing growth from 1900 to independence with growth from independence to 1992, is there some evidence of superior growth performance, with the average acceleration for the newly independent countries 0.5 percentage points faster over this period than the acceleration of the developed countries. But this suggests the growth payoff of independence comes in the very long run. Even thirty years on, growth acceleration was lower in India (by 3.3 percentage points) and Indonesia (by 2.5 percentage points) than in developed countries. Only after the growth acceleration after the ascension of President Soeharto in Indonesia the mid-1960s (twenty years postindependence) and the growth acceleration in India of the late 1970s (thirty years postindependence) did their accelerations outperform the developed countries.

Third, Table 4.2 demonstrates the huge variability in postindependence growth outcomes. Compared to the developed countries over the longest period—roughly forty-five years pre- and post-independence—two countries had dramatically outperformed the developed countries with growth accelerations of 2.9 (Korea) and 3.8 (Taiwan) percentage points larger; two countries had roughly similar performance with exactly the same acceleration (India) and .5 percent (Indonesia), and two had accelerated less than the developed countries, with Ghana experiencing an absolute deceleration of 2.3 percentage points and the Philippines accelerating only 0.5 percentage points—1 percentage point less than the developed economies.

We only have historical data for two Latin American countries that experienced independence in the early 1800s—Brazil (1822) and Mexico (1810). Since Maddison's data begins only in 1820 (for a large number of individual countries) we can only do difference estimates.

Table 4.3 Estimates of Post-Independence Growth Differences for Brazil and Mexico

	1820	1850	1870	1820–1850	1820–1870
Brazil	670	711	740	0.2%	0.2%
Mexico	760	668	710	–0.4%	–0.1%
Average				–0.1%	0.0%
Europe	1220	1498	1898	0.7%	0.9%
ARS	1236	2056	2626	1.7%	1.5%
Difference with Europe				–0.8%	–0.9%
India, Indonesia	572.5	602	608	0.2%	0.1%
USSR, China	637		773		0.4%
Developing	604.75		690		0.3%
Difference with developing countries				–0.3%	–0.1%

Table 4.3 shows the growth rates for Brazil and Mexico from 1820 to 1850 and 1870 compared to various other countries. Their growth rates are substantially slower than those in Europe, slower than the other "areas of recent settlement" (United States, Canada, Australia), and even slightly slower than India and Indonesia (which were not independent) and USSR and China, which were.

Episodic Analysis Using Recent (Post-1960) Data: Absolute Growth Differences

In this subsection we address the same empirical question using roughly the same technique. However, because we lack data before independence for many of the "newly independent" countries, instead of the difference of differences analysis we will just use differences in the growth performance of the newly independent countries and the growth over the same period of comparator groups of countries. We use two comparison groups: the trade weighted average of OECD countries, and all other developing countries (not in the midst of an independence episode).[8]

The basic result (Table 4.4) is that newly independent countries grew substantially slower than the OECD countries and about the same as all other developing countries. At every horizon the average and median growth of the newly independent countries was about 1 percent per annum *slower* than the OECD countries. This is striking because it implies that not only are these countries not gaining on the

Table 4.4 Differences in Growth Rates between Newly Independent and Other Countries

Gained Independence From:	N	10 Year			20 Year			Maximum Available Years		
			Difference			Difference			Difference	
		Growth of Newly Independent Countries (%)	OECD (%)	Independent (%)	Growth of Newly Independent Countries (%)	OECD (%)	Independent (%)	Growth of Newly Independent Countries (%)	OECD (%)	Independent (%)
France/Belgium	18									
Average		1.2	–2.9	–1.0	0.9	–2.3	–0.8	–0.1	–2.4	–0.9
Median		0.8	–3.2	–1.5	1.0	–2.3	–0.9	0.1	–2.3	–0.8
UK	27									
Average		3.1	0.4	1.7	2.2	0.1	1.4	1.8	–0.2	1.2
Median		2.7	0.2	0.6	2.0	–0.2	1.3	1.6	–0.3	1.0
Other	7									
Average		1.0	–1.0	–0.2	1.2	–0.9	0.6	1.2	–0.9	0.6
Median		–0.6	–2.0	–1.3	0.8	–1.6	0.1	0.8	–1.6	0.2
All	52									
Average		2.1	–0.9	0.5	1.6	–0.9	0.5	1.1	–1.1	0.4
Median		1.8	–0.9	–0.1	1.7	–1.1	0.3	0.7	–1.6	–0.2
Using different sample of countries and data										
All	61									
Average		2.2		–.6						
Median		2.8		–.7						

Source: Appendix 1.

OECD, but they are actually falling further and further behind. Compared to other developing countries the growth of newly independent countries growth is about the same—*average* growth is slightly higher (by about 0.5 percentage points at each horizon) but *median* growth is slightly lower at ten years and in the long run. This implies that while a few newly independent countries did very well, the *typical* newly independent country fared about the same as if there had been no independence episode. There are also differences based on the former colonialist, with French colonies doing substantially worse and British colonies doing substantially better—but this is perhaps explained by the fact that in this sample all the French independences are in Africa while the former British colonies are spread between Africa, Caribbean, and Asia Pacific region.

Episodic on Independence: Recent Difference of Differences

There are many fewer countries for which the national income data exists both before and after independence. We have two sources of data. One is the Maddison (1995) historical data, which has data going back to 1950 for five countries in addition to those with long historical series in Table 4.2. The second is the standard data source on constant price, local currency GDP per capita for countries for which the data go back in time both for the newly independent country and the comparators. This means the second set are mainly countries for which independence was more recent, which are, in turn, usually much smaller than the average country.

For those recently independent countries, growth is slower before than after independence. For the sample of twenty-six countries with data the average (median) ten-year growth jumps from 1.5 percent (1.2 percent) before independence to 2.0 percent (2.7 percent) after. Over this same period in which these countries gained independence, the continuously independent countries' growth rates actually decelerated, growing 0.8 percent slower. Therefore the difference of differences suggests that the newly independent countries grew roughly 1 percentage point faster postindependence than the comparator developing countries.

This difference, however, does not suggest that all of the gain was a large growth spurt, as the newly independent countries on average grew faster by only 0.6 percentage points in their first ten years postindependence than did the continuously independent countries. But they grew 1.2 percent faster than the comparators since these in-

Table 4.5 Before and After and Difference of Differences Estimates of Circa-1960 Independences

		10 Years			1950 to t, t to End of Data		
			Differences of Differences (%)			Differences of Differences (%)	
Country	Year of Independence	Before and After (%)	Developed	Latin America	Before and After (%)	Developed	Latin America
Morocco	1956	–1.70	–2.00	–0.90	–0.20	0.40	1.00
Côte d'Ivoire	1960	2.40	1.80	2.60	–1.40	–0.90	0.00
Kenya	1963	2.00	1.50	1.50	0.20	0.90	1.40
Tanzania	1961	1.80	1.30	1.70	–0.50	0.10	0.80
Zaire	1960	3.20	–3.80	–3.00	–4.30	–3.80	–2.90
Average		0.26	–0.24	0.38	–1.24	–0.66	0.06

Table 4.6 Episodic Analysis of Recent Independences, 10-Year Before and After and Difference of Differences

			10-Year Horizon	
Country	Year of Independence	From	Before and After (Acceleration Positive) (%)	Difference of Differences with "Old Independent" Developing Countries (%)
Cape Verde	1975	Portugal	6.9	8.9
Malta	1964	Britain	5.6	5.0
Angola	1975	Portugal	3.4	5.4
Guyana	1966	Britain	3.4	3.1
Kenya	1963	Britain	2.1	1.1
Uganda	1962	Britain	1.8	0.8
Malawi	1964	Britain	1.6	0.9
Fiji	1970	Britain	1.3	2.6
Nigeria	1960	Britain	0.9	–0.4
Seychelles	1976	Britain	0.3	2.5
Zaire	1960	Belgium	–0.5	–1.7
Bahamas	1973	Britain	–1.9	0.6
Comoros	1975	France	–2.2	–0.2
Papua New Guinea	1975	Australia	–2.5	–0.4
Belize	1981	Britain	–2.7	–1.4
Trinidad & Tobago	1962	Britain	–3.6	–4.5
Mozambique	1975	Portugal	–3.8	–1.7
Guinea-Bissau	1973	Portugal	–7.4	–4.8
Average			0.6	1.2
Median			0.9	0.8

dependences mainly occurred in a period in which other countries were slowing down.

Summary of Episodic Analysis

There are three outcomes of the episodic analysis for the various periods (from the 1800s to 1980s) with various comparators.

First, in no case did independence bring an acceleration of growth relative to the developed countries. While one might have thought that freeing countries up to pursue policies in the national interest would allow them to converge more rapidly, this was not the case. The difference and the difference of differences estimates suggest that

Table 4.7 Summarizing the Episodic Analysis of Independence

				Developed				LDC			
		Before and After		Diffs in Diffs		Differences		Diffs in Diffs		Differences	
	Number of Countries	10	Long	10	Long	10	Long	10	Long	10	Long
Historical, 1900–92	6[a]	1.1	2.0	–2.5	.5			–2.1	2.5		
Historical, 1820–70	2[b]						–.9				–.1
Recent (post-1960)	52					–.9	–1.1			.5	.4
Recent (post-1960)	61									–.6	
Recent (with pre-1960 data)	5[c]	.26	–1.24	–.24	–.66			.38	.06		
Recent (mostly 1970s, 80s)	17	.6						1.2			

[a]India, Indonesia, South Korea, Taiwan, Philippines, Ghana; [b]Mexico, Brazil; [c]Morocco, Côte d'Ivoire, Kenya, Tanzania, Zaire.

postindependence countries grow *slower* relative to the developed countries than in the preindependence period for a considerable time (at least thirty years).

Second, the evidence of the growth rates of newly independent versus continually independent developing countries is mixed, with the sense that they are "about the same"—postindependence growth is neither dramatically higher nor dramatically lower than that in countries not experiencing independence. (Exceptions are those countries becoming independent in the late 1970s and 1980s.)

Third, while *on average* independence did not create an increased tendency toward convergence, there is enormous variability around these "average" results. Postindependence, some countries grew very rapidly and did in fact converge on the income of the leaders (South Korea, Taiwan, and Singapore). Some just muddled along. Other countries actually saw income *fall* precipitously after independence.

Case Study: The Caribbean

Two difficulties with attempting to estimate the impact of independence are, first, that those countries that are still dependent are by and large atypically small, and second, by being dependent, do not have easily available comparable income data. This has bedeviled our efforts to estimate the growth of still dependent countries as the counterfactual for the newly independent countries. However, within the Caribbean there is something of a natural experiment, as there are a large number of entities that are reasonably similar in size, that share geographic features by being in or bordering the Caribbean, and hence that one might expect to have reasonably similar outcomes on other grounds. However, some have become independent relatively recently (since the 1960s), while others gained independence many years ago (Haiti was the first, in 1804).

Table 4.8 shows the interesting, if well known, fact that median GNP per capita is 3 times higher in the still dependent countries than in the recently independent countries ($15,000 versus $4,500). The median is nearly an entire order of magnitude higher in dependents than the old independents (which includes Haiti and Cuba).

Variability in Performance: Countries versus Regions

To this point the analysis has shown that sovereign countries have done no better economically than countries that lack sovereignty. The gain of political sovereignty has, at the very least, not been an unmitigated blessing. This might suggest that the lesson of disintegration is

Table 4.8 Level of GDP per Capita within the Caribbean: Still Dependents, Recent Independents, and Old Independents

Country	Independent From	PPP GDP Per Capita
Still dependent		
Anguilla	—	8,200
Aruba	—	28,000
Bermuda	—	33,000
British Virgin Islands	—	16,000
Cayman Islands	—	24,500
French Guiana	—	6,000
Guadeloupe	—	9,000
Martinique	—	11,000
Netherlands Antilles	—	24,400
Puerto Rico	—	10,000
Virgin Islands	—	15,000
Average		16,827
Median		15,000
Recent independents		
St. Kitt	Britain	7,000
Antigua	Britain	8,200
Belize	Britain	3,200
St. Lucia	Britain	4,500
St. Vincent	Britain	2,800
Dominica	Britain	4,000
Suriname	The Netherlands	3,400
Grenada	Britain	4,400
Bahamas	Britain	15,000
Barbados	Britain	14,500
Guyana	Britain	4,800
Jamaica	Britain	3,700
Trinidad	Britain	9,500
Average		6,538
Median		4,500
Old independents		
Cuba	—	1,700
Dominican Republic	—	5,700
Haiti	—	1,800
Average		3,067
Median		1,800

that it "does no harm"—the losses from new borders and the poten tially diminished market size *can* be more than compensated for by better policies, but *on average* the combination of lost market size and policy-setting capacity has been a wash. However, this ignores the very important point of the *variance* of growth rates. It may well be that the lack of full or partial policy sovereignty does not guarantee higher growth rates. Rather, limited policy sovereignty sacrifices the best outcomes to eliminate the worst. Let us present two suggestive pieces of evidence: comparison of standard deviations of growth rates across regions within a country versus across countries, and the performance if newly independent countries after the break-up of the USSR.

States within Countries (India, United States) versus Countries

To some extent growth rates of various countries are arbitrary, in so far as boundaries are arbitrary. There is no deep historical necessity or compelling logic to many of the national boundaries that exist today: they were often imposed by contingencies of history or by colonial powers with no regard for on-the-ground realities. So, even though India contains approximately the population of sub-Saharan Africa (SSA) and Latin America and the Caribbean (LAC) *combined,* India is *one* country whereas there are seventy-five countries in our sample (below) in SSA and LAC. This is not because India is any more geographically or economically homogenous than regions of LAC or of SSA. Similarly, the United States, which began as a federation of independent sovereigns, has states that are larger (in terms of both population and market size) than most other countries. One could easily imagine that, had history taken a different course, various states of India or the United States would have been independent countries. In this sense, one can compare the variability of growth performance across the states of India or the United States—which have, to a large extent, ceded sovereignty to the nation—with the variability of countries to see how much the variance of growth outcomes is reduced by a commitment to deep integration.

Table 4.9 shows the standard deviations of the growth rates across fourteen major states of India and fifty states of the United States for various periods with the standard deviations of the growth rates of countries within regions. The standard deviation of growth across states is .6 percentage points. Every region in the developing world has a standard deviation at least *three times* as high. Interestingly, countries within Western Europe—which have moved increasingly toward arrangements that limit nation-state sovereignty—have a standard deviation of growth nearly as small as India.

Table 4.9 Variability of Growth Rates across the States of India Versus across Countries within Regions

		Standard Deviation of Growth Rates			
Country/Region	*N*	1960s (%)	1970s (%)	1980s (%)	1960–92 (%)
U.S. (States)	50				.63[a]
India	14	0.8	1.2	1.4	0.6
Countries within regions					
Middle East, North Africa	19	1.7	2.5	1.0	4.2
East Asia, Pacific	19	2.4	2.5	2.3	2.3
Eastern Europe	6	1.5	1.4	1.9	1.9
Sub-Saharan Africa	46	2.5	3.4	1.9	1.9
Latin America and Caribbean	29	1.6	2.0	1.2	1.9
Western Europe	17	1.2	1.1	0.9	0.7

Sources: U.S. Census for population and BEA for real State GSP; Indian state data are from Datt and Ravallion, India Growth and Poverty Project, 1954–94. Other countries are from PWT5.6.
[a]1986–2000 for U.S.

We are aware that we are pointing out the obvious. If people, capital, and goods are allowed to move freely across regions, then the scope for the very worst growth outcomes, which are often the result of predatory states, are precluded. On the other hand, it is not the case that *mean* growth in India was high, so presumably some states might also have pursued *better* economic policies than chosen by the center.

Breakup of the USSR

Again, an obvious point from the economic collapse that followed the demise of the Soviet empire and the USSR in particular was not only that there was an economic catastrophe, but also that the magnitude of the fall varied widely across the newly independent countries. The peak-to-trough fall in income that followed the creation of the new countries varied from merely the levels of the U.S. Great Depression (the Baltics, Uzbekistan, Belarus), to those whose income fell roughly in half (Russia, Khazakastan, Kyrgyz Republic), to those who did even worse. Obviously the "benefit" of being part of the USSR was that, although growth was low on average, the worst extremes had been averted and the variance of outcomes was reduced. As the postinde-

Table 4.10 Variability in the Economic Collapse of the FSU Countries

Country of Former USSR	Percentage Fall, Peak to Trough (%)	Peak	Trough In data
Uzbekistan	–26.5	1989	1995
Lithuania	–35.4	1989	1993
Estonia	–36.2	1989	1994
Belarus	–39.5	1989	1995
Russia	–42.6	1989	1996
Kazakhstan	–48.0	1988	1995
Latvia	–49.0	1989	1993
Kyrgyzstan	–52.9	1990	1995
Turkmenistan	–57.0	1988	1996
Ukraine	–57.8	1989	1996
Moldova	–66.0	1989	1996
Armenia	–68.3	1985	1993
Tajikistan	70.4	1988	1996
Azerbaijan	–73.2	1987	1996
Georgia	–80.6	1985	1994

pendence period proceeds there will likely be increasing divergence amongst the areas of the former Soviet Union.

The same is true, if perhaps to a lesser extent, in Eastern Europe. Now that the region is no longer under the Soviet Union umbrella some Eastern European countries are doing reasonably well (Poland, Hungary, Slovenia), while others are doing badly (e.g., Romania), and others formerly "within the Soviet sphere" have disintegrated even further. The (involuntary) integration of the Eastern European countries with the USSR appears to have reduced the variability in outcomes they experienced while possibly hampering their average growth.

An Empirical Investigation: Market Size and Policy Independence

In our theoretical section we argued that independence would likely impact growth through two factors: the change in the secure market size and the change in the economic policies that the new independence allows. In this section we explore these factors empirically. We concentrate on the first twenty years of postindependence experience and try to explain the factors that account for the different growth experiences across countries. We take as our dependent variable the cumulative rate of growth of newly independent countries expressed in annual terms during the first twenty years after independence. This provides us with a sample of fifty-one countries.

To measure the decline in secure market size that a country underwent due to independence we calculate the percentage decline in secure market access. This is done by calculating the ratio of the distance-weighted GDP of the secured economic area lost because of independence (composed of the colonizer and the other colonies that were part of the same sovereign jurisdiction) to the total secured market before independence (composed of the area lost plus the internal distance-weighted GDP of the newly independent country):

$$\text{Secure market lost} = \frac{[\text{DWGDP(colonizer)} + \text{DWGDP(other ex-colonies)}]}{[\text{DWGDP(newly independent)} + \text{DWGDP(colonizer)} + \text{DWGDP(other ex-colonies)}]}.$$

We take this as a measure of the size of the reduction in secure market access for any producer in the newly independent economy. The variable is bound between zero and one and takes high values when the loss of market access is large. We used the CIA World Factbook for 2001. GDP figures are for 1999. In the same spirit, we also consider whether a country became landlocked as a consequence of its independence. We therefore calculate a dummy variable, which takes the value of 1 if this is the case.

As a measure of domestic policies we use the black market premium. We chose this variable because it indicates a failure to achieve macro balance and thus complicates international economic integration.[9] This variable is available for forty-four out of the fifty-one countries in our sample. We also consider the number of revolutions during the first twenty years of independence as a measure of problems in setting domestic policies.

Finally, we control for the initial level of GDP and for the rate of growth of the trade-weighted countries during the first twenty years of independence of each of our observations. The results are presented in the Table 4.11 below.

The results broadly show the importance of the reduction in market size as an explanatory variable for growth in the postindependence period. The typical country in the sample lost 78 percent of the secured market. The estimated coefficient, which varies between 0.25 and 0.43, implies that for the average newly independent country the impact of a smaller market size implied a growth rate of about 2 to 3

Table 4.11 Determinants of New Independents' Growth

	Average GDP per capita growth rate (independent to independent+20 years)									
	(1)	(2)	(3)	(4)	(5)	(6)	(7)	(8)	(9)	(10)
Dependent variable										
log(GDP per capita at independence)	0.0057	0.0040	0.005328	0.005809	0.0009	0.0021	0.0028	0.0006	−0.0006	0.0008
	1.26	0.93	1.16	1.24	0.21	0.44	0.56	0.13	−0.13	0.17
Trading partners GDP pc growth (%)	0.0089	0.0047	0.002886	0.004159	0.0058	0.0036	0.0047	0.0053	0.0044	0.0075
	2.02	1.1	0.56	0.79	1.51	0.72	0.9	1.05	0.9	1.54
New landlock	−0.0050				−0.0043	−0.0059	−0.0083	−0.0047	−0.0062	−0.0043
	−0.5				−0.55	−0.67	−0.9	−0.55	−0.73	−0.5
Share of market lost (colonizer + other colonies/own + colonizer + other colonies)	−0.0344				−0.0433	−0.0354	−0.0250	−0.0392	−0.0390	−0.0365
	−2.36				−3.39	−2.03	−1.43	−2.28	−2.33	−2.14
Revolutions (total)		−0.0024			−0.0029			−0.0017	−0.0023	−0.0025
		−3.11			−4.09			−1.62	−2.89	−3.14
Black market premium (average)			−3.83E−05			−5.35E−05		2.69E−05		
			−2.06			−2.85		−1.1		
Black market premium (higher than median = 14.87)				−0.0106			−0.0140		−0.0109	
				−1.54			−2.02		−1.7	
Constant	−0.0209	−0.0175	−0.02756	−0.0320	0.0373	0.0227	0.0101	0.0343	0.0507	0.0250
	−0.54	−0.48	−0.69	−0.78	1.03	0.53	0.22	0.81	1.16	0.5
R^2	0.2101	0.2423	0.17	0.1334	0.4242	0.2892	0.2229	0.3365	0.3645	0.315
Adjusted R^2	0.1414	0.1939	0.1077	0.0684	0.3602	0.1956	0.1184	0.2289	0.2615	0.2248
Number of observations		51	51	44	44	51	44	44	44	44

Continued on next page

Table 4.11 Determinants of New Independents' Growth, continued

	Mean	Standard Deviation	Minimum	Maximum
Summary statistics				
Average GDP per capita growth rate (independent to independent+20 years)	0.0146	0.0215	–0.0221	0.0650
log(GDP per capita at independence)	6.9134	0.7169	5.7137	9.2437
Trading partners GDP per capita growth (%)	2.8283	0.6959	1.2135	4.6012
New landlock	0.1818	0.3902	0	1
Share of market lost (colonizer + other colonies/own + colonizer + other colonies)	0.7808	0.2033	0.0867	0.9819
Revolutions (total)	3.1364	3.9918	0	16
Black market premium (average)	0.5	0.5058	0	1

		(1)	(2)	(3)	(4)	(5)	(6)	(7)
Correlation matrix								
Average GDP per capita growth rate (Independent to Independent+20 years)	(1)	1						
log(GDP per capita at independence)	(2)	0.1639	1					
Trading partners GDP per capita growth (%)	(3)	0.1786	–0.2865	1				
New landlock	(4)	–0.2295	–0.3608	–0.0461	1			
Share of market lost (colonizer + other colonies/own + colonizer + other colonies)	(5)	–0.1777	–0.2113	0.3055	0.3887	1		
Revolutions (total)	(6)	–0.4058	–0.2295	–0.1121	0.0434	–0.276	1	
Black market premium (average)	(7)	–0.3106	–0.0357	–0.3979	–0.1179	–0.2727	0.2649	1

Note: t-statistics below coefficient

percent slower. A one standard deviation change in market size would explain about a 0.6 percent growth difference over 20 years.

Revolutions and black market premia also have significant effects on the growth experience of the newly independent countries. Each additional revolution lowered growth by about 0.2 percent over the twenty-year period. Notice that the mean number of revolutions is 3.1 with a standard deviation of 3.9. Hence, a one standard deviation difference would account for growth differences of about 0.8 percent.

We estimated the effect of the black market premium in two ways. First, we calculated the average black market premium over the twenty-year period. We also created a dummy variable that is equal to one for countries with above-average black market premia. Both measures are significant in most specifications. The estimated effect implies that countries with black market premia above the median grew on average 1 percent less than those with smaller premia.

Interestingly, in this sample we observe no convergence, nor is the growth of the trading partners a significant determinant of the growth experience of individual countries. Once account is made of the decline in the secured market, the newly landlocked countries do not significantly underperform, even though the estimated coefficient is insignificant but consistently negative and equal to about –0.5.

In sum, the data seem to suggest that the reduction in secured market size is an important determinant of the growth experience after independence, as are the potentialities for new forms of economic and policy problems associated with the formation of the new country.

It could be argued that these two effects are not independent. Countries that would suffer a greater collapse in their secured market size may face greater difficulties in stabilizing their economies postindependence. If this were the case, the estimated coefficients would be biased toward zero. One way to address this possibility is to use a two-stage process. In the first stage we estimate equations for the black market premium and for the number of revolutions, and in the second stage we use the estimated values in the regression for growth. As Table 4.12 shows, the estimated effects remain significant, and the estimated coefficient almost doubles in size.

Table 4.12 Determinants of New Independents' Growth, Total Effect of Market Size

	OLS Regressions (First Stage)		IV Regressions: Average GDP per capita growth rate (independent to independent+20 years)	
	Black Market Premium (Average)	Revolutions (Total)		
	(1)	(2)	(3)	(4)
Dependent variable				
log(GDP per capita at independence)	20.45405	−0.483553	−0.009246	−0.002407
	0.42	−0.41	−0.83	−0.36
Trading partners GDP per capita growth (%)	−115.2695	−0.813258	0.004125	−0.004605
	−3.03	−0.89	0.54	−0.53
New landlock	6.424908	0.764755	−6.95E−05	−0.005645
	0.09	0.45	−0.01	−0.53
Share of market lost (colonizer + other colonies/own + colonizer + other colonies)	−297.3103	−6.727303	−0.075638	−0.059146
	−2.22	−2.1	−1.8	−2.14
Revolutions (total)			−0.008426	
			−1.66	
Black market premium (average)				−0.000135
				−2.08
Island	−196.5339	−3.153242		
	−2.33	−1.56		
Constant	530.9817	14.53779	0.152306	0.101594
	1.45	1.66	1.22	1.29
R^2	0.375	0.2267		
Adjusted R^2	0.2929	0.125		
Number of observations	44	44	44	44

Equations (3) and (4): Instruments for Revolutions and BMP: New Landlock, Share of Market Lost and Island

Note: t-statistics below coefficient.

Conclusion and Future Extensions

The literature on border effects suggests that the creation and elimination of borders have significant economic consequences. The last sixty years have seen a tripling of the number of sovereign states with their associated borders. Sovereignty implies the right to restrict trade and migration, the power to issue money, the discretion to regulate and set macro policies, and the discretion to enforce contracts. Integration agreements can be interpreted as attempts between sovereign states reciprocally to renounce some of these rights in order to facilitate economic activity.

This chapter has tried to use the historical record of disintegration in order to derive some lessons for the integration process. We find that countries that became independent in general saw their growth rates decline relative to those of OECD countries, meaning that independence did not facilitate convergence. Also, the comparison to still dependent entities suggests that the costs of sovereignty may not be trivial. The evidence from the Caribbean suggests that the old independent countries are poorest while the still dependent are richest. However, in comparison to developing countries that were already independent, the results are less clear. There is a big increase in variance in the performance of newly independent countries: some are doing very well while others have deteriorated very significantly.

The econometric evidence suggests that the impact of sovereignty on growth depends on the balance between two forces: on the one hand, the reduction in secure market access, which includes the possibility of migrating to other regions of the sovereign jurisdiction; on the other, the change in the quality of policies. These may move the economy to a more open economic stance in order to compensate for the reduction in the size of the secure market. Singapore, Slovenia, and the Baltic states may be examples of this. Alternatively, political economy problems may translate into internal difficulties that close off the economy. We find that the black market premium helps explain the relative performance of newly independent states.

Our tentative conclusion is that integration agreements have the potential to increase the size of the secured market and thus increase incomes. However, it is critical that these agreements improve the quality of domestic policies. Arrangements that deteriorate the overall policy framework may in fact limit the effective market size by reducing the space of contractible arrangements within the country, within the union, or among the economic links to the rest of the world. Earlier attempts at integration in the Americas may have had some of these negative effects.

It would be interesting to shed some further light on the aspects of integration that are important for income by analyzing the relative growth performance of newly independent states that maintained certain features of integration. For example, some countries, such as the Caribbean and the CFA (Communauté Financière Africaine, or Cooperation Financière en Afrique Centrale) Franc Zone in Africa, established currency unions after independence. Others kept free trade areas with their former colonizers and neighbors. How does their performance compare to that of countries that adopted a more unilateral approach to integration? Did these arrangements facilitate effective integration or did they limit it? What is the relative importance of trade arrangements vis-à-vis currency unions? How significant are migratory flows in facilitating income convergence? Is this the mechanism that makes some of the still dependent entities so rich? Is it fiscal transfers?

The experiment with political disintegration is perhaps the most significant policy event of the last fifty years. It is an experience that should shed light on many current debates. Yet the impacts seem remarkably under-investigated and the returns to further exploration seem high.

References

Alesina, Alberto, Enrico Spolare, and Romain Wacziarg. 2000. "Economic Integration and Political Disintegration." *American Economic Review* 90 (5): 1276–96.

Anderson, James E., and Eric Van Wincoop. 2001. "Gravity with Gravitas: A Solution to the Border Puzzle." National Bureau of Economic Research, Cambridge, MA.

Bradford, Scott, and Robert Z. Lawrence. 2003. "Paying the Price: The Costs of Fragmented International Markets." Photocopy.

Clemens, Michael, and Jeffrey Williamson. 2002. "Closed Jaguar, Open Dragon: Comparing Tariffs in Latin America and Asia before World War II." Photocopy. (December).

Edwards, Sebastian, and I. Igal Magendzo. 2002. "A Currency of One's Own? An Empirical Investigation on Dollarization and Indpendent Currency Unions." Photocopy.

Engel, Charles, and John H. Rogers. 1996. "How Wide is the Border?" *American Economic Review* 86 (5): 1112–25.

European Commission. 1988. "The European Challenge 1992: Benefits of a Single Market" (Ceccini Report).

Frankel, Jeffrey A., and David Romer. 1999. "Does Trade Cause Growth?" *American Economic Review* 89 (3) (June): 379–99.

Frankel, Jeffrey A., and Andrew K. Rose. 2000. "Estimating the Effect of Currency Unions on Trade and Output." National Bureau of Economic Research Working Paper no. 7857. Cambridge, MA.

Helliwell, John. 1998. *How Much Do National Borders Matter?* Washington, DC: Brookings Institution.

Helliwell, John, and Ross McKitrick. 1998. "Comparing Capital Mobility across Provincial and National Borders." National Bureau of Economic Research Working Paper no. 6624. Cambridge, MA.

Maddison, Agnus. 1995. "Monitoring the World Economy: 1820–1992." Organization for Economic Cooperation and Development, Development Centre Studies. Paris: OECD.

McCallum, John. 1995. "National Borders Matter: Regional Trade Patterns in North America." *American Economic Review* 85 (3): 615–23.

Obstfeld, Maurice, and Kenneth Rogoff. 2000. "The Six Major Puzzles in International Macroeconomics: Is There A Common Cause?" In *National Bureau of Economic Research Macroeconomics Annual 2000*, pp. 339–390. Cambridge, MA: National Bureau of Economic Research.

Parsley, David C. and Shang-Jin Wei. 1996. "Convergence to the Law of One Price Without Trade Barriers or Currency Fluctuations." *Quarterly Journal of Economics* 111: 1211–36.

———. 2000. "Explaining the Border Effect: The Role of Exchange Rate Variability, Shipping Costs and Geography." National Bureau of Economic Research Working Paper no. 7836. Cambridge, MA.

———. 2001. "Limiting Currency Volatility to Stimulate Goods Market Integration." National Bureau of Economic Research Working Paper no. 8468. Cambridge, MA.

Pritchett, Lant. 2003. "A Conclusion to Cross National Growth Research: A Foreword 'To the Countries Themselves.'" In *Explaining Growth: A Global Research Project*, edited by Gary McMahon and Lyn Squire. New York: Palgrave Macmillan.

Rodriguez, Francisco, and Dani Rodrik. 2001. "Trade Policy and Economic Growth: A Skeptic's Guide to the Cross-National Evidence." In *NBER Macroeconomic Annual 2000*, edited by Ben S. Bernanke and Kenneth Rogoff. Cambridge, MA: MIT Press.

Sachs, Jeffrey, and Andrew Warner. 1995. "Economic Reform and the Process of Global Integration." *Brookings Papers on Economic Activity* 1: 1–118.

Notes

1 Other methods and sources give different numbers, but with the same direction. Alesina, Spolare, and Wacziarg (2000) report 69 in 1920, 89 in 1950, and 192 in 1995.

2 By contrast, Anderson and Van Wincoop (2001) argue that the McCallum approach (1995) significantly overestimates the effect because of the small size of the Canadian economy relative to that of the United States. They estimate the effect to cause a reduction of trade of "only" 44 percent.

3 This view is shared by Obstfeld and Rogoff (2000), who find that, while high elasticities of substitution across finely disaggregated items can account for some of the home bias puzzle in quantities (so that small barriers inducing relatively small price differentials could explain large quantity differences with little welfare loss), the results on prices are much harder to explain.

4 More recently, Edwards and Magendzo (2002) examined the impact of international currency unions and "strict dollarization" and found some effects of higher growth rates of international currency unions—but the results were strongly determined by a few small countries.

5 Rodriguez and Rodrik (2001) challenge this result.

6 Pritchett (2003) illustrates the dangers of this confusion, as growth regressions on *policy outcomes* (results of the mapping of the state of the world into a particular policy action) will not give reliable inference about the growth impacts of underlying *policies* (the mapping itself).

7 Australia, Austria, Belgium, Canada, Denmark, Finland, France, Germany, Italy, Japan, Netherlands, New Zealand, Norway, Sweden, Switzerland, the United Kingdom, and the United States.

8 We also did the calculations comparing newly independent countries to countries that are: (1) in the same income quartile, (2) with similar export structure (e.g., minerals, manufacturers), (3) similarly in the tropics (or not), and (4) similarly landlocked (or not).

9 This variable is readily available, and according to Rodriguez and Rodrik (2001) it captures the bulk of the explanatory power of the Sachs and Warner (1995) openness variable.

5

The Old and New Regionalism: Benefits, Costs, and Implications for the FTAA

Robert Devlin and Paolo Giordano

Introduction

Since the days of independence Latin American countries have witnessed repeated attempts to "get together" in political and/or economic terms. The early postwar integration initiatives that grew up in the era of import substitution industrialization (ISI) strategies tended to stall in the 1970s, and collapsed in the 1980s under the weight of their own shortcomings and the debt crisis. However, just when it appeared that the region's proclivity for integration was being eclipsed by the shift in the development paradigm popularized by the "Washington Consensus," there emerged a renewed interest in regional integration in the 1990s that continues unabated today (IDB 2002).

The contemporary critics of regional integration have generally staked out their primary concerns in arguments that are not unlike those that underpinned earlier postwar critiques; for example, welfare losses due to trade diversion, negative effects on third parties, and systematic degradation of the world trading system. Meanwhile, the arguments supporting regional integration in the 1990s turned on many issues not heard of during the Old Regionalism. This distinction is captured by Ethier (1998a) in his article "The New Regionalism." He highlights the big differences between regional approaches then and now which makes the traditional critique a risk rather than a near certainty. More to the point, Ethier emphasizes the New Regionalism's potential for strengthening openness, structural reform, and compatibility with a healthy multilateral system.

One major new dimension of integration emerging in the 1990s is north-south integration. A notable manifestation of this is the pursuit of a Free Trade Area of the Americas (FTAA) agreement, which began in 1995 and aims to finish negotiations by 2005. Again, the idea of hemispheric free trade is not new.[1] In the First International Americas Conference of 1890 there was a proposal from the U.S. Congress to discuss a common currency and a customs union. Once again in 1960 the governor of New York, Nelson Rockefeller, proposed a hemispheric free trade area and the following year the U.S. undersecretary of commerce proposed the elimination of impediments to trade and movement of capital in the Americas. In 1964 a subcommittee in the U.S. Congress reflected on the desirability of a Western Hemisphere common market while a leading U.S. senator pointed to the strategic importance of creating a hemispheric trading area in the face of increasing ties in Europe (Dell 1966: 32). Pointedly, these initiatives and ideas came from the United States, not Latin America.

That the FTAA in some ways reverses that trend is a telling characteristic of the New Regionalism. The FTAA emerged as a centerpiece of the December 1994 Miami Summit. However, the issue of trade reached the agenda only a few months before the summit itself, and only with considerable difficulty. Indeed, the FTAA emerged largely from pressure of Latin American governments, which were reluctant to assume the summit's extensive commitments for cooperation without the central platform of a free trade initiative (Hayes 1996).

As late as the mid-1980s a free trade area involving North America would have been politically inconceivable. Indeed, Latin Americans traditionally were concerned about an excessive inflow of U.S. private capital and opposed to placing "the limited industry that Latin America has been able to establish at the mercy of United States competition" (Dell 1966). Those concerns generally have been alleviated, although echoes of this refrain can still be heard in some quarters.

The difference between the Old and New Regionalisms lies in objectives and instruments on the one hand and outcomes on the other. To understand some of the logic of the FTAA for Latin America as well as its potential pitfalls, lessons can be learned from the debates surrounding both episodes of integration. With this in mind, this chapter: (1) highlights and contrasts the objectives and instruments of the two episodes, (2) reviews the theoretical and empirical literature that spans the two episodes and examines regional and hemispheric outcomes in trade and integration, and (3) muses about how an FTAA would fit into the dynamics of the New Regionalism and explores some policy issues that should be taken into account given past experiences.

Old and New Regionalism: Objectives and Instruments

Objectives

Table 5.1 presents the stylized objectives of the Old versus New Regionalisms. The similarities generally are linked to the generic characteristics of almost any regional integration scheme.[2] The differences, however, are the factors that most condition outcomes and should be the major focus of attention in the discussion about regionalism.

Following Ethier (1998a; 1998b), what makes the New Regionalism so different from the Old is the policy framework that it is supporting. The old supported a highly protectionist ISI model that was inward looking in intent and single minded in approach. As Echevarria (1997: 79–102) points out, import substitution was “the main—really the only—goal of integration.” It was anticipated that costs associated with limited regional liberalization would be offset by special and differential treatment for smaller economies, industrial planning, and financing. The parties were politically sensitive to issues of balance between small and big countries and much less sensitive to whether their partners were democracies or authoritarian regimes. Finally, no reciprocal bilateral agreements were pursued with industrialized countries, and only a handful of countries were members of GATT.

From the above perspective, the New Regionalism turns the Old Regionalism on its head (Devlin and Estevadeordal 2001). The New Regionalism is an integral part of the structural adjustment process that is designed to make the economies more market oriented, open, outward looking, and internationally competitive in a modern democratic institutional setting. It has combined regional elimination of tariffs with very substantial unilateral and multilateral opening. This three-tier process is aimed at minimizing the costs of trade diversion and, coupled with other domestic structural reforms, makes the regional market an enabling environment for achieving export growth, diversification, and international competitiveness. The New Regionalism has not been very attentive to the issue of balance between partners, but has been fostering democracy as a condition for participation. Finally, there is an increasing disposition to formally link up with industrialized countries through regional free trade areas (FTAs), but also in the World Trade Organization (WTO), in which all countries are now active members.

Table 5.1 Old and New Regionalism in Latin America: Objectives and Stylized Facts

Old	New	Similar	Different
Policy framework			
Support import-substitution industrialization	Support structural reforms		•
Support authoritarian or democratic regimes	Support democratic regimes only		•
Static issues			
Create a preferential regional market	Create preferential regional market	•	
Create home market-like access	Create home market-like access	•	
Improve terms of trade	Improve terms of trade	•	
Maintain / increase external protection	Reduce external protection		•
Promote trade diversion	Minimize trade diversion		•
Scope: goods only	Scope: goods, services, investment, intellectual property, etc.		•
Dynamic issues			
Rationalize protected industries & achieve economies of scale	Rationalize protected industries & achieve economies of scale	•	
Promote investment	Promote investment	•	
Control/limit FDI	Attract FDI		•
Absorb unemployed / underemployed resources	More efficiency criteria		•
Limit regional competition	Promote regional competition		•
Limited concern for competitiveness and exports	Promote competitiveness and exports		•
Non-traditional effects			
Non-traditional effects: none	Lock-in; signaling; non-trade cooperation		•
Improve regional bargaining power	Improve international bargaining power		•

Continued on next page

Table 5.1 Old and New Regionalism in Latin America: Objectives and Stylized Facts, continued

Old	New	Similar	Different
Systemic issues			
Respond to regional blocs	Respond to regional blocs	•	
GATT consistency (enabling clause)	GATT/WTO consistency (Article XXIV and GATS V)	•	
South-south exclusively	South-south & north-south		•
Marginal role in GATT	Strong role in GATT/WTO		•
Institutional issues			
Bureaucracy-led process	Politically-led process		•
Heavy institutional structure	Light institutional structure		•
Industrial planning	Market–based		•
Structural balance among partners	Avoid radical imbalance		•

Source: Authors' own assessment.

Instruments

The primary tool of the Latin American Free Trade Area (LAFTA, 1961) was the creation of a free trade area, while the Central American Common Market (CACM, 1960) and the Andean Group (1969) utilized a common market.[3] In the New Regionalism the major subregions (CACM, Andean Community, and MERCOSUR) are pursuing customs unions on the road to eventual common market, and there are numerous bilateral and multilateral free trade areas in execution and negotiation. Meanwhile, the North American Free Trade Area (NAFTA, 1994) is a pioneering FTA with unprecedented scope and depth. As described in Table 5.2, the instruments applied in the Old and New Regionalisms present a stark contrast.

Trade Coverage. The Old Regionalism focused on goods trade. As demonstrated by Table 5.3, most of the new agreements cover a broad range of second-generation trade disciplines, many of them going beyond borders to affect domestic policy and reinforce structural reform. The approach follows the precedents to which Latin America was exposed by NAFTA. While many of NAFTA's provisions—as well as those in Canadian, U.S. and EU reciprocal bilateral agreements—are very much "WTO-plus," south-south second-generation agreements typically do this in a more limited way. However, some dimensions of the New Regionalism are not yet even incorporated into the WTO, such as competition policy, investor-state dispute resolution, and labor and environmental standards.

Regional Trade Liberalization. This is the typical starting point of regional integration. The Old Regionalism was marked by complex and laborious liberalization exercises, with Central America being an interesting exception for a time. The classic example was LAFTA, with exclusively positive lists, in which liberalization had to be negotiated line by line and product by product. The Andean Group advanced on this formula with automatic liberalization of somewhat more than 50 percent of tariff lines (substantially less on trade). But in both cases actual liberalization schedules were organized in "small steps" and de facto or de jure excluded very sizeable amounts of trade.[4] In the New Regionalism liberalization schedules are typically automatic on 90 percent or more of tariff lines over a period of ten years. An extreme example is MERCOSUR, under which roughly 95 percent of tariff lines were liberalized in just four years. Figure 5.1 presents the tariff elimination process for a sample of agreements in the New Regionalism.

Table 5.2 Old and New Regionalism in Latin America: Main Instruments

Old	New
Trade coverage	
Focus on goods liberalization	Goods and new second-generation issues (services, intellectual property rights, government procurement, etc.)
Trade liberalization in goods	
Positive lists or limited automatic schedules[1, 2] Extensive exceptions (>10 percent[3])[1, 2]	Negative lists and automatic schedules Very limited exceptions (<10 percent)[3]
Rules of origin	
Simple rules across tariff universe	Complex rules and families of rules of origin
Common external tariffs	
Average > 40 percent[4] and high standard deviation[2, 5]	Average < 15 percent[4] and moderate standard deviation
Industrial planning	
Extensive[1, 2, 5]	None (market-based)
Special and differentiated treatment	
Extensive[1, 2, 5]	Minimalist
Restrictions on participation of foreign direct investment in integration	
Important (formal or informal)[1, 2, 5]	National treatment
Dispute settlement	
None[1, 2,5]	Incipient
Institutions	
Extensive (European model)[1, 5]	Scaled down or non-existent

Source: Authors' own assessment.
1. Latin American Free Trade Area (LAFTA).
2. Andean Community (former Andean Pact).
3. Tariff lines.
4. Tariff level.
5. Central American Common Market (CACM).

Rules of Origin. Rules of origin in the Old Regionalism were nonexistent or very simple, with the same rule across the tariff universe. In the New Regionalism rules of origin have been influenced by the NAFTA model and are more complex. These new rules of origin typically apply three tests (change of tariff heading, technical specifications, and regional contents) in different combinations across the tariff universe. While

Table 5.3 New Regionalism: Provisions in Selected Trade Agreements in the Americas

	MERCOSUR	Canada-Costa Rica	Chile-Mexico	Costa Rica-Mexico	NAFTA	Ecuador-Chile	G-3	Chile-MERCOSUR	Mexico-Nicaragua	Canada-Chile	Mexico-North Triangle	Bolivia-MERCOSUR	CARICOM-Dominican Republic	Andean Community	Chile-Central America
Tariff elimination	•	•	•	•	•	•	•	•	•	•	•	•	•	•	•
a) Positive MFN list of exemptions	•	•	•	•	•	•	•	•	•	•	•	•	•	•	•
b) Automatic tariff elimination schedule	•	•	•	•	•	•	•	•	•	•	•	•	•	•	•
CET	•													•	
Common customs measures	•		•	•										•	
HS-rules of origin	•	•	•	•	•				•	•	•		•	•	•
SPS measures	•	•	•	•	•	•	•	•	•		•	•	•		•
Technical barriers to trade	•	•	•	•	•	•	•		•		•		•		•
Investment	BE		•	•	•	•	•	•	•	•	•		•	•	•
Investor-state dispute settlement		•	•		•		•		•	•	•				
Services	BE	•	•		•	BE	•	•	•	•	•	BE	•	•	•
Temporary entry of business persons		•	•	•	•		•		•	•	•		•		•
Government procurement			BE	•	•	BE	•		•				BE		•
Intellectual property rights	BE	•	•	•			•	•	•		•		•	•	
Anti-dumping/ countervail	BE	•		•	•	•		•	•	•	•	•	•	•	•
Competition policy	SA	•								•				•	•
Dispute settlement	SA	•	•	•	•	•	•	•	•	•	•	•	•	•	•
Labor / environment	BE	•			SA					SA					
Special and differential treatment	•					•		•				•	•	•	

Source: IDB (2002) and OAS SICE.

Notes: SA = side agreement; BE = best endeavor to define in the future: the parties shall explicitly seek to develop disciplines in these areas in the future; HS: harmonization system.

*The parties agreed to a reciprocal exemption from the application of anti-dumping.

Figure 5.1a New Regionalism: Speed of Intra-regional Tariff Liberalization

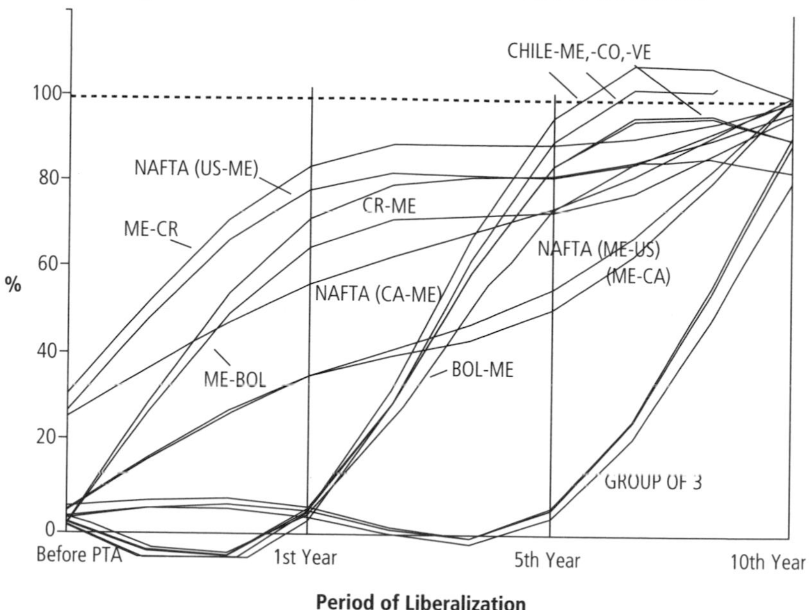

Figure 5.1b Percentage of Trade under Full Liberalization

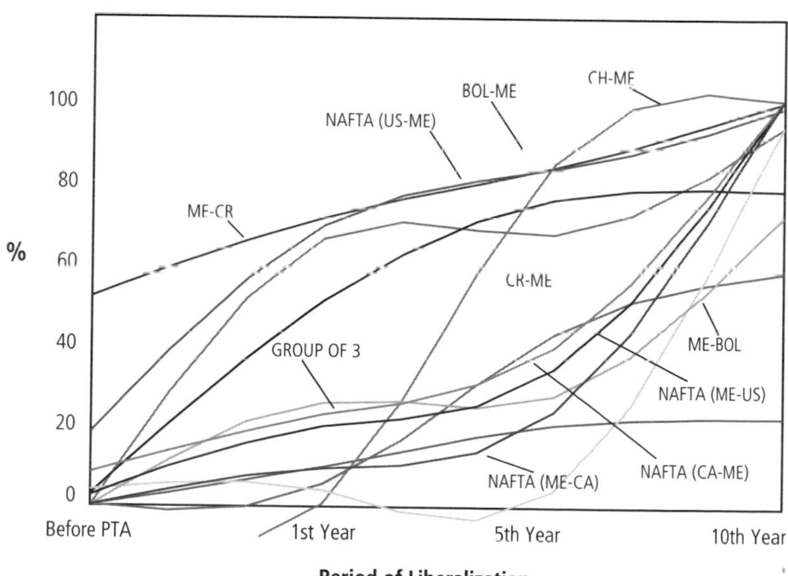

Source: Devlin and Estevadeordal (2001).

perhaps providing for flexibility, they also are more difficult to administer, less transparent, and can be a very effective tool of protectionism.

Common External Tariffs (CETs). In the Old Regionalism, agreement on a CET involved maintenance of very high, or even increasing, levels of external protection. Dispersion was typically high: for example, the range of the CET in Central America was 12 to 80 percent. In the contemporary episode the formation of CETs in Central America, the Andean Community, and MERCOSUR has been an integral part of the dramatic, unilateral liberalization that took place in 1985–95, when average tariffs fell from over 40 percent to about 12 percent. Meanwhile, CETs typically have ranged from 0 to 20 percent. However, in both episodes full implementation of the CETs has proven elusive for the countries, and they are far from achieving full customs unions.

Industrial Planning. In the Old Regionalism governments actively promoted schemes that supported sectoral planning of the regional market. The most flexible was LAFTA, with private sector negotiations for sectoral agreements. The most systematically planned by official authorities was the Andean Group; however, the planning resulted in only very limited results. In contrast, the New Regionalism is market based.

Special and Differential Treatment (S&D). S&D was a tense political issue in South America, where Bolivia, Ecuador, and Paraguay were the main protagonists. For instance, in LAFTA they pushed for, and won, special treatment in the form of an agreement that allowed negotiation of accelerated tariff concessions from their partners, lagged liberalization on their part, liberal safeguards, tolerance for protectionist policies in sectors "important" for development, and best endeavors of other partners to mobilize finance for development. Nevertheless, the smaller economies' concerns about being disadvantaged vis-à-vis their bigger, more industrialized neighbors, coupled with fears about the costs of trade diversion, were sources of friction in the LAFTA negotiations. This dissatisfaction was shared by the other Andean countries and contributed to their breakaway into the Andean Group in 1969. The Andean Group not only strengthened industrial programming but enshrined S&D in the agreement. Ecuador and Bolivia got first shot at producing goods not yet produced in the subregion, and enjoyed free market access immediately. An Andean Development Bank was also established. Not withstanding some overhang of the old S&D in the Andean countries, the New Regionalism handles asymmetric capacities mostly through slightly more favorable liberalization schedules plus technical assistance programs in the case of north-south integration.

Treatment of Foreign Direct Investment (FDI). During the first integration episode there was general suspicion of foreign multinationals. This was formally expressed only in the Andean Group, whose famous Article 24 restricted, among other things, the access of FDI and its remittances. In the New Regionalism national treatment is the standard rule and many countries have extensive incentives to attract FDI.

Dispute Settlement. None of the agreements have had formal dispute settlement.[5] Diplomacy in one form or another was the way problems were resolved, with costs in terms of transparency and precedent setting. Since the 1990s, agreements have tended to incorporate formal dispute-settlement mechanisms, but with still patchy application in south-south integration agreements.

Institutions. Finally, in terms of institutions, the Old Regionalism modeled itself after Europe. The most comprehensive structures were in the Andean Group and the CACM, where industrial programming and balanced outcomes received very high political priority. All the agreements used intergovernmental forums for decision making and executive functions and had technical secretariats. The secretariat in the Andean Group was especially powerful and exercised a considerable degree of autonomy in proposing measures and supporting implementation. Central America, like the Andean Group, had a subregional development bank and an institute for technological development. In the New Regionalism, both groups streamlined their traditional regional institutional structures, while all others have relatively simple intergovernmental arrangements. Indeed, in some ambitious agreements such as MERCOSUR there is probably a need to make institutional arrangements much more robust.

In sum, in the Old Regionalism the only agreement that for the most part followed through in the full deployment of trade liberalization instruments was CACM. While it had remarkable success, by 1970 the group imploded, largely as a result of a war between El Salvador and Honduras. LAFTA concessions made only very limited progress. In 1980 LAFTA was abandoned for a new initiative, the Latin American Integration Association (LAIA), that aimed mostly at partial preferences, ratifying the scaled-back approach that was happening anyway. Finally, the Andean Group never achieved a free trade area or customs union, and industrial programming was limited, with petrochemicals being the most significant. Meanwhile, the New Regionalism has been very successful in eliminating tariffs on regional trade and introducing a broad array of new trade-related disciplines. The issues of depth, implementation, and compliance regarding these new disciplines have, however, been uneven in the south-south accords. Moreover, the subregions are a long way from their customs unions and/or common market objectives, and indeed the Andean Community and MERCOSUR have seen their forward momentum stalled.

Formal Analysis of the Benefits and Costs of Regional Integration

In the eras of both the Old and New Regionalisms the critique of regional integration agreements (RIAs) revolved around customs-union theory. In the former episode, development economists supportive of regional integration tended to argue that the theory had limited applicability to the problems of developing countries. In the contemporary debate almost all economists are supportive of multilateral liberalization. However, proponents of RIAs argue that regionalism is complementary. In fact the potential costs highlighted by customs union theory, while a relevant consideration, are minimized in the new policy framework; and the theory fails to capture not only dynamic effects, but also important political economy considerations related to structural reform.

Static Effects

Trade Creation and Diversion in Perfect Competition

The seminal contribution of Viner (1950) shows that the impact of an RIA is ambiguous. Preferential trade liberalization results both in trade creation (the substitution of a lower-cost source of supply from a member country for a higher-cost domestic source of supply) and in trade diversion (the substitution of a higher-cost source of supply from a member country for a lower-cost source of supply from third country). In the environment of high protection that is characteristic of ISI, one could easily deduce that net trade diversion would be the outcome of regional integration.

The criticism of customs-union theory in development circles was widespread in the early Post-War period (Dell 1963; Wionczek 1966). In the words of Balassa (1966: 30), "the objective function of the traditional theory of customs unions exemplified in the absolutist approach is the attainment of static efficiency, while the objective function relevant for developing countries is the maximization of the rate of growth." Linder (1966: 39) also challenged the relevance of trade creation criteria noting that "trade diversion enables the concentration of scarce foreign exchange on input imports, thereby enhancing the capacity use and growth." Meanwhile, Meade (1955) and Lipsey (1957) show in a general equilibrium framework that a trade-diverting customs union may be welfare improving if the reduction of consumer prices offsets the efficiency costs of trade diversion. Finally, Kemp and Wan (1976) also demonstrated that RIAs can result in welfare-enhancing outcomes, while Freund and McLaren (1999) show that trade creation and diversion may materialize even prior to the entry into force of the RIA.

Under the New Regionalism the debate on customs-union theory intensified. Initially the controversy focused on the relevance of trade diversion (Summers 1991; Krugman 1991; Bhagwati 1993). Later, Venables (2003) demonstrates how north-south integration is less susceptible to trade diversion than south-south schemes. Bhagwati and Panagariya (1996) took the debate to another dimension, demonstrating that even when trade creation outweighs trade diversion (the triangle effects) it is possible that a single country could lose on account of an adverse income-distribution effect arising from tariff revenue distribution (rectangle effects). But Pomfret (1997) neatly highlighted the limits of the static theory, which does not consider the terms-of-trade effects, presence of scale economics, dynamic effects, political economy objectives, systemic issues, or institutional forms of RIAs. In a nutshell, the debate on static trade creation and diversion is only part of the story, and probably not the most important part from the standpoint of development policy in the age of the New Regionalism.

Terms of Trade

Mundell (1964) paved the way for a theory of preferential trade policy based on the possibility of member countries manipulating the terms of trade.[6] Theoretically, this entails costs for the rest of the world. However, in a second-best world it is plausible that the effects of RIAs compensate for the adverse impacts that arise from rents created by a multilateral trading system that selectively restricts trade in sectors in which developing countries display comparative advantages and in which oligopolistic market power exists. From a developing country policy perspective there is a rationale for increasing international bargaining power. However, there are also potential risks of conflicts among partners that may stem from the change of intra-regional terms of trade (Bhagwati and Panagariya 1996).

Economies of Scale and Imperfect Competition

RIAs allow the exploitation of economies of scale, which results in lower costs of production (Corden 1972). Milner (1997) differentiates the demand for regional integration according to the regional scope of scale economies, which in turn defines the optimal extension of the RIA. The rationale for regional liberalization hinges on the reciprocal exchange of market access concessions in sectors with economies of scale or where intraindustrial trade expansion induces lower adjustment costs. These arguments are particularly suitable to explain the willingness of small countries to enter into RIAs (Casella 1995).

Imperfect competition models usually reveal larger welfare gains from RIAs than those arising in perfect competition (Baldwin and Venables 1995). In this framework preferential trade can induce three broad types of effects. The adjustment of firms in the RIA brings about the multiplication of varieties, sustains intraindustry trade, reduces transport costs, and ends up in a "domestic market effect" (Helpman and Krugman 1989). Increasing competition also puts pressure on domestic firms to reduce market power and segmentation, preventing welfare-reducing price discrimination strategies. The full materialization of these effects depends above all on the implementation of deep integration policies (Lawrence 1995). Economies of scale were certainly an objective of the Old Regionalism, while this and the pro-competitive effects of integration fit well into the objectives of the New Regionalism.

Estimating the Static Effects of Regional Integration

A new emerging empirical literature has mitigated the early traditional concerns about the effects of the Latin American RIAs. The impact of regional integration policies has been estimated with different techniques such as simple trade indicators,[7] gravity models,[8] computable general equilibrium models,[9] and specific analysis of price effects[10] and of tariff revenue effects,[11] some of them discussed at length in Winters (2001a).

Under the Old Regionalism, intra-LAFTA trade shares climbed from a modest 9 percent in 1960 to 13 percent in 1980 (Figure 5.2). The increase in intra-regional export intensity was also rather modest, from 1.4 percent in 1960 to 3.4 percent in 1980 (Table 5.4). Trade in

Figure 5.2 Intra-Regional Trade in Latin America, 1960–2000; Intra-Regional Trade as % of Total Trade

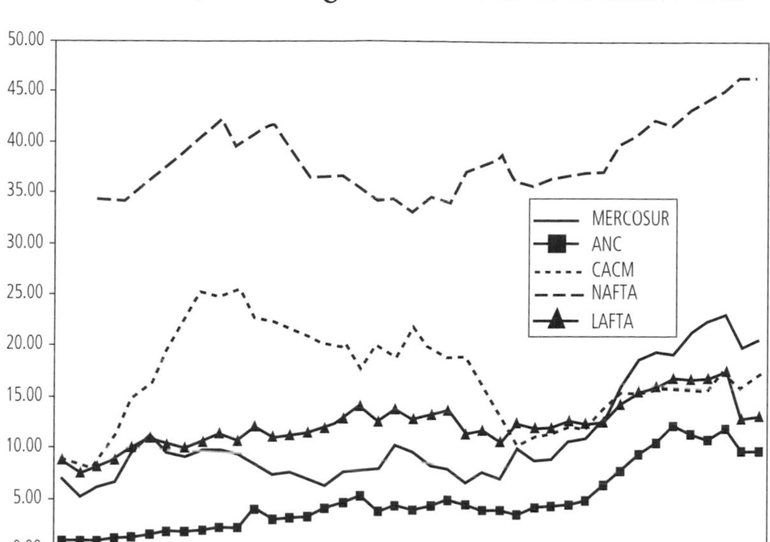

Sources: Author's calculations; IMF-Direction of Trade Statistics (2003) and UN-COMTRADE data (2003).

Notes: ANC: Andean Community (former Andean Pact)
CACM: Central American Common Market
LAFTA: Latin American Free Trade Area
MERCOSUR: Common Market of the South
NAFTA: North American Free Trade Area (The indicator shows Mexico's trade in NAFTA)

commodities grew faster than trade in goods subject to preferences, and the share of negotiated products in intra-regional imports remained as low as 40 percent (Langhammer and Hiemenz 1991). Aitken and Lowry (1973) found evidence of gross trade creation, although a more accurate investigation with a comparable gravity model reversed this conclusion (Endoh1999).

In the Andean Pact—the best paradigmatic example of the Old Regionalism—intra-regional trade shares rose marginally from 2 percent in 1969 to 4 percent in 1980 and peaked at 12 percent in 1998 (Figure 5.2). Trade intensity increased rather modestly under the Old Regionalism, while the New Regionalism has been more effective in promoting trade intensity (Table 5.4). The New Regionalism also in-

Table 5.4 Trade Intensity in Latin America Regional Integration Agreements, 1960–2000

Flow	Country / Region	1960	1970	1980	1990	2000
X	CACM	19.4	79.0	98.7	103.4	48.8
M	CACM	19.2	77.4	93.2	93.4	53.6
X	Costa Rica	7.8	66.6	118.6	71.8	32.0
M	Costa Rica	10.3	69.7	71.4	84.3	30.4
X	El Salvador	30.7	91.4	107.0	200.2	187.9
M	El Salvador	35.9	92.3	161.4	145.7	79.7
X	Guatemala	13.4	111.1	128.6	176.6	64.8
M	Guatemala	17.7	79.4	75.8	85.0	51.5
X	Honduras	35.0	33.0	42.9	20.6	26.8
M	Honduras	20.9	75.1	47.4	74.8	45.3
X	Nicaragua	10.3	74.1	69.3	86.3	43.4
M	Nicaragua	10.6	76.7	141.3	90.5	105.7
X	ANC	0.5	1.9	4.2	10.6	16.1
M	ANC	0.4	1.8	3.2	8.6	15.0
X	Bolivia	0.1	2.3	4.3	13.9	34.5
M	Bolivia	1.5	0.9	3.7	4.7	9.2
X	Colombia	0.8	5.1	11.2	16.8	34.8
M	Colombia	0.3	2.1	5.6	11.4	26.5
X	Ecuador	3.5	3.9	5.9	16.0	15.9
M	Ecuador	0.6	5.1	4.2	11.4	25.7
X	Peru	1.2	1.8	6.8	15.2	12.2
M	Peru	0.6	3.6	1.8	9.2	14.2
X	Venezuela	0.3	1.4	3.0	8.6	12.8
M	Venezuela	0.6	0.8	4.0	7.9	17.8
X	MERCOSUR	3.5	7.0	7.3	13.1	19.6
M	MERCOSUR	3.7	7.2	6.8	13.6	20.0
X	Argentina	5.9	8.9	9.1	18.9	30.8
M	Argentina	4.0	10.7	10.5	21.1	30.4
X	Brazil	4.4	12.5	13.4	22.2	28.8
M	Brazil	5.1	7.8	8.8	23.8	29.5
X	Paraguay	12.5	19.8	19.4	41.3	43.2
M	Paraguay	9.9	13.6	31.5	22.3	41.4
X	Uruguay	0.9	5.4	16.4	39.9	32.7
M	Uruguay	4.7	16.9	18.6	30.8	33.4
X	LAFTA	1.4	2.8	3.4	4.9	2.7
M	LAFTA	1.6	2.8	3.0	4.8	2.8
M	LAFTA	1.6	2.8	3.0	4.8	2.8
X	Argentina	3.2	6.1	5.9	10.8	9.7
M	Argentina	2.7	5.6	5.1	11.5	7.1
X	Bolivia	2.1	2.3	8.4	18.4	8.5
M	Bolivia	2.4	3.5	6.4	13.8	9.8
X	Brazil	1.5	3.8	5.7	5.8	5.3

Continued on next page

Table 5.4 Trade Intensity in Latin America Regional Integration Agreements, 1960–2000, continued

Flow	Country / Region	1960	1970	1980	1990	2000
M	Brazil	2.7	3.0	3.5	6.8	4.7
X	Chile	1.2	3.4	5.7	5.7	4.1
M	Chile	2.6	4.9	5.5	7.6	7.2
X	Colombia	0.2	2.0	3.3	4.2	4.4
M	Colombia	0.3	2.2	3.6	5.8	5.3
X	Ecuador	1.5	2.5	4.2	4.5	3.4
M	Ecuador	0.5	2.9	2.8	7.1	6.9
X	Mexico	0.2	2.2	1.2	2.0	0.7
M	Mexico	0.0	0.7	1.1	1.3	0.9
X	Paraguay	5.7	9.8	10.4	16.6	13.5
M	Paraguay	3.6	5.6	11.7	9.9	11.1
X	Peru	1.6	1.6	3.5	5.9	3.2
M	Peru	1.2	4.1	2.6	7.9	6.0
X	Uruguay	0.5	3.3	8.6	16.1	10.2
M	Uruguay	4.1	7.2	8.4	15.0	10.0
X	Venezuela	1.5	1.3	1.9	2.9	2.0
M	Venezuela	0.4	1.1	1.9	3.9	3.9
X	NAFTA	3.1	3.0	3.9	3.8	3.9
M	NAFTA	3.0	3.0	4.0	4.3	4.5

Sources: Author's calculations, IMF-Direction of Trade Statistics (2003) data.
Notes: IR (Intra-regional): flows to RIA partners.
XR (Extra-regional): flows to non-RIA partners.
ANC: Andean Community (former Andean Pact)
CACM: Central American Common Market
LAFTA: Latin American Free Trade Area
MERCOSUR: Common Market of the South
NAFTA: North American Free Trade Area (The indicator refers to Mexico's trade intensity inside and outside of NAFTA)
Following Anderson and Norheim (1993), the export intensity index is defined as:

$$I_{ij} = \frac{X_{ij} / X_i}{M_j / \sum_{k \neq i} M_k} = \frac{x_{ij}}{m_j}$$

where:
I_{ij} is the intensity index of exports from country i to country (or region) j;
X_{ij} are exports from i to j;
X_i are total exports from i;
M_k are total imports to country k, and
x_{ij} is the share of partner j on exports of country i; and
m_j is the share of imports of partner j on world imports (net of i's imports given that a country cannot export to itself).

duced regional intraindustrial trade. The intra-regional IIT index increased from 7 in 1980 to 30 in 1997; in contrast, the extraregional index remained low (2 in 1980 and 7 in 1997) (Table 5.5). Echevarria (1997) argued that unilateral opening *cum* regional integration were central factors behind the expansion of intra-regional trade flows in the 1990s. Applying a gravity model he concluded that trade creation dominated trade diversion, although the latter occurred in some sectors (Cernat 2001).

In the CACM, intra-regional trade shares and intensity ratios initially rose rapidly (from 7 percent in 1960 to 22 percent in 1980, and from 19 in 1960 to 95 in 1980, respectively) (Figure 5.2; Table 5.4). Under the New Regionalism the dynamism was less: intra-regional shares rose from 12 percent in 1990 to 17 percent in 2000, while trade intensity decreased from around 100 percent to 50 percent. The Old Regionalism promoted substantial intraindustry trade, while under the New Regionalism the noticeable increase was seen in extraregional flows (Table 5.5), which is partly related to the U.S. Caribbean Basin Initiative. Aitken and Lowry (1973) found evidence of gross net trade creation in the period of the Old Regionalism, but this conclusion was controversial.[12] In a very comprehensive study Cline (1978) included in his analysis the effects of economies of scale, unemployment, foreign exchange savings, and dynamic effects. He found that the static effects represented 1.9 percent of the GDP, with the benefits as a result of the fact that exchange savings dominated all other effects.[13] Although all countries have enjoyed net welfare benefits from the CACM, their distribution was very unequal. This imbalance was ultimately a deathblow to what otherwise was an impressive performance.

Turning to agreements born in the era of the New Regionalism, NAFTA has undergone some early comprehensive assessments (Hufbauer and Schott 1993). Intra-regional trade expanded vigorously from 37 percent of the total in 1990 to 46 percent in 2000 (Figure 5.2), but trade intensity did not increase (Table 5.3). Mexican intraindustry trade in NAFTA rose substantially from 34 percent in 1990 to 60 percent in 1997 (Table 5.5). Analysts seem to converge on the conclusion that the extraordinary expansion of intra-regional trade flows did not take place at the expense of the rest of the world. This is confirmed by a detailed study of trade flows at the sectoral level (Krueger 1999) and by the application of a gravity model (Soloaga and Winters 1999). A general equilibrium model allowed Francois and Shiells (1994) to find

Table 5.5 Intra-Industry Trade in Latin American Regional Integration Agreements, 1980–1997

Flow	Country / Region	1980	1985	1990	1995	1997
IR	CACM	31.0	36.7	25.7	33.9	33.3
XR	CACM	2.9	3.8	7.2	6.8	17.0
IR	Costa Rica	33.7	37.3	26.5	33.6	32.0
XR	Costa Rica	4.3	6.6	11.2	11.6	33.3
IR	El Salvador	40.0	43.4	29.8	42.4	41.4
XR	El Salvador	5.4	4.6	3.3	5.6	7.5
IR	Guatemala	37.0	42.3	30.0	39.7	41.5
XR	Guatemala	1.7	4.3	7.2	5.7	7.5
IR	Honduras	16.5	8.2	8.2	12.9	15.0
XR	Honduras	1.7	1.0	3.5	2.3	6.5
IR	Nicaragua	11.4	4.1	10.2	11.7	8.0
XR	Nicaragua	1.4	0.2	0.1	1.7	10.3
IR	ANC	7.2	7.0	11.3	28.7	30.2
XR	ANC	2.8	3.9	7.6	8.4	6.7
IR	Bolivia	1.4	22.9	0.7	7.5	8.9
XR	Bolivia	0.3	2.2	0.8	4.1	2.7
IR	Colombia	9.5	8.3	14.0	33.7	34.8
XR	Colombia	5.1	5.4	6.8	11.2	8.3
IR	Ecuador	6.2	11.1	6.2	26.6	26.3
XR	Ecuador	0.5	0.4	1.1	2.2	3.6
IR	Peru	5.1	5.0	4.8	7.1	9.2
XR	Peru	1.8	2.9	2.4	3.0	4.4
IR	Venezuela	8.0	6.5	13.8	31.9	35.8
XR	Venezuela	3.0	4.5	12.2	11.0	7.8
IR	NAFTA	14.4	50.2	34.4	56.8	60.0
XR	NAFTA	6.4	8.8	14.6	16.5	15.3
IR	MERCOSUR	17.0	21.1	36.7	47.9	51.2
XR	MERCOSUR	10.7	15.7	18.8	15.5	15.1
IR	Argentina	23.1	27.0	47.4	54.9	56.6
XR	Argentina	6.8	9.4	14.4	10.7	8.9
IR	Brazil	17.1	20.8	38.8	50.3	53.2
XR	Brazil	13.7	17.9	20.8	18.0	18.2
IR	Paraguay	0.8	0.3	2.6	3.1	5.7
XR	Paraguay	0.6	0.5	1.2	0.4	0.6
IR	Uruguay	18.4	22.9	27.6	36.8	34.5
XR	Uruguay	2.0	2.2	3.0	2.1	2.5

Sources: Author's calculations based on data from Feenstra (2000).
Notes: IR (Intra-regional): flows to RIA partners.
XR (Extra-regional): flows to non-RIA partners.
CACM: Central American Common Market
ANC: Andean Community (former Andean Pact)
LAFTA: Latin American Free Trade Area
MERCOSUR: Common Market of the South
NAFTA: North American Free Trade Area (The indicator shows Mexico's intra-industry trade inside and outside of NAFTA)

Continued on next page

Table 5.5 Intra-Industry Trade in Latin American Regional Integration Agreements, 1980–1997 continued

Following Grubell and Lloyd (1975), for every single country the trade-weighted intra-industry trade index (IIT) is calculated for each single partner *i* and sector *j* according to the following formula:

$$IIT = \sum_{i=1}^{m} \propto \left(\frac{X_i + M_i}{\sum X_i + \sum M_i} \right) \propto \left(\sum_{j=1}^{n} \propto \left(\frac{X_j + M_j}{\sum X_j + \sum M_j} \right) \propto \left(1 - \frac{|X_j - M_j|}{X_j + M_j} \right) \right)$$

where M_{ij} and X_{ij}, respectively, are imports to and imports from country *i* of product *j*. Calculations were performed using data aggregated at 4-digit level of the SITC (rev. 2). Regional figures are weighted averages of the national indexes, using the relative share of each country in the total intra- and extraregional trade of the selected region as weight. Intra-regional trade refers to trade occurring with regional partners, extraregional trade refers to trade with the rest of the world.

that all members would gain, particularly Mexico, with welfare gains between 1 and 5 percent.

MERCOSUR generated very animated debates. Intra-regional trade shares experienced explosive growth, rising from 11 percent in 1990 to a peak of 23 percent in 1998 (Figure 5.2). Intra-regional trade intensity grew from 13 in 1990 to around 20 in 2000 (Table 5.4), while the intra-regional IIT index rose from 37 in 1990 to 51 in 1997 (Table 5.5). Yeats (1997) concluded that the regional orientation of exports rose faster in products for which member countries do not have comparative advantages and hence inferred the existence of trade diversion. This conclusion has been challenged by Nogues (1996), who stressed the actual existence of intra-regional comparative advantages. Meanwhile, Devlin (1997) and Nagarajan (1998) noted that if the analysis includes imports the regional bias is mitigated by the effects of unilateral liberalization, supporting a conclusion that trade creation probably outweighs trade diversion. In addition, Giordano (2001) shows that the reorientation of regional trade hinged on the divergent path of the intra- and extra-regional real effective exchange rates, a conclusion supported by the gravity model analysis of Soloaga and Winters (1999).

Dynamic Effects

Growth Effects

The growth effects of RIAs are the main concern of policymakers. If RIAs create conditions for greater efficiency in the production of capital-intensive goods, then they lead to a temporary increase in the rate of return of capital and to greater investment, which lasts until the economy reaches a new steady-state equilibrium. In Europe, the magnitude of these dynamic effects was found to be significantly greater than that of static ones (Baldwin 1989).[14] Considering a panel of developing countries, Vamvakidis (1998) finds that nondiscriminatory openness considerably boosts growth while RIAs do not. However, the data do not include the 1990s, and only suggest that the Old Regionalism did not produce significant growth. In contrast, using firm-level data López-Córdova and Moreira (2002) found that NAFTA had a positive impact on productivity in Mexico.

Foreign Direct Investment

As mentioned, in the Old Regionalism FDI was viewed with great suspicion (Brecher and Bhagwati 1981). But FDI may benefit host countries through demonstration effects, increases in competition, export channels, backward and forward efficiency effects, or knowledge spillovers arising from labor mobility. In contrast with the past, the attraction of FDI through an enlarged market has become a primary objective of the New Regionalism (Ethier 1998a).

In the Vinerain perspective, the location of FDI in regional markets is largely a response to trade diversion and the need to jump trade barriers. This motivation, while still present, is less powerful today in the era of the New Regionalism. International trade and FDI are in fact increasingly complementary (Markusen and Maskus 2001). The location of FDI in RIAs can be motivated by correct price signals (Motta and Norman 1996), leading to vertical integration of production networks that in turn stimulates productivity, exports, and dynamic welfare gains.

Using a gravity model on panel data, Levy Yeyati, Stein, and Daude (2002) found large and significant positive effects related to the enlargement of source and host markets through RIAs, but also the presence of significant negative effects due to the dilution of existing preferences. Meanwhile, empirical investigations of Latin American cases have focused largely on NAFTA or MERCOSUR (Chudnovsky and Lopez 2001; Vodusek 2001).

Asymmetric Distribution

The determinants of the spatial allocation of economic activity are the object of a growing body of literature (Ottaviano and Puga 1997; Fujita, Krugman, and Venables 1999), which gave new breath to the old models of cumulative causation (Myrdal 1957; Hirschman 1958). Puga and Venables (1997) show that agglomeration economies induce developing countries to compete for being the first country to access north-south agreements and that a slow response may produce industrial backwardness. Ben David (1996) demonstrates the existence of catching-up effects promoted by trade integration among developed countries, but the World Bank (2000) finds little evidence of this effect among developing countries. It appears that north-south integration offers better opportunities than south-south initiatives in terms of income convergence (Venables 1999).

Nontraditional Gains

Despite the importance of credibility issues, nontraditional gains from regional integration have only been explored recently (Fernandez and Portes 1998). Indeed governments engaged in a broad reform strategy need additional policy tools to insure the irreversibility of trade liberalization (Devlin and Estevadeordal 2001). RIAs may in fact help lock in trade liberalization through legal commitments of a treaty and the cost of exclusion (Whalley 1998). It can be argued that binding trade policies multilaterally is the preferable option. However, scaled-down regional initiatives facilitate a gathering of like-minded countries and a better focus on incentives.[15]

When the adjustment cost of the entry into the RIA is significant, it functions as a signal that governments are committed to liberalization. But RIAs could also signal bad policy; for example, if there is a deterioration of the institutional setting of an RIA in terms of efficiency or enforcement of rules. The New Regionalism has generally played a positive role in signaling commitment to structural reforms, albeit unevenly. NAFTA comes the closest to a best practice in the region. In contrast, in the Old Regionalism signaling was contradictory, and this perhaps helps to explain its failure to advance (Devlin and Estevadeordal 2001).[16]

Overall, RIAs are an instrument to hedge the risk of delay or failure of multilateral trade negotiations (Perroni and Whalley 1994) or to achieve deeper market access in areas not adequately disciplined by the WTO (Hindley and Messerlin 1993). Compared to the WTO, in which more than 140 members are represented, the reduced number of like-minded countries in RIAs facilitate the coordination of negotiating positions (Khaler 1995), greater voice for small countries, and cooperation in noncommercial areas.

RIAs also have a role in the construction of diplomatic alliances. In fact, trade liberalization produces security externalities that may be internalized through the creation of an RIA (Schiff and Winters 1998). Old initiatives in Latin America perhaps failed partly because they were not grounded on strong enough common political motivations as a result of nationalism and authoritarianism. Today Latin America generally shares many fundamental common goals, such as democracy, peace, and structural reform with somewhat similar initial conditions.

The production of a diverse array of public goods is indeed an advantage that RIAs have over unilateral MFN liberalization (Johnson 1965; Cooper and Massell 1965). Theoretically the provision of a public good could be reached through a mix of taxes and subsidies. But in the developing world budget constraints and commitment issues can make an RIA a more effective political economy tool for the creation of regional public goods. Under the Old Regionalism the preference for industrialization was the principal regional public goods offered by integration initiatives. Under the New Regionalism the scope for production of regional public goods has markedly expanded, ranging from the coordination of regional infrastructure, to bloc negotiations, macroeconomic coordination, and capacity building in trade-related issues (Devlin and Estevadeordal 2003).

Increasing trade interdependence through successful regional liberalization provides endogenous incentives for cooperation in the production of regional public goods. It has been argued that this can be achieved without trade preferences through ad-hoc commitments (Winters 2001b). But this view largely overlooks the importance of trade in promoting the sustainability of common incentives to pursue noneconomic objectives or, in the words of Garcia and Glocker (2000), in fueling "integration by stealth." Devlin, Estevadeordal, and Krivonos (2002) find that "trade and cooperation nexuses" in RIAs can advance regional public goods better than initiatives that exclude trade.

Multilateral Systemic Effects

Multilateral Negotiations

In the 1990s, attention has increasingly shifted toward the systemic effects of RIAs on the multilateral trading system, or the question of whether the proliferation of RIAs is a building bloc or a stumbling bloc (Bhagwati 1993). One issue in these analyses is to understand whether the number of trading blocs provides an incentive to increase external tariffs. Krugman (1993) argued that the development of a world composed of just a few trading blocs is not a desirable outcome. The choice between a free trade area and a customs union may provide specific incentives in setting external tariffs (Richardson 1993, 1995), but overall, there is no empirical evidence that RIAs are in fact generally promoting the adoption of higher external protection (Foroutan 1998). Indeed, Devlin and Estevadeordal (2001) show that in Latin America the New Regionalism has reinforced the opening process underway since the late 1980s.

Another issue is related to the incentives for RIAs enlargements. Baldwin (1993) coined the term "domino regionalism" to show that the incentives to join increase as RIAs grow larger as the blocks endure.[17] However, it is less clear why existing members should benefit from new accessions. In fact, as membership increases the benefits from market access decline and the trade-off between deepening and enlargement turns unfavorable to deepening. There also can be FDI dilution effects for current members (IDB 2002). Winters (2001b) argued that the proliferation of RIAs simply raises the incentives for countries to enter into a "gang," but the existence of a compelling incentive does not make a gang a good thing. The crucial factors are the efficiency of the gang and its promises for growth. When presenting the characteristics of open regionalism (ECLAC 1994; Yi 1996), or when attempting to progressively and smoothly adjust to the competition in world markets (Frankel and Wei 1996), it seems that RIAs may provide an economically and politically enabling environment for an increasing integration in the multilateral system.

Because multilateral negotiations are a gradual, round-by-round process toward global free trade, RIAs also could help sustain multilateralism. First, countries can push for multilateral rounds to erode preferences, as was seen in the multilateral strategy of the United States in the face of integration in Europe. Additionally, WTO-plus RIAs can set the stage for the inclusion of new issues in multilateral rounds, as shown by the example of NAFTA when partners, having assumed the cost of certain disciplines, tried to multilateralize them in Geneva (IDB 2002). Finally, successful multilateral rounds may induce regional approaches because the reduction of tariffs worldwide increases the role of geography in determining trade patterns (Ethier 1998a).

Hub-and-Spoke Systems

The issue of the proliferation of preferential trade agreements in a hub-and-spoke (H&S) configuration is one of the most relevant issues for Latin American countries in light of the growing interest of Canada, the United States, and the EU in bilateral FTAs.[18] Wonnacott (1996) argued that the H&S system is welfare reducing for spoke countries because they fail to benefit from market access with each other and, in turn, become less attractive for FDI. In contrast, the center maximizes welfare.

Kowalczyk and Wonnacott (1992) illustrated that the center has incentives to expand membership as its welfare increases. The incentives of the spoke countries are ambiguous and depend on the complementarity or substitutability of exports of existing and potential members of the H&S system. If exports are substitutes, there may be divergent incentives and lack of interest in a more welfare-enhancing plurilateral agreement encompassing the hub and all the spokes.

Transaction Costs

From the policymaking perspective, a key issue is to understand how transaction costs impact on the efficiency of RIAs and on the political-economy incentives that may undermine freer multilateral trade through the proliferation of trade-diverting agreements (Levy 1997; Krishna 1998). Although it is theoretically plausible that regionalism leads to the weakening of multilateralism, the specific characteristics of the New Regionalism may guarantee greater complementarity. The systemic impact of an RIA depends on geography,[19] strategic interactions,[20] institutional structure, the choice between free trade areas or customs unions,[21] and specific regulations, such as rules of origin, that can alter the actual rate of protection and the political-economy incentives for further liberalization.[22]

Endogenous Regionalism

Finally, reversing the perspective, RIAs may be seen as an endogenous response to the challenge of integration in the world trading system. Freund (1998) demonstrated that the welfare gains from RIAs are in fact inversely correlated with the level of the MFN tariff, while Ethier (1998a) coined the term "New Regionalism," a paradigm of which north-south agreements, such as the FTAA, are the strongest expression.

Ethier (1998b) formally demonstrates that self-exclusion from the multilateral trading system is an inefficient—although politically sustainable—equilibrium. Nevertheless, his analysis highlights complementarity between the multilateral system and regionalism. Assuming that the production of intermediate goods has a positive externality for a developing country, multilateral trade liberalization raises the level of the positive externality and increases the interest in reforms in the South. Moreover, north-south RIAs, although characterized by a small preferential margin, nonetheless induce greater foreign direct investment for the production of intermediate goods and end up furthering interests in liberalizing reforms, including at the multilateral level.

Harrison, Rutherford, and Tarr (2001) demonstrate that reciprocal liberalization can be preferable to a unilateral approach, particularly when tariffs reach certain low levels. This explains the signature characteristic of the New Regionalism: unilateral, multilateral, and reciprocal regional liberalization have progressed in tandem. Freund (2002) shows that there is a trade-off between reciprocity and credibility (the dilemma of the Old Regionalism). As preferences granted are positively related to preferences received, countries may extract greater concessions if they have high external barriers. But if trade barriers are too high, free trade commitments are not credible. Her test for reciprocity in a wide array of RIAs confirms that there is strong evidence of reciprocity in north-north and in south-south agreements, but not in north-south ones. This suggests that north-south RIAs may allow developing countries to benefit from concessions in areas other than market access when they pursue comprehensive agreements, as in the FTAA or the EU Association Agreements (Giordano 2002).

Implications for the FTAA

The FTAA is part of a much larger, hemispheric summit process. Preparatory work began in 1995 involving thirty-four democratic countries of the hemisphere. WTO consistency requires that trade liberalization eliminate tariffs on goods and barriers to services on "substantially all trade." The multilateral rules also demand a transition period of about ten years, although a limited amount of liberalization could be extended beyond that to perhaps twelve to fifteen years.

Formal negotiations have progressed steadily and are well positioned from a technical standpoint to finish by the target date of December 2004. This could contribute to the credibility of the eventual emergence of an FTAA and hence create anticipatory effects in trade (and investment) in the hemisphere. Thus it is in Latin America's interest that the FTAA process enjoys a credible final stage of negotiations presided over by a Brazil-U.S. copresidency.

Negotiations reflect a very ambitious agreement covering virtually all modern areas of trade, with labor and environmental standards looming in the background because of the force of the template appearing in the United States' new Trade Promotion Authority. The possibility of an ambitious agreement allows one to muse about the FTAA with respect to the broader analysis of the costs and benefits of regional integration.

Static Issues

Given that FTAA countries mimic to some degree the pattern of international comparative advantage, an agreement should create a sizeable amount of new trade. Indeed, computable general equilibrium simulations by the IDB (2002) suggest that an FTAA would generate significant export growth for Latin America, primarily in labor-intensive sectors. In this context one could anticipate that the FTAA would be a vehicle to promote intraindustry trade. The experience of the Old and New Regionalisms would suggest that countries such as Brazil with extensive industrial bases and home markets should be especially well positioned to take advantage of the opportunities for intraindustry trade arising from an FTAA.

However, to achieve these results a difficult trade-off must be accomplished. North America would have to eliminate trade impediments on some "sensitive" sectors, especially agriculture and food processing. Meanwhile, Latin America would have to provide inducements by trading off not only reciprocal elimination of its higher tariffs on goods, but also significant liberalization in new issue areas such as services, intellectual property, and investment. However, the new areas are politically sensitive in the South, where they have been for the most part subject to only minimal liberalization or none at all.

Important elements of trade (and investment) creation for Latin America in an FTAA are the establishment of reciprocal rules and a dispute-settlement mechanism. These elements are a way to obtain guarantees on market access, including preferences that have been granted unilaterally but can be withdrawn in the same way and over which the countries have little voice and no neutral recourse for settling disputes.

An FTAA would be anchored by North America, which consists of relatively open, world-class economies. Hence an FTAA should reduce residual trade diversion in existing subregional agreements by exposing them to a greater spectrum of international comparative advantage (IDB 2002). However, while external tariffs have fallen very sharply in Latin America, they still are relatively high and dispersed. So one can expect trade diversion to materialize with the rest of the world. But the welfare costs for Latin America may not be too high vis-à-vis the status quo.[23]

External tariffs and preferences are not the only source of trade diversion: NAFTA-like rules of origin, in addition to being difficult to administer, have been a vehicle for protection because of their specificity.[24] Restrictive rules of origin could be a problem, particularly for South America where there is considerable extrahemispheric importing. The costs of trade diversion can be reduced by lowering third-party tariffs. This can be done unilaterally, by pursuing extraregional trade agreements (the Mexican strategy after NAFTA) and by encouraging liberalization in the WTO. Aside from reducing trade diversion, an additional incentive for lowering tariffs through unilateral or extraregional approaches is competition with North America in an FTAA.

One serious issue is the loss of tariff revenue and income-redistribution effects that come from asymmetric north-south external tariff structures. This is one of the "entry fees" that Latin American countries must pay to capture the benefits of North American partners. The Caribbean, and to a lesser extent Central America, are especially dependent on tariff revenue. Fiscal reform to substitute tariff revenue and the lowering of average external protection—issues which must be dealt with anyway in an era of globalization—are the responses needed to minimize these costs.

Dynamic Effects

If an FTAA opens and secures market access in North America in a substantial number of areas where the Latin America's exploitation of its international comparative advantage is still being frustrated, it should stimulate investment, growth, and employment through expansion of exports that tend to be relatively labor intensive. But it also will have a contractionnary effect on some import-competing industries, especially capital-intensive ones.

Again, countries now want to attract FDI, in particular through north-south integration. The FTAA will be a huge market of 800 million people anchored by a vibrant North American economy and a rules-based trading system. Hence it should be a major channel of new FDI. But the effects will not be even, because of the consequences of dilution effects, clustering in certain geographic locations, and welfare losses due to fiscal competition among countries to attract foreign firms. The IDB (2002) illustrates the significant impact that the creation of the FTAA could have on FDI across the Western Hemisphere, with countries such as Argentina "winning" and Mexico "losing" as a result of dilution effects.

In theory, trade and investment in north-south integration would be expected to contribute in the long run to convergence and improved income distribution in Latin America. But in the short to medium term, outcomes can be ambiguous (IDB 2002). Lessons from the European experience are only partially relevant because its political commitment to deep integration generated finance of collective convergence mechanisms that are not typical of FTAs. Relevant lessons of both the Old and New Regionalisms are that when left to market forces (1) the dynamic impact of regional integration can be very uneven between and within countries, (2) market segmentation and imperfect information can leave unexploited opportunities for investments, which can foster more completeness of the regional market, (3) productivity gains can be a one-off event if not followed up by proactive promotion of competitiveness and exports, and (4) the reallocation of resources will create losers and requirements for transitional aid and social protection.

Of course, these problems can be serious in an FTAA with thirty-two developing countries and with subregions that have had little commercial contact with each other in the past. To address them, countries will have to explore proactive national competitiveness and local development programs, as well as transition assistance, without distorting trade. This is motivated by competition and equity considerations, but it also has a political-economy dimension, since the Old and New Regionalisms also show that serious imbalances within and between partners can create domestic political resistance and thereby disrupt a regional initiative offering potential net gains (IDB 2002).

Nontraditional Gains

An FTAA anchored by North America clearly would be a major signal to investors of the region's commitment to structural reform. It also would be an excellent vehicle for lock-in since north-south agreements are less prone than south-south accords to reversals (IDB 2002). These intangibles—not a minor consideration in the current uncertain environment of the region—could lower risk premia for private investors and stimulate much-needed growth.

An FTAA could drive extensive institutional modernization that modern trade disciplines can foster and that competition can induce. However, the institutional requirements for implementing these disciplines are complex, costly, and skill intensive. Moreover, certain disciplines adopted may be of marginal benefit or even generate net costs for some countries, especially smaller ones, until certain development thresholds are met. This suggests the usefulness of extended transitions into certain disciplines or even some type of *de minimis* arrangement.

Regional public goods also could increase in an FTAA. Currently most regional public goods are emerging out of subregional integration agreements where trade and investment links have tightened and generated externalities. An FTAA could stimulate lagging hemispheric cooperation and strengthen the United States' commitment to the region in areas beyond business as such. One important cooperative arrangement already achieved is that participation in an FTAA will be conditioned by democratic government.

Macroeconomic Considerations

While not covered in this chapter, a lesson of the Old and New Regionalisms is that macroeconomic instability is a major threat to trade, investment, and political cohesion in regional integration. Moreover, integration agreements themselves can contribute to this instability. Loss of tariff revenue through tariff elimination and trade diversion can create fiscal imbalances. Surges of capital inflows *cum* real exchange overvaluation is a formula for external vulnerability and debt crisis, disincentives to exports, and unanticipated reduction of protection for domestic import substitutes. Meanwhile, financial-services integration may advance faster than prudential regulation. In sum, in an FTAA liberalization would face serious sequencing issues given the different pace of structural reform in the thirty-two developing countries.

FTAA Institutional Issues

The Old Regionalism was top heavy in institutions and bureaucracy. The New Regionalism is paper thin in both. The heterogeneity of development among FTAA countries suggests that a happy medium will be needed. At a minimum, a small and highly professional technical and administrative secretariat would help countries, implement disciplines, monitor development effects and balance (basic principles of the FTAA ministers), and provide ongoing support for the future evolution of the agreement. Given the volatility of Latin American economies some consideration will probably be given to the politically thorny issue of transparent safeguards in transition periods and even after the agreement is in place.

Good and sustainable agreements require good negotiations and implementation. Capacities in this area are also very asymmetric between North and South. Fortunately, the FTAA negotiations are incorporating an innovative program to mobilize technical assistance. The plan involves support for development of national capacity-building strategies and a coordinating mechanism among donors to channel resources in a timely way.

Systemic Issues

The Multilateral System

A plausible scenario, as long as structural adjustment is at the center of development in the region, is that the FTAA and the multilateral system will "talk to each other" and generate positive synergies. An FTAA would be too big and its countries' liberalization credentials too important for it not to fulfill its official promise of WTO consistency. The FTAA process, moreover, is intimately linked to the progress of negotiations in Doha because certain important FTAA agenda items such as antidumping, export subsidies, and domestic support in agriculture are important, but difficult to treat in a regional forum. Fortunately, tariffs and quotas can be treated in an FTAA and these are the main trade distorting measures in hemispheric agricultural trade (IDB 2002).

On the other hand, the creation of an FTAA that is significantly WTO-plus could be used by the United States (perhaps in alliance with Latin America) as a negotiating tool in Geneva to push forward a liberalizing agenda just as was done with NAFTA in the Uruguay Round. Regarding the Doha Round, the United States has been far from passive, tabling aggressive proposals to reduce agriculture subsidies and to eliminate industrial goods tariffs by 2015. The FTAA could give it a bigger stick. It also could stimulate more attention to perfecting multilateral rules for regional integration. Meanwhile, any WTO-plus agreement would prepare the Latin American countries for further liberalization in the multilateral forum.

Of course, Europe risks losing market share, as actually happened with Mexico in NAFTA. Hence if an FTAA emerges, Europe will be under greater pressure to realize its official strategy of creating FTAs with all the subregions (in addition to its actual FTAs with Chile and Mexico). An FTAA undoubtedly would also raise the intensity of Europe's interest in a successful Doha Round and would probably further stimulate Asia's growing interest in regionalism as well as Japan's interest in an ambitious Doha Round.

The spaghetti-bowl form of the New Regionalism is a legitimate concern. An ambitious FTAA would help clean it up, since the FTAA is supposed to absorb agreements of lesser scope and depth. While it remains to be seen how ambitious it will be, there is the additional difficult problem of making operational the absorption principle.

Hub-and-Spoke Agreements

One dimension of the increasing presence of north-south agreements is a growing number of bilateral negotiations in the hemisphere that parallel the FTAA negotiations. These raise risks and opportunities (IDB 2002). Agenda setters can use bilateral negotiations to energize the FTAA negotiations and spark laggards by signaling their commitment to liberalizing market access and setting precedents that mirror the comprehensive, balanced, and development-oriented principles of the FTAA. In this way bilaterals could be a building block. On the other hand they also can be used to maximize bargaining power and set precedents that reflect narrow geopolitical and mercantilist interests. This could either erode the welfare benefits of an FTAA or block its realization, leaving in its place a welfare-inferior hub-and-spoke system that further aggravates the spaghetti bowl. In the real world bilaterals probably contain an element of both approaches and the balance is hard to predict, but developments here clearly merit watching.

Exclusion

A " gang effect" is already evident in the FTAA process, exclusion could be costly for the dissenting country and, depending on who is excluded, for others as well if it creates political instability in the hemisphere. Hence, maintaining the spirit of hemispheric community and consensus is important for a welfare-enhancing FTAA.

Subregional Integration

An FTAA, especially a comprehensive one, would test the political and economic relevance of subregional integration schemes with deep objectives, which have stalled in recent years, especially MERCOSUR. The FTAA is not a substitute for a well designed, successful, deep subregional integration scheme, and indeed it could be argued that there are positive synergies so that both should be pursued simultaneously and coexist in the framework of a strong, rules-based, multilateral system.

Again, an FTAA would reduce risks of trade diversion in the subregions. It also would establish a floor from which they would have to deepen "to survive." Meanwhile, a deep, subregional integration agreement would strengthen member countries and the FTAA. Members of the subgroup would be better able to combine factors of production to compete through a more powerful free flow of resources than would emerge in the hemispheric agreement. They could cooperate in technology, marketing, development of productive chains, and other enterprises. Macroeconomic stability could be enhanced through coordination efforts or even monetary unions. A customs union or common market with a solid bloc negotiation would also serve to enhance bargaining power in the negotiation and the future evolution of the agreement after 2005. Another consideration is that deep integration schemes implicate more than business issues. They have a strong political dimension (in which business provides cohesion) that provides them with a comparative advantage for addressing neighborhood issues that are unlikely to be addressed by an FTAA. Successful resolution of neighborhood issues would contribute to a more stable hemisphere for an FTAA.

These considerations, however, assume that the subregional agreements can progressively deepen toward their common market objectives over a reasonable time frame. If not, the costs of living with partially completed commitments and half structures may exceed the benefits, making the absorption by the larger hemispheric accord a welfare-enhancing option.

Conclusion

In conclusion, an FTAA raises many important economic and strategic questions. Precise answers must await an agreement, the configuration of its trade-related disciplines and institutional arrangements. One thing is clear: The FTAA process is one of the best expressions of Ethier's (1998a) New Regionalism.

References

Aitken, Norman, and William Lowery. 1973. "A Cross-Sectional Study of the Effects of LAFTA and CACM on Latin American Trade." *Journal of Common Market Studies* 11 (June): 326–36.

Anderson, Kym, and Hege Norheim. 1993. "History, Geography and Regional Economic Integration." In *Regional Integration and the Global Trading System*, edited by K. Anderson and R. Blachurst. Geneva: Harvester Wheatsheaf.

Balassa, Bela. 1966. "Towards a Theory of Economic Integration." In *Latin American Economic Integration*, edited by M. Wionczek. New York: Praeger.

———. 1967. "Trade Creation and Trade Diversion in the European Common Market." *Economic Journal* 77: 1–2.

Baldwin, Richard. 1989. "The Growth Effects of 1992." *Economic Policy: A European Forum* 9: 247–81.

———. 1993. "A Domino Theory of Regionalism." National Bureau of Economic Research Working Paper no. 4465, Cambridge, MA.

Baldwin, Richard, and Anthony J. Venables. 1995. "Regional Economic Integration." In *Handbook of International Economics*, vol. 3, edited by G. Grossman and K. Rogoff, pp. 1597–644. Amsterdam: Elsevier.

Ben David, Dan. 1996. "Trade and Convergence among Countries." *Journal of International Economics* (40): 279–98.

Bhagwati, Jagdish. 1993. "Regionalism and Multilateralism: An Overview." In *New Dimensions in Regional Integration*, edited by J. de Melo and A. Panagariya. Cambridge: Cambridge University Press.

Bhagwati, Jagdish, and Arvind Panagariya. 1996. "Preferential Trading Areas and Multilateralism: Strangers, Friends or Foes?" In *The Economics of Preferential Trade Agreements*, edited by J. Bhagwati and A. Panagariya, pp. 1–78. Washington, DC: American Enterprise Institute Press.

Brecher, Richard, and Jagdish Bhagwati. 1981. "Foreign Ownership and the Theory of Trade and Welfare." *Journal of Political Economy* 89 (June): 497–511.

Cadot, Olivier, Jaime de Melo, and Marcelo Olarreaga. 1996. "Regional Integration and Lobbying for Tariffs against Non-Members." Centre for Economic Policy Research Discussion Paper no. 1448, London.

Casella, Alessandra. 1995. "Large Countries, Small Countries and the Enlargement of Trade Blocks." National Bureau of Economic Research Working Paper no. 5365, Cambridge, MA.

Cernat, Lucian. 2001. "Assessing Regional Trade Arrangements: Are South-South RTAs More Trade Diverting?" *Global Economic Quarterly* 2 (July–September): 235–59.

Chang, Won, and L. Alan Winters. 1999. "How Regional Blocs Affect Excluded Countries: The Price Effects of MERCOSUR." World Bank Policy Research Working Paper no. 2157, Washington, DC.

Chudnovsky, Daniel, and Andrés Lopez. 2001. *El boom de la inversión extranjera directa en el Mercosur*. Buenos Aires: Siglo Veintiuno and Red Mercosur.

Cline, William. 1978. "Benefits and Costs of Economic Integration in Central America." In *Economic Integration in Central America*, edited by W. Cline and C. Delgado, pp. 59–124. Washington, DC: Brookings Institution.

Cooper, Charles, and Benton Massel. "Towards a General Theory of Customs Unions for Developing Countries." *Journal of Political Economy* 73: 461–76.

Corden W. Max. 1972. "Economies of Scale and Customs Union Theory." *Journal of Political Economy* 80: 465–72.

Dell, Sydney. 1963. *Trade Blocs and Common Markets*. New York: Alfred A. Knopf.

———. 1966. *A Latin American Common Market?* London: Royal Institute of International Affairs.

Devlin, Robert. 1997. "En defensa del Mercosur." *Archivos del Presente 7*: 171–75.

Devlin, Robert, and Antoni Estevadeordal. 2001. "What's New in the New Regionalism in the Americas?" In *Regional Integration in Latin America and the Caribbean: The Political Economy of Open Regionalism*, edited by V. Bulmer-Thomas. London: ILAS-University of London.

———. 2003. "Trade and Cooperation: A Regional Public Goods Approach." Inter-American Development Bank, Washington, DC. Photocopy.

Devlin, Robert, Antoni Estevadeordal, and Ekaterina Krivonos. 2002. "The Trade and Cooperation Nexus: How does the MERCOSUR-EU Process Measure Up?" In *An Integrated Approach to the European Union-Mercosur Association*, edited by P. Giordano, pp. 79–122. Paris: Chaire Mercosur de Sciences Po.

Echevarria, Juan José. 1997. "Trade Flows in the Andean Countries: Unilateral Liberalization or Regional Preferences?" Paper presented at the Annual World Bank Conference on Development in Latin America and the Caribbean, "Trade, Towards Open Regionalism," Washington, DC.

Economic Commission for Latina America and the Caribbean (ECLAC). 1994. *Open Regionalism and Economic Integration*. Santiago: ECLAC.

Endoh, Masahiro. 1999. "Trade Creation and Trade Diversion in the EEC, the LAFTA and the CMEA: 1960–1994." *Applied Economics* 31 (February): 207–16.

Estevadeordal, Antoni. 1999. "Negotiating Preferential Market Access: The Case of NAFTA?" Inter-American Development Bank, INTAL-ITD-STA Working Paper Series no. 3, Washington, DC.

Estevadeordal, Antoni, and Kati Suominen. 2003. "Rules of Origin in FTAs in Europe and in the Americas." Inter-American Development Bank, Washington, DC.

Ethier, Wilfred. 1998a. "The New Regionalism." *Economic Journal* 108: 1149–61.

———. 1998b. "Regionalism in a Multilateral World." *Journal of Political Economy* 106: 1214–45.

Feenstra, Robert C. 2000. "World Trade Flows, 1980–1997, with Production and Tariff Data." University of California, Davis. Photocopy.

Fernandez, Raquel, and Jonathan Portes. 1998. "Returns to Regionalism: An Evaluation of Non-Traditional Gains from Regional Trade Agreements." *World Bank Economic Review* 2: 196–220.

Foroutan, Faezeh. 1998. "Does Membership in a Regional Preferential Trade Arrangement Make a Country More or Less Protectionist?" Policy Research Working Paper no. 1898, World Bank, Washington, DC.

Francois, Joseph, and Clinton Shiells. 1994. *Modeling Trade Policy Applied General Equilibrium Assessments of North American Free Trade.* Cambridge: Cambridge University Press.

Frankel, Jeffrey A. 1997. *Regional Trading Blocs in the World Economic System.* Washington, DC: Institute for International Economics.

Frankel, Jeffrey A., and Shang-Jin Wei. 1996. "Regionalization of World Trade and Currencies: Economics and Politics." In *The regionalization of the world economy*, edited by J. A. Frankel, pp. 189–226. Chicago: University of Chicago Press.

Freund, Caroline. 1998. "Multilateralism and the Endogenous Formation of PTAs." International Finance Discussion Papers no. 614, Board of Governors of the Federal Reserve System, Washington, DC.

———. 2002. "Reciprocity in Free Trade Agreements." World Bank, Washington, DC. Photocopy.

Freund, Caroline, and John McLaren. 1999. "On the Dynamics of Trade Diversion: Evidence from Four Trade Blocs." Board of Governors of the Federal Reserve System, Washington, DC. Photocopy.

Fujita, Masahisa, Paul Krugman, and Anthony Venables. 1999. *The Spatial Economy: Cities, Regions and International Trade.* Cambridge, MA: MIT Press.

Garcia, Herrero, and G. Glocker. 2000. "Options for Latin America in a Globalized World: A Regional Monetary Union versus Dollarization." European Central Bank, Frankfurt. Photocopy.

Giordano, Paolo. 2001. "The Political Economy of Regional Integration in MERCOSUR." Ph.D. Dissertation, Institut d'Etudes Politiques de Paris.

Giordano, Paolo, ed. 2002. *An Integrated Approach to the European Union-Mercosur Association*. Paris: Chaire Mercosur de Sciences Po.

Grubel, Herbert, and Peter Lloyd. 1975. *Intra-Industry Trade, the Theory and Measurement of Trade in Differentiated Products*. London: Macmillan.

Gupta, Anju, and Maurice Schiff. 1997. "Outsiders and Regional Trade Agreements among Small Countries: The Case of Regional Markets." Policy Research Working Paper no. 1847, World Bank, Washington, DC.

Harrison, Glenn, Thomas Rutherford, and David Tarr. Forthcoming. "Trade Policy Options for Chile: the Importance of Market Access." *Integration and Trade* and *Economie Internationale*.

Hayes, Margaret. 1996. *Building the Hemispheric Community: Lessons from the Summit of the Americas Process*. Washington, DC: Inter-American Dialogue.

Helpman, Elhanan, and Paul Krugman. 1989. *Trade Policy and Market Structure*, Cambridge, MA: MIT Press.

Hindley, Brian, and Patrick Messerlin. 1993. "Guarantees of Market Access and Regionalism." In *Regional Integration and the Global Trading System*, edited by K. Anderson and R. Blackhurst. Geneva: Harvester Wheatsheaf.

Hirschman, Albert. 1958. *The Strategy of Economic Development*. New Haven: Yale University Press.

Hufbauer, Gary, and Jeffrey Schott. 1993. *NAFTA: An Assessment*. Washington, DC: Institute for International Economics.

Inter-American Development Bank (IDB). 1995–2002. *Trade and Integration in the Americas, Periodic Notes*. 8 vols. Integration and Regional Programs Department, Inter-American Development Bank, Washington, DC.

———. 2002. *Economic and Social Progress in Latin America 2002 Report, Beyond Borders: The New Regionalism in Latin America*. Washington, DC: Inter-American Development Bank.

Johnson, Harry. 1965. "The Economic Theory of Protectionism, Tariff Bargaining and the Formation of Customs Unions." *Journal of Political Economy* 73: 256–83.

Kemp, Murray, and Henry Wan. 1995. "An Elementary Proposition Concerning the Formation of Customs Unions." *Journal of International Economics* 6: 95–7.

Khaler, Miles. 1995. *International Institutions and the Political Economy of Integration*. Washington, DC: Brookings Institution.

Kowalczyk, Carsten, and Ronald Wonnacott. 1992. "Hubs and Spokes, and Free Trade in the Americas." National Bureau of Economic Research Working Paper no. 4198, Cambridge, MA.

Krishna, Kala, and Anne O. Krueger. 1995. "Implementing Free Trade Areas: Rules of Origin and Hidden Protection." In *New Directions in Trade Theory*, edited by A. Deardoff, J. Levinsohn, and R. Stern, pp. 149–70. Ann Arbor, MI: University of Michigan Press.

Krishna, Pravin. 1998. "Regionalism and Multilateralism: A Political Economy Approach." *Quarterly Journal of Economics* 113: 227–51.

Krueger, Anne O. 1993. "Rules of Origin as Protectionist Devices." National Bureau of Economic Research Working Paper no. 4352, Cambridge, MA.

———. 1995. "Free Trade Agreements versus Customs Unions." National Bureau of Economic Research Working Paper no. 5084, Cambridge, MA.

———. 1999. "Trade Creation and Trade Diversion under NAFTA." National Bureau of Economic Research Working Paper no. 7429, Cambridge, MA.

Krugman, Paul. 1991. "The Move Towards Free Trade Zones." In *Policy Implications of Trade and Currency Zones*, edited by the Federal Reserve Bank of Kansas City, pp. 7–42. Kansas City, MO: Federal Reserve Bank of Kansas City.

———. 1993. "Regionalism versus Multilateralism: Analytical Notes." In *New Dimensions in Regional Integration*, edited by J. de Melo and A Panagariya, pp. 58–78. Cambridge: Cambridge University Press.

Langhammer, Rolf, and Ulrich Hiemenz. 1991. *Regional Integration among Developing Countries: Survey of Past Performance and Agenda for Future Policy Action*. Washington, DC: World Bank.

Lawrence, Robert. 1995. *Regionalism, Multilateralism and Deeper Integration*. Washington, DC: Brookings Institution.

Levy, Philip, "A Political Economy Analysis of Free Trade Agreements." *American Economic Review* 87: 506–19.

Levy Yeyati, Eduardo, Ernesto Stein, and Christian Daude. 2002. *Regional Integration and the Location of FDI*. Inter-American Development Bank, Washington, DC. Photocopy.

Linder, Staffan. 1966. "Customs Unions and Economic Development." In *Latin American Economic Integration: Experiences and Prospects*, edited by M. Wionczek. New York: Praeger.

Lipsey, Richard. 1957. "The Theory of Customs Unions: Trade Diversion and Welfare." *Economica* 24: 40–6.

López-Córdova, Ernesto, and Mauricio Mesquita Moreira. 2002. Regional Integration and Productivity: the Experiences of Brazil and Mexico. Inter-American Development Bank, Washington, DC. Photocopy.

Markusen, James, and Keith Maskus. 2001. "General Equilibrium Approaches to the Multinational Firm: A Review of Theory and Evidence." National Bureau for Economic Research Working paper no. 8334, Cambridge, MA.

Meade, James. 1955. *The Theory of Customs Unions.* Amsterdam: North-Holland.

Milner, Helen. 1997. "Industries, Governments, and Regional Trade Blocks." In *The Political Economy of Regionalism*, edited by E. Mansfield and H. Milner, pp. 77–106. New York: Columbia University Press.

Motta, Massimo, and George Norman. 1996. "Does Economic Integration Cause Foreign Direct Investment?" *International Economic Review* 37: 757–83.

Mundell, Robert A. 1964. "Tariff Preferences and the Terms of Trade." *Manchester School of Economic and Social Studies* 32: 1–13.

Myrdal, Gunnar. 1957. *Economic Theory and Under-Developed Regions.* London: Gerald Duckworthand Co.

Nagarajan, Nigel. 1998. "On the Evidence for Trade Diversion in MERCOSUR." *Integration and Trade* 6: 3–34.

Nogues, Julio. 1996. "Does MERCOSUR's Trade Performance Raise Concerns about the Effects of Regional Trade Arrangements? NO." Buenos Aires. Photocopy.

Ottaviano, Gianmarco, and Diego Puga. 1997. "Agglomeration in the Global Economy: A Survey of the 'New Economic Geography.'" Centre for Economic Policy Research Discussion Paper no. 356, London.

Padoan, Pier Carlo. 1997. "Technology Accumulation and Diffusion: Is There a Regional Dimension?" World Bank Policy Research Working Paper no. 1781, Washington, DC.

Panagariya, Arvind. 1996. "The Free Trade Area of the Americas: Good for Latin America?" *World Economy* 19: 485–515.

Perroni, Carlo, and John Whalley. 1994. "The New Regionalism: Trade Liberalization or Insurance?" National Bureau of Economic Research Working Paper no. 4626, Cambridge, MA.

Pomfret Richard. 1997. *The Economics of Regional Trading Arrangements.* Oxford: Oxford University Press.

Puga, Diego, and Anthony J. Venables. 1997. "Preferential Trading Arrangements and Industrial Location." *Journal of International Economics* 43: 347–68.

Richardson, Martin. 1993. "Endogenous Protection and Trade Diversion." *Journal of International Economics* 34: 329–24.

———. 1995. "Tariff Revenue Competition in a Free Trade Area." *European Economic Review* 39: 1429–37.

Rivera-Batiz, Luis, and Paul Romer. 1991. "Economic Integration and Endogenous Growth." *Quarterly Journal of Economics* 106: 531–55.

Robinson, Sherman. 1989. "Multisectoral Models." In *Handbook of Development Economies*, edited by H. B. Chenery and T. N. Srinivasan. Amsterdam: North-Holland.

Robinson, Sherman, and Karen Thierfelder. 1999. "Trade Liberalization and Regional Integration: The Search for Large Numbers." International Food Policy Research Institute Discussion Paper no. 34, Washington, DC.

Schiff, Maurice, and L. Alan Winters. 1998. "Regional Integration as Diplomacy." *World Bank Economic Review* 12: 271–96.

Soloaga, Isidro, and L. Alan Winters. 1999. "Regionalism in the Nineties: What Effect on Trade?" World Bank Policy Research Working Paper no. 2156, Washington, DC.

Summers. Lawrence. 1991. "Regionalism and the World Trading System." In *Policy Implications of Trade and Currency Zones*, edited by the Federal Reserve Bank of Kansas City, pp. 295–301. Kansas City, MO: Federal Reserve Bank of Kansas City.

Vamvakidis, Athanasios. 1998. "Regional Trade Agreements versus Broad Liberalization: Which Path Leads to Faster Growth, Time-Series Evidence." International Monetary Fund Working Paper no. 40, Washington, DC.

Venables, Anthony. 1999. "Integration Agreements: A Force For Convergence or Divergence?" World Bank Policy Research Working Paper no. 2260, Washington, DC.

Venables Anthony. 2003. "Regionalism and Development." In *Bridges for Development*, edited by R. Devlin and A. Estevadeordal, pp. 51–74. Washington, DC: Inter-American Development Bank.

Viner, Jacob. 1950. *The Customs Union Issue*. Washington, DC: Carnegie Endowment for International Peace.

Vodusek, Ziga, ed. 2001. *Foreign Direct Investment in Latin America: The Role of European Investors*. Washington, DC: Inter-American Development Bank.

Whalley, John. 1998. "Why Do Countries Seek Regional Trade Agreements?" In *The Regionalization of the World Economy*, edited by J. A. Frankel. Cambridge, MA: National Bureau of Economic Research.

Willmore, Larry. 1976. "Trade Creation, Trade Diversion and Effective Protection in the Central American Common Market." *Journal of Development Studies* 12: 396–414.

Winters, L. Alan. 1996. "Regionalism versus Multilateralism." World Bank Policy Research Paper no. 1687, Washington, DC.

———. 2001a. "Regionalism for Developing Countries: Assessing the Costs and Benefits." In *Regionalism and Globalization: Theory and Practice*, edited by Sajal Lahiri. London: Routledge.

———. 2001b. "Regionalism and Multilateralism in the Twenty-First Century." Paper prepared for the Regional Policy Dialogue on Trade and Integration, Inter-American Development Bank, Washington, DC.

Wionczek, Miguel, ed. 1966. *Latin American Economic Integration: Experiences and Prospects*. New York: Praeger.

Wonnacott, Ronald, 1996. "Trade and Investment in an Hub-and-Spoke System versus a Free Trade Area." *World Economy* 19: 237–52.

World Bank. 2000. *Trade Blocs*. Oxford: Oxford University Press.

Yeats, Alexander. 1997. "Does MERCOSUR's Trade Performance Raise Concerns about the Effects of Regional Trade Arrangements?" World Bank Policy Research Working Paper no. 1729, Washington, DC.

Yi, Sang-Seung. 1996. "Endogenous Formation of Customs Unions Under Imperfect Competition: Open Regionalism is Good." *Journal of International Economics* 41: 153–57.

Notes

1 We thank Javier Comas for his insights on this subject.

2 These are: (1) creation of a larger preferential regional market that has (2) secure home market-like access to (3) stimulate investment and productivity through (4) rationalizing protected industries and (5) exploiting economies of scale and specialization in a way that is (6) consistent with multilateral rules. Other similarities include (7) enhanced terms of trade, (8) absorption of unemployed resources, and (9) a response to the creation of regional blocs elsewhere (principally Europe in the Old Regionalism and NAFTA in the New).

3 Note that the CACM and the Andean Pact span the two periods. However, in the early 1990s both were relaunched in the spirit of the New Regionalism with a noticeable difference in their objectives and instruments. The latter also changed its name to the Andean Community.

4 Central America was more successful as the bulk of regional trade was liberalized within five years.

5 The Andean Group established a formal court of justice in 1984 but little or no activity occurred until the 1990s.

6 In a model in which goods are substitutes he shows that for a single tariff change by one member the preferred exporting partner's terms of trade unambiguously improve, while the excluded country's deteriorate. The net effect of the active country's tariff concessions on its own terms

of trade is ambiguous, but when two countries swap preferential concessions, as in an RIA, they collectively improve their terms of trade vis-à-vis the rest of the world.

7 The simplest consists of an analysis of the evolution of intra- and extra-regional trade shares (IDB 1995–2002). Such indicators, however, overlook the influence of history and geography on the determinants of trade and depend on economic size and on the value of countries' total trade. Following Anderson and Norheim (1993), the effects of regional integration policies can be accurately traced by looking at the trade-intensity ratio. Although the index is influenced by structural factors, its change can be attributed to trade policies, as these are unlikely to change dramatically in the short run (Table 5.4).

8 Gravity models have been successfully applied to different types of flows, including intra- and extra-regional trade and foreign investment. Some models have been successfully applied to developing countries (Soloaga and Winters 1999; Estevadeordal and Robertson, this volume). Overall, RIAs researched with this technique generally do not generate evidence to suggest net trade diversion effects.

9 Robinson and Thierfelder (1999) argue that computable general equilibrium models incorporating the new growth theory invariably find that trade creation greatly dominates trade diversion. These models predict welfare gains of 1 percent of the GDP in perfect competition, 2 to 3 percent under imperfect competition, and 5 percent in the dynamic specifications. The strength of these models is that their microeconomic structure allows a detailed exploration of the sectoral effects of trade-policy reforms. Their shortcoming, however, is that they require an important amount of quantitative information that it is sometimes hard to construct in a rigorous way (Robinson 1989).

10 Very few studies address the terms-of-trade effects of Latin American RIAs. Gupta and Schiff (1997) found that the formation of the Andean Pact led to improvements of the terms of trade in some sectors. Meanwhile Chang and Winters (1999) found that MERCOSUR led to the decline of U.S. exports prices to Brazil.

11 The impact of trade liberalization on government revenue can be large for small countries or for countries that liberalize trade preferentially with a major trading partner. The loss of tariff revenue can be minimized by reducing the level of protection to third parties and by promoting a tax reform that reduces dependence on tariffs. The tariff revenue loss from regional integration is, however, a trade-off for an investment in institutional modernization that may bring additional benefits in the long run, if the investment is a wise one.

12 The analysis relied on the methodology introduced by Balassa (1967) based on the comparison of pre- and post-integration income elasticity

of total import demand. Differentiating the import demand for durable and nondurable consumer goods and intermediate goods, Willmore (1976) challenged this conclusion. He found considerable trade diversion in non-durable consumer goods, a category that accounted for 52 percent of intra-regional trade.

13 The inclusion of dynamic effects raised the figure to 3 percent, which is a substantial gain that may explain the very robust nature of the CACM.

14 The theory of endogenous growth also spurred new approaches to these dynamic issues (Rivera-Batiz and Romer 1991). In particular the researchers analyzed how RIAs can stimulate the accumulation of research and development activities that foster endogenous growth (Padoan 1997), the import and the local production of capital goods, and greater efficiency in the financial market, which leads to capital accumulation.

15 In fact the WTO may present free-riding problems that lead to less correlation between the costs and benefits of retaliation. In addition, the cost of dispute procedures in RIAs is generally lower than in the WTO and the tolerance for protectionism may therefore be reduced.

16 On one hand, governments and the private sector were firmly committed to maintaining protection, but on the other they were seeking to liberalize, albeit regionally. Hence the vehicle designed to save the ISI policy (regional integration) was undermined by the commitment to protection. In the New Regionalism governments have been more successful because the goals of regional integration and structural reform have been working in tandem rather than at cross purposes. Notwithstanding economic crises in the 1990s, most regional schemes have largely kept their commitments, especially in goods trade. North-south schemes have been superior to south-south in this regard.

17 Whalley (1998), for instance, argues that the main cost of being left out is the risk of facing trade wars without allies.

18 An H&S system features one central developed country signing agreements with many developing countries in the periphery that do not liberalize trade among themselves.

19 Considering the natural-trading-area hypothesis, Frankel (1997) addresses the issue of transport costs both theoretically and empirically. He finds that the efficiency of RIAs is correlated with the ratio of transportation costs between member and nonmember countries.

20 Many game-theoretic models that explore strategic interactions converge on the conclusion that reaching free trade is a prisoner's dilemma. If one assumes that individual countries are not able to negotiate multilateral free trade, these arguments justify RIAs as building blocs of the multilateral trading system (Winters 1996).

21 The institutional structure of RIA is a main source of transaction costs. A free trade area allows member countries to retain sovereignty over their external trade policy and to minimize the costs of trade diversion by reducing the external tariff (Richardson 1993). Aside from eliminating the need for rules of origin, a customs union avoids frictions of competition for collecting tariff revenue (Richardson 1995) and may make increasing protection more difficult. Overall, the latter is generally deemed to be a superior arrangement (Krueger 1995). In any case, the effects are principally determined by the degree of openness of the RIA and by the extent to which it favors the elimination of market segmentation.

22 Cadot, de Melo, and Olarreaga (1996) argue that the introduction of restrictive rules of origin may reduce the incentives for lowering external protection. Krueger (1993) demonstrated that restrictive rules of origin could contribute to reaching agreement on an FTA and act as a political-economy factor underlying its sustainability, but they also could provide negative incentives for multilateral trade liberalization (Krishna and Krueger 1995). It is well documented that the complexity of such rules can be an instrument of protection (Estevadeordal 1999; Estevadeordal and Suominen 2003).

23 The Caribbean Basin is already very integrated in its trade pattern with North America. South America has more import links with Europe, but differences in competitiveness with North America may not be large. Meanwhile, imports from Asia are modest, less than 10 percent of the total in the major subregions.

24 In the case of Mexico there is some evidence of diversion due to NAFTA rules of origin. The overall effect on trade has been mitigated by the fact that Mexico was already highly integrated into the U.S. production system.

PART III

Macroeconomics of the FTAA

6

The Monetary Consequences of a Free Trade Area of the Americas

Barry Eichengreen and Alan M. Taylor

Introduction

Do regional trade agreements (RTAs) encourage monetary and exchange-rate cooperation among the participating countries? There is certainly a heated debate about whether they *should*; unfortunately, theoretical analyses of policy choice do not provide an unambiguous answer to the question.[1] Nor does past experience offer much guidance. On the one hand there is Europe, where the creation of a free trade area and a customs union was followed by a succession of measures to stabilize exchange rates and coordinate monetary policies in what many observers characterize as the successive stages of a single process. On the other hand there is North America, where the completion of a free trade area nearly a decade ago has not created noticeable impetus for exchange-rate stabilization and monetary cooperation. It has not promoted serious discussion of a single North American currency, the recommendations of a few far-seeing academic visionaries to the contrary notwithstanding.[2]

These contrasting examples suggest that RTAs can have different consequences for monetary institutions and exchange-rate arrangements depending on the context and circumstances in which they are established. The question for present purposes is which context and circumstances matter. In this chapter we seek to draw out the answer and to apply it to an understanding of the monetary and exchange-rate consequences of a Free Trade Area of the Americas.

Part of that context, clearly, is political. In Europe, economic and monetary integration was envisaged from the start as part of the process of building an "ever-closer Europe," entailing not just a customs union but also a single market, and not just the closer coordination of national policies, but also the creation of supranational policy-making institutions. Europe's readiness to move from a customs union to a single market in which regulatory policies are harmonized and governance is shared altered the costs and benefits of national monetary autonomy, making monetary independence less desirable and increasing the attractiveness of exchange-rate stabilization and monetary unification.[3] A willingness to create supranational policy-making institutions like the European Commission and the European Central Bank and to convene a constitutional convention charged with creating a regional political structure through which those institutions can be held accountable have further enhanced the efficiency and legitimacy of supranational policy making. Thus, politics shaped the monetary consequences of Europe's single market by opening up institution-building options that are not obviously available in other regions. If commercial integration created a desire for monetary integration, which in turn ratcheted up the pressure for political integration as a way of ensuring the accountability of the institutions responsible for the common monetary policy (deepening and widening regional integration through a dynamic that political scientists refer to as "neofunctionalist spillovers"), then this was something to be encouraged, not resisted.

In North America, in contrast, there is little desire for political integration.[4] The three nations participating in the North American Free Trade Agreement (NAFTA) are jealous of their sovereignty. There is no discussion of a North American equivalent of the European Parliament to whom a regional central bank would be accountable. Hence, there is little willingness to contemplate a single currency for NATFA, since the monetary authority charged with its management would not be regarded as politically legitimate given its lack of accountability.[5] At the same time, there has been surprisingly little pressure (surprising, at least, when seen from a European perspective) to stabilize exchange rates, coordinate monetary policies, and discuss monetary unification. If anything, the three North American currencies, and the Mexican peso in particular, have been floating more freely since the negotiation of NAFTA than before.

Another part of the context surrounding RTAs is economic. In Europe, commercial integration led to a sharp expansion in the volume of intraregional trade.[6] Because Europe's free trade area is of long standing, there has been an opportunity for trade and production to adjust.[7] Moreover, there is the feeling (not overwhelmingly supported by evidence) that exchange rate volatility has a depressing effect on trade. Consequently, the stimulus to the volume of trade from the creation of Europe's customs union and single market augmented the number of those who saw exchange-rate stability as in their economic self-interest and lobbied accordingly (Frieden 1996).[8]

There is also the fear that exchange-rate fluctuations can produce misalignments that create an arbitrary and capricious competitive advantage for the country with the undervalued currency and a political backlash against free trade in the partner consequently experiencing an import surge.[9] Because the expansion of trade associated with the regional arrangement augments the ranks of those who benefit from cross-border transactions, it amplifies calls for exchange-rate stabilization and monetary coordination to contain the potential for a political backlash against that expansion.[10]

In North America, in contrast, the adjustment of trade and production is still underway, since NAFTA is less than a decade old. There are few special agreements, like the Common Agricultural Policy, that might be jeopardized by currency fluctuations.[11] In addition, it can be argued that trade and production are organized vertically in North America, in contrast to Europe where they are organized horizontally. Because French and German firms producing the same products compete head to head, small exchange-rate changes can have big consequences for exports and profitability. In contrast, U.S. and Mexican companies specialize in different products and different stages of the production process. Mexican producers provide inputs and assembly operations for manufactures designed and marketed in the United States. To the extent that producers in the two countries specialize in different stages of the production process, they are less likely to compete head to head, and each country will be less likely to lose business to the other as a result of exchange-rate fluctuations.[12]

If the contrast between Europe and North America offers little clear guidance as to the prospects for monetary cooperation in an FTAA, recent experience in South America confuses the picture further. The continent's most significant trade agreement, MERCOSUR, has been blessed with even less monetary cooperation than NAFTA. After Brazil's real was devalued in 1999, the Argentine economy came under pressure, and then in 2001 the dramatic collapse of Argentine convertibility has seen the real exchange rate see-saw once again. Paraguay and Uruguay, the smaller countries in the compact, have been buffeted repeatedly by these shocks emanating from their larger neighbors. Free trade has been all but lost in an increasingly complex web of exemptions adopted in response to this turbulence. The fallout from this monetary turbulence has led some to ask whether MERCOSUR is now a trade treaty in name only.

Implicit in these observations is a series of questions. Why do the monetary experiences of RTAs span such a wide spectrum? Why is MERCOSUR located at one end? Where should we place other RTAs, not only the EU, NAFTA, and MERCOSUR but also ASEAN's free trade area (AFTA) and the Australia–New Zealand agreement (ANZCER)? Finally, can this analytical mapping help us understand what lies ahead for the FTAA?

In this chapter we seek to understand the implications of RTAs for the monetary and exchange-rate arrangements of the participating countries. In addition to thinking about the composition and behavior of an FTAA, which is still a hypothetical construct, we pay special attention to the constituents of such an arrangement, in particular the NAFTA and MERCOSUR countries. We build on the theory of optimum currency areas (OCAs), augmented to include a role for regionalism, to derive a model of the determinants of exchange rate outcomes.

Following Bayoumi and Eichengreen (1997b), we focus on the determinants of bilateral exchange-rate volatility. In this framework, the volatility of the exchange rate between two currencies is a function of bilateral trade, economic openness, economic size, and the syncronicity of business cycles, as suggested by the theory of optimum currency areas.[13] An RTA can thus affect observed exchange-rate behavior through two channels. One is the trade channel: by stimulating more trade between the partners, an RTA should increase the benefits of stable exchange rates while augmenting the numbers supporting currency stabilization to facilitate yet additional cross-border transactions. The other is the political channel: participation in an RTA may create other political pressures for currency stabilization.[14]

A problem with applying the theory of optimum currency areas to Latin America is that finance may be more important than trade for explaining exchange-rate fluctuations. OCA theory focuses on the implications for the exchange rate of the current account and on how exchange-rate volatility affects trade and debt-service flows and in turn is affected by them. Latin American exchange rates are arguably more strongly affected by the capital account—by financial flows rather than trade flows. This makes it important to extend our framework to take into account the financial characteristics and vulnerabilities of RTA participants and to be certain that our conclusions still hold.

The remainder of the chapter is organized as follows. The following section introduces the empirical framework and reports the results. The subsequent sections draw out the implications of our findings for the monetary consequences of a Free Trade Area of the Americas.

Empirical Framework and Data

The theory of optimum currency areas focuses on factors that make stable exchange rates and harmonized monetary policies more or less desirable across regions and countries.[15] Among the country characteristics at the center of this analysis are: asymmetric business cycle disturbances, the extent of trade among the countries concerned, the transactions costs associated with the maintenance of separate national currencies, the degree of labor mobility, and the automatic stabilizers provided by federal governments. The last two of these characteristics are important for adjustment among regions within a country but are less obviously relevant when we consider adjustment between countries. Consequently, we focus in what follows on the first three items on this list.

We measure asymmetric disturbances as the standard deviation of the change in the log of relative output in the two countries (*sdg*). For two countries whose business cycles are relatively symmetric, the value of this measure will be small. We measure the importance of bilateral trade linkages by the average value of exports to the partner country, scaled by GDP, for the two countries concerned (*ltrade*). We measure the transactions costs associated with the maintenance of a national currency by the size of the countries, the argument being that small countries benefit the most from the unit of account, means of payment, and store of value services provided by a common currency—as well as from stabilizing the price of the domestic currency in terms of foreign exchange. We measure size as the log of the product of real GDP in U.S. dollars of the two countries (*lrgdp*). In addition, we include openness, the arithmetic average of the total trade/GNP ratios of the two countries (*open*), as a second proxy for the transactions costs associated with a fluctuating domestic currency, as suggested by McKinnon (1963).

Finally, we add a vector of RTA variables that equal unity when the two partner countries are both members of the same regional arrangement, and zero otherwise. Previous work has constructed this variable in two ways. Frankel (1997) limits his measure to the five most important RTAs. Rose (2000), on the other hand, considers also a number of smaller RTAs. (The way in which this variable is constructed, as we shall see below, turns out to make a difference.) In some specifications we constrain the effects of all RTAs to be equal (note, however, that the variable in question continues to equal unity only if both partner countries belong to the *same* RTA), while in other specifications we allow different effects of different RTAs. We also allow for trade diversion by including a vector of RTA diversion variables that equal unity when one of the two partner countries is a member of a regional arrangement, and zero otherwise.

A number of issues arise when attempting to estimate this model:

1. There is the question of whether to consider nominal or real exchange-rate variability. It is nominal variability that is arguably influenced by the authorities, but real variability that matters for the economic and political consequences. Fortunately, we obtain very similar results for both dependent variables.[16] In what follows we report results for the nominal exchange rate, since the nominal rate is the focus of policy discussions.
2. There is the fact that the dependent variable (*sdce*, the five-year centered moving average of the standard deviation of the change in the log nominal exchange rate) is truncated at zero and that a substantial number of observations are heaped on that value. We therefore estimated the relationship using both a linear model and a Tobit model. The estimated coefficients were virtually identical, and since the linear model allows us to handle endogeneity and display correct standard errors, we show only these results henceforth.[17]
3. There is the fact that bilateral trade is endogenous and that it is affected by participation in an RTA and potentially, following earlier arguments, by the variability of the exchange rate.[18] We address this by simultaneously estimating a gravity model of bilateral trade. The volume of trade (*ltrade*) is a function of the standard deviation of the exchange rate (*sdce*, the dependent variable in our exchange-rate equation, which is therefore treated as simultaneously determined), the standard arguments of the gravity model (the size of the countries, distance, contiguity, and common language), and the same vector of RTA variables included in our exchange-rate variability regressions. Using the arguments of this trade equation as instruments in our exchange-rate equation addresses the possibility of reverse causality—that trade is affected by exchange-rate volatility.[19]

4. There is the possibility that the consequences for exchange rate policy of an RTA will depend not just on the volume but also the structure of trade. This is suggested by the comparison of Europe and NAFTA in Part II of this book. Kenen (1969) similarly suggests that the attractiveness of exchange rate stabilization and monetary unification will depend on the (dis)similarity of the trade structures of the potential partners.[20] In our analysis of exchange rate variability, we therefore consider the structure as well as the volume of trade using a measure of trade dissimilarity (*dissim*).
5. Finally, there is the fact that this framework addresses trade largely to the exclusion of financial flows. We address this limitation below.

We draw data from the International Monetary Fund's *Direction of Trade* and *International Financial Statistics*, *Penn World Tables* 5.6, Statistics Canada's *World Trade Analyzer*, the World Bank's *World Development Indicators*, and the OECD's *Main Economic Indicators*. The *Direction of Trade* database provides our measures of bilateral trade, size, distance, and country-specific attributes (e.g., common language and border), while the *Penn World Tables* allow us to construct our measures of exchange-rate volatility, business-cycle dispersion, openness, and monetization, and the *World Trade Analyzer* forms the basis of our measures of the similarity or dissimilarity of exports and of multilateral resistance.[21] *World Development Indicators*, *Main Economic Indicators*, and *International Financial Statistics* are used for information on the level and composition of external debts.

Baseline Results

The baseline results in Table 6.1 are consistent with the theory of optimum currency areas. In the gravity model regressions, trade increases with size, common border, and common language, and falls with distance and exchange rate volatility, as expected. In the exchange-rate-volatility regressions, volatility rises with the dispersion of business cycles and economic size and falls with the volume of bilateral trade, again as expected. There is no evidence that more open economies have more stable rates, controlling for size (which is also related to the propensity to trade).[22]

The negative coefficient on the volume of bilateral trade in the exchange-rate equation is worth further attention, since it would be convenient to be able to argue that an RTA that stimulates bilateral trade naturally produces more stable bilateral rates. The coefficient in question is robust and well determined. (Recall that we have controlled for

Table 6.1 Basic Model of Trade and Exchange Rate Volatility

	Full Sample (1)	Full Sample (2)	Full Sample (3)	OECD Pairs (4)	OECD Pairs (5)	OECD Pairs (6)	FTAA Pairs (7)	FTAA Pairs (8)	FTAA Pairs (9)
(a) IV Gravity Model of ltrade									
sdce	–0.164 (1.0)	–0.232 (1.4)	–0.148 (0.9)	–7.205 (7.1)	–7.235 (7.2)	–5.820 (5.6)	0.576 (1.7)	0.223 (0.7)	0.161 (0.5)
lrgdp	1.190 (42.2)	1.180 (41.7)	1.225 (43.4)	1.262 (25.9)	1.262 (25.9)	1.217 (26.6)	1.315 (17.7)	1.124 (14.5)	1.127 (14.6)
ldist	–1.218 (155.0)	–1.279 (159.8)	–1.283 (161.1)	–0.940 (54.0)	–0.940 (53.4)	–0.931 (48.5)	–1.549 (52.3)	–1.796 (59.7)	–1.798 (60.0)
border	0.431 (13.8)	0.425 (13.7)	0.422 (13.8)	0.000 (0.0)	–0.005 (0.2)	0.032 (1.2)	0.137 (2.5)	0.085 (1.5)	0.089 (1.6)
comlang	0.714 (47.5)	0.715 (47.4)	0.706 (47.0)	0.326 (12.7)	0.324 (12.6)	0.314 (12.5)	0.854 (24.5)	1.269 (33.8)	1.272 (33.9)
regional	0.811 (16.5)	—	—	0.095 (2.5)	—	—	1.578 (23.4)	—	—
regional_div	–0.084 (7.0)	—	—	0.014 (0.8)	—	—	–0.514 (14.1)	—	—
rta	—	–0.419 (9.9)	—	—	0.066 (1.9)	—	—	0.497 (2.1)	—
rta_div	—	0.146 (12.3)	—	—	–0.021 (1.3)	—	—	–0.259 (4.2)	—
eu	—	—	–0.061 (1.2)	—	—	0.075 (1.7)	—	—	—
nafta	—	—	0.761 (3.8)	—	—	0.220 (3.1)	—	—	–1.494 (4.5)
merco	—	—	1.634 (13.9)	—	—	—	—	—	1.358 (6.9)
asean	—	—	0.214 (2.2)	—	—	—	—	—	—
anzcer	—	—	1.398 (11.6)	—	—	–0.247 (2.5)	—	—	—
eu_div	—	—	0.686 (35.1)	—	—	0.032 (1.5)	—	—	—
nafta_div	—	—	0.239 (7.8)	—	—	–0.423 (11.0)	—	—	–0.312 (4.7)
merco_div	—	—	0.305 (6.8)	—	—	—	—	—	–0.039 (0.4)
asean_div	—	—	–0.020 (0.5)	—	—	—	—	—	—
anzcer_div	—	—	–0.109 (2.5)	—	—	–0.402 (7.9)	—	—	—

Continued on next page

Table 6.1 Basic Model of Trade and Exchange Rate Volatility, continued

	Full Sample (1)	Full Sample (2)	Full Sample (3)	OECD Pairs (4)	OECD Pairs (5)	OECD Pairs (6)	FTAA Pairs (7)	FTAA Pairs (8)	FTAA Pairs (9)
(b) IV Model of sdce									
ltrade	–0.035 (82.1)	–0.034 (80.0)	–0.033 (79.8)	–0.014 (27.3)	–0.014 (27.2)	–0.014 (28.0)	–0.059 (25.4)	–0.042 (21.9)	–0.042 (21.8)
lrgdp	0.043 (89.4)	0.041 (88.1)	0.041 (88.1)	0.021 (43.5)	0.021 (43.2)	0.022 (44.2)	0.068 (26.5)	0.048 (22.6)	0.049 (22.8)
sdg	1.138 (65.5)	1.132 (65.3)	1.128 (65.1)	0.297 (8.8)	0.301 (8.9)	0.287 (8.5)	2.455 (25.9)	2.447 (26.0)	2.431 (25.8)
open	0.000 (8.8)	0.000 (8.9)	0.000 (9.0)	0.001 (29.8)	0.001 (29.5)	0.001 (30.5)	–0.001 (6.0)	–0.001 (3.3)	0.000 (2.9)
regional	0.087 (14.5)	—	—	–0.014 (9.1)	—	—	0.244 (14.9)	—	—
rta	—	0.001 (0.1)	—	—	–0.013 (8.1)	—	—	0.368 (7.6)	—
eu	—	—	–0.034 (4.0)	—	—	–0.015 (9.4)	—	—	—
nafta	—	—	–0.003 (0.0)	—	—	–0.033 (2.3)	—	—	–0.085 (0.9)
merco	—	—	0.669 (15.8)	—	—	—	—	—	0.541 (9.5)
asean	—	—	0.021 (1.4)	—	—	—	—	—	—
anzcer	—	—	0.035 (0.7)	—	—	0.054 (7.2)	—	—	—
N	149067	149067	149067	8190	8190	8190	11652	11652	11652

Notes: In the IV gravity model of ltrade the instruments for sdce are sdg and open. Country and time dummies in all specifications. In the IV model of sdce, ltrade is instrumented using ldist, border, comlang, time and country dummies. Nicaragua omitted due to hyperinflation.

the possibility of reverse causality running from exchange-rate volatility to trade.) One can think of several economic mechanisms through which trade would produce more stable exchange rates; for example, it could encourage foreign-exchange-market transactions, resulting in more liquid and stable currency markets.[23] Frankel and Rose (1998), in a related analysis, show that more bilateral trade leads to more synchronized business cycles in the two partner countries. The question, for present purposes, is whether the effect in question is large or small. We return to this below.

Of particular interest are the coefficients on the RTAs. In the gravity model, the results in columns 1 and 2 are consistent with those of previous investigators. Rose's comprehensive RTA measure generates a significant positive coefficient, suggesting that RTAs are trade creating. In contrast, the more selective Frankel measure, which is limited to the five principal RTAs, generates a negative coefficient; this is the same result as in Frankel (1997).

Further disaggregation may help to explain this contrast. When we disaggregate the five large RTAs (Table 6.1, column 3), we find that the negative effect (evidence that participation in an RTA reduces trade) is driven by the EU.[24] However, this negative coefficient is eliminated (it becomes statistically indistinguishable from zero) when we add a vector of trade-diversion variables for cases in which one member of a country pair but not the other belongs to a particular RTA. We include this vector of trade-diversion variables in all of the specifications that follow. The results also appear to vary across developed and developing country subsamples. In the OECD regressions (columns 4 through 6), RTAs appear to weakly encourage trade, but the impact in the FTAA subsample (columns 7 through 9) is larger. FTAA trade appears to be more sensitive to distance and borders than OECD trade, as one might expect if transport infrastructure is weaker in the developing world. FTAA trade, in contrast, seems less sensitive to exchange-rate volatility.

Our main interest is in the exchange-rate regression, with trade now treated as endogenous. Here we find sharply different effects of different regional arrangements. The RTA coefficient, which should now be interpreted as capturing nontrade ("political") effects since we are controlling for trade separately, is uniformly positive, and significantly so when we use the comprehensive Rose measure. In apparent contradiction of pure OCA logic, the formation of RTAs has evidently been associated with *increased* exchange-rate volatility. This impact has not been uniform, however. The coefficient is significantly negative for the EU, and it is also significantly negative for NAFTA when we limit the sample to OECD countries. In contrast, we obtain a large and positive coefficient for MERCOSUR, in both the full sample and the FTAA sample.[25] Evidently, the MERCOSUR free trade area has created political pressures that have done little to promote and, if anything, have obstructed monetary cooperation. This is no surprise in light of MERCOSUR's checkered history. But these political effects may not be the entire story, since MERCOSUR also created trade and hence presumably generated economic pressure for monetary cooperation. Which influence mattered more?

For some regions like the EU, both the expansion of intra-RTA trade and RTA-related political pressure could make for more stable exchange rates, while for other regions like MERCOSUR the two factors work in opposite directions. Consider the full sample results. The indirect effect is the impact of MERCOSUR on the volume of trade (1.67 according to column 3) times the impact of trade on exchange-rate variability (–0.05). While this effect is not inconsequential, the product of the two terms is small (–0.09). The direct effect on exchange rate variability (the "political" effect, which captures all other reasons why exchange rate variability may be larger or smaller in a particular region or FTAA) is 0.71 for the MERCOSUR countries. The direct effect is thus seven times the size of the indirect effect: the trade channel is swamped by the "political" channel.[26]

It would be provocative to be able to argue that the additional trade generated by participation in an RTA works to stabilize exchange rates. We find some evidence to this effect, since more bilateral trade is consistently associated with less bilateral exchange-rate volatility, ceteris paribus. But this channel is swamped by other factors. For MERCOSUR, those other factors work in the direction of greater volatility.

Extensions

In Table 6.2 we consider extensions of the basic model, restricting our attention to the full sample of data due to space constraints. We focus on the exchange-rate volatility equation, maintaining the same first-stage gravity equation estimated in Table 6.1, Regression 3. The results reinforce our conclusion that NAFTA and especially MERCOSUR have been associated with pressure for less exchange-rate stabilization than was seen in the EU project.

Table 6.2 Extended Model of Exchange Rate Volatility

IV Model of sdce	(1)	(2)	(3)	(4)
ltrade	–0.024 (43.8)	–0.004 (4.8)	–0.012 (17.6)	–0.012 (18.0)
lrgdp	0.037 (58.2)	0.026 (26.7)	0.024 (29.1)	0.025 (29.9)
sdg	1.317 (63.1)	1.351 (36.9)	1.355 (48.7)	1.362 (48.9)
open	–0.0001 (3.9)	–0.0028 (35.7)	–0.0025 (41.6)	–0.0025 (41.2)
dissim	0.122 (38.7)	0.058 (11.4)	0.036 (8.9)	0.040 (9.7)
av_totaldebt/gnp	—	0.002 (57.4)	0.002 (65.3)	0.002 (65.5)
av_shorttermdebt /totaldebt	—	0.001 (3.5)	—	—
gdp_size	—	—	—	–0.016 (8.4)
eu	–0.049 (5.4)	—d	–0.092 (6.8)	–0.095 (7.0)
nafta	–0.040 (0.6)	—d	–0.102 (1.4)	–0.105 (1.4)
merco	0.645 (14.4)	0.533 (10.5)	0.593 (12.4)	0.596 (12.5)
asean	–0.014 (0.9)	–0.094 (4.0)	–0.044 (2.0)	–0.054 (2.5)
anzcer	–0.001 (0.0)	—d	–0.090 (0.7)	–0.087 (0.6)
N	103181	39082	63169	63169

Notes: "d" denotes dropped due to missing data. ltrade is instrumented using ldist, border, comlang, time and country dummies. The full sample is used. Nicaragua omitted due to hyperinflation.

In Regression 1 we add a variable that measures the similarity in the composition of exports (*dissim*), which has some additional effect on reducing the volatility of exchange rates over and above its association with the volume of trade.[27] Looking at the RTA dummies, we see that this extension now demonstrates the EU discouraging trade but encouraging exchange-rate coordination (where the second effect was insignificantly different from zero for the full sample in Table 6.1), providing stronger support than before for the hypothesis that the political channel played an important role in the European Monetary Union.[28]

In contrast, the effects of NAFTA are unchanged. NAFTA still appears to generate modest trade but statistically insignificant exchange-rate coordination effects, as if the tendency for more extensive trade links to create economic pressure for exchange rate stabilization dominates political influences, operating in either direction. MERCOSUR appears to operate very differently from the EU, producing significantly more trade but also significantly more exchange-rate volatility.

In Regressions 2 through 4 we add financial variables to our exchange-rate volatility equation in order to address the possibility that finance as well as trade shapes policies toward the exchange rate. One could imagine, for example, that countries with large amounts of short-term debt find it more difficult to hold the exchange rate stable since they are less able to raise interest rates to prevent the exchange rate from weakening. At the same time, countries with large amounts of debt may have a stronger desire to stabilize the exchange rate in order to avoid destabilizing balance-sheet effects, especially when much of the debt in question is denominated in foreign currency (the "fear of floating" syndrome).[29]

We therefore added to the exchange-rate equation the external debt/GNP ratio and the short-term/total external debt ratio, as tabulated by the World Bank.[30] In Regression 2, for the sample of countries and years for which both variables are available (we do not have data on short-term debt for OECD countries), it appears that more heavily indebted countries and countries with larger shares of short-term obligations in total external debt have more volatile exchange rates.[31] We are able to expand the sample to include the OECD countries by dropping short-term debt, as in Regression 3.[32] Doing so changed none of the other results. Alternatively, we were able to gather foreign debt as a share of total debt from IMF sources. The results suggest that countries with larger shares of foreign debt have more volatile exchange rates, other things remaining equal.[33] But our key finding—that while more bilateral trade encourages exchange-rate stabilization, the political effects of RTA participation do not, at least in the Western Hemisphere—is unaffected by these extensions. True, the MERCOSUR dummy is somewhat smaller in these regressions, around 0.5 compared 0.7 in Table 6.1, suggesting that considerations relating to trade structure, multilateral resistance, and debt can explain some part of the MERCOSUR countries' unusually high levels of exchange-rate variability. But most of that additional variability remains unexplained.

In Regression 4, we entertain the possibility that Europe is different because it is made up of a number of relatively large, similarly sized economies well positioned to negotiate symmetrical arrangements to stabilize their exchange rates. It has been hypothesized that a number of countries of roughly comparable size will have substantial effects on one another, and hence that they will tend to gain significantly from coordinating.[34] The ancillary hypothesis, informed by European experience, is that symmetrical forms of coordination to which both countries contribute are more likely to produce stable rates than asymmetric arrangements in which the small country is forced to unilaterally accept the monetary policy dictates of its larger neighbor. We therefore added to our specification an asymmetry-of-size variable (*gdpsize*), defined as the absolute value of the difference in GDP between the two countries, normalized by the average of their two GDPs.

Contrary to the hypothesis, this variable enters with a negative coefficient: two countries are more likely to have a relatively stable bilateral rate when one is much larger than the other. It could be objected that the symmetry-leads-to-stability argument holds only for large countries and not small ones; we therefore constructed an alternative measure by multiplying the previous variable by the average size of the two countries.[35] Again, the resulting variable entered negatively, contrary to the null; countries of similar size appear less likely to stabilize their bilateral rates, ceteris paribus. But the key point is that none of our other results was substantively affected by this extension.

What Exchange Rate Regime for the Western Hemisphere?

None of the preceding disputes that exchange-rate volatility can be a problem for a regional arrangement—that it may negatively affect trade and, by conferring an arbitrary and capricious competitive disadvantage on some national producers, that it may provoke a protectionist backlash against liberalization. It would be convenient to be able to argue, building on the observation that more open economies prefer more stable currencies, that additional trade automatically produces additional exchange-rate stability, but our results suggest that the magnitude of this effect is small. It would be convenient were greater trade within the region to create political pressure for exchange-rate stabilization, but our results suggest that there can be a gap between aspiration and realization. To be sure, in Europe the aspiration to limit exchange-rate flexibility has been realized by a series of monetary arrangements, culminating in EMU, which significantly reduced exchange-rate volatility over and above what might have been predicted on the basis of the volume of trade. In NAFTA, in contrast, there is little evidence of an analogous effect. Among the MERCOSUR countries, any such aspiration has been frustrated: exchange rates have been consistently more volatile, not less, than the volume of intraregional trade and other factors would lead one to expect.

What can the FTAA countries do about this? There is a literature on institutions and practices for macroeconomic coordination suggesting initiatives for better harmonizing macroeconomic policies and outcomes with the goal of stabilizing bilateral rates. Countries can agree to regular meetings and procedures for exchanging information on economic conditions and objectives; this will minimize the danger that they will pursue inconsistent policies because they hold inconsistent assumptions.[36] They can engage in policy adjustments that may be undesirable in isolation but are mutually advantageous when undertaken simultaneously. They can appeal to international pressure for policy reforms that meet political resistance at home. And they can extend financial support to partner currencies that come under speculative pressure.

We are skeptical that these approaches to policy coordination would be productive in the FTAA context. Different information sets hardly seem to be the main reason that policy inputs and macroeconomic outputs (such as the movement of exchange rates) differ so sharply across the countries of the Southern Cone and the Western Hemisphere. There already exist mechanisms for information sharing and assessment at the multilateral and regional levels, including IMF surveillance, IDB projections, and ELCA forecasts.

Indeed, the members of MERCOSUR already possess a structure for policy coordination under the provisions of the Treaty of Ouro Preto, ratified in 1994. An agreement among ministers and central bank governors reached in 2000 established targets and procedures for the convergence of debts, deficits, and levels of public debt.[37] Governments created the High Level Macroeconomic Monitoring Group made up of senior officials from ministries of finance and central banks (analogous to the EU's Economic and Financial Committee) to monitor macroeconomic developments in member countries and advance proposals for policy coordination. The Andean countries have developed similar arrangements. But little has come of all this. The problem is not inadequate institutionalization, in other words; it is the lack of a political and economic context in which those institutions can operate effectively or, simply put, lack of will. As Buti and Giudice (2002: 30) put it, "given the lack of discernible penalties and rewards, it is unclear how the supranational dimension could enhance the incentives to abide by the agreed rules."

Nor do we think that the problem in MERCOSUR has been, or that in an FTAA it would be, the inability of the participating countries to engage in mutually advantageous policy trades. The reason that Argentina was unwilling to follow a tighter fiscal policy in 2001 was not Brazil's unwillingness to follow a looser monetary policy, or vice versa.[38] In the context of an FTAA, meaningful policy trades would presumably involve adjustments in U.S. monetary policy in return for adjustments in fiscal policy involving much of Latin America. But, while the U.S. Federal Reserve Board may at times take international conditions into account when making interest rate decisions, this is hardly a dominant consideration. Nor is it easy to imagine circumstances in which it would be heavily influenced by events in Latin America only.

While mechanisms for exerting peer pressure are better developed in Europe than in the Western Hemisphere, even there their efficacy has been limited. Europe has negotiated an international treaty (the Maastricht Treaty, or Treaty of European Union) that makes explicit provision for mutual surveillance. It benefits from the existence of an international institution, the European Commission, which can undertake central monitoring and act as fair broker. Yet, in the summer of 2002, by appealing to another EU institution (the Council of Ministers, made up of national heads of state), France and Germany were able to rebuff the commission's attempts to send letters to their governments warning of excessive budget deficits, as provided for under the terms of the Stability and Growth Pact. The point is not that peer pressure is impossible, but rather that it is only one, and often a minor, factor affecting domestic policy formulation.[39] Even in Europe, where mechanisms for applying it are highly developed and heavily institutionalized, it is not always effective. Governments, especially those of consequential countries with political leverage, can resist its application. To put the point another way, if the pressure applied by the U.S. government, the IMF, and the markets for Argentina to get its fiscal house in order did not suffice in 1998–2001, it is hard to imagine that a regional surveillance exercise, conducted under the aegis of MERCOSUR or an FTAA, would be significantly more effectual.[40]

Finally, there is the argument for financial supports in the context of an RTA. These were famously provided in Europe through the Short-Term and Very-Short-Term Financing Facilities of the European Monetary System. Financial supports were provided by the United States to Mexico in the context of NAFTA—first a contingency facility in November 1993 to deal with trouble if the NAFTA vote went wrong, then a second contingency arrangement put in place in July and August 1994 in anticipation of postelection troubles in Mexico, and finally bilateral support in 1995 through the U.S. Treasury's Exchange Stabilization Fund. The ASEAN countries similarly negotiated an ASEAN Swap Arrangement (ASA) to supplement their regional trade initiative; together with China, Japan, and South Korea they agreed in 2000 to the Chiang Mai Initiative (CMI), an expanded network of swap and repurchase agreements.

But there are reasons to doubt that countries with strong currencies and ample reserves will really be prepared to offer extensive support to their weak-currency counterparts under the terms of such arrangements. They will do so only if they are confident that their resources will not be squandered, only if they are assured that the obligation to intervene is accompanied by surveillance capable of anticipating and heading off crises, and only if it is accompanied by conditionality that leads to strong adjustment in the crisis country that will reassure the markets and maximize the likelihood of prompt repayment of any swaps. Otherwise, strong-currency countries will be unlikely to commit significant resources to supporting weak regional currencies, statutory commitments to do so or not. Even in Europe, where the commitment to collective currency pegs was exceptionally strong, mutual surveillance and conditionality were less than effective, resulting in limits on the extent of actual support. Germany obtained an opt-out from the provision of the EMS Articles of Agreement obliging it to intervene without limit in support of its partners, reflecting fears of the costs of unlimited interventions and what unlimited support might imply for its creditworthiness. Participants in the ASEAN Swap Arrangement could similarly opt out of that arrangement.[41] Under the Chiang Mai Initiative activation of the swap is similarly at the discretion of the lender. It is not an unconditional commitment.

The essence of the matter is that governments are no more inclined than commercial banks to lend freely and unconditionally. Market participants, conscious of this reluctance to lend freely, are unlikely to be deterred by promises of official support from attacking weak currencies. An international lender of last resort who lends freely to support weak currencies remains a pipe dream in a world of sovereign states; it is a thin reed on which to hang hopes of exchange-rate stabilization, in the Western Hemisphere or elsewhere. And if strong conditions have to be attached to international loans, both the lenders and borrowers are likely to prefer that these be formulated by a third party such as the IMF rather than by, for example, the U.S. government, which would then become the focus of populist vitriol. If there is going to be outside support for exchange rates, in other words, it is more likely to come from the multilaterals than bilaterally in the context of an RTA.[42]

The bottom line is that neither MERCOSUR nor an FTAA is likely to provide a platform for a collective currency stabilization agreement. Financial supports will remain limited. And, if there is one lesson of recent experience, it is that currency bands and pegs are fragile and crisis prone in an environment of open capital markets, democratic politics, and limited multilateral support—which is precisely the environment in which exchange rate policy will be formulated in the Western Hemisphere.

Small countries like Ecuador and El Salvador can eliminate the exchange rate problem by eliminating the exchange rate—by dollarizing unilaterally. Our empirical results confirm that small countries that trade disproportionately with one partner, such as the United States, would find eliminating all exchange-rate variability by adopting the currency of that larger partner relatively attractive. But there is little indication that larger countries such as Mexico, Brazil, or even Argentina find this option attractive on economic and political grounds. To reconcile dollarization in these countries with our empirical results, one would have to appeal to an out-of-sample nonlinearity missed by our empirical model. Some would say that this is not inconceivable: countries that have shown scant regard for keeping their exchange rates stable might suddenly find a very hard regime attractive as a way of tying their hands where all other approaches to monetary management have failed.

We should say a few words about the idea of a monetary union for MERCOSUR (or other RTAs) or a single currency for the Western Hemisphere. Those words can be quite few: there is no indication that the United States would be prepared to give Canada, Mexico, and other countries in the hemisphere seats on the Federal Reserve Board, much less abolish the board in favor of a hemispheric central bank. However appealing the idea of a monetary union may be to economic theorists, we regard it as social science fiction.[43] It is easier to imagine a single currency for MERCOSUR, but only slightly. As noted in our introduction, European monetary integration is part of a larger process of political integration. Countries like Germany were prepared to countenance the additional uncertainty about future monetary policy associated with the transition from the Bundesbank to the ECB because of the value they attached to the larger European project. In addition, there exist in Europe transnational institutions of collective governance (such as the European Parliament) to hold the ECB accountable for its actions and to lend political legitimacy to the single monetary policy. Suffice it to say that none of these conditions prevails in the Western Hemisphere, nor will they any time soon.

Economic Gaps Versus Political Gaps

One way of illustrating the importance of the economic versus political origins of monetary coordination is to examine the predictions of our model. The exchange-rate-volatility equation can be used to construct fitted values to see where each country pair in the sample should sit in terms of predicted volatility, our measure of regime choice. (We show here the forecast of the *sdce* equation, which may take negative values; a value below zero should be read as implying a desire to fix.)

The fitted values from our model compound economic and political effects. The former are included via the measures of bilateral trade, size, and so on; the latter are measured as the RTA-specific desire for exchange-rate stabilization (or volatility) unexplained by economic effects. Figure 6.1 offers a summary of the model's predictions based on the full sample of data from Regression 4 in Table 6.2. Box plots summarize the distribution of fitted values for the exchange-rate-volatility measure. We divide the sample into the five major RTA zones and other pairs. The Western Hemisphere stands out: compared to the rest of the world, and controlling for trade and other economic factors, the impact of RTAs is definitely not to reduce exchange-rate volatility (as in the case of NAFTA) and may even increase it (as in the case of MERCOSUR). Monetary noncooperation is the rule in the FTAA zone. In contrast, ASEAN and ANZCER seem to have almost as much preference for fixing as the EU, gauged from of the distribution of fitted values.[44]

Counterfactual exercises can show exactly how important political factors are in the FTAA zone as an obstacle to monetary coordination. Imagine that we could impose the EU's level of "political willingness" to cooperate on the MERCOSUR countries. We compute this by adding the difference between the EU and MERCOSUR terms to the fitted values. The new implied distribution of exchange-rate volatilities is then shown in the box plots labeled "MERCOSUR (CF-EU)."[45] The implications are clear: the failure to engage in monetary cooperation in MERCOSUR is not obviously a function of economic variables. The countries do not have unusual size, trade, composition, or other economic characteristics that militate against monetary cooperation; in this respect they are reasonably similar to the EU. Rather, the sources of the cooperation deficit lie elsewhere.

Figure 6.1 Predicted Exchange Rate Volatility and MERCOSUR-with-EU-"Politics" Counterfactual

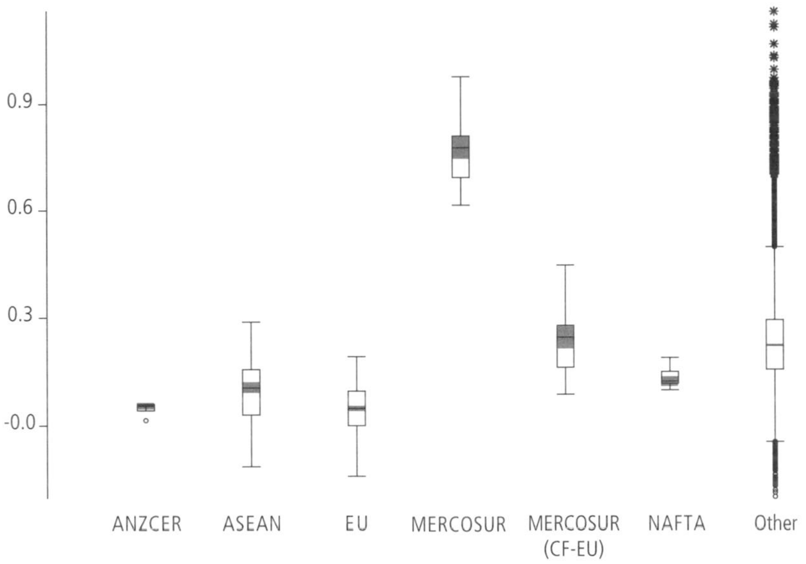

Note: Plot of *sdce* fitted values by RTA. MERCOSUR (CF-EU) counterfactual based on Table 2, column 4.

This is not to say that monetary cooperation, even monetary union, is impossible except in Europe. Europe was special in that political will supplemented compelling economic reasons for coordination. Other regions may be following a similar path, although none of them is as far along that path as Europe is today. It may be possible to envisage a future in which the FTAA goes down that path as well, although doing so takes some imagination. For the present, in any case, there is little sign of the necessary will.

A Modest Proposal

Having ruled out alternatives for cooperation ad seriatim, we are led to conclude that floating exchange rates in the Western Hemisphere are here to stay in the medium term. This conclusion may not be comfortably reconciled with the desire for more extensive trade, but it is the reality.

Is the implication a council of despair—that exchange-rate instability will continue to slow efforts to promote regional trade liberalization?

Not necessarily. An exchange rate that adjusts smoothly to differences in national economic conditions can be part of the solution rather than part of the problem. In particular, gradual adjustments that eliminate disequilibria smoothly are preferable to discrete, disruptive changes of formerly pegged rates precipitated by crises. We now argue that the more widespread adoption of inflation targeting in the region will go some way toward ensuring such adjustment and thereby limiting exchange-rate tensions.[46]

The argument, in a nutshell, is that a credible policy of inflation targeting provides a nominal anchor for expectations and that, with an anchor for expectations, exchange rates will settle down. Market participants will no longer have reason to believe that inflation today is a leading indicator of inflation tomorrow because the authorities have explicitly committed to low inflation, because they will pay a political price if they miss that target, and because they will have to provide an explanation for any passing failure.[47] Speculation in the foreign exchange market will become stabilizing rather than destabilizing.

The association between exchange-rate stability and inflation targeting has not been analyzed much previously. The one study of which we are aware, by Kuttner and Posen (2001), uses data for forty-one developing and emerging-market economies, relating measures of exchange-rate volatility to whether or not a country targets inflation (and to measures of central bank autonomy and the declared exchange-rate regime). While inflation targeters display lower levels of exchange-rate volatility (as measured, alternatively, by the standard deviation of the exchange rate, its kurtosis, and various measures of its range), the differences are not statistically significant.

To marshal additional evidence, we added to our exchange-rate-volatility regressions dummy variables for whether countries target inflation, as shown in Table 6.3. We used the comprehensive tabulation of inflation targeting around the world from Mishkin and Schmidt-Hebbel (2001) to construct two variables: one that equals unity when one of two partner countries targets inflation, and another that equals unity when both countries have adopted this monetary regime. Alternatively, we used the J. P. Morgan classification. Since inflation targeting is one possible alternative to attempting to peg the exchange rate (though it is not the only one—another alternative is to resist the temptation to articulate an explicit monetary policy operating strategy), we controlled for the choice of exchange-rate regime when testing for the effects of this inflation-targeting variable.

Table 6.3 Extended Model of Exchange Rate Volatility with Inflation Targeting

IV Model of sdce Inflation Targeting Measure	(1) Mishkin and Schmidt–Hebbel	(2) J. P. Morgan
ltrade	0.001 (0.5)	0.002 (0.7)
lrgdp	0.018 (4.8)	0.018 (4.9)
sdg	2.310 (15.8)	2.307 (15.8)
open	–0.0028 (11.7)	–0.0028 (11.5)
dissim	0.1175 (5.6)	0.1155 (5.5)
inflation targeting in one country	–0.075 (3.2)	–0.048 (1.8)
inflation targeting in both countries	–0.036 (2.3)	–0.048 (2.9)
average reinhart–rogoff peg measure	0.035 (7.1)	0.034 (7.0)
eu (dropped) (dropped)		
nafta	–0.117 (1.1)	–0.119 (1.1)
merco	0.468 (7.6)	0.464 (7.6)
asean	–0.090 (1.5)	–0.096 (1.6)
anzcer	–0.123 (0.8)	–0.117 (0.8)
N	4709	4709

Notes: "d" denotes dropped due to collinearity. ltrade is instrumented using ldist, border, comlang, time and country dummies. Inflation targeting variables are instrumented via probit using average M2/GDP, average total debt/GNP, and average law and order measures. The full sample is used. Nicaragua omitted due to hyperinflation.

Of course, the decision to target inflation may be endogenous. In particular, the literature on inflation targeting in open economies points out that countries with more volatile exchange rates may find it more difficult to inflation target because, inter alia, the domestic price level will be more difficult to forecast and exchange-rate fluctuations will have disruptive output effects.[48] In addition, countries with deeper financial markets, less short-term debt, and a history of policy transparency are more likely to inflation target (transparency being the sine qua non of inflation targeting). Thus, there is the danger that countries with these characteristics may both prefer to inflation target and enjoy more stable exchange rates, but that the causal connection between inflation targeting and exchange rate stability is weak. We therefore instrumented our dummy variables for inflation targeting using a first-stage probit regression in which the independent variables were the M2/GNP ratio as (a measure of financial depth), the short-term debt/GNP ratio, and *Transparency International's* measure of transparency and corruption. The results are suggestive: we find that countries that target inflation have significantly less volatile exchange rates, even after controlling for a variety of other economic and financial determinants of realized volatility and even after adjusting for the endogeneity of the regime.[49]

One interpretation of these results is that inflation targeting is a better way of delivering relatively low levels of exchange rate instability, ex post, than pegging the nominal rate. Pegs, no matter how hard, have historically had a tendency to collapse, unleashing pent-up volatility. Our results thus suggest that a credible agreement by FTAA partners to move to inflation targeting (and perhaps to agree on a common inflation target) may go some way toward limiting the tension between floating exchange rates and the pursuit of regional trade liberalization.

This last sentence includes two important qualifications. The first piece of critical wording is "some way." Although the coefficient on the MERCOSUR dummy is reduced in size with the addition of the inflation-targeting variables (from 0.7 or 0.5 in earlier results to 0.4), it does not go to zero. Lack of inflation-targeting capability alone, in other words, does not explain the exceptional exchange-rate volatility of the MERCOSUR countries. Conceivably, this volatility could be diminished via the institutional and other changes necessitated by inflation targeting, but such counterfactuals lie outside the model presented here.[50]

The second bit of critical wording is "credible." While not a few developed countries have successfully pursued inflation-targeting policies for some years, can this strategy be credibly applied to the FTAA as a whole? Some readers will point to seemingly hopeless cases, such as Argentina in 2002, and question whether inflation targeting is feasible in Latin America.[51]

The older literature on inflation targeting (e.g., Eichengreen et al. 1999) points to central bank independence and the absence of chronic budget deficits as key prerequisites for credible inflation targeting. If the central bank is not independent, it will not be able to credibly subordinate other goals to the pursuit of low inflation. And if chronic budget deficits are a problem, the country will eventually become subject to unpleasant monetary arithmetic. Public-sector deficits will have to be monetized by the central bank to avert the inevitable funding crisis, whether the central bank likes it—and is independent—or not. Thus, Latin American countries in which these prerequisites are absent are unlikely to be able to inflation target. Monetary autonomy will therefore translate into relatively high levels of exchange-rate instability that will be difficult to reconcile with the desire for regional trade liberalization.

The potential for a funding crisis perhaps warrants the most attention. In many recent crises, the problem has been not simply the size of deficits but the structure of the debt. In Brazil, in particular, high levels of short-term debt meant that if investors refused to roll over the government's maturing obligations except at very high interest rates, the debt burden might quickly become unsustainable, even in the face of very impressive primary budget surpluses. And, if the central bank refused to monetize the debt, the government might be forced into default, which would wreak havoc with bank balance sheets and force the central bank to engage in lender-of-last-resort intervention, with inflationary consequences. Two cases in point are the recent crisis in Argentina and the crises a century ago in both Argentina and Brazil.

We can think of this as the Fiscal Dominance Mark II critique of inflation targeting. Credible inflation targeting requires not just the absence of chronic deficits (the absence of Fiscal Dominance Mark I) but also success at lengthening the maturity structure of the domestic debt and de-linking it from exchange rates and short-term interest rates, so that shocks to confidence cannot cause a debt run-off (the absence of "Fiscal Dominance Mark II"). Otherwise, the reduction in exchange-rate volatility delivered by the authorities' embrace of inflation targeting may be no more than a temporary blessing.

Goldstein (2002) has described the menu of policies that countries should follow in order to be free of Fiscal Dominance Mark II. They should manage the maturity and currency composition of the public debt, resisting the temptation to limit short-run funding costs by incurring short-term, foreign-currency denominated debt that will come back to bite them in the long run. They need to regulate the banking system to limit currency mismatches on commercial bank balance sheets. They may need to use tax and regulatory policies to prevent the banks from funding themselves in dollars and simply passing that exposure on to the corporate sector, which will be thrust into bankruptcy when the exchange rate depreciates, in turn bringing the banks tumbling down. With careful pursuit of such policies, it is argued, inflation targeting will become widely feasible in Latin America.

The limitation of this prescription is that it ignores the role of history in shaping monetary conditions. In this respect Argentina and

Uruguay, where there were no capital controls and dollar-denominated bank accounts are prevalent, may be very different from Brazil and Chile, where more restrictive policies toward the current account have bequeathed a less difficult environment for inflation targeting. Pesification can conveniently remove the legacy of earlier policies, but only by dealing a sharp blow to confidence, the same variable that inflation targeting is designed to enhance.

The question is whether high levels of liability dollarization, inherited from the past, merely complicate the conduct of inflation targeting, requiring the central bank to perhaps attach a higher weight to the exchange rate (whose depreciation not only signals future inflation, as in any other open economy, but also threatens destabilizing balance-sheet effects, which will depress output at the same time inflation accelerates). Or does the liability-dollarization problem in fact render open-economy inflation targeting infeasible? Does it amplify the destabilizing effects of exchange-rate fluctuations so dramatically that the authorities cannot permit the exchange rate to move at all, in which case they might as well dollarize de jure as well as de facto? Or is this extreme case as rare as it is extreme: are there still some advantages of exchange-rate flexibility and, by implication, of inflation targeting in all but the most highly dollarized economies? The advocates of this last position point to Peru, a highly dollarized economy that nonetheless has been able to reap benefits from floating-cum-inflation targeting and suggest hopefully that even other highly dollarized Latin American countries will be able to follow its example (see Berg, Borensztein, and Mauro 2002).

Many extensions of our analysis are clearly possible; the few we have considered leave our central results unchanged. To address the objection that our results fail to control adequately for the dollarization problem just noted, we added the M2/GDP ratio to the regressions of Table 6.3.[52] The results were not significantly altered; although the M2 ratio had a negative and significant coefficient (indicating that high liability dollarization and low financial depth are associated with greater exchange-rate volatility, as expected), the coefficients on the RTAs barely budged, and the MERCOSUR politics dummy remained highly significant.[53]

Another potential objection is that MERCOSUR is still a young RTA compared to, inter alia, the EU. Perhaps RTAs deliver more exchange-rate stability after some years than at inception. To test this we included a dummy variable that equaled unity during the first five years of an RTA agreement. Immature RTAs did have significantly higher exchange-rate volatility in our sample (the coefficient on the new dummy variable was 0.3), but the MERCOSUR dummy remained around 0.36 and statistically significant at the 99 percent confidence level.

Finally, it might be objected that all we are doing is capturing the propensity of certain countries to experience exchange-rate crises that are associated with unusually high levels of volatility. Perhaps, leaving these crisis periods aside, MERCOSUR has been able to avoid outlandish exchange-rate volatility, and what we have really pointed out is the need simply to understand the political economy of the crisis problem in these countries. To address this possibility, we excluded observations with very high volatility. When we dropped observations for which *sdce* was greater than two, little changed. When we excluded all observations for which *sdce* was greater than one, the key results were actually strengthened. While the coefficient on the MERCOSUR dummy fell from 0.4 to 0.1, it was still highly significant at standard confidence levels. In addition, in this truncated sample the negative coefficients on the two inflation-targeting variables were both significant at the 99 percent confidence level (and negative as before). Evidently, the tendency for inflation targeting better to reconcile monetary autonomy with exchange-rate volatility does not hinge on the contrast with a few crisis prone countries during episodes of highly unstable exchange rates, a subsample that does not begin to satisfy the preconditions for successful inflation targeting; it obtains also when these crisis episodes are omitted and the sample is limited to countries with reasonably stable exchange rates.

Conclusion

Our short-run diagnosis, then, is that floating is here to stay in the Western Hemisphere, although dollarization remains a wildcard, mainly for small countries such as those of Central America with especially heavy dependence on trade with the United States. If yearnings for an "ever closer" FTAA develop over time (the EU-politics counterfactual), then the monetary calculus could change. On purely economic grounds, there is no reason why the Western Hemisphere should be more or less inclined toward monetary union than Western Europe.[54] The question is how to get there. But looking to Europe now as a model would be a mistake. Our findings suggest that Europe's single market was a stepping stone to monetary union because of a special constellation of political forces that created an overwhelming desire for exchange-rate coordination and monetary union. This desire was far in excess of any other countries' wishes for exchange rate stability based on economic criteria alone.

There is little in these results to suggest that other RTAs possess attributes rendering them similarly ripe for monetary coordination.[55] In fact, NAFTA and MERCOSUR, which include the larger economies in the Western Hemisphere, show the least inclination in these matters. The best that can be hoped for in the short run is better individually managed monetary policies that credibly deliver improved exchange-rate stability, be it by inflation targeting or other means.

Appendix

In the following list of variables, sources are in parentheses; "Rose" denotes Andrew Rose's data set from his website, data7web.dta; PWT denotes Penn World Tables version 5.6; WTA denotes variables derived from World Trade Analyzer; WB denotes the World Bank's World Development Indicators CD-ROM.

sdce: five-year (centered) moving average of standard deviation of the change in the log nominal exchange rate (PWT)

ltrade: log of bilateral trade value (Rose)

lrgdp: log of product of real GDPs (Rose)

ldist: log of linear distance (Rose)

border: dummy for adjacent countries (Rose)

comlang: dummy for common language (Rose)

regional: dummy for (bilateral) RTA, i.e., EU, NAFTA, ASEAN, MERCOSUR, ANZCER, U.S.-Israel, Caricom, CACM, SPARTECA (Rose)

rta: dummy for "Big-5" RTAs: EU, NAFTA, ASEAN, MERCOSUR, ANZCER

open: average of two countries' openness, defined as (X+M)/GDP (PWT)

dissim: sum of squared differences between bilateral pairs in manufactured export shares over thirty-four BEA industrial classifications (WTA)

av_totaldebt/gnp: average of two countries' total debt divided by GNP (WB)

av_shorttermdebt/totaldebt: average of two countries' short-term debt divided by total debt (WB) *gdp_size*: asymmetry of countries measured by the absolute value of the difference in real GDPs divided by average of real GDPs (PWT)

m2: average of two countries' M2-to-GDP ratios (PWT)

In addition to these variables we used inflation-targeting dummy variables (defined in the text) from two distinct sources; a hardness-of-peg measure from Reinhart and Rogoff (2002); a transparency and corruption measure from Transparency International; and dummies for intra-RTA trade for the following regions: OECD, FTAA, EU, NAFTA, MERCOSUR, ASEAN, and ANZCER.

References

Arroyo, Heliodoro Temprano. 2002. "Latin America's Integration Processes in the Light of the EU's Experience with EMU." Economic Paper no. 173, Directorate-General for Economic and Financial Affairs, European Commission, Brussels. (July).

Baier, Scott, and Jeffrey Bergstrand. 2002. "On the Endogeneity of International Trade Flows and Free Trade Agreements." Clemson University and University of Notre Dame. Photocopy.

Bayoumi, Tamim, and Barry Eichengreen. 1993. "Shocking Aspects of European Monetary Unification." In *Adjustment and Growth in the European Monetary Union,* edited by Francesco Giavazzi and Francisco Torres, pp. 193–230. Cambridge: Cambridge University Press.

———. 1997a. "Is Regionalism Simply a Diversion? Evidence from the Evolution of the EC and EFTA." In *Regionalism versus Multilateral Trade Arrangements,* edited by Takatoshi Ito and Anne Krueger, pp. 141–68. Chicago: University of Chicago Press.

———. 1997b. "Optimum Currency Areas and Exchange Rate Volatility: Theory and Evidence Compared." In *International Trade and Finance: New Frontiers for Research,* edited by Benjamin J. Cohen, pp. 184–215. Cambridge: Cambridge University Press.

Berg, Andrew, Eduardo Borensztein, and Paolo Mauro. 2002. "An Evaluation of Monetary Regime Options for Latin America." International Monetary Fund Working Paper no. 02/211 (December), Washington, DC.

Buiter, Willem. 1999. "The EMU and NAMU: What is the Case for a North American Monetary Union?" *Canadian Public Policy* 25:285–305.

Buti, Marco, and Gabriele Giudice. 2002. "EMU's Fiscal Rules: What Can and Cannot Be Exported?" European Commission (February). Photocopy.

Carmichael, Ted. 2002. "Canada's Dollarization Debate." Special Report, J. P. Morgan Securities Canada, Toronto (May 24).

Chriszt, Michael. 2000. "Perspectives on a Potential North American Currency Union." *Federal Reserve Bank of Atlanta Economic Review* 85:29–38.

Courchene, Thomas J., and Richard G. Harris. 1999. *From Fixing to Monetary Union*. C. D. Howe Institute (June), Toronto.

DeLong, J. Bradford, and Barry Eichengreen. 2002. "Between Meltdown and Moral Hazard: The International Monetary and Financial Policies of the Clinton Administration." In *American Economic Policy in the 1990s*, edited by Jeffrey A. Frankel and Peter Orszag, pp. 191–254. Cambridge, MA: MIT Press.

Devereux, Michael, and Philip Lane. 2001. "Understanding Bilateral Exchange Rate Volatility." University of British Columbia and Trinity College, Dublin. Photocopy.

Eichengreen, Barry. 1996. "A More Perfect Union: The Logic of Economic Integration." *Essays in International Finance* no. 198, International Finance Section, Department of Economics, Princeton University (June).

———.1998. "Does MERCOSUR Need a Single Currency?" National Bureau for Economic research Working Paper no. 6821 (December), Cambridge, MA.

———. 2001. "International Monetary Options for the Twenty-First Century." *Annals of the American Academy of Political and Social Sciences* 579: 11–26

———. 2002. "International Monetary Options for the 21st Century." *Annals of the American Academy of Political and Social Science* 579: 11–21.

Eichengreen, Barry, Paul Masson, Miguel Savastano, and Sunil Sharma. 1999. "Transition Strategies and Nominal Anchors on the Road to Greater Exchange-Rate Flexibility." *Princeton Studies in International Finance* no. 213, International Finance Section, Department of Economics, Princeton University.

Eichengreen, Barry, and Yung Chul Park. 2002. "Why Has There Been More Financial Integration in Europe Than East Asia?" University of California, Berkeley. Photocopy.

Feenstra, Robert C. 2000. *World Trade Flows, 1980–1997*. University of California Davis. CD-ROM.

Fernández-Arias, Eduardo, Ugo Panizza, and Ernesto Stein. 2002. "Trade Agreements, Exchange Rate Disagreements." Inter-American Development Bank (March), Washington, DC. Photocopy.

Frankel, Jeffrey A. 1997. *Regional Trading Blocs in the World Economic System*. Washington, DC: Institute for International Economics.

Frankel, Jeffrey A., and Andrew K. Rose. 1998. "The Endogeneity of the Optimum Currency Area Criteria." *Economic Journal* 108: 1009–25.

Frieden, Jeffry. 1996. "The Impact of Goods and Capital Market Integration on European Monetary Politics." *Contemporary Political Studies* 29: 193–222.

Frieden, Jeffry, Piero Ghezzi, and Ernesto Stein. 2000. "Politics and Exchange Rates: A Cross-Country Approach to Latin America." Working Paper no. R-421 (October), Inter-American Development Bank, Washington, DC.

Giavazzi, Francesco, and Alberto Giovannini. 1989. *Limiting Exchange Rate Variability: The European Monetary System*. Cambridge, MA: MIT Press.

Goldstein, Morris. 2002. *Managed Floating Plus*. Washington, DC: Institute for International Economics.

Grubel, Herbert. 1999. "The Case for the Amero: The Economics and Politics of a North American Monetary Union." Fraser Institute (October), Vancouver. Photocopy.

Hausmann, Ricardo, Ugo Panizza, and Ernesto Stein. 1999."Why Do Countries Float the Way They Float?" Inter-American Development Bank, Washington, DC. Photocopy.

Heston, Alan et al. 1994. The Penn World Table, Version 5.6. National Bureau of Economic Research, Cambridge, MA (November). http://nber.harvard.edu.

Kenen, Peter B. 1969. "The Theory of Optimum Currency Areas: An Eclectic View." In *Monetary Problems of the International Economy*, edited by Robert A. Mundell and Alexander K. Swoboda, pp. 41–60. Chicago: University of Chicago Press.

Krugman, Paul. 1993. "Lessons of Massachusetts for EMU." In *Adjustment and Growth in the European Monetary Union,* edited by Francesco Giavazzi and Francisco Torres, pp. 241–61. Cambridge: Cambridge University Press.

Kuttner, Kenneth, and Adam Posen. 2001. "Beyond Bipolar: A Three-Dimensional Assessment of Monetary Frameworks." *International Journal of Finance and Economics* 6: 369–87.

Machinea, José Luis. 2002. "Exchange Rate Instability in MERCOSUR: Causes, Problems and Possible Solutions." Inter-American Development Bank, Washington, DC (July). Photocopy.

McKinnon, Ronald. 1963. "Optimum Currency Areas." *American Economic Review* 53: 717–25.

Meyer, Lawrence, Brian Doyle, Joseph Gagnon, and Dale Henderson. 2002. "International Coordination of Macroeconomic Policies: Still Alive in the New Millennium?" International Finance Discussion Paper no. 723, Board of Governors of the Federal Reserve System, Washington, DC.

Mishkin, Frederic, and Klaus Schmidt-Hebbel. 2001. "One Decade of Inflation Targeting in the World: What Do We Know and What Do We Need to Know?" National Bureau for Economic Research Working Paper no. 8397 (July), Cambridge, MA.

Mundell, Robert A. 1961. "A Theory of Optimum Currency Areas." *American Economic Review* 51: 657–65.

Mussa, Michael. 2002. *Argentina and the Fund: From Triumph to Tragedy.* Washington, DC: Institute for International Economics.

Reinhart, Carmen M., and Kenneth S. Rogoff. 2002. "The Modern History of Exchange Rate Arrangements: A Reinterpretation." National Bureau for Economic Research Working Paper no. 8963 (May), Cambridge, MA.

Rogoff, Kenneth S. 2002. "Managing the World Economy." *The Economist* (August 1).

Rojas-Suarez, Liliana. 2002. "Toward a Sustainable FTAA: Does Latin America Meet the Necessary Financial Preconditions?" Institute for International Economics (January), Washington, DC. Photocopy.

Rose, Andrew K. 2000. "One Money, One Market: The Effect of Common Currencies on Trade." *Economic Policy* 15:7–33.

Rozemberg, R., and G. Svarzman. 2002. "El proceso de integración Argentina-Brasil en perspectiva: Conflictos, tensiones y acciones de los gobiernos." Inter-American Development Bank, Washington, DC. Photocopy.

Shin, Kwanho, and Yunjong Wang. 2002. "Trade Integration and Business Cycle Co-Movements: The Case of Korea with Other Asian Countries." Korean Institute for International Economic Policy Working Paper no. 02–08, Seoul.

World Bank. *World Development Indicators.* Washington, DC: World Bank.

Notes

The authors thank Calvin Ho and David Jacks for research assistance and Guillermo Calvo, Ernesto Stein, and Andrés Velasco for helpful comments. Eichengreen acknowledges the support of a "Crossing Borders Grant" from the University of California, Berkeley. Taylor gratefully acknowledges the support of the Chancellor's Fellowship at the University of California, Davis. All errors are ours.

1 See Chapter 7 by Powell and Sturzenegger in this volume.

2 For a sampling of academic ruminations, see Buiter (1999), Chriszt (2000), Courchene and Harris (1999), and Grubel (1999).

3 Eichengreen (1996) has made this argument repeatedly in earlier work.

4 See Carmichael (2002). To be sure, there are some signs of neofunction-

alist spillovers; for example, the expansion of trade has created pressure for the liberalization of labor and capital flows. The United States has pushed to improve the access of its banks to the Mexican financial sector, while Mexico has pushed to regularize the employment of Mexican citizens in the United States. But the process has limits, political limits in particular.

5 And, similarly, there is reluctance on the part of Canada and Mexico to contemplate the option of seats on an expanded Federal Reserve Board, since there still would be no mechanism through which the members of the Board could be held accountable to the Canadian and Mexican polities. Buiter (1999) discusses the possibility of a supranational monetary policy committee with representatives from all three countries. He notes that absent the regional equivalent of the European Parliament, the Canadian parliament would be able to call only its own national representative(s) to account. The non-Canadian majority on the committee presumably would be under no obligation to respond to questions from Canada's elected or appointed officials.

6 See for example the evidence in Bayoumi and Eichengreen (1997a).

7 Because commercial integration has extended from a free trade area to a customs union and a single market, the pressure for adjustment has been particularly strong.

8 Further empirical support for this regularity, drawn from Latin American data, is in Frieden, Ghezzi, and Stein (2000).

9 For an analysis in the context of Argentine-Brazilian relations in the wake of the 1999 devaluation of the Real, see Rozemberg and Svarzman (2002). Fenandez-Arias, Panizza, and Stein (2002) suggest that to the extent that an RTA allows members to export to their partners goods that are not competitive on international markets, leaving no outlet for them when the partner currency depreciates, such tensions will be larger still. They provide evidence that this is a problem in practice.

10 This assumes, of course, that regional arrangements are necessarily trade creating, or at least that they stimulate trade within the RTA more than they stimulate trade with the rest of the world. As an empirical matter it is not obvious that this is an accurate assumption; we will have more to say about it below.

11 While economists would question the wisdom of the Common Agricultural Policy (CAP), it was, for better or worse, one of the European Community's first concrete economic achievements. Its structure, which created separate floors in terms of domestic currency for agricultural prices in each member state, meant that exchange-rate fluctuations could wreak havoc with its operation by greatly strengthening the incen-

tives for cross-border arbitrage (Giavazzi and Giovannini 1989).

12 The vertical versus horizontal structure of trade is clearly not the only factor shaping the competitive impact of bilateral exchange-rate fluctuations. Fernandez-Arias, Panizza, and Stein (2002) focus on the degree of protection in the RTA partner producing the final good, suggesting that when exports are destined mainly for a highly protected RTA partner there may be little scope for reallocating them to third markets in the event of a depreciation.

13 There have been a variety of extensions of this approach, for example Devereux and Lane (2001).

14 Or, conceivably, against, as we shall see below.

15 The seminal references are Mundell (1961), McKinnon (1963), and Kenen (1969).

16 As was the case in Bayoumi and Eichengreen (1997) for a more limited sample of (high-income) countries.

17 Tobit two-stage results with uncorrected standard errors are available from the authors upon request.

18 In addition, there is the possibility that the decision to join an RTA is endogenous, as argued by Baier and Bergstrand (2002). Addressing this possibility would be complex, since we are already dealing with a system of equations. We leave this extension to future work.

19 As always, the estimates are only as reliable as the instruments. In practice, the measure of business-cycle conformance and openness included in the exchange-rate equation are the instruments for exchange rates in the trade equation, while distance, contiguity, common language, and time and country dummies are the instruments for bilateral trade in the exchange-rate equation.

20 He had in mind that when countries specialize in the production of distinct goods, the prices of which are affected very differently by disturbances, asymmetric shocks are more likely, increasing the attractions of an independent monetary policy and a fluctuating exchange rate. We have in mind that when countries specialize in the production of distinct goods, exchange-rate fluctuations lead to less substitution between them, placing less pressure on competitiveness, net exports, and profitability. Thus, while the mechanisms are different, the implications are the same.

21 The appendix provides more precise definitions of the variables contained in our data set.

22 This result may indicate that more open economies, although they face costs from volatility, also benefit from the shock absorption of a flexible

rate, and the benefits appear to outweigh the costs for a given country size.

23 Eichengreen and Park (2002) report evidence that greater bilateral trade is associated with greater financial integration as measured by the BIS statistics on consolidated international bank claims, by country.

24 Again, this is the same result as in Frankel (1997).

25 We also find a positive coefficient for the ASEAN and ANZCER RTAs, indicating some political resistance to exchange-rate stabilization. Future writing should address ASEAN, ASEAN+3, and various subgroupings, given the debate over the question of the desirability of monetary integration in Asia.

26 It is not central to this discussion, but we should note in passing that, even in columns 4 through 7 for the OECD where we find the two channels working in harmony, again the "political" channel for the EU swamps the trade channel.

27 We did not find a significant association between *dissim* and *ltrade* in the gravity equation, leading us to omit this variable from our specification and retain the Table 6.1 gravity model for further analysis.

28 See the literature inspired by Frankel and Rose (1998), in which the synchronicity of business cycles and not the volatility of exchange rates is the dependent variable. In that context, Shin and Wang (2002) find that the similarity of exports (intraindustry trade in particular) is positively associated with business cycle coherence.

29 For theory and evidence to this effect, see Hausmann et al. (1999). Note further that in order to draw implications from these arguments for the connections between the formation of a free *trade* agreement and exchange-rate volatility, it is also necessary to have views of how an RTA will affect these financial variables. Some will argue that an RTA that encourages countries to trade more heavily with one another will also encourage them to engage in more cross-border investment with one another, and vice versa. There is some limited evidence of this in the literature on the determinants of direct foreign investment (see for example Frankel 1997), but little evidence of which we are aware on the connections between trade and portfolio capital flows. Casual observation suggests no single pattern: whereas regional integration in Europe has significantly stimulated the volume of cross-border capital flows, analogous initiatives in Asia have had much more limited financial effects (Eichengreen and Park 2002).

30 Both variables are taken from the World Bank's *World Development Indicators* CD-ROM. Note that the sample size drops significantly when we add this variable. Ideally, one would also want a measure of the currency denomination of the debt, but such information is not readily available.

31 There are some interesting contrasts between the results for the full sam-

ple and the potential members of an FTAA. While total indebtedness is associated with more variable exchange rates in both instances, the effect of a shorter maturity structure is negative in the FTAA subsample, reversing the full sample finding. Conceivably, short-term debt could be disproportionately denominated in foreign currency, heightening the risk of destabilizing balance-sheet effects if the exchange rate is allowed to move, but the data do not permit one do to more than speculate about this possibility.

32 We also included additional data on total debt/GNP from the OECD's *Main Economic Indicators*.

33 Interestingly, that positive and significant coefficient goes to zero for the FTAA subsample.

34 We owe this idea to Andrés Velasco.

35 The variable now is simply the absolute value of the difference in the GDPs of the two countries.

36 The information-exchange rationale for international policy coordination is discussed in Meyer et al. (2002).

37 We provide more details on these targets below.

38 One can imagine an argument that modest policy adjustments in these directions would have benefited both countries. The argument would be that tighter fiscal policy in Argentina would have bolstered investor confidence in both countries, while looser monetary policy in Brazil would have stimulated aggregate demand throughout the region.

39 Some European observers would not reach equally pessimistic conclusions about the efficacy of mutual surveillance. See for example Buti and Giudice (2002). But even they would acknowledge that "it is not clear whether the political-economy factors which underpinned the success of Maastricht consolidation can be recreated in Latin America" (p. 1).

40 NAFTA's experience is consistent with this view. In fact, U.S. Treasury and Federal Reserve Board officials discussed the need for a standing consultative mechanism to anticipate exchange-rate problems within the RTA in 1993, and soon thereafter they launched the North American Framework Agreement and North American Financial Group with Canada (see DeLong and Eichengreen 2002). Suffice it to say that neither mechanism played much of a role in heading off the Mexican crisis or managing its consequences.

41 Opting out in the event of "exceptional financial circumstances" was permitted from the inception of the ASA, and in 1992 the right to opt out became effectively unlimited.

42 It could be argued that MERCOSUR countries might be more willing to provide financial support to one another precisely in order to free them-

selves from the scrutiny of the IMF. Thus, there were suggestions in Argentina in 2001 of perhaps obtaining financial assistance from Brazil. But, to the extent that the various economies of the Southern Cone tend to come under market pressure at the same time (as when the United States raises interest rates and capital flows to emerging markets dry up), this is unlikely to be a solution. There is also the fact that Brazil is several times larger than the other MERCOSUR countries combined, making it hard to see how it could be effectively supported by its partners (Machinea 2002).

43 Here, we are speaking of a single currency for a hemisphere that is managed by an independent central bank on whose board sit representatives of all the participating countries. The previous paragraph deals with the other case, in which countries unilaterally adopted the currency of a larger neighbor without also seeking a voice in the formulation of the joint monetary policy.

44 On this basis we might conclude that discussions of monetary cooperation—even monetary unification—in those regions may not be unrealistic, since the "political" effects do not offset, and if anything support, the case for coordination. But such is not true, in any case, of the potential members of an FTAA.

45 CF refers to counterfactual.

46 This argument that regional free trade may more effectively be encouraged by floating than by fragile, temporarily pegged rates is also advanced by Rojas-Suarez (2002), although she does not make the link to inflation targeting.

47 We define inflation targeting as a monetary policy operating strategy with four elements: an institutionalized commitment to price stability as the primary goal of monetary policy; mechanisms rendering the central bank accountable for attaining its monetary policy goals; the public announcement of targets for inflation; and a policy of communicating to the public and the markets the rationale for the decisions taken by the central bank. Institutionalizing the commitment to price stability lends credibility to that objective and gives the central bank the independence needed to pursue it. Mechanisms for accountability make this pursuit politically acceptable and impose costs on central banks that are incompetent or behave opportunistically. Announcing a target for inflation and articulating the basis for the central bank's decisions allows these mechanisms to operate.

48 A review of reviews on open-economy inflation targeting is Eichengreen (2001).

49 Volatility is also less if both countries inflation target. One could object that in a world of medium-run "purchasing power parity" (PPP), tar-

geting one nominal variable such as the inflation rate is no different than targeting another such as the exchange rate. However, this is not a tautology at shorter horizons, and our exchange rate measure uses a five-year window, a span short enough to allow ample deviations from PPP.

50 There is one other reason to worry about the extent to which an optimistic outlook on inflation targeting and exchange-rate volatility can be attached to the results in Table 6.3. Recall that this option is being considered in opposition to a hard-peg solution, and imagine a pair of current FTAA members suffering from acute "fear of floating," one of which is thinking of inflation targeting. The country would gain a modest amount of stability if they target (the coefficient is about –0.1), but they will *also* experience a change in exchange-rate regime that might offset this gain, according to the coefficient on the Reinhart-Rogoff measure (moving from a peg = 1 to a float = 4 would offset half of the inflation target benefits, if we multiply 3 by 0.04 and divide by 2; though moving to intermediate regimes might not). The conceptual difficulty here is that pegging is an exchange-rate-based regime, but floating is not a "regime" at all, and more accurate specification of the objective function (such as inflation target) is needed, as Guillermo Calvo and others have frequently pointed out. Our inflation-target measures capture this in some way, but we admit this only scratches the surface of the tradeoff between exchange-rate and inflation-target based stabilization plans.

51 Others worry that inflation targeting in Brazil may have collapsed in a burst of inflation between the time of writing and the publication of this volume.

52 Averaged across the two countries.

53 Of course, reverse causality is a problem for this interpretation. A long history of monetary and exchange-rate instability in these countries has encouraged currency substitution and financial underdevelopment, leading one to question the true exogeneity of the M2/GDP ratio.

54 We are not alone in drawing this inference. See also Rogoff (2002), who writes: "Since 1945, the number of currencies in the world has increased roughly twofold, almost proportionately to the number of countries. I believe that at some point later this century there will be consolidation, ending perhaps in two or three core currencies, with a scattered periphery of floaters. Getting there, and managing macroeconomic policy with less exchange-rate flexibility, is one of the major *political and economic challenges* of the next era of globalization" (emphasis added).

55 Although some, like ANZCER, might conceivably become contenders.

7

Macroeconomic Coordination and Monetary Unions in an *n*-Country World: Do All Roads Lead to Rome?

Andrew Powell and Federico Sturzenegger

Introduction

Mundell (1961), McKinnon (1963), and Poole (1970) provided path-breaking theoretical models for the analysis of when countries should consider adopting a common currency. These publications gave rise to what are now referred to as the optimal currency area (OCA) conditions. OCA theory has hence become an essential element in the toolkit of international economists and there is now a wide literature.[1]

However, most OCA models are essentially two-country, suggesting when a country should "fix" to the other—which is often thought of as the rest of the world. Such models are thus restrictive in analyzing important issues. One set of unaddressed considerations is the effect on a third country when two other trading partners form a monetary union; how two current members of a monetary union are affected if a third, fourth, and fifth country join in; and (hence) what the optimal membership of a monetary union might be for a particular country. These are not simply interesting theoretical issues but they are also of significant practical importance. In the context of the European Monetary Union, twelve countries have now adopted the single currency, while three EU members have stayed out. The EU enlargement process implies a very large number of potential new eligible members. In Latin America, two countries have recently dollarized (Ecuador and El Salvador), while the majority have adopted more flexible regimes with floating exchange rates. A recurring theme is a common regional currency—for example, among countries in MERCOSUR.[2]

The decision of El Salvador to dollarize has effects on other countries in Central America, and if another country in the region dollarized that would likewise affect El Salvador. If the Southern Cone adopted a single currency, that would be a very significant development for the whole of South America and beyond. To date, there does not appear to be a simple theoretical framework capable of analyzing the externalities of one country's decisions on others in a multicountry setting that might be made applicable to these real-world examples.

A second issue insufficiently addressed by current OCA theory is the interplay of monetary unions with trade and free trade areas (FTAs). Economists have a strong belief in the benefits of trade integration. Yet this unusual consensus within the profession has not been matched by advances at the implementation stage when protectionist forces have tended to delay the process of trade integration. The link between trade and monetary integration is a subtle one. The common view might be that trade integration is a necessary condition for monetary integration. However, others might argue that monetary integration might provide the impulse for trade liberalization and counter the protectionist forces.

The interplay between these two reforms is then highly significant. Again, Europe and the Americas provide interesting contrasts. In the former, a single currency came about only after a significant deepening of trade integration, whereas in the case of the Americas there is a dollarization debate in Latin America that at times appears quite independent of the debate regarding an FTAA. NAFTA is deepening trade integration in the north but there is less talk of a single currency among the current three partners. MERCOSUR attempted to deepen trade integration in the South and, although as mentioned a common currency has been a recurring theme, Argentina in particular has also flirted with the idea of dollarization.

This chapter constitutes a first attempt at developing a simple framework potentially capable of considering these various different interaction effects. We develop what might be considered a "reduced-form" version of an OCA model and extend it to the case of *n* countries. More specifically, our model might be described as "the factor approach (or more loosely capital asset pricing model) meets OCA."

We assume countries are affected by four types of shocks: idiosyncratic and systemic shocks, both real and monetary in nature. We then develop equations for GDP volatility as a function of simple underlying characteristics of countries and, in particular, their dependence on systemic shocks (a type of beta coefficient), the size (volatility) of the idiosyncratic shocks, and the choice of exchange rate regime. While we label shocks as real or monetary, they can be interpreted more widely as shocks to which it would be desirable for the exchange rate to respond, and shocks that might shift the nominal exchange rate away from some desired path (in terms of GDP stabilization), respectively. This relatively simple framework allows us to consider the effect of a monetary union in a subset of countries on the members of the union and on other countries. We can also compare the case of a monetary union in which monetary policy, and hence exchange rates, respond to the shocks to members of the union with the case of "dollarization" in which monetary policy and exchange rates are assumed to be governed by U.S. (or the anchor country) characteristics. We illustrate these points in a set of simulations.

We introduce trade integration and free trade areas as we posit that countries that are more integrated will have a more similar dependence on the systemic factors. Hence if an FTA increases integration, we then have a link between trade and monetary integration. Broadly speaking, the greater the degree of trade integration in a currency union, the lower is the cost of a single currency between members. We illustrate that the establishment of an FTA may then increase the argument for a currency union. At the same time, however, if a subset of countries forms an FTA, increasing the incentives for those countries to form a currency union, then this may have a deleterious effect on other countries that are left out.

We also provide a first empirical application of the model—to Latin America. We conduct a principal-component analysis to obtain the systemic factors and the dependence of countries on those factors—the "factor loadings." We then estimate, using a vector autoregression technology, the volatility of the idiosyncratic real and nominal shocks. This analysis yields some interesting if preliminary results.

The chapter is organized as follows. In the next section, we provide the basic theoretical model. In the third section we consider a set of initial simulations regarding currency unions and dollarization. In the fourth section we present the empirical application to Latin America, and the final section concludes.

The Model

A Reduced-Form OCA

Our model is a reduced form version of the OCA conditions inspired by the early work of Mundell and Poole that we think nests many views regarding the costs and benefits of currency unions. We start with an initial output equation for a single country *i* of the form:

$$\Delta GDP_i = \Delta R_i - \alpha \Delta S_i. \tag{1}$$

In this specification, real shocks ΔR_i, which affect output directly, can be smoothed by exchange-rate adjustments ΔS_i. Here, α is the smoothing effect of the exchange-rate movement. In this specification, the exchange rate refers to the nominal exchange rate, which is determined by a "monetary approach to the exchange rate" equation as follows,

$$\Delta S_i = \Delta GDP_i - \Delta M_i, \tag{2}$$

where, as expected, a positive monetary shock results in an exchange rate depreciation. Combining (1) and (2) we get

$$\Delta GDP_i = \frac{1}{1+\alpha} \Delta R_i + \frac{\alpha}{1+\alpha} \Delta M_i, \tag{3}$$

which applies to countries under float. Under a fix regime we have simply:

$$\Delta S_i = 0, \tag{4}$$

The benefit of choosing a float is that the exchange rate can act as a shock absorber in the case of real shocks but also introduces the possibility of monetary shocks that tend to move the exchange rate away from this smoothing motion. In this specification, real shocks can be terms of trade, productivity, or capital-flow disturbances (sudden stops). Monetary shocks can relate to money-supply disturbances or changes in money demand not related to the real side of the economy. The important aspect of our monetary shocks is that they are shocks that drive the exchange rate away from desired changes given the confluence of real shocks.[3] Relating the model to the early work of Mundell and others, a country that suffers large "monetary" shocks may then find it should fix, whereas a country that has low monetary shocks but suffers large "real" shocks should float and use the exchange rate to smooth those real disturbances.

A potential criticism of this set-up is that there appears to be no room for independent monetary policy. However, for those that believe that independent monetary policy can be employed to respond perfectly to real shocks without suffering monetary shocks, this view can be translated simply into our model with the assumption that the monetary shocks have a low variance and the alpha parameter is large. Then, GDP volatility is close to zero under a float even in the presence of real shocks. However, a more general view might be that there are certain limitations to using monetary policy in this way and that monetary variables may not be totally within the control of the monetary authorities.[4]

Another view, stressed by Calvo (see, for example, Calvo 2002) focuses on the severity and importance of "sudden stops." In our model, a sudden stop might be thought of as a systemic real shock. As such, shocks impact the real economy through a decline in available funds for investment and in general require a significant current-account adjustment. These are then shocks to which it would generally be advantageous to respond with exchange-rate flexibility.[5] To the extent that a group of countries suffer from such a shock simultaneously implies that the cost of a monetary union between those countries would be low, although if an individual country were more prone to such a sudden stop then individual exchange-rate flexibility would clearly be an advantage.

A Factor Approach to OCA

In the previous analysis we referred to one country in isolation. The extension to many countries entails tracking the exchange rates between countries. Suppose there are $n+1$ countries (i.e., $n+$ country i). Our equation for GDP is

$$\Delta GDP_i = \Delta R_i - \alpha \sum_{j=1}^{n} \frac{1}{n} \Delta S_{ij}, \tag{5}$$

where ΔR_i is a real shock that hits country i and where the real shock has both a systemic and an individual component:

$$\Delta R_i = \beta_i^R \varepsilon_w^R + \varepsilon_i^R. \tag{6}$$

Each country is affected directly by individual shocks ε_i^R or in response to world shocks ε_w^R with adjustment coefficient β_i^R. Exchange-rate changes are governed by the monetary approach to the exchange rate such that the nominal exchange rate is affected by changes in relative outputs and relative monetary supply. Thus

$$\Delta S_i = (\Delta GDP_i - \Delta GDP_j) - (\Delta M_i - \Delta M_j). \tag{7}$$

Where the relative money shock has, in similar vein to the real shocks, systemic and independent components, then

$$\Delta M_i = \beta_i^M \varepsilon_w^M + \varepsilon_i^M. \tag{8}$$

Equations (7) and (8) imply that exchange-rate movements are driven by real and monetary shocks. In order to express the exchange-rate movement only in terms of these shocks, we first compute the difference in GDP movements of countries i and j. From equation (5):

$$\Delta GDP_i - \Delta GDP_j = \Delta R_i - \Delta R_j - \frac{\alpha}{n}\sum_{k=1}^{n} (\Delta S_{ik} - \Delta S_{jk}). \tag{9}$$

However, from our setup it follows that $\Delta S_{ij} = \Delta S_{ik} - \Delta S_{jk}$ and hence this simplifies to:

$$\Delta GDP_i - \Delta GDP_j = \Delta R_i - \Lambda R_j - \alpha \Delta S_{ij}. \tag{10}$$

We can then substitute this expression into equation (5) to obtain:

$$\Delta GDP_i = \Delta R_i - \frac{\alpha}{1+\alpha}\frac{1}{n}\sum_{j=1}^{n} [(\Delta R_i - \Delta R_j) - (\Delta M_i - \Delta M_j)]. \tag{11}$$

This makes clear that for a country that has asymmetric real shocks (i.e., where its real shocks are different from the other n countries), a floating exchange rate has a dampening role. On the other hand, a country that has asymmetric monetary shocks (e.g., where individual monetary shocks are large), a floating exchange rate may imply greater shocks to GDP relative to a fixed one. Substituting in for the specification of the real and monetary shocks, we can write that:

$$\Delta GDP_i = \frac{1}{1+\alpha}(\beta_i^R + \frac{\alpha}{n}\sum_{j-1}^{n} \beta_j^R)\varepsilon_w^R + \frac{\alpha}{1+\alpha}\frac{1}{n}\sum_{j=1}^{n} \varepsilon_j^R + \frac{1}{1+\alpha}\varepsilon_i^R$$
$$\frac{\alpha}{1+\alpha}\sum_{j=1}^{n}\frac{1}{n}(\beta_j^M - \beta_j^M)\varepsilon_w^M - \frac{\alpha}{1+\alpha}\sum_{j=1}^{n}\frac{1}{n}\varepsilon_j^M + \frac{\alpha}{1+\alpha}\varepsilon_i^M. \tag{12}$$

We will identify welfare with the inverse of GDP volatility. Given that the systemic shocks and the individual shocks are all independent, GDP volatility is now relatively straightforward in this world of n+1 floating currencies. This turns out to be[6]

$$\sigma^2_{GDP_i^{Float}} = \left(\frac{1}{1+\alpha}\right)^2 \sigma^2_{\varepsilon_i^R} + \left(\frac{1}{1+\alpha}\right)^2 \left[\beta_i^R + \frac{\alpha}{n}\sum_{j=1}^{n}(\beta_j^R)\right]^2 \sigma^2_{\varepsilon_w^R} + \left(\frac{\alpha}{1+\alpha}\right)^2 \sigma^2_{\varepsilon_i^M} + \left(\frac{\alpha}{1+\alpha}\frac{1}{n}\right)^2 \left[\sum_{j=1}^{n}(\beta_i^M - \beta_j^M)\right]^2 \sigma^2_{\varepsilon_w^M}. \tag{13}$$

On the other hand, if there is one world currency, then we have

$$\Delta GDP_i^{Fix} = \Delta R_i = \beta_i^R \varepsilon_w^R + \varepsilon_i^R. \tag{14}$$

The volatility under a one world currency is given by

$$\sigma^2_{GDP_i^{Fix}} = \beta_i^{R^2} \sigma^2_{\varepsilon_w^R} + \sigma^2_{\varepsilon_w^R}. \tag{15}$$

Comparing this to the equation for GDP volatility under floating rates, we can see that floating reduces GDP volatility derived from a country's own asymmetric real shocks (idiosyncratic or systemic, but where betas are different) to the extent that (is positive. But floating also introduces greater GDP volatility stemming from the monetary shocks in other countries (that affect exchange rates domestically) and a country's own asymmetric monetary shocks.

Partial Monetary Unions

This simple set-up is useful in that it also allows us to consider what happens when two or more countries form a currency union. If two countries decide to adopt the same currency, then the basic equation for GDP movements remains the same except for the fact that now one currency disappears:

$$\Delta GDP_{i(k)} = \Delta R_i - \alpha \sum_{j \neq k}^{n-1} \frac{1}{n} \Delta S_{i(k)j}, \tag{16}$$

where we assume that i merges with k, indicated by the subscript $i(k)$. We assume symmetry in that all countries are of equal size and hence have equal weight regarding how the common exchange rate of a monetary union is determined. Denoting $\Delta M_{i(k)} = \Delta M_{k(i)}$ as the monetary shock of the monetary union between countries i and k, the common exchange-rate movement is given by

$$\Delta S_{i(k)j} = \begin{cases} 0 & \text{if } j = k, \\ \dfrac{\Delta GDP_{i(k)} + \Delta GDP_{k(i)}}{2} - \Delta GDP_j - (\Delta M_{i(k)} - \Delta M_j) & \text{if } j \neq k\,. \end{cases} \tag{17}$$

We will assume that the movement of the joint exchange rate follows the same rules, with a systemic and an individual component for the real shocks and monetary shocks. Following standard theories of finance, the beta of the currency union is then simply the average of the two individual-country betas and the individual shock of the currency union is just the average individual-country shocks. Let us define:

$$\Delta R_{i(k)} = \frac{1}{2}(\beta_i^R + \beta_k^R)\varepsilon_w^R + \frac{1}{2}(\varepsilon_i^R + \varepsilon_k^R), \tag{18}$$

and

$$\Delta M_{i(k)} = \frac{1}{2}(\beta_i^M + \beta_k^M)\varepsilon_w^M + \frac{1}{2}(\varepsilon_i^M + \varepsilon_k^M). \tag{19}$$

With this notation, for the case $j \neq k$, we can write:

$$\Delta S_{i(k)j} = \frac{1}{1+\alpha}[(\Delta R_{i(k)} - \Delta R_j) - \Delta M_{i(k)} - \Delta M_j)], \tag{20}$$

where we use the fact that $\Delta S_{i(k)l} = \Delta S_{k(i)l}$ and $\Delta S_{i(k)l} - \Delta S_{jl} = \Delta S_{i(k)j}$. We can then write the change in GDP, if i and k fix, as a function of the real and monetary shocks as follows[7]

$$\begin{aligned}\Delta GDP_{i(k)} = {} & \left\{\beta_i^R - \frac{\alpha}{1+\alpha}\frac{1}{n}\sum_{j\neq k}^{n-1}\left[\frac{1}{2}(\beta_i^R + \beta_k^R) - \beta_j^R\right]\right\}\varepsilon_w^R - \frac{\alpha}{1+\alpha}\frac{1}{n}\sum_{j\neq k}^{n-1}\varepsilon_j^R \\ & + \left(1 - \frac{1}{2}\frac{n-1}{n}\frac{\alpha}{1+\alpha}\right)\varepsilon_i^R + \frac{1}{2}\frac{n-1}{n}\frac{\alpha}{1+\alpha}\varepsilon_k^R \\ & + \left\{\frac{\alpha}{1+\alpha}\frac{1}{n}\sum_{j\neq k}^{n-1}\left[\frac{1}{2}(\beta_i^M + \beta_k^M) - \beta_j^M\right]\right\}\varepsilon_w^M \\ & - \frac{\alpha}{1+\alpha}\frac{n-1}{n}\frac{1}{2}\varepsilon_i^M - \frac{\alpha}{1+\alpha}\frac{n-1}{n}\frac{1}{2}\varepsilon_k^M + \frac{\alpha}{1+\alpha}\sum_{j\neq k}^{n-1}\frac{1}{n}\varepsilon_j^M.\end{aligned} \tag{21}$$

The variance of GDP is then given by:

$$
\begin{aligned}
\sigma^2_{GDP_{i(k)}} = {} & \left\{\beta_i^R - \frac{\alpha}{1+\alpha}\frac{1}{n}\sum_{j\neq k}^{n-1}\left[\frac{1}{2}(\beta_i^R + \beta_k^R) - \beta_j^R\right]\right\}^2 \sigma^2_{\varepsilon_w^R} \\
& + \left(\frac{\alpha}{1+\alpha}\frac{1}{n}\right)^2 \sum_{j\neq k}^{n-1}\sigma^2_{\varepsilon_j^R} + \left(1 - \frac{1}{2}\frac{n-1}{n}\frac{\alpha}{1+\alpha}\right)^2 \sigma^2_{\varepsilon_i^R} \\
& + \left(\frac{1}{2}\frac{n-1}{n}\frac{\alpha}{1+\alpha}\right)^2 \sigma^2_{\varepsilon_k^R} + \left(\frac{\alpha}{1+\alpha}\frac{n-1}{n}\frac{1}{2}\right)^2 \sigma^2_{\varepsilon_i^M} \\
& + \left\{\frac{\alpha}{1+\alpha}\frac{1}{n}\sum_{j\neq k}^{n-1}\left[\frac{1}{2}(\beta_i^M + \beta_k^M) - \beta_j^M\right]\right\}^2 \sigma^2_{\varepsilon_w^M} \\
& + \left(\frac{\alpha}{1+\alpha}\frac{n-1}{n}\frac{1}{2}\right)^2 \sigma^2_{\varepsilon_k^M} + \left(\frac{\alpha}{1+\alpha}\frac{1}{n}\right)^2 \sum_{j\neq k}^{n-1}\sigma^2_{\varepsilon_j^M}.
\end{aligned}
\tag{22}
$$

This equation can be extended to the case in which more than two countries decide to conform to a monetary union. If the monetary union is between three countries, for example i, k and l, then the exchange-rate equation is calculated including real and monetary shocks with the betas defined as

$$
\beta_{i(k,l)} = \frac{1}{3}\beta_i + \frac{1}{3}\beta_k + \frac{1}{3}\beta_l, \tag{23}
$$

The exchange rate of the union also reflects the individual shocks that hit the members. Let us define $\varepsilon_{i(k,l)}$ as follows:

$$
\varepsilon_{i(k,l)} = \frac{1}{3}\varepsilon_i + \frac{1}{3}\varepsilon_k + \frac{1}{3}\varepsilon_l. \tag{24}
$$

In this way, we can use this approach to consider partial monetary unions including $x+1$ of the $n+1$ countries. The general equation for the GDP volatility for this case is:

$$
\begin{aligned}
\sigma^2_{GDP_{i(k,\ldots,x)}} = {} & \left\{\beta^R_i - \frac{\alpha}{1+\alpha}\frac{1}{n}\sum_{j\neq k,\ldots x}^{n-x}\left[\frac{1}{x+1}(\beta^R_i+\beta^R_k+\ldots\beta^R_x)-\beta^R_j\right]\right\}^2\sigma^2_{\varepsilon^R_w} \\
& + \left(\frac{\alpha}{1+\alpha}\frac{1}{n}\right)^2\sum_{j\neq k\ldots x}^{n-x}\sigma^2_{\varepsilon^R_j} + \left(1-\frac{1}{x+1}\frac{n-x}{n}\frac{\alpha}{1+\alpha}\right)^2\sigma^2_{\varepsilon^R_i} \\
& + \left(\frac{1}{x+1}\frac{n-x}{n}\frac{\alpha}{1+\alpha}\right)^2(\sigma^2_{\varepsilon^R_k}+\sigma^2_{\varepsilon^R_l}+\ldots\sigma^2_{\varepsilon^R_x}) \qquad (25) \\
& + \left\{\frac{\alpha}{1+\alpha}\frac{1}{n}\sum_{j\neq k}^{n-1}\left[\frac{1}{x+1}(\beta^M_i+\beta^M_k+\ldots\beta^M_x)-\beta^M_j\right]\right\}^2\sigma^2_{\varepsilon^M_w} \\
& + \left(\frac{\alpha}{1+\alpha}\frac{n-1}{n}\frac{1}{x+1}\right)^2(\sigma^2_{\varepsilon^M_k}+\sigma^2_{\varepsilon^M_l}+\ldots\sigma^2_{\varepsilon^M_x}) \\
& + \left(\frac{\alpha}{1+\alpha}\frac{n-x}{n}\frac{1}{x+1}\right)^2\sigma^2_{\varepsilon^M_i} + \left(\frac{\alpha}{1+\alpha}\frac{1}{x+1}\right)^2\sum_{j\neq k\ldots x}^{n-x}\sigma^2_{\varepsilon^M_j}.
\end{aligned}
$$

Although this formula is long it is fairly simple to interpret. It shows that as the number of countries forming a monetary union increases, if the betas are very different, then the exchange rate will not reflect well the systemic real shocks that hit country i (first term). This makes intuitive sense, as the exchange rate in a very large monetary union of diverse members will do little to smooth the systemic shocks of individual members. On the other hand, the effect of the individual real shocks of countries not in the union become less important (second term) as they affect less and less the exchange rate of the union, which is increasingly driven by its members. Also, the exchange rate of the union is going to reflect to a lesser deree the individual real shocks of country i (third term) and hence smooth output less efficiently. There is a positive effect as the exchange rate will also reflect to a lesser degree the individual monetary shocks of the countries of the union (the fifth term). The fourth term reflects the asymetric monetary shocks: the best case for monetary union is one in which the effect of the union is to generate an average beta close to the average beta of the $n+1$ countries. The final term indicates that when the number of countries in the union increase then the individual monetary shocks of countries not in the union become less important as they affect to a lesser degree the exchange rate of the union. Note that as x tends to n, this equation collapses to the equation for output volatility for the one-world-currency case.

Fixing to an Anchor Currency

Alternatively, countries may choose to coordinate by fixing to a particular country that can provide some credibility enhancement. We will refer to this country as the United States. The purpose of this section is to provide the sequence of volatilities as more and more countries peg to the same currency. As always we start with our canonical output equation

$$\Delta GDP_{i(US)} = \Delta R_i - \alpha \sum_j^n \frac{1}{n} \Delta S_{USj}, \tag{26}$$

In this case, we can write that

$$\Delta GDP_{i(US)} = \Delta R_i - \sum_j^{n-1} \frac{1}{n} \frac{1}{1+\alpha} \{(\Delta R_{US} - \Delta R_j) - (\Delta M_{US} - \Delta M_j)\}, \tag{27}$$

and going through the same procedure as above, we find the variance of output fixing to the U.S. dollar:

$$\begin{aligned}
\sigma^2_{GDP_{i(US)}} = {} & \left\{\beta_i^R - \frac{\alpha}{1+\alpha}\frac{1}{n}\sum_{j \neq k}^{n-1}(\beta_{US}^R - \beta_j^R)\right\}^2 \sigma^2_{\varepsilon_w^R} + \left(\frac{\alpha}{1+\alpha}\frac{1}{n}\right)^2 \sum_{j \neq k}^{n-1} \sigma^2_{\varepsilon_j^R} \\
& + \left\{\frac{\alpha}{1+\alpha}\frac{1}{n}\sum_{j \neq k}^{n-1}(\beta_{US}^M - \beta_j^M)\right\}^2 \sigma^2_{\varepsilon_w^M} \\
& + \sigma^2_{\varepsilon_i^R} + \left(\frac{\alpha}{1+\alpha}\right)^2 \sigma^2_{\varepsilon_{US}^R} + \left(\frac{\alpha}{1+\alpha}\right)^2 \sigma^2_{\varepsilon_{US}^M} \\
& + \left(\frac{\alpha}{1+\alpha}\frac{1}{n}\right)^2 \sum_{j \neq k}^{n-1} \sigma^2_{\varepsilon_j^M}
\end{aligned} \tag{28}$$

If now a second country dollarizes then the extension is reasonably straightforward, and if x countries plus country i dollarize then we obtain the following equation for output volatility:

$$\begin{aligned}\sigma^2_{GDP_{i(US)}} = & \left\{\beta^R_i - \frac{\alpha}{1+\alpha}\frac{1}{n}\sum_{j\neq k,\dots x}^{n-x}(\beta^R_{US}-\beta^R_j)\right\}^2\sigma^2_{\varepsilon^R_w} \\ & + \left(\frac{\alpha}{1+\alpha}\frac{1}{n}\right)^2\sum_{j\neq k}^{n-x}\sigma^2_{\varepsilon^R_j} + \sigma^2_{\varepsilon^R_i} + \left(\frac{\alpha}{1+\alpha}\frac{n-x}{n}\right)^2\sigma^2_{\varepsilon^R_{US}} \\ & + \left\{\frac{\alpha}{1+\alpha}\frac{1}{n}\sum_{j\neq k,\dots x}^{n-x}(\beta^M_{US}-\beta^M_j)\right\}^2\sigma^2_{\varepsilon^M_w} \\ & + \left(\frac{\alpha}{1+\alpha}\frac{n-x}{n}\right)^2\sigma^2_{\varepsilon^M_{US}} + \left(\frac{\alpha}{1+\alpha}\frac{1}{n}\right)^2\sum_{j\neq k,\dots x}^{n-1}\sigma^2_{\varepsilon^M_j}.\end{aligned} \tag{29}$$

Dollarization then eliminates the dependence of output volatility on the local monetary shock, replacing it with U.S. monetary shocks, but will import volatility to the extent that real and monetary shocks are asymmetric. As the number of countries that dollarize increases, the importance of the asymmetric real shocks increases (there are more terms in the first summation), but the importance of U.S. monetary shocks diminishes. As x tends to n, this equation collapses onto that for the one-world-currency (fixed) case.

A Set of Simulations

The Model in Action to Illustrate Different Possibilities

In this section we report the results of a set of simulations of the model. Our aim is to understand the implications for GDP volatility under different exchange-rate regimes of different constellations of parameter values. The model is simple but extremely general in that by varying a parsimonious set of variables we obtain very different results. The different parametrizations we adopt below are detailed in Table 7.1. The simulations are labeled somewhat suggestively according to the flavor of the results obtained.

G-3

In the first simulation, the size of the individual real shocks are the same as the size of the individual nominal shocks (all equal to one). The α parameter is set to 0.5, implying that a floating rate can substantially

Table 7.1 Model Parameters for Simulation Exercise

	G3	EMU	Dollarization	Currency Union versus Dollarization
α	0.5	0.5	0.5	0.5
β_i^R	1	0.25	0.75	0.75
β_i^M	1	1	1	1
$\sigma_{\varepsilon_i^R}$	1	1.5	2	1
$\sigma_{\varepsilon_i^M}$	1	10	50	10
$\sigma_{\varepsilon_w^R}$	1	1	1	1
$\sigma_{\varepsilon_w^M}$	1	1	0.75	1
β_{US}^R	1	0.75	1	0.75
β_{US}^M	1	1	1	1
$\sigma_{\varepsilon_{US}^R}$	1	1	1	1
$\sigma_{\varepsilon_{US}^M}$	1	5	2.5	2

smooth the real shocks. In this simulation all the betas for all the countries are set equal to one and the volatility of the shocks are also the same across countries. Figure 7.1 graphs one country's GDP volatility: (1) when that country forms a monetary union with an increasing number of partners (the number of partners is the X axis); (2) versus pegging to one of the other countries (let us call it the United States although in this simulation the United States is just another country—the number of countries pegged to the United States is the X axis); versus (3) a floating rate. Remember that fixing to the U.S. anchor and forming a monetary union both converge to the case of one world currency as the number of countries that fix increases. It is clear that floating is best in terms of the lowest GDP volatility, followed by a partial monetary union, followed by a one world currency, and finally fixing to the United States. A monetary union is preferred to fixing to the U.S. currency, since in a monetary union with two members the monetary policy more closely reflects the real shocks of those two members. However, in this case in which floating is optimal, the cost of a monetary union (that one country's monetary policy does not reflect that country's real shocks) outweighs the benefit in terms of the diversification of "harmful" monetary shocks. Hence as the number of members of the monetary union rises, the cost of the monetary union increases. In this G-3 inspired simulation, in which harmful nominal shocks are no higher than the real shocks, the best policy is to float.

Figure 7.1 G3

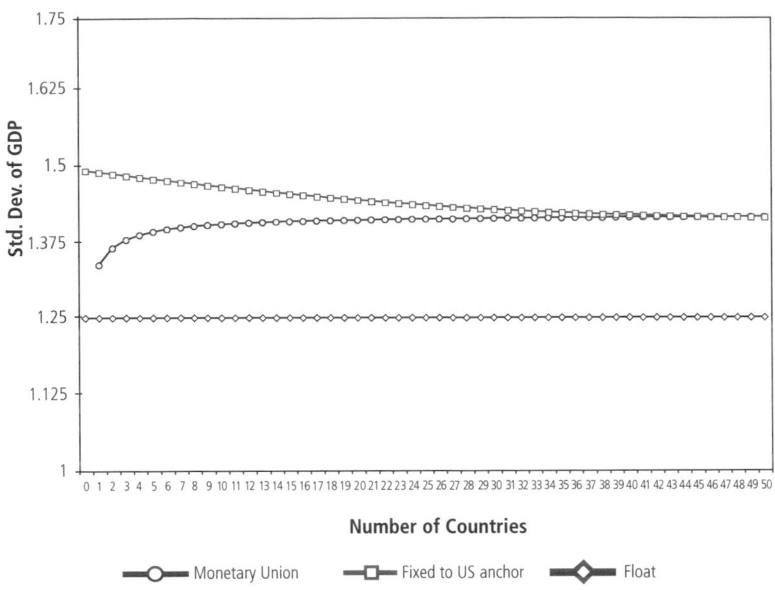

EMU

In this second simulation we make various changes. We assume that the anchor country has relatively smaller nominal shocks and the other countries higher nominal shocks.[8] We also assume that the anchor country has a dependence on the systemic real factor that is higher than the other countries (0.75 versus 0.25). We assume that the other countries all have the same, lower, dependence on the systemic real factor. The idea here is that the anchor is a more "systemic" country than the other countries and also has smaller individual monetary shocks. We tentatively suggest that these stylized facts might be thought of as modeling Europe. Here we find, as illustrated in Figure 7.2, that the best policy is a monetary union. A monetary union is now superior to floating as the benefit of diversifying the nominal shocks outweighs the cost of adopting a monetary policy that does not fit one's own characteristics, as given by the real shocks. In common with results on diversification of financial assets, it is noticeable how quickly the standard deviation of output drops as a few more countries join the monetary union. After some seven or eight countries join, virtually all the benefits of a monetary union are dissipated. In this simulation, pegging to the anchor is better than floating as the anchor has considerably lower

Figure 7.2 EMU

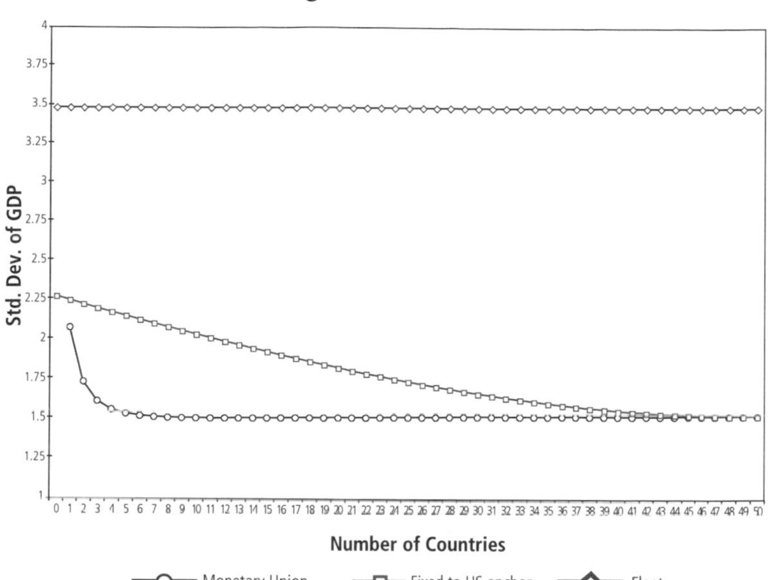

monetary shocks. Again, as more and more countries fix, both options of a monetary union and fixing to the anchor converge on the standard deviation of the one world currency. We then label this simulation EMU, as the model with this set of assumptions yields the result that a monetary union is indeed optimal.

Dollarization

In the third simulation we increase the nominal (monetary) volatility substantially, thus increasing the relative attractiveness of the anchor's (U.S.) currency . In this case, as illustrated in Figure 7.3, dollarization is the preferred option. Floating, of course, yields the highest GDP volatility, and while a currency union diversifies some of the individual monetary shocks, fixing to the low nominal volatility country (the United States) is clearly preferred. We note that this relative attraction of dollarization decreases as more countries fix and dollarization and a monetary union converge again on the output volatility of a one world currency.

Currency Union or Dollarization: Size Matters

In Figure 7.4, we fine-tune the costs and benefits of a currency union relative to dollarization to illustrate an interesting case. Here the indi-

Figure 7.3 Dollarization

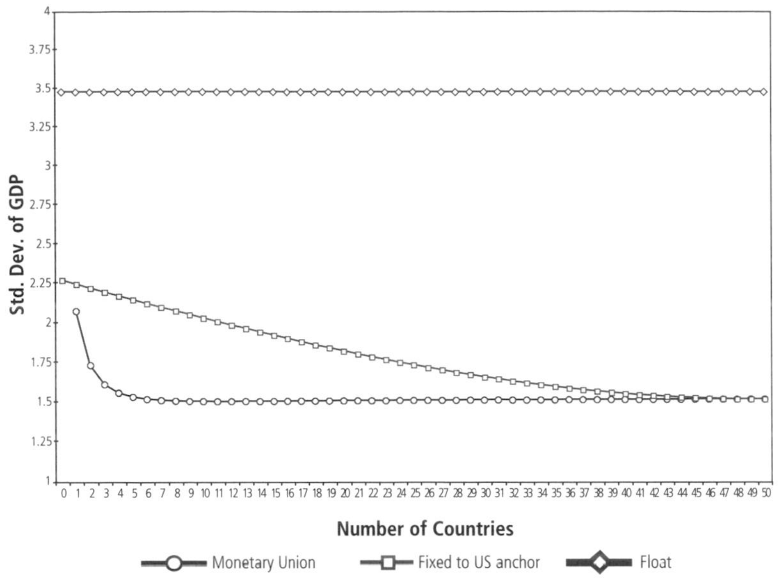

Figure 7.4 Currency Union vs. Dollarization

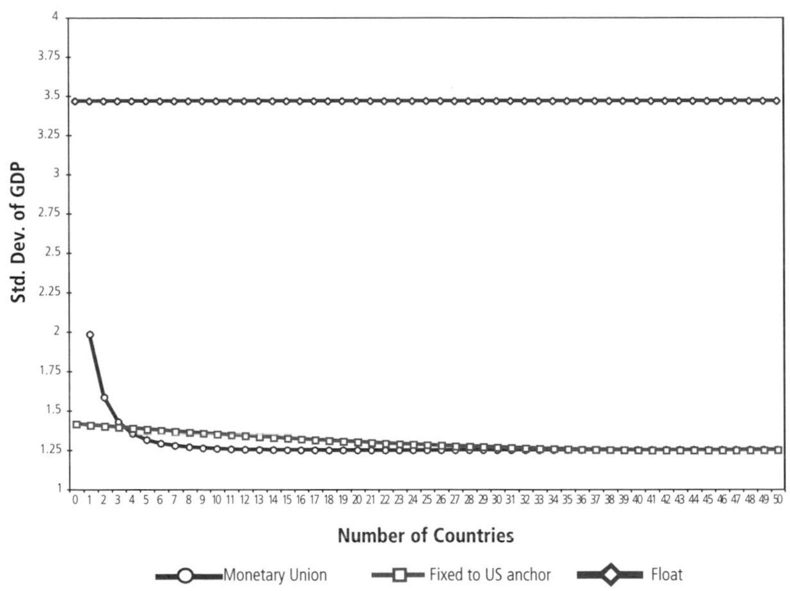

vidual nominal volatility is lower than in Figure 7.3 and the two curves cross. This implies that if we consider a country dollarizing or forming a monetary union with a single partner, then dollarization is preferred. This result is obviously driven by the lower individual nominal volatility assumed for the United States. However, after a critical number of countries have entered the currency union is preferred. In this case output volatility of a monetary union with five countries (country *i* plus four partners) is lower than that if those five countries dollarize. Now the diversifcation effect of the currency union has reduced substantially the problem of the high individual nominal volatility, and in the union, the monetary policy more closely reflects the real shocks of the its members—whereas with dollarization monetary policy reflects the real shocks of the United States.

This result may give rise to a coordination problem. Suppose there are six countries in a world of fifty that might either dollarize or eventually form a currency union, but that the technology of union formation is such that only two countries can first enter and only subsequently can their union be extended. The problem is that the initial two or three countries would prefer dollarization over the alternative of a small currency union. Hence, if the decision of each country is to dollarize today versus forming a currency union with one or two partners in the hope of convincing others to join later, then the decision today might be to dollarize. A union with six members may never get off the ground even though it is the preferred solution for the whole group.

On Endogenizing the Effect of Trade Integration

As suggested in the introduction, we might posit that the "real betas" of two countries that are more integrated will be more similar than those of two countries that do not trade very much. This idea may provide a link between trade agreements and monetary agreements. Also, for a group of countries that join a currency union, we might posit that the "monetary betas" could also converge. This would be a way of making operational Mundell's idea that the traditional OCA criteria are to a large extent endogenous.[9]

To illustrate this possibility, we consider a monetary union between a country that has a real beta of 0.75 and a group of countries that have dispersed real and monetary betas. The distribution of real betas for these other countries is uniform between 0.1 and 0.9. We then shrink the dispersion of that distribution toward 0.75. The result is illustrated

Figure 7.5 Endogenizing the Betas

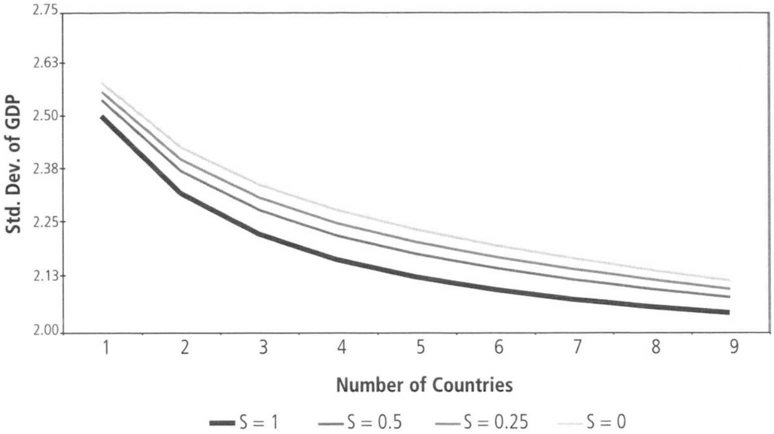

in Figure 7.5, and more detail on the parameterization is given in the appendix in Table 7.3. In Figure 7.5, the variable *S* summarizes the dispersion of the distribution with a S = 1 implying total uniformity (all betas equal to 0.75) and S = 0 represents a uniform distribution in the interval 0.1 to 0.9. As the real betas converge, the GDP volatility falls. We might posit that forming a currency union might speed this convergence process. This means that as a currency union is formed between a divergent group, the relevant curve may not be the curve with divergent betas, but rather the betas may converge and output volatility may fall to one of the lower curves depicted in Figure 7.5. This graph then illustrates the potential importance of endogenous convergence between members of a currency union.

An Application to Latin America

In this section we report the results of the empirical exercise of applying our model and applying it to Latin America. We identify the systemic shocks and the factor loadings for countries to those systemic shocks by conducting a principal-component analysis based on the first difference of GDP and then on exchange-rate movements in six countries across Latin America and the United States over the period 1980–99.[10] In this exercise we consider just the first principal factor, and in both cases this explains close to 40 percent of the variation. The dependencies to the first principal factor across the different countries are then used as the beta coefficients in our simulations, and the first

Table 7.2 Model Parameters for Country Applications

	Mexico	Brazil	Chile
α	0.5	0.5	0.5
β_i^R	0.20	0.37	0.45
β_i^M	0.39	0.31	0.17
$\sigma_{\varepsilon_i^R}$	3.36	3.20	3.23
$\sigma_{\varepsilon_i^M}$	23.47	68.50	9.41
$\sigma_{\varepsilon_w^R}$	1.86	1.86	1.86
$\sigma_{\varepsilon_w^M}$	9.47	9.47	9.47
β_{US}^R	0.25	0.25	0.25
β_{US}^M	0.31	0.31	0.31
$\sigma_{\varepsilon_{US}^R}$	1.86	1.86	1.86
$\sigma_{\varepsilon_{US}^M}$	9.47	9.47	9.47

principal factors from this analysis are then the systemic real and monetary shocks, respectively. The theoretical model and the empirical exercise could of course be extended to multiple factors—to more orthogonal systemic shocks and hence other corresponding sets of beta coefficients. We leave this for future work.

We then conduct a vector autoregression for each country in which we have one equation for the log change in GDP and a second equation for the log change in the nominal exchange rate against the U.S. dollar. In the autoregression we introduce the principal components as exogenous variables. We then interpret the residuals from these regressions as the individual real and monetary shocks respectively. Table 7.2 provides a summary of the variables and their values for the different countries employed in this exercise. Finally we set the α parameter equal to 0.5 as in the simulations above. In fact, we find that the spirit of the results are not very sensitive to different values of the α parameter in terms of the effects on output volatility of the relative exchange-rate arrangements. Given the number of assumptions, the results should of course be taken as suggestive rather than definitive.

Mexico

We first consider the case of Mexico. Mexico, as can be seen from Table 7.2, has higher individual monetary shocks relative to the average, relatively low individual real shocks, and the lowest real beta (dependence on the real systemic shock principal component). It is therefore not surprising that floating is the worst exchange-rate regime choice

Figure 7.6 Mexico

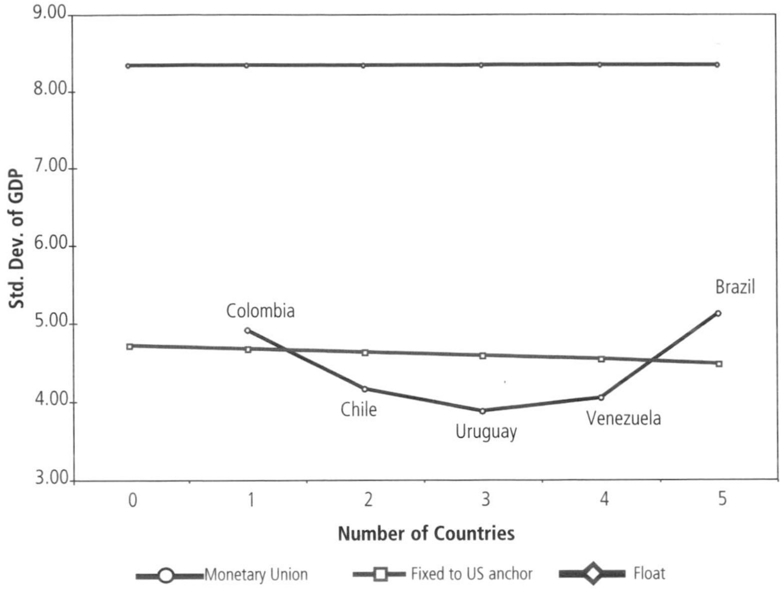

for Mexico. Figure 7.6 illustrates that forming a monetary union lowers GDP volatility, and we find that a currency union including Colombia, Chile, and Uruguay is the best on offer. While Colombia has a higher real beta, its individual monetary shocks are low. Gains are also to be had in extending the union to Chile and Uruguay, which also have low individual monetary shocks. However, incorporating Venezuela, and especially Brazil, with their higher individual monetary shocks, worsens the output volatility of the union for Mexico. Dollarizing also lowers GDP volatility for Mexico and indeed is slightly better than a union with Colombia. However, the optimal policy for Mexico is a union with Colombia, Chile, and Uruguay.

Brazil

Turning to the case of Brazil, Table 7.2 shows that Brazil has average levels of the beta parameters, a low value for the individual real shock, but a high value for the individual monetary shock. Here, due to the higher individual monetary shocks, the benefits of dollarizing or joining a currency union are substantially increased relative to floating. Figure 7.7 shows that for the case of Brazil, extending the union to all five other countries provides benefits—the full extension of the union

Figure 7.7 Brazil

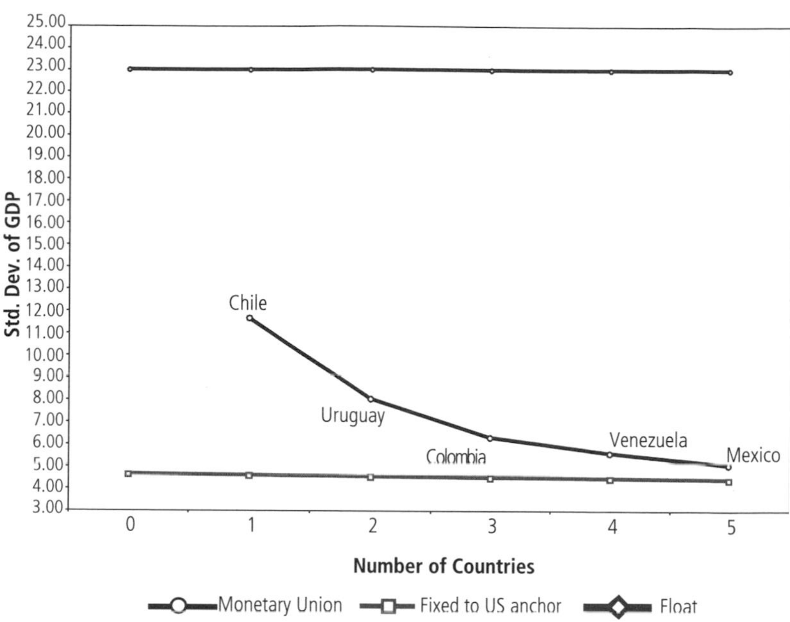

working to diversify Brazil's individual monetary shocks. However, the optimal policy, according to these strictly economic criteria, is dollarization, which is preferred even compared to the currency union including all countries.

Chile

A simulation for the case of Chile is illustrated in Figure 7.8. Chile has a relatively high value for the real beta, a low value of the monetary beta, and low real and monetary individual shocks. Dollarization is worse than floating for Chile. However, a monetary union with Colombia is the preferred option and output volatility is only slightly increased if Uruguay is also admitted. However, if Brazil is added to the currency union, then the union becomes worse for Chile than floating or even dollarizing. If we change the order of inclusion such that we have Colombia, Uruguay, Mexico, Venezuela, and Brazil, then, as before, a union with Colombia or with Colombia and Uruguay is preferred. Adding Mexico and Venezuela serves to increase GDP volatility, although it remains just below the GDP volatility of floating. Adding Brazil makes GDP volatility for much Chile higher than floating.

Figure 7.8 Chile

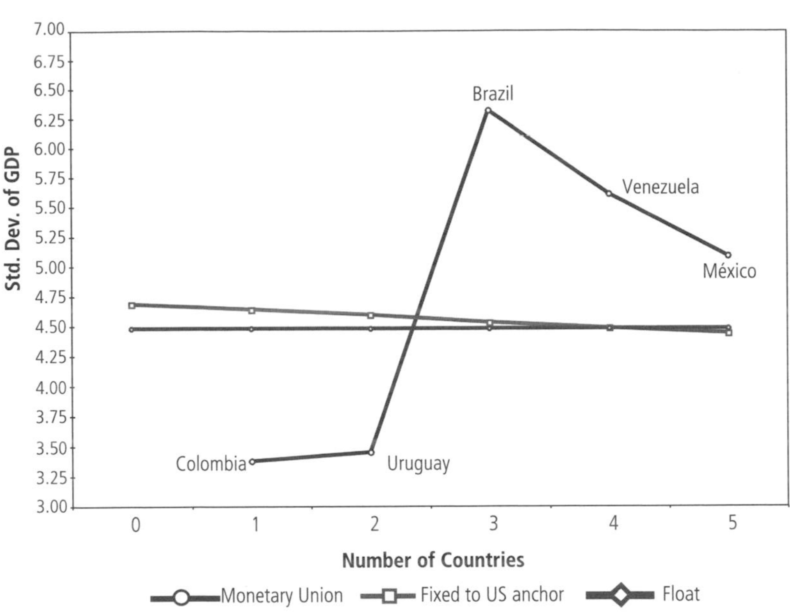

Exchange-Rate Disagreements

This empirical exercise illustrates some of the potential conflicts regarding exchange-rate arrangements in Latin America. For example, according to this strictly economic exercise, Brazil should prefer to dollarize, Mexico would like to have a currency union with Colombia and Chile, but Chile would prefer to have Colombia and Uruguay in a union and not include Mexico. If we are considering just currency union, while Brazil would prefer a union with all seven members, neither Chile nor Mexico would wish to have Brazil in a union at all. Of course, these results should only be considered highly tentative and by no means definitive, but they give some flavor to the types of conflicts that might be present. It is perhaps not so surprising that despite the repeated debates about currency unions in the region, little has actually happened.

Endogenous Betas and Reducing Individual Monetary Shocks

Again, these results assume that the beta coefficients and especially the individual monetary shocks remain constant despite the changes in monetary regimes discussed. We might for example expect the monetary betas and the real betas to converge with greater integration.

Figure 7.9 Mexico: Endogenizing Betas and Reducing the Individual Monetary Shocks

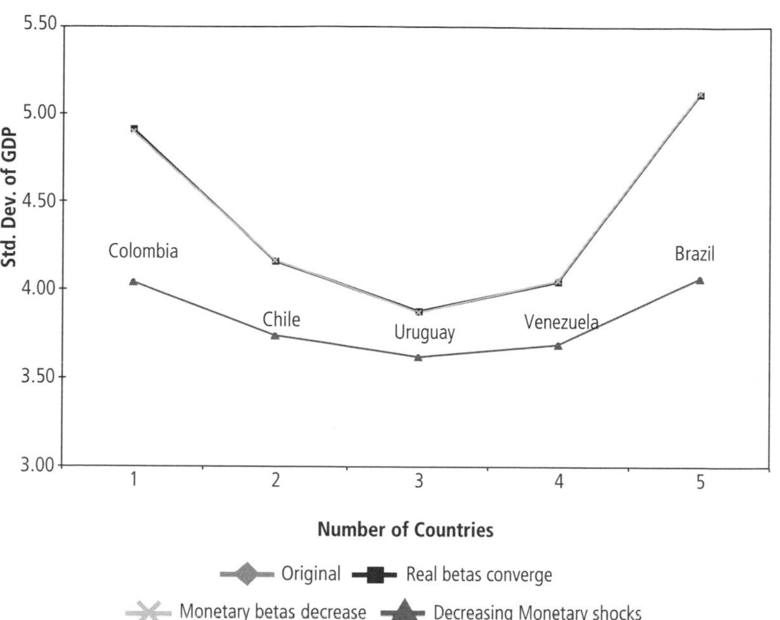

Moreover, it might also be argued that a multinational central bank in charge of the monetary policy of a currency union would boost central bank independence and credibility and thus reduce the size of the individual monetary shocks.[11] We can also use the model to attempt to gauge how important these effects are. In Figures 7.9–7.11 we consider the convergence of the real betas, the monetary betas, and the reduction in size of the individual monetary shocks for Mexico, Brazil, and Chile, respectively. Specifically, we set the real betas and then subsequently the monetary betas all equal to their average values, then reduce the individual monetary shock size of Brazil, Mexico, and Venezuela half-way toward that of Chile as a result of a monetary union.[12] The figures tell a similar story.

The convergence of the betas appears insignificant in terms of reducing the GDP volatility, but reducing the size of the individual monetary shocks has a sizeable impact. Of course, if such a change could be affected under another regime, then the attractiveness of that regime would also rise. For example, if the recent adoption of inflation targeting in Mexico and Brazil led to a reduction in individual monetary

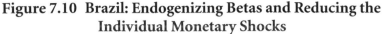

Figure 7.10 Brazil: Endogenizing Betas and Reducing the Individual Monetary Shocks

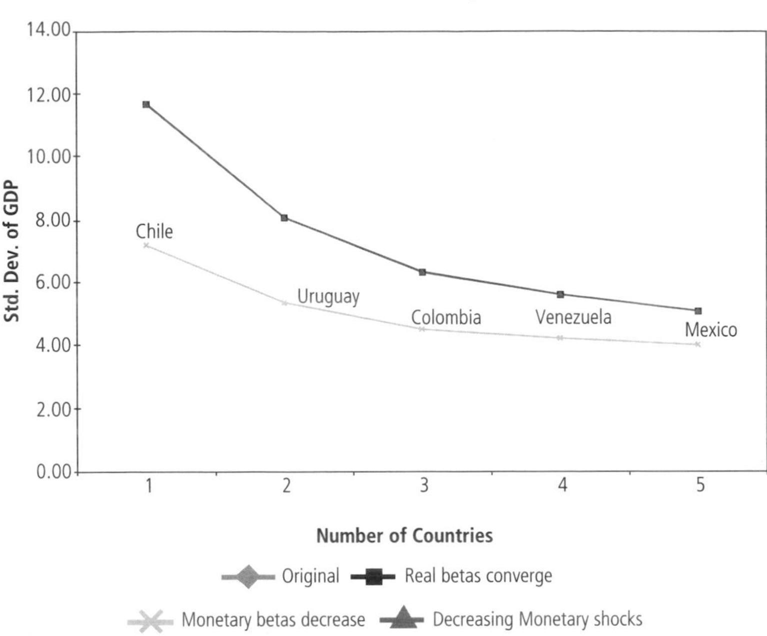

shocks along Chilean lines, then floating would become more attractive. In fact, we suggest that this result supports the view that greater emphasis should be placed on the governance structure of central banks. If a multinational central bank provides a way to enhance the independence and credibility of monetary policy, then the results here suggest that option would provide a significant boost to the attractiveness of a regional currency.

Conclusions

In this chapter we have developed a simple theoretical framework that might be thought of as a reduced form of the OCA conditions capable of being extended to an *n*-country world. The model combines a CAPM or factor approach with systemic and individual shocks, with the idea that for some sorts of shocks it is valuable to have exchange-rate flexibility (the real shocks) whereas for other (monetary) shocks flexibility may represent a cost.

A set of simulations shows the model in action. We illustrate how, by varying the parameters of the model, different cases can be analyzed and, perhaps most importantly, how one country's decisions

Figure 7.11 Chile: Endogenizing Betas and Reducing the Individual Monetary Shocks

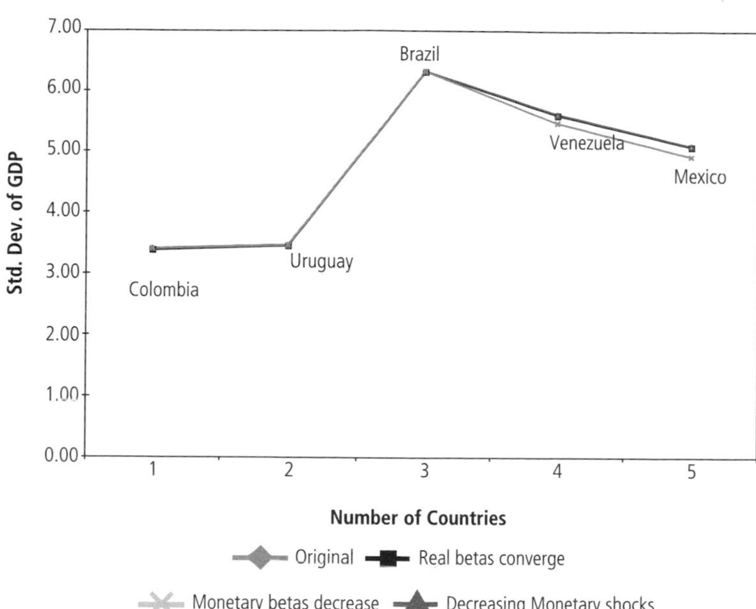

may impact on others' GDP volatility. Depending on parameter values, floating, a monetary union, or dollarization might be the best option for a particular country. Interestingly, as more countries join a currency union, there is a tradeoff between the diversification effect (diversifying individual monetary shocks) against a cost of including more countries with different sensitivities to the systemic real shock—the real betas. One possibility is that dollarization might be preferred to a small union but that a larger union with a greater diversification of the individual monetary shocks is most desirable. Depending on the technology of union formation, this might imply a coordination problem among countries.

We have also explored how, if trade and monetary integration affects the betas' coefficients, then a currency union may be more attractive. For example, if trade integration implies a convergence of the real betas and monetary integration implies a convergence of the monetary betas, the cost of a union is reduced. The advent of an FTAA might then be thought of as sparking greater trade integration and hence a convergence of the real betas in the context of our model.

Finally, we have conducted a first empirical exercise considering six countries in Latin America. Specifically, for Mexico, Brazil, and Chile we have compared dollarization to different country combinations in a currency union between the six countries to floating. The results, based strictly on these economic criteria, suggest that Brazil should prefer to dollarize, Mexico would like to have a union with Colombia and Chile, and Chile would prefer to have a union with Colombia and Uruguay but to exclude Mexico. If we are considering just currency unions, Brazil would prefer to include all six countries, but neither Chile nor Mexico would wish to include Brazil. For Chile, the gains of entering the preferred union over floating are small, whereas the gains for Mexico and especially Brazil from their preferred unions, (or dollarizing) are quite significant. The results then indicate the potential for significant conflict when it comes to exchange-rate arrangements in the region. This may be part of the reason little has happened regarding exchange-rate coordination.

Finally, we have investigated how these results might change if the beta coefficients converge to their average values for these countries as, for example, an FTAA is formed and a regional currency union is put in place. We also compute what would happen, perhaps as a result of the formation of a multi-national central bank, if the individual monetary shocks in Brazil, Mexico, and Venezuela (the high individual monetary shock countries of the group) are reduced. We find that the convergence of the betas leads to virtually no change in our results—it is just not quantitatively important. However, we find a very significant gain from the reduction in individual monetary shocks. We conclude therefore that when it comes to analyzing the potential costs and benefits of a regional currency union, the emphasis should be placed on the potential benefits of enhancing the governance structure of a multinational central bank that might increase monetary policy credibility and reduce the size of individual monetary shocks, whereas less emphasis should be placed on the costs of a lack of trade integration.

We consider this chapter to be a first attempt at applying this general theoretical framework to a practical example. We offer the results as suggestive rather than definitive, and hope that the theoretical ideas of how to model OCA conditions in a very simple way may provoke further interest in trying to pin down the real and monetary individual and systemic shocks and how they might be best estimated in practice. We believe the theoretical framework could be substantially developed and used to analyze a set of interesting questions in multi-country versions of OCA theory and in many practical applications.

Appendix Table 7.3 Model Parameters for Endogenizing the Betas

Parameter	Value	Countries	$\sigma = 0$		$\sigma = 0.2$		$\sigma = 0.5$		$\sigma = 1$	
			β^R	β^M	β^R	β^M	β^R	β^M	β^R	β^M
α	0.5	1	0.10	1	0.26	1	0.43	1	0.75	1
$\sigma_{\varepsilon_i^R}$	1.5	2	0.20	1	0.34	1	0.48	1	0.75	1
$\sigma_{\varepsilon_i^M}$	7.5	3	0.30	1	0.34	1	0.53	1	0.75	1
$\sigma_{\varepsilon_w^R}$	2	4	0.40	1	0.34	1	0.58	1	0.75	1
$\sigma_{\varepsilon_w^M}$	1	5	0.50	1	0.34	1	0.63	1	0.75	1
β_{US}^R	0.75	6	0.60	1	0.64	1	0.68	1	0.75	1
β_{US}^M	1	7	0.70	1	0.71	1	0.73	1	0.75	1
$\sigma_{\varepsilon_{US}^R}$	1	8	0.80	1	0.79	1	0.78	1	0.75	1
$\sigma_{\varepsilon_{US}^M}$	0	9	0.90	1	0.86	1	0.83	1	0.75	1

Appendix Table 7.4 Endogenous Betas and Reduced Individual Monetary Shocks

	Mexico		Brazil		Chile
	Original	Reduced Monetary Shock	Original	Reduced Monetary Shock	
α	0.5	0.5	0.5	0.5	0.5
β_i^R	0.20	0.20	0.37	0.37	0.45
β_i^M	0.39	0.39	0.31	0.31	0.17
$\sigma_{\varepsilon_i^R}$	3.36	3.36	3.20	3.20	3.23
$\sigma_{\varepsilon_i^M}$	16.44	23.47	38.95	68.50	9.41
$\sigma_{\varepsilon_w^R}$	1.86	1.86	1.86	1.86	1.86
$\sigma_{\varepsilon_w^M}$	9.47	9.47	9.47	9.47	9.47
β_{US}^R	0.25	0.25	0.25	0.25	0.25
β_{US}^M	0.31	0.31	0.31	0.31	0.31
$\sigma_{\varepsilon_{US}^R}$	1.86	1.86	1.86	1.86	1.86
$\sigma_{\varepsilon_{US}^M}$	9.47	9.47	9.47	9.47	9.47

References

Bayoumi, Tamim. 1994. "A Formal Theory of Optimum Currency Areas." International Monetary Fund Staff Papers 42: 537–54.

Bayoumi, Tamim. and Barry. Eichengreen. 1994. "Monetary and Exchange Rate Arrangements for NAFTA." *Journal of Development Economics* 43: 125–65.

Bean, Charles R. 1992. "Economic and Monetary Union in Europe." *Journal of Economic Perspectives* 6: 31–52.

Buiter, Willem. 1999. "Optimal Currency Areas: Why Does the Exchange Rate Matter?" Sixth Royal Bank of Scotland/Scottish Economic Society Annual Lecture, University of Cambridge. Photocopy.

Calvo, Guillermo. 2002. "Explaining Sudden Stop, Growth Collapse and BOP Crisis: The Case of Distortionary Output Taxes." Paper prepared for the Annual International Monetary Fund Research Conference, Mundell Fleming Lecture, November 7.

Carrera, Jorge, and Federico Sturzenegger. 2000. *Coordinación de políticas macroeconómicos en el mercosur*. Buenos Aires: Fondo de Cultura Económica.

Masson, Paul, and Mark P. Taylor.1994. "Optimal Currency Areas: A Fresh Look at the Traditional Criteria." In *Varieties of Monetary Reform*, edited by Pierre Siklos, pp. 23–44. Boston: Kluwer.

McKinnon, Ronald I. 1963. "Optimum Currency Areas." *American Economic Review* 53: 717–25.

Mundell, Robert A. 1961. "A Theory of Optimum Currency Areas." *American Economic Review* 51: 657–75.

Poole, William. 1970. "Optimal Choice of Monetary Policy Instruments in a Simple Stochastic Macromodel." *Quarterly Journal of Economics* 84: 197–216.

Willett, Thomas D. 1999. "The OCA Approach to Exchange Rate Regimes: A Perspective on Recent Developments." Paper presented at the conference "Should Canada and the U.S. Adopt a Common Currency?" Western Washington University, April 30.

Endnotes

We are grateful for comments from Guillermo Calvo, Ernestto Stein, Alan Taylor, Andrés Velasco, and participants at the brainstorming session in Cambridge, MA, and the "FTAA and Beyond: Prospects for Integration in the Americas" conference in Punta del Este, Uruguay.

1 See for example Bayoumi (1994) for a formal model of OCAs, Bayoumi and Eichengreen (1994) on OCA and Nafta, Bean (1992) on OCA and Europe, Buiter (1999) on OCA and the United Kingdom, and Masson and Taylor (1993) and Willett (1999) for more recent reviews.

2 See Carrera and Sturzenegger (2000).

3 We note that this set-up abstracts from the ever-growing list of "new considerations" that various authors have suggested should be included within OCA theory. Willett (1999) includes as (new) considerations "optimal public finance, the degree of international currency substitution, the new classical view of policy effectiveness, the informativeness of price and quantity signals, the controllability of the money supply, time inconsistency problems, and credibility issues.

4 As Buiter (1999) puts it, perhaps too strongly, "objections to UK (EMU membership) are based on the misapprehension that independent monetary policy, and the associated nominal exchange rate flexibility, can be used effectively to offset or even neutralize asymmetric shocks. This 'fine-tuning delusion' is compounded by a failure to understand that, under a high degree of international financial integration, market determined exchange rates are primarily a source of shocks and instability" (quoted from the abstract of the paper).

5 We note however that this assumes that the shock is exogenous to the exchange rate regime in place. We come back to these endogeneity issues below. We also assume balance-sheet effects are not too large.

6 In equation 13, we assume n is sufficiently large that terms of the order $(1/n)^2$ tend to zero. In other words, given independence of individual shocks the effect of the j countries' individual shocks are fully diversified.

7 Note that this equation combines the real shocks that directly hit i with the movement of the monetary union's currency given by the shocks to hit the member countries.

8 The anchor country is labeled the United States in the graph but we could equally think of it as Germany. In other words, fixing to the anchor would be adopting German monetary policy whereas in a monetary union the monetary policy reflects the shocks of the whole monetary area.

9 Of course, a similar argument could be made for dollarization—the betas of a country adopting the U.S. currency might converge to U.S. values.

10 The six countries are Brazil, Chile, Colombia, Mexico, Uruguay, and Venezuela. We do not include Argentina due to the fixed exchange rate during the period of analysis.

11 In contrast to other countries that have adopted inflation targeting, the central banks of Brazil and Mexico lack formal independence and specific legislation setting out their policy objectives. With a currency union, we might expect some institutional advances for the common central bank and less political interference in policy making.

12 While this is arbitrary, it seems reasonable as a way of capturing the potential credibility gain.

PART IV

Negotiating the FTAA Agreement: Traditional and New Issues

8

Prospects and Challenges for the Liberalization of Agricultural Trade in the Western Hemisphere

Mario Berrios, Jaime Granados, Marcos S. Jank, Josefina Monteagudo, and Masakazu Watanuki

Introduction

Since the establishment of the General Agreement on Tariffs and Trade (GATT), agriculture[1] has been the most controversial and slowest moving sector in trade negotiations. The heavy protection granted to the sector in the form of both tariff and nontariff barriers is typically associated with economic and strategic concerns such as price volatility (and hence farmers' income volatility), the importance of agricultural self-sufficiency, and the sociocultural value of preserving rural areas.

For most Western hemispheric countries agriculture is a sensitive, complex, and heterogeneous sector, and its relevance and meaning vary from country to country. Agricultural trade in the hemisphere totals US$200 billion and accounts for approximately 30 percent of the world's agricultural trade and 9 percent of total trade in this region. Overall, it absorbs a considerable portion of the economically active population, and represents a high percentage of GDP and exports. For small economies, for example for most of the Caribbean countries, this means a strong dependence on preferential or duty-free access agreements such as the Generalized System of Preferences (GSP) or the Lomé-Cotonou Agreements between the European Union (EU) and the African, Caribbean, and Pacific Group of States. The elimination of subsidies is a sensitive issue for the "net food importers" countries, since they depend heavily on low-cost food imports and consequently resist the elimination of export incentives in the developed world such as agricultural export and credit subsidies and food aid mechanisms. For medium-sized economies such as Brazil and Argentina, agriculture is a competitive sector with strong potential to generate trade surpluses. These countries can be expected to demand further liberalization. For large economies such as the EU, the United States, and Japan, agriculture is a politically sensitive sector due to the pressure that lobby groups exert on the lawmaking process. As a result, agriculture is a strategic issue for all American countries for both regional and multilateral trade negotiations.

Right now, Western Hemisphere countries are engaged in one of the most ambitious negotiations: the Free Trade Area of the Americas (FTAA). Agriculture is considered to be a pivotal component of this negotiation, since many countries believe that there will be an FTAA only if a strong agricultural package is agreed upon. Achieving a final balance will be a very difficult task because of the complex political and economical factors involved.

In this chapter we seek to address what we believe are the most important issues in agricultural trade negotiations while recognizing that other topics, such as biotechnology, are gaining in importance. As in many other papers of this nature, we do not address nontariff measures (NTMs), even though we fully acknowledge their importance and their impact on agricultural trade flows. The lack of accurate information on NTMs prevents us from factoring them into our analysis, making this an issue for further research. The chapter has been divided into four sections. The first section provides an overview of the structure and direction of agricultural trade within the Western Hemisphere (WH). The second section measures the level of tariff protection in agricultural products. The third section assesses the impact that the liberalization of intrahemispheric agricultural trade would have on Latin American and Caribbean (LAC) countries. Finally, the fourth section provides some reflections on the challenges faced by the agricultural sector in the Western Hemisphere.

Structure and Direction of Agricultural Trade in the Western Hemisphere

Although the importance of agriculture varies from country to country, this sector of the economy is very important throughout the hemisphere. In the LAC region, agriculture encompasses a sizable share of the GDP. In the developed countries of North America, its relative share is much smaller. While the agricultural GDP in the United States accounted for 1.2 percent in 1999, it accounted for 31.6

percent in Nicaragua and 29.2 percent in Paraguay. Furthermore, while the farm sector in the United States employs 2.1 percent of the labor force (World Bank 2001), it employs 46.1 percent in Guatemala and 34.4 percent in Paraguay. These statistics only reinforce the well-known existence of an inverse relationship between the size of the farm labor force of a country and the country's degree of economic development. A similar relationship exists for the importance of intra-WH agricultural trade for developed and developing countries in the region. Our results show that intra-WH agricultural trade accounted for only 6.2 percent of total U.S. trade, while it accounted for 36 percent in Paraguay and 28 percent in Guatemala.

This section provides an overview of the composition and structure of agricultural exchanges in the hemisphere. We assessed, from a dynamic perspective, the concentration and direction of both intra- and extra-hemispheric agricultural trade. Finally, we explored complementarity indexes in agricultural trade.

Composition of Agricultural Trade in the Western Hemisphere

We started identifying the major exporting and importing countries as well as the principal groups of products that were traded in the region in year 2000. The analysis was performed by aggregating all agricultural products at the six-digit level of the Harmonized System (HS) into a subset of forty-three groups. Then, we performed a more disaggregated analysis.

Trade Concentration

Figure 8.1 shows that intrahemispheric agricultural trade is highly concentrated in a homogeneous group of countries dominating both export and import activities. Specifically, eight of the top ten trading countries play a role as both top importers and top exporters. The United States is by far the most important trading country as both importer and exporter, accounting for almost 40 percent of the whole hemispheric trade in agricultural products. Canada, Mexico, Brazil (imports), and Argentina (exports) constitute a second group of principal traders. The third group is comprised of countries accounting for 5 percent of total U.S. intrahemispheric imports and exports.

Other countries that are not part of the top-ten group of traders also deserve special attention. These comprise two groups: net food exporters and net food importers.[2] In the first group, research results

Figure 8.1 Agricultural Trade in the Western Hemisphere: Top 10 Exporters and Importers (2000)

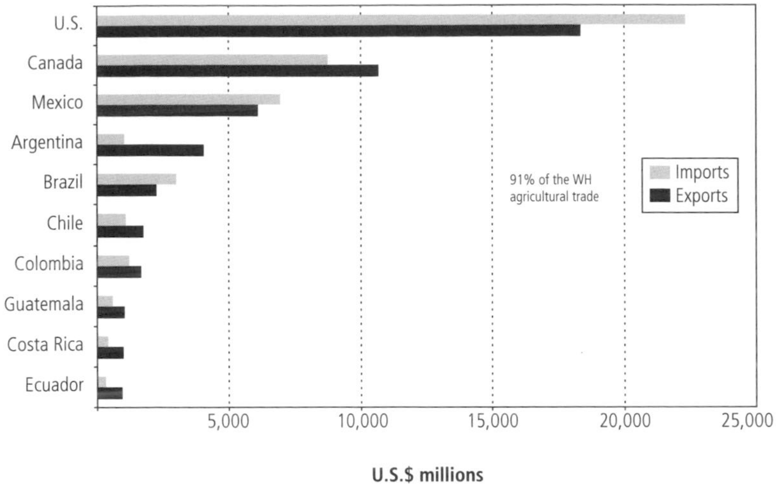

U.S.
Canada
Mexico
Argentina
Brazil
Chile
Colombia
Guatemala
Costa Rica
Ecuador
91% of the WH agricultural trade
Imports
Exports
5,000 10,000 15,000 20,000 25,000
U.S.$ millions

Source: Integration and Regional Programs Department (INT)–IDB calculations based on IDB (2001).

identify Argentina and Chile. The second group of countries includes St. Vincent, Peru, Dominican Republic, Grenada, Barbados, Dominica, Venezuela, and St. Kitts and Nevis. Experience reveals that the net exporters usually present a strong interest in the liberalization of agricultural trade. On the other hand, the net importers are more prone to develop different arguments concerning agricultural trade reforms, usually in relation to the treatment of agricultural export subsidies.

Key Features of the Composition of Intra-WH Agriculture Trade

The United States has been identified as the largest agricultural exporter and importer. At a commodity-specific level, grains (barley, maize, rice) and soybeans are its most exported commodities, and beverages and coffee its largest imports. Live animals and bovine meat are Canada's main agricultural exports, and processed grains and vegetables its principal agricultural imports. Vegetables and beverages are Mexico's top exports, while its main imports are grains (barley, maize, rice) and bovine meat. Product competition seems to be primarily concentrated in the grain and meat subsectors. At the aggregate level, 52 percent of intrahemispheric exchanges are concentrated in ten sectors, with grains (barley, maize, rice) accounting for 6.3 percent (US$3.2 billion) of agricultural intrahemispheric trade; beverages for 5.6 percent (US$2.9 billion); bovine meat and grains (wheat and malt) for 5.5 percent each (US$2.8 billion per sector); vegetables for 5.2 percent (US$2.7 billion); coffee and processed grains for 5 percent each (US$2.6 billion per sector); food preparation for 4.9 percent (US$2.5 billion); potatoes, tomatoes and onions for 4.5 percent (US$2.3 billion); and tropical fruits for 4 percent (US$2.1 billion).

On a product-specific basis (individual tariff lines), the main exchanged commodities in the WH are coffee (US$2.1 billion, 4.1 percent of the total hemispheric agricultural trade), maize (US$ 1.9 billion, 3.7 percent of the total), bovine meat (US$1.8 billion, 3.5 percent of the total), wheat and meslin (US$1.8 billion, 3.5 percent of the total), and live bovine animals (US$1.5 billion, 2.9 percent of the total).

Export Intensity Indexes in WH Agriculture Trade

Using the database developed by Feenstra (2000), we examined the dynamics of agricultural exchange and geographic bias in trade in the WH from 1980 to 1997. We used the export intensity indexes[3] proposed by Anderson and Norheim (1993). These indexes examine the evolution of the geographical concentration of trade and map out the structural factors that link the economies through trade agreements. We adjusted these export intensity indexes and developed an Agriculture Export Intensity Index (AEII). The AEII, defined here as the measurement of the degree of regional integration, is constructed as the ratio between the share of a country's agricultural exports to a region and the region's importance in terms of total world agricultural imports.

A unitary index indicates no geographical bias, meaning that the share of the country's agricultural exports to the region is the same as the share of the region's world agricultural imports. If the AEII is higher (lower) than one, then the country has higher (lower) bilateral trade than would be expected based on the partner's share in world trade. The empirical results are summarized in graphical terms.[4]

Figure 8.2 displays the results of calculations for extra- and intra-hemispheric agricultural export intensity of WH countries. In terms of extra-WH agricultural export intensity, WH agricultural exports with respect to the rest of the world gradually declined from an index of 0.85 in 1980 to 0.75 in 1997. This downward trend was observed during a period when no significant improvement occurred in terms of global market access conditions for agriculture goods.

Figure 8.2 Agricultural Export Intensity Index (AEII) in the Western Hemisphere

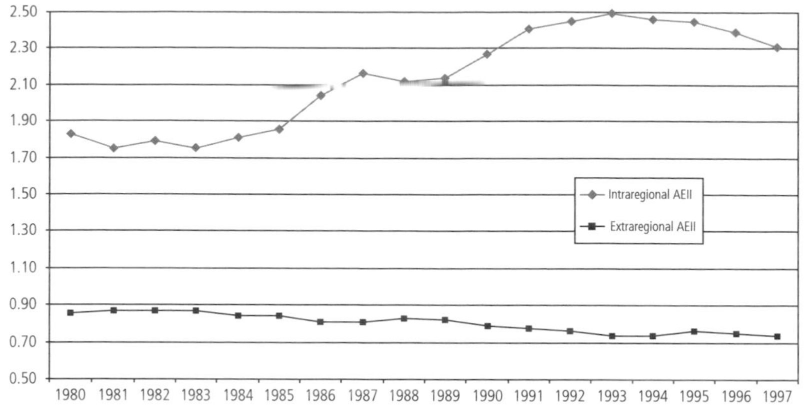

Source: INT-IDB calculations based on IDB (2001).

In an opposite direction, at the intraregional level, new regional trade agreements (RTAs) within the FTAA (i.e., NAFTA and MERCOSUR) did introduce important reforms with the goal of liberalizing most trade in agriculture. Also, previous agreements (i.e., the CACM and the Andean Community) either reactivated or renegotiated further measures to liberalize agricultural trade. We concluded that during the period studied, intrahemispheric agricultural exports increased moderately relative to a non–geographically biased concentration of trade.

Another exercise was conducted for specific RTAs within the WH. This exercise also showed export intensity values within regions greater than one. In addition, the value of the indexes increased in the 1980s and has either stabilized or further increased in recent years. This pattern was more evident among the RTAs between smaller and less developed countries. For example, calculations made for the year 1997 placed CARICOM with the highest level of intraregional trade concentration (AEII of 45), followed by CACM (27), the Andean Community (12), MERCOSUR (10), and NAFTA (3.5). In a longer-run perspective (1980–97), all regional groups presented an increasing AEII trend, with the exception of the CACM.[5]

Trade Complementarity

We explore now trade complementarity for the ten most traded products of the agricultural subsectors in the hemisphere. The methodology used follows Drysdale (1988) where complementarity indices reveal the extent to which one country's export pattern matches another country's commodity import pattern in relation to world trade on a sector basis.[6]

Under this type of analysis, a high specialization in two countries' exports and imports translates into an overall high complementarity in the sector. We would expect low complementarity between two countries that specialize in the exports of the same product groups since neither county would exhibit high import specialization in any of the products in that sector. In this framework, a complementarity index with a value greater than one thus suggests certain degree of similarity between the exports (supply) of country *i* and the imports (demand) of country (or region) *j*, relative to the world pattern of imports. A value close to zero implies a poor match between *i*'s exports and *j*'s imports. A value of the index close to one suggests that import and export specialization of both countries is similar to that of the world.

We should note that in this analytical framework we consider, as a by-product from the computation of complementarity indices, the export and import specialization indices. These indices measure the relative importance of each product in the subsector in regard to a country's exports or imports. Country specialization indices quantify the importance (of exports or imports) of each product within a sector with respect to the product's importance in the sector's world trade. An index greater than one means that, on average, the country under study is relatively more specialized in exporting (or importing) the specific product than all other exporters (or importers).

Using the COMTRADE database,[7] specialization indices were calculated for main exporting agricultural subsectors in the hemisphere (grains, beverages, bovine meat, vegetables, coffee, fruit, oilseeds, live animals, swine meat, and sweeteners). For the period 1991–2000, the empirical results reveal increasing complementarity in the following subsectors: grains (U.S. exports to NAFTA and to the hemisphere), bovine meat (Argentina's exports to the United States, MERCOSUR, and to the hemisphere), fruit (U.S. exports to NAFTA and to the hemisphere), oilseeds (Brazil's exports to the hemisphere) and sweeteners (U.S. exports to NAFTA and to the hemisphere).

To summarize the empirical results of agriculture trade complementarity, we classify the trends in complementarity as increasing (grains, bovine meat, fruits, oilseeds, sweeteners), stable (beverages, coffee) and declining (vegetables, oilseeds, live animals, pork meat) in the 1991–2000 period. The results suggest that: first, when increasing trade complementarity is observed it occurs mostly between the supplying country and its sub-regional and hemispheric markets; second, decreasing trade complementarity is more observed between the supplying country and the U.S. subregional and hemispheric markets; and third, oilseeds is the only product showing both an increasing complementarity between Brazilian supply and hemispheric demand and a decreasing complementarity between Brazilian supply and import demand from the U.S. and MERCOSUR countries.

Tariff Protection and Market Access in the Western Hemisphere

Despite the achievements of the (Uruguay Round Agreement on Agriculture) URAA, agriculture continues to be the most protected sector in the world economy.[8] Although ad valorem tariffs continue to be the main instrument for trade protection, agricultural products are unique in that they are also protected through specific and mixed tariffs, tariff rate quotas (TRQs), sanitary restrictions, domestic and export subsidies, and NTMs (price bands, licensing, standards, prohibitions, state trading enterprises, etc.). In this section various methods are used to measure the level of tariff protection in agricultural products. New indicators to evaluate tariff protection in bilateral trade and RTAs are introduced.

Comparative Tariff Structure

Overall, the average tariff on agricultural products in the WH is 16 percent.[9] With average tariffs of over 20 percent, Barbados, the Bahamas, Mexico, Dominica, the Dominican Republic, and Canada have the highest ad valorem equivalents (AVE).[10] Nicaragua, Chile, Guatemala, and Bolivia hold the lowest average tariffs—below 10 percent (see Appendix A, p. 288).

Comparing the mean and the median of a country's tariff schedule may provide more valuable insights into the agricultural trade policy of different countries. Most WH countries have close mean and median tariffs. MERCOSUR countries in particular have experienced a strong convergence in their agricultural tariffs. Their means are all near 12 percent, their medians are exactly 13 percent, and their standard deviations are about 6 percent. Andean countries have means and medians between 10 percent and 17 percent and dispersions below 6.5 percent. This shows that the whole agricultural sector has been encompassed in the late 1980s process of liberalization with no exception. Nevertheless, in countries such as the United States, Canada, and

Mexico, the median is far lower than the mean. This indicates the simultaneous presence of a large number of tariff lines far below the mean and a few tariff lines with very high rates (usually a very small group of politically sensitive products with tariffs above 50 percent), commonly called "tariff peaks."

Another important way to measure tariff protection is to consider the type of tariff applied. Tariff barriers in agriculture are based not only on ad valorem tariffs, but also on the extensive use of specific and mixed tariffs[11] and TRQs. NAFTA countries particularly stand out with their use of this kind of tariff. More than 43 percent of U.S. tariffs are non–ad valorem, followed by Canada with 27 percent and Mexico with 5 percent. Some Caribbean countries such as Antigua, Barbados, and the Bahamas also widely apply specific tariffs, resulting in higher protection according to the level of competitiveness of the exporting country. All other Latin American countries use only ad valorem tariffs, with the exceptions of El Salvador and Guatemala.

Measuring Tariff Protection for Sensitive Export Products

A country that mainly exports raw sugar and bananas is not interested in the overall level of tariffs imposed by another partner, but only in the tariffs imposed on its main exports. In fact, this country will concentrate on the additional access it can gain for its primary traded products through international negotiations. Statistical aggregates such as means, medians, and dispersions do not measure the real importance and levels of tariff protection on very specific and sensitive products.

Weighted averages are a good technique to capture the actual level of tariff protection, since these take into account the proportional relevance of sensitive products rather than treat all products equally. Given that our purpose is to measure trade protection, imports and exports could be used to weight the faced tariffs. However, using import values produces a downward bias because the imports of items facing high tariffs will have little weight, as these high tariffs are likely to create "trade-chilling" effects by restraining or even impeding trade. For example, even though the Brazilian sugar industry is very competitive, representing 57 percent of the WH total sugar exports, it only accounts for approximately 10 percent of U.S. total sugar imports because of the high above-quota tariff applied to sugar imports. Thus, weighted-average tariffs should depend on the importer tariffs and the composition of a country's total exports to the world (not the exports between partners). This approach emphasizes those tariffs in importing countries that are of greatest importance for exporting countries, and provides a dynamic view of the level of protection that each country imposes and faces with respect to its trading partners. Another advantage of this approach is that by using global export values, potential trade gains are incorporated, providing a more accurate picture of each country's relative competitiveness.[12]

Comparing Tariff Protection

In addition to the analysis of tariff barriers faced by agricultural products, the effects of trade liberalization preferential tariffs should also be taken into consideration.

Most-Favored-Nation versus Preferential Tariffs

During the last decade more than thirty bilateral and multilateral RTAs have been negotiated in the Western Hemisphere. These agreements have significantly increased trade between partners by providing preferential or duty-free access to a large portion of hemispheric trade. When these preferential agreements are taken into consideration a different picture of tariff protection emerges. For example, the U.S. average imposed tariff on its NAFTA partners, Canada and Mexico, is approximately 40 percent lower than its MFN average. It is also interesting to note that most of the so-called small economies—Caribbean and Central American countries—experience a significant decrease in the level of tariff protection because of the unilateral preferential access granted by the United States for the few commodities that make the bulk of their exports, such as coffee, cocoa, sugar, and bananas. This provides a striking example of how a reduction in the tariffs faced by a few sensitive products can significantly impact the overall level of tariff barriers faced by a country. However, in the case of many South American countries, preferential access does not notably decrease the overall agricultural tariff barriers (since these agreements do not provide access to sensitive products). The point is that using MFN rates to measure tariff protection may create, in some cases, an upward bias.

Evaluating Tariff Protection in a Bilateral Agreement: The Relative Tariff Ratio Index

The Relative Tariff Ratio Index (RTR), originally developed by Sandrey (2000) and further expanded by Wainio and Gibson (2002) and Gehlhar and Wainio (2002), is an index that measures the effects of trade liberalization in a bilateral negotiation. The index considers the bilateral protection between two countries, where each tariff line of country A is weighted by the total exports to the world for the same tariff line of country B, and vice versa. The index is constructed as the ratio between a country's faced tariffs in the numerator and its imposed tariffs in the denominator.[13] In general, a ratio close to one means that both countries have similar tariff protection, and thus face and impose comparable barriers. However, this does not reflect the levels of tariffs, only their relative ratios. A ratio of 3.9 between the US and Mexico means that for every percentage point that Mexico faces in the United States, the United States faces 3.9 points in Mexico (see Appendix B, p. 290). The main advantage of the RTR index is that it summarizes a large amount of trade-flow and tariff-level data into a concise number, which can be easily interpreted. Therefore it can be used as a practical tool to appraise progress in a free trade agreement and as a starting point to identify potential sectors on which negotiators should focus. A next step would be to calculate several years to capture trends, since one year may not be fully representative.

Evaluating Tariff Protection in a Regional Integration Agreement: the "Regional Export Sensitive Tariff" Index

Building on the RTR index, Jank, Fuchsloch, and Kutas (2002) propose an extension of this index at the regional level. The Regional Export Sensitive Tariff Index (REST) aggregates all tariffs faced and imposed by each country at the regional level into a single indicator, representing a ratio of the weighted value of those tariffs.[14] The index measures each country's faced tariffs from its partners weighted by its total exports in the numerator, and each country's imposed tariffs weighted by the total exports of all its partners in the denominator, calculated one by one, based on a potential RTA. Each combination of tariffs and share of export ratios for one country is weighted by the relative importance of total exports from the region in the case of faced tariffs, and total imports in the case of imposed tariffs. Both the RTR and the REST indexes can be used to gauge the concessions that each country would make relative to those it would receive in the event of the elimination of trade barriers. The advantage of the REST index is that it can go far beyond the bilateral level to address the important issue of liberalization at a regional or multilateral level.

However, the REST index has two important limitations, and is more of a pragmatic tool than an elegant academic measure. First, the REST index is based on tariffs and therefore does not take NTMs into account. Second, the index fails to incorporate the effects of elasticity and trade substitution that may occur once barriers decrease. It assumes that the totality of a country's sectoral exports will go uniformly to all its partners in the regional agreement. This is somewhat implausible, especially in the case of exports from big to small economies. However, the index is influenced largely by each country's sensitive exports to its most important partners, giving marginal importance to other products and countries. Thus, the REST index contrasts countries' competitive products with major trading partners' barriers.

In sum, the advantages presented by a practical and concise figure that provides a measurement for sensitive products tariff barriers in a regional agreement far outweigh any of the limitations mentioned. Therefore, the index could be used in negotiations to provide a valid and useful way to measure the "mercantilist progress" and "balanced concessions" that are behind most regional trade negotiations.

Finally, when RTAs already exist, preferential tariffs—or zero tariffs—have to be used to calculate the index. This is the case because existing RTAs have already created trade and thus MFN tariffs would induce bias in an index that is trying to gauge the level of distortion in trade flows produced by high tariff rates. Only trade data from non-MERCOSUR countries were used, for instance, to compute the Argentinean MFN REST in the WH. As a result the Argentinean MFN REST value measures the concessions that the country makes relative to those it receives while only taking into account the WH countries outside the MERCOSUR agreement. The same approach was used for the Andean Community, CACM, and NAFTA countries. It should be emphasized that such a concern does not exist when preferential tariffs are used to calculate the REST. So, when calculating the preferential REST for the Western Hemisphere, each country was weighted against all others in the hemisphere.

Figure 8.3 displays the faced tariff for agricultural products. Most countries experience a significant decrease in the regional agricultural tariff level when preferential agreements are taken into consideration. When considering MFN figures, Brazil's agricultural exports face the highest barriers in the hemisphere. Looking at preferential faced tariffs, it is interesting to note that the U.S. agricultural preferential faced tariff is actually higher than the MFN tariff. This is the case because the MFN calculations for "regional" tariffs do not take into consideration trade between existing RTA members (NAFTA members in this case). The preferential tariff ends up being higher because the United States still faces some protection on agricultural exports from other NAFTA members. It has been pointed out that the United States has provided relatively more access than it has gained from its NAFTA partners.

Our analysis of trade liberalization continues with the analysis of the results for the MFN and preferential REST index for the whole economy, industrial sector, and agriculture. Table 8.1 provides an easy visual interpretation in which REST index figures from 0.8 to 1.2 represent similar tariff protections and are depicted in bold. REST index

Table 8.1 Regional Export Sensitive Tariffs (REST) Index by Sectors in the Western Hemisphere (MFN and Preferential, HS-6, 2000)

	MFN			Preferential		
REST	All	Industrial	Agricultural	All	Industrial	Agricultural
MERCOSUR						
Argentina	**0.9**	0.4	1.2	0.7	0.3	**1.1**
Brazil	0.7	0.3	2.2	0.7	0.3	2.2
Paraguay	**0.9**	0.7	0.7	1.8	0.6	1.4
Uruguay	1.4	**0.9**	1.7	**1.1**	0.7	1.5
NAFTA						
Canada	1.7	4.2	0.5	0.4	13.3	0.3
Mexico	0.7	**0.9**	0.4	0.2	0.2	0.3
U.S.	1.4	3.6	0.7	3.2	11.7	2.5
Others						
Chile	**0.9**	**0.8**	1.7	**1.0**	**0.8**	1.9
Dom. Rep.	**1.1**	0.4	1.7	**1.0**	0.3	1.5
Panama	**1.0**	**1.1**	0.6	**0.9**	**1.0**	0.5
CACM						
Costa Rica	1.6	1.4	**0.8**	**1.2**	**1.2**	0.6
Guatemala	2.8	1.8	1.3	2.7	1.7	1.4
Honduras	**1.2**	**0.8**	0.6	**0.8**	0.5	0.5
Nicaragua	5.5	3.6	1.9	4.0	2.5	1.5
El Salvador	2.4	2.1	1.3	1.3	**0.9**	**1.1**
Andean						
Bolivia	**0.8**	0.7	**1.1**	**0.8**	0.7	**1.1**
Colombia	0.7	0.5	**0.8**	0.4	0.3	0.6
Ecuador	0.7	0.6	0.6	0.6	0.5	0.6
Peru	0.5	0.5	0.6	0.3	0.3	0.4
Venezuela	0.4	0.4	1.9	0.5	0.4	1.8
CARICOM	0.5	0.3	**0.9**	0.4	0.2	0.6

Source: INT-IDB calculations based on IDB (2001).

Figure 8.3 Agricultural Tariff Protection Faced by Countries in the Western Hemisphere (MFN and Preferential, HS-6, 2002)

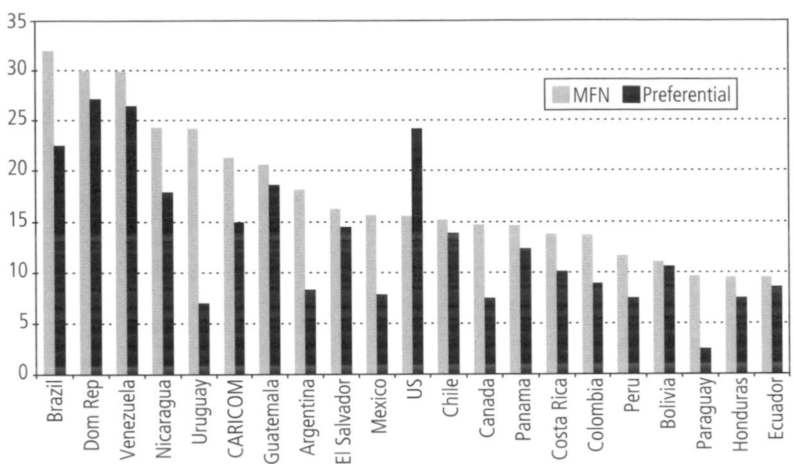

Source: INT-IDB calculations based on IDB (2001).

numbers above 1.2 characterize higher faced than imposed weighted tariffs, therefore indicating a protectionist reality that could be reversed (depicted in gray). When the index is below 0.8 it denotes lower faced than imposed tariffs, and therefore a country that would be a net liberalizer in that sector (symbolized in dark gray).

In general, a REST ratio close to one can be interpreted as an overall evenness between a country's tariff regime and that of its regional partners. Consequently, the objective of RTAs' negotiations could be to progress towards REST values that are close to one for all partners. This does not necessarily mean that all tariffs should be close to zero. It rather implies that countries will have equivalent access for their most sensitive products exports at the regional level.

Agricultural Sector

Figure 8.4 presents the calculation of the REST index for agricultural products using MFN and preferential tariffs. The figure shows very clearly that NAFTA, the Caribbean, and most Andean countries impose higher weighted MFN tariffs than they face in the WH (REST below one). The biggest face-off is Mexico and Canada, where high tariffs imposed on a very small group of key products are significant

Figure 8.4 Regional Export Sensitivity Tariffs (REST) Index for Agricultural Trade in the Western Hemisphere (HS6 2000)

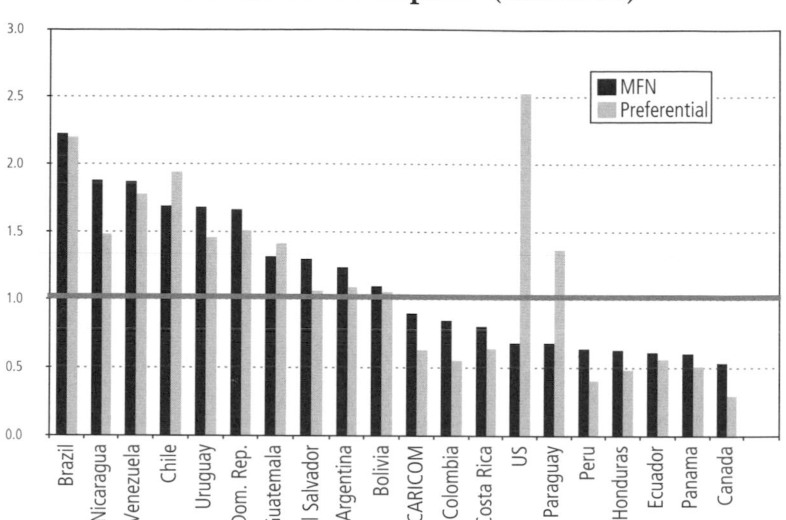

to potential FTAA partners. In other words, these countries are net liberalizers within the integration process in terms of agricultural tariff protection.

On the other hand, Chile and most MERCOSUR and Central American countries would obtain net gains in terms of agricultural market access. Brazil would rank first in this process above Uruguay, Chile, and Argentina as a result of the very high tariffs faced by Brazil's sensitive products such as sugar, orange juice and tobacco, especially in the United States. There are no major differences between the MFN and preferential REST figures for most countries other than the United States and Paraguay. In fact, as we have mentioned previously, the United States has provided more access in agriculture trade to its NAFTA partners than it has received. Paraguay's preferential REST index is higher because, while it has provided virtually free access to its MERCOSUR partners, it still encounters some tariff barriers.

In summary, it is important for all WH countries to consider the potential gains of balanced FTAA negotiations for the different sectors as well as the setbacks that they could face in the absence of this agreement. It is our opinion that the REST index has the potential to become a powerful tool to help negotiators understand the dynamics that underlie tariff barriers and trade flows for sensitive products in any regional or multilateral trade negotiation process.

Evaluating Agricultural Reform under an FTAA

In this section we evaluate the economic effects that a deep agricultural reform in the WH would have on LAC countries. We use an applied general equilibrium model. The model allows for the simulation of the effects on LAC countries of the elimination of three policy instruments that distort world prices and restrict agricultural trade flows: tariffs (ad valorem plus ad valorem-equivalent estimations), domestic support, and export subsidies. The effects of agricultural reform in the WH are measured as the difference between a full, sector-wide liberalization, and full liberalization that excludes agriculture. By completely eliminating the main barriers to trade in agriculture within the WH, the results also provide a measure of the costs LAC countries incur from protectionism in agriculture.

The Computable General Equilibrium Model

The model belongs to a class of multiregion, multisector, comparative static Computable General Equilibrium (CGE) models. All regions are fully endogenized and linked through trade.[15] The model deals with the real side of the economy and does not consider financial or monetary markets.

Our static CGE model extends beyond standard versions in three areas. First, it is widely acknowledged that a greater liberalization or the creation of RTAs has dynamic effects resulting from economies of scale, technical changes, technological spillovers, specialization, and increased investment. In order to capture some of these dynamic effects, we extend our model to consider trade-productivity links. Our second extension is the inclusion of economies of scale in manufacturing industries. Scale economies are modeled by introducing a fixed cost component in the cost function. Our third extension of the model is the inclusion of domestic farm programs in place in the Western Hemisphere. In addition to tariffs and export subsidies, we incorporate the producer support estimate (PSE) from the OECD. In the model, PSEs are modeled either as price wedges, which affect output decisions, or as lump-sum income transfers to farmers, which do not directly affect production decisions but which influence households' purchasing power.

Our model is constructed on the basis of the individual country or regional social accounting matrix for each region. The sectoral breakdown includes sixteen agriculture-related sectors comprising primary and processed foods and ten nonagricultural sectors.[16] The base year of the model is 1997. The rest of the model follows the standard trade-focused CGE models.[17] As with many static CGE models, our model does not capture capital accumulation, institutional changes, or other policies that often come along with liberalization reforms. The simulation results reported in this section should not be interpreted as actual forecasts of the reform effects, but rather as useful tools for identifying key issues, especially for the most affected and sensitive sectors.

Structure of Trade-Distorting Measures in the Model

The previous sections discussed agricultural trade and the protection measures applied in the region in some detail, and this section briefs the structure of agricultural protection used in our CGE model, which gives a crucial understanding of the simulation results.

With respect to tariffs, we focus on ad valorem tariffs as well as AVEs of specific and mixed tariffs and TRQs levied by Canada, the United States, and Mexico.[18] In terms of MFN ad valorem tariffs, processed foods are more protected than are primary agricultural products. Import-sensitive products are heavily protected, even though the degree of protection varies considerably across countries. Canada imposes very high tariffs on sensitive products such as dairy (133.4 percent) and poultry meat (66.2 percent). Although the United States has a low weighted-average tariff, it levies high protection on dairy products (22.2 percent), oilseeds and soybeans (19.3 percent), and beverages and tobaccos (17.6 percent). Mexico has the highest average tariff (26.4 percent), and imposes high tariffs on sugar (89.8 percent), poultry meat (68.3 percent), and wheat (76.0 percent). Central America and the Caribbean have the second highest MFN average tariff (18.2 percent). Chile has a uniform tariff rate of 11 percent. With a relatively high average protection (14.5 percent), the Andean Community has the second lowest protection deviation after Chile. MERCOSUR is still an incomplete customs union, as the applied MFN tariffs between Argentina and Brazil differ slightly. Besides MFN protection, the model incorporates the main preferential and trade agreements in place in the hemisphere.[19]

The model also incorporates agricultural domestic support measured by the OECD PSE.[20] Grains (including wheat and other cereal grains) receive the largest amount of support, accounting for over 64 percent of the total agricultural producer support in the United States and 79 percent in Mexico. Grains also record the highest domestic support rates (PSE rates)—wheat in Canada (14.9 percent) and the United States (34.2 percent), and other cereal grains in Mexico (23.7 percent).[21] Other agricultural sectors receiving sizable domestic support include oilseeds and soybeans (13 percent in the United States).

Finally, export subsidies are introduced into the model based on the WTO notifications in 1997. Most countries in the WH only provide export subsidies for a small group of selected agricultural products. The United States allocates almost all subsidies in dairy products with a subsidy rate of 15 percent.[22] The targeted sector in Mexico is sugar (33.1 percent), and in Central America and the Caribbean vegetables and fruits are the targeted sectors (5.8 percent). In the Andean Community, subsidy rates are marginal (less than 1 percent).

Policy Simulations

In order to evaluate the costs of trade-distorting policies in agriculture and the potential gains from their elimination for LAC countries, we quantify the effects of eliminating each of three policy instruments of agricultural support at the hemispheric level. A fourth simulation examines the cumulative effects of these reforms.

These policy shocks would generate different effects on the economy. In our first simulation, the elimination of tariffs reduces the price of imports and causes domestic firms to adjust the production technology along their production possibility frontiers. While tariff elimination reduces government tariff revenue, it raises household real income, as domestic commodity prices decline. Regarding domestic support, in our second simulation we consider two policy variables: fixed per-unit ad valorem subsidies to inputs and outputs, and lump-sum income transfer to farm households.[23] The elimination of the ad valorem subsidies directly raises the prices of domestic production, and this influences firms' or farmers' production decisions. On the other hand, the elimination of the lump-sum transfer causes household income to decline, but has no direct effect on prices. Both measures reduce government expenditures on firms and households. As domestic prices rise, household real income declines. Exports also decrease. The elimination of export subsidies in our third simulation removes price advantages to exporters. Domestic producers lose competitiveness in global markets, and exports decrease.

Results

In analyzing the effects of the reforms we mainly focus on exports. There are two major factors behind trade effects: the initial level of protection, especially in the United States, and the countries' initial trade linkages. The higher the initial protection and the smaller the trade linkage at benchmark, the larger will be the impact. The sixteen agricultural sectors are aggregated into two macrosectors: primary agriculture and processed foods.[24]

Experiment 1: Tariff Elimination

Tariff elimination increases agricultural exports from LAC countries to the Western Hemisphere by 11 percent. As processed food sectors are more protected than primary agriculture within the hemisphere, they enjoy a faster export growth of 15 percent compared to 7 percent. By product, LAC countries expand exports of poultry meat and beverages and tobaccos by more than 20 percent. Exports of sugar jump by 19 percent and oilseeds and soybeans by 16 percent. Wheat exports show the lowest growth rate (2.3 percent), followed by bovine animals (4.2 percent). Figure 8.5 presents the effects of agricultural reform on LAC exports to the hemisphere market by policy shock.

Figure 8.5 Impact of Hemispheric Agricultural Reform on Latin America's Exports to the Western Hemisphere (Percentage Change from Base Year)

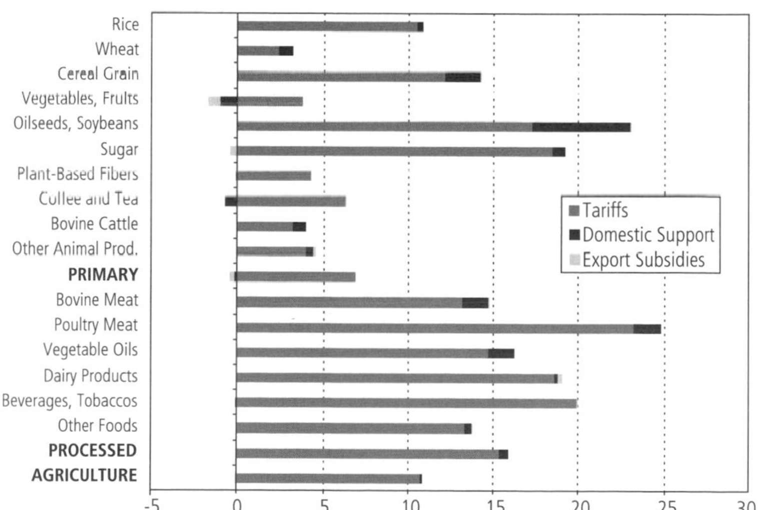

Source: Monteagudo and Watanuki (2002).

All countries in the hemisphere benefit from the creation of a hemispheric free trade area in agriculture. Brazil and Chile experience the largest export growth, largely due to the low initial market access to the United States. Central American/Caribbean and Andean countries, with preferential treatments in the United States, experience lower export growth rates of 9 percent and 8 percent respectively, and increased exports mainly to LAC markets. Mexico's exports, which already enjoy free access to its NAFTA partners, grow by 5 percent. The United States also benefits, as exports expand by 12 percent, mainly to non-NAFTA countries.

Figure 8.6 shows the impact on intrahemispheric exports of the agricultural reform by policy shock. In all countries, processed food industries enjoy booming exports relative to primary exports and to nonagricultural industries, which mostly decrease. Processed food exports grow by more than 15 percent in MERCOSUR countries and Chile. They increase by 12 percent in Central American/Caribbean countries and by 10 percent in Andean countries. Primary agricultural exports increase at slower rates, ranging from 3 percent in Mexico to 13 percent in Chile. The different growth dynamism across sectors leads to an export specialization toward agriculture—processed foods—at the cost of nonagricultural products. The intensity of this

Figure 8.6 Impact of the Hemispheric Agricultural Reform on Exports to the Western Hemisphere (Percentage Change from Base Year)

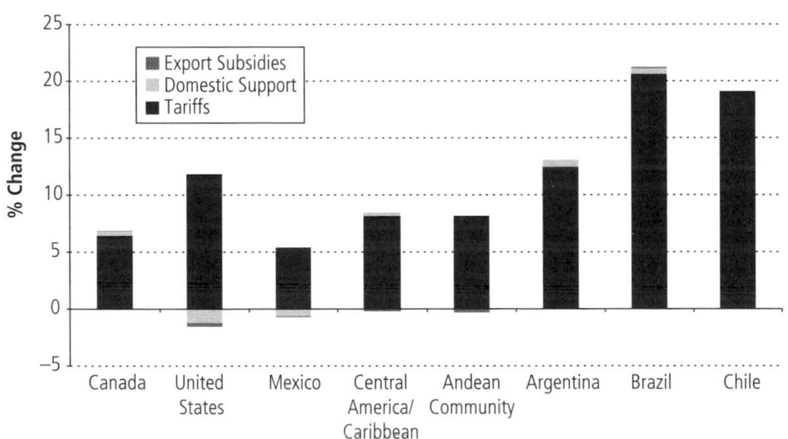

Source: Monteagudo and Watanuki (2002).

change varies across countries: Andean countries have the least uneven export composition shift among LAC countries, while MERCOSUR countries and Chile undergo the largest composition shift toward processed foods.

Experiment 2: Elimination of Domestic Support

The elimination of domestic support enhances LAC agricultural exports to the WH by only 0.15 percent, with a mixed impact of –0.2 percent for primary agriculture and 0.6 percent for processed foods. MERCOSUR countries benefit the most, with an increase in agricultural exports over 0.6 percent, while NAFTA countries, the users of domestic support in the WH, suffer a decline in total exports (–3 percent in the United States, –1.4 percent in Canada, and –0.6 percent in Mexico). For LAC countries, the most benefited sectors are oilseeds and soybeans, whose exports increase by 5 percent, followed by cereal grains (2.0 percent increase) and poultry meat (1.6 percent).

The simulation exercises show the nondiscriminatory effects associated with the elimination of domestic support, benefiting partners outside the agreement. In particular, the reform leads to an increase in U.S. wheat imports from the rest of the world by 40 percent, paddy rice by 15 percent, and oilseeds by 20 percent. Likewise, the EU also benefits from the nondiscriminatory effects, as its exports to NAFTA increase by 0.8 percent.

Experiment 3: Elimination of Export Subsidies

The elimination of export subsidies has a small negative impact on LAC exports. Due to the nondiscriminatory nature of the effects, nonuser LAC countries are not much affected, while exports from LAC users—Mexico, Central America and the Caribbean, and the Andean Community—decrease as domestic producers reduce exports along their supply curve in the face of declining domestic prices of exports. Exports of processed foods to the WH marginally increase (0.1 percent), whereas exports of primary agriculture decline by 0.3 percent. Exports of vegetables and fruits decline the most (0.8 percent), followed by sugar (-0.5 percent), while dairy products increase exports by a small 0.3 percent.

Although the region's exports as a whole are rarely affected, the impact varies by sector and by country or region. In Central America and the Caribbean, vegetable and fruits suffer an export decline of 3.6 percent. Similarly, in the Andean Community, sugar exports drop by 1.3 percent and vegetables and fruits by 1.2 percent. Total exports of dairy products from the United States and sugar in Mexico decrease by 6 percent; exports to the hemisphere decrease by 16 percent in both countries.

Experiment 4: Elimination of All Agricultural Protection and Support
The effects of the full agricultural reform in the WH are nearly the sum of the individual policy reform effects. Agricultural exports from LAC countries to the Western Hemisphere expand by 10.7 percent. Processed foods exports increase by 16 percent, a rate more than twice that of the primary goods exports. Among processed foods, poultry meat enjoys the highest export growth (25 percent), followed by beverages plus tobaccos (20 percent) and dairy products (19 percent). Among primary exports, oilseeds and soybeans expand the fastest (23 percent), followed by sugar (18 percent).

The reforms activate agricultural trade among blocs in the hemisphere. MERCOSUR increases exports to NAFTA by 22 percent and to the Andean Community by 32 percent. NAFTA and the Andean Community raise exports to MERCOSUR by 21 percent and 11 percent, respectively. Processed foods are the leading commodities traded between MERCOSUR and NAFTA, and exported from MERCOSUR to the Andean Community.

Effects on World Prices of Agricultural Products

Figure 8.7 shows the impact of the policy reforms on global agricultural prices. The elimination of tariffs leads to an average increase in global agricultural prices by a mere 0.3 percent. World prices for rice rise the most (0.5 percent), followed by cereal grains (0.4 percent) and sugar (0.4 percent). For most products, the elimination of domestic support more than doubles the increase in agricultural prices, compared to the tariff elimination scenario. Under this reform, prices for oilseeds and soybeans increase the most (2.9 percent), followed by wheat (2.2 percent) and cereal grains (1.6 percent). The elimination of export subsidies has almost no effect on world prices. The simultaneous elimination of all trade-distorting barriers in agriculture increases world prices by 0.5 percent. World prices of oilseeds and soybeans experience the highest growth (3.0 percent), followed by wheat (2.0 percent).

Implications of the Findings

The results show that the aggregate effects on LAC economies of agricultural reform are, on average, modest, although the impact differs

Figure 8.7 Impact of Hemispheric Agricultural Reform on Global Commodity Prices (Percentage Change from Base Year)

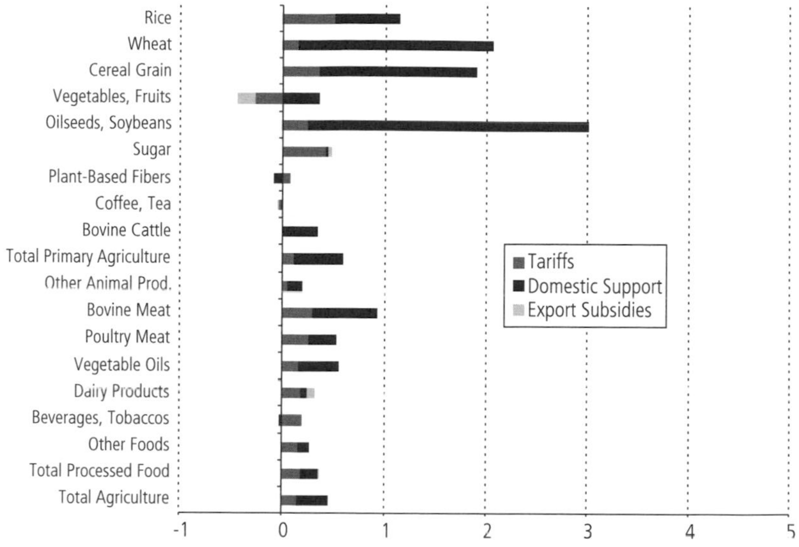

Source: Monteagudo and Watanuki (2002).

by partner and sector. The fact that tariffs are the protection measure more widely applied by all partners, together with their discriminatory nature, helps to explain why tariff elimination has a bigger impact on LAC countries than do the other two protection measures. The high protection of processed foods across countries induces a high export growth and export specialization in these products. Southern Cone countries, with low preferential access to the U.S. market and a strong competitiveness in processed foods relative to other LAC countries, benefit most.

While all members gain from agricultural reform in the hemisphere, the simulation results reveal a free-rider problem associated with the reform of domestic and export subsidies in the context of RTAs. The discriminatory nature of tariff elimination makes it a central issue to be negotiated at the regional level. However, the nondiscriminatory nature of the other two measures make negotiations more difficult at the regional level, as third parties outside the agreement will benefit equally from the reform. This indicates that domestic support and export subsidies seem to be pressing issues to discuss at the multilateral level.

Conclusions and Reflections

This chapter has provided evidence of an increasing degree of intrahemispheric agricultural trade concentration vis-à-vis trade with the rest of the world. As we first pointed out, the hemisphere has proved to be a more receptive and dynamic market for regional agricultural commodities during the last decade. Two key elements of these dynamics are unilateral liberalization and RTAs, which have improved market access conditions.

Trade in agriculture, however, is far from homogeneous across the hemisphere. On the contrary, the composition of hemispheric trade shows that only a few countries capture a very large portion of intrahemispheric trade and, likewise, only a handful of commodities make up most of that trade. Intrahemispheric trade to date also shows an important degree of complementarity. For purposes of further liberalization, this warrants two immediate observations: first, incorporating more commodities into these dynamics may bring considerable additional gains to trade and welfare, (our data proves this), but, second, achieving the required degree of openness may become a difficult internal political battle in many—perhaps all—of the countries of the hemisphere.

Even though agricultural trade policies have been the subject of trade reform during the last decade, many farmers are still shielded by high levels of tariff and nontariff protection. Despite excessive levels of tariff protection having been considerably eliminated, agricultural protection is still twice as high as industrial protection. The presence of very high peak tariffs in many countries poses a challenge for further liberalization. NTMs, by means of price bands, licensing, TRQs, arbitrary sanitary and phytosanitary measures, and other technical barriers hinder more trade from taking place. In addition, there is the widespread perception that export subsidies and other trade-distorting measures, including domestic support and other measures with an effect equivalent to export subsidies, may also be creating hurdles to freer trade.

The results of our analysis suggest that the most important challenge to further trade liberalization in the hemisphere is tariff protection. Many products of interest to LAC countries face high tariff levels in most of the hemisphere, predominantly in the large, rich and developed markets of the North. High tariff levels have particularly affected Brazilian and Argentinean exports.

With regard to trade liberalization, countries are now engaged in several processes. Countries are following a two-fold strategy including regional approaches (FTAA negotiations being the most important, albeit not the only one) and multilateral talks in the WTO. These two parallel initiatives provide countries with a unique opportunity more fully to exploit their individual natural comparative advantages.

Past agricultural negotiations have been complex. Ongoing negotiations face equally challenging tasks, and new and varied issues arise frequently. Since this chapter has focused on trade flows, protection, and the economic impact of liberalizing agriculture in the hemisphere, we summarize some of the most important future tasks for FTAA countries.

The WTO/FTAA Dilemma

Both regional and multilateral negotiations will discuss (at least) these three most important topics in agricultural negotiations: market access, export subsidies, and domestic support. Progress in each area might be subject to different dynamics, opportunities, and limitations.

Market Access

Our data show that the foremost trade barrier in the WH is tariff protection. The presence of specific and mixed tariffs, price bands, peaks, and tariff escalation impedes trade in agricultural products and a full realization of the natural comparative advantages of Latin America and some Caribbean countries. An FTAA is expected to eliminate tariffs on "substantially all trade" (as mandated by Article XXIV of GATT of 1994). Our trade concentration and tariff protection data allow us to induce that political problems are likely to arise only in a handful of products subject to high protection. Our figures suggest that under free trade conditions intrahemispheric agricultural exports are bound to rise considerably; however, NTMs can present an obstacle to these gains from tariff elimination. Although our study does not assess the impact of these practices, there is a stated commitment on behalf of the FTAA authorities to tackle this issue and eliminate nontariff barriers.

Experience in trade agreements signed recently in the hemisphere indicates that many sensitive agricultural products are subject to different types of special treatment, such as TRQs. Sensitive products typically have been subject to TRQs for a smoother transition to free trade. The size of in-quota quantities may increase while levels of the in-quota tariffs may decrease periodically. The viability of this instrument as a way of reaching agreement in sensitive agricultural products in an FTAA is an idea worth exploring. But the administration of TRQs around the world has posed problems for agricultural traders.[25] Countries have several ways of administering TRQs, leading to quota-rent issues and a lack of uniformity and transparency. Given the extensive use of TRQs in the multilateral context as a result of the tariffication commitments under the URAA, WTO countries are currently discussing the administration of TRQs. Hopefully, new disciplines for administering TRQs are expected as a result of this new round. This is to say that these multilateral endeavors with TRQs may be used as inputs for dealing with transitional TRQs that may be negotiated as a result of an FTAA.

In essence, an FTAA brings the promise of major changes in tariff policies for agricultural products. The largest economic benefits accrue from this process alone. NTMs may be regulated and kept under tighter control as a result of the FTAA negotiations. If TRQs are eventually used as a transitional measure, their administration may be subject to disciplines similar to those expected of the new multilateral negotiations in WTO.

Export Subsidies

Simulation results indicate that export subsidies are less of a problem in agricultural trade in the WH. Not only do they affect a small group of products, but also total amounts by country are relatively low. In addition, trade ministers stated in the San Jose Declaration (March 1998)[26] their clear intention of eliminating export subsidies that affect agricultural products in the WH. Likewise, in Toronto (1999), ministers agreed to work together in the context of the current multilateral negotiations to eliminate export subsidies worldwide.[27]

This seems to suggest that export subsidies are a policy instrument under control in the WH. There are two dimensions of the export subsidies, however, that pose challenges to negotiators. These are the issues of exports of subsidized products to non-FTAA countries and imports of subsidized products into FTAA markets from non-FTAA countries. The extraregional dimensions of these two issues very easily lead to the idea that they may be better dealt with under current multilateral negotiations. That may be so for the most part. Yet there are other factors in the hemisphere that should not be overlooked.

One is the fact that many countries demand assurances within the FTAA that imports from and exports to non-FTAA countries will not affect their ability to compete with their nonsubsidized goods. The other is that there are net food importers in the hemisphere for whom the idea of completely banning the possibility of sourcing food in cheaper, distorted international markets is something that must be carefully considered. Whether the economic repercussions for these countries are offset by agricultural trade creation is a question for further research. These two issues entail new political challenges, and for strategic reasons many countries have stated publicly that they are willing to move forward on them in the WTO context.[28] Trade ministers have also repeatedly stated their willingness to continue discussions on these issues in the context of FTAA.[29]

Domestic Support

Farm support and other trade-distorting domestic support measures are also important issues in any agricultural negotiation, and indeed have been some of the most difficult in both multilateral and hemispheric trade fora. Several countries in the hemisphere provide farm support,[30] yet no LAC countries provide the levels that the United States and Canada provide to their farmers.[31] Worldwide, very high levels of subsidization prevail and distort agricultural trade.[32] Our evidence leads us to believe that domestic support plays a limited role in the overall magnitude of agricultural trade: estimated free trade gains remain almost the same whether domestic support is phased out or not. This does not mean that reducing the trade-distorting effect of some types of domestic support is not economically and politically important for discrete sectors in certain countries. The approval of support measures for six additional years in the United States[33] in recent months only compounded the levels of discomfort in many Latin American and Caribbean countries. Some large countries have argued publicly that many of these issues are better dealt with in the WTO and other relevant fora than in the FTAA negotiating process. Yet again, trade ministers in the Western Hemisphere have recently restated their willingness to continue discussions on all measures that distort trade in agriculture, including measures that have an effect equivalent to export subsidies,[34] in the context of FTAA negotiations.

Other Distorting Measures in Trade of Agricultural Products

Many countries have addressed other policy instruments that may have trade-distorting effects on agricultural flows. Among those instruments are export tax differentials, state trading companies, food aid, export credits, export insurance credits and other export inducements. While our study does not address these specific instruments, other studies have found that many of them do have a distorting effect equivalent to that of export subsidies.[35] As evident in the chapter on agriculture in the FTAA draft agreement,[36] there is no agreement on these issues. Once again, some countries have stated their preference for discussing these issues in what they consider to be other "appropriate fora." Other countries, however, want a regional answer.

Unraveling the Spaghetti Bowl

One of the systemic challenges that the FTAA raises is how to streamline the so-called spaghetti bowl—the vast network of trade arrangements currently in effect or envisaged among countries of the WH. More than forty such agreements were negotiated during the last four decades.[37] This spaghetti bowl implies that negotiators have to figure out a way to integrate into the FTAA several tariff elimination programs, varying rules of origin, differing documentary requirements and standards, and so on.

Globalization Anxieties

The discussion thus far has failed to capture the animosity that takes place in every country where liberalization of trade in agricultural commodities is debated. Farmers are particularly effective at mobilizing public opinion worldwide. In fact, this is a sector whose lobbying efforts are almost always successful. In addition, many other sectors of civil society join farmers in expressing their concerns about, and outright opposition to, free trade in agricultural products. Countries face a tremendous political challenge on this front. Creativity is part of the answer to this challenge; mobilization of actual and potential winning sectors is another part. Many of the globalization anxieties will not vanish unless the agreement shows effective gains and opportunities for farmers, and unless governments implement adequate policies to support farming. We offer this chapter as a contribution to the former. The latter, however, is a daunting task, and falls beyond the scope of our study.

Coping with Asymmetries and Adjustment Costs

The size, economic, cultural, and political differences among FTAA countries create additional complications. Some of the salient features of the FTAA negotiations seek to level the playing field somewhat.[38] Negotiating in subregional groups first (CARICOM, CACM, MERCOSUR, and the Andean Community) is another strategy to increase the clout of LAC countries in these and other negotiations. Countries with smaller economies have tried to obtain concessions in their favor and so far they have succeeded to a considerable degree.[39] As stated by ministers in all FTAA declarations, it is likely that there will be a general recognition of these asymmetries. It is also likely that some countries will have to face the challenge of various adjustment costs, either fiscal or structural. Equally challenging is the fact that many LAC countries still have to stabilize their macroeconomic conditions and start implementing structural adjustment measures.

Some claim, correctly, that the FTAA process has already started to deliver some of these goods.[40] Moreover, ministries of trade approved in Quito (November 2002) the Hemispheric Cooperation Program.[41] At this stage, the Hemispheric Cooperation Program provides only an institutional umbrella for the development of specific projects financed by donor countries and international financial organizations. This is a good start, but concrete results are still to be seen. On a more optimistic note, an FTAA might have a catalytic effect, generating pressures to achieve better policy outcomes.

Appendix A: Table 8.2 Trade and Tariff Structure in Agriculture in the Western Hemisphere

Country	Trade Balance in US$ Thousands	# of Tariff Lines		Frequency Distribution of Tariff Rates					Main Statistics				
		Ad Val	Non Ad Val[a]	0%	0–15%	15–30%	30–50%	>50%	Mean	Median	St Dev	Max	TRQs
MERCOSUR													
Argentina	9,494,815	940	—	79	564	296	1	—	12.7	13.0	5.9	32.0	—
Brazil	8,050,652	940	—	79	565	296	—	—	12.6	13.0	5.8	27.0	4
Paraguay	302,221	945	—	79	576	286	4	—	12.3	13.0	5.6	30.0	—
Uruguay	579,329	908	—	77	552	279	—	—	12.4	13.0	5.6	23.0	—
NAFTA													
Mexico	(2,101,401)	1,016	53	30	496	427	62	54	23.3	15.0	37.8	260.0	68
Canada	4,142,472	979	362	538	656	46	3	98	22.4	3.0	63.1	538.0	123
U.S.	14,237,485	989	747	372	1,083	161	59	61	11.4	3.7	32.0	350.0	376
Andean Comm.													
Bolivia	169,664	873	—	15	858	—	—	—	9.8	10.0	1.3	10.0	0
Colombia	1,441,657	881	—	—	280	601	—	—	14.5	15.0	5.5	20.0	66
Ecuador	1,117,100	865	—	20	268	577	—	—	14.3	15.0	5.7	20.0	21
Peru	(258,173)	900	—	—	530	314	56	—	17.1	12.0	6.5	30.0	0
Venezuela	(1,309,192)	865	—	—	278	591	—	—	14.6	15.0	5.4	20.0	59
CACM													
Costa Rica	1,241,539	1,138	—	238	796	—	64	40	13.8	14.0	20.0	162.0	73
Guatemala	919,306	811	60	208	215	388	—	—	9.2	10.0	6.5	20.0	31
Honduras	98,404	869	—	—	425	426	13	5	11.5	15.0	8.4	55.0	0
Nicaragua	141,281	869	—	197	638	18	7	9	7.3	10.0	7.4	76.7	17
El Salvador	(90,269)	937	25	217	217	429	49	—	11.2	15.0	8.9	40.0	37

Continued on next page

Appendix A: Table 8.2 Trade and Tariff Structure in Agriculture in the Western Hemisphere, continued

Country	Trade Balance in US$ Thousands	# of Tariff Lines: Ad Val	Non Ad Val[a]	Frequency Distribution of Tariff Rates: 0%	0–15%	15–30%	30–50%	>50%	Main Statistics: Mean	Median	St Dev	Max	TRQs
Others													
Chile	1,567,390	747	—	—	747	—	—	—	9.0	9.0	—	9.0	0
Dominican Republic	(327,892)	778	—	—	229	277	272	—	21.2	25.0	10.6	35.0	0
Panama	(67,856)	1,334	—	67	455	723	48	41	15.0	15.0	20.8	300.0	57
Caribbean Community													
Antigua and Barbuda	(73,457)	999	19	218	246	208	327	—	17.3	20.0	14.7	45.0	0
Trinidad and Tobago	(49,375)	1,000	24	389	80	245	284	2	16.6	15.0	16.7	75.0	0
St. Lucia	(43,929)	1,024	—	285	238	173	328	—	16.5	10.0	16.0	45.0	0
St. Kitts and Nevis	(27,211)	998	22	257	257	120	364	—	17.5	10.0	16.3	40.0	0
Jamaica	(133,611)	1,021	—	410	61	224	321	5	17.2	15.0	17.0	75.0	0
Grenada	(19,639)	1,015	1	120	351	219	324	—	18.2	15.0	15.1	40.0	0
Dominica	(8,666)	579	439	159	55	78	287	—	22.7	25.0	17.9	45.0	0
Barbados	(94,877)	886	27	—	349	194	246	97	36.6	20.0	51.6	243.0	37
Bahamas	(615,499)	676	—	152	788	—	—	3	25.4	30.0	17.6	260.0	0
St. Vincent	(4,874)	1,007	13	117	392	228	270	—	17.0	10.0	15.0	40.0	0
Sum or Average	38,277,394	926	60	144	442	261	113	14	16.0	14.1	15.4	98.9	9[illegible]9
EU-15	(4,625,098)	1,227	852	845	505	513	136	80	18.3	11.5	24.5	251.6	2[illegible]6

Sources: IDB-INT calculations based on IDB (2001).
[a]Non–ad valorem = sum of all specific and mixed rates.

Appendix B: Table 8.3 US MFN and Preferential RTR Index for Western Hemisphere Countries (HS-6, 2000)

	MFN Tariffs			Preferential Tariffs		
RTR	All	Agr	Ind	All	Agr	Ind
Argentina	1.5	0.8	4	1.8	0.8	9.8
Brazil	1.5	0.4	5	1.8	0.4	14.3
Paraguay	1.4	1.5	2	1.6	1.5	8.9
Uruguay	0.8	0.5	2	1	0.6	5.1
Canada	1.7	2.9	1.1	4.6	3.5	—
Mexico	3.9	4.2	3.6	9.2	3.5	16.5
Chile	3.2	1.1	5.4	4.2	1.1	9.6
Dom Rep	1	0.6	4	1.2	0.7	12.9
Panama	1.6	2.1	3.4	2.7	3.3	10.2
Costa Rica	0.8	1.5	1.2	1.7	2.3	5.5
Guatemala	0.4	0.8	1.2	0.5	1	5.7
Honduras	1.1	2	2.5	1.9	2.9	8.4
Nicaragua	0.2	0.5	1.3	0.2	0.5	14.4
El Salvador	0.6	1	0.7	0.8	1.1	2.1
Bolivia	2.3	1.2	5	6.5	2.1	—
Colombia	2.3	1.6	3	8.2	2.8	—
Ecuador	1.7	2.4	2	13.6	9	—
Peru	2.9	1.9	3	39.1	5.3	—
Venezuela	4	0.5	4.4	4.4	0.5	4.8
CARICOM	2.5	1.1	5.4	4.4	1.7	14.9
EU	1.1	0.9	1	1.1	0.9	1

Sources: IDB-INT calculations based on IDB (2001).
Note: Canada's imposed tariff is equal to zero, so the RTR index approaches infinity.

References

Agricultural Market Access Database. 2001. Release 2.0 (Fall/Winter), http://www.amad.org/.

Anderson, Kym, and Hege Norheim. 1993. "Is World Trade Becoming More Regionalized?" *Review of International Economics* 2 (1): 91–109.

Berrios, Mario. Forthcoming. *Composition and Direction of Agricultural Trade in the Western Hemisphere.* Washington, D.C.: Inter-American Development Bank.

Drysdale, Peter. 1988. *International Economic Pluralism: Economic Policy in East Asia and the Pacific.* New York: Columbia University Press.

Feenstra, Robert. 2000. "World Trade Flows, 1980–1997, with Production and Tariff Data." University of California Davis. Photocopy.

Gehlhar, Mark, and John Wainio. 2002. "A Reevaluation of Processed Food Tariffs Facing Exporters: Implications for Liberalization." Paper prepared for the Fifth Annual Conference on Global Economic Analysis, June 5–7, Taipei, Taiwan.

Gibson, Paul, John Wainio, Daniel Whitley, and Mary Bohman. 2001. "Profiles of Tariffs in Global Agricultural Markets." Agricultural Economic Report no. 796, Economic Research Service, United States Department of Agriculture (January).

Granados, Jaime. 2002. "Ecuador en las negociaciones de acceso a mercado del ALCA." In *ALCA: Riesgos y oportunidades para el sector productivo ecuatoriano*. Quito: CORDES.

Hertel, Thomas. 1997. *Global Trade Analysis: Modeling and Applications.* Cambridge: Cambridge University Press.

Iglesias, Enrique. 2000. "Statement at the Fifth Meeting of FTAA Ministers Responsible for Trade." Toronto, Canada, November 1999. Inter-American Development Bank, Economic Commission for Latin America and the Caribbean, and Organization of American States.

Inter-American Development Bank (IDB). 2000. Hemispheric Trade and Tariff Database. Version 2000.

———. 2001. Hemispheric Database, Free Trade Area of the Americas. Version 1.0e.

International Agricultural Trade Research Consortium. 2000. "Issues in Reforming Tariff-Rate Imports Quotas in the Agreement on Agriculture in the WTO." Commissioned Paper no. 13. http://agecon.lib.umn.edu/.

Jank, Marcos S., Ian Fuchsloch, and Géraldine Kutas. 2002. "Agricultural Liberalization in Multilateral and Regional Trade Negotiations." Paper presented at the seminar "Agricultural Liberalization and Integration: What to Expect from the FTAA and the WTO?" Special Initiative on Integration and Trade, Integration and Regional Programs Department, Inter-American Development Bank, Washington, DC, October.

Monteagudo, Josefina, and Masakazu Watanuki. 2002. "Evaluation of the Potential Effects of Agricultural Reform in Regional Negotiations: FTAA and MERCOSUR-EU Agreement." Paper presented at the seminar "Agricultural Liberalization and Integration: What to Expect from the FTAA and the WTO?" Special Initiative on Integration and Trade, Integration and Regional Programs Department, Inter-American Development Bank, Washington, DC, October.

Organization for Economic Cooperation and Development (OECD). 2001. *State Trading Enterprises in Agriculture.* Paris.

———. 2002. *Agricultural Policies in the OECD Countries: Monitoring and Evaluation.* Paris.

Sandrey, Ron. 2000. "The Relative Tariff Ratio Index." Working Paper no.7, New Zealand Trade Consortium.

Thompson, Wyatt. 2001. *An Analysis of Officially Supported Export Credits in Agriculture.* Paris: Organization for Economic Cooperation and Development.

Wainio, John, and Paul Gibson. 2001. "U.S. Exports Face High Tariffs in some Key Markets, USDA/ERS." *Food Review* 3 (24): 29–39.

———. 2002. Market Access: "Tariff Reform within the Free Trade Area of the Americas (FTAA)." Economic Research Service, United States Department of Agriculture, Washington, DC.

World Trade Organization. 1995. "The Results of the Uruguay Round of Multilateral Trade Negotiations, The Legal Texts. Member's Notifications and Member's Trade Policy Reviews." Geneva.

World Bank. 2001. *World Development Indicators.* Washington, DC.

Notes

The authors acknowledge the assistance of Ian Fuchsloch, Reuben Kline, Géraldine Kutas, Luis San Vicente, and Henry Vega.

1 The definition of agriculture used in this chapter follows the definition provided by the World Trade Organization (WTO) in the URAA.

2 Net food importers/exporters are those countries whose agricultural imports/exports represent at least 70 percent of their agricultural trade.

3 The export intensity index of country *i* with country *j* is defined as:

$$IX_{ij} = \frac{X_{ij} / X_i}{M_j / (WM - M_i)}$$

where: $X_{i,j}$ = exports of country *i* to *j*, X_i = total exports from country *i*, M_j = total imports by country *j*, WM = total world imports, and M_i = total imports by country *i*.

4 Since we computed the intensity index for trading groups, the formula was slightly adjusted to avoid double counting of exports and imports among partners (see Anderson and Norheim 1993). For a full account of numerical results see Berrios (2003).

5 The AEII declined 1.3 percent during the sample period; nonetheless, it is the second most highly concentrated RTA.

6 Following Drysdale (1988), the complementarity index of a given sector between two countries (C_{jk}) is defined as the sum across the sector's commodities ($k = 1, \ldots, n$) of the product of country *i*'s export specialization index (R_{ik}) times country or region *j*'s import specialization index of

commodity k (D_{jk}), weighted by the share of commodity k in the sector's world imports.

$$R_{ik} = \frac{x_{ik} / x_i}{T_k / T}$$

where, x_{ik} : i's exports of k; x_i : i's total sector exports; T_k : world imports of k; T: total sector world imports.

$$D_{jk} = \frac{m_{jk} / m_j}{T_k / T}$$

where, m_{jk} is j's imports of k; m_j is j's total sector imports.

Thus, $C_{ij} = \sum_{k}^{n} \left(R_{ik} \cdot D_{jk} \cdot \frac{T_k}{T} \right)$

7 The COMTRADE database includes information for over 130 countries, some of which have been reporting exports and imports by commodity and partner country to the United Nations since 1962. The data are recorded according to six internationally recognized trade and tariff classifications.

8 Gibson et al. (2001) estimate that the simple global average for most-favored-nation (MFN) bound tariff on agricultural imports will exceed 60 percent even after all the cuts that countries carry out through the URAA.

9 The data used in this section correspond to year 2000 from the Agricultural Market Access Database (2001).

10 The methodology followed in this study to convert specific and mixed tariffs into AVEs was to divide the product's specific rate by its import price. In this case the price was calculated by dividing the value of imports by the quantity of imports. Where no trade data were available, the price of the closest related product was used.

11 Specific tariffs are calculated as a percentage or a fixed amount per volume units (i.e., kilograms), and consequently result in higher protection levels the more competitive the exporting country (lower import prices result in higher ad valorem equivalents). As a result of the "tariffication" effort of the URAA, many products that used to be protected with import quotas are now protected through TRQs. In this case, lower "within-access commitment" rates are set for specified quantities, and higher "over-access commitment" rates are set for quantities that exceed

the quota. The in-quota tariff would be the tariff rate up to the quota limit, and the over-quota tariff is the higher duty rate.

12 To calculate the weighted average tariffs, each country's tariff lines and trade flow data were aggregated according to the HS at the six-digit level. The over-quota tariff rate was used when TRQ tariffs were aggregated at the six-digit level. Wainio and Gibson (2001) have stressed that TRQs do, in most cases, represent a binding constraint on additional trade. As such, over-quota rates give a more accurate account of the level of protection provided by the tariff schedule and should be used to reflect the overall restrictive nature of a country's trade policy. However, it should be noted that this might overestimate the impact of TRQs in cases in which in-quota rates are not 100 percent utilized for a product. Nevertheless, any approach entails some kind of bias: using the simple mean underestimates while using maximum overestimates the effect of TRQs.

13

$$RTR_{AB} = \frac{\sum_{i}^{n}\left(X_i^B \cdot Y_i^A\right)}{\sum_{i}^{n}\left(X_i^A \cdot Y_i^B\right)}$$

Where A, B = Countries A and B; X_i= AVE tariff rate for product i; and Y_i = share of exports of product i in total exports.

14

$$REST_A = \frac{\sum_{R \neq A}^{N}\left\{\left(X_R^A / X_T^A\right)\sum_{i=1}^{n} x_i^R \cdot y_i^A\right\}}{\sum_{R \neq A}^{N}\left\{\left(M_R^A / M_T^A\right)\sum_{i=1}^{n} x_i^A \cdot y_i^R\right\}}$$

Where $A, B, C, \ldots, N$ = member countries of an RTA and R is any country; x_i^A = maximum ad valorem equivalent tariff rate at HS-96 level for tariff line i in country A; y_i^A = share of exports of i in total exports; M_R^A = country A's total imports from country R; M_T^A = country A's total imports from all RTA countries; X_R^A = country A's total exports to country R; and X_T^A = country A's total exports to all RTA countries.

15 The model includes ten regions: Canada, the United States, Mexico, Central America and the Caribbean, the Andean Community, Argentina, Brazil, Chile, the EU, and the rest of the world.

16 The sixteen agricultural sectors are: grains, wheat, cereal grains, vegetables and fruits, oilseeds and soybeans, sugar, plant-based fibers, coffee and tea, bovine cattle, other animal products, bovine meat, poultry

meat, vegetable oils, dairy products, beverages and tobaccos, and other food products. Sectors are based on the Global Trade Analysis Project (GTAP) classification, 1997 dataset, version 5.0, as described in Hertel (1997).

17 For more detail on the model structure, refer to Monteagudo and Watanuki (2002).

18 For single countries, the MFN ad valorem tariff equivalents are estimated as simple averages of the tariff line schedules in each sector. For regional blocs, they are estimated as simple averages of the tariff lines across countries. Tariffs are estimated on the basis of the eight-digit tariff line schedule of the HS.

19 Our calculations are based on IDB (2000). We include six RTAs: NAFTA, CACM, CARICOM, the Andean Community, MERCOSUR, Grupo de los Tres (Mexico, Colombia, and Venezuela); three bilateral agreements: MERCOSUR-Chile, Canada-Chile, and Mexico-Chile; and four unilateral preferential arrangements: three U.S. arrangements (the Generalized System of Preferences; the Andean Trade Preference Act; and the Caribbean Basin Initiative) and Canada's preferential arrangement (the General Preferential Tariff).

20 Based on availability of data from OECD sources, in the Western Hemisphere only Canada, the United States, and Mexico apply domestic support.

21 The domestic support rate is the amount of domestic support divided by sectoral production value.

22 This is measured by the total amount of export subsidies received by each product over exports value of that product.

23 Because the model uses fixed input-output coefficients for intermediate inputs, the elimination of input and output subsidies works the same way.

24 Primary agriculture includes grain, wheat, cereal grains, vegetables and fruits, oilseeds and soybeans, sugar, plant-based fibers, coffee and tea, bovine cattle, and other animal products. Processed foods include bovine meat, poultry meat, vegetable oils, dairy products, beverages and tobaccos, and other food products.

25 See International Agricultural Trade Research Consortium (2000).

26 See San Jose Ministerial Declaration, March 1998, Annex II.

27 See Toronto Ministerial Declaration, November 1999, paragraph 21.

28 See, for instance, Canada's position at www.dfait-maeci.gc.ca.

29 See Buenos Aires and Quito Trade Ministerial Declarations, Annex I in both cases.

30 According to the WTO Agreement on Agriculture, the following countries have bound commitments on domestic support: Argentina, Brazil, Canada, Colombia, Costa Rica, Mexico, the United States, and Venezuela (see WTO 1995).

31 Recently Mexico has also increased the amount of support to farmers (see OECD 2002).

32 OECD (2002).

33 The U.S. Farm Security and Rural Investment Act of 2002.

34 See Buenos Aires and Quito Trade Ministerial Declarations, Annex 1, paragraphs B and 15, respectively.

35 See, for instance, OECD (2001) and Thompson (2001).

36 See the new Draft FTAA Agreement, www.ftaa-alca.com.

37 For a thorough discussion, see Chapter 13 in this volume and Granados (2002).

38 Decisions are by consensus; the negotiations are a single undertaking; the Tripartite Committee (composed of the Inter-American Development Bank, the United Nations Economic Commission for Latin America and the Caribbean, and the Organization of American States) provides impartial technical support to the FTAA process and technical assistance to smaller countries, etc.

39 All of the FTAA Ministerial Declarations and derestricted documents provide a clear indication of how proactive smaller economies have been in promoting their particular interests. See the FTAA website at www.ftaa-alca.com.

40 Statement made by Enrique Iglesias at the Fifth Meeting of FTAA Ministers Responsible for Trade. Toronto, Canada, November 1999.

41 See Quito Ministerial Declaration, Annex 1.

9

Regionalism and Trade in Services in the Western Hemisphere: A Policy Agenda

Aaditya Mattoo and Pierre Sauvé

Introduction

While a large literature has investigated the costs and benefits of integration agreements for trade in goods, hardly any analysis exists of the implications of such agreements for services.[1] Such a gap is surprising given the strong growth over the last decade and a half in the number of regional trade agreements featuring detailed disciplines on trade and investment in services. The recent proliferation of trade agreements covering services offers tangible proof of heightened policy interest in the contribution of efficient service sectors to economic growth and development and of a growing appreciation of the gains likely to flow from the progressive dismantling of impediments to trade and investment in services.

Regional attempts at developing trade rules for services have paralleled efforts at framing similar disciplines in the World Trade Organization (WTO) under the aegis of the General Agreement on Trade in Services (GATS). Because they typically have been negotiated in a concurrent fashion, regional and multilateral efforts at services rule making have tended to be closely intertwined processes, with much iterative learning by doing, imitation, or reverse engineering. Experience gained in developing the services provisions of regional trade agreements (RTAs) has built up significant negotiating capacity in participating countries, providing expertise available for deployment in a multilateral setting.

The proliferation of regional initiatives has provided governments with significant policy space in which to experiment with various approaches to rule making and market opening in the area of services trade. In particular, the regional route has afforded governments the ability to pursue policy approaches differing from those emerging from the incipient multilateral framework under the GATS. Because the GATS itself remains incomplete, with negotiations pending in a number of key areas (e.g., emergency safeguards, subsidies, government procurement, domestic regulation), such regional experimentation has generated a number of useful policy lessons in comparative negotiating and rule-making dynamics.

Countries in the Western Hemisphere have devoted considerable effort in recent years to developing, both in the FTAA negotiations per se but also in the context of several concurrent (and at times partly overlapping) integration agreements, rules aimed at governing the process of services trade liberalization in the region. Such efforts have come in the wake of far-reaching changes in many countries' services and investment policy frameworks over the last decade. For many countries in the hemisphere, the FTAA negotiations offer the opportunity to pursue, deepen, or lock in some (or much) of the policy virtue practiced domestically in recent years and to reap the signaling benefits likely to flow from such policy consolidation.

The FTAA is without a doubt a very ambitious undertaking, bringing together countries that account for a significant share of global services trade. Several countries in the hemisphere are also major players in the WTO/GATS process. Because the final phase of the FTAA negotiating process (between 2003 and 2005) will coincide—and in certain ways compete, including in terms of the deployment of scarce negotiating resources—with the scheduled completion of negotiations on services proceeding under the WTO's Doha Development Agenda (DDA) single undertaking,[2] it is important that countries in the hemisphere clearly formulate the extra value added (which could be characterized as "GATS-plus" outcomes in terms of both market access and rule design) they seek to achieve at the regional level. Given the sheer size of the FTAA, it is doubtful that merely replicating GATS at the hemispheric level (the seeming objective of a number of key players in the negotiations, including Brazil) could meet the challenge of a value-adding agreement. Absent such added value (the scope for which will in part be determined outside the realm of services), it is unclear whether the hemispheric process will be able to sustain the level of political commitment required for its successful completion.

This chapter seeks to inform the policy choices required to generate a value-adding FTAA outcome on services. It does so by focusing on two core issues. First, it asks whether and how the treatment of services liberalization must be made to adapt to some of the defining characteristics of services trade. Simply put, do the economics of services trade differ sufficiently from trade in goods as to require different policy instruments and approaches?

Second, turning to political economy considerations, the chapter addresses a range of negotiating issues arising from the treatment of services trade in selected regional agreements and their possible relevance to the FTAA process. It does so by distilling, based on a comparison between GATS and a sample of twenty-three regional trade agreements featuring services provisions (sixteen of which involve countries from the Western Hemisphere), some of the key lessons emerging from the recent *practice* of services trade liberalization at the regional level.

An attempt at such comparative analysis can be useful in helping to shape expectations surrounding possible outcomes of hemispheric negotiations in the services field and to test the relevance of some of the conceptual considerations examined in part one. Such comparative analysis may also help negotiators and policy analysts identify in a timely manner some of the potential roadblocks to a value-adding FTAA package of rules and commitments in services and suggest some of the means available for overcoming them.

Economic and Benefits of Preferential Services Liberalization: Conceptual Considerations

Is services trade[3] so different from trade in goods that we need to modify the conclusions reached so far as regards the economic effects of preferential liberalization?[4] In particular, what would happen if a country liberalized services trade faster in the regional context than at the multilateral level? And if a country were to secure preferential access to foreign goods markets, would the benefits justify granting preferential access in services to its home market?

Addressing first the efficiency effects of unilateral policy choice in a particular services market, this chapter seeks answers to two key questions: In its independent choice of services policy, is a country likely to improve upon the status quo by liberalizing on a preferential basis? And is preferential or nonpreferential liberalization likely to produce larger welfare gains?

Gains from Services Liberalization and Domestic Reform

Removing barriers to trade in services in a particular sector is likely to lead to lower prices, improved quality, and greater variety.[5] As in the case of trade in goods, restrictions on trade in services reduce welfare because they create a wedge between domestic and foreign prices, leading to a loss to consumers that is greater than any benefit to producers and government.[6] Empirical studies generally support this contention.[7] Since many services are inputs into goods production, the inefficient supply of such services acts as a tax on production and prevents the realization of significant gains in productivity. Furthermore, as countries reduce tariffs and other barriers to trade, effective rates of protection for manufacturing industries may become negative if they continue to be confronted with input prices that are higher than they would be if services markets were competitive.

A major benefit of liberalization is likely to be access to a wider variety of services whose production is subject to economies of scale. Consumers derive not only a direct benefit from diversity in services such as health care, restaurants, and entertainment, but also an indirect benefit because a wider variety of more specialized producer services, such as telecommunications and finance, can lower the costs of both goods and services production. Estimates of benefits vary for individual countries—from under 1 percent to over 50 percent of GDP—depending on the initial levels of protection and the assumed reduction in barriers. Moreover, the gains from liberalizing services may be substantially greater than those from liberalizing trade in goods because current levels of protection in many countries are higher and because liberalization could create greater spillover benefits. For instance, one model finds that the welfare gains from a 50 percent cut in services-sector protection would be five times larger than those from nonservice-sector trade liberalization.

Dynamic effects may also be significant. Certain service industries clearly possess growth- generating characteristics. A competitive and well-regulated financial sector leads to the efficient transformation of savings to investment, ensuring that resources are deployed wherever they have the highest returns and facilitating better risk sharing in the economy. Improved efficiency in telecommunications generates economy-wide benefits, as this service is a vital intermediate input and also crucial to the dissemination and diffusion of knowledge. Business services such as accounting and legal services are important in reducing transaction costs.

In all such sectors, greater foreign participation and increased competition together imply a larger scale of activity and hence greater scope for generating the special growth-enhancing effects. Even without scale effects, the import of foreign factors that characterizes service-sector liberalization could still have positive effects because they are likely to bring technology with them.[8] Econometric evidence confirms that openness in services influences long-run growth performance.[9] While these estimates indicate that there are substantial gains from liberalizing key services sectors, however, it would be wrong to infer that these gains can be realized by a mechanical opening up of services markets.

Poorly designed reform programs in services can substantially undercut the benefits of liberalization. For example, if privatization of state monopolies is conducted without the introduction of competition, the result may be merely transfers of monopoly rents to private (sometimes foreign) owners. If increased entry into financial sectors is not accompanied by adequate and prudent supervision and full competition, the result may be insider lending and poor investment decisions. If policies to ensure universal service are not put in place, liberalization need not improve access to essential services for the poor. If there are no measures to address the costs of adjustment in factor markets, liberalization could create social and political difficulties. Managing reforms of services markets therefore requires complementing trade opening with appropriate regulation.

Compared to the status quo, a country is likely to gain from preferential liberalization of services trade at a particular point in time—as distinct from the more ambiguous conclusions emerging for goods trade. The main reason is that barriers to services trade are often prohibitive and not revenue generating, so there are few costs of trade diversion.

Preferential versus Nonpreferential Liberalization

As in the case of goods trade, nonpreferential liberalization is likely to produce larger gains than preferential liberalization ceteris paribus. Nonpreferential liberalization is superior because it does not in any way bias consumer choice and allows consumers to import from the most competitive source. The ability of nonpreferential liberalization to more readily secure access to the most efficient suppliers of services is a matter of some importance given the crucial infrastructural role many services perform and the strong influence such intermediate inputs can exert on economy-wide performance.

Turning to the economics of international cooperation in services trade, it bears asking whether there can be circumstances in which a country is more likely to benefit from cooperation in a plurilateral (or regional) forum than in a multilateral forum. Three main arguments can be made in favor of a regional or plurilateral approach.

First, participants in a regional or plurilateral agreement may gain at the expense of the rest of the world either through improved terms of trade in competitive markets or by shifting rents toward participants' firms in oligopolistic markets—unless excluded countries retaliate by concluding similar agreements. There may also be gains over time if there are dynamic economies—for instance, if a larger protected regional market offers the opportunity to learn by doing and develop comparative advantage in new areas.

Second, more efficient bargaining is possible in a regional or plurilateral context than in the multilateral context: there is less concern that outsiders will be able to free ride on the reciprocal exchange of concessions than if there were a general MFN obligation. Ceteris paribus, the desirability of discriminatory arrangements would be greater, the more serious the free-rider problem for non-discriminatory arrangements. Under these circumstances, preferential trading arrangements may make some political sense as a second best alternative.

However, apart from the possible efficiency costs of departing from the MFN principle, another concern raised by preferential arrangements is that they tend to undermine the security of trade concessions. A country's willingness to pay for a concession may be undermined if it fears that its partner might subsequently grant preferred access to someone else. Faced with this possibility it would offer less for the concession in the first place and fewer mutually beneficial deals would be struck. The MFN obligation protects the value of any negotiated concessions against future erosion through discrimination and thus brings benefits to the bargaining process. Moreover, as discussed in this chapter, there may be sectors in which multilateral bargaining can help overcome the disincentives to negotiate arising from asymmetrics in political commitment or market size at play in regional settings.

Third, regulatory cooperation may be more desirable—and likely more feasible—among a subset of countries than if pursued on a global scale. However, there is little, if any, empirical guidance on the payoffs to regulatory cooperation. What are the costs and benefits of deeper harmonization of regulatory standards and/or the establishment of mutual recognition agreements (MRAs)? The lack of empirical evidence complicates the task of deciding on the scope and depth, as well as the geographical reach and the institutional form, of cooperation. If national standards are not optimal, then regional and/or international harmonization can be a way of improving national standards, as has happened with the Basle accord on capital adequacy. In such situations, the best partners for regulatory cooperation are likely to be those with the soundest regulatory framework. Such partners may not always be found within regional compacts. Moreover, standards can at times be captured by protectionist interests, in which case convergence around best-practice regulatory practice can serve as a purely liberalizing device.

There are gains from regulatory cooperation, but also costs. The former will dominate where national regulation can be improved.[10] One can thus think of *optimum regulatory areas* that define the set of countries for which aggregate welfare would be maximized by regulatory convergence.[11] However, whether an individual country benefits from regulatory convergence or harmonization, and its willingness to participate in such an area, depends on where the standard is set—which in turn will determine who will bear the costs of transition.[12] This chapter's discussion of the practice of regionalism in services suggests that attempts at regulatory convergence can also face significant hurdles at the regional level.

An important general caveat applies, however, to each of the above three arguments: the sequence of liberalization matters more in services than it does in the case of goods trade. In particular, the benefits of eventual nonpreferential liberalization may be different if it is *preceded* by preferential liberalization. This is because location-specific sunk costs of production are important in many services, so that even temporary privileged access for an inferior supplier can translate into a long-term advantage in the market. Thus, while the elimination of preferences may lead to a relatively painless switch to more efficient sources of goods supply, the entry of more efficient service providers may be durably deterred if their competitive advantage does not offset the advantages conferred by incumbency. Such considerations seem particularly relevant for the many countries (especially developing countries) that mainly export goods and import services.[13] The challenge for policy makers is thus to ensure that proper attention is paid to promoting greater market contestability in the context of both domestic reform efforts (e.g., domestic liberalization and privatization) and trade and investment liberalization.

Regional versus Multilateral Approaches to Services Liberalization: Lessons from Practice

As countries in the Western Hemisphere enter the last stages of negotiations toward an FTAA, they are confronted by a number of different models for international agreements on services. Despite several years of continuous work, the latest draft negotiating text suggests that much remains to be decided as regards the core architecture of rules for services, with the GATS/MERCOSUR and North American Free Trade Area (NAFTA) models battling for the soul of FTAA negotiators.[14] Throughout the draft (and heavily square-bracketed) FTAA text,[15] one can identify competing provisions lifted from NAFTA and GATS. GATS itself need not be regarded as cast in stone, and it may be possible to negotiate improvements to it during the current round of multilateral negotiations.

In addressing questions of design, negotiators must begin by asking: what should be expected from an international agreement governing services trade? Even though the main challenges in services liberalization are domestic in nature, and despite the fact that, as with goods trade, unilateral reform efforts carry the greatest potential payoffs, international agreements can assist in three important ways by helping achieve greater transparency through rules that require mutual openness, heightened credibility of policy through legally binding commitments, and efficient protection and regulation through rules that favor the choice of superior policy instruments.

Realizing the benefits of international agreements necessarily implies giving up a certain degree of flexibility; for example, the ability to exclude certain sectors or modes of supply, to limit transparency, to reverse liberalization, to discriminate between trading partners in favor of national providers and across modes of delivery, and to use domestic regulations to discriminate. The challenge for many countries involved in hemispheric negotiations is to reap the benefits of stronger rules and more open markets in services agreements while retaining negotiating flexibility to pursue market access objectives in areas such as agriculture that are heavily protected in other countries.

Key Disciplines: Convergence and Divergence

While RTAs covering services come in many different shapes and sizes, they tend to feature a common set of key disciplines governing trade and investment in services that are also found in GATS, albeit with differing burdens of obligation (see Table 9.1). Areas of greatest rule-making convergence between the multilateral and regional levels relate to the agreements' scope of coverage (where carve-outs in respect of air traffic rights and public services tend to define the norm): disciplines on transparency, national treatment, most-favored-nation treatment, as well as disciplines on payments and transfers, monopolies and exclusive service providers, and general exceptions. Considerable similarities also exist between the multilateral and regional levels as regards the need for sectoral specificity (i.e., sectors requiring special treatment in annexes). Lesser convergence (and more limited regional progress) can be observed in areas of rule making that have posed difficulties in a GATS setting. These include issues such as nondiscriminatory quantitative restrictions (market access in GATS-speak), domestic regulation, emergency safeguards, and subsidies.

The principles of most-favored-nation and national treatment constitute two of the most basic building blocks to any agreement on services, just as they do in the goods area. As with GATS, very few RTAs set out such principles in unqualified form,[16] regardless of whether they are framed as general obligations (which is the case for MFN in virtually all agreements and for national treatment in agreements pursuing a negative-list approach to liberalization) or as obligations that apply solely in sectors in which liberalization commitments are positively undertaken.

As may be expected given the regulatory intensity of services trade, transparency disciplines are common to all RTAs covering services. These typically stipulate, as is the case under GATS, an obligation to publish relevant measures and notify new (or changes to existing) measures affecting trade in services and to establish national inquiry points to provide information on measures affecting services trade upon request. One innovation over GATS is the provision that some RTAs, particularly in the Western Hemisphere, make for members to afford the opportunity (to the extent possible, i.e., on a "best-endeavors" basis) for prior comment on proposed changes to services regulations.

While RTAs covering services typically address nondiscriminatory quantitative restrictions that impede access to services markets (addressed under Article XVI of GATS), many agreements, particularly those concluded in the Western Hemisphere and modeled on NAFTA, are weaker than GATS, committing parties solely to making such measures fully transparent in annexes listing nonconforming measures and to a best-endeavors approach as regards their progressive dismantling in future. In contrast, under GATS, WTO members

Table 9.1 Key Disciplines in RTAs Covering Services

Agreements	MFN Treatment	National Treatment	Market access (N-D QRs)[a]	Domestic Regulation	Emergency Safeguards	Subsidy Disciplines	Government Procurement	Rule of Origin (Denial of Benefits)
GATS	Yes	Yes	Yes	Yes	Future	Future negotiations	Future negotiations	Yes
NAFTA	Yes	Yes	Yes	Yes*	No	No	Separate chapter	Yes
Canada-Chile	Yes	Yes	Yes	Yes*	No	No	No	Yes
Chile-Mexico	Yes	Yes	Yes	Yes*	No	No	No	Yes
Bolivia-Mexico	Yes	Yes	Yes	Yes*	Future	No	Separate chapter	Yes
Costa Rica–Mexico	Yes	Yes	Yes	Yes*	Future	No	Separate chapter	Yes
Mexico-Nicaragua	Yes	Yes	Yes	Yes*	No	No	Future negotiations	Yes
Mexico–Northern Triangle[b]	Yes	Yes	Yes	Yes*	Future	No	No	Yes
Central America–Dominican Republic	Yes	Yes	Yes	Yes*	Future	Future negotiations	Separate chapter	Yes
Central America–Chile	Yes	Yes	Yes	Yes*	No	No	Separate chapter	Yes
Group of Three	Yes	Yes	Yes	Yes*	No	No	Separate chapter	Yes
MERCOSUR	Yes	Yes	Yes	Yes	No	Future negotiations	Future negotiations	Yes
Andean Community	Yes	Yes	Yes	Yes*	No	No	No	Yes
CARICOM	Not specified	Yes	Not specified	Yes*	Yes	No	No	Yes
CARICOM–Dominican Republic	Yes	Yes	Yes	Yes*	Future	No	Separate chapter	Yes
Central American Economic Integration	Not specified	No general article	No	No	No	No	No	Not specified

Continued on next page

Table 9.1 Key Disciplines in RTAs Covering Services, continued

Agreements	MFN Treatment	National Treatment	Market access (N-D QRs)[a]	Domestic Regulation	Emergency Safeguards	Subsidy Disciplines	Government Procurement	Rule of Origin (Denial of Benefits)
EU	Yes	Yes	Yes	Yes	No	Yes (covered under competition disciplines)	Yes	Yes
Europe Agreements	Yes	Yes	No	Yes	No	Yes (under competition disciplines)	No	Beneficiaries specified through definition of "undertakings"
EU-Mexico	Yes	Yes	Yes	No (provisions on regulatory carve-out and recognition)	No	No	Separate chapter	Yes
EFTA-Mexico	Yes	Yes	Yes	Yes	No	No	No	Not specified
EFTA-Singapore	Yes	Yes	Yes	Yes	No	Requests for consultations to be given sympathetic consideration	Separate chapter	Yes
Japan – Singapore	No	Yes	Yes	Yes	No	No	Separate chapter	Yes

Continued on next page

Table 9.1 Key Disciplines in RTAs Covering Services , continued

Agreements	MFN Treatment	National Treatment	Market access (N-D QRs)[a]	Domestic Regulation	Emergency Safeguards	Subsidy Disciplines	Government Procurement	Rule of Origin (Denial of Benefits)
ASEAN Framework Agreement on Services	Yes	Yes	Yes	Not specified	Yes	No	No	Yes
ANZCER	MFN for excluded sectors	Yes	Yes	Yes	No	Export subsidies prohibited Other subsidies excluded	No	Yes
U.S.-Jordan U.S.-Jordan		Yes	Yes	Yes	No	Future negotiations	Yes	Yes

*Rules on domestic regulation are set out more narrowly (in most cases they apply only to the licensing and certification of professional services suppliers)

[a]Nondiscriminatory quantitative restrictions.

[b]Honduras, Guatemala, and El Salvador.

undertake policy bindings in sectors, subsectors, and modes of supply against which market access commitments are scheduled. Many other RTAs, such as MERCOSUR and the various RTAs to which EU members are party, introduce a prohibition on the introduction of new nondiscriminatory quantitative restrictions on any scheduled commitment and sector, mirroring a similar requirement under GATS.

The argument has been made that RTAs in the services field provide scope for creating optimum regulatory areas, the presumption being that the aggregate adjustment costs of regulatory convergence and policy harmonization are likely to be smaller when foreign regulatory preferences are similar and regulatory institutions broadly compatible. Both sets of conditions are more likely on balance to obtain among countries that are "closer" in physical and/or cultural/historical terms.[17] In practice, however, it is notable that the broad intersection between domestic regulation and services trade has tended to prove intractable (just as it has under GATS) even among the smaller subset of countries engaging in RTAs.

In many instances, RTAs address domestic regulation with a focus on procedural transparency to ensure that regulatory activity does not lead to disguised restrictions on trade or investment in services, an approach analogous to that found in Article VI of GATS.

With the exception of the EU itself and of agreements reached between the EU and countries in Central and Eastern Europe in pre-EU accession mode, no RTA has to date made tangible progress in delineating the possible elements of a necessity test aimed at ensuring broad proportionality between regulatory means and objectives (as is potentially foreseen under the GATS Article VI section 4 mandate, but on which progress at the negotiating table has, with the exception of accountancy disciplines agreed upon by WTO members in 1999, been limited to date).

Similarly, with few exceptions (e.g., in the EU context as well as the ANZCERTA), little significant tangible progress has been registered in regulatory harmonization. It is notable that neither NAFTA nor the many NAFTA-type agreements reached in the Western Hemisphere contain an article on domestic regulation per se in their services chapters. Rather, such agreements feature more narrowly drawn disciplines relating to the licensing and certification of professionals.[18] Moreover, even though a number of RTAs, notably those concluded in the Western Hemisphere, call on members to recognize, at times on the basis of explicit timetables (as in NAFTA in the case of foreign legal consultants and the temporary licensing of engineers), foreign educational credentials and professional qualifications in selected professions, progress in concluding mutual recognition agreements has proven slow and difficult, particularly when pursued between countries with federal political systems.

The experience to date with regulatory convergence and cooperation at the regional level does not provide clear-cut evidence in support of the argument advanced by Mattoo and Fink (2002) on optimum (regional) regulatory areas. Given that any attempt at reaching MRAs in the services area (as with goods-related MRAs) is almost by definition likely to involve a limited number of participating countries, it is not altogether clear that RTAs offer a superior alternative to that available to WTO members under Article VII of GATS.[19]

With few exceptions, RTAs similarly have made little headway in tackling the key "unfinished" rule-making items on the GATS agenda. This is most notably the case for disciplines on an emergency safeguard mechanism and subsidies for services, about which governments confront the same conceptual challenges, data limitations, and political sensitivities at the regional level as they do on the multilateral front. It is interesting to note, for instance, that the countries of Southeast Asia, which have been amongst the most vocal proponents of an emergency safeguard mechanism in GATS, have not adopted such a provision within the ASEAN Framework Agreement on Services. To date, only members of CARICOM (in Protocol II) in the Western Hemisphere have adopted (but not yet used) such an instrument, and questions remain as to the operational feasibility of an emergency safeguard mechanism in services trade. Elsewhere, NAFTA has provided one example of sectoral experimentation (in financial services) with safeguard-type measures.[20]

Regarding subsidies, with the exception of the EU (including its pre-accession agreements with countries in Central and Eastern Europe) and of ANZCERTA, the adoption of regional disciplines in the services area has proven elusive, particularly in countries with federal political systems given the extent of subnational policy activism in this area. Whereas a number of RTAs (e.g., MERCOSUR) replicate the call, made in GATS, to develop future disciplines on subsidies in services trade, others, notably NAFTA and numerous NAFTA-type agreements in the Western Hemisphere, specifically exclude subsidy practices from coverage.[21]

More progress has been made at the regional level in opening up government procurement markets for services, though this has tended to be achieved through negotiations in the area of government procurement per se (as with the WTO's Government Procurement Agreement) rather than addressed in services negotiations.[22] The approach taken in RTAs is for the most part very similar to that adopted in the WTO of nondiscrimination among members within the scope of scheduled commitments and procedures to enhance transparency and due process. RTAs whose members are all parties to the Government Procurement Agreement, such as EFTA and the Singapore-Japan FTA, specifically mention its relevant articles, and most agreements concluded in the Western Hemisphere basically replicate its disciplines at the regional level. However, it bears noting that unlike the Government Procurement Agreement, which applies in principle to purchases by both state and subnational governments, many RTAs provide for binding government procurement disciplines at the national level only.[23]

The Treatment of Investment in Services: Establishment and Nonestablishment Rights

Starting with NAFTA in 1994, an increasing number of RTAs have sought to complement disciplines on cross-border trade in services (modes one and two of GATS) with a more comprehensive set of parallel disciplines on investment (rules governing both the protection and liberalization of investors and their investments in goods- and services-producing activities) and the temporary movement of business people (related to goods and services trade and investment generically).[24]

One important difference in approaches to services trade between (and among) RTAs and GATS concerns the interplay between cross-border trade and investment in services. At the multilateral level, the GATS (and the WTO more broadly) does not contain a comprehensive body of investment disciplines (GATS is silent, for instance, on matters of investment protection) but incorporates investment in services ("commercial presence" in GATS-speak) as one of four modes of service delivery (see Table 9.2).

A GATS-like approach has been followed in a number of RTAs, notably by MERCOSUR members and many RTAs concluded outside the Western Hemisphere (e.g., ASEAN Framework Agreement on Services, U.S.-Jordan FTA). This approach contrasts with that taken by

Table 9.2 Key Features of RTAs Covering Services

Agreements	Scope/Coverage[a]	Negotiating Modality	Treatment of Investment in Services	Right of Nonestablishment	Ratchet Mechanism
GATS	Universal	Positive-list approach	Covered as "commercial presence" (mode 3)	No	No
NAFTA	Universal	Negative-list approach	Separate chapter	Yes	Yes
Canada-Chile	Universal	Negative-list approach	Separate chapter	Yes	Yes
Chile-Mexico	Universal	Negative-list approach	Separate chapter	Yes	Yes
Bolivia-Mexico	Universal	Negative-list approach	Separate chapter	Yes	Yes
Costa Rica-Mexico	Universal	Negative-list approach	Separate chapter	Yes	Yes
Mexico-Nicaragua	Universal	Negative-list approach	Separate chapter	Yes	Yes
Mexico–Northern Triangle[b]	Universal	Negative-list approach	Separate chapter	Yes	Yes
Central America–Dominican Republic	Universal	Negative-list approach	Separate chapter	Yes	Yes
Central America–Chile	Universal	Negative-list approach	Separate chapter	Yes	Yes
Group of Three	Universal	Negative-list approach	Separate chapter	Yes	Yes
MERCOSUR	Universal	Positive-list approach	Separate Protocols	No	No
Andean Community	Universal	Negative-list approach	Covered as "commercial presence"	No	No
CARICOM	Universal	Negative-list approach	Covered as "commercial presence" and in separate chapters (on right of establishment and movement of capital)	No	No

Continued on next page

Table 9.2 Key Features of RTAs Covering Services, continued

Agreements	Scope/Coverage[a]	Negotiating Modality	Treatment of investment in services	Right of Nonestablishment	Ratchet Mechanism
CARICOM–Dominican Republic	Universal	Negative-list approach	Separate chapter	Yes	No
Central American Common Market	Construction services	Positive-list approach	Not specified	No	No
EU	Universal	Negative-list approach	Treated as freedom to establish	Yes	No
Europe Agreements	Universal	Negative-list approach	separate chapter	Yes	No
EU-Mexico	Universal (audio-visual services explicitly excluded)	Standstill (+ future negotiation of commitments à la GATS)	Covered as "commercial presence" and under a separate investment chapter	No	No
EFTA–Mexico	Universal	Positive-list approach	Covered as "commercial presence" and under a separate investment chapter	No	No
EFTA–Singapore	Universal	Positive-list approach	Covered as "commercial presence" and under a separate investment chapter	No	No

Continued on next page

Table 9.2 Key Features of RTAs Covering Services, continued

Agreements	Scope/Coverage[a]	Negotiating Modality	Treatment of Investment in Services	Right of Nonestablishment	Ratchet Mechanism
Japan-Singapore	Universal	Positive-list approach	Covered as "commercial presence" and under a separate investment chapter	No	No
ASEAN Framework Agreement on Services	Universal	Positive-list approach	Covered as "commercial presence" and under a separate investment chapter	No	No
ANZCER	Universal	Negative-list approach	Covered as "commercial presence" but no common disciplines on investment	Yes	No
U.S.-Jordan	Universal	Positive-list approach	Covered as "commercial presence"	No	No

[a] In this column, the term "universal" excludes air transport and in certain cases cabotage in maritime services.
[b] Honduras, Guatemala, and El Salvador.

NAFTA and the NAFTA-type RTAs, in which investment rules and disciplines covering both matters of investment protection (as typically treated under bilateral investment treaties) and liberalization (typically with respect to both pre- and post-establishment matters), combined with investor-state and state-to-state dispute settlement provisions, apply in a generic manner to goods and services in a separate chapter. The latter agreements thus feature services chapters that focus solely on cross-border delivery (modes one and two of GATS), complemented by separate chapters governing the movement of capital (investment) on the one hand, and the temporary entry of business people on the other.[25]

A number of RTAs, such as the Japan-Singapore FTA, CARICOM, and the EFTA-Mexico and EFTA-Singapore FTAs, address investment in services both under the commercial presence mode of supply (in their services chapters) as well as in separate chapters dealing with investment, the right of establishment, or the movement of capital (see Table 9.2).

As Table 9.2 indicates, RTAs featuring generic investment disciplines typically provide for a right of nonestablishment (i.e., no local presence requirement as a precondition to supply a service, subject to the right to reserve and list existing nonconforming measures) as a means of encouraging greater volumes of cross-border trade in services. While such an obligation, for which no GATS equivalent exists,[26] was initially crafted (starting with NAFTA) before the Internet became a tangible commercial reality, they may nonetheless prove particularly well suited to promoting e-commerce and encouraging countries to adopt less onerous restrictions on cross-border trade whilst achieving legitimate public policy objectives (e.g., prudential supervision and consumer protection).

With very few exceptions (of a mainly sectoral nature), RTAs covering services typically adopt a liberal "rule of origin" (via a provision on denial of benefits), meaning the benefits of RTA treatment are typically denied only to juridical persons who do not conduct substantial business operations in a member country. In practice, the adoption of a liberal rule of origin implies that the postestablishment treatment of what in many instances represents the most important mode of supplying services in foreign markets—investment—is nonpreferential for third-country investors as regards liberalization commitments.[27] Stated differently, under a liberal rule of origin for services and investment, third-country investors can in most instances take full advantage of the expanded market opportunities afforded by the creation of an RTA by establishing operations within the region.[28] An RTA with such a rule can thus extend privileges to outsiders in a manner equivalent to MFN treatment in a multilateral setting.

The above consideration may to some extent explain the observed readiness that a number of governments participating in RTAs have shown to subsequently extend (either immediately or in a progressive manner) regional preferences on an MFN basis under GATS. This may reflect a realization both that preferential treatment may be harder to confer in services trade (and may indeed be economically undesirable with regard to investment) and that multilateral liberalization may offer greater opportunities to secure access to the most efficient suppliers, particularly of infrastructural services likely to exert significant effects on economy-wide performance.[29]

A readiness to extend RTA preferences on an MFN basis in GATS (or to extend such preferences in RTAs concluded with other countries) is most noticeable amongst countries of the Western Hemisphere, the majority of which have tended to lock in the regulatory status quo prevailing in their investment regimes by virtue of adopting a negative-list approach to liberalization in the RTAs to which they are party (see below).

Modalities of Liberalization: Negative versus Positive-List Approaches

Two major approaches towards the liberalization of trade and investment in services have been manifest in RTAs and in the WTO: the positive list or "bottom-up" approach (typically a hybrid approach featuring a voluntary, positive, choice of sectors, sub-sectors and/or modes of supply in which governments are willing to make binding commitments together with a negative list of nonconforming measures to be retained in scheduled areas), and the negative list or "top-down," "list it or lose it" approach. While both negotiating modalities can produce (and indeed have in some instances produced) broadly equivalent outcomes in liberalization terms, it can be argued that the two approaches generate a number of qualitative differences of potential significance from both domestic and international governance points of view.[30]

While the debate over these competing approaches appears settled in the GATS context, it is useful to recall these differences, as the issue is still very much alive in the FTAA context and as WTO members contemplate the scope that may exist in the current negotiations for making possible improvements to the GATS architecture.

Under a GATS-like, positive (or hybrid) approach to scheduling liberalization commitments, countries agree to undertake national treatment and market access commitments specifying (through reservations in scheduled areas) the nature of treatment or access offered to foreign services or foreign service suppliers.[31] Under such an approach, countries retain the full right to undertake no commitments. In such instances, they are under no legal obligation to supply information to their trading partners on the nature of discriminatory or access-impeding regulations maintained at the domestic level.

A related feature of GATS that tends to be replicated in RTAs that espouse a bottom-up approach to liberalization is to afford countries the possibility of making commitments that do not reflect (i.e. are made below) the regulatory status quo (a long-standing practice in tariff negotiations that was replicated in a GATS setting).

The alternative, "top-down" approach to services trade and investment liberalization is based upon the concept of negative listing, whereby all sectors and nonconforming measures are to be liberalized unless otherwise specified in a transparent manner in reservation lists appended to an agreement. Nonconforming measures contained in reservation lists are then usually liberalized through consultations or, as in GATS, periodic negotiations.

It is interesting to note that, despite the strong opposition that such an approach generated when first mooted by a few GATT contracting parties during the Uruguay Round, the negative-list approach to services liberalization has in recent years been adopted in a large number of RTAs covering services. Canada, Mexico, and the United States pioneered this approach in NAFTA in 1994. Since NAFTA took effect, Mexico has played a pivotal role in extending this liberalization approach and similar types of disciplines (i.e., right of nonestablishment) on services to other RTAs it has signed with countries in South and Central America.[32]

A number of distinguishing features of negative listing can be identified. First, such an approach enshrines and affirms the up-front commitment of signatories (subject to reservations) to an overarching set of general obligations. This is currently the case under GATS solely with respect to the agreement's provisions on MFN treatment (Article II, with scope for one-time exceptions) and transparency (Article III), with all other disciplines applying in an à la carte manner to sectors and modes of supply on those terms inscribed in members' schedules of commitments.[33]

A second, and perhaps more immediately operational, defining characteristic of negative listing lies in its ability to generate a standstill, or to establish a stronger floor of liberalization by locking in the statutory or regulatory status quo. Such an approach, therefore, avoids the GATS pitfall of allowing a wedge to arise between applied and bound regulatory or statutory practices.[34]

A third important governance-enhancing feature arising from the adoption of a negative-list approach is the greater level of transparency it generates. The information contained in reservation lists will be important to prospective traders and investors, who value the one-stop-shopping attributes of a comprehensive inventory of potential restrictions in foreign markets. They are also likely to benefit home-country negotiators, assisting them in establishing a hierarchy of impediments to tackle in future negotiations. Such information can in turn lend itself more easily to formula-based liberalization, for instance by encouraging members to agree to reduce or progressively phase out "revealed" nonconforming measures that may be similar across countries (e.g., quantitative limitations on foreign ownership in airlines).[35]

Fourth, the production of a negative list may help to generate a useful domestic policy dialogue between the trade negotiating and regulatory communities, thereby encouraging countries to perform a comprehensive audit of existing trade- and investment-restrictive measures, benchmark domestic regulatory regimes against best international practices, and revisit the rationale for, and most efficient means of satisfying, domestic policy objectives.

A fifth liberalizing feature found in a number of RTAs using a negative-list approach to liberalization consists of a ratchet mechanism (see Table 9.2), whereby any autonomous liberalization measure undertaken by an RTA member between periodic negotiating rounds is automatically reflected in that member's schedule of commitments or lists of reservations. Such a provision typically aims at preventing countries from backsliding with respect to autonomously decreed policy changes. It may also facilitate the provision of negotiating credit for autonomous liberalization, an issue currently under discussion in the GATS context. It has been argued that provisions of this type exert positive effects on the investment climate of host countries by signaling to foreign suppliers the host countries' commitment not to reverse the (liberalizing) course of policy change.[36]

Two potential pitfalls arising from the use of negative listing have been identified. First, such an approach may be administratively burdensome, particularly for developing countries. Such a burden may be mitigated by allowing for progressivity in the completion of members' negative lists of nonconforming measures.[37] The costs of compliance must also be weighted against some of the benefits in governance and best regulatory practices described above.

A second concern relates to the fact that the adoption of a negative list implies that governments ultimately forgo the right to introduce discriminatory or access-impairing measures in future, including in sectors that do not exist or are not regulated at the time of an agreement's entry into force. To assuage these concerns whilst promoting the transparency-enhancing properties associated with the use of negative listing, the suggestion has been made to encourage countries (including possibly in the WTO context) to exchange (as they have in the Andean Community and are considering doing within MERCOSUR) comprehensive and nonbinding lists of nonconforming measures.[38]

Limits to Gravity? Assessing the Depth of Regional versus Multilateral Liberalization in Services Trade

With the notable exception of land transportation issues, in which physical proximity stands out as a determinative facilitating feature, RTAs have generally made little progress in opening up those service sectors that to date have proven particularly difficult to address at the multilateral level.

Most RTAs have tended to exclude the bulk of air transportation services (with the notable exception of the EU for intra-EU traffic) from their coverage. Limited progress has similarly been achieved at the regional level in sectors in which particular policy sensitivities arise—such as maritime transport, audio-visual services, and the movement of service suppliers—or in which the scope for meaningful liberalization was limited (by technology or market structure/ownership considerations) at the time of RTA negotiations, such as in the case of energy services until recently.

Similarly, advances in regulatory convergence and/or harmonization and mutual recognition in services, while a common objective of many RTAs, continue to prove difficult to achieve at the regional level. There have, of course, been a number of instances of tangible forward movement in the RTA context, notably within the EU and ANZCERTA (where, however, progress has been slow, for instance with regard to the recognition of professional qualifications, even in the context of common labor market policies or integrated single markets[39]), as well as in North America (where MRAs have been concluded in a number of professions, notably accountancy, architecture, and engineering, but with highly variable degrees of compliance by subnational licensing bodies).

Moreover, while a number of RTAs have gone beyond GATS as regards the treatment of mode-four trade (for instance with respect to the broader range of professional categories benefiting from temporary entry privileges under NAFTA as compared to the GATS) and, in the process, drawn much needed policy attention to the essential trade-facilitating role that labor mobility provisions can play alongside trade and investment liberalization, they have nonetheless been prone to encountering many of the political sensitivities on display at the multilateral level in the area of labor mobility.

In some instances, it appears that RTAs may simply have been overtaken by events at the multilateral level. Thus, in the key infrastructural areas of basic telecommunications and financial services, GATS has achieved a higher level of bound liberalization than that on offer in most RTAs.[40] In part, this may simply reflect timing issues. For instance, the conditions required to contemplate far-reaching liberalization in basic telecommunications services were generally not ripe at the time that NAFTA was completed in 1993, whereas the required constellation of political, regulatory, and technological forces obtained at the time the GATS Agreement on Basic Telecommunications was concluded in 1997.

Experience under both the telecommunications and the financial services agreements also suggests that, in some sectors, the political economy of multilateral bargaining, with its attendant gains in critical mass, may help overcome the resistance to liberalization arising in the narrower or asymmetrical confines of regional agreements.

Lessons from the Practice of Regionalism in Services: A Preliminary Synthesis

The following key points arise from the preceding analysis:[41]

- RTAs tend to show broad commonality, both among each other and vis-à-vis GATS, as regards the standard panoply of disciplines directed toward the progressive opening of services markets. In some instances, however, GATS disciplines go further than those found in a number of RTAs.

- Starting with NAFTA in 1994, an increasing number of RTAs have in recent years sought to complement disciplines on cross border trade in services with a more comprehensive set of parallel disciplines on investment and the temporary movement of business people.[42]
- RTAs featuring comprehensive or generic investment disciplines typically provide for a right of nonestablishment as a means of encouraging cross-border trade in services. Such a provision, for which no GATS equivalent exists, might prove particularly well suited to promoting e-commerce.
- With very few exceptions, RTAs covering services typically feature a liberal "rule of origin" or denial of benefits clause extending preferential treatment to all legal persons conducting substantial business operations in a member country. In practice, the adoption of a liberal stance in this regard implies that the postestablishment treatment of what in many instances represents the most important mode of supplying services in foreign markets—investment—is nonpreferential as regards third-country investors.
- RTAs covering services tend to follow two broad approaches to the modalities of services trade and investment liberalization. A number of them replicate the GATS model of a positive-list or hybrid approach to market opening, whereas others pursue a negative-list approach. While both approaches can in theory generate broadly equivalent outcomes in liberalization terms, as a practical matter a negative-list approach can be more effective and ambitious in producing liberalization. Further, the process of "getting there" tends to differ, with a number of good governance-enhancing features associated with negative listing, most notably in terms of transparency.
- A number of governments participating in RTAs, particularly those adopting a negative-list approach to liberalization, have shown a readiness to subsequently extend regional preferences on an MFN basis under GATS. This may reflect the realizations that preferential treatment may be harder to confer in services trade (and is indeed perhaps economically undesirable with regard to investment) and that multilateral liberalization may offer greater opportunities of securing access to the most efficient suppliers, particularly of infrastructural services likely to exert significant effects on economy-wide performance.

- RTAs have generally made little progress in tackling the rule-making interface between domestic regulation and trade in services. Indeed, many RTAs feature provisions in this area that are no more fleshed out and, in some instances, are weaker or more narrowly drawn than those arising under GATS.
- RTAs tend to be viewed as offering greater scope for making speedier headway on regulatory cooperation in services trade, notably in areas such as services-related standards and the recognition of licenses and professional or educational qualifications. Despite the greater initial similarities in approaches to regulation and greater cross-border contact between regulators that geographical proximity can afford, progress in the area of domestic regulation has been slow and generally disappointing even at the regional level.
- With a few exceptions, RTAs have made little headway in tackling the key "unfinished" rule-making items on the GATS agenda. This is most notably the case regarding disciplines on emergency safeguards and subsidies for services, where governments confront the same technical challenges or political sensitivities at the regional level as they do on the multilateral front. More progress has been made at the regional level in opening up procurement markets for services, though such advances have tended to be made in procurement negotiations rather than in the services field.
- With the notable exception of land transportation issues, where physical proximity stands out as a determinative facilitating feature, RTAs have generally made little progress in opening up those service sectors that have proven difficult to address at the multilateral level (e.g., air and maritime transport, audio-visual services,[43] movement of service suppliers, and energy services). In the key infrastructural areas of basic telecommunications and financial services, GATS has in fact achieved a higher level of bound liberalization than that on offer in most RTAs. The latter result suggests that, in some sectors, the political economy of multilateral bargaining, with its attendant gains in critical mass, may help overcome the resistance to liberalization arising in the narrower or asymmetrical confines of regional negotiations.

Concluding Remarks: Elements of a "GATS-Plus" Hemispheric Compact on Services

This depiction of progress to date in services liberalization at the regional level suggests that expectations of significant forward momentum and path-breaking results in an FTAA context should probably be tempered. Because of the sheer diversity of sectors and the complexity of regulations and institutions in play, experience shows that services trade liberalization tends to occur in small increments that consist more often of policy consolidation than of de novo market opening, regardless of the negotiating setting. Another reason for tempering expectations is that hemispheric attempts at crafting a regime for services trade and investment confront many of the same difficulties—conceptual and practical—encountered at the multilateral level. This is true in terms of both market access and outstanding rule-making challenges.

Moreover, whereas bilateral agreements, particularly those negotiated along north-south lines, can (and are often used to) generate demonstration effects on new or more controversial issues, such as investment, environment, or labor (so-called "tactical" regionalism), the sheer size of a "super-regional" agreement such as the FTAA may well be an obstacle to policy innovation. This may be so to the extent that some of the key (and largest) protagonists in the talks—Brazil, Canada and the United States notably—may feel that the political capital required to achieve policy innovation on thorny rule-making issues or to open up sensitive sectors may be better expended and generate greater benefits in a multilateral setting. At the same time, and more positively, the size of the FTAA, and the collective influence its member countries exert in the WTO, also suggests that scope may exist for migrating "best" FTAA practices to Geneva.

Despite the challenges posed by the above political economy considerations, the FTAA process affords services negotiators policy space in which to harness more fully the potential of service sector reforms whilst achieving a GATS-plus outcome in both liberalization (market access) and rule making. This chapter concludes with a consideration of what that space could usefully and realistically be.

Agreeing on the Architecture of FTAA Rules on Services and Investment

Somewhat surprisingly, several years into the FTAA negotiations, the foremost issue remains how to structure services provisions and how to link disciplines on services and investment. It is over this issue that the clash between the approaches of MERCOSUR and GATS tends to be fiercest. Such a debate is far from trivial, as its resolution could largely determine whether and how an FTAA services compact can hope to generate a value-adding, GATS-plus outcome.

Indeed, it is debatable whether a codification of the GATS approach at the hemispheric level can add significant value to the status quo. Prospective FTAA signatories are all members of the WTO, and hence already subject to GATS rules and liberalization modalities. The main rationale for replicating the GATS/MERCOSUR approach at the hemispheric level arguably would be to achieve a higher level of bound liberalization than that on offer at the multilateral level. Such a question, however, can only be resolved at the negotiating table.

Adopting a NAFTA-type architecture, which would consist of a complementary set of disciplines on cross-border trade in services, together with separate chapters featuring generic (non–services-specific) disciplines on the movement of capital/investment and of service suppliers, would likely impart a different (and novel) dynamic to the FTAA process. By affirming the conceptual equivalence between the movement of capital and of labor under trade agreements, such an architecture could enhance prospects for a richer harvest of liberalization undertakings in both areas, particularly in labor mobility. It would also provide additional negotiating leverage to developing country *demandeurs* of greater exports of labor services. Countries that would rather segment the treatment of investment into its goods and services components may well be short-changing themselves.

Treating investment in goods and services in a generic manner would also move away from the artificial (and largely political/bureaucratic) distinctions drawn between goods and services and between trade and investment since the early days of the Uruguay Round. Such a distinction bears no relation to the manner in which globally integrated firms deploy their assets in today's economy. As many, if not most, leading manufacturing firms are typically also service-providing firms, it makes little sense to subject them to two sets of rules depending on the nature of the cross-border activity being carried out.[44]

Opposition to a NAFTA-type architecture is often rooted in the mistaken belief that such a framework necessarily operates on the basis of a negative-list approach to liberalization. In reality, a NAFTA-type architecture can be implemented regardless of the chosen modalities for scheduling liberalization commitments. It can, indeed, coexist with either a positive- or negative-list approach. While either of these two approaches can be compatible with a given liberalization outcome, the process of "getting there" tends to favor negative listing.

However, should FTAA negotiators ultimately opt, in part on precautionary regulatory grounds, for a GATS-like hybrid approach to scheduling, they should consider a GATS-plus obligation that, while keeping with the voluntary nature of bound commitments, would still oblige signatories to commit to the regulatory status quo. That is, an FTAA should not tolerate the existence of a mercantilistic wedge to apply between bound and applied regulation, as such a practice sends potentially troubling signals to prospective investors on the nature of competitive conditions prevailing postentry.

Three additional issues relating to the chosen architecture for services and investment warrant the attention of FTAA negotiators. The first relates to the desirability of embedding a right of nonestablishment into the agreement. Doing so would help promote greater doses of cross-border trade and a concomitant convergence in underlying regulatory frameworks (for prudential or consumer protection reasons) that such trade requires. Creating a stronger presumption against forced establishment requirements as preconditions for serving domestic markets could prove particularly useful for the continued growth of e-commerce within the hemisphere.

A second practice worth replicating at the hemispheric level concerns the use of a ratcheting mechanism whereby any unilateral liberalization of trade and investment in services decreed between negotiating rounds is automatically reflected in countries' schedules of commitments (or reservations lists). Such a mechanism was pioneered in NAFTA and is found in a number of RTAs involving countries in the Western Hemisphere. Adopting such a provision could provide a useful anchor for developing an FTAA system of credit for autonomous liberalization, an issue on which GATS has made progress, in part because it allows countries to bind at less than the status quo.

A final governance-enhancing issue where useful and precedent-setting headway could be made at the hemispheric level concerns the protection of acquired rights. The FTAA should include a general obligation ensuring that service providers already established in a market should not suffer a loss of rights due to the enactment of the agreement.

Promoting Greater Labor Mobility

Countries in the Western Hemisphere, particularly developing countries, have a strong interest in the movement of labor, their relatively abundant factor of production. There is good reason to believe that the liberalization of such movement even on a temporary basis could produce substantial welfare gains for all countries. Estimates by Walmsley and Winters (2002) suggest that allowing an increase in temporary access equivalent to 3 percent of the OECD population for developing country service suppliers could produce global income gains of about US$156 billion—greater than the gains from the abolition of all merchandise trade barriers.[45] The large potential gains justify a comprehensive coverage of this mode in international negotiations despite the significant political difficulties in facilitating greater labor mobility.

It is desirable that international agreements be comprehensive in their coverage of the temporary movement of natural persons and not exclude any category of skill or type of employment.[46] All measures affecting such movement would fall within the scope of the agreements. Comprehensiveness of coverage does not, of course, prejudge the depth of liberalizing commitments and rules, which would be the subject of negotiations.

There is currently no dedicated negotiating group on labor mobility in the FTAA context. Such a shortcoming needs to be corrected if a more balanced outcome on the treatment of factor movement is to be secured. As things currently stand, the issue of services trade continues to be as pigeon-holed as it is in GATS, reflecting first and foremost the lukewarm attitude of the United States government toward greater developing country demands in this sensitive area.[47] As noted above, consideration should be given to placing labor mobility on par with investment in any FTAA services compact. Moreover, efforts should be directed to facilitating temporary entry privileges and dedicated visa procedures (i.e., FTAA visas) to five categories of natural persons: business visitors, traders and investors, intracompany transferees, professionals, and nonprofessional essential personnel. The last category, which was not covered under Chapter 16 of NAFTA, holds potentially significant promise for developing country exporters, particularly in sectors (such as construction) in which the ability to deploy workers with various skill categories holds the key to effective access in foreign markets.

Strengthening Regulatory Transparency

Transparency is desirable because it helps reduce transaction costs for the private sector, promotes accountability and good governance, and facilitates international trade negotiations. Its importance to services is especially critical given the regulatory nature of impediments to trade in the sector. Transparency has two dimensions. One regards existing policies, and the other regards future changes in policy as well as processes leading to such changes.

Most agreements promote transparency on the first dimension by obliging countries to make public all measures of general application. Less progress has been made to date on the latter dimension. The FTAA could break important new ground by featuring an obligation for member countries to provide prior notification. Because of the administrative burden such an obligation can entail, an obligation of this sort could be phased in progressively according to countries' levels of development. Alternatively, FTAA signatories could seek agreement on transparency dealing with various aspects of government regulatory processes and procedures, to which countries could subscribe, in whole or in part, on a voluntary basis. The model for such an approach was provided by the WTO Understanding on Commitments in Financial Services.

It is likely that the negotiation of liberalization commitments in highly regulated sectors or in sectors subject to particular types of market failure (e.g., network-based industries prone to monopolistic or oligopolistic market structures and the abuse of dominance by major suppliers) requires the adoption of additional regulatory principles, including in the realm of transparency. Such sectoral experimentation should be encouraged in an FTAA setting. It is likely to be a central component of any determined push to secure deeper market-opening commitments in sectors such as energy (electricity, oil, and gas pipelines), environmental services (water distribution), or transport (especially air transport).

It bears recalling that an agreement's approach to scheduling liberalization commitments can have a major bearing on the extent to which trading partners are informed about the existence of restrictive measures. GATS compels members to list all impediments only in a positive list of scheduled sectors. The freedom of GATS members not to list particular service sectors, or to specify "unbound" for particular modes, allows them to exclude such sectors or modes from the agreement's coverage without shedding any light on the restrictive measures they maintain in these sectors and modes. Agreements modeled on NAFTA's negative-list approach to liberalization typically compel parties to list all nonconforming measures at both national and subnational levels within prescribed time limits. Failure to list nonconforming measures entails their full and automatic liberalization.

Improved mechanisms to enhance transparency are vitally important. In principle, the adoption of either a negative-list approach or a comprehensive positive-list approach would represent a strong commitment to transparency across the board. The requirement to reveal all nonconforming measures in all sectors is inherent in a negative list approach, and the transparency benefits are matched by a positive-list approach only if it obliges members to list all sectors. One desirable approach to be considered in the FTAA context is that taken by the Andean Community and being contemplated under MERCOSUR, whereby each member produces comprehensive lists of restrictive measures that are made available to all other members.

An international agreement along the above lines could help promote domestic transparency in services regimes while overcoming the reluctance of countries to reveal their restrictions unilaterally. One question is whether such lists should take the form of legally binding schedules of commitments , as contemplated in the Andean Community and under MERCOSUR. While there would be significant gains in terms of policy certainty, this approach does create a link between transparency and bindings so that the unwillingness to bind (or to bind the status quo) translates into an unwillingness to reveal. All parties to an FTAA could therefore agree to submit comprehensive "mock schedules" describing all nonconforming measures, with no sector or mode of supply excluded. These schedules need not have legal status and would serve only to enhance transparency of services regimes and help countries perform an informed audit of domestic regulatory practices.

Addressing Regulatory Impediments to Trade and Investment in Services

Services agreements must create a framework of rules that address forms of protection more complex and less visible than tariffs. These include, first, a variety of quantitative restrictions ranging from cargo sharing in transport services, to limits on the number of (foreign) suppliers in telecommunications and banking, to restrictions on the movement of service-providing personnel that affect trade in all services. Second, there are numerous forms of discrimination against foreign providers, including taxes, subsidies, and less favorable access to essential facilities such as ports, airports, or telecommunications networks.

Finally, there is a subtle class of measures that are neither quotas nor explicitly discriminatory but that nevertheless have a profound effect on services trade. These are domestic regulations such as qualification and licensing requirements.

Both NAFTA and GATS recognize the potential for nondiscriminatory, quantitative barriers to restrict the contestability of service markets. While NAFTA does not prohibit the latter measures, they must nonetheless be listed in an annex for transparency purposes and parties shall endeavor to eliminate them through future negotiations. Under GATS and MERCOSUR, all quantitative restrictions (discriminatory and nondiscriminatory) are covered by the market access provision, which prohibits such restrictions in scheduled sectors unless a member has listed them in its schedule. The GATS/MERCOSUR approach should be replicated in an FTAA context, subject to the obligation suggested above that bound commitments (under either a positive or negative list) reflect the regulatory status quo.

Developing countries have much to gain from strengthened multilateral disciplines on domestic regulations for at least two reasons. First, the development of such disciplines can play a role in promoting and consolidating domestic regulatory reform. The experience with the WTO's Telecommunications Services Reference Paper is an example of this possibility. Second, such disciplines can equip developing country exporters to address regulatory barriers to their exports in foreign markets. Furthermore, unless disciplines are developed to deal with licensing and qualification requirements, market access commitments on the movement of skilled natural persons ranging from architecture and engineering to health care—areas in which several developing countries in the Western Hemisphere have clear export interests—will have only notional value. Similar concerns arise in other regulation-intensive services sectors.

The diversity of services sectors and the difficulty in making certain policy-relevant generalizations have tended to favor sector-specific approaches to the interface between domestic regulation and services trade. However, even though services sectors differ greatly, the underlying economic and social reasons for regulatory intervention do not. Directing rule-making efforts in response to these reasons may provide the basis for the creation of meaningful disciplines on domestic regulation. Such a route may be particularly attractive at the regional level given the lesser likelihood and desirability of pursuing harmonization and mutual recognition at the multilateral level.

The economic case for regulation in all services sectors arises essentially from market failures attributable primarily to three kinds of problems: natural monopoly or oligopoly, asymmetric information, and externalities. Market failure due to natural monopoly or oligopoly may create trade problems because incumbents can impede access to markets in the absence of appropriate regulation. Because of its direct impact on trade, this is the only form of market failure that needs to be addressed directly by trade disciplines. The relevant GATS provision, Article VIII dealing with monopolies, is limited in scope. As a consequence, in the context of the WTO's basic telecommunications negotiations, a reference paper with its pro-competitive principles was developed in order to ensure that monopolistic suppliers would not undermine market access commitments. FTAA negotiators need to examine how far these principles can be generalized to a variety of other network services, including transport, environmental services, and energy services.[48]

In all other cases of market failure, trade disciplines do not need to address the problem per se, but rather to ensure that domestic measures to deal with the problem do not serve unduly to restrict trade. The same is true for measures designed to achieve social objectives. Such trade-restrictive effects can arise from a variety of technical standards, prudential regulations, and qualification requirements in professional, financial, and numerous other services, as well as from the granting of monopoly rights to complement universal service obligations in services such as transport and telecommunications.

The trade-inhibiting effect of this entire class of regulations is best disciplined by complementing the national treatment obligation with a variant of the so-called necessity test. Such a test is already part of the recently established disciplines in the accountancy sector under GATS. This test essentially leaves governments free to deal with economic and social problems provided that any measures taken are not more trade restrictive than necessary to achieve the relevant objective. It would seem desirable to use the test to create a presumption in favor of economically efficient choice of policy in remedying market failure and in pursuing noneconomic objectives. For instance, in the case of professionals such as doctors, a requirement to requalify likely would be judged unnecessary since the basic problem, inadequate information about whether they possess the required skills, could be remedied by a less burdensome test of competence. There is little doubt that progress in this area is likely to be difficult, fraught as it is with political and bureaucratic sensitivities. In today's environment of considerably heightened civil society activism, domestic regulators are becoming increasingly opposed to the subjection of sovereign regulatory conduct to a market access/trade prism.

Every effort should be made in an FTAA context to introduce some measure of discipline on nondiscriminatory conduct. Doing so would ensure some measure of proportionality between regulatory objectives and the means to achieve them. The sad tale of blocked Mexican access to the U.S. trucking market under NAFTA is a stark reminder of how domestic regulation can all too easily be captured by protectionist interests and translate in demands that are patently more burdensome than necessary to secure compliance with legitimate public policy objectives.[49]

Liberalizing Government Procurement of Services

There are many good reasons to liberalize government procurement, though experience, both in the WTO and in regional agreements, shows that most countries (developed and developing) are reluctant immediately to accept full liberalization of procurement of services. Still, such liberalization holds the key to meaningful access for many service-providing firms that are otherwise subject to few other formal barriers to entry. If countries are unwilling to give up the right to protect, then at least they could agree to bind the margins of preference granted to national suppliers and to make these margins subject to unilateral or negotiated reductions in a manner analogous to tariffs. Government procurement stands out as one of the areas in which the chances of securing a WTO-plus outcome at the hemispheric level is greatest, given that only two of the thirty-four countries taking part in FTAA negotiations, Canada and the United States, are signatories of the WTO's Government Procurement Agreement.

One of the most important services sectors in the context of government procurement, and one in which several countries in the Western Hemisphere have a significant stake, is construction. All signatories to the Government Procurement Agreement have accepted its disciplines in this sector above a certain threshold value. Yet under GATS, members have usually not bound themselves to grant market access to the supply of construction services through the presence of natural persons, except for certain limited categories of intracorporate transferees. The assurance that workers temporarily can be moved to construction sites would greatly increase the benefit of nondiscriminatory government procurement for developing countries. The same applies to procurement of other services, such as software and transport. FTAA negotiators should seek to ensure that any agreed market-access package in a particular services market features a procurement complement, either as additional commitments in the services chapter or as separate commitments under a generic procurement chapter. Moreover, because meaningfully contesting local procurement markets typically implies a local presence on the part of foreign bidders, the liberalization of investment regimes can usefully underpin procurement liberalization.

Opting for Liberal Rules of Origin for Services

Under international law the nationality of a company is typically determined by its country of incorporation. However, this criterion of incorporation has been deemed to be inadequate for certain purposes. For example, it may accord nationality to corporations that are incorporated in a country for tax avoidance or related purposes, but do no business or have no assets in that country. This perceived inadequacy is reflected in many bilateral and plurilateral trade and investment agreements and in bilateral tax treaties.[50] Article V of GATS states that a juridical person constituted under the laws of a party to a regional agreement shall be entitled to treatment granted under such an agreement provided it engages in substantive business operations in the territory of the parties to such an agreement. But in an agreement involving only developing countries, more favorable treatment may be granted to juridical persons owned or controlled by natural persons of the parties to such an agreement.

Most regional agreements extend benefits to all investors and service providers that are nationals or permanent residents of a member country or are incorporated under the laws of a party. Ownership or control is not the primary criterion. NAFTA requires that service providers, regardless of nationality, either carry out substantial business operations in the territory of any party (for cross-border trade in services) or be incorporated in and carry out substantial business operations in a member country (for investment) in order to receive NAFTA treatment. In addition to incorporation, the EC requires that entities conduct substantial business operations within member countries. The "single-passport" approach adopted by numerous services-related EC directives generally affords foreign-established entities nondiscriminatory terms of access to EC markets.[51] MERCOSUR adopts a similar rule of origin. It defines the service supplier of another member as constituted or otherwise organized under the law of that member and engaged in substantial business interests in the territory of that member or any other member.

Again, rules of origin play a critical role in determining the degree to which regional trading arrangements discriminate against nonmember countries, and hence the extent of potentially costly trade and investment diversion. When levels of protection differ between participating countries, the effective preference granted to a trading partner depends on the restrictiveness of the rule of origin. In the extreme, if one participant has a completely open market, the adoption of a liberal rule of origin by the other participants is equivalent to MFN liberalization.[52]

While suffering from the bargaining handicaps of the MFN principle—it lessens the incentive to negotiate a preferential agreement and potentially reduces negotiating leverage vis-à-vis third countries—a liberal rule of origin nonetheless minimizes the costs of trade and investment diversion and is economically efficient. Accordingly, the FTAA should adopt such a rule in the realm of services (including for investment).

References

Baier, S. L., and J. H. Bergstrand. 2001. "International Trade in Services, Free Trade Agreements, and the WTO." In *Services in the International Economy*, edited by R. M. Stern. Ann Arbor: University of Michigan Press.

Baldwin, R. 2000. "Regulatory Protectionism, Developing Nations and a Two-Tier World Trade System." Centre for Economic Policy Research Discussion Paper Series 2574 (October):1–39.

Coe, D. T., E. Helpman, and A.W. Hoffmaister. 1997. "North-South R&D Spillovers." *Economic Journal*, 107: 134–49.

Commission of the European Communities. 2002. "The State of the Internal Market for Services: Report from the Commission to the Council and the European Parliament." Presented under the first stage of the Internal Market Strategy for Services, COM(2002)41 Final, Brussels (July 30).

Copeland, B. R. 2002. "Benefits and Costs of Trade and Investment Liberalization in Services. " In *Trade Policy Research 2002*, edited by J. M. Curtis and D. Ciuriak, pp. 107–218. Ottawa: Department of Foreign Affairs and International Trade, Government of Canada.

Ethier, W. 1982. "National and International Returns to Scale in the Modern Theory of International Trade." *American Economic Review* 72 (June): 492–506.

Frankel, J., E. Stein, and S. Wei. 1995. "Trading Blocs and the Americas: The Natural, the Unnatural and the Supernatural." *Journal of Development Economics* 47: 61–96.

Glassman, C. A. 2000. "Customer Benefits from Current Information Sharing by Financial Services Companies." Study prepared for the Financial Services Roundtable, December.

Hamilton, B., and J. Whalley. 1984. "Efficiency and Distributional Implications of Global Restrictions on Labour Mobility: Calculations and Policy Implications." *Journal of Development Economics* 14: 61–75.

Hart, M., and P. Sauvé. 1997. "Does Size Matter? Canadian Perspectives on the Development of Government Procurement Disciplines in North America." In *Law and Policy in Public Purchasing*, edited by B. Hoekman and P. Mavroidis, pp. 203–21. Ann Arbor: University of Michigan Press.

Hoekman, B. and C. Primo Braga. 1997. "Protection and Trade in Services: A Survey." *Open Economics Review* 8: 285–308.

Hoekman, B., and P. Sauvé. 1994. "Liberalizing Trade in Services." World Bank Discussion Paper no. 243, Washington, DC.

Leroux, E. 1995. *Le libre-échange nord-américain et les services financiers*. Collection Minerve, Montréal: Editions Yvon Blais.

Mattoo, A., and C. Fink. 2002. "Regional Agreements in Services: Some Conceptual Issues." World Bank, Washington, DC. Photocopy.

Mattoo, A., R. Rathindran, and A. Subramanian. 2001. "Measuring Services Trade Liberalization and its Impact on Economic Growth: An Illustration." World Bank Policy Research Working Paper no. 2380, Washington, DC.

McLaren, J. 1997. "Size, Sunk Costs, and Judge Bowker's Objection to Free Trade." *American Economic Review* 87 (June): 400–20.

———. 1999. "A Theory of Insidious Regionalis." Department of Economics, Columbia University (June). Photocopy.

Organization for Economic Cooperation and Development (OECD). 2002a. *GATS: The Case for Open Services Markets*. Paris.

———. 2002b. "The Relationship between the Multilateral Trade System and Regional Trade Agreements: Government Procurement." TD/TC/WP(2002)24 (15 April), Paris.

———. 2002c. "The Relationship Between Regional Trade Agreements and the Multilateral Trading System: Investment." TD/TC/WP(2002)18, Paris.

———. 2002d. "Labour Mobility in RTAs," TD/TC/WP(2002)16, Paris.

Panagariya, A. 2000. "Preferential Trade Liberalization: The Traditional Theory and New Developments." *Journal of Economic Literature* 38 (2): 287–331.

Pena, M. A. 2000. "Services in MERCOSUR: The Protocol of Montevideo." In *Services Trade in the Western Hemisphere: Liberalization, Integration and Reform*, edited by S. M. Stephenson, pp. 154–68. Washington, DC: Trade Unit of the Organization of American States and Brookings Institution Press.

Robert, M., P. Sauvé, and K. Steinfatt. 2001. "Negotiating Investment Rules: Possible Scenarios for an EU-MERCOSUR Agreement." Institut d'Etudes Politiques, Paris. Photocopy.

Robinson, S., Z. Wang, and W. Martin. 1999. "Capturing the Implications of Services Trade Liberalization." Paper presented at the Second Annual Conference on Global Economic Analysis, GL Avernaes Conference Center, Ebberup, Denmark, June 20–22.

Salazar-Xirinachs, J. M., and M. Robert. 2001. *Toward Free Trade in the Americas.* Washington, DC: Organization of American States and Brookings Institution Press.

Sapir, A. 1998. "GATS 1994–2000." *Journal of World Trade* 33: 51–66.

Sauvé, P. 1996. "Services and the International Contestability of Markets." *Transnational Corporations* 5 (1) (April): 37–56.

———. 2000. "Making Progress on Trade and Investment: Multilateral vs. Regional Perspectives." In *Services Trade in the Western Hemisphere: Liberalization, Integration and Reform*, edited by S. M. Stephenson, pp. 72–85. Washington, DC: Trade Unit of the Organization of American States and Brookings Institution Press.

———. 2002. "Completing the GATS Framework: Safeguards, Subsidies and Government Procurement." In *Development, Trade and the WTO: A Handbook,* edited by B. Hoekman, A. Mattoo, and P. English, pp. 326–35. Washington, DC: World Bank.

Sauvé, P., and B. Gonzalez-Hermosillo. 1993. "Implications of the NAFTA for Canadian Financial Institutions." C. D. Howe Institute Commentary no. 44 (April), Toronto.

Sauvé, P., and K. Steinfatt. 2001. "Financial Services and the WTO: What Next?" In *Open Doors: Foreign Participation in Financial Systems in Developing Countries*, edited by R. E. Litan, P. Masson, and M. Pomerleano, pp. 351–86. Washington, DC: World Bank, International Monetary Fund, and Brookings Institution Press.

Sauvé, P., and C. Wilkie. 2000. "Investment Liberalization in GATS." In *GATS 2000: New Directions in Services Trade Liberalization*, edited by P. Sauvé and R. M. Stern, pp. 331–63. Washington, DC: Harvard University Center for Business and Government and Brookings Institution Press.

Schiff, M., and W. Chang. forthcoming. "Market Presence, Contestability, and the Terms-of-Trade Effects of Regional Integration." *Journal of International Economics.*

Silver, S. 2002. U.S. "Under Pressure over Mexican Trucking." *Financial Times*, November 4.

Snape, R. and M. Bosworth. 1996. "Advancing Services Negotiations." In *The World Trading System: Challenges Ahead*, edited by J. Schott, pp. 185–203. Washington, DC: Institute for International Economics.

Stephenson, S. M. 2001a. "Services." In *Toward Free Trade in the Americas*, edited by J.-M. Salazar-Xirinachs and M. Robert, pp. 163–85. Washington, DC: Trade Unit of the Organization of American States and Brookings Institution Press.

———. 2001b. "Deepening Disciplines for Trade in Services." Organization of American States Trade Unit Studies, Analyses on Trade and Integration in the Americas (March), Washington, DC.

———. 2002. "Regional Versus Multilateral Liberalization of Services." *World Trade Review* 1 (2) (July): 187–209.

Thompson, R. 2000. "Formula Approaches to Improving GATS Commitments." In *GATS 2000: New Directions in Services Trade Liberalization*, edited by P. Sauvé and R. M. Stern, pp. 473–86. Washington, DC: Harvard University Center for Business and Government and Brookings Institution Press.

Walmsely, T., and L. A. Winters. 2002. "Relaxing the Restrictions on the Temporary Movement of Natural Persons: A Simulation Analysis." University of Sussex. Photocopy.

Winters, L. A. 1996. "Regionalism versus Multilateralism." World Bank Policy Research Working Paper no. 1687, Washington, DC.

———. 2001. "Harnessing Trade for Development." University of Sussex. Photocopy.

Wonnacott, P., and R. Wonnacott. 1981. "Is Unilateral Tariff Reduction Preferable to a Customs Union? The Curious Case of the Missing Foreign Tariffs." *American Economic Review* 71 (4) (September): 704–14.

World Bank. 2000. *Trade Blocs*. New York: Oxford University Press.

———. 2001. *Global Economic Prospects*. Washington, DC.

World Trade Organization (WTO). 2001. "Market Access: Unfinished Business—Post Uruguay Round Inventory." Special Study no. 6, Geneva.

Notes

1 One recent paper by Baier and Bergstrand (2001) does seek to examine the implications of a free trade agreement in services, but their assumptions limit the value of the results. Services are assumed to differ from goods because they have higher or prohibitive transport costs—but strangely, only when transported across continents while transport costs

are zero between countries on the same continent. Not surprisingly, continental FTAs in services are found to be desirable—a conclusion similar to the finding by Frankel, Stein, and Wei (1995) for trade in goods. The only other difference examined between trade in goods and services is that the latter face a higher level of protection in services.

2 Negotiations on services predate the DDA, having resumed (alongside talks on agriculture) in January 2000 as foreseen under the Uruguay Round's built-in agenda.

3 This section draws on Fink and Mattoo (2002).

4 The analysis of preferential agreements in services requires an extension of conventional theory in two ways. First, since services trade often requires proximity between the supplier and the consumer, we need to consider preferences extended not just to cross-border trade, but also to foreign direct investment and foreign individual service providers. Second, preferential treatment could be granted not through tariffs, which are rare in services trade, but through discriminatory restrictions on the movement of labor and capital (e.g., in terms of quantity or share of foreign ownership), and a variety of domestic regulations, such as technical standards and licensing and qualification requirements.

5 The following review draws upon World Bank (2001, Chapter 3).

6 This is strictly true in static models without market imperfections—such as monopolistic market structures, internal and external economies of scale, or other distortions. The presence of imperfections opens up a plethora of possibilities in which the effects of trade policies are typically indeterminate, depending on the prior distortion.

7 See Hoekman and Braga (1997) for a review.

8 See Ethier (1982) and Copland (2001).

9 Robinson, Wang, and Martin (1999).

10 Coe, Helpman, and Hoffmaister (1999) present empirical evidence demonstrating the impact of technology diffusion—in their case through trade in goods—on total factor productivity growth. In principle, the same should hold true for technology that is diffused through factor flows

11 After controlling for other determinants of growth, countries that fully liberalized the financial services sector (in terms of the three dimensions noted above) grew, on average, about 1 percentage point faster than other countries. An even greater impetus on growth was found to come from fully liberalizing both the telecommunications and the financial services sectors. Estimates suggest that countries that fully liberalized both sectors grew, on average, about 1.5 percentage points faster than other countries.

12 The aggregate adjustment cost of regulatory convergence depends on the distance between the policy-related standards of the countries. The costs are likely to be smallest when foreign regulatory preferences are similar and regulatory institutions are compatible. The benefits of eliminating policy differences through harmonization depend on the prospects of creating a truly integrated market, which depends on the "natural distance" between countries, and that in turn depends on physical distance, legal systems, language, and so on.

13 In the definition of an optimal regulatory area, it must also be recognized that cooperation fora can be a vehicle to exchange information on different experiences with regulatory reform and to identify good regulatory practices. This form of cooperation can be especially useful for regulating new services in sectors with continuous technical change. Developing countries may then have an interest in cooperating with advanced industrial countries that have the longest experience with regulatory reform and/or where the newest technologies are often introduced first.

14 This issue can be thought of as the outcome of bargaining. The incentive to make regulations converge may depend on the relative market size, with the small country having more to gain. This may explain why small countries acceding to the EU agree to bear the full cost of transition. Furthermore, the sequence matters: where the standard is set will depend on which sets of countries negotiate first—for example EU fifteen and then Eastern European countries, or all together, and so on.

15 It should be noted that the process of regulatory convergence itself could involve sunk costs of transition. The sequence in which a country chooses to harmonize its regulations with different trading partners is not irrelevant. One reason is that the sequence of harmonization may influence the bargaining power of different country groupings in the negotiation over where the harmonized standard should be set. For example, the countries in Eastern Europe that are acceding to the EU one by one could arguably have had a greater say in the EU-wide standard in specific areas if they had been original members, had negotiated collectively, or both. Thus, harmonization first at the MERCOSUR level and then at the FTAA or multilateral level could imply different costs and produce a different outcome from direct harmonization at the broader level.

16 The following objectives for services negotiations within the FTAA were set out in the San Jose Declaration of March 1998: to establish disciplines to progressively liberalize trade in services so as to permit the achievement of a hemispheric free trade area under conditions of certainty and transparency, and to ensure the integration of the smaller economies into the FTAA process. In the preparatory phase (March 1995 to March 1998), it had been agreed to focus on six elements: sectoral coverage,

MFN treatment, national treatment, market access, transparency, and the denial of benefits. During the first phase of negotiations (June 1998 to November 1999), members of the Negotiating Group on Services discussed in depth the scope of a future agreement in services and these six elements. At the end of 2000, the negotiating group finalized a draft text containing proposed language for these and other related issues. At their sixth meeting (Buenos Aires, April 7, 2001) the Ministers Responsible for Trade representing the thirty-four countries participating in the FTAA process instructed "the Negotiating Group on Services to submit to the Trade Negotiations Committee, its recommendations on modalities and procedures for negotiations by April 1, 2002, for its evaluation by the TNC during its first meeting following that date, in order to initiate negotiations no later than May 15, 2002." The latest draft FTAA text on services can be found at http:// www.globalservicesnetwork.com.

17 Only the MERCOSUR Protocol and Decision 439 of the Andean Community provides that no deviation from MFN and national treatment be allowed among members to the two integration groupings.

18 Whereas similar GATS language states that the measures in question should not be a restriction to the supply of a service under any of the four GATS modes, the NAFTA-type agreements narrow this requirement to the cross-border supply of a service. No comparable provision can be found in these agreements' investment chapters. Meanwhile, in ANZCER, language on licensing and certification is not legally binding but rather hortatory in nature.

19 Indeed, Article VII of GATS arguably allows greater initial selectivity in the choice of partners in regulatory harmonization, whereas RTAs allow for convergence between countries whose regulatory fit may not always be optimal. There is, of course, one important difference between RTAs and GATS insofar as preferential treatment (including in regulatory matters) can be fully protected under Article V of GATS, whereas WTO members must be prepared under Article VII to extend recognition privileges to all members willing and able to satisfy national regulatory requirements.

20 Under the terms of NAFTA's chapter on financial services, Mexico was allowed to impose market share caps if the specific foreign ownership thresholds agreed to—25 and 30 percent respectively for banks and securities firms—are reached before 2004. Mexico may only have recourse to such market share limitations once during the 2000–04 period and may only impose them for a three-year period. Under no circumstances may such measures be maintained after 2007. It bears noting that Mexico has not to date made use of such provisions even as the aggregate share of foreign participation in its financial system is today significantly higher than the thresholds described above. See Sauvé (2002).

21 The EFTA-Singapore FTA requires that sympathetic consideration be given to requests by a party for consultations in instances in which subsidy practices affecting trade in services may be deemed to have injurious effects. The Japan-Singapore New Partnership Agreement features generic provisions on subsidies applicable to both goods and services trade.

22 Still, it bears recalling that despite notable progress in RTAs, government procurement practices continue in most instances to be the province of discriminatory practices. In the case of NAFTA, for instance, despite the fact that the scope of covered purchases was quadrupled when compared to the outcome of the 1987 Canada–United States FTA, covered entities only represented a tenth of North America's civilian procurement market at the time of the agreement's entry into force. See Hart and Sauvé (1997).

23 For a fuller discussion of the treatment of government procurement in RTAs, see OECD (2002b).

24 For a fuller account of the treatment of investment and the movement of labor in RTAs, see OECD (2002c and d).

25 Such movement is usually defined as comprising four distinct categories to which preferential temporary entry privileges are bestowed: business visitors, traders and investors, intracompany transferees, and professionals.

26 It could be argued that such a provision is somewhat implicit in GATS insofar as the agreement only allows member countries to maintain local presence requirements in scheduled sectors (under modes 1 and 2) to the extent that such nonconforming measures are explicitly inscribed in their schedules. No such discipline, however, applies to sectors that do not appear in members' GATS schedules or in those modes of supply in which WTO members remain unbound. In contrast, the right to nonestablishment is a general obligation under the NAFTA, against which reservations to preserve existing nonconforming measures can be lodged.

27 It bears recalling, however, that a number of economic factors (e.g., the scale economies arising from a larger regional market) and policy variables (e.g., the maintenance of discriminatory sectoral rules of origin within an RTA) can affect global patterns of investment, as discussed in OECD (2002c).

28 Indeed, the aim of attracting greater volumes of FDI, including from third-country sources, is often a central objective of RTAs. For this reason, there are generally few instances in which the benefits of an RTA in the investment field are restricted to juridical persons that are owned or controlled by nationals of a member country. Among the RTAs reviewed in this note, only the MERCOSUR and the Andean Pact feature such restrictions.

29 See Sauvé (2000).

30 The purpose of the ensuing discussion is to note such differences without advocating any implicit hierarchy of policy desirability. Both approaches have strengths and weaknesses. The governance-enhancing aspects of negative listing have, however, been noted by several observers. See in particular Sauvé (1996); Snape and Bosworth (1996); World Trade Organization (2001); and Stephenson (2002).

31 Members of MERCOSUR adopted one slightly different version of the positive-list approach with a view to liberalizing services trade within the region. According to MERCOSUR's Protocol of Montevideo on Trade in Services, annual rounds of negotiations based on the scheduling of increasing numbers of commitments in all sectors (with no exclusions) are to result in the elimination of all restrictions to services trade among the members of the group within ten years of the entry into force of the protocol. The latter has yet to enter into force. See Stephenson (2001a) and Pena (2000).

32 The Andean Community has adopted a somewhat different version of the negative-list approach. Decision 439 on Trade in Services specifies that the process of liberalization is to begin when comprehensive (nonbinding) national inventories of measures affecting trade in services for all members of the Andean Community are finalized. Discriminatory restrictions listed in these inventories are to be lifted gradually through a series of negotiations, ultimately resulting in a common market free of barriers to services trade within a five-year period set out to conclude in 2005.

33 It bears noting, however, that most RTAs that employ a negative-list approach to liberalization feature so-called "unbound" reservations, listing sectors in which members wish to preserve the right to introduce new nonconforming measures in future. In many RTAs, particularly those modeled on NAFTA, such reservations nonetheless oblige member countries to list existing discriminatory or access-impairing measures whose effect on foreign services or service suppliers might in the future be made more burdensome.

34 The suggestion has been made that WTO Members could address this issue in GATS without revisiting the agreement's negotiating modality by agreeing to a new framework provision whose purpose would be to encourage governments to reflect the statutory or regulatory status quo in their scheduled commitments (whilst keeping with the voluntary nature of such commitments). See Sauvé and Wilkie (2000).

35 See Sauvé (1996).

36 See Hoekman and Sauvé (1994) and Stephenson (2001b).

37 In NAFTA, for instance, subnational governments were initially given an extra two years to complete their lists of nonconforming measures pertaining to services and investment. NAFTA parties subsequently decided not to complete the lists at the subnational level, opting instead for a standstill on existing nonconforming measures. Compliance with the production of negative lists has similarly been problematic elsewhere in the Western Hemisphere, as a number of agreements were concluded without such lists being finalized and without firm deadlines for doing so. The inability of "users" to access the information contained in the negative lists to such agreements deprives the latter of an important good-governance-promoting feature.

38 See Sauvé and Wilkie (2000) for a fuller depiction of such a proposal.

39 For a detailed analysis of problems encountered in realizing the European Union's single market program for services, see Commission of the European Communities (2002). Negotiations in GATS on financial services, and notably the development of the GATS Understanding on Commitments in Financial Services, took advantage of insights gained in addressing financial market opening at the regional level. This was particularly the case under NAFTA, whose Chapter 14 addressed (in 1993) a range of issues that would feature prominently in negotiations of the WTO's 1997 Financial Services Agreement. See Sauvé and Gonzalez-Hermosillo (1993); see also Leroux (1995) and Sauvé and Steinfatt (2001).

40 For instance, EU member countries had not yet put in place the procompetitive regulatory framework required to achieve an integrated market for telecommunication services.

41 It bears noting that the stylized facts summarized here depict broad trends. Such trends may obtain even as the treatment of specific rulemaking issues and/or the degree of liberalization achieved in specific sectors or with regard to particular modes of supplying services may show greater variance. The large number of RTAs covering services and the even greater number of individual sectors such agreements encompass obviously complicates attempts at making broad analytical generalizations. For instance, one can note the tendency for NAFTA members, particularly Canada and the United States, to take on liberalization commitments broadly in line with what was being contemplated (and would later be bound) under GATS in a majority of sectors even as particular sectoral liberalization initiatives, for instance in the fields of land transportation (bus and truck services) or specialty air services, were being pursued exclusively on a regional level.

42 For a fuller account of the treatment of investment and the movement of labor in RTAs, see OECD (2002c).

43 While such a result obtained within the great majority of RTAs, some agreements, notably the Chile–Mexico FTA, the Chile–MERCOSUR FTA, or the United States–Jordan FTA, did achieve some measure of liberalization in audio-visual services.

44 Such an artificial distinction (separate rules governing investment in goods and services) was incorporated most recently in the Chile–European Union FTA, creating a tactical precedent supportive of the EU's push for investment rules (on manufacturing only) under the WTO Doha Development Agenda.

45 Hamilton and Whalley (1984) found that the elimination of all restrictions on labor mobility could produce gains exceeding existing worldwide GNP.

46 GATS provides no guaranteed access for mode-four suppliers; access is determined by the nature of each member's specific commitments. Generally, mode-four commitments are quite restrictive, tend to mostly concern intracorporate transferees, and are often subject to economic needs tests. While mode four covers service suppliers at all skill levels, members' commitments tend to be limited to higher-skilled categories such as managers, specialists, and professionals. Access under mode four can also be affected by MFN exemptions and licensing requirements, including recognition of qualifications, as well as restriction under mode three. There are no specific provisions in GATS for facilitated entry, although individual countries' specific commitments may include measures to facilitate entry. Chapter 16 of NAFTA deals with the movement of businesspersons. The agreement is limited to temporary entry, defined negatively as being "without the intent to establish permanent residence," and applies only to citizens of parties. Access is basically limited to four higher skills categories: traders and investors, intracompany transferees, business visitors, and professionals (detailed definitions are provided). However, these groups are not limited to services and may include persons in activities related to agriculture or manufacturing. Labor certification or labor-market assessments and tests are removed for all four groups. However, work permits are required for traders and investors, intracompany transferees, and professionals, but not business visitors. While visas are still required, fees for processing applications are to be limited to the approximate cost of services rendered. Dispute-settlement provisions cannot be invoked regarding a refusal to grant temporary entry unless the matter involves a pattern of practice and the business person has exhausted the available administrative remedies. Under NAFTA, the United States provides Trade NAFTA (TN) visas for professionals that last for one year and are renewable. Criteria include that: the profession is on the NAFTA list, the candidate meets the specific criteria for that profession, the prospective position requires someone in

that capacity, and the candidate is going to work for a U.S. employer. Canadians can receive TN status at the port of entry on presentation of a letter from a U.S. employer, but Mexicans must currently arrange for their employer to file a labor condition application (although this requirement will expire in January 2004), and then they must apply for a visa at the U.S. Embassy in Mexico. Under NAFTA, the United States applies a quota of 5,500 to Mexican professionals, due to expire on 1 January 2004. Canada has chosen not to set a quota on the temporary entry of Mexican professionals. NAFTA, furthermore, extends duty-free privileges to the tools of the trade (e.g. computers, software, samples, and promotional material) imported on a temporary basis by professionals covered under the agreement's chapter Temporary Entry of Business People.

47 The U.S. private sector is itself a strong *demandeur* on a relaxation of government restrictions on the temporary movement of business people. A challenge is for developing-country FTAA negotiators to build a prochange coalition with U.S. and Canadian private-sector interests. On U.S. business attitudes on this question, see the website of the U.S. Coalition of Service Industries at www.uscsi.org, which features the Coalition's services priorities for the FTAA.

48 Work on this issue has been initiated jointly by the OECD and World Bank, and a preliminary set of papers can be accessed from the following website: www.worldbank.org/trade.

49 See Silver (2002).

50 Bilateral investment treaties negotiated between certain OECD countries and developing countries may include ownership or control as the primary or as additional factors for determining the origin of a corporation. The bilateral investment treaties of countries such as France, Germany, and the United Kingdom rely primarily on the incorporation criterion, "referring to control or substantial interest only in specific contexts, such as the grant of national treatment to investments by nationals of a party." Those of the United States use a combination of incorporation and substantial interest, while other countries such as Switzerland focus only on control.

51 The EC maintains discriminatory rules of origin for professional practice by limiting the benefits of mutual recognition described above to EC nationals. The same applies to the temporary entry privileges obtaining for business people under the FTA and NAFTA, which are reserved for member countries' citizens.

52 Not surprisingly, participants who seek to benefit from preferential access to a protected market would argue for restrictive rules of origin.

10

Tackling International Anticompetitive Practices in the Americas: Implications for the Free Trade Area of the Americas

Julian L. Clarke and Simon J. Evenett

Introduction

In the context of the negotiations for a Free Trade Area of the Americas, it has been proposed that nations in the region enact and enforce a law against private anti-competitive practices. This chapter examines some of the factors that are pertinent to assessing the merits of such a proposal, especially as it relates to laws against cartelization and against so-called hardcore cartels.

The first three sections describe the status of the ongoing negotiations on competition policy in the FTAA and, given our focus on hardcore cartels, defines and characterizes them. More importantly, the fourth section contains accounts of recent initiatives in competition policy in the United States, Brazil, Mexico, Chile, Peru, and Canada. Each account includes an overview of any revisions to national competition legislation during the 1990s, the record of enforcement against hardcore cartels during that time frame, and any proposals advanced for future national and regional initiatives to combat hardcore cartels within the proposed FTAA. As well as providing important context, this part of the study will enable an assessment of the feasibility of national enforcement actions against hardcore cartels in Latin America.

The fifth section of this chapter is more quantitative in nature and aims to provide some estimates of the costs and benefits of national anticartel enforcement. Specifically, it examines whether the magnitude of overcharges borne by Latin American economies from one prominent international hardcore cartel—the long-lasting vitamins cartel—differs systematically across nations according to the presence of an active anticartel enforcement regime. The policy implications of this quantitative analysis, plus the first part of the study, are summarized in a final section.

It is worth noting in passing that this chapter will not cover such competition policy matters as mergers and acquisitions, or the relationship between trade and competition policies more generally, except where discussion of those topics is germane to the focus on hardcore cartels.

Negotiations on Competition Policy in an FTAA

At the Summit of the Americas in Miami, Florida, December 9–11, 1994, thirty-four Latin American nations met to discuss their mutual interest in a broad range of issues ranging from trade to the environment and even women's issues.[1] The group met again in Denver the following year to discuss the specifics of a future trade agreement. Their work at these two summits evolved into the draft version of FTAA. The participating countries, listed in alphabetical order, are: Antigua and Barbuda, Argentina, the Bahamas, Barbados, Belize, Bolivia, Brazil, Canada, Colombia, Chile, Costa Rica, Dominica, Dominican Republic, Ecuador, El Salvador, Grenada, Guatemala, Guyana, Haiti, Honduras, Jamaica, Mexico, Nicaragua, Panama, Paraguay, Peru, St. Kitts and Nevis, St. Lucia, St. Vincent and the Grenadines, Suriname, Trinidad and Tobago, United States, Uruguay and Venezuela.

The draft agreement has evolved significantly since its inception, and has not yet been finalized. The excerpts quoted in this document contain square brackets, which indicate text that is still being debated and may be excluded or amended before the FTAA is finally adopted. Because some countries have chosen to keep their FTAA proposals confidential, other primary sources (such as country submissions to the Working Group on the Interaction between Trade and Competition Policy [WGTCP] at the World Trade Organization [WTO] and to the Organization for Economic Cooperation and Development [OECD] Global Forum on Competition), in addition to various secondary sources by other authors, are used in this analysis to determine national priorities.

The FTAA negotiating group began working on the competition chapter in 1997. The results of the workshop set out a broad agenda for the negotiations that followed. In general, the negotiating parties agreed that they should aim for free competition within the constraints of existing multilateral commitments. To this end, there was agreement that each country should create a specialized and independent agency capable of applying and reviewing competition policy. The principles of transparency and nondiscrimination were to be respected and the philosophy of positive comity was to underlie all the measures adopted. In particular, it was clear at the Brazil Workshop in 1997 that parties were aware from the beginning that inexperienced Latin American countries would require special assistance in adhering to the requirements of a competition agreement and that any competition framework would have to serve the dual purpose of educating members about competition and promoting and enforcing competition.[2] There is no explicit reference to a desire to harmonize the laws of the various members, but there is a proposed requirement to grant legal personality to complainants from member states in the local jurisdictions of other members, and a desire to create a forum for dispute settlement between members.

In 2002 the FTAA Negotiating Group on Competition Policy compiled an inventory of domestic laws and regulations pertaining to competition policy in the Western Hemisphere. This inventory was part of a broader study on existing competition regimes in Latin America. It showed that

> thirteen (13) countries in the hemisphere have legislation and institutions on free competition: Argentina (1919, amended in 1946 and 1980, and currently under review), Brazil (1962, amended in 1990 and revised in 1994), Canada (1889, and subsequent legislation and amendments), Colombia (1959, supplemented in 1992), Costa Rica (1994), Chile (1959, amended in 1973 and revised and incorporated in 1979), Jamaica (1993), Mexico (1934, replaced in 1992), Panama (1996), Peru (1991, modified in 1994 and 1996), Uruguay (2001), Venezuela (1991) and United States (1890 and subsequent other legislation and amendments).
>
> Furthermore, Bolivia, Ecuador, Honduras, El Salvador, Guatemala, Nicaragua, Dominican Republic, and Trinidad and Tobago are actively designing and debating respective draft legislation on the issue.[3]

The Draft Agreement on Competition Policy[4] is divided into nine sections: Competition Law, Regulatory Principles, Legal Monopolies, Institutional Provisions, Review Mechanism, Dispute Settlement, Technical Assistance, Transitional Measures, Confidentiality. It seems that 2002 was a busy year for the FTAA negotiating group for competition policy because the text of the agreeement was amended substantially between May and November. An analysis of the differences between the May and November drafts provides useful insight into the direction being taken by the negotiators. For example, the May draft stipulates that parties would be allowed to exclude certain cartels from their obligations under the agreement. Section 1.3.3 stated that "[[. . . . After the entry into force of this Agreement, the Parties shall make an [annual] notification to the Committee provided for in point 3.5 of any new exclusion or extended exclusion or category of authorization related to hard core cartels.]]" Interestingly, the reference to hardcore cartels disappeared from the November version, which is somewhat stricter in terms of the right of parties to exempt or exclude certain anticompetitive agreements. The latter draft states requires exclusions to be reviewed periodically by the member country or by a subregional entity to determine whether they remain necessary:

> [1.3 Any exclusions or exceptions from the coverage of national or subregional competition measures shall be transparent and [should] be reviewed periodically by the Party or subregional entity to evaluate if they are necessary to achieve their overriding policy objectives. [After the entry into force of this Agreement, the parties shall make a notification to the Committee provided for in point 3.5 [3.2] of any new or extended exclusion or exemption.]][5]

The review committee mentioned in the last sentence is a nonbinding mechanism that, it must be stressed, does not prejudge any disputes that may arise under the dispute settlement provisions outlined elsewhere in the draft FTAA.

Another interesting point of comparison in the documents is the extent to which cooperation is enforced. In the May draft, under the heading Anti-Competitive Conduct with Cross-Border Impact, the language regarding enforcement cooperation against hardcore cartels is hortatory rather than binding. It asks the parties to the agreement only to "consider cooperating in investigating and taking appropriate action, carrying out joint investigations, where appropriate."[6] There is no *obligation* to cooperate in enforcement. This issue is highlighted again in Section 1.2.2:

> If there is evidence that anticompetitive practices are being carried out in the territory of a Party, and that these practices negatively affect the interests of another Party, and in the event that such activities are not permitted under the competition law of the Party in which they are occurring, the competition authority of the affected Party *may request* [italics added] that the competition authority of the other Party investigate and, as appropriate, take appropriate action, pursuant to its own legislation.[7]

To reiterate, in this earlier draft there is no obligation for parties to cooperate in the investigation of any type of cross-border, anticompetitive conduct. The use of the words "may request" indicates this lack of a binding commitment upon signatories in this regard. The party receiving such a request is not obligated to comply with it, nor is there any route by which a party affected by cross-border, anti-competitive measures originating in another party's territory can seek compensation for damages caused.[8]

The November draft is equally weak on the issue of enforcement. While paying lip service to the principles of notification and comity, it leaves open the final question of whether or not parties will be able to take action based upon requests from a fellow FTAA member. Section 4.3.3 states clearly that "[nothing in this provision limits the discretion of the requested Party's competition authority under its competition laws and enforcement policies as to whether to undertake enforcement activities with respect to the anticompetitive activities identified in a request (positive comity)].[9]

In sum, it seems that one of the principal obligations of a potential FTAA competition agreement is to enact some form of legislation against private anticompetitive practices, of which hardcore cartels are a leading example. The next section provides a brief account of what these cartels are.

Hardcore Cartels

The term hardcore cartels has acquired a special significance since the OECD members agreed to the nonbinding 1998 Recommendation on such cartels. According to the OECD, a hardcore cartel is "an anticompetitive agreement, anticompetitive concerted practice, or anticompetitive arrangement by competitors to fix prices, make rigged bids (collusive tenders), establish output restrictions or quotas, or share or divide markets by allocating consumers, suppliers, territories, or lines of commerce."[10]

Interestingly, the FTAA definition of anticompetitive behavior is almost a replica of the OECD definition. Looking at the latest DACP we see that anticompetitive behavior has been defined as "[...anticompetitive agreements, anticompetitive concerted practices or anticompetitive arrangements by competitors to fix prices, make rigged bids (collusive tenders), establish output restrictions or quotas, or share or divide markets by allocating customers, suppliers, territories or lines of commerce]."[11]

Perhaps the most important distinction between the definition of a traditional cartel and that of a hardcore cartel is the repeated reference to the phrase "anticompetitive" in the definition of the latter.[12] This raises the issue of whether a cartel could be pro-competitive, that is, whether a cartel's formation could result in lower prices for purchasers. Some Chicago-school scholars have pointed out that, as a theoretical matter it is possible for a cartel—under certain specific circumstances—to result in large enough cost reductions that prices paid by purchasers actually fall.[13] The relevance of this theoretical observation for policy discourse has not been established in the available empirical evidence on recently prosecuted private international cartels. It should be noted that hardcore cartels exist in both the government and private sector and that they may be either national or international in scope. This chapter is concerned with hardcore cartels in the private sector and, where possible, focuses on cartels that are international in character.

Agreements formed between conspirators in a cartel are, by definition, explicit. Often, meetings between the cartel conspirators are documented and the exact nature of the conspiracy is laid out in considerable detail in agreements between all cartel members. Hardcore cartels are characterized by secretive behaviour. The cartel operators tend to hide documentation outside of the jurisdictions in which they conspire, making the task of prosecuting them difficult unless the cooperation of competition agencies and judiciaries in other countries can be counted upon. Cartels also tend to organize in countries in which competition laws are lax or nonexistent. These countries form so-called safe havens for the conspirators.[14]

Hardcore cartels distort competition in markets by conspiring to fix prices and quantities and by segregating markets. In doing so they harm customers who are forced to pay higher prices for goods and services, tending to restrict choice as well as the availability of products. The rents garnered by the cartel conspirators amount to a transfer from the customer. The net result of this rent seeking is normally waste and certainly inefficiency in the affected market. Finally, hardcore cartels are often international in the sense that their effects are felt simultaneously in many jurisdictions or their membership is drawn from firms located in more than one economy.

Measures against hardcore cartels range from orders to discontinue this form of anticompetitive behavior to fines and the imprisonment of executives. It appears that there are limits to the effectiveness of national enforcement efforts against international hardcore cartels for a number of reasons. Efforts in one jurisdiction, especially when the jurisdiction in question is small, may have a negligible impact upon the overall conspiracy.[15] Moreover, firms may be reluctant to apply for corporate leniency in a country with a small economy if doing so jeopardizes the profits garnered by cartelizing in larger jurisdictions abroad, especially if the original leniency application decision is eventually made public.

Cartels became the focus of much attention in international discussions on competition policy during the late 1990s. Since 1993, the United States Department of Justice has prosecuted more than forty private international cartels. During the same period, many Latin American countries reinvigorated their competition regimes and enforcement capacities to cater to large-scale privatization in their economies. Countries such as Mexico, Brazil, and, to an extent, Peru, promoted competition policies during this decade as a means of ensuring that domestic market reforms were not eroded by the power of formerly state-run enterprises.

The prosecution of international cartels in the United States during the 1990s formed the first investigative challenge for many of the newly restructured Latin American competition agencies. Confessions of cartel members in the United States indicated that conspiracies by firms to fix prices and output were distorting markets not just in the United States, but also in certain Latin American economies. Brazil, for example, found itself to be host to the Latin American corporate headquarters of the perpetrators of the vitamins cartel.[16]

More generally, enforcement activities against cartels in the 1990s also took place in Brazil, Mexico, Peru, and Canada. In Brazil, Mexico, and Canada, action against cartels was prompted at least in part by the U.S. Department of Justice investigations.[17] In Peru, action was taken against domestic cartels, including the notorious poultry cartel,[18] but no enforcement actions in Peru were undertaken against international cartels. The enforcement activities of these Latin American countries against international cartels revealed the scope of industries affected by cartelization and raised the concern that previous enforcement actions undertaken in Latin American countries may not have been of a magnitude sufficient to deter future cartelization.

In addition, the attempts of the Latin American countries to investigate anticompetitive behavior were hampered by constraints on information sharing between enforcement agencies. The deficiencies of national and regional legislation in the area of cartel enforcement were partially responsible for the initiatives on competition policy that have appeared in the proposed legislation of both MERCOSUR and the FTAA.

Competition Laws and Experience with Cartel Enforcement in Selected Nations in the Americas

This section contains brief accounts of a number of national initiatives in competition law, its enforcement—especially as it relates to hardcore cartels—and certain proposals made in international fora on matters related to competition policy.

The United States of America

The first U.S. competition law was the Sherman Act of 1890. The first section of that act criminalizes "hardcore cartel activity, price-fixing, bid-rigging and market allocation agreements."[19] The United States has the strictest penalties in the region to deter this form of anticompetitive conduct, and can punish conspirators with fines and prison terms. Fines are based on a complicated formula involving 20 percent of the affected commerce for the period of the conspiracy plus a multiplier, based on a "culpability score" that, among other factors, takes the previous violations of antitrust law by a firm into account. The culpability score then informs the multipliers, which are added to the original fine, thus potentially increasing it drastically. The base fine of US$35,090,000 imposed upon Mitsubishi for its part in the graphite electrodes cartel, for example, was increased to $134,000,000 by the time the culpability score and the multipliers had been factored in.[20]

Prison terms are likewise included in the arsenal of weapons available to antitrust enforcers in the Unites States. These prison terms may be imposed on foreign nationals as easily as upon U.S. citizens. As evidence of this it is worth noting that over twenty defendants have been sentenced to incarceration for one year or longer with an average prison term of fifteen months. Six Swiss and German executives from F. Hoffmann-La Roche AG and BASF AG were convicted for their role in one conspiracy alone, and all served time in U.S. prisons.[21]

The U.S. Department of Justice relies on a "carrot-and-stick" approach to uncovering and prosecuting hardcore cartels. The punishments, as outlined above, are severe. The question may well be asked, therefore, what is the carrot? The department induces companies to come forward and confess their role in a cartel in return for a full or partial amnesty on punishments. This grant of leniency can extend to all officers, directors, and employees of the company who choose to cooperate with the authorities. Full leniency applies only to the first company to come forward with a confession of involvement in a cartel. Moreover, amongst other conditions, such leniency will only be granted if there is no preexisting investigation by the antitrust authorities.

The success of this approach, which has been in operation since 1993, is described in reports by the Department of Justice such as the following:

> Under the old policy, the Division obtained roughly one amnesty application per year. Under the new policy, the application rate has jumped to more than one per month. Moreover, the application rate has surged over the last year to better than two per month, and to over four per month in the first three months of this fiscal year. As a result of this increased interest, the Division frequently encounters situations where a company approaches the government within days, and in some cases less than one business day, after one of its co-conspirators has secured its position as first in line for amnesty.[22]

Since 1993, the Department of Justice has prosecuted around forty international cartels across a range of industries. In 2001, seventy-percent of the companies charged were firms based outside the United

States and roughly thirty-three percent of the individual defendants were foreign nationals.[23] The scope of U.S. enforcement activity in this area dwarfs that of any other country in the region.

In terms of international cooperation, the United States has worked closely with enforcement officials in certain countries, notably Canada with which it has a Mutual Legal Assistance Treaty that covers antitrust matters as well as other intergovernmental agreements. Moreover, the Antitrust Division of the Department of Justice has signed antitrust cooperation agreements with competition agencies in Japan, Brazil, Israel, Mexico, Australia, Germany, Canada and the European Union.[24] The Department of Justice has also made use of the international police force, Interpol, to detain and to extradite criminals wanted for antitrust crimes undertaken, or having effects in, the United States.[25]

These considerations appear to have informed the U.S. position on the competition chapter in the FTAA. The United States believes that cooperation among the FTAA parties is important for the propagation of competition law and policy development. It does not advocate the harmonization of competition law,[26] but does, however, recommend technical assistance on competition policy and law enforcement. The United States further believes that the DACP should mandate that each country have a competition agency at the national or subregional level responsible for the enforcement of antitrust laws within its jurisdiction. These agencies should be subject to independent judicial review and operate according to the core principles of transparency, due process, and nondiscrimination.[27]

Brazil

In 1994 Brazil passed a new competition law (no. 8.884) which converted the Administrative Council for Economic Defense and the Brazilian Administrative Antitrust Tribunal into independent agencies.[28] In institutional terms, a president and a board of commissioners govern the council. The president is a former federal judge with a background in international law, and the majority of the commissioners are economists and lawyers drawn from Brazilian universities. This reorganization is part of a concerted effort to maintain the independence of the competition body from the government interference that had plagued competition authorities in the past.[29]

Brazil offers a carrot-and-stick approach to enforcement of competition law that mirrors that used by the United States. The two competition agencies that support the Administrative Council for Economic Defense in Brazil—the Secretariat for Economic Monitoring and the Secretariat for Economic Law—are able to impose fines, recommend imprisonment (of between two and five years for cartel members), and offer leniency as an inducement to conspirators who may wish to confess to their involvement in a cartel.[30]

Brazil prosecuted approximately ten hardcore cartels during the 1990s, not all of which were international in character. The industries affected included steel, orange juice, lysine, vitamins, maritime transportation, aluminum, and even gasoline stations. Brazil claims, however, that its enforcement ability during this period was hampered by lack of cooperation from the United States. Brazil was tipped off to the operation of the vitamins cartel, for example, by the unilateral enforcement actions of its U.S. colleagues. Brazilian competition agents discovered that the headquarters for the vitamin conspirators in Latin America were located within Brazil only upon reading about the U.S. prosecution of the conspiracy,[31] and then were frustrated to find that the United States was unwilling to share more information on the cartel because of legal constraints on confidential information. This left the Brazilians to piece together the conspiracy based solely upon hints and informal cooperation from their U.S. counterparts.[32]

After its experience investigating and prosecuting the vitamins cartel, Brazil's submissions to international and regional fora has been characterized by proposals encouraging cooperation between countries. In October 1999 the Brazilians signed an agreement with the United States for the informal exchange of information between their antitrust enforcers.[33] A recent bilateral agreement with Russia contained similar provisions,[34] and Brazil's proposal to MERCOSUR on competition policy also encourages cooperation in broad terms. It is in its proposal to the FTAA that Brazil is most specific about its requirements, stating that: "the development of mechanisms aiming at promoting cooperation and information exchange among antitrust authorities" is one of its four negotiating goals.[35]

Mexico

The Federal Competition Commission of Mexico was created in 1993 as an independent body charged with overseeing competition in the marketplace.[36] As in Brazil, the competition agency evolved as a means of ensuring competition in the wake of the concurrent privatization of state-run enterprises.[37] The commission contains a decision-making body called the Plenum, which is also entrusted with the task of notifying authorities of criminal conduct in antitrust matters. It should be noted that any form of implicit or explicit collusion is per se illegal under Mexican law and that the commission is not obliged to prove distortions to markets as a result of any conspiracy it uncovers; cartels are assumed to be damaging in all cases.[38] Judicial sanctions take the form of fines; prison sentences are not included in the catalogue of permitted punishments available to Mexican prosecutors.[39]

The commission's brief expanded beyond the enforcement of competition in privatized industries to encompass other forms of anticompetitive conduct. Turning once more to the vitamins cartel, we observe that information about its existence in Mexico came to light in a press release by the U.S. Department of Justice regarding its investigation into this decade-long conspiracy. Mexico initiated an investigation into the branch offices of the same companies under investigation in the United States. Unlike their Brazilian counterparts, the Mexican antitrust authorities did not seek information from the United States, but rather approached the conspirators themselves to gain confessions and employed other investigatory tactics.

The main drawback of Mexico's competition legislation is that it does not provide for corporate leniency, which restricts its ability to successfully uncover and prosecute cartels.[40] Thus, the carrot-and-stick strategy favored by the United States cannot be applied in Mexico. That Mexican antitrust agencies are less successful in uncovering cartels because of the absence of a leniency provision, and that the Mexicans themselves suspect as much, is made clear in the words of the Mexican submission to the WGTCP: "the legal framework does not provide for leniency programs and so the CFC [Federal Competition Commission of Mexico] frequently lacks elements to detect collusive agreements. It also faces some opposition to information and document requirements needed to compile legal evidence to substantiate proceedings."[41] Mexico's ambitions for competition policy in the FTAA, therefore, may be inferred from its experience in prosecuting cartels as well as from its submissions to international bodies regarding competition policy. In fact, Mexico's submission to the OECD Global Forum on Competition in 2001 lists three areas in which it envisages the need for further initiatives: competition advocacy at a social level, the inability to impose requests for cooperation outside Mexican borders and the ability of competition authority to deal with dynamism and progress.[42] To this end,

> The FCC has promoted coordination with other countries' competition authorities to exchange experiences and apply techniques of analysis of competition in a global context. This coordination has led to the negotiation and subscription of international treaties and agreements. Similarly, there has been active and prominent participation in international fora in which the topics of competition and best practices are discussed, among them are the OECD, WTO, UNCTAD and EFTA. These actions provide the FCC with better tools to protect Mexican interests.[43]

Chile

Chile's competition enforcement regime is founded on a law from 1973, Decree Law 211, that "created diverse organizations in charge of the prevention, correction and repression of commercial practices that might harm freedom of competition in economic activities. These agencies are: the Economic National Prosecutor´s Office, the Resolutory Commission, the Central Preventive Commission, and the Regional Preventive Commissions."[44]

The antitrust authority is independent of the government, and the National Economic Prosecutor is also independent from the other three commissions. Penalties may take the form of either fines or imprisonment. Unlike the Mexican law, Chilean law insists that the burden of proof lies with the anticompetition agency. The latter must show that there has been an anticompetitive agreement and, importantly, that damage has resulted from it. Leniency programs are not mentioned.[45]

Chile considers that cooperation is an issue that should be addressed at a regional level, as evidenced by its recent agreements with Canada and Costa Rica. A memorandum of understanding signed between the three governments aims at harmonizing the enforcement of competition laws. [46] To date, however, there is no evidence that Chile has cooperated on antitrust matters with other countries (or that other countries have cooperated with Chile) in practice. Moreover, there is no record of international cartels being prosecuted in Chile. The Chilean antitrust bodies are intensely involved in mergers and acquisitions, and Chile's appeal for technical assistance—an adjunct to its submission to the OECD in 2002—focuses on the complexity of merger requirements rather than on the enforcement actions against cartels.[47]

Peru

The Peruvian Free Competition Commission operates as a unit within the National Institute of Defence of Competition and Protection of Intellectual Property, which was established in 1991. The Free Competition Commission operates under Legislative Decree Number 701, which is a "law of elimination of monopoly, control and restrictive practices of free competition [which] establishes the prohibition of abusive practices of a dominant position as well as the restrictive practices of competition which involve the concerted action of two or more competitors in the market."[48] Article 6 of the same decree lists the anti-competitive criteria as including

> a) direct or indirect agreement among competitors to fix prices or other commercial conditions or services; . . . (c) the allocation of production quotas; d) agreement on the quality of products, as long as they do not correspond to national or international standards and have a negative effect on the consumer; . . . h) agreement to limit or control production, distribution, innovations and technical development; . . . j) Other cases of similar effect.

Penalties for cartelization include imprisonment and fines. There is no mention in legislation or enforcement practice of a leniency program.[49]

Peru's experience in prosecuting hardcore cartels is somewhat limited. The most important hardcore cartel case that the Peruvian competition authorities have faced was the poultry cartel. The cartel was preceded by the overproduction of baby chickens, which depressed prices. The unique nature of the Peruvian poultry industry prevented international competitors from playing a major part in it. Some 80 percent of total chicken production in Peru is traded live and only 20 percent is slaughtered chicken. Most slaughtered chicken is sold in refrigerated form to supermarkets and there is a small market for frozen chicken, which is traded mostly in the southern highlands of the country. The only opening for international trade is in the market for frozen chicken in the South, which is a small segment of the overall chicken market.[50] The lack of international competition made it easy for domestic Peruvian producers to organizc and operate a cartel based on price fixing through output controls on poultry. The cartel, which included nineteen firms trading in the market for live chickens, developed anticompetitive mechanisms to suppress and eliminate competitors in the markets of metropolitan Lima and Callao.

Lengthy and detailed investigation by the Peruvian authorities found that the conspiracy had been explicitly managed through a "statistics committee" run by the poultry industry. They determined that the conspiracy breached Decree 701, which sanctioned any business practice that generated *or could generate* the effect of restricting or hindering competition. In addition, the conspirators were in breach of an amendment, Decree 807, which states in article 6h that the "agreement to limit or to control production volumes is an anticompetitive practice."[51] The decree establishes the maximum fine for anti-competitive behavior to be one thousand taxing units. Taxing Units are set by the Ministry of the Economy and generally vary between US$900 and 1000.00 per unit depending upon the exchange rate. There is no prison term for anticompetitive behavior.[52] In its prosecution of the poultry case, the Free Competition Commission respected the confidentiality of business information. Fines were eventually imposed upon twenty-one conspirators and the amount of each fine was not higher than 10 percent of their sales through the distribution centers, amounts that were later reduced on appeal.

Peru's submissions to international competition forums have stressed the need for technical assistance in the analysis of mergers and determination of market dominance but do not focus in detail on cartels. None of Peru's submissions concern either the regional application of competition policy or the problems of enforcement against international cartels.

Canada

Canada's main competition authority is the Competition Tribunal. It came into being in 1986 as a result of reforms to competition policy enacted by the Canadian Parliament. During the late 1990s the Canadian Parliament renewed the brief of the competition authority to give it increased powers:

The committee's preliminary findings are that the government, after consulting with the public, should consider whether to do the following:

- modify the abuse of dominant position provision (section 79) to deal with predatory pricing and price maintenance;
- introduce guidelines on abuse of dominant position and conspiracies;

- make the price discrimination provisions reviewable;
- permit private individuals to make applications to the Competition Tribunal;
- introduce an interim cease and desist order;
- create a two-track approach for agreements relating to conspiracies (section 45);
- reevaluate the minimum thresholds for reviewing a merger.[53]

The Canadians have been actively supporting initiatives to combat anticompetitive practices in their submissions to the FTAA, and have proposed substantial amendments to the existing DACP. These have been summarized in the FTAA Inventory of Rules and Regulations as follows:

> The proposed framework (submitted by Canada) includes an obligation from signatory countries to adopt or maintain a competition law and to establish or maintain an independent and impartial competition agency authorized to take appropriate action and to advocate competition in regulated sectors. The framework also includes an obligation for countries to adhere to general principles of transparency, nondiscrimination and procedural fairness, as well as mechanisms to promote enforcement cooperation and coordination. Consultation mechanisms and peer review are also part of the proposal. In addition, the negotiating group considered the topic of competition policy in smaller economies and economies without competition regimes, and concluded terms of reference for further study. In the area of technical assistance, the Bureau participated in technical sessions, including one on competition issues related to the deregulation of the electricity sector, in general as well as in Ontario and Alberta.

The draft chapter on competition policy consolidates all countries' proposals and shows that consensus has yet to be reached on many issues.[54]

Canada's enforcement record against hardcore cartels is strong but does not yet compare with that of the United States. Between 1993 and 1999, the Canadian Competition Bureau prosecuted several international cartels that were found to be in breach of the Canadian

Competition Act. These cartels operated in eleven industries and included most of the famous hardcore cartels prosecuted by the United States during the same period. The markets for bulk vitamins, citric acid, sorbates, choline chloride, sodium gluconate, graphite electrodes, lysine, fax paper, pipe, chemical insecticides, and biological insecticides were all victimized by cartels in Canada at some point during this period.[55]

Penalties for the conspirators, who were both companies and individuals, ranged from fines to prison sentences. Dr Roland Bronnimann, chief executive of Hoffman-La Roche, for example, was personally fined Can$250,000 for his role in the bulk vitamins cartel, in addition to the fine of $48,000,000 which was imposed upon his company. Other executives were not fortunate enough to escape with just a fine. Mr. Russell Cosburn, a former executive of Chinook Group Ltd., was imprisoned for nine months and ordered to serve a further fifty hours of community service for his role in the choline chloride cartel. This punishment was in addition to a fine of Can$2,250,000 imposed on Chinook Group Ltd. itself.

Despite this enforcement record, Canada has made no specific proposals on hardcore cartels in the FTAA negotiations. Moreover, in its 2002 submissions to the WTO[56] Canada refrained from making any proposals for multilateral disciplines on hardcore cartels, submitting only questions about the form of a future agreement. Similarly, Canada's draft of the DACP, which can be found on the web site of its Competition Tribunal, has no proposed wording on anticompetitive conduct with cross-border impacts. The section is simply left blank.[57] This is in contrast with its submission of no less than four proposals on core principles as they relate to competition policy between 2001 and 2002,[58] and two on voluntary cooperation in the year 2002 alone.[59]

Potential Lessons from these National Experiences

What can be learned from these countries' experiences with cartel enforcement since 1990? First, the countries in the Western Hemisphere differ markedly in the nature and extent of their competition laws. Although each of the countries examined above has some form of competition legislation, there are a number of Latin American countries that at present do not. Countries such as Paraguay, Belize, Nicaragua, Guatemala, Honduras, the Dominican Republic, and Costa Rica have not yet enacted any form of competition legislation. These points are important to bear in mind when considering proposals in an FTAA that would require each member to enact and enforce certain competition laws.

Second, enforcement of competition law throughout the region is patchy. Since 1990 the United States has prosecuted nearly forty international cartels, Canada one-third of this amount, Brazil only three, and Peru and Chile have yet to prosecute a single international cartel (the poultry cartel in Peru was a domestic one). The pecuniary penalties against participating in a hardcore cartel are bounded by legislation in several Latin American countries, and while these bounds may have been high in comparison to pecuniary penalties for other crimes committed in those countries, they are in fact quite low when compared to the profits typically made by cartel operators during their conspiracies. These relatively low fines call into question whether the penalties are sufficiently high to deter cartelization in the first place. Furthermore, some Latin American countries appear reluctant to impose fines and/or jail terms on individuals responsible for operating and organizing a hardcore cartel, which similarly weakens the deterrent effect.

Third, enforcement in most Latin American countries suffers from the absence of the carrot-and-stick approach that has been used to prosecute cartels in the United States since the 1970s. So successful has the U.S. leniency program been since it was revised in 1993 that it has resulted in a more than tenfold year-on-year increase in the number of applicants for amnesty.[60] The inability of most Latin American competition authorities to extend leniency to potential conspirators has reduced the number of cartels uncovered within their jurisdictions.

Although there are some examples of formal or informal cooperation between competition agencies in the region, the preponderance of investigations are carried out by a single competition authority acting alone; admittedly, a few of these investigations did have their genesis in oblique or second-hand information gleaned from competition authorities abroad or from press reports of their activities.

The International Vitamins Cartel

By way of introduction to an analysis of the impact of the vitamin cartel on international trade, we provide a brief account of the international vitamins cartel without unnecessarily repeating the detailed accounts that can be found elsewhere.[61] This cartel has been described as "wheels within wheels" by Connor (2001), principally because it comprised a series of interrelated conspiracies to manipulate the markets of at least eight vitamins and four associated chemical compounds.

The cartel started in 1989 when two European vitamin manufacturers—Hoffman-LaRoche and BASF—agreed to gradually increase the price of vitamins A and E and to a geographic division of the world's markets for these two substances.[62] Roche and BASF controlled over seventy percent of sales in these markets and subsequently successfully co-opted their principal rivals, Rhone-Poulenc and Eisai. By 1991, these four companies essentially controlled the world price for vitamins A and E, a situation they were able to sustain until 1999 when the conspiracy was prosecuted by the U.S. antitrust authorities.

The conspirators' success encouraged them to widen the scope of the cartel to include other vitamins and other producers. By the end of the 1990s, twenty-two manufacturers one time or another had been a part of the twelve "wheels" (cartels) within the overall vitamins conspiracy.[63] So extensive was the price fixing within these markets that the European Commission branded the entire vitamins industry a single conspiracy.[64] Table 10.1 lists the durations of eight such "wheels." It is noteworthy that five of these conspiracies lasted until (at least) 1998, potentially distorting international markets throughout almost the entire 1990s. In contrast, the cartel in vitamins B1, B6, and folic acid fell apart in 1994, largely as a result of competition from Chinese exporters that were not members of the cartel.

In late 1998, Rhone-Poulenc sought corporate leniency from U.S. antitrust authorities for its participation in the vitamins cartel. It has been argued that Rhone-Poulenc's decision was prompted by the earlier indictment by U.S. authorities of Lonza for the latter's participation in the vitamins B3 cartel. Another factor may well have been the United States' well-publicized investigation into the lysine and citric acid cartels, which included scrutiny of firms that also produced vitamins.[65]

Table 10.2 lists the names and locations of the headquarters of the sixteen firms that, according to U.S. federal indictments in 1999, participated in the vitamins conspiracy.[66] This subsequent American enforcement action resulted in fines of $10.5 million, $5 million, $500 million, $225 million, $72 million, $40 million, $25 million, $13 million, and $2 million for Lonza, Chinook, Hoffman-La Roche, BASF, Takeda, Eisai, Daiichi, Degussa, and Reilly/Vitachem, respectively.

The European Commission's investigation into this cartel's activities revealed a slightly different set of cartel members and estimates of each wheel's duration (see Table 10.3). Four additional companies were found to have participated in this cartel: Kongo Chemical Co. (headquartered in Japan), Solvay Pharmaceuticals (headquartered in

Table 10.1 Conspirators Forming Eight Global Cartels to Fix the Prices of Selected Compounds, 1990–1999

Duration of cartel	1990–99	1990–99	1991–94	1991–95	1991–98	1991–98	1989–98	1989–96
Products	A&E	B12	B1, B6 & Folic	C & B2	B5	Beta Carotene	Niacin	Choline Chloride
Cartel Members	Roche BASF Rhone Eisai	Rhone Hoechst	Roche Takeda Daiichi	Roche BASF Takeda E. Merck	Roche BASF Daiichi	Roche BASF	Degussa Lonza Napera	Chinook Mitsui DuCoa BASF Akzo UCB

Source: Connor (2001: 307).

Table 10.2 Companies Mentioned in U.S. Federal Indictments and the Locations of Their Headquarters

Company	Country
Akzo	Netherlands
BASF	Germany
Chinoook	Canada
Daiichi	Japan
Degussa	Germany
DuCoa	USA
Eisai	Japan
Hoechst	Germany
Lonza	Switzerland
Merck	Netherlands
Mitsui	Japan
Napera	USA
Rhone-Poulenc	France
Roche	Switzerland
Takeda	Japan
UCB	Belgium

Source: U.S. Department of Justice Press Releases 1999–2000.

the Netherlands), Sumitomo (headquartered in Japan), and Tanabe (headquartered in Japan.) The EC enforcement action resulted in the following fines for nine firms: Hoffman-La Roche, €462 million; BASF, €296.16 million; Takeda, €37.06 million; Eisai, €13.23 million; Daiichi, €23.4 million; Merck, €9.24 million; Aventis, €5.04 million; Solvay Pharmaceuticals, €9.1 million; and Takeda, €37.06 million.[67]

This brief account of the international vitamins cartel would be incomplete without some mention of the role that Chinese exporters are said to have played in disrupting some of the cartel's wheels.[68] Chinese firms remained outside the cartel and their exports of vitamins and polyvitamins surged after 1991 (see Figure 10.1). These exports rose from just under $100 million in 1990 to nearly $350 million in 1995 before falling back to approximately $250 million in 1997, and then rose sharply to over $350 million in 2000 (all of these import values were measured in year 2000 in U.S. dollars).[69] It has been claimed that Chinese exports were an important factor in the breakdown in 1994 of the cartel in Vitamins B1 and B6 and in folic acid.[70]As will become clear, in estimating the effect of the vitamins cartel's formation on the value of vitamins exported from countries where the conspirators

Table 10.3 Cartels Uncovered in the EC Investigation

Vitamin	Participants	Duration* From	Duration* To
Vitamin A	Roche, BASF, Rhone-Poulenc (Aventis)	September 1989	February 1999
Vitamin E	Roche, BASF, Rhone-Poulenc (Aventis), Eisai	September 1989	February 1999
Vitamin B1 (Thiamine)	Roche, Takeda, BASF	January 1991	June 1994
Vitamin B2 (Riboflavin)	Roche, BASF, Takeda	January 1991	September 1995
Vitamin B5 (Calpan)	Roche, BASF, Daiichi	January 1991	February 1999
Vitamin B6	Roche, Takeda, Daiichi	January 1991	June 1994
Folic Acid (B)	Roche, Takeda, Kongo, Sumika	January 1991	June 1994
Vitamin C	Roche, BASF, Takeda, Merck	January 1991	August 1995
Vitamin D3	Roche, BASF, Solvay Pharmaceuticals, Rhone-Poulenc (Aventis)	January 1994	June 1998
Vitamin H (Biotin)	Roche, Merck, Lonza, Sumitomo, Tanabe, BASF	October 1991	April 1994
Beta Carotene	Roche, BASF	September 1992	December 1998
Carotinioids	Roche, BASF	May 1993	December 1998

Source: F. Arbault et al. (2001: 32).
*The duration of each company's participation in a cartel need not necessarily be the same.

maintained their headquarters, this chapter attempts to control for the effect of Chinese vitamins exports.

With these facts in mind we turn to our theoretical rationale for an analysis of the vitamin cartel's effects on international trade flows and discuss the way in which our empirical analysis has been implemented.[71]

Effect of Cartelization on Prices and Total Revenues or Sales

Theoretical analyses of cartel behavior invariably focus on the conspiracy's effects on the prices charged to buyers, rather than on the effects on total revenues (or total sales) of the cartel members.[72] For our

Figure 10.1 Chinese Exports of Vitamins and Polyvitamins (1985–2000)

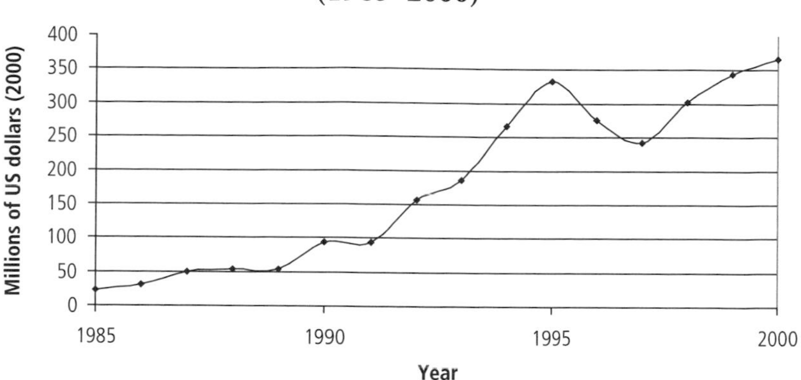

current purposes, this emphasis is unfortunate as international trade data on the price of vitamins is much more scarce than data on the *total value* of purchases by buyers located in one economy from firms or sellers located in another economy. Assuming a given price elasticity of the good in question, the implications of a cartel's decision to raise prices in a market for the value of total sales by cartel members in that market can be readily ascertained. If the demand for a good is price inelastic, then an increase in price will generate an increase in total revenues. What is more, because demand falls when prices rise, one can also conclude that the percentage increase in total revenues that result from the formation of the cartel bounds from below the price increase that is caused by the conspiracy. These considerations are pertinent to analysis of the international vitamins cartel because a detailed study of the vitamins-producing sector has concluded that the demand for different types of vitamins is indeed price inelastic.[73]

Establishing a Benchmark for Trade Flows in the Absence of Cartelization

It is thus clear how total sales in a market—be it domestic or foreign—can be distorted by the creation of a cartel. This begs the question of what benchmark level of sales would have prevailed in the absence of the cartel. In the international trade context, such a benchmark is important because it establishes the value of exports from one nation's firms to another nation's buyers as it would have been in the absence of the cartel. Fortunately, the study of such bilateral trade flows is well advanced in international trade research and provides a benchmark that can be implemented empirically.

One of the few—perhaps the only—robust empirical regularity in the analysis of international trade flows is known as the gravity equation. This equation relates the total value of one nation's imports from another nation positively to the levels of national income of both countries and negatively to the distance between them.[74] Over the last twenty-five years our understanding of the theoretical underpinning of the gravity equation has deepened[75] and empirical analyses of this equation have become more sophisticated.[76] What follows draws upon this substantial body of research into bilateral trade flows. Specifically, this paper adopts a standard formulation of the gravity equation. Denote:

M_{ij}^{v} as the total value of country *i*'s imports of vitamins (v) from country *j*;
Y_j^v as the total value of country *j*'s production of vitamins (v);
Y_i as country *i*'s national income or gross domestic product;
Y_j as country *j*'s national income or gross domestic product;
Y_W as the world's total income or gross product;
M_{ij} as the total value of all country *i*'s imports from nation *j*.

Following Anderson's theoretical analysis of the gravity equation,[77] in the absence of barriers to international trade flows, with balanced trade in each nation and each country's buyers have identical and homothetic preferences, one can derive the following two expressions for the gravity equation:

$$M_{ij}^{v} = \left(\frac{Y_i}{Y_w}\right) y_j^v \tag{1}$$

$$M_{ij} = \left(\frac{Y_i}{Y_w}\right) Y_j \tag{2}$$

Equation 1 refers to the gravity equation for a single good (v) and equation 2 refers to the gravity equation for a nation's total imports. Dividing 2 by 1 and rearranging yields

$$M^{v}_{ij} = M_{ij} = \left(\frac{y^{v}_{j}}{Y_{j}}\right) \tag{3}$$

In this formulation, then, country *i*'s imports of vitamins from country *j* would rise 1 percent if the proportion of country *j*'s national output

$$\left(\frac{y^{v}_{j}}{Y_{j}}\right)$$

that is devoted to vitamins production rose by 1 percent also. Furthermore, any factor that leads to a 1 percent reduction in the overall bilateral level of trade between nations *i* and *j* will, in this formulation, lead to *i*'s imports of vitamins from *j* falling by the same percentage. As these predictions were derived in the absence of a cartel, they can form the basis of a benchmark for international trade in vitamins.

Finally, taking logarithms of equation 3 yields

$$\ln(M^{v}_{ij}) = \ln(M_{ij}) + \ln(y^{v}_{j}) - \ln(Y_{j}) \tag{4}$$

which takes a convenient linear form amenable to econometric estimation.

Econometric Strategy

This econometric strategy has two goals. First, by using data on imports by Latin American nations of vitamins before and after the vitamin cartel was formed, one can examine whether the cartel's formation results in a systematic change in the value of bilateral imports of vitamins from that predicted in equation 4 above. As argued earlier, so long as the demand for vitamins is price inelastic and the conspiracy resulted in higher prices, then, if all else is equal, the observed value of country *i*'s vitamins imports (M^{v}_{ij}) should rise after the cartel's formation. In essence, the analysis uses the intertemporal variation of the trade data in vitamins to identify the effect of the cartel's formation.

Second, it is possible to examine whether the impact of the cartel's formation on the total value of a nation's vitamins imports (M^{v}_{ij}) depends on whether that nation's cartel enforcement regime is active or not. Again, several Latin American nations' enforcement agencies actively prosecuted cartels in the 1990s. Moreover, two of these nations (Chile and Peru) only established active competition enforcement authorities after the cartel's formation, providing an opportunity to examine whether the imports of vitamins responded to the creation of such an authority. Therefore, this chapter uses both cross-sectional and intertemporal variation to identify the effects of cartel enforcement on the value of trade in cartelized vitamins.

A time subscript (denoted by t) to each of the variables in equation 4 is added to indicate the year that each (data) observation refers to. Furthermore, to take account of the effect on cartelized imports of competition from Chinese sources, another independent variable, denoted C_t, is included to represent the total exports of Chinese vitamins to all destinations in a given year t. This variable proxies for the marginal costs of production of vitamins in China, assuming that lower marginal costs of production in China would translate—holding other factors constant—into higher Chinese exports to all foreign markets.

Next, four parameters were formed to discriminate between the years before and since the cartel was formed, and between those nations with active cartel enforcement regimes (A) and those non-active enforcement regimes (NA). In our case, the first wheel of the vitamin cartel was formed in 1989, implying that 1990 was the first complete year when vitamins trade was distorted by the cartel's formation. Thus 1990 was taken as the threshold year when the cartel's effects were first fully felt. One can, then, denote these four parameters by A_{1990}, A_{1990}, NA_{1990}, and NA_{1990}, respectively. These four parameters, along with variable and a random error term $\ln(M^v_{ij}) = \ln(M_{ij}) + \ln(y^v_j) - \ln(Y_j)$, could be added to equation 4 to form the following estimating equation:

$$\ln(M^v_{ijt}) = I_{it}A_{1990} + (1 - I_{it})NA_{1990} + I^*_{it}A_{1990} + (1 - I^*_{it})NA_{1990} + \beta_1\ln(M_{ijt}) + \beta_2\ln(y^v_{jt}) + \beta_3\ln(Y_{jt}) + \beta_4\ln(C_t) + \varepsilon_{ijt} \quad (5)$$

Where β_1,β_2,β_3 and β_4 are other parameters to be estimated also, I_{it} takes a value of one if country i has an active enforcement regime in year t (where t is before 1990) and zero otherwise, and I^*_{it} takes a value of one if country i has an active enforcement regime in year t (where t is after 1989) and zero otherwise. In this formulation an economy that commences active cartel enforcement in 1993 will, for example, see I_{it} take a value of zero throughout and I^*_{it} takes a value for years before 1993 and a value of one from 1993.

If equation 5 were confronted with data and estimates of the parameters A_{1990}, NA_{1990}, A_{1990}, NA_{1990} recovered, then the estimated differences $(NA_{1990} - NA_{1990})$ and $(A_{1990} - A_{1990})$ would reveal whether the cartel's formation leads import values to rise faster in nations without active cartel enforcement regimes than in nations that have such regimes. Before discussing the econometric estimation in some detail, we describe certain matters relating to data collection.

Data Collection

We identified above the following eight economies in which the headquarters of the members of the vitamins cartel are located: Belgium, Canada, France, Germany, Japan, the Netherlands, Switzerland, and the United States. Each of these economies exported substantial amounts of vitamins over the years 1985–99. The goal is to examine how these trade flows were distorted—if at all—by the creation of the vitamins cartel. The vitamins exports of other nations where the overseas subsidiaries of the cartel members were based may also have been affected by the formation of this international conspiracy, but lacking detailed data on the location of such subsidiaries, the analysis here focuses only on the exports of vitamins by the eight economies listed above.

Data on vitamins imports by all of the Latin American economies was collected for the years 1985–99. Statistics Canada's *World Trade Analyzer*, which employs the United Nations' classification of economies and customs territories, was used to identify all of the potential vitamins importers in Latin America. A further adjustment was made to the set of importers: those economies that had in the year 2000 a population of less than 5 million people or a national income that was below US$5 billion were deleted.[78] The rationale for this step, which is often taken in studies using the gravity equation, was that such "smaller" economies tend to have unrepresentative trading patterns. Indeed, concerns about the irregular nature of the trading partners of the small Caribbean island economies accounts for this study's focus on the Latin American economies in the first place.

The sample assembled contains annual observations from 1985 to 1999 on the total value of vitamins imports by each (remaining) importer from each of the eight vitamins exporters identified earlier. The value of each importer's total purchases of vitamins can be downloaded from the *World Trade Analyzer* database. The four-digit code for the product line that corresponds to trade in vitamins and polyvitamins is 5411. No other product line at this level of disaggregation that included the word vitamins in the title or descriptor was found. Moreover, further disaggregation of trade in vitamins was not possible with this database. All of its recorded import values are reported in current U.S. dollars and, consequently, each observation was converted into a common base year, specifically year 2000 U.S. dollars. This was accomplished by using the U.S. price deflator for gross domestic product (the so-called U.S. GDP price deflator), which is available on the World Bank's *World Development Indicators* web site.

Data on each importing economy's total purchases of all goods from a given exporter—that is, the observations on M_{ijt}—were also obtained from the *World Trade Analyzer* database. The absence of production data for vitamins in the eight exporting economies necessitated the construction of a proxy variable for y^v_{jt}. As total sales of vitamins by firms located within a given nation j equals the sum of its total sales within nation j and its total sales abroad, the observed level of total vitamins exports by economy j was used as a proxy for y^v_{jt}. Furthermore, for each nation i, one netted out economy i's total imports of vitamins from j's total annual exports of vitamins, so creating a proxy for y^v_{jt} that is denoted by $y^v_{-i,\,jt}$.[79] The final piece of international trade data collected was annual data on the total value of Chinese exports of vitamins, again obtained from the *World Trade Analyzer* database.

Data on the gross domestic product of each exporter was taken from the *World Development Indicators* database. A full set of such GDP data was available for each vitamins exporter except Germany, where GDP data was only available after 1992. The *Penn World Tables* database was the source of the German GDP data before 1992 and, before reunification, only GDP data on West Germany was used.[80]

The last step in data collection was to identify those economies in which there was some evidence of active cartel enforcement. For each importer in the sample, the extensive number of submissions to the OECD's 2001 and 2002 Global Forums on Competition were examined to see if that importer reported any cases of cartel enforcement activity that resulted in fines or some other form of sanction, or in an order to cartel members to cease their conspiracy.[81] If there was such evidence then the importer is classified as having an active cartel enforcement regime in the years since 1985 or the year its anticartel law came into force, whichever is later. Four jurisdictions in the sample were identified as having an active cartel enforcement regime: Brazil and Chile (whose anticartel laws were passed before the vitamins cartel came into effect), Peru (whose anticartel law came into effect in 1991), and Mexico (whose anticartel law came into effect in 1993.)

As far as creating the indicator variables, introduced in equation 5 above, three cases can be distinguished. First, in an economy in which such enforcement activity was reported in OECD documentation and the economy's anticartel legislation came into force before 1990, the indicator variable I_{it} switches from its default value of zero to one for every year since that legislation came into force, and the indicator variable I^*_{it} takes a value of one for every year in the 1990s. Second, in an economy in which evidence of cartel enforcement activity was found and the economy's anticartel legislation came into force during or since 1990, then the indicator variable I_{it} takes a value of zero throughout and the indicator variable I^*_{it} switches from its default value of zero to one for every year since the legislation came into force. In the third case, in which there is no evidence of cartel enforcement by an economy's authorities, both indicator variables I_{it} and I^*_{it} take a value of zero in every year.

This investigation-based measure of the presence of an active cartel enforcement regime is not without its drawbacks. For instance, the binary nature of the indicator does not take into account the differences in the intensity of cartel enforcement efforts among those nations that do have active enforcement regimes. Probably the best defense of the indicators employed here is that they do discriminate between nations on the basis of whether any cartel enforcement activity is reported at all to the international antitrust community that attends or follows meetings at the OECD. Arguably, a national cartel enforcement regime is unlikely to have a strong deterrent effect if members of the community—some of whom advise corporations—do not know of a regime's record in tackling price-fixing conspiracies and the like.

Econometric Concerns and Estimation Procedure

We now have a sample of Latin American importers of vitamins. It might be tempting to confront equation 5 with data from each sample and use standard ordinary least squares techniques to recover the relevant parameters. However, this would ignore several important econometric concerns.

First, many of the observed levels of vitamins imports (M^v_{ijt}) equal zero—especially in the poorest importing nations. As the logarithm of zero is undefined, this would pose a considerable problem. Often, this problem is—to put it politely—sidestepped by assuming that a dollar's worth of imports actually occurred, which yields a defined value of the dependent variable, namely the logarithm of one. However, there is something very unsatisfactory about assuming that a positive level of bilateral trade exists when the measured data reveals that it does not. Consequently, this analysis takes another tack, eliminating those observations with zero trade from the sample and arguing that the theory predicts positive levels of vitamins trade and that it is most likely—if ever—to fit the data in a setting in which positive amounts of trade exist. This step of eliminating the zero trade observations reduces the number of observations in the sample to 1319.

The second econometric problem is that since vitamins imports (M^v_{ijt}) are an element of total bilateral imports (M_{ijt}), there must be a contemporaneous correlation between the error term ε_{ijt} and M_{ijt}, implying that ordinary least squares procedures will generate inconsistent estimates. To break this contemporaneous correlation the variable M_{ijt} is lagged by one year, essentially creating the variable M_{ijt-1}.[82] A similar but slightly different concern relates to the variable C_t. Here a reduction in the formal or informal trade barriers to vitamins might result in both an increase in country *i*'s vitamins imports from nation *j* and from China. This would induce a positive correlation between ε_{ijt} and C_t, again potentially resulting in inconsistent estimates from ordinary least squares. To break this contemporaneous correlation, C_t is lagged by one year, using data on last year's total Chinese exports of vitamins to all export destinations, C_{t-1}.

Again, our proxy for country *j*'s production of vitamins (y^v_{jt}) is—in the absence of direct data on the production of vitamins—country *j*'s total export of vitamins in year *t* (net of its vitamins) exports to country *i*. This variable too could be contemporaneously correlated with the error term, and so $y^v_{-1,jt}$ is lagged by one year also. This is the third adjustment to equation 5.

In the light of the foregoing remarks the so-called base econometric specification[83] taken to the data is:

$$\ln(M^v_{ijt}) = I_{it}A_{1990} + (1 - I_{it})NA_{1990} + I^*_{it}A_{1990} + (1 - I^*_{it})NA_{1990} + \beta_1\ln(M_{ijt-1}) + \beta_2\ln(y^v_{-i,jt-1}) + \beta_3\ln(Y_{jt}) + \beta_4\ln(C_{t-1}) + \varepsilon_{ijt} \quad (6)$$

It is worth noting that the base specification does not include a direct role for the distance between countries *i* and *j*, which is the traditional proxy for international transportation costs in gravity equation

Table 10.4 Latin American Imports of Vitamins (Estimation Results for Baseline Equation)

Parameter		Specification Number, Parameter Estimates, and t Statistics					
		1		2		3	
Name of Parameter	Predicted Sign of Parameter Estimate	Parameter Estimate	t Statistic	Parameter Estimate	t Statistic	Parameter Estimate	t Statistic
Constant for all years	?	1.42	1.29				
Constant for precartel years	?			4.71	3.17		
Constant for cartel years	?			5.19	3.27		
Constants for pre-1990							
Enforcer	?					4.74	3.20
Nonenforcer	?					4.22	2.86
Constants for post-1990							
Enforcer	?					5.14	3.26
Nonenforcer	?					4.66	2.95
Last year's total imports from exporter	+	0.91	34.20	0.91	34.44	0.84	28.42
Exporter's national income	–	–0.78	–19.96	–0.79	–20.23	–0.72	–17.34
Proxy for exporter's total vitamins production	+	0.95	26.96	0.95	27.16	0.96	27.54
Last year's total vitamins exports from China	–	–0.13	–2.98	–0.32	–4.41	–0.34	–4.75
Number of observations		1319		1319		1319	
R^2		0.57		0.57		0.58	

studies. However, it should be noted that higher levels of such costs would reduce total bilateral imports, so reducing M_{ijt-1}. More generally, many time-invariant and time-varying determinants of bilateral imports of vitamins (such as bilateral exchange rates and distance) will also affect total bilateral imports, so the latter variable (ie. M_{ijt-1}) can act as a control for a number of potentially important determinants of vitamins imports.

A final econometric concern is that the estimation results may be sensitive to outliers. This issue has been systematically explored in a related gravity-equation analysis[84]—which also made extensive use of dummy variables—and it was found that the inclusion of outliers substantially affected the estimated parameters of interest. In that study only when the 10 percent of the sample that had the largest (in absolute value) residuals were deleted was a semblance of parameter stability restored. The same concern was explored here by trimming 1 percent, 2.5 percent, 5 percent, 10 percent, and 20 percent of the sample, and examining the stability of the parameter estimates as more and more outliers were removed. We now turn to a discussion of the consequences of such "trimming" for the parameter estimates, among other outcomes.

Econometric Findings and Their Economic Implications

Table 10.4 reports the estimated parameters for the base specification (specification 3) and two more parsimonious specifications (specifications 1 and 2). The latter specifications do not discriminate between importers on the basis of the presence of an active anticartel enforcement regime as the base specification does. Moreover, specification 1 in Table 10.4 does not discriminate between the years before and after the formation of the cartel. All of the specifications do include the same slope variables, namely the "gravity like" variables, and the same control for the exports of vitamins from China. One of the interesting findings in Table 10.4 is the relatively similar estimates for the parameters of the slope variables. Moreover, the estimated parameters for the three gravity variables have the correct sign and are statistically significant.

In Table10.4 the parameter estimates for the total value of Chinese exports to all foreign destinations (which is the proxy for the marginal cost of vitamins production in China) is negative and statistically significant. In the base specification (3), the estimated parameter on Chinese exports implies that a 10 percent increase in Chinese vitamins exports reduces the total value of vitamins imports from cartel members by 3.4 percent. To the extent that the latter reduction represents a

Table 10.5 Latin American Imports of Vitamins (Sensitivity to Outliers)

Parameter		Specification Number, Parameter Estimates, and t Statistics											
		3		4		5		6		7		8	
Name of Parameter	Predicted Sign of Parameter Estimate	Parameter Estimate	t Statistic	Parameter Estimate	t Statistic	Parameter Estimate	t Statistic	Parameter Estimate	t Statistic	Parameter Estimate	t Statistic	Parameter Estimate	t Statistic
Constants for pre-1990													
Enforcer	?	4.75	3.21	5.35	3.81	5.11	3.84	3.81	3.10	3.66	3.32	4.26	4.50
Nonenforcer	?	4.22	2.86	4.86	3.46	4.64	3.50	3.39	2.76	3.18	2.89	3.83	4.[illegible]4
Constants for post-1990													
Enforcer	?	5.14	3.27	5.80	3.88	5.55	3.93	4.14	3.16	3.92	3.34	4.58	4.65
Nonenforcer	?	4.67	2.96	5.38	3.59	5.15	3.64	3.78	2.88	3.60	3.07	4.27	4.34
Last year's total imports from exporter	+	0.35	28.42	0.87	30.50	0.87	32.45	0.88	35.01	0.86	38.65	0.90	46.33
Exporter's national income	–	–0.73	–17.34	–0.76	–1914	–0.78	–20.85	–0.80	–22.80	–0.80	–25.82	–0.83	–31.24
Proxy for exporter's total vitamins production	+	0.96	27.54	1.00	30.03	1.05	32.82	1.08	36.01	1.10	40.74	1.13	47.53
Last year's total vitamins exports from China	–	–0.34	–4.75	–0.38	–5.55	–0.39	–5.92	–0.33	–5.40	–0.32	–5.83	–0.38	–8.18
Number of observations		1319		1306		1286		1253		1187		1055	
Percentage of observations removed as outliers		0		1		2.5		5		10		20	
R^2		0.5848		0.6185		0.6530		0.6962		0.7530		0.8316	

Table 10.6 Latin American Imports of Vitamins and Anticartel Enforcement Regimes (Percentage Increase after Cartel is Formed)

Specification	3	4	5	6	7	8
Percentage of outliers deleted from original sample	0	1	2.5	5	10	20
Percentage increase in imports in jurisdictions *with* active anticartel regimes	48.72	56.08	56.13	38.60	29.63	38.07
Percentage increase in imports in jurisdictions without active anticartel regimes	56.04	68.61	66.90	46.63	52.93	56.38
Additional increase in imports in jurisdictions without active anticartel regimes	7.31	12.53	10.77	8.03	23.29	18.31

Note: Results based on Table 10.5 specifications.

fall in the prices that the cartel members charge Latin American consumers, this finding highlights how openness to trade goes some way to undermine the anticompetitive impact of international hardcore cartels.

In contrast to the stability of the slope parameters in all specifications, there do appear to be considerable differences across specifications in the estimated values of the indicator variables (A_{1990}, NA_{1990}, A_{1900}, NA_{1990}). Nevertheless, there is one consistent pattern in the estimated parameters. In both specifications 2 and 3 the formation of the cartel leads to an increase in the estimated value of the relevant regression constant, which—given the price inelasticity of the demand for vitamins—is consistent with the hypothesis that the cartel has been able to raise the price of vitamins.

As noted in the last subsection, the estimated value of constant terms or dummy variables in gravity equation studies can be very sensitive to the presence of outliers. To explore this matter further, outliers were systematically removed from the sample and the parameters reestimated. Table 10.5 reports the parameter estimates for each of these sensitivity checks, listed as specifications 4 through 8 (specification 3 repeats the base specification with the full sample and is reported for reference). Examination of the estimated constants in Table 10.5 reveals that in both cases (when an importer had an active cartel enforcement regime and when it did not), the estimated total value of vitamins imports increases after the formation of the cartel in 1989. Moreover, the explained variation increases monotonically with the percentage of outliers removed from the sample.

To provide further interpretation, Table 10.6 calculates the implied percentage increase in the import bills of those Latin American economies that have *never* had an active cartel enforcement regime and contrasts that percentage increase with the comparable increase in a jurisdiction that had an active regime *before and after* the international vitamins cartel was formed. In specifications 4 through 8, irrespective of the amount of outliers removed, after the vitamins cartel was formed import bills rose more in those Latin American jurisdictions that did not have active cartel enforcement regimes. Taking as given the claim that the demand for vitamins is price inelastic, this finding implies that prices of vitamins rose more than eight percentage points more in those jurisdictions without active anticartel enforcement regimes. It would appear, therefore, that this particular international cartel deliberately discriminated across jurisdictions on

Table 10.7 Overcharges Paid on Imports of Vitamins (1989–1999)

	Overcharges (US$million)
Active anticartel regimes	
Brazil	239.149
Mexico	192.526
Chile	50.121
Peru	24.492
Inactive anticartel regimes	
Argentina	85.417
Colombia	63.577
Venezuela	52.437
Honduras	29.926
Ecuador	17.149
Guatemala	12.047
Paraguay	5.285
Costa Rica	4.421
Bolivia	3.996
Dominican Republic	3.553
El Salvador	3.128
Nicaragua	1.388
Panama	0.787
Total overcharges in these countries	789.398

the strength of their anticartel enforcement regimes. If this is the case, then it suggests that there is a price to be paid for nonenforcement or under-enforcement of anticartel laws in Latin America.

The econometric estimates can be taken a step further to compute a lower bound (strictly an underestimate[85]) of the overcharges paid by each Latin American jurisdiction on its vitamins imports. These estimated overcharges are reported in Table 10.7 and were calculated using the most conservative set of parameter estimates, specifically those from specification 6 in which 5 percent of the original sample was removed as outliers. Throughout the 1990s the overcharges on vitamins imports paid by the 17 Latin American economies in the sample is at least US$789 million (in year-2000 dollars). The amount of overcharges paid varies considerably from just under a quarter of a billion U.S. dollars for Brazil to under a million for Panama. Moreover, in ten of the seventeen Latin American economies considered here, the overcharges on vitamins imports exceeded $10 million, implying overcharges on this cartel alone of over a million dollars per year.

Table 10.8 Deterrent Effects of Active Cartel Enforcement

Active anticartel regimes	Reduction in overcharges due to *active* cartel enforcement (US$million)
Brazil	45.913
Mexico	28.394
Chile	9.622
Peru	4.447

Inactive anticartel regimes	Reduction in overcharges due to *inactive* cartel enforcement (US$million)
Argentina	13.758
Colombia	10.240
Venezuela	8.446
Honduras	4.820
Ecuador	2.762
Guatemala	1.940
Paraguay	0.851
Costa Rica	0.712
Bolivia	0.644
Dominican Republic	0.572
El Salvador	0.504
Nicaragua	0.224
Panama	0.127

The parameter estimates from the most conservative specification (6) can also be used to estimate the likely increase in overcharges that an active cartel enforcer would have paid if that jurisdiction did not have a cartel enforcement regime. In effect, this quantifies—for the case of the international vitamins cartel—the value of active cartel enforcement. More precisely, in the case of this one international hard-core cartel it provides an estimate of the deterrent effect of active national anticartel enforcement. These estimates are presented in the upper panel of Table 10.8. If Brazil did not enforce it's anticartel laws, then the likely overcharges on vitamins imports would have been approximately US$45 million per year higher. This amounts to a saving of approximately US$5 million per year for 1990–98, when the cartel was known to be in operation. It is also worth noting that in 2000 the Brazilian government spent US$10.96 million on the enforcement of all of its competition laws, implying that—had similar levels of state expenditure prevailed during 1990–98—the reduced overcharges on vitamins imports alone would have paid for just under half of that expense. The comparable total reduction in overcharges in Mexico, Chile, and Peru were in excess of US$28 million, US$9 million, and US$4 million, respectively. In the light of the magnitude of the estimated savings, perhaps the question ought not to be whether Latin American countries can afford to have active anticartel enforcement regimes but rather whether they can afford *not* to have such regimes.

The estimated parameters from specification 6 can also be used to calculate how much smaller certain Latin American nations' overcharges would have been if their import bills had increased by the percentage experienced in those jurisdictions with active anticartel enforcement regimes. Of course, this calculation can only be performed for those nations that do not have active enforcement regimes. The results are reported in the lower panel of Table 10.8. As this table makes clear, in the case of the international vitamins cartel, failing to actively enforce an anticartel regime was particularly costly for Argentina, Columbia, and Venezuela.

To summarize, the econometric specifications employed here—which were based on the traditional gravity equation—performed well in the sense that all of the parameter estimates of the standard slope variables had the correct sign and were highly statistically significant. Moreover, the finding that import bills rose more (in percentage terms) in jurisdictions that do not actively enforce anticartel regimes seems to be very robust to the exclusion of outliers, as these jurisdictions saw their import bills rise by at least eight percentage points more than those with such regimes. Given the magnitude of vitamins imports by Latin American economies, this difference translates into millions of dollars less in overcharges for those nations (Brazil, Chile, Mexico, and Peru) that actively enforced their anticartel laws at some point in the 1990s. These reductions in overcharges are a tangible and quantifiable measure of the benefits of targeting hardcore cartels through national competition policies, adding to the benefits created by another deterrent effect of such policies, namely the disincentive to form a cartel in the first place.

Policy Implications for the FTAA Negotiations

Competition policy has tended not to be a priority for Latin American policymakers interested in international trade and regional integration. However, such matters are likely to grow in prominence as negotiations on a potential Free Trade Area of the Americas intensify.

Moreover, initiatives on competition policy at the World Trade Organization in the context of the Doha Development Agenda will further raise the profile of private anticompetitive practices and the national and international measures that can be taken to tackle them.

In the context of an FTAA, it has been proposed that signatories agree to enact and enforce laws against anticompetitive corporate practices. An important question, therefore, is whether such a binding obligation will benefit Latin American economies. Two criteria might be employed when assessing the relative merits of such an initiative: feasibility and economic desirability. This chapter has discussed both criteria in the context of national anticartel laws, which are some of the most prevalent laws against certain private anticompetitive practices.

The experiences of Brazil, Mexico, and Peru in enforcing their anticartel laws clearly demonstrate that enforcement actions against cartels are no longer the sole preserve of industrialized countries such as the United States and Canada. Latin American economies appear to have marshaled the expertise and resources necessary to tackle hardcore cartels, suggesting that the feasibility requirement has been met.

Turning now to assessing the desirability of enacting and enforcing national anticartel law, we employ our estimates of the potential benefits of national anticartel enforcement. Specifically, the empirical evidence suggests that the international vitamins cartel inflicted higher overcharges on those jurisdictions without active anticartel enforcement regimes. Such is the magnitude of vitamins imports into Latin America that active anticartel enforcement appears to have saved certain nations in the region millions of U.S. dollars per year. In the case of Brazil, the reduction in overcharges from the vitamins cartel alone was equal to just under half of the state expenditures for enforcement of all of its competition laws. As it is unclear why other national and international cartels would not be deterred in a manner similar to the international vitamins cartel, these findings suggest that the reduction in overcharges on those cartels that do have the audacity to form would go a long way to offset—if not to completely offset—any implementation costs associated with enforcing these laws.

In sum, these latter considerations point to the desirability of adopting provisions to enact and enforce national anticartel laws. That said, a number of important caveats should be borne in mind. First, the likely net benefits of any FTAA agreement on competition policy matters will depend critically on the provisions contained therein. For example, if such an agreement contains many sectoral exemptions, then the expected benefits are likely to be reduced. Second, the discussion here has focused on the ongoing costs and benefits of an already established anticartel enforcement regime. There may well be costs associated with creating such a regime from scratch that ought to be factored into any comprehensive economic evaluation of competition policy. Such costs could, of course, be mitigated by technical assistance measures, capacity building initiatives, and aid. Third, it should be recognized that this study is based on an analysis of one long-lasting and prominent international hardcore cartel. Future studies may arrive at different findings or, indeed, they may reinforce or strengthen the conclusions reached here. Even so, this chapter's analysis reveals that adopting anti-cartel laws have saved some Latin American countries' purchasers millions of dollars per year.

Appendix: Table 10.9 Fines Accruing to U.S. and International Firms in Breach of the Sherman Act through January 2003

Antitrust Division
Sherman Act Violations Yielding a Fine of US$10 Million or More

Defendant (FY)	Product	Fine (US$ Millions)	Geographic Scope	Country
F. Hoffmann-La Roche, Ltd. (1999)	Vitamins	$500	International	Switzerland
BASF AG (1999)	Vitamins	$225	International	Germany
SGL Carbon AG (1999)	Graphite Electrodes	$135	International	Germany
Mitsubishi Corp. (2001)	Graphite Electrodes	$134	International	Japan
UCAR International, Inc. (1998)	Graphite Electrodes	$110	International	U.S.
Archer Daniels Midland Co. (1997)	Lysine & Citric Acid	$100	International	U.S.
Takeda Chemical Industries, Ltd. (1999)	Vitamins	$72	International	Japan
Bilhar International Establishment (2002)	Construction	$54	International	Liechtenstein
Daicel Chemical Industries, Ltd. (2000)	Sorbates	$53	International	Japan
ABB Middle East & Africa Participations AG (2001)	Construction	$53	International	Switzerland
Haarmann & Reimer Corp. (1997)	Citric Acid	$50	International	German Parent
HeereMac v.o.f. (1998)	Marine Construction	$49	International	Netherlands
Sotheby's Holdings Inc. (2001)	Fine Arts Auctions	$45	International	U.S.
Eisai Co., Ltd. (1999)	Vitamins	$40	International	Japan
Hoechst AG (1999)	Sorbates	$36	International	Germany
Showa Denko Carbon, Inc. (1998)	Graphite Electrodes	$32.5	International	Japan
Philipp Holzmann AG (2000)	Construction	$30	International	Germany
Arteva Specialties (2003)	Polyester Staple	$28.5	International	Luxembourg
Daiichi Pharmaceutical Co., Ltd. (1999)	Vitamins	$25	International	Japan

Continued on next page

Appendix: Table 10.9 Fines Accruing to U.S. and International Firms in Breach of the Sherman Act through January 2003, continued

Antitrust Division

Sherman Act Violations Yielding a Fine of US$10 Million or More

Defendant (FY)	Product	Fine (US$ Millions)	Geographic Scope	Country
Nippon Gohsei (1999)	Sorbates	$21	International	Japan
Pfizer Inc. (1999)	Maltol/Sodium Erythorbate	$20	International	U.S.
Fujisawa Pharmaceuticals Co. (1998)	Sodium Gluconate	$20	International	Japan
Dockwise N.V. (1998)	Marine Transportation	$15	International	Belgium
Dyno Nobel (1995)	Explosives	$15	Domestic	Norwegian Parent
F. Hoffmann-La Roche, Ltd. (1997)	Citric Acid	$14	International	Switzerland
Merck KgaA (2000)	Vitamins	$14	International	Germany
Degussa-Huls AG (2000)	Vitamins	$13	International	Germany
Akzo Nobel Chemicals, BV (2001)	Monochloracetic Acid	$12	International	Netherlands
Ueno Fine Chemicals Industry, Ltd. (2001)	Sorbates	$11	International	Japan
Eastman Chemical Co. (1998)	Sorbates	$11	International	U.S.
Jungbunzlauer International AG (1997)	Citric Acid	$11	International	Switzerland
Lonza AG (1998)	Vitamins	$10.5	International	Switzerland
Morganite, Inc. (2003)	Carbon Products	$10	International	British parent
Akzo Nobel Chemicals, BV & Glucona, BV (1997)	Sodium Gluconate	$10	International	Netherlands
ICI Explosives (1995)	Explosives	$10	Domestic	British Parent
Mrs. Baird's Bakeries (1996)	Bread	$10	Domestic	U.S.
Ajinomoto Co., Inc. (1996)	Lysine	$10	International	Japan
Kyowa Hakko Kogyo, Co., Ltd. (1996)	Lysine	$10	International	Japan

Source: USDOJ. Available online at http://www.usdoj.gov/art/public/criminal/12557.htm.

References

Anderson, J. 1979. "A Theroetical Foundation for the Gravity Equation." *American Economic Review* (69): 106–11.

Arbault, F., S. Suurnakki, F. Peiro, B. Nijs, P. Bridgeland, G. Berger, M. Lindroos, and E. Marteil. 2001. "Commission Adopts Eight New Decisions Imposing Fines on Hardcore Cartels." *Competition Policy Newsletter* no.1 (February), European Commission, Brussles.

Brazilian Ministry of Justice and Ministry of Finance. 2000. *Annual Report on Competition Policy Developments in Brazil.* Brasilia. www.oecd.org /dataoecd/52/49/2406761.pdf.

———. 2002. *Competition Policy in Brazil, 2002.* Brasilia.

Clarke, J., and S. Evenett. Forthcoming. "The Deterrent Effects of National Anti-Cartel Laws: Evidence from the Vitamins Cartel." *Antitrust Bulletin.*

Connor, J. M. 2001. *Global Price Fixing: Our Customers Are the Enemy.* Boston: Kluwer Academic Publishing.

Considera, C. M., and C. P. Teixeira. N.d. "Brazil's Recent Experience in International Cooperation." Secretariat for Political Economy, Brazilian Ministry of Finance, Brasilia.

Correa, P. 2001. "Discovering Leads: The Recent Brazilian Experience." Secretariat for Economic Monitoring, Brazilian Ministry of Finance, Brasilia.

Deardorff, A. V. 1998. "Determinanats of Bilateral Trade: Does Gravity Work in a Neoclassical World?" In *The Regionalization of the World Economy,* edited by J. A. Frankel. Chicago: University of Chicago Press.

Eaton, J., and S. Kortum. 2003. "Technology, Geography, and Trade," *Econometrica.*

Evenett, S. J. 2002."The Impact of Economic Sanctions on South African Exports." *Scottish Journal of Political Economy* 49 (5) (November).

Evenett, S. J., and W. Keller. 2002. "On Theories Explaining the Success of the Gravity Equation." *Journal of Political Economy,*11(2) (April): 281–316.

Evenett, S., M. C. Levenstein, and V. Suslow. 2001. "International Cartel Enforcement: Lessons from the 1990's." *World Economy* (September).

Dick, A. R. 1992. "Are Export Cartels Efficiency Enhancing or Monopoly Promoting: Evidence from the Webb-Pomerene Experience." *Research in Law and Economics* 14: 89–127.

First, H. 2001. "The Vitamins Case: Cartel Prosecutions and the Coming of International Competition Law." *Antitrust Law Journal*: 711–29.

Free Trade Areas of the Americas (FTAA). 1994. *Declaration of Principles.* Miami Summit of the Americas. http://www.sice.oas.org/ftaa/miami /sadope.asp.

———. 2001. *Inventory of Domestic Laws and Regulations Relating to Competition Policy in the Western Hemisphere.* Negotiating Group on Competition Policy.

———. 2002a. *Inventory of Domestic Laws and Regulations Relating to Competition Policy in the Western Hemisphere.* Negotiating Group on Competition Policy.

———. 2002b. *Draft Agreement on Competition Policy.* Negotiating Group on Competition (November). http://www.ftaa-alca.org/ftaadraft/eng /ngcpe_1.asp.

———. 2003. *Report on Development and Enforcement of Competition Policy and Laws in the Western Hemisphere.* Negotiating Group on Competition Policy.

———. 2002. *Hardcore Cartels.* Submission to the World Trade Organization's Working Group on the Interaction Between Trade and Competition Policy (WT/WGTCP/W201).

Government of Canada. 2000. *Proposal from Canada for the FTAA Agreement on Competition Policy.* http://www.sice.oas.org/geograph/north/cnpocp1 _e.asp.

Government of Chile. 2001. *Organization and Function of Competition Entities.* Submission to the OECD's Global Forum on Competition Policy (CCNM/GF/COMP/WD(2001)26.

———. 2002. *Capacity Building and Technical Assistance.* Submission to the OECD's Global Forum on Competition Policy (CCNM/GF/COMP /WD(2002)21.

Government of Mexico. 2001. *Merger Enforcement.* Submission to the Organization of Economic Cooperation and Development's Global Forum on Competition (CCNM/GF/COMP/WD).

———. 2002. *Hard Core Cartels.* Communication from Mexico to World Trade Organization's Working Group on the Interaction Between Trade and Competition Policy (WG/WGTCP/W/196).

———. 2002. Submission to the OECD's Global Forum on Competition. (CCNM/GF/COMP/WD(2002)21).

Government of Peru. 2001. Submission to the OECD's Global Forum on Competition. (CCNM/GF/COMP/WD) 2001.

Government of the United States of America. N.d. *Summary of the United States Negotiating Positions in the FTAA.* FTAA Negotiating Group on Competition Policy. http://www.sice.oas.org/geograph/north/uspocp _e.asp.

———. 2003. "A Summary Overview of the Antitrust Division's Criminal Enforcement Program." Speech delivered at the New York State Bar

Association Annual Meeting, New York. http://www.usdoj.gov/atr/public/speeches/200686.htm.

Hammond, S. D. 2002. "A Review of Recent Cases and Developments in the Antitrust Division's Criminal Enforcement Program." Speech delivered at the conference "Antitrust Issues in Today's Economy." http://www.usdoj.gov/atr/public/speeches/10862.htm.

Helpman, E., and P. Krugman. 1985. *Market Structure and Foreign Trade.* Cambridge, MA: MIT Press.

Hummels, D., and J. Levinsohn. 1995. "Monopolistic Competition and International Trade: Reconsidering the Evidence." *Quarterly Journal of Economics* 110 (3) (August): 799–836.

International Competition Policy Advisory Committee to the U.S. Attorney General and Assistant Attorney General for Antitrust (ICPAC). 2000. *Final Report.* United States Department of Justice, Washington, DC.

Landes, W. M. 1983. "Optimal Sanctions for Antitrust Violation." *University of Chicago Law Review* 50: 2, 652–78.

Organization for Economic Cooperation and Development (OECD). 2000. Policy Brief: Hard Core Cartels. Paris.

———. 2001. *Policy Brief: Using Leniency to Fight Hard Core Cartels.* Paris.

Organization of American States Foreign Trade Information System (SICE). 1997. *Summary and Conclusions.* Meeting of the Americas Third Business Forum of the Americas, Belo Horizonte, Brazil, May. http://www.sice.oas.org/ftaa/BELO/FORUM/WORKSHOPS/SUCON5_E.asp.

United Nations Conference on Trade and Development (UNCTAD). 2002. *Recent Important Competition Cases in Developing Countries.* Trade and Development Board TD/B/COM.2/CLP/26 (April). Geneva.

United States Department of Justice. 1999–2000. Press Releases. Various speeches pertaining to the international vitamins cartel. Available online at http://www.usdoj.gov/atr/public/speeches/speeches.htm.

Notes

1 See FTAA (1994).

2 Organization of American States Foreign Trade Information System (1997).

3 FTAA (2002a).

4 FTAA (2002b).

5 FTAA (2002b).

6 FTAA (2002b), Section 1.2.1.

7 FTAA (2002b), Section 1.2.2.

8 FTAA (2002b), Section 5.2 of the DCAP states: "The Dispute Settlement Mechanism of the FTAA shall *not* be applicable for challenging or reviewing the administrative or [judicial] [jurisdictional] decisions of Parties with respect to competition law and policy."[italics added]

9 FTAA (2002b), Section 4.3.3

10 See OECD (2000). Notice here that the definition of hardcore cartels is being discussed, not the important issue of the sectoral scope and practices covered by the OECD Recommendation. The latter is discussed in section 6 below.

11 See FTAA (2002b), Section 1.4.1.

12 See FTAA (2002b), Section 1.4.1.

13 See Landes (1983) for such a claim. Another logical possibility is for the formation of a cartel to increase the sum of consumer and producer surplus, and not just the former. For some empirical evidence on this matter, see Dick (1992).

14 See Clarke and Evenett (forthcoming).

15 See Evenett, Suslow, and Levenstein (2001) for a fuller explication of this point.

16 UNCTAD (2002).

17 Government of Mexico (2002).

18 Government of Peru (2001).

19 Ibid.

20 Ibid.

21 Ibid.

22 Hammond (2003).

23 Hammond (2002).

24 Ibid.

25 Ibid.

26 Government of the United States of America (n.d.).

27 Ibid.

28 Considera and Teixeira (n.d.).

29 Government of Brazil (2000).

30 According to the Brazil (2002), fines are levied on both companies and individuals and are based upon the company's gross pretax revenue, which, according to Article 23 of the Brazilian Antitrust Legislation,

"shall by no means be lower than the advantage obtained from the underlying violation, if assessable."

31 UNCTAD (2002).

32 Correa (2001).

33 Ibid.

34 Considera and Teixeira (n.d.).

35 Ibid.

36 Government of Mexico (2002).

37 Government of Mexico (2001).

38 Ibid.

39 FTAA (2001).

40 For more on the topic of leniency please refer to OECD (2001).

41 Government of Mexico (2002).

42 Government of Mexico (2001).

43 Ibid.

44 Government of Chile (2001).

45 Childe (2002).

46 FTAA (2003).

47 Ibid.

48 Government of Peru (2002).

49 Ibid.

50 Government of Peru (2001).

51 Ibid.

52 Ibid.

53 FTAA (2001).

54 Ibid.

55 ICPAC (2000), Annex 4-C.

56 Government of Canada (2002).

57 Government of Canada (2000)

58 Hammond (2003).

59 Connor (2001) and First (2001).

60 Hammond (2003).

61 See Connor (2001) and First (2001).

62 See Connor (2001: note 58, at 305–6).

63 See Connor (2001).

64 See Arbault et al. (2001).

65 See Connor (2001: 368–9).

66 See United States Department of Justice Press Releases (1999–2000).

67 See Arbult *et al.* (2001).

68 See Connor (2001: 306).

69 The source of this data on Chinese exports of vitamins is the Statistics Canada *World Trade Analyser Database.* Product line number 5411 in this database refers to trade in vitamins and polyvitamins.

70 See Connor (2001: 306).

71 The former is similar to the position taken in Clarke and Evenett (forthcoming), though the empirical implementation of this chapter differs in important respects.

72 It is straightforward to show that the change in consumer surplus caused by the cartel's formation is (in magnitude) larger than the increase in total revenues of the cartel members. Therefore, any estimates of the changes in the total value of sales of the cartelized product in a given market will also provide a lower bound on the harm done by the cartel's formation to consumers in that market.

73 For a discussion of the price inelasticity of the demand for vitamins see Connor (2001).

74 The analogy to the determinants of the force between two masses in the physical sciences is deliberate.

75 See Anderson (1979), Helpman and Krugman (1985), Deardorff (1998), and Eaton and Kortum (2003).

76 See Hummels and Levinsohn (1995) and Evenett and Keller (2002).

77 Anderson (1979).

78 The World Bank's *World Development Indicators* database was used to discern whether an economy was too "small" on either criterion.

79 This adjustment is needed because the dependent variable in our econometric analysis—the value of nation *i*'s imports of vitamins from nation *j* in a given year *t*—is obviously a component of the total exports of vitamins by nation *j* to all destinations.

80 This widely used cross-country dataset can be accessed at http://datacentre2 .chass.utoronto.ca/pwt.

81 See the recent annual reports of the national competition authorities to the OECD's Committee on Competition Law and Policy for evidence of cartel enforcement activity at http://www1.oecd.org/daf/clp/Annual_reports /1999–00.htm. See documentation for the 2001 OECD Global Forum on

Competition at http://www1.oecd.org/daf/clp/GFC_October2001/. See documentation for the 2002 OECD Global Forum on Competition at http://www.oecd.org/oecd/pages/home/displaygeneral/0,3380,EN-document-0-nodirectorate-no-20–24303–0,00.html#title0.

82 Furthermore, the value of the dependent variable in year (t-1) was subtracted from M_{ijt-1}. Thus the variable M_{ijt-1} is the lagged value of all non-vitamins imports by nation i from nation j.

83 More parsimonious specifications—that do not take into account the timing of the formation of the cartel or whether a nation has an active cartel enforcement regime—are taken to the data also, see the following section.

84 See Evenett (2002).

85 The parameter estimates enable the change in the total value of imported vitamins to be calculated. The overcharges on vitamins imports caused by the cartel equal the change in the price multiplied by the post-cartelization quantity of vitamins imports. With a downward sloping demand curve and a positive price increase caused by the cartel, then the estimated change in the total value of imported vitamins must exceed the level of overcharges. (Of course, the level of overcharges is itself less than the loss of consumer surplus due to cartelization.)

PART V

The Political Economy of the FTAA

11

The United States and a Free Trade Area of the Americas: A Political-Economic Analysis

I. M. (Mac) Destler

The administration of George W. Bush started strongly on trade policy. In the spring of 2001, the president affirmed in Quebec City strong U.S. support for a Free Trade Area of the Americas. In the fall, his trade representative (USTR), Robert Zoellick, led in achieving international agreement to launch the WTO "Doha Round." And not only did the administration renew the quest for "fast-track" trade negotiating authority (now renamed trade promotion authority, or TPA), but it won House approval of TPA legislation by a razor-thin vote of 215 to 214 in December 2001.

In 2002, however, the Bush administration diverged sharply from the liberal-trade path, granting substantial new protection to the U.S. steel industry. Bush was responding to an industry in distress (due to imports and other causes), and the action was broadly consistent with the GATT-WTO right of a nation to invoke temporary trade "safeguards." Nonetheless, the magnitude of the protection, and the reported prominence of electoral calculations in its motivation, provoked a vociferous international outcry. This was followed by a new U.S. farm law that reversed the trend toward reducing agricultural subsidies. This action seemed not just politically driven but blatantly hypocritical given the longstanding U.S. advocacy of subsidy reduction in international trade negotiations. Both of these actions struck hard at the interests of Brazil, the most important U.S. partner in an FTAA. And taken together, they fueled regional and global skepticism about whether the United States would prove willing to sustain the political pain necessary to open politically sensitive markets.

In the second half of 2002, the administration moved to restore its free trade luster. In late July, Zoellick tabled a sweeping global proposal to curb farm subsidies and agricultural tariffs. A week later, Congress completed action on TPA, with its strong margin in the Senate made possible by a broad new commitment to help trade-displaced workers. Then on November 26, the USTR unveiled a broad proposal to the WTO for a "tariff-free world . . . on industrial and consumer goods by 2015."[1] Free trade action continued into 2003, with the release in February of a comprehensive U.S. offering to eliminate most industrial and agricultural tariffs immediately upon an FTAA's entry into force.[2]

Which of these approaches to trade will prove to reflect the "real United States," or the "real George W. Bush administration?" Were the protectionist actions of early 2002 an aberration, perhaps even justified as necessary steps to win House votes for TPA?[3] Or do they accurately reflect the proclivities of an administration whose economic policies appear to many Washington insiders to be overridingly driven by partisan politics, even more so than those of Bush's highly political predecessor? In the end, will the president be listening to his talented and committed trade negotiator, Robert Zoellick, or to his astute and personally closer political adviser, Karl Rove?

These questions, of course, speak not just to the FTAA negotiations, but also to the Doha talks with which FTAA is intertwined. This chapter centers on the talks within the Western Hemisphere. Some of the political problems it will highlight apply equally to the WTO round, but one bears particularly on the American neighborhood. This is the relatively modest magnitude of U.S. trade with American nations south of Mexico. In winning approval for trade-liberalizing agreements that provoke resistance from import-impacted industries, U.S. leaders (like their counterparts elsewhere) typically seek support from internationalist business interests that are significantly engaged in foreign markets and see major gains in their further opening. If current engagement is modest, so too may be the political energy they will bring to support of an FTAA.

And that is precisely the situation. As the United States moves toward serious trade bargaining with its hemispheric partners, it confronts an inevitable asymmetry. For many Latin American countries, the North American colossus is *the* market they depend on and need to sell to. For the United States, the hemisphere outside of NAFTA is of modest importance in trade terms.

Problem One: Limited Stakes

Taken as a whole, U.S. economic engagement with potential FTAA members is large and growing. In 1991, U.S. trade with other Western Hemisphere nations was already one-third of the global total, or 33.7 percent to be precise (see Table 11.1). By 2001, this share had risen by 6 points, to 39.7 percent. This is a lower proportion than that for the bulk of other nations in the Americas. But given the fact that the six largest economies with whom the U.S. trades are in the Eastern hemisphere, and given the further fact that Korea, Taiwan, Singapore, and four separate EU nations rank higher in U.S. merchandise trade totals than does any Latin nation south of Mexico, 39.7 percent of the total is impressive. To paraphrase what George Ball said in another context, propinquity really propinques.

But there is a catch. The preponderant share of that trade is with Canada and Mexico, and hence already covered by NAFTA. In 2001, NAFTA trade was 83 percent of the U.S. hemispheric total, up from about 80 percent for Canada and Mexico in 1991. More remarkably, virtually the entire growth in the Western Hemisphere share of U.S. trade over the past decade can be attributed to the explosion of bilateral trade with Mexico, which grew from 7.1 to 12.5 percent of the U.S. world total. The remainder came from a .8 percent increase in the world share of U.S. trade with Canada. Trade with all other American nations grew in absolute terms, but was stagnant as a portion of the global total—6.8 percent in 1991 and 6.7 percent in 2001.

Of course, NAFTA brought to North America not only open trade, but also open investment. And if one looks at this sphere of economic activity, the current distribution within the hemisphere is somewhat different. Of the US$1.4 trillion dollars in cumulative U.S. direct investment overseas at the end of 2001, US$191 billion (13.8 percent) was in NAFTA countries and US$217 billion (15.7 percent) elsewhere in the hemisphere, including US$36 billion (2.6 percent) in Brazil. If one narrows that to the US$376 billion in U.S. global *manufacturing* investment, the NAFTA share rises to 19.5 percent and that of the rest of the hemisphere plunges to 6.9 percent. Within the latter, however, Brazil's share rises to 4.1 percent, or US$15.5 billion.[4]

Still, the hemispheric shares of overall U.S. direct investment (29.6 percent) and investment in manufacturing (26.4 percent) are smaller than the trade share cited above (39.7 percent). The bulk of both trade and manufacturing investment is with NAFTA partners Canada and

Table 11.1 U.S. Merchandise Trade with Western Hemisphere Nations, 1991–2001 (In Millions and Percentage of World Total)

	World	Western Hemisphere	NAFTA	Latin America and the Caribbean	Central/ South America	Canada	Mexico	Brazil
1991								
Exports	414,083	148,935	118,782	63,257	30,153	85,678	33,104	6,106
Imports	491,020	156,036	124,540	62,988	31,496	93,048	31,492	6,842
Total	905,103	304,971	243,322	126,245	61,649	178,726	64,596	12,948
% of World	—	33.7	26.9	13.9	6.8	19.7	7.1	1.4
2001								
Exports	718,762	322,282	264,490	158,973	57,792	163,309	101,181	15,790
Imports	1,145,927	418,345	350,939	199,610	67,406	218,735	132,204	14,467
Total	1,864,689	740,627	615,429	358,583	125,198	382,044	233,385	30,257
% of World	—	39.7	33.0	19.2	6.7	20.5	12.5	1.6
2001/1991								
Exports	1.74	2.16	2.23	2.51	1.92	1.91	3.06	2.59
Imports	2.33	2.68	2.82	3.17	2.14	2.35	4.20	2.11
Total	2.06	2.43	2.53	2.84	2.03	2.14	3.61	2.34

Source: U.S. Department of Commerce, Bureau of Economic Analysis (2002b).

Notes: Exports and imports are adjusted to balance of payment basis, excluding military.

Mexico. Hence, the preponderance of U.S. economic activity in the Western Hemisphere is already covered by a free trade agreement. So the United States is already reaping most of the benefits of open trade and investment in the Americas.

This is not to say, of course, that there is no further fruit to be harvested. U.S. exports to key South American countries have in fact declined over the past few years, due in part to crises in key economies such as Argentina and Brazil. Beyond this hopefully short-term phenomenon, U.S. trade with South American countries, Brazil in particular, seems atypically low, and would doubtless grow if they were brought within a free trade arrangement. Drawing on a model developed by Jeffrey Frankel (1997), Jeffrey Schott and Gary Hufbauer (2001) estimate that had Brazil been in an FTA with the United States in the year 2000, trade between the two countries would have been triple its actual level, US$90 billion rather than US$30 billion.[5] This would raise it to around 5 percent of the U.S. total—still only two-fifths of Mexico, but above the Asian newly industrialized countries and about the level of Germany, the largest U.S. trading partner in the European Union.

But potential benefits seldom translate into active political engagement by those who might realize them, especially when they are diffused throughout the region and across the U.S. economy, and hard for any specific export interest to be confident of in advance. "Exporters. . .are unlikely to expend the same energy to achieve a conjectural gain as their [protected] adversaries will to preserve a current market."[6] Thus we do not see pro-trade activism surrounding FTAA, for example, comparable to that surrounding the conferral of permanent normal trade relations status for China, when U.S. business saw not only future gains but a domestic political threat to the current level of market access. FTAA therefore lacks a robust political base in the United States. Current U.S. trade interest in the Americas, outside of NAFTA, is insufficient to generate strong political activity from those who would benefit from its expansion. The same is true of actual and potential U.S. investors in the region. Internationalist economic interests within the United States are unlikely to provide sufficient political support for approval of an FTAA agreement.

Moreover, the lack of strong business interest makes FTAA vulnerable to those pressing other trade agendas. House Democrats, led by Representative Charles Rangel (D-NY), presented an alternative fast-track bill last fall that included forty-odd detailed pages of separate negotiating objectives for the FTAA and bilateral pacts. These included stronger demands on labor, environmental, and social issues than did parallel language in the bill for the WTO Doha Round. And when the House Republican leadership was looking for swing Republican votes to pass their fast-track bill, the textile provisions of the Andean Trade Preference Act were among those targeted, to the dismay of both Rangel and Ways and Means Committee Chair William Thomas (R-CA).

Finally, there is a particular problem in the agricultural sphere. On balance, U.S. farm groups have been backers of trade liberalization and a key part of the pro–free trade coalition. However, their primary market-opening target is across the Atlantic. They see major gains in global exports if the European Union can at last be brought to make major modifications in its Common Agricultural Policy, particularly its export subsidies. Brazil, of course, sees the United States as a key potential market for *its* agricultural production, as does Argentina. But U.S. farmers are most reluctant to make market-opening and subsidy-reducing concessions in the FTAA context (seen as "unilateral disarmament") until they get satisfaction in the Doha Round.

Problem Two: Entrenched Redoubts of Protection

Over the past half-century, the U.S. economy has been liberalized to a remarkable degree. Tariffs are very low. The Multi-Fiber Arrangement (MFA) is approaching its demise. Yet there remain exceptions: hardy market restrictions have survived the overall liberalization trend. Three areas stand out, all of particular interest to Latin American producers, and all hard to crack.

Most prominent, perhaps, are restrictions on specialized agricultural products, among which oranges and sugar stand out. Neither is a big factor for the overall U.S. economy, but the former is concentrated in Florida, key to the presidential election of 2000 (and perhaps that of 2004), and production of the latter is sufficiently scattered—cane producers in the south, beet sugar in certain northern locations—that it has managed to retain a quota system that has raised prices and facilitated the growth of corn-sweetener production as well.

The TPA legislation does not rule out barrier reduction in this sector, but it contains provisions designed to make it difficult. Section 2104(b)(2) of the law, entitled Special Consultations on Import Sensitive (Agricultural) Products, requires the USTR to identify products meeting certain criteria, consult with the trade and agriculture committees of Congress about them, notify these committees of any intentions "to seek tariff liberalization in the negotiations," and provide "the reasons for seeking such tariff liberalization." This must be done prior to the onset of negotiations or "as soon as practicable" if they are identified for possible liberalization thereafter.[7]

There is also a special, albeit less onerous, requirement on textiles, traditionally the strongest antiliberalization force in U.S. trade politics. Over the past decade, the industry has made a partial accommodation with trade liberalization, with the politically dominant manufacturers of fiber and fabric jettisoning their longtime alliance with domestic apparel producers. Clothmakers' support of NAFTA was won through an ingenious rule of origin, the "triple transformation test."[8] But tariffs on textile products from other nations remain high on average, and the textile industry will resist their removal unless it sees substantial gains in hemispheric sales for its fiber and fabric.

Section 2104(c) of the TPA law provides that before negotiating on "textiles and apparel products with any country, the President shall assess whether [U.S. Uruguay Round textile/apparel tariffs] are lower than the tariffs bound by that country and whether the negotiation provides an opportunity to address any such disparity." The president is then required to consult with the House Ways and Means and Senate Finance Committees on "whether it is appropriate" for the United States "to agree to further tariff reductions."

Finally, there is the knotty matter of trade remedy laws, antidumping in particular. Many Latin countries, like others around the world, see these U.S. laws as tilted in favor of domestic producers and against foreign competitors, a view that finds support in the fact that only 5 percent of cases are rejected because the Commerce Department finds there has been no dumping (see Table 11.2).[9] In practice, these laws are employed by a rather narrow segment of U.S. industry: steel producers alone have initiated 46 percent of all cases over the past two decades. However, some other industries are interested in having these laws available, and the vast majority is indifferent. Hence the pattern widespread in trade politics of vociferous support not effectively balanced by those whose interest lies on the other side.

Responding to this one-sided pressure, Congress has shown itself particularly resistant to changes in antidumping laws. In its initial consideration of the TPA legislation in May 2002, the Senate passed—over the Bush administration's opposition—the Dayton-Craig amendment, which would have subjected any negotiated changes in these laws to a separate up-or-down vote. Such a provision was viewed as effectively

Table 11.2 U. S. Anti-Dumping Cases and Results, 1980–2001

Year	Total	Cases Withdrawn	Cases in Progress	Cases Completed	Cases Affirmed		No Dumping		No Injury	
					Number	Percentage	Number	Percentage	Number	Percentage
1980	21	9	0	12	4	33.3	1	8.3	7	58.3
1981	15	4	0	11	7	63.6	1	9.1	3	27.3
1982	65	24	0	41	14	34.1	3	7.3	24	58.5
1983	46	5	0	41	19	46.3	5	12.2	17	41.5
1984	74	41	0	33	9	27.3	6	18.2	18	54.5
1985	66	16	0	50	29	58.0	2	4.0	19	38.0
1986	71	7	0	64	44	68.8	3	4.7	17	26.6
1987	15	1	0	14	9	64.3	0	0.0	5	35.7
1988	42	0	0	42	22	52.4	3	7.1	17	40.5
1989	23	3	0	20	14	70.0	0	0.0	6	30.0
1990	43	2	0	41	19	46.3	5	12.2	17	41.5
1991	53	4	0	49	24	49.0	2	4.1	23	46.9
1992	99	11	0	88	45	51.1	1	1.1	42	47.7
1993	42	6	0	36	19	52.8	2	5.6	15	41.7
1994	43	3	0	40	21	52.5	1	2.5	18	45.0
1995	14	1	0	13	8	61.5	0	0.0	5	38.5
1996	20	0	0	20	17	85.0	1	5.0	2	10.0
1997	16	1	0	15	8	53.3	0	0.0	7	46.7
1998	36	0	0	36	22	61.1	0	0.0	14	38.9
1999	61	4	0	57	24	42.1	1	1.8	32	56.1
2000	51	0	7	44	27	61.4	5	11.4	12	27.3
2001	69	5	53	11	2	18.2	0	0.0	9	81.8
Total	985	147	60	778	407	52.3	42	5.4	329	42.3

Note: All suspended cases are counted as completed and affirmative.
Source: Destler (1995); *The Year in Trade* by USITC; Federal Register.

blocking any changes in these laws, and went contrary to the bargain at Doha, where U.S. willingness to put them on the table was a key concession in bringing East Asian and developing countries on board. At administration insistence, the Dayton-Craig amendment was replaced in conference by a much weaker procedural requirement. But the message was clear—the administration would face trouble if it made major concessions in this area.

None of these entrenched interests represented a major force in the U.S. economy, but the leverage of each was enhanced by the fracturing of the longstanding bipartisan consensus supporting trade liberalization in the United States.

Problem Three: Narrow, Partisan Base

Since the 1960s, most Democrats have found it hard to vote for trade liberalization, particularly in the House of Representatives. The biggest single reason, of course, has been the strong resistance of organized labor to most trade-liberalizing legislation. During the Kennedy administration, the AFL-CIO was still in the free trade camp, as labor had been earlier in the century. A decade later, it had moved to a trade-restrictive stance. The United Auto Workers followed during that industry's crisis of 1979–82.

In the 1990s a new ingredient entered the trade-politics mix—prominent demands that trade agreements include provisions regarding enforcement of trade and environmental standards by U.S. trading partners.[10] These issues were raised forcefully in 1991, when the Bush administration needed an extension of fast-track authority to pursue NAFTA and the Uruguay Round negotiations. They gained further prominence in 1992 and 1993 when candidate and then President Bill Clinton conditioned his support of NAFTA on the negotiation of side agreements addressing labor and environmental issues.

Clinton's trade representative, Mickey Kantor, successfully accomplished this objective, leading to NAFTA's enactment in 1993 but leading also to trade-policy stalemate in 1994, when conflict with business over administration interest in further pursuit of labor and environmental concerns led to removal of fast-track extension from the legislation implementing the Uruguay Round agreements. Three years later, the determination of business and Republicans to exclude most labor and environment issues from the 1997–98 fast-track extension bill alienated all but a small minority of Democrats, and the House was unable to garner a majority in its support.

As late as 1994, two-thirds of House Democrats and three-fourths of Senate Democrats voted for the legislation implementing the Uruguay Round Agreements that established the World Trade Organization. By November 1997, however, the number of Democrats willing to back the Clinton fast-track bill had shrunk to around fourty-five, about 21 percent of the House total belonging to that party. It dropped to twenty-nine Democrats the next year, when Speaker Newt Gingrich forced a vote on the legislation as a means of exploiting Democratic divisions on the issue in the upcoming midterm election. At the Seattle meeting of the WTO a year later, protests were driven by concerns over trade's impact on labor and environmental standards around the world.

The year 2001 offered a new opportunity to bridge this divide. Business and House Republicans recognized that some compromise was required. A reasonably broad spectrum of Democrats (albeit well under a majority) seemed willing to explore common ground as well. The TPA legislation as passed did represent such a compromise. "Labor and the environment" is the eleventh of seventeen "principal trade negotiating objectives," and additional labor and environmental goals are set forth in a separate subjection (2102[c]) entitled "promotion of certain priorities."

Unfortunately, TPA came to a House in which partisan polarization had been deepening for many years. Party positions on issues had become clearer, centrist representatives fewer, and trust across the aisle an increasingly scarce commodity. As a result, the legislative process was less and less the "Congress in committees," reaching for bipartisan consensus, that Woodrow Wilson made famous in the late-nineteenth century and that dominated through most of the twentieth. Rather, basic legislative decisions were increasingly made in the caucus of the majority party and ratified thereafter by committees voting along partisan lines.

For the most part, trade policy resisted this pattern well into the nineties. Major bills were drafted in the Ways and Means Committee and supported by senior leaders from both parties. Senior committee Democrats entered the 2001 debate over TPA assuming that this process would be pursued that year, at least to explore whether bipartisan accord was possible on terms acceptable to the administration. The Bush White House, moreover, signaled on several occasions that it wanted such a cross-party compromise process to proceed.

But Chairman Thomas had other ideas. He realized he needed some Democratic votes, but decided early that negotiating with ranking members Charles Rangel (D-NY) and Sander Levin (D-MI) would not yield an acceptable result. When the latter approached him on the floor and asked when they were going to talk, Thomas reportedly responded, only half in jest, "I consider you the enemy on this issue." Instead, the chairman negotiated with three junior pro-trade Democrats, whose leader, Cal Dooley (D-CA), was not even a member of Ways and Means. Thomas reached a reasonable compromise with them on the sensitive labor and environment issues, but in a way that shut the senior Democrats out of the process until he confronted his committee with a fait accompli. This gave both Ways and Means Democrats and fence-sitting members of that party generally every incentive to vote no. Underscoring the breach was the negative vote of Robert Matsui (D-CA), the senior Ways and Means Democrat who was floor leader in the fight for NAFTA in 1993. This, in turn, forced House Majority Whip Tom Delay (R-TX) to put the screws on Republicans who had never before backed free trade.[11] It also inflated the power of protectionist interests, as illustrated when the final swing vote was cast by a Carolina Republican in exchange for a commitment tightening textile restrictions in the U.S. trade agreement with Andean nations.

In contrast to the divisive House process, the Senate crafted a bipartisan package with path-breaking new aid to trade-displaced workers, broadening the legislation's appeal to Democrats. This enabled TPA passage in that chamber by a broad sixty-six to thirty margin, and when the bill emerged from conference with most of those provisions intact, the number of House Democrats in favor rose from twenty-one to twenty-five. But none of the senior Ways and Means Democrats was among them. Unlike prior major trade legislation, the process of enacting TPA has not created a bipartisan support consensus in the House. And as long as that is absent, with approval hanging on a handful of votes, entrenched protectionist interests will have enhanced power.

Problem Four: Erosion of the Hemispheric Dream

Finally, support for an FTAA is undercut by the fading of the vision of the late 1980s and early 1990s, a vision of a hemisphere of free, open, and increasingly prosperous market democracies. Economic disaster in Argentina, political turmoil in Venezuela, policy uncertainty with the new Lula government in Brazil, and the general failure of liberal economic policies to bring broad, hemispheric welfare gains of the sort achieved in East Asia and Chile (and, to a lesser degree, Mexico) all have tarnished the vision, replacing hope with doubt. In the United States, as elsewhere, there is not today the excitement about the potential of the hemisphere that seemed present at Miami eight years ago.

So are the prospects hopeless? Surely not. While the politics of 2001/02 inflated the power of producer-based protectionism, such traditional political resistance to imports is actually weaker in the United States than it has ever been.[12] Many import-impacted interests have already adapted substantially to the rise in imports triggered by NAFTA and by lower overall trade barriers in general. At the same time, the steady internationalization of the U.S. economy has increased business stakes in open markets at home as well as abroad.

The antiglobalization coalition in the United States proved weaker than many expected in the 2001/02 trade-legislative struggle, and is unlikely to be able to make FTAA into the same symbolic threat that it effectively portrayed south of the border in 1993.[13] This will be particularly true if the final agreement, or parallel hemispheric action, includes constructive steps on the social agenda.

An ambitious FTAA agreement, one that really removes barriers to trade across the board, will certainly encounter serious resistance in the United States and it will not engender overpowering business support. But it can win. After all, NAFTA won, despite a formidable coalition and a national movement against it. And it may provide some lessons for the broader agreement.

Lesson One: It Is More Than Economics

The initial impetus for NAFTA was political, not economic. When Carlos Salinas de Gortari first signaled his surprising decision to cast his economic lot with the devil to the north, it was not business interests or the USTR that leaped to embrace him. They saw problems more than opportunities. Rather, it was Secretary of State James Baker, and above all President George H. W. Bush, who saw opportunity for a historic movement in Mexico's economic and political orientation. And when NAFTA was in deep trouble three years later, it was raised from the near-dead not by the business community but when a second president, Bill Clinton, embraced it and pushed for it. Business support was necessary, of course, and in the end it came through strongly. It was essential for NAFTA advocates to refute the negative economic argument about the "giant sucking sound" of jobs being pulled south, but securing the relationship with Mexico was also an important argument helping to push the agreement over the top.[14]

U.S. commitment to an FTAA had similar origins. When the idea was raised in the Clinton administration's new National Economic Council, it stalled there. So the senior Latin America aide on the National Security Council staff, Richard Feinberg, went to Vice President Al Gore and persuaded him that an offer to host a hemispheric summit was just the thing to make his December 1993 NAFTA follow-up speech in Mexico City a success.[15] Once Al Gore gave the speech and the invitation was accepted, preparations inevitably centered on a free trade agreement as the capstone of the new hemisphere.

As the debate over an actual FTAA becomes serious in the United States, the economic case will need to be folded within a broader political-strategic argument, highlighting the value of building a more congenial, democratic, and prosperous neighborhood. The agreement will need to be presented as part of a broader strategy for hemispheric progress within the framework of the twenty-three parallel objectives established by the Miami summit, and must involve issues from promoting democracy and human rights, to eradicating poverty, to guaranteeing sustainable development.[16] Nor would it hurt if hemispheric leaders could find a way to add collaboration on antiterrorism to the mix.

Lesson Two: Reach Across the Political Divide

If the narrow margin of TPA's enactment inflated the power of special interests, the obvious remedy is to broaden the political base for trade liberalization in general and for FTAA in particular. In particular, the USTR needs to reach out to senior Democrats within the broad Congressional consultation process mandated by the TPA legislation. They were alienated in 2001/02, but they still showed interest in engagement. Even as Ways and Means Democrats were being shunted aside, Sander Levin, the ranking minority member of the Subcommittee on Trade, was the only member of Congress to travel to Doha for the pivotal talks there in November 2001.

Fortunately, 2003 has offered opportunity to renew cooperation across party lines. No major trade legislation is pending, but U.S. negotiation of FTAs is accelerating. Completed agreements with Singapore and Chile were reviewed by the House Ways and Means Committee in bipartisan session, after Democrats unanimously insisted that this customary procedure be maintained. Thereafter, each was approved in July in a strong vote, with seventy-five Democratic supporters including Rangel, Levin, Matsui, and the party's two top chamber leaders, Nancy Pelosi (D-CA) and Steny Hoyer (D-MD).

This probably represented something of a high-water mark: the FTA nearing completion with Central American nations faced far fiercer opposition from labor. Still, cooperation on Singapore and Chile suggests a potential for fairly broad Democratic support of a completed FTAA.

Of course, Republicans were not of one mind on how much to seek Democratic support. Their recapture of the Senate in November 2002 reinforced the tendency among some to build legislative victories mainly along partisan lines. Further, Senate Democrats are now in a weaker position to demand attention. The biggest base-broadening measure in the TPA law—the expansion of Trade Adjustment Assistance for workers—was enacted after Senate Majority Leader Tom Daschle (D-SD) embraced the issue and exploited his control over the upper chamber's agenda to delay consideration of the TPA until the bipartisan compromise was well advanced. He *might* have been able to use the lesser powers of a minority leader to achieve the same result in the closely divided Senate, since it takes only forty-one votes to block legislation through unlimited debate. But the administration and Senate Republicans would likely have been much more resistant on the details.

As the 2004 election approaches, moreover, Democrats may also be less disposed to cooperate and more inclined to press their differences. Prominent among postmortem critiques of Democrats' losing election performance in 2002 was their alleged failure to draw clear policy distinctions with the Republicans. An exception was Senator Mary Landrieu (D-LA), whose campaign used reports of a "secret deal" by the Bush administration to increase sugar imports from Mexico to help turn the tide in a close December run-off election.[17] In the summer of and fall of 2003, most Democratic presidential contenders, vying for the backing of organized labor, were attacking Bush administration trade policies, stressing in particular the need for stronger labor and environmental standards in future U.S. trade deals.

But Congress will not vote on an FTAA until well after the 2004 election. Whatever its outcome, one can hope that leaders can replicate the spirit of a Ways and Means Committee meeting shortly after the 2002 election. As Zoellick testified on a range of issues, according to one perceptive reporter, "Swords were sheathed" and Zoellick praised "Rangel, Levin and other Democrats for various good deeds on behalf of free trade."[18]

Latin nations can contribute by looking for steps they might take on issues of particular concern to Democrats. For example, the more they can demonstrate genuine interest in cooperation on environmental and labor issues—not necessarily tied to the specifics of an FTAA, but at minimum involving commitments on the same timetable—the more they can strike positive relations with groups in the United States that espouse these concerns and with members of Congress who respond to these groups.

The USTR can also make a virtue of necessity by assiduously respecting the special consultation provisions on sensitive agricultural provisions, textiles, and anti-dumping laws. Any major U.S. concessions on these politically dicey issues will need to be sold to Congress in any case. Few legislators are likely to endorse them until the eleventh hour when they see the gains for other U.S. interests and when FTAA supporters become actively engaged in the ratification campaign. But they need to be apprised of the possibilities and to begin thinking seriously about the substance and politics of these issues. A base can be built for positive final action if most key legislators can be persuaded to hold their fire until they see the final package, and if that package is an FTAA in fact as well as name.

Lesson Three: Mobilize the Trade Winners

Economic interests will not be enough to carry the politics of an FTAA, but they will be a significant component of any winning campaign. Just as it was necessary for NAFTA advocates to counter Ross Perot's "giant sucking sound" metaphor about jobs, there will be a need to highlight the positive economic side of hemisphere-wide trade liberalization for specific U.S. firms and workers. At a general level, such argumentation is important to refute the common notion that trade liberalization hurts people more than it helps, and to give politicians who want to back trade liberalization a specific, hard-nosed excuse for doing so. But such an argument gains specific credibility when particular economic interests are visibly active in supporting it. It makes the interest-group politics a two-sided game.

Export opportunities are one part of any pro-FTAA story, but by no means the only one. In addition to those who sell abroad, there is the overlapping group of those who invest abroad and see an FTAA as locking in consistent rules to protect this activity. There are also important stakeholders on the import side of the equation. Household consumers obviously benefit from trade liberalization, and as Edward Gresser has noted, tariffs are a regressive tax that hit hardest those least able to pay.[19] On rare occasions, price increases sparked by import barriers can actually provoke a consumer revolt, as when sugar price rises, combined with corruption issues, led to a House vote against renewal of statutory quota legislation in 1974.[20]

More frequently, organizers against import restrictions can build on the fact that, in the words of Douglas Irwin, "businesses are consumers too."[21] This suggests that FTAA supporters should look to build a coalition including the soft drink and candy manufacturers who use sugar, the retail chains that sell orange juice, and the manufacturers (such as those of automobiles) for whom steel is a key input. With the deepening of global U.S. economic interdependence, the number and stakes of such antiprotection interests can only increase.

Lesson Four: Sweeten the Pot

U.S. trading partners throughout the hemisphere can increase the number of winners by bargaining strategically, with an eye to creating and strengthening political allies within the U.S. political system. Brazil, for example, has deep interests in the opening of U.S. markets for agricultural products—orange juice is a prime example. It faces, of course, the unfortunate fact that their competitor here is concentrated in Florida, revealed as the ultimate "swing state" in presidential politics in the 2000 election. It may well be true that, overall, given its location, the state of Florida stands to benefit enormously from the expanded commerce an FTAA will bring. But again, this is the sort of potential interest that is hard to mobilize as a counterweight to those who see an imminent danger of invasion of their markets.

Suppose, however, that Brazilian authorities decided to look for a way to increase U.S. business stakes in a real FTAA. Suppose they find that the way to do so is to strike a comprehensive deal facilitating inward foreign investment. U.S. business might well find this to be something worth fighting for, and to get it they might back U.S. concessions on sensitive agricultural imports or, for example, antidumping law.[22]

Even more ambitiously, Brazil and the United States might make a joint strategic decision to lead in shaping an FTAA and to reinforce one another in the process. Brasilia could ally with Washington in backing major agricultural liberalization in the Doha Round because the South American giant would gain enormously from European and East Asian market opening and because it would help the United States grant Brazil access to key U.S. farm product markets. The United States would recognize Brazil's status as "first among equals" in Latin America, and treat U.S.-Brazil bargaining for an FTAA the same way that it sees U.S.-EU bargaining in global talks—as the necessary foundation for agreement.

This may seem unlikely in the wake of the unsuccessful Cancun Ministerial Meeting of the WTO in September 2003. At that gathering, Brazil seemed to move in another direction, leading the Group of 21 developing nations against the U.S. and the EU, using their modest agricultural concessions to stoke the fierce third-world resistance to the draft communiqué. But even as that meeting was breaking up in disagreement, Brazil was showing signs of wanting to move toward compromise. Further, its Brazilian activism at Cancun gave it the credibility to serve as an effective broker for the developing world in rescuing the Doha talks and negotiating a global agremeent.

Lesson Five: Renew the Vision

Properly managed and publicized, U.S.-Brazil cooperation could also make the FTAA talks into a broad, historic event—the two American continents coming together in a venture involving not just commerce but democratization, economic stability, and human welfare. The emphasis on poverty alleviation by Brazil's new "populist" president, Luiz Inácio Lula da Silva, could enormously add to the appeal of such a construction within the United States. In the end, support must come from both the micropolitics of specific issues and the macropolitics of the overall construction. Any campaign to negotiate, enact, and implement an FTAA agreement will need to pinpoint and mobilize specific interests that will gain. But for reasons stated at the outset of this paper, these will not suffice to overcome the resistance of entrenched "losers."

The failure at Cancun makes it most unlikely that a strong FTAA agreement can be reached by the January 2005 deadline, since major U.S. agricultural concessions depend on a prior breakthrough in the global farm talks. In the short run, then, much of the U.S. political game may well be damage limitation. During the U.S. presidential election in 2004, FTAA advocates must organize to block, for example, campaign commitments by either party's candidate in 2004 to protect strategically located product interests from FTAA (or Doha) barrier reduction. Pro-trade business organizations must decide in advance to unite in denouncing any such commitment, if made. But it will be far easier for them to do so if hope for an attainable FTAA agreement is maintained during the 2004 campaign—an FTAA connected not just with economic gains but with a better life for citizens of the hemisphere.

The danger is not so much that such losers will mobilize and overturn, through Congressional rejection, a completed FTAA. It is rather that U.S. political leaders will back away from negotiating a *real* FTAA in the first place. The core challenge, therefore, is to persuade the Bush administration and/or its successor that an FTAA that really does free up the preponderance of hemispheric trade is negotiable with U.S. trading partners, is in the broad U.S. interest, and would prove to be a truly historic achievement. The President who is (re-)elected in 2004 must be persuaded that this can be something big, with which his or her name would be forever identified, to his or her enduring credit.

Without a vision, FTAA may indeed perish. But it need not. With commitment at the top and assiduous political effort from its supporters, it will not.

References

Bergsten, C. Fred. 2002. "A Renaissance for U.S. Trade Policy?" *Foreign Affairs* (November/December): 86–98.

Destler, I. M. 1995. *American Trade Politics*. 3d ed. Washington, DC: Institute for International Economics.

Destler, I. M., and John S. Odell. 1987. "Anti-Protection: Changing Forces in United States Trade Politics." Policy Analysis no. 21 (September), Institute for International Economics, Washington, DC.

Destler, I. M., and Peter J. Balint. 1999. "The New Politics of American Trade: Trade, Labor, and the Environment." Policy Analysis no. 58 (October), Institute for International Economics, Washington, DC.

Feinberg, Richard. 1997. *Summitry in the Americas: A Progress Report*. Washington, DC: Institute for International Economics.

Gresser, Edward. 2002. "Toughest on the Poor: America's Flawed Tariff System." *Foreign Affairs* (November/December).

Hockstader, Lee, and Adam Nossiter. 2002. "GOP Outmaneuvered in La. Runoff." *Washington Post*, 9 December.

Horlick, Gary. 2002. Presentation at the Inter-American Dialogue Conference, "Bridging the Divide: Toward a Consensus on Free Trade in the Americas," Washington, DC, 23 November.

Irwin, Douglas A. 1996. *Three Simple Principles of Trade Policy*. Washington, DC: American Enterprise Institute Press.

Krugman, Paul. 1993. "The Uncomfortable Truth About NAFTA: It's Foreign Policy, Stupid." *Foreign Affairs* (November/December).

Mayer, Frederick. 1998. *Interpreting NAFTA: The Science and Art of Political Analysis*. New York: Columbia University Press.

Nelson Report. 26 February 2003. Samuels International Associates, Inc., Washington, DC.

Schott, Jeffrey J. 2001. *Prospects for Free Trade in the Americas*. Washington, DC: Institute for International Economics.

U.S. Department of Commerce, Bureau of Economic Analysis. 2002a. "U.S. Direct Investment Position Abroad on a Historical-Cost Basis, 2001." *Survey of Current Business* (July): Table 2.2. http://www.bea.doc.gov/bea/ARTICLES/2002/07July/0702dip.pdf.

U.S. Department of Commerce, Bureau of Economic Analysis. 2002b. U.S. International Transactions Accounts Data. http://www.bea.gov/bea/international/bp_web/list.cfm?anon=256.

U.S. Department of Commerce, Bureau of Economic Analysis. 2002c. "U.S. Net International Investment Position at Yearend 2001." Press Release. Washington, DC. http://www.bea.doc.gov/bea/newsrel/intinvnewsrelease.htm.

U.S. Executive Office of the President, Office of the U.S. Trade Representative. 2003. "U.S. Advances Bold Proposals in FTAA Negotiations to Create World's Largest Free Market in 2005." Press Release, 11 February. Washington, DC. http://www.ustr.gov/releases/2003/02/02–08.pdf.

U.S. Public Law 107–210. 107th Cong., H.R. 3009, 6 August 2002. *Trade Act of 2002.*

U.S. Trade Representative and U.S. Department of Commerce. 2002. "U.S. Proposes Tariff-Free World, WTO Proposal Would Eliminate Tariffs on Industrial and Consumer Goods by 2015: Duty-Free Trade Would Help Consumers, Producers, Poor." Press Release, 26 November. Washington, DC. http://www.ustr.gov/releases/2002/11/02–112.pdf.

Notes

1 http://www.ustr.gov/releases/2002/11/02–112.

2 http://www.ustr.gov/releases/2003/02/02–08.

3 Bergsten (2002).

4 U.S. Department of Commerce, Bureau of Economic Analysis (2002a).

5 Schott (2001: 96).

6 Destler (1995: 5).

7 Public Law 107–210.

8 To qualify for duty-free treatment under NAFTA, an apparel product entering the United States must have the three processes of fiber, cloth, and clothing manufacture all carried out in a NAFTA country.

9 See also Destler (1995: 168).

10 Destler and Balint (1999).

11 From the Uruguay Round onward, at least fifty House Republicans had voted against every major piece of trade-liberalizing legislation. Thirty-three had even voted for a 2000 resolution to require the United States to

withdraw from the WTO! The partisan strategy of the 2001 House leadership brought this number down to twenty-three on the critical December 2001 vote.

12 For the fuller argument, see Destler and Balint (1999: 1–9).

13 Mayer (1998: Chap. 7).

14 Cf. Krugman (1993).

15 Feinberg (1997: 55–61, 206–7).

16 For the Miami documents, see the appendices to Feinberg (1997).

17 "The day after Bush's campaign visit to the state last Tuesday, Landrieu's campaign began airing an ad charging that the White House had struck a 'secret deal' to double Mexican sugar imports to the United States.The imports would hurt Louisiana's 27,000 sugar farmers and the state's $1.7 billion sugar industry. The ad hung on a slender thread of evidence: a single, unsourced article in the Mexican newspaper *Reforma*. The White House denied the existence of any such 'deal' to flood the United States with cheap Mexican sugar. Nonetheless, the point seemed to hit home, dovetailing with Landrieu's message that she would put 'Louisiana first' while [Republican candidate Suzanne] Terrell—by now appearing in television ads side by side with the president—would be a rubber stamp for the administration who would disregard the state's interests. 'The momentum definitely shifted when we came out with the sugar issue,' said Mitch Landrieu, a Democratic member of the state's House of Representatives who served as a key unofficial campaign operative for his older sister Mary. 'It played directly into our theme and proved our point that a senator's supposed to be for Louisiana first and Suzie [Terrell] and George Bush are linked at the hip'" (Hockstader and Nossiter 2002).

18 Rangel responded, "If I'm elected president, I'll have you as my USTR!" And Zoellick said he'd be happy to so serve. *The Nelson Report* (2003).

19 Gresser (2002).

20 Destler and Odell (1987: 10). A new quota system was put in place in 1981 by the Reagan administration in exchange for votes by Louisiana House members in favor of the president's economic legislation (Ibid., 14.)

21 Irwin (1996); see also Destler and Odell (1987: esp. Chap. 3).

22 Gary Horlick of the law firm Wilmer, Cutler, and Pickering suggested just such a possible U.S. business linkage between investment opportunities in Brazil and antidumping law in the United States at the Inter-American Dialogue Conference on "Bridging the Divide: Toward a Consensus on Free Trade in the Americas," Washington, DC, November 23, 2002.

12

The Political Economy of Economic Integration in the Americas: Latin American Interests

Marcelo de Paiva Abreu

Introduction

Trade negotiations generally are conducted on the basis of the exchange of "concessions" in the form of reciprocal reduction of protection (tariffs and nontariff barriers). It is somewhat ironic, then, that concessions offered by a given country, if adopted unilaterally, would in fact normally enhance its net welfare position. Existing levels of protection correspond to the equilibrium of national political economy processes involving the distributive impact of the costs and benefits entailed by protection. Protection persists everywhere mostly because of the lack of balance between the capacity of inefficient or high-profit domestic producers favored by protection to lobby effectively, and the relative powerlessness of consumers of expensive or lower quality domestic substitutes of imports, who bear most of the cost of protection.

To create the Free Trade Area of the Americas is to find ways to move away from the protectionism that thrives in practically every economy of the hemisphere and in the direction of an alternative zero-protection equilibrium that can be reached after a reasonable transition period. The reciprocal dismantlement of protection in the economies involved in the trade negotiations depends crucially on the mobilization of political support from groups that are likely to benefit from hemispheric integration in order to counter the political weight of those groups favored by protection that will be hurt by trade liberalization.

Commitments to liberalize can of course be ineffectual if it remains feasible to adopt unilateral discretionary policies based on actions intending to counter the effects of dumping or subsidies, or simply to safeguard domestic producers from injury due to import surges. The issue of how binding commitments concerning reduction of protection actually are, even after the FTAA is completed, is thus critical.

Each possible FTAA member is likely to favor a strategy that will minimize improved access to its own market upfront and assure prompt access to export markets of other members. The political economy of the FTAA for each future member boils down to finding an acceptable balance during the transition period between benefits for exporters and dislocation of the output of domestic producers by imports, plus the effects of trade diversion. But increased exports due to improved market access for each FTAA member correspond to inefficient output that is displaced by trade creation in other FTAA markets. Thus the political economy of the FTAA is mostly related to the political economy of protectionism in its members and, probably to a lesser extent, to the consequences of trade diversion on pre-FTAA trade.

FTAA negotiations will not, of course, be restricted to market access and will certainly include many other issues, though what those additional issues will be is not yet clear. There is, to a certain extent, a trade-off between concessions concerning access and the comprehensiveness of agreements covering other issues. Latin American countries, for instance, are certainly less than enthusiastic about agreements on environment and labor standards, issues deemed to be crucial by some interests in the United States.

The next section of this chapter centers on the marked heterogeneity of interests concerning an FTAA in the various Latin American economies. Different groups of economies are considered, with an emphasis on contrasts concerning their size, present trade structure, and trade orientation. A third section analyses the political economy of protection in different Latin American economies, underlines the important contrasts between past experiences of different economies in the transition from high protection to more liberal trade regimes, and considers possible economic reasons for such contrasts. To the extent that dismantlement of protection is bound to be, even if to a limited extent, reciprocal, reference must be made, as it is in section four, to the political economy of protection in the United States (see Chapter 11 in this volume for a fuller treatment of this topic). This is because of the weight of the United States economy in an eventual FTAA, of the terms of the Trade Promotion Authority recently approved in Washington,

D.C., and other recent trade policy decisions by the United States government concerning steel imports and a new farm bill. The fifth section considers several aspects of the process of formation of an FTAA related to liberalization schedules, comprehensiveness of offers, and reciprocal gains. Estimates of FTAA effects are reported and considered; the FTAA's comprehensiveness, in terms of the spectrum of issues that it will embrace, is analyzed; and the interaction, in terms of substance and timing, between the FTAA negotiating process and other negotiations, especially in the World Trade Organization, is considered. A final section concludes.

Contrasts in the Hemisphere: Size and Trade

Once the structural characteristics of the thirty-four possible FTAA members are duly taken into account it does not seem implausible that national interests with respect to a future FTAA should vary considerably. There are two striking features concerning composition of an FTAA as an integration initiative compared to most other integration initiatives. The first is that, in common with NAFTA, the size of its most important member is overwhelming. The gross national income corrected for different purchasing-power parities (GNI-PPP) of the United States is more than two-thirds of the total FTAA GNI-PPP and almost eight times that of Brazil, the second largest economy in a future FTAA. The United States, Brazil, Mexico, and Canada account for almost 90 percent of total FTAA GNI-PPP (see Table 12.1). The second important feature is a consequence of the first. The average size of the other FTAA members is extremely small (0.3 percent of the total GDI-PPP for thirty remaining members[1]). Any measure of concentration of GNI-PPP within the FTAA underlines this fact, in contrast with other integration initiatives that do not include the United States. The ratio between the share of the United States in FTAA's GNI-PPP and the average share of the other members is 76.3 compared to numbers in the 2.0–7.4 range for the CACM, the Andean Community, the European Union, CARICOM, and MERCOSUR. Bargaining power of members' of other initiatives, such as those of the European Union, tends to be less concentrated both because there is a group of "big" economies more or less of the same size at the core of the decision-making process, because there is not just one single, dominant economy, and because of the larger relative size of the other members.

Table 12.1 Relative Size of Participants in Selected FTA Initiatives (2000)

	European Union	Andean Community	CARICOM	CACM	MERCOSUR	NAFTA	FTAA
Date of creation	1957	1969	1973	1960	1991	1993	?
Present number of members	15	5	13	5	4	3	34
Size of total GNI-PPP in 2000 (EU=100)	100.0	6.4	0.4	1.4	19.7	128.0	158.4
GNI-PPP share of largest member in initiative's total GNI-PPP (A)	23.2 (Germany)	44.0 (Colombia)	28.2 (Trinidad Tobago)	33.6 (Guatemala)	71.3 (Brazil)	85.0 (U.S.)	68.7 (U.S.)
GNI-PPP share of second-largest member in initiative's total GNI-PPP (B)	16.2 (France)	24.6 (Venezuela)	23.1 (Jamaica)	23.4 (Costa Rica)	25.6 (Argentina)	7.6 (Mexico)	8.9 (Brazil)
GNI-PPP share of third-largest member in initiative's total GNI-PPP (C)	15.9 (UK)	21.4 (Peru)	12.8 (Barbados)	21.9 (El Salvador)	1.7 (Uruguay)	7.4 (Canada)	6.1 (Mexico)
Average GNI-PPP share of other members excluding the three largest (D)	3.7	5.0	3.6	10.6	1.4	0	0.5
Average GNI-PPP of all members excluding the largest (E)	5.5	14	6.0	16.6	9.6	7.5	0.9
F = A / E	4.2	3.1	4.7	2	7.4	11.3	76.3

Source: World Bank (2001).
Note: All gross national income estimates are adjusted for purchasing-power parities.

The larger an economy, the more likely that political economy-processes related to integration include, rightly or wrongly, the perception that the country has the bargaining power to influence the stance of bigger partners and the outcome of negotiations. The smaller an economy, the more likely it is that traditional "small-country status" and consequent lack of bargaining power is generally accepted. Coalition building may qualify this assertion, but if small economies are extremely small, as is often the case in the FTAA region, even perfect coalitions would yield blocs with very limited bargaining power.

MERCOSUR economies constitute by far the most significant share of FTAA trade and GNI-PPP, in both cases excluding NAFTA economies. They comprise about half FTAA region's non-NAFTA trade and almost two thirds of its non-NAFTA GNI-PPP (see Table 12.2). Since many of the issues under discussion in the FTAA negotiations are related to the size of markets rather than to trade exclusively, perhaps the GNI-PPP share is a better indication of national relevance in the FTAA. Still, it is important to stress the wide contrasts in the relative importance of trade for different Latin American economies. The share of total trade in GNI-PPP is less than 10 percent in MERCOSUR,

Table 12.2 Main Economic Indicators in Selected FTA Initiatives (2000)

	GNI-PPP in US$ billions[a] (A)	Total Trade in Goods US$ billions[b] (B)	A / B
NAFTA	11350	2869	.253
Canada	840	529	.628
Mexico	864	341	.395
United States	9646	1999	.207
Andean Community[c]	566	99	.175
Colombia	249	25	.100
Peru	121	14	.116
Venezuela	139	50	.360
CARICOM[d]	38	17	.447
CACM[e]	128	35	.273
MERCOSUR[f]	1747	171	.098
Argentina	448	49	.109
Brazil	1245	111	.089
Other	216	64	.296
Chile	139	35	.252
Other[g]	77	29	.377
Total	14045	3225	.230

[a]GNI-PPP in 2000 from World Bank (2001).
[b]Trade data for 2000 from International Monetary Fund (2002). Trade data for Costa Rica are for 1999 and for Haiti for 1998. For most CARICOM economies trade data are for years before 2000 as available in the IMF publications.
[c]Other members: Bolivia and Ecuador.
[d]Members: Antigua and Barbuda, the Bahamas, Barbados, Belize, Dominica, Grenada, Guyana, Jamaica, St Kitts and Nevis, St. Lucia, St. Vincent and the Grenadines, Suriname, and Trinidad and Tobago.
[e]Members: Costa Rica, El Salvador, Guatemala, Honduras, and Nicaragua.
[f]Other Members: Paraguay and Uruguay.
[g]The Dominican Republic, Haiti, and Panama.

explained by a combination of a long tradition of inwardness, the continental features of the Brazilian economy, and, especially in the case of Argentina, obstacles to the expansion of agricultural exports due to protection in developed markets. It is also very low in Colombia (10 percent) and Peru (11.6 percent). The more open economies in the hemisphere are those more dependent on the U.S. market: Canada (almost 70 percent ratio of total trade to GNI-PPP), Mexico (about 40 percent), CARICOM economies (44.7 percent), and Venezuela (36 percent). Chile (25.2 percent) and the United States (20.7 percent) are in the intermediate range.

Another important contrast between Latin American economies is the relative importance of intra-FTA trade, trade with the United States, trade within the hemisphere, and trade outside the hemisphere (see Table 12.3). Some of the economies in the Southern

Table 12.3 Main Trade Indicators in Selected FTA Initiatives (2000)

	Share of Intra-FTA Trade in Total Trade	Share of Trade with the U.S. in Total Trade	Share of Trade with Rest of Hemisphere in Total Trade	Share of Trade outside the Hemisphere in Total Trade
NAFTA	46.50	—	5.30	48.20
Canada	78.5	76.7	1.3	20.2
Mexico	82.9	80.7	3.3	13.8
United States	32.2	—	6.7	61.1
Andean Community	10.0	41.3	21.6	27.1
Colombia	15.3	42.7	15.0	27.0
Peru	9.3	28.2	19.3	53.2
Venezuela	5.9	45.0	27.6	21.5
CARICOM	11.2	38.2	12.3	49.5
CACM	11.4	47.5	13.3	27.8
MERCOSUR	20.9	20.4	11.0	47.7
Argentina	30.9	15.7	11.6	41.8
Brazil	13.9	23.5	10.8	51.8
Other				
Chile	—	18.4	30.6	51.0

Source: International Monetary Fund (2001; 2002).
Notes: Total trade includes FTA trade (exports and imports of all partners). CARICOM excludes Antigua; data are for 1999.

Cone, especially those of MERCOSUR, which are more closed, have geographically more diversified trade than those economies that are more open and nearer to the United States. This reflects the similar natural resource endowments of the United States and MERCOSUR if compared to those of most other Latin American economies.

About 80 percent of the trade of Canada and Mexico is with the United States. For CACM trade with the United States is about 50 percent, for CARICOM and the Andean Community it is around 40 percent, and for MERCOSUR and Chile it is around 20 percent. Economies such as Canada and Mexico conduct a very small share of their trade with non-NAFTA countries. With the exception of Chile and Venezuela, the share of trade of all hemispheric economies with the hemisphere, excluding the relevant FTAs and the United States, is rather small. Similarly, with the exception of Canada and Mexico, to a lesser extent the United States in relation to NAFTA, and Argentina in relation to MERCOSUR, intra-FTA trade tends to be no more than around 10 percent of total trade in most other economies.

Although the importance of trade diversion generated by preferential trade agreements is often exaggerated, it is more significant for a specific economy the higher that country's share of non-FTAA imports relative to its total imports. Similarly, the more geographically diversified is the trade of a given economy, the more likely are multilateral concerns to prevail over the regional perspective.

Contrasts between the levels of protection in different hemispheric economies are less marked than is generally taken for granted. Progress toward lower protection since the mid-1980s in Latin America has been substantial. In the late 1980s, in the more extreme cases, average tariffs considerably exceeded 50 percent and imports of many products were prohibited. Trade liberalization proceeded very fast in the early 1990s, but became somewhat bogged down after the middle of the decade, especially in southern South America. Based on simple average tariffs and not taking nontariff barriers into account (see Table 12.4) there is a small group of economies with a low average tariff level: Canada and the United States (4 to 5 percent) and CACM and Chile (5 to 8 percent). Most other average tariffs are in the 11 to 14 percent range.[2] The highest average tariffs are in the 16 to 21 percent range for Mexico and CARICOM. It is, of course, important to qualify any statement based on high simple average tariff levels by the fact that a trade-weighted tariff taking into account preferential arrangements could generate quite different numbers. Especially in the case of

Table 12.4 Tariff Protection in Selected FTA Initiatives (2001)

	Average Tariff	Standard Deviation	Coefficient of Variation	% of Tariff Lines above 15%	% of Tariff Lines above 35%
NAFTA					
Canada	4.20	7.20	1.71	11.63	0.09
Mexico	16.70	14.10	0.84	47.90	0.63
United States	4.50	11.50	2.56	3.54	0.37
Andean Community					
Colombia	11.60	6.30	0.54	23.86	0.19
Peru	13.50	3.70	0.27	16.05	0.00
Venezuela	12.00	6.00	0.50	24.26	0.00
CARICOM	17.70–20.90	11.10–15.30	0.58–0.84	35.74–71.06	8.21–25.17
CACM	5.10–7.60	6.90–9.20	1.04–1.77	0.43–24.73	0.15–1.12
MERCOSUR					
Argentina	13.40	6.60	0.49	49.98	0.40
Brazil	13.20	6.80	0.52	41.18	0.04
Other					
Chile	8.00	0.00	0.00	0.00	0.00

Source: Hemispheric Trade and Tariff Database, retrieved February 4, 2003.
Notes: For CARICOM economies information is for 1999 or 2000. CARICOM excludes the Bahamas, whose simple average tariff is 0.6%, with a standard deviation of 6.7% and a coefficient of variation of 11.17, and whose percentage of tariff lines above both 15% and 35% is 0.27%.

Mexico, given the importance of intra-NAFTA trade, the relevant weighted average tariff is much lower than the simple average tariff. Trade creation following an FTAA agreement would tend to be more important in those economies with a higher simple average tariff and lower shares of their trade with preferential trade partners.

Dispersion of the Mexican, CARICOM, and U.S. tariff is rather high if compared to that of MERCOSUR and several of the Andean economies, and as the U.S. average tariff is low, the U.S. tariff coefficient of variation is the highest in the hemisphere. The proportion of ad valorem tariff lines above 15 percent—tariff peaks—in the hemisphere varies between 3.5 percent of all ad valorem tariff lines in the United States to between 40 and 50 percent in MERCOSUR. Data presented in Table 12.4, however, only include tariff lines for which there is an ad valorem tariff. Since, especially in the case of the United States, specific duties are frequent, this omission significantly affects any assessment of protection. Data for 2000 on ad valorem equivalents of specific duties imposed in the United States indicate that the number of total U.S. tariff lines exceeding 15 percent would be almost doubled if account is taken of the ad valorem equivalent of specific duties, to reach a total of about five hundred. The number of tariff lines above 35 percent would be affected even more significantly, rising from 30 (ad valorem) to a total of 107 (ad valorem and ad valorem equivalents of specific tariffs).[3] In most Latin American economies, on the other hand, the role of specific duties is not relevant. In some Latin American economies agricultural products are significantly protected. Most of them, but not all, are net importers of agricultural products: Mexico, Venezuela, Peru, and most of Central America and the Caribbean. In Chile, Colombia, and Peru, there are price bands in operation that dampen the effect of world price fluctuations on domestic prices through the use of variable duties. The mean tariff on agricultural products in Canada and Mexico is around 22 to 23 percent, and there are also many tariff peaks, specific duties, and tariff quotas. In the Caribbean such averages are even higher.[4]

Tariff peaks in the United States are concentrated in a relatively small number of chapters. Table 12.5 shows the data for those tariff chapters in which the average ad valorem tariff is more than double the average tariff: tobacco products, footwear, textiles and clothing, dairy products, and agricultural products such as nuts, vegetables, and fruit juices. There is also a concentration of specific duties with high ad valorem equivalents in some of these chapters.[5]

Another source of distortion in the evaluation of protection in hemispheric markets refers to nontariff barriers or tariff quotas. These are more significant in the United States than in other economies in the hemisphere, affecting, for instance, trade in textiles, clothing, sugar, and tobacco.[6] There are also contingency measures such as safeguards and anti-dumping and countervailing duties that the United States can use more effectively than its partners in the hemisphere due to its bargaining power. The same applies to Section 301 and similar measures (World Trade Organization 2002). These issues are likely to be of paramount importance in the formation of an FTAA.

It is rather more difficult to single out peaks in Latin American markets, as tariff dispersion is much lower and average tariffs much higher. In MERCOSUR, for instance, there are no less than thirty-five Harmonized System chapters with average tariffs between 16 and 23

Table 12.5 Tariff Protection in the United States (2001)

Chapters of the Harmonized System	Average Tariff	Standard Deviation	Coefficient of Variation	Share of Specific Duties in Tariff Peaks	Share of Specific Duties in Tariff Peaks above 35%
04 Dairy products	12.4	5.0	0.40	69.7	100.0
07 Edible vegetables	9.0	7.6	0.84	12.5	0.0
19 Preparations of cereals	9.1	5.8	0.63	58.3	100.0
20 Preparations of vegetables	11.3	21.9	1.94	18.2	25
24 Tobacco and manuf. tobacco	90.7	156.3	1.72	40.0	33.3
52 Cotton	9.2	3.9	0.42	28.6	100.0
54 Manmade filaments	10.9	3.9	0.36	0.0	0.0
55 Manmade fibres	11.4	4.0	0.35	100.0	0.0
60 Knitted or crocheted fabrics	10.9	3.9	0.36	0.0	0.0
61 Apparel and clothing, k. & c.	12.7	8.4	0.66	21.7	0.0
62 Apparel and clothing, n.k. & n.c.	10.7	7.4	0.69	37.8	0.0
64 Footwear	14.1	14.2	1.00	35.1	24.0

Source: Hemispheric Trade and Tariff Database, retrieved February 4, 2003.

percent.[7] From the more disaggregated perspective: tariff peaks are concentrated most of all in transport equipment (31 to 36 percent)[8] as well as in dairy products, capital goods (chapters 84 and 85), and footwear (26 to 31 percent). There is also a high incidence of tariff peaks in the 21 to 26 percent range in many other chapters covering food residues, leather goods, textiles and clothing, and capital goods (other than chapters 84 and 85).[9]

A synthetic indication of the imbalances among different prospective FTAA members on the relative importance of protection affecting agricultural and nonagricultural exports and imports is the "relative tariff ratio" (RTR) (Sandrey 2000). The index is a ratio between tariffs faced by country A in country B and tariffs imposed by country A on imports from country B. Tariffs in each country are weighted by exports by the other country. In the case of RTRs for the United States,

Brazil is the extreme case among Western Hemisphere economies of divergence between agricultural products (very low RTR) and nonagricultural products (very high RTR), reflecting the protectionist stances of the United States for agricultural goods and of MERCOSUR for industrial goods (Jank, Fuchsloch, and Kutas 2002).[10]

A low tariff does not guarantee access. Antidumping has been increasingly used as an alternative to tariffs. Most antidumping activity in the Americas involves either as origin or destination the five largest economies: the United States, Brazil, Mexico, Canada, and Argentina.[11] The United States and Brazil initiated about 60 percent of all FTAA actions. Actions by the United States are heavily concentrated in base metals, while antidumping actions by other countries are more evenly distributed between sectors.

Access issues also include services, but the definition of levels of protection is considerably more complex than in the case of goods. Main gaps to bridge between the position of the United States and that of at least some of the Latin American economies involve coverage criteria and modes of delivery. Services and investment issues are closely related, especially in a context such as that of recent years, when most of the foreign direct investment flows into Latin America were directed to the provision of public services. Other controversial foreign direct investment issues include those related to compulsory local content, technology transfer, and also to Chapter 11 NAFTA-like rules involving dispute settlement between foreign investors and host governments.

Developing economies are not *demandeurs* of liberalization related to public procurement. This is made explicit in the FTAA negotiations as some of the larger Latin American economies have presented modest positive lists on the provision of services related to public procurement and long negative lists on the exclusion of goods. The objective seems to be to exclude procurement at subnational levels and to leave open the possibility of liberalizing the procurement policies of major state companies only in the long term.

The heterogeneous sizes of Latin American economies, together with differences in the export composition and in the direction of exports, go a long way in explaining why resistance to the FTAA is concentrated in MERCOSUR. The different nature of structures of protection in the United States, and in most of Latin America, adds to the difficulties. A low average tariff and many tariff peaks in the United States contrast with high average tariffs and no tariff peaks in Latin America. As the next section will show, these difficulties tend to be made even more formidable by long-standing traditions of high protection, particularly in MERCOSUR.

The Political Economy of Protection in Latin America: The Inertia of History

Lack of a sufficiently long, stable democratic tradition is an obstacle to the consolidation of transparency in electoral processes and adequate analysis of the political economy of protection using standard models. Lobby for protection without a fully working democratic regime is bound to be even less transparent than under the usually established checks and balances. It thus affects any credible estimate of mobilization of lobbying resources and its possible links to tariff formation. Political instability is bound to affect the stability of political-support functions since losses to the general population are not constrained by the usual electoral requirements that apply under democratic rules. Lack of transparency also affects any attempt to explain protection by a campaign-contributions approach or by a political-contributions approach.[12]

As the position stands, at least in some of the big Latin American economies there is a very limited tradition of open discussion of the consequences of protection in terms of costs and benefits for different sections of society. The links between the credibility of pledges by politicians and voting patterns are extremely fuzzy. This helps to explain why there is a patent lack of consciousness by different segments of the society about the distributive impact of protection.

To a large extent what appears simply as a myopic behavior is due to history. Inertial elements are of paramount importance in the political economy of protectionism in economies such as Brazil. There has been a tradition of high protection since the mid-nineteenth century. More recently, in the 1947–90 period, there was absolute protection against imports of many products. But at the same time high growth was achieved in the twentieth century, at least until the 1970s. The Brazilian experience stands as the most successful among developing economies. Growth in 1900–73 was faster only in Japan and Finland (Maddison 1989). It has been suggested that it was possible to maintain a high tariff in Brazil because higher production costs affecting exports could be significantly transferred to coffee consumers (Abreu and Bevilaqua 2000). This was due to the combination of a dominant position in the world coffee market, the importance of the coffee-export economy in the Brazilian economy as a whole, and the low price elasticity of coffee demand. Attempts to raise protection in other commodity-exporting economies raised the opposition of exporters who were price takers, rather than price makers, in their main commodity markets, and increased input prices resulted either in reduced mark ups or in reduced market shares in the world markets. It was not that Brazil was able to avoid the costs entailed by a high tariff, it was a rather a question of at least partly compensating such costs at the expense of world coffee consumers.[13] As coffee lost importance in the economy as a whole such effects tended to become weaker over time.

After the 1929–33 recession, protection in Latin America became widespread, in many cases in the form of quantitative restrictions implicit in exchange controls. The strategy of import substitution by means of high protection was adopted by many smaller Latin American economies with small shares in world commodity markets and whose market size only allowed extremely inefficient domestic production. Foreign exchange regimes adopted after World War II entailed severe anti-export bias. But it is important to recognize that to some extent such policies were the result of the contraction of traditional export markets rather than just the result of primitive reasoning by populist politicians.[14]

The attraction of direct foreign investment even in the larger economies starting in the 1950s included policies that assured that competition would be limited to few entrants protected by very high tariff walls. This has created a strange Latin American phenomenon—multinational companies that played, and continue to play, a crucial role in trying to delay trade liberalization because they have a long-established, vested interest in protection. From the mid-1960s, the more extreme version of the autarkical model started to be abandoned in many Latin American economies as there was growing concern about the sustained anti-export bias of many of the previous international economic policies. But it is wrong to say that policies became outward looking as domestic markets were opened slowly and, indeed, as a reaction to oil shocks and the following debt crisis, trade liberalization was often reversed. In the mid-1970s nominal tariffs were typically very high, and often protection was absolute due to import controls, but this was coupled with the discretionary distribution of tariff exemptions and reductions so that the collection of import duties was not very significant. Exports, on the other hand, were heavily subsidized, especially, but not exclusively, in the context of attracting foreign direct capital using fiscal rebates linked to future export performance. The spectacular increase in the share of industrial products in the total exports of economies such as Brazil from the mid-1960s to the early 1980s was a direct result of such subsidies. In a way, it is possible to say that foreign economic policy making remained very much based on pick-the-winner strategies. The differences were that there was a relay of pickers, with the military in full control for a long period, and that instead of picking winners in connection with import substitution, as until the 1960s, the scope was widened to include those who were thought to be promising future exporters. So, rent seeking, after being concentrated for a long period in import-substitution projects, and the consequent demands for protection, came to play a crucial role also in the distribution of export subsidies. Conventional wisdom regarding the links between outwardness and growth only took account of such distortions quite late .[15]

Since the late 1970s, but more markedly from the mid-1980s, trade liberalization came to be adopted as a pillar of comprehensive economic reform in most Latin American economies, even in those economies that were more reluctant to change traditionally protectionist policies. There was substantial unilateral trade liberalization, with sharp reductions in average tariffs and dismantlement of nontariff barriers. Recourse to quantitative restrictions under Article XVIII:B of the General Agreement on Tariffs and Trade, once frequent, almost disappeared. In the Uruguay Round, most Latin American countries bound 100 percent of their tariff lines on industrial products at levels that converged to a maximum of 35 percent in five years. But in most cases applied tariffs are much below bound levels.

This shift in policies was due to the recognition that import substitution had failed to provide the incentives for high growth, even in the economies in which the strategy had been more successful in the past. Imports had been reduced so much that even a further spectacular surge of import substitution (much more difficult to obtain) had no significant overall impact. Moreover, long-term costs of protection became explicit, as exports faced increasing problems due to their lack of competitiveness, which was aggravated by inefficient investment outlays in high-cost, domestically produced capital goods. Exports subsidies also became an excessive fiscal burden in a context in which there was much more competition for scarce public funding.

While commitment to trade liberalization is probably high in most of Latin America, there are important actual or potential sources of resistance to its deepening, especially in MERCOSUR. As Argentina faces its most dramatic economic crisis in its independent history, it is open to question whether commitment to more open markets in the future is feasible independent of what will be the mid-term outlook from a political point of view. The present crisis tends to undermine commitment to reform, and it is not uncommon to hear comments suggesting that Argentina's collapse was due to the reforms undertaken since the beginning of the 1990's.

Similarly in Brazil, cavalier comments regarding the shortcomings of trade liberalization coming "too-fast and too-deep" are mingled with criticisms of the excessively long period during which the exchange rate was allowed to remain overvalued in the expectation of the beneficial consequences of a comprehensive reform program that in the end was only partly implemented. Consistently with the country's laggard position in the Latin American move towards liberalization, the domestic debate on "industrial policy" shows a widespread reluctance to engage in further trade liberalization, especially in the FTAA context. The political element is perhaps paramount as there is much suspicion surrounding the decision to develop closer ties with the United States. But, in addition, the lack of economic sophistication of stances adopted by the average politician on trade matters may come as a surprise to newcomers. Mercantilist ways of thinking are pervasive, with frequent arguments on the need to redress balance-of-payments imbalances on a sector-by-sector basis through more interventionist policies seeking import substitution. The protectionist, or latently protectionist, coalition is extremely wide and includes domestic entrepreneurs, unions, and, frequently in a prominent position, multinationals seeking to protect their *chasse gardée* recovering typical past stances adopted in the golden age of import-substitution industrialization. All candidates during the recent presidential campaign emphasized the desirability of a return to more interventionist "industrial" policies. Victory of the opposition in October, 2002, shall mean, at least in principle, that the future stance on foreign economic policy is likely to be significantly less liberal than that adopted since the late 1980s, and that a revival of protectionism is not unlikely. It is true that the victorious opposition seems to have reversed rather sharply its long-standing, sweeping condemnation of orthodox macroeconomic policies. But it is unlikely that this *volte-face* will spread with the same intensity to trade policies.

The stance of multinationals concerning the political economy of protection in Latin America tends to be much more diversified today than it was in the high tariff period. There was a spectacular increase of foreign direct investment in nontradable sectors such as banking and public services. These firms have a vested interest in the opening up of the Latin American economies and particularly in the stability of the macroeconomic environment. Most of the FDI in sectors other than services was directed to plants that were not necessarily geared exclusively to the domestic markets, even in the larger economies. But it is still true that many multinational firms, especially when supplying large domestic markets, are crucial *demandeurs* of sustained protection and export subsidies and still enjoy effective protection well above 35 percent in the more protected economies.

The entrenched resistance to trade liberalization in Latin America, mostly in MERCOSUR, is matched by similar difficulties in the United States as very high protection, or other measures affecting market access of imports, affect a significant number of tariff lines. Many of these are agricultural products, and thus of special interest for MERCOSUR.

The Political Economy of Protection in the United States: Ominous Developments

Some of the features of protection in the United States that constitute important obstacles to a successful FTAA negotiation have already been indicated. In spite of the low average tariff, the United States tariff schedule includes a relative large number of tariff peaks (above 15 percent) and very high tariffs (above 35 percent) in the form of ad valorem and specific tariffs, in contrast with most other hemispheric economies. These sectors—textile and apparel and agricultural products—as well as steel products, which answer for most antidumping actions, are the more sensitive products from the U. S. viewpoint and are also the most important for its FTAA partners.

The analytical framework of many analyses of an FTAA takes at least implicitly as a matter of course that the FTAA should be an extension of NAFTA, or at least that the question can be treated as if the United States occupied a de facto hub position, with all the Latin American and Caribbean non-NAFTA economies anxious to qualify for entry. The economic policies of Latin American countries are assessed for "readiness" to enter the FTAA, as if the whole exercise could be reduced to a club-formation activity under the supervision of NAFTA members (Hufbauer and Schott 1994 and successive revisions). There is less symmetrical effort to consider readiness from the point of view of the political economy of protection in the NAFTA members, and especially in the United States, a determinant factor for the success of the preferential trade arrangement as a result of negotiations based on mutual concessions.

A number of features of the U.S. trade policy are problematic for successful FTAA negotiations. First, in spite of indications, cogently expressed already in the mid-1930's by internal critics of protectionism, that policy in the United States should seek to manage political pressures by protection-seeking lobbies rather than letting them "run wild" (Schattschneider 1935: 292–3), more recent U.S. negotiating strategy has duly reflected the strength of those sectors more "sensitive" to the competition of imports. A direct result has been the U.S. emphasis on a pick-and-choose approach to the dismantlement of tariff and, more rarely, nontariff barriers, to the detriment of a comprehensive dismantlement of protection based on reduction formulae applied without exceptions. This emphasis on selectivity has converged with a similar outlook in the European Union, with its long-standing strategy of placing high priority to resisting liberalization of trade in agricultural products. It was combined with the pressure since the 1980s, to continuous widening of the multilateral trade negotiations agenda through the inclusion of new issues, which has resulted in a significant backlog of unfinished business, mostly affecting traditional issues in relation to which developing economies, that is most of prospective FTAA members, are *demandeurs*. The expressed U.S. desire to take into account "product sensitivities"—in USTR lingo—points to the recurrence of a negotiation strategy that will leave a backlog of products or issues that are sensitive for the United States but essential to the agenda for most of the other FTAA members.

The second feature of United States trade policy that raises difficulties for a successful conclusion of the FTAA negotiation is related to uncertainty about whether U.S. commitments concerning market access are sufficiently binding. What is at stake is whether, even if mutually advantageous reciprocal tariff concessions can be made during the transition period toward a preferential trade area, the United States can assure its future partners that market access in the United States will not be prevented by antidumping, safeguard actions, or other such discretionary instruments.

Third, recent decisions on United States trade policy such as the Trade Promotion Authority signed in August, 2002, together with the safeguards affecting steel imports and the new farm bill, give an indication of the obstacles that will have to be surmounted for the successful conclusion of an FTAA. Such a radical shrinking of the "win-set"—that is, of the set of possible outcomes of international negotiations given the restrictions imposed by the domestic political economy of protection—enhances significantly the already immense bargaining power of the bigger player (Putnam 1988). But such a development may simply be overkill and thus reduce radically the likelihood of the other parties in the international negotiation accepting the signaled terms.

The approved Trade Promotion Authority removes some of the provisions of former drafts that, in the words of United States Trade Representative Robert Zoellick, would "cripple America's [*sic*] ability to open markets around the world." The Dayton-Craig Senate amendment that would have allowed Congress to veto specific provisions of trade pacts if they changed U.S. antidumping and other so-called "trade remedy" laws has dissolved. So has a previous clause on remedies to counter the allegedly unfair competition of goods produced in economies that resort to foreign-exchange devaluation. But by creating a more elaborate compulsory consultation process between USTR and Congress, Congress continues to make difficult commitments on behalf of the United States to improved access for a significant list of "import-sensitive" products, particularly agricultural goods.

The recent decision by the United States on steel safeguards does not create a concrete obstacle to negotiations. It is also true that it has been followed by many exclusions that have reduced its initial distortions. But the move underlines the vulnerability of any negotiation on access based exclusively on tariff- and nontariff-barriers bargaining. Perhaps more seriously, it underlines the inability of the United States to live up to its alleged commitment to free trade. It is true that NAFTA members have been excluded from the list of countries affected by the steel safeguards. But, besides doubts about the WTO legality of such exclusions, it is not entirely clear whether the United States would be willing to make such exclusion clauses a feature of an FTAA.

The new farm bill has dramatically increased U.S. agricultural subsidies. While the total amounts to be spent are still within the caps set in the Uruguay Round, there are doubts about whether the administration will indeed have the political clout to make use of the trigger mechanism that allows the further reduction in subsidies should world agricultural prices continue to fall and the WTO subsidy caps are exceeded. In any case, it is difficult not to see the decision as a further surrender to protectionist pressures by the U.S. administration.

These decisions boil down to "padding"—that is, increase of protection within the maximum levels multilaterally agreed so as to cut water in a prospective future negotiation. Some comments on this decision are candid: "the 2002 farm bill and the steel relief measures gave [Latin America] additional incentives to enter a regional trade pact whose rules and understandings might roll back such protectionist policies and make them less likely in the future" (Feinberg 2002). Such a view is to be deplored, especially when the Latin American economies agreed in the context of the FTAA negotiations to consider applied tariff rates as the initial tariff levels to be considered in the tariff-reduction schedules rather than those, much higher, rates bound in the Uruguay Round.

Recent developments in the trade policies of the United States toward increased protection, coupled with the evident obstacles to a reversal of such a stance in an electoral year, place the original FTAA timetable under stress. The next section puts into perspective assessments of the impact of the FTAA on trade and welfare by taking up problems raised by the negotiations. It stresses the difficulties likely to be faced concerning the pace of liberalization and comprehensiveness of the coverage of issues.

The FTAA Negotiation Process

There are several alternative estimates of the impact of an FTAA on particular economies and specific sectors from the point of view of trade and welfare, based both in the general-equilibrium and partial-equilibrium frameworks. For instance, Monteagudo and Watanuki (2002) estimated recently the impact of FTAA trade liberalization (excluding non-tariff barriers) using a computable general-equilibrium model incorporating trade-related externalities and economies of scale. They suggest that hemispheric real GDP would increase 0.55 percent, ranging from 0.3 percent for NAFTA to 2.2 percent for MERCOSUR with Chile, Central America, and the Andean Community roughly between 1.4 and 1.8 percent.[16] There would be an expansion of exports substantially higher than imports in most FTAA economies. Only Canada, Mexico, and Venezuela would be exceptions. Exports would expand 1.7 percent in NAFTA members, 4.7 percent in MERCOSUR, 5.2 percent in Chile, 4.4 percent in the Andean Community, and 6.7 percent in Central America and the Caribbean. These aggregate data, however, may hide important intercountry contrasts: for instance, Brazilian exports to the United States would increase 9 percent while Brazilian imports from the United States would increase 23.2 percent.[17] In a preliminary version of the Monteagudo and Watanuki study, the impact on bilateral imports and exports became of the same magnitude only when nontariff barriers were considered.

All these estimates, however, consider instantaneous trade liberalization and do not take into account exclusions. U.S. strategy in the FTAA negotiations is unlikely to contrast sharply with that adopted in the NAFTA negotiations. It has been shown that the tariff phase-out in the NAFTA process took longer for high-duty products and that liberalization in Mexico was correlated to liberalization in the United States for the same products, perhaps an attempt to establish narrow reciprocity at the eight-digit level (Kowalczyk and Davis 1998). This could be an indication that export interests of the United States in Mexico were concentrated in those sectors also enjoying high protection in the United States and that the likelihood of trade diversion in the Mexican market is high (Panagariya 1998).

Recent research on reciprocal Brazil-U.S. market access for goods and revealed comparative advantage[18] has shown that, at the six-digit level, to a certain extent, the relatively more competitive are Brazilian products, the higher tends to be protection in the United States market. In the Brazilian market, however, this relation is reversed, as the relatively more competitive imports from the United States tend to face lower tariffs than do the less competitive products. This is an indication that Brazilian exports to the United States tend to be more adversely affected by protection than do exports by the United States to Brazil.

The FTAA negotiation, as any other trade negotiation, involves countries endeavoring to maximize, or expedite, access to export markets of their partners and to minimize, or delay, access to its own market given an implementation time span. It has been pointed out (Panagariya 1998) that every country would tend to offer liberalization that entails trade diversion first, leaving trade-creation liberalization to the later stages of implementation. While reciprocity is an important feature of trade negotiations involving mostly big economies of not very dissimilar size, it is unlikely to have the same importance in the regional or subregional context since there are such sharp differences in the size of the economies involved (Staiger 1998).

The stance adopted by each country in international negotiation results from an internal negotiation involving interests that may see gains or losses with the implementation of the initiative (Putnam

1988). This complex domestic negotiation involves many relevant players: government, consumers, taxpayers, multinationals, trade unions, exporters, buyers of intermediate and capital goods, and domestic producers of products likely to face increased competition from imports. To break the deadlock that allows high protection to survive, it is important to be able to mobilize effectively those bound to gain from liberalization. Are there good reasons to postpone liberalization of sensitive products or, in a more extreme scenario, to exclude certain sensitive products in a too-elastic interpretation of the hazy "substantially all trade" provision for FTAs under multilateral rules?[19] U.S. reliance on a negotiating strategy that postpones more relevant liberalization—that is, liberalization that affects inefficient domestic producers—notwithstanding, a "first-things-last" strategy from a strict efficiency viewpoint may be justifiable under certain conditions. Exclusions would reduce the government political costs in facing either the impact of trade diversion on the average voter, or the opposition of coordinated import-competing sectors—that is, loss of lobby income (Grossman and Helpman 1994).[20] Bargaining over the ranking of sectors exempted would reflect the clout to bargain of different governments.

Even supposing that an analysis emphasizing the role of contributions by affected sectors is relevant to all governments in the FTAA context, more optimistic views, which would not put interpretations of what really is "substantially all trade" under undue stress, could result, for example, from substantially higher sensitivity by governments to the average voter. This would contribute to the likelihood of liberalization across the board, or at least would moderate the incentives to delay liberalization that entails trade creation.

The universal application of a formula or formulae to eliminate tariff (or tariff-equivalent) levels of protection would have been an efficient instrument to assure that different governments do not drag their feet to delay the impact of liberalization on their most protected producers. The impact of formulae as tariff-cutting criteria on tariff dispersion, a usual indicator of sensitivity, is even more rapid than on tariff levels. But the opportunity to adopt such formulae has passed, as the FTAA tariff negotiations are to be conducted on the basis of lists of products classified in different categories according the liberalization horizon: instantaneous, five years, ten years, and a residual of sensitive products. The U.S. offers are based in different lists presented to different FTAA partners. The negotiation would then tend to be of a "hub-and-spoke" character, the main differences being that there would be some possible economies of scale in the negotiating process and that trade liberalization would be simultaneous even if affecting different products in the case of each pair of countries. Other countries would prefer a regional, MFN-based approach coupled with provisions that take into account different levels of development among prospective members.

In the negotiation on services, the United States would prefer excluded sectors to constitute a negative list. Many Latin American countries would prefer a positive list, as in the WTO General Agreement on Trade in Services, as this would cope more adequately with the lack of detailed knowledge regarding the impact of liberalization on national providers of many services. In any case, there is greater Latin American reluctance to liberalize services than goods: some countries wish to consider WTO-bound commitments as an initial basis for negotiation rather than actual access conditions. Other important differences to bridge in services are the divergent views on local presence requirements and the flexibility of arrangements to accommodate movements of top managerial personnel (see Chapter 9 in this volume).

In the gray area between services and investment lie many of the thornier problems to cope with in the negotiations, especially those concerning the provision of public services, such as transparency requirements or dispute settlement between foreign investors and host economies. While most of the issues involving trade-related investment measures seem uncontroversial, attempts by Latin American economies to reopen some of the provisions of the agreements on trade-related intellectual property and subsidies reached in the Uruguay Round may be the origin of much heat. This is the case for banned performance requirements, particularly those that are export related. Substantially more complex to solve are the problems connected to different views on issues such as compulsory transfer of technology and other possible requirements related to treatment of foreign direct investment.

Agricultural subsidies are one of the main stumbling blocks faced by the negotiations as many of their adverse effects are on markets outside the FTAA. While the dismantlement of such export subsidies affecting intra-FTAA markets is feasible, their importance is limited, and it is much harder to think of substantive remedies which would counter their impact in other markets. This applies even more forcefully to other types of subsidies, and is typically an issue that is more adequately dealt with in multilateral negotiations rather than at the regional level. Similarly, antidumping and safeguards measures, which are a crucial part of the U.S. protectionist armor and are increasingly so of other big economies in the continent, if left as they stand could seriously undermine results of access negotiations. But there is more scope for regional negotiations than in the case of agriculture. Of course, attempted tit-for-tat, bilateral use of antidumping is likely to put smaller economies at a disadvantage in relation to the United States.

While the U.S. stance on some of the "new" issues has proved to be until now less sanguine than it was initially feared, it is not impossible that such a stance will harden during the negotiations as, and if, the pressure for complementary agreements à la NAFTA gains strength.

Conclusions

The importance of the obstacles in the path of successful FTAA negotiations should not be underestimated. Protectionist lobbies in the United States and in Latin America, especially in the big and more protected economies, are stronger now than they were even just a couple of years ago, and have been more successful in their bid to delay trade liberalization.

U.S. strategy based in delaying trade liberalization of sensitive products to the last possible moment, or excluding such trade from the FTA agreement, is likely to be taken as an example by other countries. Trade-creation liberalization is to be delayed and trade diversion to prevail in the shorter term. The negotiation of specific lists of products to be included in four categories, defined according a liberalization schedule and sensitiveness on a bilateral basis, is a return to the "hub and spoke" model.

Not always explicit is the difficulty faced in the FTAA negotiations that there are many existing preferences that would be adversely affected by the implementation of comprehensive trade liberalization. The erosion of subregional preferences, especially those related to the U.S. market, in the NAFTA context and also in Central America and the Caribbean may act as a deterrent for a more active approach by economies likely to be affected by a reversal of trade diversion.

The collapse of Argentina and macroeconomic instability in Brazil placed the eventual macroeconomic advantages of an FTA including the United States in a relatively secondary position in the list of possible benefits of such an integration, at least in a midterm perspective.

To the extent, however, that binding trade-liberalization commitments are made, there is a powerful implied macroeconomic discipline imposed by the sheer size of the main economy involved in the initiative. The scope for the adoption of unsustainable policies is significantly curtailed by the likely consequences on trade and foreign direct investment flows. Potential gains entailed by the reduction in interest-rate spreads are substantially higher than those related to trade. Curiously enough, the impact of these imported macroeconomic virtues has tended to play a rather secondary role in the Latin American public debate on an FTAA.

What can the United States offer to Latin America that may clinch the deal? To a large extent what can be offered by the United States that could ease the political pain of concessions by Latin America is concentrated in its list of sensitive products. This is why recent moves in the political economy of protection of the United States tend to jeopardize successful FTAA negotiations.

The bigger Latin American economies outside NAFTA are *demandeurs* of both a reduction of national discretion in the use of antidumping and safeguard measures as well as of further disciplines and scheduled elimination of agricultural subsidies, or of policies producing equivalent results. The resistance by the United States to the overhaul of such policies in a regional negotiation is substantial. The United States could always surmount such difficulties by offering a more attractive access package, but it is unclear whether this would make sense if these issues will be discussed multilaterally in Geneva.

It must be kept constantly in mind that the FTAA and the WTO negotiations are closely intertwined. This is especially relevant in connection with issues such as antidumping and agricultural subsidies, but also to a certain extent in relation to access, as MFN-improved access is bound to have important consequences on FTAA trade, especially on those all-important exporters seeking to exploit opportunities created by FTAA-induced trade diversion. Countries negotiating the FTAA will keep a very attentive eye on Geneva and, perhaps, be reluctant to clinch a hemispheric deal without a full picture of multilateral developments. This could be an additional source of pressure to delay the FTAA negotiations if the Doha Round proves to be as protracted as its predecessors and the deadline of 2005 is not binding. Many analysts believe that an inevitable consequence of the EU move to delay crucial decisions to cut support under the Common Agricultural Policy until 2007 will be a postponement of the date scheduled for the end of the

Doha Round. It is likely that this will also be relevant for the FTAA timetable of negotiations.

References

Bouët, Antoine, Lionel Fontagné, Mondher Mimouni, and Xavier Pichot. 2001. "Market Access Maps: A Bilateral and Disaggregated Measure of Market Access." Working Papers Series no. 2001–18, Centre d'Etudes Prospectives et d'Informations Internationales, Paris (December).

Brasil, Ministério de Desenvolvimento, Indústria e Comércio. O Departamento de Defesa Commercial. www.mdic.gov.br/comext/decom/decom.html.

Carvalho, Alexandre, and Andreia Parente. 1999. "Impactos comerciais da área de livre comércio das Américas." Texto para Discussão no. 635, Instituto de Pesquisa Econômica Aplicada, Brasília.

de Paiva Abreu, Marcelo. 1995. "O Nafta e as relações econômicas Brasil-EUA." In *Mercosul & Nafta. O Brasil e a Integração Hemisférica*, edited by J. P. Velloso et al. Rio de Janeiro: José Olympio.

de Paiva Abreu, Marcelo, and Afonso S. Bevilaqua. 2000. "Brazil as an Export Economy, 1880–1930." In *An Economic History of Twentieth-Century Latin America*, vol.1: *The Export Age*, edited by E. Cardenas, J. A. Ocampo, and R. Thorp. Basingstoke: Palgrave.

Dsiao, Xinshen, Eugenio Díaz-Bonilla, and Sherman Robinson. 2002. "Scenarios for Trade Integration in the Americas." Discussion Paper no. 90, Trade and Macroeconomics Division, International Food Policy Research Institute, Washington, DC (January).

Feinberg, Richard. 2002. "A Vision for the Americas." *Financial Times*, 7 August, sec. 1: 11.

Fodor, Jorge. 1975. "Perón's Policies for Agricultural Exports, 1946–1948: Dogmatism or Common Sense?" In *Argentina in the Twentieth Century*, edited by David Rock. London: Duckworth.

Grossman, Gene M., and Elhanan Helpman. 1994. "The Politics of Free-Trade Agreements." *American Economic Review* 85 (4): 667–90.

———. 2001. *Special Interest Politics*. Cambridge, MA: MIT Press.

Helpman, Elhanan. 1997. "Politics and Trade Policy." In *Advances in Economics and Econometrica: Theory and Applications*, edited by I. D. M. Kreps and K. F. Wallis. Cambridge: Cambridge University Press.

Hufbauer, Gary, and Jeffrey Schott, assisted by Diana Clark. 1994. *Western Hemisphere Economic Integration*. Washington, DC: Institute for International Economics.

International Monetary Fund. 2001. *Direction of Trade Statistics Yearbook 2000*. Washington, DC.

———. 2002. *Direction of Trade Statistics Quarterly*. Washington, DC (December).

Jank, Marcos. 2002. A Complexidade das Negociações Internacionais. *O Estado de São Paulo*, 16 April, pt. 1: 2.

Jank, Marcos, Ian Fuchsloch, and Géraldine Kutas. 2002. "Agricultural Liberalization in Multilateral and Regional Trade Negotiations." Inter-American Development Bank (September). Photocopy.

Kowalczyk, Carsten, and Donald Davis. 1998. "Tariff Phase-Outs: Theory and Evidence from GATT and NAFTA." In *The Regionalization of the World Economy*, edited by Jeffrey Frankel. Chicago: University of Chicago Press.

Kume, Honório. 2003. "ALCA: Uma análise da questão de acesso a mercado." Centro Brasileiro de Relações Internacionais, Rio de Janeiro (September). Photocopy.

Maddison, Angus. 1989. *The World Economy in the Twentieth Century*. Paris: Organization for Economic Cooperation and Development.

Monteagudo, Josefina, and Masakazu Watanuki. 2001. "Regional Trade Agreements for MERCOSUR: A Comparison between the FTAA and the FTA with the European Union." Paper presented at the Conference on Impacts of Trade Liberalization Agreements on Latin America and the Caribbean, Washington, DC, November 5–6.

Panagariya, Arvind. 1998. "Comment on Carsten Kowalczyk and Donald Davis, Tariff Phase-Outs: Theory and Evidence from GATT and NAFTA." In *The Regionalization of the World Economy*, edited by Jeffrey Frankel. Chicago: University of Chicago Press.

Putnam, Robert. 1988. "Diplomacy and Domestic Politics: The Logic of Two-Level Games." *International Organization* 43 (3): 427–60.

Rodrik, Dani. 1995. "Political Economy of Trade Policy." In *Handbook of International Economics*, vol. 3, edited by Gene M. Grossman and Kennneth Rogoff. Amsterdam: North-Holland.

Sandrey, Ron. 2000. "The Relative Tariff Ratio Index." Working Paper Series no. 7, New Zealand Trade Consortium, Wellington.

Schattschneider, E. E. 1935. *Politics, Pressures and the Tariffs: A Study of Free Private Enterprise in Pressure Politics, as Shown in the 1929–1930 Revision of the Tariff*. New York: Prentice-Hall.

Staiger, Robert W. 1998. "Comment on Carsten Kowalczyk and Donald Davis, Tariff Phase-Outs: Theory and Evidence from GATT and NAFTA." In *The Regionalization of the World Economy*, edited by Jeffrey Frankel. Chicago: University of Chicago Press.

Tavares, José. 2002. "As normas antidumping da ALCA e a agenda multilateral." Centro Brasileiro de Relações Internacionais, Rio de Janeiro. Photocopy.

World Bank. 2001. *World Development Report 2001/2002.* Washington, DC.

World Trade Organization (WTO). 1995. *Analytical Index: Guide to GATT Law and Practice.* Vol. 2, Articles XXII-XXXVIII. Geneva.

———. 2002. *Trade Policy Review: United States of America 2001.* Geneva.

Yeats, Alexander J. 1998. "Does MERCOSUR's Trade Performance Raise Concerns about the Effects of Regional Trade Arrangements?" *The World Bank Economic Review* 12 (1): 1–28.

Notes

The author thanks the participants of the preconference and conference "FTAA and Beyond: Prospects for Integration in the Americas" in Cambridge, Mass. and Punta del Este, May 31–June 1 and December 15–16, 2002, who commented on this chapter, and especially Jeff Schott and Andrés Velasco. The author also thanks Marcos Jank, Honório Kume, Eduardo Loyo, Josefina Monteagudo, Guida Piani, and Sandra Rios for their help.

1 Rising to 0.5 percent if the group of remaining thirty-one members includes Canada.

2 It should be kept in mind that reference here is always to applied tariff rates. In most Latin American economies tariff lines have been bound in the WTO at 35 percent for industrial products. For some agricultural products bound levels are higher. Applied rates are thus much below bound rates. For the United States and Canada applied rates are generally those bound in the WTO. The adoption of bound rates as a basis to start tariff reduction in the FTAA framework would be tantamount to acceptance by the United States of a grace period before trade liberalization started to be effective in Latin America.

3 Ad valorem equivalents provide lower bound estimates for the protective effect as they are lowered by tariff reductions enjoyed in the United States by preferential trade partners.

4 Data supplied by Marcos Jank. Calculations are based on data from the 2001 Hemispheric Trade and Tariff Data Base for Market Access (www.ftaa-alca.org/NGROUPS/NGMADB_E.asp), and Agricultural Market Access Database, www.amad.org.

5 It has been suggested that the abolition of tariff peaks in the United States that affect Brazilian exports of "other agricultural products and food industry" products, that is, their reduction to 15 percent ad valorem would halve the average tariff rate from 18.2 percent to 9.1 percent (Bouët et al. 2001).

6 Quite often extremely high U.S. peaks on agricultural products are hidden by inadequate disaggregation of the data. The eight-digit line

24011065 (tobacco, not stemmed or stripped, not over 35 percent wrapper tobacco, flue-cured burley, etc.) tariff is 350 percent, but at the six-digit level the internationally comparable tariff on line 240110 (wrapper tobacco) is a much more innocent-looking average of 42.5 percent (Jank 2002).

7 These are the values for Brazil.

8 This is the most extreme case of protectionist inertia in MERCOSUR. It is of interest to note, in the context of the political economy of protection, that the list of *demandeurs* of a high common MERCOSUR external tariff traditionally includes in a prominent position multinationals producing cars and capital goods that fear the loss of their cozy, protected markets. This is an important explanation for trade diversion resulting from MERCOSUR (Yeats 1998).

9 Hemispheric Trade and Tariff Database. See Jank, Fuchsloch, and Kutas (2002) for a comprehensive analysis of protection in the FTAA with emphasis on agricultural products.

10 Divergences for other MERCOSUR economies, Venezuela, and CARICOM are also substantial.

11 These economies have initiated 410 out of the total 485 actions initiated by prospective FTAA members from 1987 to 2000 (Tavares 2002). In Brazil, there is a concentration of actions involving chemical products (www.mdic.gov.br/comext/decom/decom.html).

12 See Rodrik (1995) for the standard review of alternative political-economy models. See also Grossman and Helpman (2001). Much of the political economy literature requires substantial adjustment to be applied to the formulation and implementation of commercial policy in economies with institutional characteristics rather different from those in the United States.

13 This resulted, of course, in important income transfers from consumers of imports to coffee growers.

14 Argentina's anti-export bias was not due entirely to either Perón's foolishness or his wickedness, as suggested by many analysts, but to the recognition that it was preferable to increase real wages and let the masses eat more beef than accumulate idle unconvertible assets in European central banks (Fodor 1975).

15 The relatively low shift toward trade liberalization was also related to the high priority in most Latin American economies of generating trade surpluses to service the significant foreign debt.

16 Other results (Dsiao, Díaz-Bonilla, and Robinson 2002), based on increasing returns to scale and considering only the elimination of tariffs, generate similar rates of GDP increase for most economies. But for NAFTA their estimates are higher and for Central America and the Caribbean and the Andean Community, much higher.

17 These are in line with partial equilibrium estimates by Abreu (1995) and Carvalho and Parente (1999).

18 Kume (2003).

19 There are many intricacies surrounding what is "substantially all trade" in the context of Article XXIV of GATT 1994 (World Trade Organization 1995: 824–7).

20 It is also suggested that that successful negotiations between "politically minded governments"—that is, governments that take into account political contributions by interest groups, both against and in favor of the FTA, as well as the average voter well-being—are more likely the more balanced is trade between two economies. That success in the negotiation is also more likely when the FTA results in enhanced protection—that is, when there is significant trade diversion—rather than reduced protection in most sectors. Enhanced viability of the FTA is thus related to enhanced likelihood of a loss in aggregate welfare. See also Helpman (1997).

PART VI

Assessing the Economics of the FTAA

13

Do Preferential Trade Agreements Matter for Trade? The FTAA and the Pattern of Trade

Antoni Estevadeordal and Raymond Robertson

Introduction

The complexities of multilateral trade negotiations are greatly compounded by the increasing speed in which regional trade agreements are being initiated and negotiated around the world. Even as the latest WTO round advances, the pendulum of the world trading system is once again swinging toward regional trade agreements. In the case of Latin America and the Caribbean the most ambitious regional initiative is the attempt to build a Free Trade Area of the Americas (FTAA) among thirty-four countries by 2005.

The debate among those who believe bilateral deals are dangerous distractions from the multilateral system and therefore are "stumbling blocs" and those who view them as "building blocs" that will promote broader global liberalization is alive and well, bypassing the academic circles and reaching the policy discussions. The WTO director general Supachai Panitchpakdi has warned that "à la carte regionalism" is posing a systemic risk to the global trading system. In contrast, the U.S. trade representative Robert Zoellick has argued that FTAs will trigger a beneficial process of "competitive liberalization" as a speedy route to global free trade.[1]

Academic economists have contributed relatively little to this debate thus far. Although theoretical economists have mostly favored multilateral trade liberalization (Bhagwati and Panagariya 1996) an increasing number of studies have shown the potential positive role for regional trade agreements (IDB 2002, Schiff and Winters 2003). Relevant empirical studies are even harder to find. In a controversial article, Rose (2000) challenged the conventional wisdom asserting that the role played by GATT in boosting trade was at best modest, while preferential schemes (reciprocal free trade agreements or nonreciprocal preferential arrangements such as the Generalized System of Preference, or GSP) have promoted trade expansion. In general, however, the empirical literature lacks precise estimates on how preferential trade regimes affect the pattern of bilateral trade among partners, even though this is a fundamental policy question in evaluating the effects of ambitious initiatives such as the creation in the Americas of the world's largest FTA (FTAA). As a result, it is difficult to anticipate the effects of the FTAA on trade patterns.[2]

In this chapter we take this challenge seriously. We offer three contributions to the academic and policy debate. First, from a policy perspective, it is important to highlight the difficulties of negotiating market access in the context of an FTAA. The unraveling of the "spaghetti bowl" created by the coexistence of overlapping agreements is an important challenge of a hemispheric agreement. We carefully provide the context in which we perform our empirical exercise by reviewing how FTA negotiations have advanced in the region since the mid-1980s, with an emphasis on market access negotiations, in particular tariffs and rules of origin.

This chapter also offers two empirical contributions. The first emphasizes the *relative* nature of trade costs. Theory suggests that, in a free trade agreement, bilateral trade patterns would depend on the bilateral tariff frictions among members (preferential tariffs) vis-à-vis the tariff frictions that each member faces with respect to the rest of the world (most-favored-nation [MFN] tariffs). A small but rising number of publications simultaneously account for the effects of multilateral and bilateral tariffs, and this chapter directly contributes to this work. We describe a theoretical framework building on previous work by Anderson (1979) and Anderson and van Wincoop (2000) incorporating both bilateral and multilateral resistance factors. After controlling for size and other variables, trade between two countries is a decreasing function of their bilateral trade barrier *relative to* the average barrier of the two countries to trade with all their partners. That is, the more resistant to trade with all others a country is, the more it is pushed to trade with a given bilateral partner.

Our second empirical contribution takes advantage of the *asymmetric* nature of preferential tariffs among members of a preferential trade area. Most previous work uses proxies for tariffs such as average tariff levels or dummy variables. Instead, we ground our empirical work by explicitly incorporating asymmetric tariff barriers into the familiar gravity model, following some recent empirical attempts to measure directly trade costs (Hummels 1999, Limao and Venables 2001). To our knowledge this chapter constitutes the first study to attempt to measure the direct effect of tariffs on trade patterns applying a gravity-equation model with precise measures of both preferential and multilateral tariff frictions among FTA partners and with the rest of the world. Based on this analysis we simulate some potential effects of an FTAA on the pattern of trade in the region.

The chapter is organized in six sections. First, we motivate our study with some stylized facts of the increasing regionalization of the world trading system, with special attention to the blossoming of FTAs in the Americas. Next, we describe the mechanics of preferential tariff liberalization in FTAs in the Americas since the mid-1980s, stressing the important but often forgotten role played by rules of origin. The following section suggests a theoretical framework that modifies a traditional gravity model by explicitly incorporating preferential and MFN tariff barriers. The next section discusses the empirical results, and a final section concludes by considering some policy issues with respect to the proposed FTAA.

The Rise of Regionalism around the World and the "Spaghetti Bowl" in the Americas

Starting in the mid- to late-1980s, most of the developing world began moving toward substantial market-oriented economic reforms, which included, almost without exception, unilateral trade liberalization policies. The depth of the unilateral trade reforms by most countries in the Americas is made obvious by the average MFN tariff rates, which fell from 40 percent in the mid-1980s to 10 percent in 2000. Tariff dispersion has also declined substantially—from 30 percent in the mid-1980s to an average of 10 percent in 2000—limiting the potential distortionary effects due to tariff escalation.

This process of opening up unilaterally was accompanied by liberalization efforts under the multilateral trade negotiations of the Uruguay Round. Latin America as a whole agreed to bind practically all tariff lines at around 35 percent on average.[3] A new round of negotiations was launched in Doha (Qatar) in November 2001, with further commitments to liberalize world trade.

These unilateral and multilateral efforts proceeded just as regionalism gained popularity. Nowhere has this regionalism developed faster in recent times than in Latin America during the 1990s. More than thirty new agreements have already been signed.[4] As part of the structural economic reforms implemented since the mid-1980s and throughout the 1990s, countries created a complex web of simultaneous unilateral, multilateral, and preferential (bilateral or regional) agreements to liberalize trade. The resulting so-called spaghetti bowl of trade agreements is shown in Figure 13.1.[5]

Until early 1990s, most existing FTAs in the region were "partial" agreements in the sense that they covered just a few sectors negotiated within the Latin American Integration Association (LAIA; ALADI in Spanish). A turning point in the Americas was the signature of the North American Free Trade Agreement (NAFTA) among the United States, Canada, and Mexico.

Other significant agreements followed NAFTA. Argentina, Brazil, Paraguay and Uruguay launched a customs union (MERCOSUR) in January 1995 that built upon some previously signed bilateral Complementary Economic Agreements (Acuerdos de Complementación Económica). Mexico and Chile started consolidating their positions as

Figure 13.1 The Spaghetti Bowl: Trade Agreements Signed and under Negotiation in the Americas (as of 2002)

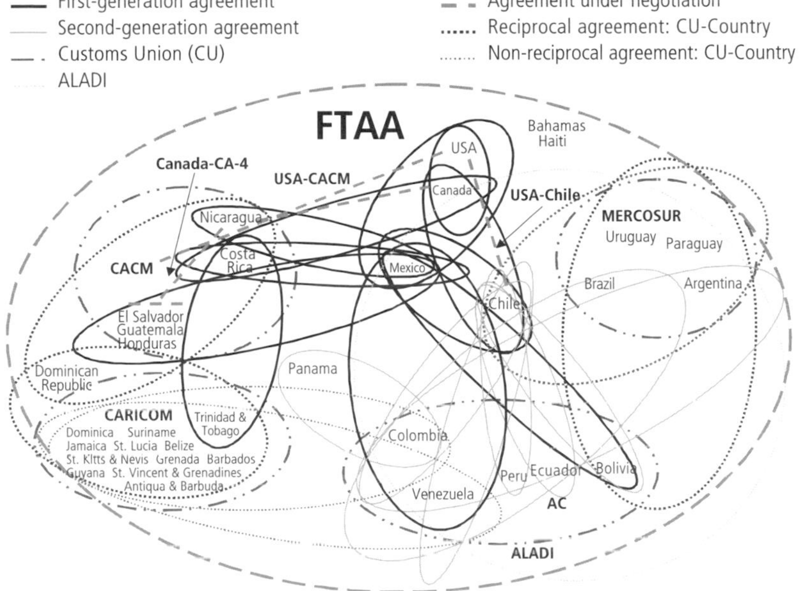

Source: IDB (2002).

strategic trade hubs in the region in the mid-1990s. In 1994, Mexico secured three important agreements, based on the NAFTA model, with Colombia and Venezuela (known as the G-3 Agreement), Costa Rica, and Bolivia. Building on this momentum, Mexico concluded agreements with Nicaragua in 1997 and the Northern Triangle in 2000, and successfully broadened and deepened its agreement with Chile in 1998.

The other trade hub in the Americas, Chile, acquired its status by gradually building a complete network of agreements. It signed its first and most basic agreements with Mexico in 1991, Venezuela in 1992, Colombia in 1993, and Ecuador in 1994. This network expanded with Chile's 1996 association agreement with MERCOSUR and 1998 agreement with Peru. The broadest expansion in the scope of Chilean agreements came in 1996 when it signed a free trade agreement with Canada that almost completely mimicked NAFTA. Subsequently, Chile's 1998 revisions to its agreement with Mexico were based on the NAFTA model, as were its 1999 accords with the countries of the Central American Common Market. Most recently, Chile has concluded free trade agreements with the European Union and United States and signed the first-ever transpacific FTA with South Korea in February 2003. In addition, other countries deepened the intraregional liberalization of older agreements, such as the Andean Pact (renamed Andean Community in 1997, including Colombia, Venezuela, Bolivia, Ecuador, and Peru), CARICOM, and the Central American Common Market.

This regional dynamic continues full force. Negotiations toward the most ambitious initiative for economic integration ever to take place in the hemisphere—an FTAA agreement—are advancing as scheduled toward the 2005 deadline. Those negotiations, however, have not stopped countries in the region from simultaneously pursuing other bilateral negotiations. This is especially true for the largest player in the region, the United States. As of March 2003, the United States had in place FTAs with Canada, Mexico, and Israel, and had concluded negotiations with Singapore and Chile. The U.S. Congress has been notified of negotiations with Central America, Morocco, the South African Customs Union, and Australia. The United States is also considering entering into an FTA with South Korea, Taiwan, New Zealand, Egypt, and at least three members of ASEAN (Indonesia, Philippines, and Thailand) under the Enterprise for ASEAN Initiative. Many others are willing to wait in line.

On the other side of the Atlantic, the European Union is proceeding with its enlargement policy and a somewhat more timid bilateral trade policy. The European Union has negotiated full-fledged, reciprocal FTAs with several countries in Latin America. The most far-reaching process to date has been the Economic Partnership, Political Coordination and Cooperation Agreement between Mexico and the European Union. The broad framework agreement was signed in 1997 and led to the signing of a comprehensive free trade agreement between the two parties in 1999. Framework cooperation agreements with MERCOSUR in 1995 and Chile in 1996 were signed to open negotiations to establish full FTAs. Negotiations were formally launched in April 2000, and Chile completed negotiations and signed an FTA agreement with the EU in May 2002.

Although most of these initiatives are reciprocal trade agreements, several countries in the Americas still are beneficiaries of important nonreciprocal agreements or "one-way" preferential arrangements. These are generally preferences granted by the United States and Canada under the Andean Trade Preferences Act, the Caribbean Basin Initiative, and the GSP regime. Also, several countries are beneficiaries of the European Union GSP regime and special agreement with the Caribbean. Under those regimes, not all products in all countries are entitled to preferential treatment.

Negotiating Preferential Market Access in the Americas: Preferential Tariff Liberalization and Rules of Origin

When negotiating an FTA, countries must first negotiate schedules for dismantling internal tariffs (preferential tariffs among FTA members) vis-à-vis the tariffs applied to third parties (MFN tariffs) and then agree on a system of rules of origin. Those two basic buildings blocs have evolved in Latin America since the late 1980s. These changes now constitute important precedents for FTAA negotiations. We therefore review this evolution and summarize some recent literature in order to evaluate the impact of both instruments on the pattern of trade. We follow our discussion of the evolution of tariffs and rules of origin with a brief review of the empirical literature in order to provide context for the empirical work that follows.

Preferential Tariff Liberalization

Market access negotiations under the "old regionalism" used a fixed preferential tariff below the MFN tariffs. Unilateral and multilateral tariff reductions progressively eroded the difference between the preferential tariff and the MFN tariffs, reducing the initial margins of preference. In order to maintain those margins constant over time, countries continuously had to renegotiate the agreements. Alternatively, some agreements were negotiated by means of preferential tariff reductions as a percentage of current MFN applied rates, which also kept the margins of preference constant over time.

Today, most FTAs in the region include tariff elimination mechanisms that are relatively quick, automatic, and nearly universal in terms of product coverage. The tariff elimination process follows prespecified timetables generally ranging from immediate elimination to a ten-year phase out, with some special phase-out periods for "sensitive" products. Negotiations usually begin with an agreement on a base rate or base level from which phase-out schedules will be applied. Those base rates usually coincide with the MFN applied rates to third parties at the time of negotiations. Although tariffs will be fully dismantled under most trade agreements currently in force (exceptions are between 5 and 10 percent), the tariff phase-out programs vary widely across agreements. For some agreements, more than 50 percent of the products become tariff free during the first year of implementation of the agreement. For others, those percentages will not be reached until the fifth year or much later.

The structure of these phase-out schedules for some agreements is illustrated in Figure 13.2. The evolution of MFN tariffs vis-à-vis the result of this process of preferential liberalization from 1985 to 1997 is presented in Figure 13.3. This figure compares the average MFN rate for eleven Latin American countries with the average preferential rate that each country applies to all partners in this group under different bilateral or regional trade agreements. It shows in a particularly striking way the simultaneous lowering of external and internal barriers, which minimizes the probability for trade diversion. Finally, Figure 13.4 estimates the percentage of tariff lines that will be fully liberalized by 2005 as a result of implementing existing tariff liberalization programs. It has been estimated that 80 percent of total intrahemispheric trade will be liberalized by 2005, the year in which an FTAA is expected to enter into force (IDB 2002). Since GATT/WTO rules require that liberalization cover "substantially all trade," the bulk of the difficulties in negotiating tariff liberalization in an FTAA will involve around 10 percent of current intraregional trade flows, allowing for a margin of around 10 percent of trade being eventually excepted from the agreement.

Figure 13.2 Preferential Tariff Liberalization in Selected FTAs in Latin America: Phase-Out Schedules (% Tariff Lines)

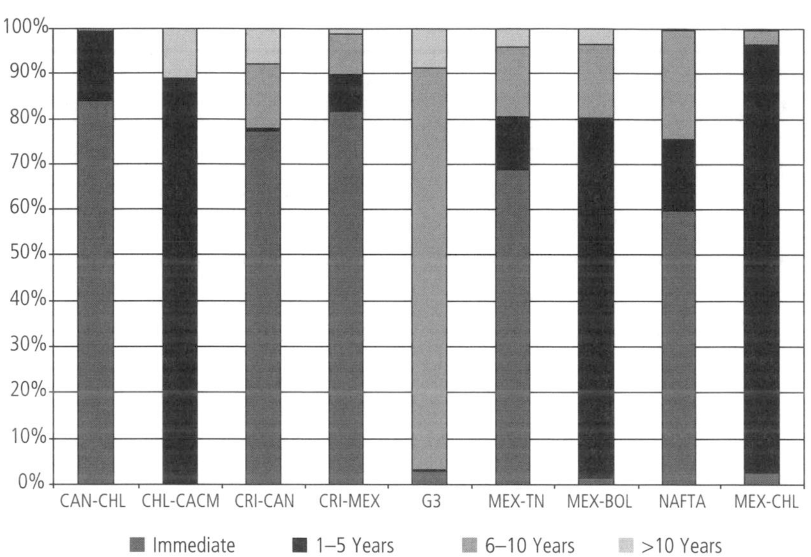

Source: Authors' calculations based on official texts.

Rules of Origin

The counterparts to tariffs are the rules-of-origin provisions. Trade preferences only apply to goods originating in the FTA region. Rules of origin are an important but often forgotten aspect in the analysis of FTAs, but they are necessary to prevent trade deflection.[6] They specify the conditions that goods must meet in order to be deemed as "originating" and hence be eligible for preferential tariff treatment.

Rules of origin vary widely depending on the agreements. While the simpler rules rely on a single, uniform criterion across all products, such as those in ALADI-type agreements, the more complex agreements, such as NAFTA, use a general rule plus additional specific rules negotiated at the product-specific level, combining in different ways three methods to establish "substantial transformation." Those methods can be defined in terms of a "tariff-shift" approach, a "value-added" criterion, or a "technical test." The use of these different criteria can vary widely across agreements, as illustrated in Figure 13.5.[7]

Since rules of origin can be used as effective instruments to deter transshipment of goods within an FTA, they can be used for purposes

Figure 13.3 MFN and Preferential Tariff Liberalization in Latin America (1985–1997) (in Percent)

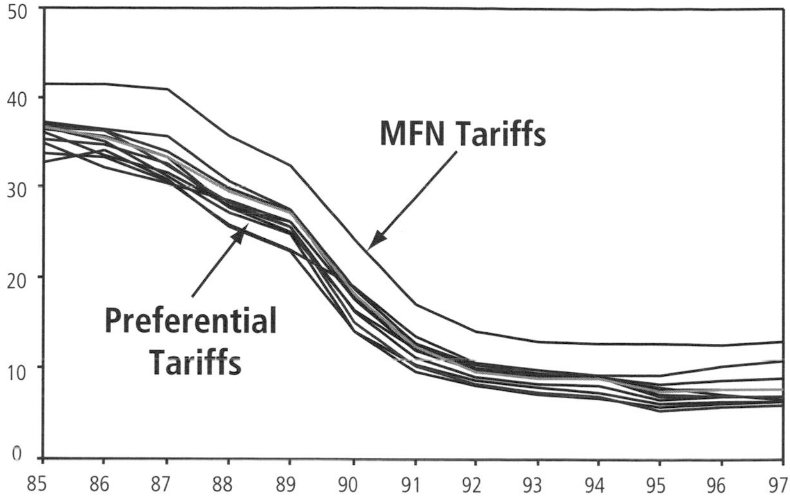

Source: IDB (2002).
Note: MFN Tariffs represents the simple average of the Most Favored Nation tariffs applied by the following 11 Latin American countries (based on country averages): Argentina, Bolivia, Chile, Colombia, Ecuador, Mexico, Paraguay, Peru, Uruguay and Venezuela. Preferential Tariffs represents the average preferential tariff that each country applies to the other countries in this sample under different regional trade agreements. Calculations include only ad valorem tariffs.

beyond that of averting trade deflection. Indeed, with the lowering of tariff and nontariff barriers and the concomitant proliferation of FTAs around the world, they arguably have become a widespread and potentially powerful trade policy instrument.[8]

In theoretical terms, an FTA without rules of origin could be expected to result in dramatic changes in trade patterns due to a rise in transshipment through the country with the lowest tariff. Without them, an FTA would be highly liberalizing given that the lowest tariff would apply to each import category. However, in the presence of stringent rules, the potential for an FTA to boost trade between the members will likely be moderated by the rise in the cost of inputs for the intra-FTA final-goods producers—which decreases final-goods production and lowers the final-goods producers' derived demand for intra-FTA inputs, undercutting intra-FTA trade in both inputs and final goods (Ju and Krishna 1998).[9]

Figure 13.4 Preferential Tariff Liberalization by 2005 in Selected FTAs in Latin America (Percent of Items to be Tariff-Free)

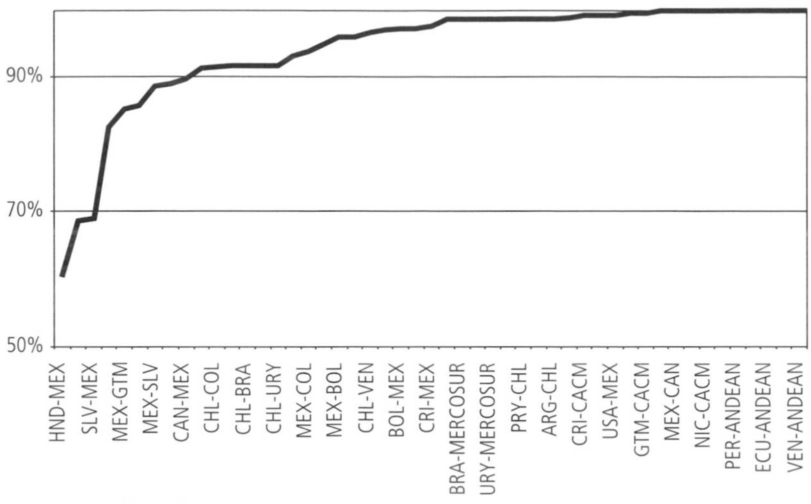

Source: IDB (2002).

The potential effects of restrictive rules of origin have three immediate implications for the theoretical debate over the potential trade effects of FTAs. First, rules of origin can reduce the utilization rates of the FTA-provided preferences. Second, they can hamper FTA-induced trade liberalization, undercutting the trade effect that tariff lowering between the FTA partners would have in an FTA with loose rules. Third, the relevance of rules of origin per se—and thereby their importance as a constraint on commerce—decreases with the lowering of MFN tariff barriers across FTA members. These issues have moved some analysts to suggest that the expanding spaghetti bowl of overlapping FTAs and rules of origin regimes should either be accompanied by the prinicple of open regionalism by simultatneously lowering MFN tariffs or else replaced by a partial or full customs union.[10]

However, the theoretical literature is hard pressed to specify the exact level at which rules of origin are loose enough to keep input prices low or restrictive enough for the price of inputs to rise to unsustainable heights and for the negative effects of trade diversion to kick in (Ju and Krishna 1998). As such, the relationship between the restrictiveness of rules of origin and intra-FTA trade flows in intermediate and final goods is relegated to an empirical matter.

Figure 13.5 Preferential Tariff Liberalization in Selected FTAs in Latin America: Rules of Origin

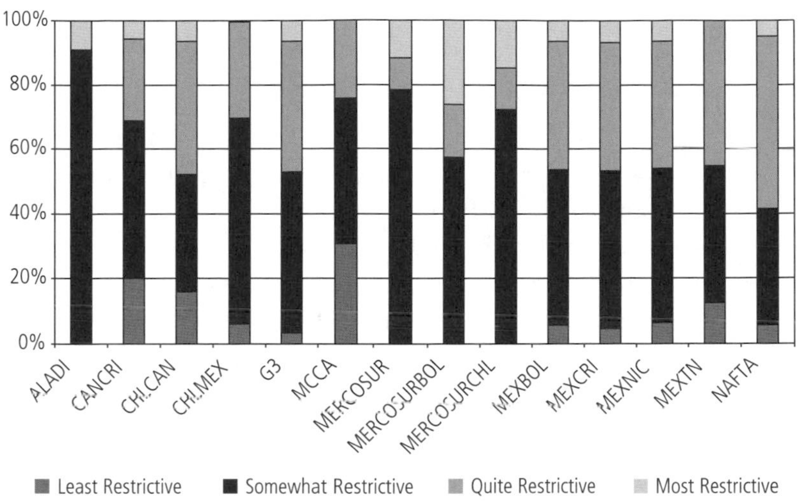

Source: Authors' calculations based on Estevadeordal and Suominen(2003).

Results from the Empirical Literature

The empirical literature that evaluates the effects of preferential tariff liberalization on trade mainly focuses on trade creation and trade diversion.[11] Within this rather large body of literature,[12] we focus on the growing interest in using the gravity-model framework to measure the effects of trade costs on the pattern of trade. In standard gravity models, trade costs are typically assumed to be a function of a number of geographical variables, especially distance and other cultural or political factors. Distance is one of the most successful variables in terms of its impact and statistical significance in this class of models.[13]

Trade costs, however, are also associated with policy measures as part of a free trade area (low tariff costs among members) or a currency union (low transaction costs among members). The vast majority of these studies have explored the effects of preferential trade agreements on trade via the inclusion of dummy variables for trade agreements. Aitken's study (1973) pioneered in employing this technique. More recently, Frankel (1997) provides an extensive analysis of regional trade agreements based almost solely on this technique. He found, for example, that the formation of the EC raised trade among European countries by about 65 percent, and MERCOSUR and the

Andean Community promoted trade by 150 percent among their partners. Similar impacts of FTAs or regional trading blocs on trade have been confirmed by an extensive number of studies that use an FTA dummy in a gravity framework.

Relatively few studies, however, have incorporated explicit measures of tariffs into a gravity equation, and we found none that uses preferential tariffs. For example, Linnemann and Verbruggen (1991), Oguledo and MacPhee (1994), Di Mauro (2000), Tamirisa (1999), and Estevadeordal, Frantz, and Taylor (2002) are some of the few publications that explicitly incorporate MFN tariff measures. These elasticity estimates are important because they help address concerns over the effects of the agreement on the composition of trade, such as trade diversion or trade creation.[14] Table 13.1 summarizes estimates from several of these studies. Since most of them measure tariffs indirectly, they may be subject to measurement error that could bias the estimates downward. We include this table to provide a benchmark for our empirical results.

Economic analysis of rules of origin has been relatively limited in terms of both formal modeling and empirical testing. Empirical evidence, for its part, is scarce given the difficulties of operationalizing rules of origin—translating the complex technical requirements into a variable that serves as a measure of their stringency. The pioneering works surveyed in Estevadeordal and Suominen (2003), however, clearly illustrate the dampening effect of the technical and administrative requirement of rules of origin on trade. Brenton and Manchin (2002) estimate that in 1999, whereas the EU's GSP theoretically covered 99 percent of EU imports from eligible countries, only 31 percent of exports were shipped under preferential rates because of the EU's restrictive rules and the costs of compliance with those rules. Appiah (1999) finds that rules of origin distort trade flows, diverting resources from their most efficient uses and undercutting global welfare. Estevadeordal and Miller (2002) document "missed preferences"—utilization rates below 100 percent—between the United States and Canada due to the tightening of the pre-FTA rules of origin under NAFTA launched in 1994. Cadot et al. (2002) attribute the mere 64 percent utilization rate of NAFTA preferences in part to rules of origin, and also show that stringent rules have undermined Mexican exports to the United States. Canadian producers were reported to have opted to pay the tariff rather than go through the administrative hurdles to meet the rules already in the context of the NAFTA predecessor, the U.S.-Canada FTA (Krueger 1995).

Table 13.1 Effects of Free Trade Agreements and Tariffs on Trade Flows

Study	Dependent Variable	Estimation Method	Estimated FTA/ Tariffs Effect	
	Effects of Free Trade Agreements on Trade			
Coe et al. (2002)	Log Total Trade	Nonlinear Cross Sect.	Avg 1975–2000	0.71
	Log Total Trade	Nonlinear Cross Sect.	2000	0.64
	Log Total Trade	OLS Panel	1975–2000	0.55
Aitken (1973)	Log Exports	OLS Cross Sect.	Avg. 1960–67	0.23
			1967	0.57
Melitz (2001)	Log Total Trade	OLS Cross Sect.	Range: Min	1.03
			Range: Max	1.24
Carrere (2002)	Log Imports	IV Panel	EU	0.29
Frankel and Rose (2002)	Log Total Trade	OLS Cross Sect.	Range: Min	1.16
			Range: Max	1.31
Rose (2002)	Log Total Trade	OLS Panel	Range: Min	0.94
			Range: Max	1.50
	Effects of Tariffs on Trade			
Linneman and Verbruggen (1991)	Log Exports	OLS Cross Section	Range: Min	−1.53
			Range: Max	−2.15
Baier and Bergstrand (2001)	Log Total Trade	Differenced Cross Section	Range: Min	−2.71
			Range: Max	−4.49
Estevadeordal, Frantz, and Taylor (2002)	Log Total Trade	OLS Panel	Range: Min	−0.84
			Range: Max	−1.68

Estevadeordal (2000) has documented in the case of NAFTA the interaction between the degree of stringency of rules of origin and the speed of preferential tariff liberalization, stressing the importance of considering rules of origin as key policy instruments in the design and implementation of FTAs. In the case of NAFTA, the study finds that the origin regime clearly performed its main role as an instrument against trade deflection, based on a strong and statistically significant correlation between the MFN tariff differential and the degree of restrictiveness imposed by the rules. In addition, there is evidence that those sectors with more restrictive rules had associated longer tariff phase outs, and therefore rules of origin and phase-out periods could be viewed as complementary instruments of a discriminatory tariff policy. However, a more sophisticated interpretation of this result would be the existence of a substitution effect. Longer phase outs are usually applied to the "most sensitive sectors" with high levels of tariff protection, and although those tariffs would be eventually eliminated at the end of the tariff phase out, the origin requirement would remain in place, eventually providing the protective effects of the original tariffs.[15] Borrowing the language of the endogenous protection literature, one could conclude that the same forces that push for tariff protection also push for more stringent origin rules. In the sections that follow, we shift the focus back to tariffs to take a first step in estimating the effects of tariffs on trade flows and generating some predictions for how an FTAA could affect the pattern of trade within the hemisphere.

The Model

Trade negotiations in Latin America are complex and involve asymmetric trade barriers that depend both on bilateral and average tariff rates as well as on rules of origin regulations. In this section we describe a model that emphasizes the *relative* and *asymmetric* nature of some trade costs and, for the sake of simplicity, we focus on tariffs as our policy variable. In a free trade agreement, bilateral trade patterns would depend on the bilateral tariff frictions among members (preferential tariffs) vis-à-vis the tariff frictions that each member faces with respect the rest of the world (e.g., MFN tariffs). Trade between two countries, after controlling by size and other variables, is decreasing in their bilateral trade barrier relative to the average barrier of the two countries to trade with all their partners. That is, the more resistant to trade with all others a country is, the more it is pushed to trade with a given bilateral partner. Also, by explicitly measuring bilateral and multilateral tariff liberalization, the model also introduces an important asymmetry, since as shown in the previous section preferential tariff rates vary considerably *over* and *between* partners.

Since we are focusing on the effects of regional trade agreements on national imports and exports, it is helpful to begin with the assumption that all goods are differentiated by place of origin and that each country produces only one good. We next follow Anderson and Van Wincoop (2000) and assume that consumers have identical, homothetic preferences that can be approximated with a constant elasticity of substitution (CES) utility function. For example, consider the following function for consumers in country j consuming goods z from country i

$$\left(\sum_i \beta_i^{1/\sigma} z_{ij}^{(\sigma-1)/\sigma}\right)^{\sigma/(\sigma-1)} \tag{1}$$

which is maximized according to the budget constraint

$$\sum_i p_{ij} z_{ij} = y_j. \tag{2}$$

The σ represent the constant elasticity of substitution between goods from each country, β_i are positive consumption weights (summing over i to one), p_{ij} are the prices of region i goods in country j, and finally y_j represents the nominal income of consumers in country j. Maximizing this system yields the country j's demand function for goods produced by country i:

$$\frac{y\beta_i p_i^{1-\sigma}}{\sum_i^N \beta_i p_i^{1-\sigma}} = z_i p_i \text{ or } \frac{y\beta_i p_i^{-\sigma}}{\sum_i^N \beta_i p_i^{1-\sigma}} = z_i \tag{3}$$

For the sake of intuition, assume that the elasticity of substitution is greater than one. Then imports from country i (defined as $z_i p_i$) are a decreasing function of the own price and an increasing function of the price of substitutes. They are also a positive function of home income and the preference parameter beta.

At this point it is useful to incorporate explicitly tariffs and distance, which reduce the price that the producer receives and increase the price that importing consumers pay. We can formalize this relationship defining the importing price p_i as

$$p_i = \pi_i \tau_i \delta_i \tag{4}$$

which decomposes the price into the exporter's price, the tariff, and distance (respectively). As pointed out by Anderson (1979), equation 3 implies that bilateral trade is increasing in the average resistance measures of the importer (tariffs and distance) because higher average tariffs and greater average distance from trading partners push any given bilateral trade higher (furthermore, $\partial z_i / \partial p_j > 0$).

To complete the framework, we now turn to the production side. Higher tariffs and distance discourage bilateral trade, but average exporter tariffs and distance also matter. To illustrate how they affect trade, we assume that demands are independent across countries for each exporter's good j. That is, we rule out third-party exports. Each exporter will face the sum of demand curves in equation 3 as the total demand. Since costs are not distinguished by destination, the exporter in country i maximizes

$$\sum_j^N \pi_j z_j(\pi_j) - C\left(\sum_j^N z_j\right). \tag{5}$$

The first-order condition equates marginal revenue with marginal costs in each market:

$$\pi_j \frac{\partial z_j}{\partial \pi_j} + z_j = \frac{\partial C}{\partial z_j} \frac{\partial z_j}{\partial \pi_j} \quad \forall j. \tag{6}$$

Given imperfect competition, this condition leads to the familiar Ramsey Rule

$$\frac{\pi_j - C'(Z)}{\pi_j} = \frac{1}{\varepsilon} \tag{7}$$

in which ε is the absolute value of the price elasticity of demand. Exporters would prefer to sell less (charge higher prices) to importers. The price elasticity of demand, $\frac{\partial z}{\partial \pi} \cdot \frac{\pi}{z}$, can be expressed as

$$\sigma + \frac{(1-\sigma)\beta_i \pi_i^{1-\sigma}}{\sum_i^N \beta_i \pi_i^{1-\sigma}} \tag{8}$$

which is a decreasing function of π when $\sigma > 1$.

Exporters consider their home market as one of the *N* markets. Higher average tariffs and distance decrease the elasticity of home demand, making firms want to charge a higher price by selling less at home. The result is that the residual supply of exports will be greater, suggesting that higher average exporter tariffs and distance will increase bilateral trade.

The final step toward our estimation equation is to incorporate exporter income. Equation 7 can be expressed as

$$\pi_i = C'(Z)\left(\frac{\varepsilon}{\varepsilon - 1}\right) \tag{9}$$

Economies of scale suggest that marginal costs are decreasing in total output. Thus, the price is falling with total output. Since trade is an inverse function of price, trade is an increasing function of exporter market size.

This offers an additional motivation for focusing on asymmetry: the role of the traditional gravity-model elements are not symmetric because they depend on whether a country is an exporter or an importer.

Furthermore, the role of average tariffs and average distance are not symmetric. Higher average distance and tariffs of the importing country increase bilateral trade for importers and exporters, but there is no reason to believe that these effects are of a similar magnitude.

The theory sketched here identifies the key element of the traditional gravity equation and suggests how each variable should affect bilateral trade. We therefore consider the estimation equation

$$\begin{aligned}\ln x_{ij} = {} & \alpha + \vartheta_1 \ln\delta_{ij} + \vartheta_2 \ln\tau_{ij} + \vartheta_3 \ln y_i + \vartheta_4 \ln y_j + \vartheta_5 \ln\overline{\delta}_j \\ & + \vartheta_6 \ln\overline{\tau}_j + \vartheta_7 \ln\overline{\delta}_i + \vartheta_8 \ln\overline{\tau}_i + \varepsilon_{ij}\end{aligned} \tag{10}$$

in which the variables are defined as above. One contribution of this chapter is our inclusion of asymmetric trade barriers (τ) along with distance (δ). These variables enter both as the level of tariffs and distance between the two countries and the average tariff level and distance for the importing country *j*.

Our discussion of the increasing regionalization of the world trading system also suggests that bilateral tariffs, as preferential tariffs, are considered relative to the MFN tariff or the average tariff level. The model above suggests that, for the importing country, increasing the difference between the bilateral tariff and the importing country's average tariff will reduce bilateral trade. Therefore, we include both the bilateral tariff and the ratio of the bilateral tariff to the average tariff when estimating our gravity equation. We will, of course, also consider the effects of including the traditional gravity variables, such as exchange rates, language, border, island, and being landlocked. We also explore the effects of various interaction terms and regional effects in the next section.

Empirical Analysis

The major data collection effort of this paper has consisted in constructing from original sources the preferential bilateral tariff rates for all possible bilateral relations among the twenty-nine countries included in our sample, in addition to the MFN rates that each country applies to the rest of the world. The data has been collected on a yearly basis for the period 1985–97. All data come directly from the tariff-liberalization schedules of existing FTA agreements at every point in time. In a few cases, due to the lack of data, we had to make some simplifying assumptions to have a completely balanced panel. A description of the data set as well as the methodology regarding other standard variables used in gravity-model estimates can be found in the Appendix.

We present the empirical analysis in four sections. First, we motivate our focus on asymmetry by contrasting the symmetry of trade and the asymmetry of tariffs. Second, we present our basic cross-section results. Third, we present panel estimates. We conclude with some estimates of how a projected Free Trade Agreement of the Americas would affect both imports and exports of the participating members.

Symmetry of Trade and Asymmetry of Tariffs

Trade patterns are generally symmetric: bilateral exports are generally an excellent predictor of bilateral imports. Figure 13.6a illustrates the symmetry of trade in 1999. One country's exports to a given partner explain about 80 percent of the variation of that country's imports from the same partner (the R^2 value is 0.803).

Tariffs, in contrast, are generally not symmetric. Figure 13.6b illustrates this point. In 1999, a given country's tariffs explain less than 40 percent of the variation in its partner's tariffs toward them. The symmetry of tariffs increases over our sample. Prior to 1990, one country's tariffs account for less than 1 percent of the variation in the partner's tariffs. The implication of this asymmetry is that average trade barriers introduce possibly significant measurement error when they are used as proxies for partner-specific tariffs. This measurement error would bias the estimated effects of tariffs towards zero, suggesting that the literature that relies on average tariffs underestimates the real impact of tariffs on trade.

Cross Section Approaches

We begin with equation 10 and add variables that are now standard in the gravity equation: controls for being landlocked, sharing a common language, being an island, and sharing a common border. The relatively few studies that employ specific tariffs use the form ln(1+tariff/100). We follow this convention. We restrict the sample to the 1985–97 period due to the availability of data.

Table 13.2 contains the central cross-section results. As expected, the GDP of the importer and the exporter have strong effects on trade. Distance and being landlocked discourages trade, and having a common border or a common language increases trade. Tariffs significantly reduce trade. Our estimated tariff coefficient in the baseline regression in the first column of results is –0.313, which is much smaller than the estimates from our comparison studies.

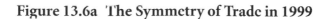

Figure 13.6a The Symmetry of Trade in 1999

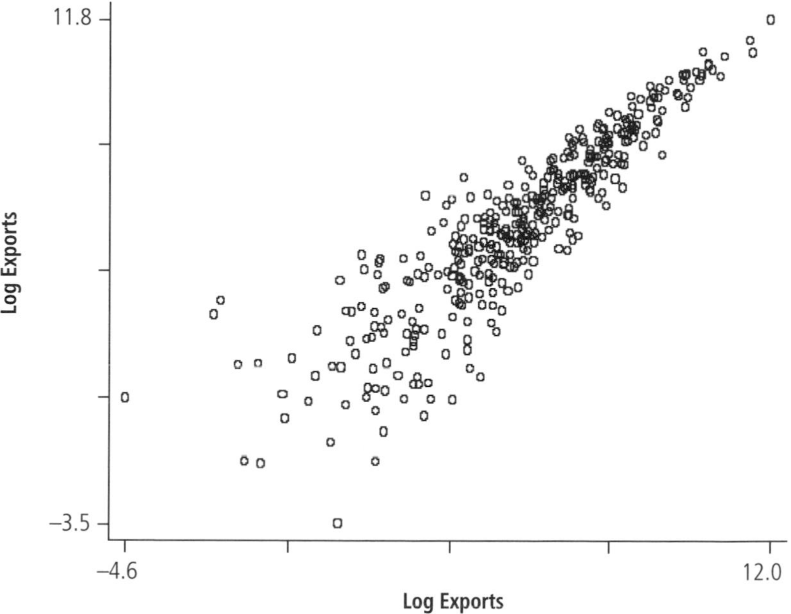

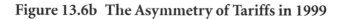

Figure 13.6b The Asymmetry of Tariffs in 1999

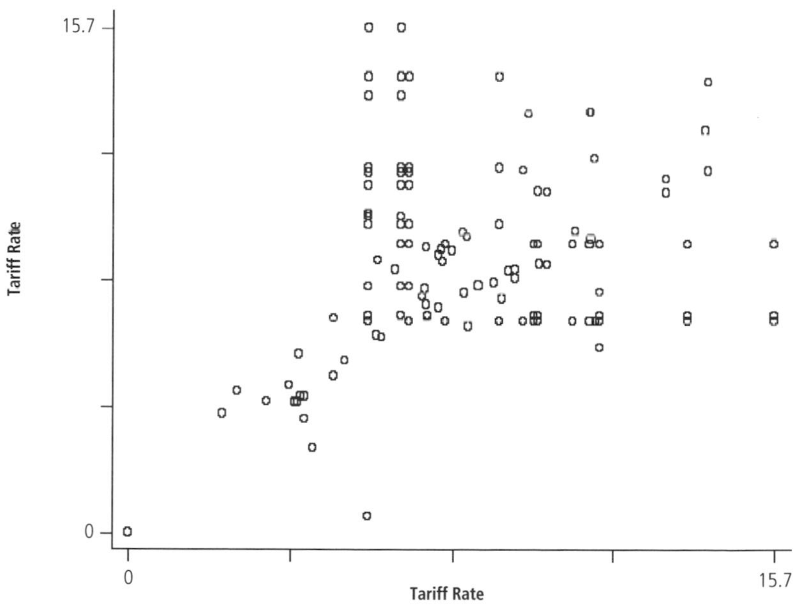

Source: Authors' calculations.

In column 2 we introduce the multilateral resistance measures. The exporter's average tariff and average distance from other trading partners seems to have a significant and positive effect on trade, as the theory above suggests. The importer's average distance does not have a statistically significant effect on bilateral trade in column 2, but the bilateral tariff/average tariff ratio has a significant and negative coefficient. As expected, the more preferential the bilateral tariff relative to the importer's average tariff, the more trade occurs between the trading partners.

Since we have multiple years of data, we consider two alternative controls for time. In Table 13.2, we alter our basic gravity model by including a linear time trend (column 3) and individual year effects (column 4). We considered a time trend because trade increases over our sample period. Surprisingly, neither the time trend nor the interaction of the time trend and tariffs are significant. The estimate of the tariff effect is similar when the trend is not interacted with tariffs or when year effects are included (results not shown).

When the tariff is interacted with the year effects, however, the tariff coefficient increases. The year effects (not shown) are all significant. The interaction between tariffs and the year effect (using 1985 as the omitted year) is only significant for 1986–89 and ranges from 0.924 (in 1989) to 1.656 (in 1988), but shows no pattern of change over the sample period. The tariff effects remain robust in sign and significance, and generally in magnitude, when different time controls are included.

We explore the robustness of our results in several ways. Our tariff estimate remains very stable when we omit the average distance measures. We also replaced the average distances of the importer and the exporter with the Baier and Bergstrand (2001) remoteness index. The remoteness measure itself emerges significantly, which is consistent with earlier studies. Including this index does not affect our estimated tariff coefficient, suggesting that the tariff estimate is robust to alternative measures of distance. We also explored the effect of exchange-rate volatility. We find that real exchange-rate volatility has an unexpected positive effect on trade volumes, but this effect is imprecisely estimated. We did note that including real exchange rate volatility slightly raises our estimate of the tariff effect, but the estimated tariff effect is within the range of the estimates presented in Table 13.2.

The experience of the different regions in our sample—notably North America, Europe, and Latin America—varied through our sample period. We therefore explored the robustness when we include

Table 13.2 Tariff Liberalization and Bilateral Trade in Latin America (Cross Section Estimates)

	Resistance Measures	Trend x Tariff	Year Effects	FTAA
Log tariff	–0.772	–0.886	–1.743	–0.794
	(5.34)**	(4.46)**	(6.28)**	(4.49)**
Time trend		0.002		
		(0.19)		
Trend x log tariff		0.041		
		(0.84)		
FTAA countries				0.345
				(5.72)**
FTAA countries x log tariff				–0.597
				(2.18)*
Log GDP importer	0.798	0.799	0.801	0.805
	(107.16)**	(105.59)**	(104.85)**	(107.30)**
Log GDP exporter	0.943	0.941	0.947	0.965
	(133.38)**	(130.22)**	(123.43)**	(116.29)**
Log distance	–0.891	–0.892	–0.908	–0.903
	(32.21)**	(31.55)**	(30.46)**	(29.94)**
Bilat. tariff/avg. importer tariff	–0.305	–0.312	–0.281	–0.202
	(9.46)**	(9.32)**	(7.44)**	(5.08)**
Exporter avg. world tariff	2.628	3.015	0.221	–5.485
	(8.41)**	(3.89)**	(0.13)	(2.74)**
Log ave. dist importer to world	–0.114	–0.129	–0.098	–0.222
	(1.44)	(1.6)	(1.18)	(2.64)**
Log ave. dist exporter to world	0.535	0.525	0.617	0.594
	(7.52)**	(7.01)**	(6.89)**	(6.64)**
Common border	0.807	0.804	0.795	0.78
	(15.18)**	(15.36)**	(15.09)**	(14.86)**
Either is landlocked	–0.665	–0.663	–0.661	–0.661
	(20.99)**	(20.85)**	(20.74)**	(20.90)**
Either is an island	–0.028	–0.026	–0.032	0.023
	(0.92)	(0.85)	(1.04)	(0.72)
Common language	0.198	0.194	0.202	0.151
	(6.08)**	(5.93)**	(6.14)**	(4.47)**
Constant	–12.151	–11.983	–12.282	–10.829
	(14.17)**	(13.69)**	(13.36)**	(12.22)**
Year effects?	No	No	Yes	Yes
Year x tariff effects?	No	No	Yes	No
Observations	9709	9709	9709	9709
R^2	0.84	0.84	0.84	0.84

* Significant at 5%.
** Significant at 1%.

various regional controls. Specifically, we included controls for when a North American country (the United States or Canada) is an importer or an exporter. We find that these controls have a very small effect on the magnitude of our tariff coefficient. We also dropped all European countries from the sample. Our tariff estimate remained very close to –0.80 and statistically significant. Including dummy variables for pairs in which a European country is an exporter or an importer does not affect the sign or significance of the tariff coefficient, but it does increase the absolute magnitude of the effect. That is, tariffs have a larger negative effect on trade (more than 50 percent larger) when the European controls are included. This seems to be the only control that affects our tariff estimates. We hope to explore more fully the ramifications of the European effect in future research.

Since we have a particular interest in the Americas, we also allowed the tariff effect to differ for pairs in which both countries are Latin American. Including a control for Latin American pairs, as well as the tariff interaction term, does not significantly affect the main tariff effect. The marginal effect of tariffs on intra-Latin American trade seems large and significant, suggesting that reducing tariffs within Latin America would have much larger effects on trade within Latin America than would global tariff removal. The total effect (standard error) for Latin America is –1.891 (0.254). This is not surprising, given the fact that tariffs in Latin America are generally higher than in the rest of our sample.

Our primary emphasis here, however, is the effect of an FTAA. Latin American countries may be interested in lowering barriers among themselves, but one significant motivation of joining the FTAA is to secure access to Canadian and U.S. markets. We therefore consider the possible effects of an FTAA by including a dummy variable for FTAA countries (the United States., Canada, and Latin America) and interacting this variable with the tariff. These results are shown in the last column of Table 13.2. FTAA countries already trade more, even with our other controls. The main effect of the FTAA tariff remains similar to previous columns. The marginal tariff effect is negative, significant, and nearly equal to the main tariff effect in magnitude. This is consistent with the idea that the potential trade effects of an FTAA could be large even if other countries (e.g., Europe) are not included.

Panel Data Approaches

Most gravity models in the current literature have been estimated using cross-section data. The increasing availability of panel data and estimation techniques have also begun to affect the gravity literature (Matyas 1997, Soloaga and Winters 2001, Carrere 2002). These papers suggest that controlling for country-specific effects in gravity models is important. To explore the effects of panel estimation with our sample, and in particular to test for the robustness of the tariff effect, we first estimated a random-effects model using ordinary least squares (OLS). We found a larger coefficient on the tariff effect, but the other variables are generally similar to those estimated in previous tables. We chose not to report these results, however, because the random-effects specification may not adequately control for sample heterogeneity. We formally tested the random-effects specification using a Hausman test. Our results reject the random-effects specification. Table 13.3 contains the results that emerge when we include country-specific (not pair-specific) effects. This specification now passes the Hausman specification test, but the tariff estimate remains virtually identical to our earlier estimate. Although larger, our tariff effects seem generally robust to panel specification.

We also explored the effects of interacting the tariff term with a dummy for Latin American pairs. We found that the tariff effect is reduced, although it remains negative and significant. The total effect (standard error) for Latin America was –1.870 (0.149), which is very similar to our previous estimates. This is also consistent with higher tariffs in Latin America than in the rest of the world. Column 2 of Table 13.3 contains the results when FTAA controls are included in the panel specification. These results again suggest large potential gains from an FTAA because the marginal effect of the FTAA tariff is approximately equal to the main tariff effect.

To pursue the tariff effect in FTAA countries further, we restricted the sample to just the FTAA countries. These results are found in the last two columns of Table 13.3. Latin America experienced a great deal of trade liberalization in the 1990s. It is possible that these countries signed so many bilateral agreements because the cost of doing so was not large. That is, many agreements may have been signed between countries that traded relatively little. In periods of rapid trade liberalization, this bias could create the impression that lowering tariffs lowered trade.

To explore this possibility, we replaced the current tariff with the lagged tariff and again restricted the sample to just FTAA pairs. Using lagged tariffs generates a result very similar to those found in previous tables. The magnitude, however, is slightly smaller than the total

Table 13.3 Tariff Liberalization and Bilateral Trade in Latin America (Initial Panel Estimates)

	Country Fixed Effects	FTAA	FTAA	FTAA
Log tariff	–0.902	–0.603	0.007	
	(10.32)**	(5.38)**	–0.02	
Lagged log tariff				–1.268
				(3.14)**
FTAA countries		–0.115		
		(0.55)		
FTAA countries x log tariff		–0.688		
		(4.24)**		
GDP importer	0.707	0.707	0.283	0.238
	(21.65)**	(21.67)**	(3.51)**	(2.70)**
GDP exporter	0.113	0.12	–0.093	–0.009
	(3.36)**	(3.57)**	(1.2)	(0.11)
Log distance	–0.463	–0.586	–1.051	–1.06
	(7.18)**	(7.52)**	(6.76)**	(6.97)**
Tariff differential	–0.814	–0.735	–1.444	–1.233
	(10.94)**	(8.81)**	(6.42)**	(5.46)**
Avg. world tariff	1.159	–0.613	0.724	–0.611
	(0.71)	(0.36)	(0.18)	–0.15
Ln avg. dist partner world	–8.163	1.685		
	(8.37)**	(1.73)		
Ln avg. dist reporter world	8.072	–1.625	1.328	1.412
	(8.23)**	(1.66)	(5.71)**	(5.90)**
Common border	0.799	0.718	0.712	0.7
	(6.31)**	(5.47)**	(3.12)**	(3.14)**
Either is landlocked	0.203	0.205	0.252	0.273
	(0.46)	(0.46)	(0.29)	(0.32)
Common language	0.623	0.613	0.52	0.476
	(5.57)**	(5.56)**	(1.53)	(1.43)
Year effects?	Yes	Yes	Yes	Yes
Year x tariff effects?	No	No	Yes	Yes
Country fixed effects?	Yes	Yes	Yes	Yes
Observations	9269	9269	1872	1728
Number of pairs	713	713	144	144

* Significant at 5%.
** Significant at 1%.
Note: Tariff Differential is the difference between the country's bilateral tariff and the country's average mean tariff to the rest of the world.

effect found in the previous columns. The potential for increasing trade seems to be statistically significant with a tariff coefficient greater than one when lagged tariffs replace contemporary tariffs in the panel regression.

We also experimented with the Arellano-Bond estimator for dynamic panel data (Arellano and Bond 1991). In our estimation, which generated results very similar to those obtained with other approaches, we consistently rejected the hypothesis that the over-identifying restrictions were valid. The estimation results also suggested the presence of first-order serial correlation. Therefore, we decided to employ an estimation approach that allows us directly to estimate and test the degree of serial correlation in the error terms.

Table 13.4 contains results from the fixed-effects model (using country-pair fixed effects) that tests and adjusts for first-order serial correlation. The modified Bhargava, Franzini, and Narendranathan (1982), or BFN, test statistic for serial correlation in balanced panel data is shown at the bottom of each column. This statistic falls short of the suggested minimum Durbin-Watson bound, suggesting serial correlation. The statistic also falls above the suggested maximum value for the random walk-test statistic, leading us to reject the random-walk hypothesis. Therefore, we adjust our estimation using the estimated correlation coefficient (also shown at the bottom of each column).

Compared to earlier estimates, the estimated lagged tariff effects in the first two columns of Table 13.4 are somewhat higher. Including the multilateral resistance measures does not have a large effect on the estimated tariff effect. The multilateral resistance measures emerge in the expected way. The larger the difference between the importer's bilateral and average tariff, the less bilateral trade occurs. The contemporaneous exporter's average world tariff is positive, but the lagged value is negative and of nearly the same magnitude.

The estimates for the FTAA area are found in the second column, where we interact the tariff (and lagged values) with an FTAA dummy variable. These results suggest that the early effects of reducing tariffs would be higher in Latin America, but the second lagged value is significant and positive, raising questions about the long-term effects of tariff reduction. A similar result emerges when we restrict the sample to only the FTAA countries. The initial effect of the tariff change is positive, but the second lag is positive and significant, suggesting some mitigation of the tariff change on trade flows in the long run. The sum of the two estimates, however, is still negative, suggesting an increase in trade when tariffs fall in the Americas.

The last two columns of Table 13.4 contain the results from the differenced model. As when pair-specific dummy variables are included, the constant effects of distance, language, island, border, and being landlocked drop out when the data are differenced. We include year

Table 13.4 Tariff Liberalization and Bilateral Trade in Latin America (Panel Estimates Controlling for Serial Correlation)

	Levels	Levels	Differences	Differences
Log tariff	0.571	0.782	1.251	1.378
	(2.67)**	(2.86)**	(6.99)**	(6.16)**
First lag	–1.548	–1.434	–1.351	–1.103
	(6.11)**	(4.44)**	(7.76)**	(4.93)**
Second lag	0.101	–0.24	–0.277	–0.32
	(0.57)	(1.08)	(1.69)	(1.54)
FTAA x log tariff		–0.507		–0.393
		(1.21)		(1.15)
First lag		–0.287		–0.819
		(0.56)		(2.36)*
Second lag		0.818		0.211
		(2.45)*		(0.68)
GDP importer	0.601	0.601	0.593	0.595
	(13.90)**	(13.90)**	(13.82)**	(13.94)**
First lag	–0.179	–0.178	0.48	0.45
	(4.16)**	(4.16)**	(11.28)**	(10.61)**
GDP exporter	0.247	0.254	0.149	0.149
	(6.16)**	(6.30)**	(3.48)**	(3.51)**
First lag	–0.192	–0.186	–0.096	–0.112
	(4.63)**	(4.49)**	(2.26)*	(2.65)**
Tariff differential	–0.306	–0.319	–0.292	–0.252
	(2.06)*	(2.11)*	(1.99)*	(1.68)
First lag	–0.023	–0.066	–0.297	–0.203
	(0.15)	(0.41)	(2.03)*	(1.37)
Avg world tariff	1.598	1.571	–1.097	–2.101
	(2.15)*	(2.11)*	(0.53)	(1.01)
First lag	–1.411	–1.355	5.912	4.853
	(2.31)*	(2.22)*	(3.14)**	(2.54)*
Constant	–2.478	–2.578	0.027	0.011
	(4.01)**	(4.17)**	(1.49)	(0.62)
Correlation coefficient	0.086	0.086	0.163	0.068
Modified BFN DW	1.828	1.828	1.864	1.863
Observations	7130	7130	7130	7130
Number of pairs	713	713	713	713

* Significant at 5%.
** Significant at 1%.
Note: Tariff Differential is the difference between the country's bilateral tariff and the country's average mean tariff to the rest of the world.

effects and two lags of differenced log exports. All right-hand side variables are represented by a contemporaneous and lagged differenced value. We test for serial correlation of the error terms using the

BFN modified Durbin Watson statistic as described above. We reach the same conclusions with the differenced estimates and therefore use the same correction procedure.

The results in the last two columns of Table 13.4 tell a story similar to the first two columns. Contemporaneous changes in tariffs are correlated with higher trade, perhaps suggesting endogeneity. The lagged values, however, are negative, significant, and hardly affected by the inclusion of the multilateral resistance measures. We also focus on the FTAA countries by first interacting an FTAA dummy variable with the change in tariffs in column 4. The result is somewhat similar to the earlier tables, except here the effect of a change in tariffs seems slightly larger in the FTAA countries. Given the higher tariffs in Latin America relative to the rest of the world, these results may suggest that an FTAA agreement could have a significant and positive effect on trade volumes in the region.

Our estimates seem to be toward the upper end of the estimates from previous studies shown in Table 13.1. One possible explanation for this is that previous studies use less precise measures of tariffs, which could bias the previous estimates downward. The implication of our results is that trade agreements may have a larger positive effect on trade volumes than was previously expected. We now use our estimates to generate some predictions for how an FTAA would affect bilateral trade patterns.

Counterfactual Scenarios

One of the most pressing questions about the FTAA is that of how trade patterns will be affected. In particular, nations are especially interested in how exports and imports are expected to change. To predict how an FTAA would affect trade flows, we relied on our dynamic panel estimates from column 2 of Table 13.4. We are most interested in comparisons between three statistics: the actual level of imports or exports, the model's prediction of the level of imports or exports, and the effect that an FTAA would have on the predicted level of exports.

To generate the predicted values of pairwise trade, we simply constructed the linear projection of the estimation equation presented in column 2 of Table 13.4 (adding in pair-specific fixed effect). To generate the predicted effects of NAFTA tariff removal, we first subtracted the product of the tariff effect and the tariff (including all lagged terms). Since by our specification the bilateral tariff/average tariff ratio would also go to zero for FTAA countries, we then subtracted the product of the coefficient and the ratio for each pair. If FTAA tariffs all go to zero, then each FTAA member's average tariff would also be affected. Therefore, we calculated the new average tariffs that would be in place if only FTAA member tariffs went to zero and subtracted the product of this change with the estimated effect of the average tariff on trade (again, including lags). This process produces the expected change in each pair's trade volume. To illustrate the effect on imports and exports we summed the predicted value of trade over all partner countries for importers and exporters, respectively.

The effects on exports as a share of GDP for all FTAA countries are shown in Figure 13.7. The United States, Canada, and Mexico trade the most. The model generally fits very well for most countries (as seen by the closeness of the first and second bars for each country). The main exception to this good fit is Mexico, which both exports and imports more than predicted by the model. Not surprisingly, Mexican and U.S. exports would increase relatively more than Canadian exports if the FTAA brought all tariffs to zero.

The effects on imports are shown for all FTAA countries in Figure 13.8. Again the fit of the model, as illustrated by the closeness of the first and second columns for each country, is generally very good. The model underpredicts trade for Bolivia and overpredicts trade for Canada, which may suggest some nonlinearities that we are not capturing. The changes in imports, however, seem relatively large for many Latin American countries.

To get a clearer sense of the expected change in imports and exports by country, Figure 13.9 shows the log difference in the model's predicted trade flow and the FTAA predicted values. Mexico, Peru, Bolivia, and Venezuela have the largest predicted increases in import shares, while Canada and the United States have the smallest. Mexico and Venezuela have the largest predicted increases in export shares.

One result emerges immediately from Figure 13.9. The model predicts a larger percentage increase in the import shares than the export shares for all Latin American countries, while the reverse is true for the United States and Canada. This result probably reflects the fact that the United States and Canada have initially smaller tariff levels than most of the Latin American countries.

Conclusions

As the Americas approach the deadline for negotiating an FTAA, the question of how trade patterns may be affected becomes increasingly

Figure 13.7 Export Shares of GDP by FTAA Country

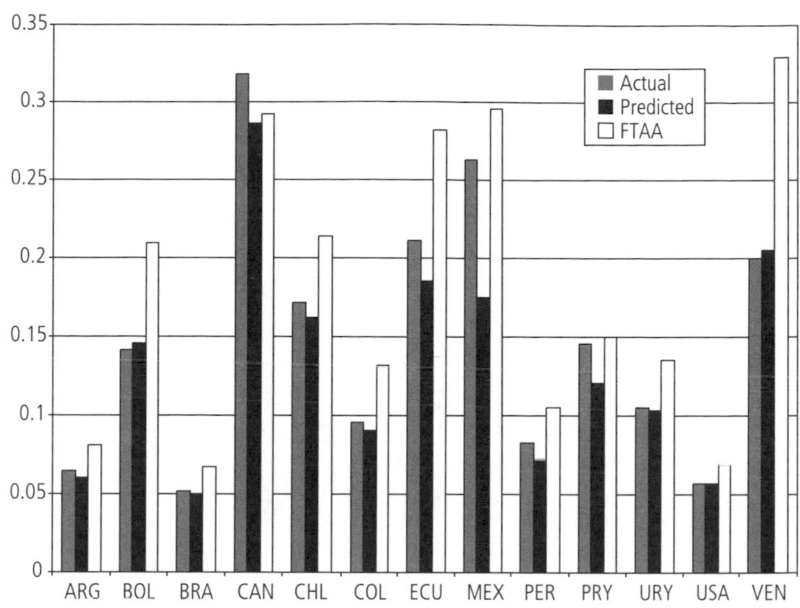

Source: Authors' calculations.

Figure 13.8 Import Shares of GDP by FTAA Country

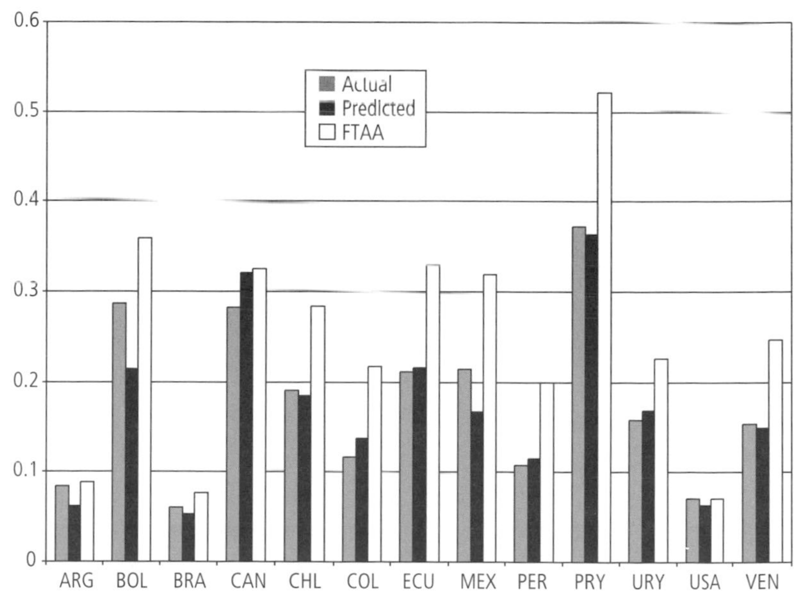

Source: Authors' calculations.

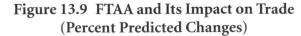

Figure 13.9 FTAA and Its Impact on Trade (Percent Predicted Changes)

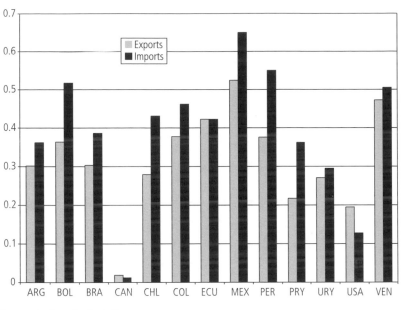

Source: Authors' calculations.

important. This chapter takes four steps toward understanding the potential implications of an FTAA on trade patterns.

We began by reviewing the evolution of trade agreements in the Americas. Trade agreements are complex in that they involve both negotiations about tariff levels and rules of origin. We focused on the evolution of both of these key components of trade agreements, which generated several characteristics of tariffs. Tariffs are generally asymmetric, since, even in reciprocal agreements, countries do not always match their partner's tariff levels. Tariffs are also important relative to average tariff levels, and countries in the Americas have largely focused on negotiating preferential tariffs. We also emphasized the importance of rules of origin and note again here that this is a fertile area for future research.

Given the fact that tariffs are asymmetric and depend on both bilateral and average tariff levels, we then described a theoretical model that illustrates how these characteristics can be expressed in the context of the gravity equation. The advantage of this model is that it provides guidance on the expected values in our empirical work.

In our empirical work, several results stand out. We employed very specific tariff data to estimate the effects of tariffs on trade. Not surprisingly, we find that our precise data generate estimates of the effects of tariffs that are in the upper range of those found in the literature. We find that our estimates are robust to a large number of different specifications. We find that the tariff-reducing effect of trade is larger in the Americas than in our full sample. Our results seem to be robust to alternative measures of distance, regions, and time effects.

Several recent studies have found that appropriately treating dynamics in the context of gravity models is important. We have provided some evidence that is consistent with this argument, and used dynamic tariff estimates to generate predictions for changes in trade flows with an FTAA. We find that our model does reasonably well in predicting both imports and exports. Therefore, we use our estimates to generate some preliminary predictions about how trade would change if an FTAA reduced tariffs to zero among member countries. Our predictions suggest that changes in trade could be very substantial. Generally, imports for Latin American countries are predicted to rise more than exports. The reverse is true for the United States and Canada. While this result is most likely due to the differences in initial tariff levels, it could also help explain some of the resistance to an FTAA in some countries.

Appendix

The dataset used in this study covers the period from 1985 to 1997 and the following countries: Argentina, Bolivia, Brazil, Colombia, Chile, Ecuador, Mexico, Paraguay, Peru, Uruguay, Venezuela, United States, Canada and the European Union (fifteen countries). The standard gravity variables (bilateral trade values, GDP, distance, dummy variables for common border, common language, and being landlocked) come from standard sources in the gravity literature, and in particular from Andrew Rose's data set from his website, data7web.dta, complemented by trade data from the United Nations COMTRADE database. All MFN tariff data have been collected from official national statistical sources and regional secretariats. All preferential tariff data have been collected directly from original tariff schedules of regional and bilateral trade agreements (reciprocal and nonreciprocal) signed and implemented during this period (1985–97). It includes bilateral and regional agreements signed under the LAIA framework among Latin American countries (Acuerdos de Renegociación del Patrimonio Histórico, Acuerdos Comerciales, Acuerdos de Complementación Económica, Acuerdos Regionales); the North-American Free Trade Agreement among United States, Canada and Mexico; and the non-reciprocal preferential agreements between Latin American countries and the United States, and between Latin American countries and the European Union under the Generalized System of Preferences. A full, detailed appendix can be obtained directly from the authors.

References

Aitken, N. D. 1973. "The Effect of the EEC and EFTA on European Trade: A Temporal Cross-Section Analysis." *American Economic Review* 63 (5): 881–92.

Anderson, J. E. 1979. "A Theoretical Foundation for the Gravity Equation." *American Economic Review* 69 (1) (March): 106–16.

Anderson, J. E., and E. Van Wincoop. 2000. "Gravity with Gravitas: A Solution to the Border Puzzle." *American Economic Review* 93 (1): 170–192.

Appiah, A. J. 1999. "Applied General Equilibrium Model of North American Integration with Rules of Origin." Ph.D. Dissertation, Simon Fraser University, Canada.

Arellano, M., and S. Bond. 1991. "Some Tests of Specification for Panel Data: Monte Carlo Evidence and an Application to Employment Equations." *Review of Economic Studies* 58 (2) (April): 277–97.

Baier, S. L., and J. H. Bergstrand. 2001. "The Growth of World Trade: Tariffs, Transport Costs, and Income Similarity." *Journal of International Economics* 53 (1) (February): 1–27.

Bergsten, C. F. 1997. "Open Regionalism." In *Whither APEC: The Progress to Date and Agenda for the Future.* Washington, DC: Institute of International Economics.

Bhagwati, J., and A. Panagariya. 1996. *The Economics of Preferential Trade Agreements.* Washington, DC: American Enterprise Institute.

Bhargava, A., L. Franzini, and W. Narendranathan. 1982. "Serial Correlation and the Fixed Effects Model." *Review of Economic Studies* 49 (4) (October): 533–49.

Brenton, P., and M. Manchin. 2002. *Making EU Trade Agreements Work: The Role of Rules of Origin.* Centre for European Policy Studies Working Document no. 183 (March), Brussels.

Cadot, O., A. Estevadeordal, J. de Melo, A. Suwa-Eisenmann and B. Tumurchudur. 2002. "Assessing the Effect of NAFTA's Rules of Origin." The World Bank, Washington, DC. Photocopy.

Clausing, K. A. 2001. "Trade Creation and Trade Diversion in the Canada United States Free Trade Agreement." *Canadian Journal of Economics* 34 (3) (August): 677–96.

Coe, D. T., A. Subramanian, and N. T. Tamirisa, with R. Bhavrani. 2002. *The Missing Globalization Puzzle.* International Monetary Fund Working paper WP/02/171, Washington, DC.

Devlin, R., and A. Estevadeordal. 2001. "What's New in the New Regionalism in the Americas?" In *Regional Integration in Latin America and the Caribbean: The Political Economy of Open Regionalism,* edited by V. Bulmer-Thomas. London: Institute of Latin American Studies.

Di Mauro, F. 2000. *The Impact of Economic Integration on FDI and Exports: A Gravity Approach.* Centre for European Policy Studies Working Document no. 156 (November), Brussels.

Duttagupta, R. 2000. "Intermediate Inputs and Rules of Origin: Implications for Welfare and Viability of Free Trade Agreements." Ph.D. Dissertation, University of Maryland, College Park.

Estevadeordal, A. 2000. "Negotiating Preferential Market Access: The Case of the North American Free Trade Agreement." *Journal of World Trade* 34 (1) (February): 141–66.

Estevadeordal, A., B. Frantz, and A. M. Taylor. 2003. "The Rise and Fall of World Trade, 1870–1939." *Quarterly Journal of Economics* 118 (2): 359–407.

Estevadeordal, A., and E. Miller. 2002. "Rules of Origin and the Pattern of Trade between U.S. and Canada." Integration, Trade and Hemispheric Issues Division, Inter-American Development Bank, Washington, DC.

Estevadeordal, A., and K. Suominen. 2003. "Rules of Origin: A World Map and Trade Effects." Inter-American Development Bank, Washington, DC. Photocopy.

Ethier, W. 1998. "The New Regionalism." *Economic Journal* 108 (449) (July): 1149–61.

Frankel, J. A., with E. Stein and S.-J. Wei. 1997. "Regional Trading Blocs in the World Economic System." Washington, DC: Institute for International Economics.

Frankel, J. A., and A. K. Rose. 2002. "An Estimate of the Effect of Common Currencies on Trade and Income." *Quarterly Journal of Economics* 117: 437–66.

Hummels, D. 1999. "Towards a Geography of Trade Costs." Department of Economics, Purdue University. Photocopy.

Inter-American Development Bank (IDB). 2002. "Beyond Borders: The New Regionalism in Latin America." Inter-American Development Bank Economic and Social Progress Report, Washington, DC

Ju, J., and K. Krishna. 1998. *Firm Behavior and Market Access in a Free Trade Area With Rules of Origin.* National Bureau of Economic Research Working Paper no. 6857, Cambridge, MA.

Krishna, K., and A. O. Kruger. 1995. "Implementing Free Trade Areas: Rules of Origin and Hidden Protection." In *New Directions in Trade Theory*, edited by A. Deardorff, J. Levinsohn, and R. Stern. Ann Arbor: University of Michigan Press.

Krueger, A. O. 1999. *Trade Creation and Trade Diversion under NAFTA*. National Bureau of Economic Research Working Paper no. 7429, Cambridge, MA.

Limao, N., and A. Venables. 2001. "Infrastructure, Geographical Disadvantage, Transport Costs, and Trade." *World Bank Economic Review* 15 (3): 451–79.

Linnemann, H., and H. Verbruggen. 1991. "GSTP Tariff Reduction and Its Effects on South-South Trade in Manufactures." *World Development* 19 (5) (May): 539–51.

Matyas, L. 1997. "Proper Econometric Specification of the Gravity Model." *World Economy* 20 (3) (May): 363–68.

Mélitz, J. 2001. "Geography, Trade and Currency Union." Discussion Paper Series No. 2987, Center for Economic Policy Research (October).

Oguledo, V. I., and C. R. MacPhee. 1994. "Gravity Models: A Reformulation and an Application to Discriminatory Trade Agreements." *Applied Economics* 26: 107–20.

Redding, S., and A. Venables. 2000. "Economic Geography and International Inequality." Centre for Economic Policy Research Discussion Paper, London.

Romalis, J. 2001. "NAFTA's Impact on North American Trade." Graduate School of Business, University of Chicago. Photocopy.

Rose, A. K. 2002. "Do We Really Know that the WTO Increases Trade?" Centre for Economic Policy Research Discussion Paper 3538, London.

Shiff, M., and L. A. Winters. 2003. *Regional Integration and Development.* Oxford: Oxford University Press.

Soloaga, I., and L. A. Winters. 2001. "Regionalism in the Nineties: What Effect on Trade?" World Bank Policy Research Working Paper 2156, Washington, DC.

Tamirisa, N. T. 1999. "Exchange and Capital Controls as Barriers to Trade." International Monetary Fund Staff Papers 46: 69–88. Washington, DC.

United Nations Conference on Trade and Development. 2001. "Improving Market Access for Least Developed Countries." United Nations Conference on Trade and Development DITC/TNCD/4. Geneva.

Wonnacott, P. 1996. "Beyond NAFTA—The Design of a Free Trade Agreement of the Americas." In *The Economics of Preferential Trading Agreements*, edited by J. Bhagwati and A. Panagariya, pp. 79–107. Washington, DC: American Enterprise Institute Press.

World Bank. 2000. *Trade Blocs*. Oxford: Oxford University Press.

Yeats, A. J. 1998. "Does MERCOSUR's Trade Performance Raise Concerns about the Effects of Regional Trade Arrangements?" *World Bank Economic Review* 12 (1): 1–28.

Notes

We have benefited from comments at the IDB/INTAL-Harvard pre-conference, Cambridge, MA, May-June 1, 2002 and the IDB/INTAL-Harvard Final Conference in Punta del Este, December 2002. In particular, we thank our discussant Caroline Freund for her valuable comments. All errors are ours.

1 *Financial Times*, 19 November 2002.

2 We use in this chapter indistinctively free trade area (FTA) and preferential trade area (PTA). For our purposes, two countries entering into a free trade agreement will eventually converge to an intraregional zero-tariff zone. However, both countries will impose tariffs on each other on a preferential basis (below rates applied on an MFN basis) during the phase-out period. Those phase-out or tariff-elimination programs are in most cases asymmetric.

3 This is especially significant when compared to the existing levels of tariff bindings before the Uruguay Round began. In Latin America, only 38 percent of tariff lines for industrial products were bound, equivalent to 57 percent of imports. For agricultural products, the percentages were 36 and 74, respectively.

4 This count does not include existing residual preferential regimes with partial coverage of products from previous decades, i.e., partial agreements under the LAIA (or ALADI) framework.

5 See Ethier (1998) and Devlin and Estevadeordal (2001) for a discussion of the concept of New Regionalism.

6 Rules of origin would be unnecessary in a customs union with a common external tariff that covered the whole tariff universe. However, in practice, rules of origin are widely used in customs unions, either as a transitory tool in the process of moving toward a common external tariff, such as in MERCOSUR, or as a more permanent means of covering product categories for which reaching agreement is difficult, for instance due to large tariff differentials between the member countries.

7 A detailed analytical survey of rules of origin regimes in FTAs around the world can be found in Estevadeordal and Suominen (2003).

8 Indeed, that governments forego negotiating simple regional value-added rules, and, rather, engage in prolonged, contentious bargaining over highly complex and different types of rules of origin, suggests that rules of origin play a role beyond resolving the trade deflection problem.

9 The costs of production may be compounded by the fact that rules of origin are based on the harmonized system, which was not designed with a consideration for the determination of origin. For instance, a product may undergo a substantial transformation in practice yet fail to alter its tariff classification, and hence fail to meet the Change of Tariff Classification test.

10 See Bergsten (1997) and Wonnacott (1996).

11 There is a large literature based on general equilibrium models that estimates the impact of trade liberalization, including scenarios of regional trade agreements, on trade that we do not review here.

12 For a review of studies concerning Latin America and the Caribbean see Inter-American Development Bank (2002).

13 Most studies also include other variables in other to capture the role of history, culture, politics, etc. Frankel (1997) provides a good survey of this literature.

14 A lively debate has recently emerged regarding some important agreements in the Americas. See for example Krueger (1999), Clausing (2001), and Romalis (2001) on NAFTA or Yeats (1998) and Soloaga and Winters (1999) on MERCOSUR.

15 See an extension of this result in Cadot et al. (2002)

14

A Virtuous Circle? Regional Tariff Liberalization and Scale Economies in Transport

David Hummels and Alexandre Skiba

Introduction

It is common when analyzing the effects of trade liberalization to take other trade frictions as given. This is consistent with a modeling strategy that focuses on how and where goods are produced, but ignores the manner in which they are shipped from location to location. But of course, arbitrage does not happen magically. It requires inputs in the form of transportation, warehousing, and distribution in foreign markets.

These inputs are not limited to transportation services in the traditional sense. They may also include information services—learning about foreign markets as well as coordination and communication between home and abroad. Jones and Kierzkowski (1990) note that "service links" of this sort are especially important when the trade in question involves fragmenting production processes across countries.

These service links are subject to potentially large and increasing returns to scale. For example, a multinational firm wishing to sell into a foreign market may pay high fixed costs in order to gather market information, tailor product specifications to local standards, or establish centers for distribution and after-sales service. In each case, the average cost of the service link is decreasing as foreign sales volume increases. It follows that tariff liberalization, by expanding foreign sales volume, may have a virtuous side effect. The cost of service links drop, reinforcing the tariff liberalization.

In this chapter we focus specifically on the transportation link. The circumstantial evidence for investigating scale economies in shipping can be seen by examining freight costs for large versus small exporters.

Consider Japan and the Ivory Coast, equi-distant from the west and east coasts of the United States, respectively. Shipping costs from the Ivory Coast to the United States are twice as high as those from Japan, even after adjusting for differences in the commodity composition of trade.[1]

What is the source of scale economies in shipping? One possible source lies in the domestic trade infrastructure built up by each country. Ports (and the internal road or rail system necessary to reach them) tend to be large, lumpy investments. If the fixed costs are large enough, increased trade scale will benefit the investing country directly, and perhaps some of its trade partners, through lowered shipping costs.

Scale economies may also operate at the level of the country pair and the trade route. The capacity of a modern ocean liner is large relative to the quantities shipped by most exporters. As a consequence, goods are almost never shipped point to point directly between the exporter and importer. Instead, a vessel may stop in a dozen ports in many different countries. Table 14.1 displays two typical port-of-call itineraries for vessels between North and South America.[2] Each route involves five or more countries and multiple stops within each. Considering all exporting routes to the United States, the median number of countries visited by each ocean liner on a single route is ten.

Table 14.1 Liner Vessel Itineraries

Mediterranean Shipping, USASA Service		Libra, ASANG Service	
Chiara, Voyage 487A		TMM Guadalajara, Voyage 4	
Location	Date	Location	Date
Veracruz, Mexico	Thu Jun 6	Buenos Aires, Argentina	Sun Jun 9
Altamira, Mexico	Sat Jun 8	Itajai, Brazil	Wed Jun 12
Houston, TX, USA	Sun Jun 9	Santos, Brazil	Fri Jun 14
New Orleans, LA, USA	Tue Jun 11	Rio de Janeiro, Brazil	Sun Jun 16
Freeport, Bahamas	Tue Jun 18	Puerto Cabello, Venezuela	Sun Jun 23
Cartagena, Colombia	Sat Jun 22	Veracruz, Mexico	Sat Jun 29
Buenaventura, Colombia	Mon Jun 24	Altamira, Mexico	Sun Jun 30
Callao, Peru	Fri Jun 28	Houston, TX, USA	Tue Jul 2
Guayaquil, Ecuador	Fri Jun 28	New Orleans, LA, USA	Thu Jul 4
Arica, Chile	Mon Jul 1		
Antofagasta, Chile	Tue Jul 2		
Valparaiso, Chile	Wed Jul 3		
Talcahuano, Chile	Mon Jul 8		

As trade quantities increase it is possible to more effectively realize gains from four sources. First, a densely traded route allows for effective use of hub-and-spoke shipping economies—small container vessels move quantities into a hub where containers are aggregated into much larger and faster containerships for longer hauls. Examples include the European hub of Rotterdam, as well as Asian hubs in Singapore and Hong Kong.[3]

Second, the movement of some goods requires specialized vessels. Examples include ships specialized to move bulk commodities, petroleum products, refrigerated produce, and automobiles. Increased quantities allow the introduction of these specialized ships along a route. Similarly, larger ships will be introduced on heavily traded routes, and these ships enjoy substantial cost savings relative to older, smaller models still in use. (One source of scale advantage is in crew costs, which are roughly independent of ship size.)

A historical example of these effects in combination can be seen in the introduction of containerized shipping. Containerized shipping is thought by many specialists to be one of the most important transportation revolutions in the twentieth century. The use of standardized containers provides cost savings by allowing goods to be packed once and moved over long distances via a variety of transport modes (truck, rail, ocean liner, rail, then truck again) without being unpacked and repacked.

Despite these advantages, containerized shipping did not diffuse immediately throughout the world. Instead, it was first introduced in the United States in the 1960s, then on U.S.-Europe and U.S.-Japan routes in the late 1960s and 1970s, then to developing countries from the late 1970s onward. In Figure 14.1 we display the share of liner tonnage that was containerized for U.S. imports in 1979, 1983, 1991, and 1997. Each data point represents a major trade route, and we graph the container share against the sum of country GDPs on that route. This graph shows a few interesting, broad patterns. The degree of containerization varies markedly across regions and is positively correlated with route GDP, and most of the growth in this period occurs on smaller GDP routes. Note also that containerization experienced the most pronounced increases on the route involving the west coast of South America.

An obvious explanation for this slow diffusion lies in the fixed costs of adoption. To make full use of containerization requires container-ready ocean liners and ports adapted to container use (specialized

Figure 14.1 Share of Containerization for U.S. Imports from Latin America by Trade Route

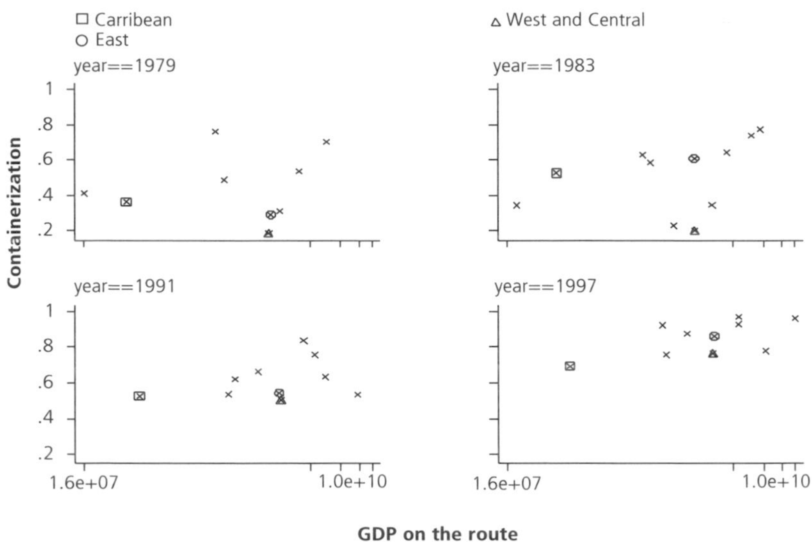

cranes, storage areas, and railheads). Building container ports typically requires large capital expenses, and will not be undertaken unless a large volume of trade can be moved through them. Similarly, shipping companies will not dedicate a container-ready ocean liner to a route unless there is a sufficient volume of trade along that route. Finally, the full benefit of containerization may not be enjoyed unless it is combined into hub-and-spoke systems at the regional level that allow the matching of differently sized ships to appropriate route lengths. Thus, adoption of a revolutionary shipping technology such as containerization depends on the scale of trade at the level of the exporter and on the exporting route.

A third source of scale benefits lies in pro-competitive effects on pricing. Many trade routes are serviced by a small number of liner companies that have traditionally been organized in formal cartels called "liner conferences." Whether these companies successfully exert market power in pricing shipping services is an open question. Some authors have used contestability theory to argue that the small number of participants is in no way indicative of their market power. However, this point has never adequately been addressed empirically, and at least one study (Fink, Mattoo, and Neagu 2002) has found evidence that freight rates are sensitive to regulatory changes meant to constrain collusive behavior by liner conferences. Supposing that freight prices do include significant monopoly markups, it is possible that increasing trade quantities would lead to entry and have a pro-competitive effect on prices.[4]

If scale effects operating through hub-and-spoke economies, specialized ships, and pro-competitive effects on prices are important, we expect to see a negative relationship between shipment quantities and measured freight rates. A fourth source of scale benefits appears only as an implicit cost of trade. Recent work by Hummels (2001) argues that lags in shipping time can be a serious deterrent to trade. He shows that each additional day lag in shipping time reduces the probability of sourcing from a particular exporter by 1 percent. Conditional on exporting, each additional day lag in shipping time imposes costs of 0.8 percent ad valorem. By increasing quantities along a route, the frequency of ship visits rises, lowering implicit time costs of trade.

All four arguments suggest that shipping scale economies are a regional public good. That is, increases in trade between the United States and Argentina benefit these partners, but also the other countries (Brazil, Venezuela, Caribbean) lying along the route. It follows that countries may prefer to see tariff liberalization concentrated among regional neighbors.

This chapter proceeds in two main sections. First we sketch a model that describes the interaction between the scale of trade and shipping costs. In the model, a monopoly shipper decides whether to pay a fixed cost in order to adopt a lower marginal cost shipping technology. The quantity of trade along a route determines which technology is chosen; tariffs increase trade quantities, making it more likely that the low marginal cost technology is chosen. Liberalizing countries thus face a complementary reduction in shipping costs.

This model is consistent with the introduction of specialized vessels along a route as well as the addition of shipping capacity in order to reduce shipping lags. It is also consistent with the development of hub-and-spoke networks provided that the shipper in question is a monopolist able to internalize the externalities of such a network. In order to keep the model simple, we have not incorporated pro-competitive effects on freight prices, though we think these effects may be at least as important as the shipping-capacity decision we highlight here. (In any case, our empirical exercise cannot distinguish the two channels.)

The model suggests the two sorts of empirical analysis that we explore in the subsequent section. First, we directly estimate the effects of shipping scale (at the level of the exporter and the exporting route) on technology adoption and shipping frequency. We examine the adoption of containerized shipping from 1976 to 1995, relating it to the scale of trade. We also estimate the sensitivity of shipment frequency to shipment quantities. Combining these with Hummels' (2001) estimates of time-cost savings provides a second source of scale gains in shipping.

In our second empirical analysis, trade quantities and shipping costs are jointly determined. We estimate this joint dependence and find strong evidence for scale economies in shipping. Increasing trade quantities (at the level of shipments, aggregate bilateral trade, and aggregate regional trade) reduces shipping costs. The identification strategy relies on bilateral variation in tariff rates as an exogenous determinant of trade quantities, precisely the same policy experiment as is conducted under regional liberalization such as an FTAA.

The model and empirical analysis in this chapter are entirely positive in focus. The concluding section describes some normative implications that follow. These implications include the possibility that, with route-specific scale economies in trade, selective regional liberalization may lead to greater gains from trade than would broad multilateral liberalization.

The Model

In this section we describe a model in which the quantity of trade and the level of transportation costs is jointly determined. To focus on this interaction we consider a partial equilibrium model of trade in a homogeneous final good to keep the trade side of the model as simple as possible, and introduce a monopoly shipper that makes decisions about which technology to use and how to price transportation services. These decisions are affected by variation in parameters such as the size of the market and the tariffs set by the importer.

There are two countries, an importer and an exporter of the good. We assume that exporting firms are perfectly competitive price takers with constant marginal costs p. The importing country has excess (import) demand for the good of

$$q = a - bp^* \tag{1}$$

The price that a consumer faces is the price of the good times the tariff and plus the transportation cost:

$$p^* = pt + f \tag{2}$$

Substituting for the price from equation 2 into equation 1 allows us to construct a derived demand for transportation services in terms of the freight rate:

$$q = (a - bpt) - bf \tag{3}$$

For convenience denote the intercept of the transportation demand curve as $\tilde{a}$:

$$\tilde{a} = a - bpt \tag{4}$$

A higher tariff (or a higher goods price) represents an inward shift of the transportation demand curve. Rewriting equation 3 using equation 4 yields the inverse transportation demand curve as

$$f = \frac{\tilde{a} - q}{b} \tag{5}$$

The monopolist has a cost function:

$$C = F + cq \tag{6}$$

Facing demand given by equation 5, profit maximization implies a monopoly freight rate charged to exporting firms of

$$f = \frac{1}{2}\left(\frac{\tilde{a}}{b} + c\right) \tag{7}$$

The price charged by the shipper depends positively on the intercept—lowering a tariff leads to a parallel outward shift in the demand for transportation services. At the initial freight price this represents a drop in the elasticity of transportation demand, and so the reduced tariff causes the monopoly markup to increase.

We can now examine the effects of a tariff reduction on the quantity imported. Given import demand and the monopoly shipper's optimal freight price we solve for the quantity imported as

$$q = \frac{1}{2}\left(a - bpt - bc\right) \tag{8}$$

Comparing equation 8 to equation 3 allows us to see the direct and indirect effects of tariff reductions on import quantities. If the freight price is fixed and independent of the tariff, inspection of equation 3 shows that any change in tariffs will have an effect on the quantity of the traded goods given by $\partial q / \partial t = -bp$. (The higher the price of the good that is being shipped and the more elastic the demand for that good, the greater is the impact of a change in a tariff on the quantity.) Incorporating the monopolist's pricing decision in equation 8, we see that a tariff change has a smaller effect on import quantity: $\partial q / \partial t = -bp / 2$. The reason is that the tariff reduction lowers the elasticity of transportation demand and causes the monopolist to charge a higher markup over marginal cost. This indirect effect operating through the markup unravels half of the tariff reduction. In other words, tariff reductions are associated with increased shipping costs.

The two technologies available to the monopoly shipping firm are

$$\begin{Bmatrix} F = 0; c > 0 \\ F > 0; c = 0 \end{Bmatrix} \tag{9}$$

The first technology requires no fixed costs, but has a positive marginal cost per unit shipped. The second requires a fixed payment, but has no marginal cost per unit. We choose these for simplicity, but the demonstration extends readily. One can more generally think about our setup in incremental terms—a reduction in marginal costs of *c* can be purchased with an incremental investment of *F*. Thus one can think of this choice either as a single yes/no decision on, for example, port infrastructure, or one can think of the choice in terms of a menu of ship sizes from which the shipper can select.

Examining the first-order condition we see that, for a given tariff (and corresponding level of demand), the monopoly would charge a lower price when adopting the low marginal cost technology. The difference is given by

$$f_{\text{low MC}} - f_{\text{hi MC}} = -\frac{c}{2} \tag{10}$$

Inducing the shift to the lower marginal cost technology would therefore lower trade costs and further increase trade. The simple point is that tariff reductions can increase the scale of trade to such an extent that the monopolist prefers a high fixed cost, low marginal cost shipping technology.

The technology choice in turn has an effect on the quantity traded. If the tariff reductions are insufficient to induce adoption of the high fixed cost technology then transportation prices and import quantities are given by equations 7 and 8. Quantities traded are increasing, but at a slower rate than if the freight rate were fixed. However, if tariff reductions are sufficient to induce adoption of the low marginal cost shipping technology, there is a discrete downward jump in the freight price charged. The size of the jump is given by equation 10. This has a corresponding upward jump in the quantity traded.

This model is very simple but it yields several interesting conclusions. In the single technology case (or when tariff reductions are small), tariff liberalizations result in higher shipping costs because they give greater markup power to monopolists. In fact, the monopoly shipper unravels half of a tariff reduction through increased markups.

If the choice of shipping technology is made endogenous, then sufficiently large tariff liberalizations will be reinforced by shipping-cost reductions. Once the scale of trade is large enough, the monopoly shipper complements the tariff reduction by adopting a lower marginal cost technology and consequently offering lower prices.

These two possibilities are starkly at odds, and suggest an interesting empirical question: do we anticipate higher or lower shipping costs on heavily traded routes? Lower shipping costs suggest that shippers may respond to liberalizations by adopting lower marginal cost technologies.

Empirics

In this section we provide several exercises inspired by the underlying model. First, we examine whether changes in shipping technology are a function of the scale of trade. In particular, we analyze the adoption of containerized shipping and the frequency of port visits. Both have the characteristic of a technology that raises fixed costs but lowers marginal costs of shipping, either explicitly (containerization) or implicitly (through time savings). Second, we examine whether these technological changes, and others we cannot measure directly, show up in lowered freight rates for heavily traded shipping routes.

In each case there is an issue of identification. Nearly any model of trade will predict causality running from trade costs to trade quantities—high shipping costs impede trade. Similarly, trade and transportation infrastructure will obviously be positively correlated (in the same sense that factory output is positively correlated with the number of workers or the capital stock that a factory uses). Several studies have emphasized the strong link between the quality of domestic transportation infrastructure and trade volumes, but neither indicate which way the causality runs, nor do they address issues of scale.[5]

Our innovation is to suggest that equilibrium trade quantities feed back on trade costs through the adoption of increasing returns to scale shipping technology. The key to the estimation strategy is using tariffs and country size variation to trace out exogenous variation in trade quantities. Scale effects on technology choice, and their corresponding effect on freight costs, can then be appropriately identified.

Containerization

UNCTAD's *Review of Maritime Transport* reports the number of container "lifts"—that is, the number of inbound and outbound containers handled by ports in each country. Its data span 1976–95, with a focus on developing countries. This is an ideal period to examine. Containerization was initially introduced in the early 1960s in the United States, and spread rapidly throughout OECD countries in the 1960s and 1970s. However, outside of the OECD, adoption of containerization took place between the late 1970s and the early 1990s.

The dependent variable is the (log) number of container lifts for each country *j*, in levels, and scaled by the value of *j*'s trade (imports plus exports) worldwide. We regress this on the value of *j*'s trade, and the value of worldwide trade for counties along *j*'s trade routes.

Calculating the trade along *j*'s route is a little tricky as a country *m* may frequently but not always lie on the same shipping itinerary with the country *j* in question. Accordingly, we weight country *m*'s trade by

Table 14.2 Adoption of Containerization

	Volume of Trade[b]		
Dependent Variable[a]	Country	Route Weighted	Number of Observations
Container lifts	11.16	–0.02	597
	(4.75)	(0.08)	
Container lifts/trade value	2.73	0.001	597
	(0.93)	(0.016)	

Note: All variables are in logs and mean differenced by country.
[a]Both regressions include year fixed effects.
[b]Volumes of trade are instrumented by corresponding GDPs.

the frequency with which vessels visiting *j* also visit *m*. We then sum the weighted trade values over all countries to get *j*'s trade "route." Our trade values may be endogenous to the use of the improved shipping technology (containers), so we instrument using *j*'s GDP and the (similarly) weighted sum of GDPs for countries along *j*'s trade routes. We estimate with country fixed effects to isolate changes corresponding to trade growth, and include year dummies to pick up trends.

The results are displayed in Table 14.2. Countries with a large volume of trade use containers more intensively. Countries that expand the scale of trade via GDP growth and tariff reductions see a substantial increase in the use of a revolutionary shipping technology. However, the route effects evident in Figure 14.1 appear not to matter in the regression specification that includes own trade.

Shipment Frequency and Time Lags

Suppose that ocean-going vessels could be costlessly scaled up or down in size without sacrificing any operating efficiencies. Then the size of shipments between a country pair, or along a route, would not affect the frequency of vessel visits. One could simply utilize small ships on small-scale routes, large shipments on large routes, and have these ships visit daily. However, if vessel scale does matter, shippers must examine the scale of cargo available to be moved and adjust accordingly. One dimension of adjustment is vessel size. Another dimension of adjustment is the frequency of visits, that is, having a containership visit once a month rather than once a week, or daily.

These adjustments can be very costly. Hummels (2001) estimates that time lags associated with shipping are equivalent to almost 1 per-

Table 14.3 Trade Scale and Time Lags in Shipping

	Dependent Variable: Time to U.S.	
Distance shipped	0.64	0.56
	(0.02)	(0.02)
Exporter trade quantity	–0.1	–0.12
	(0.01)	(0.01)
Route trade quantity	–0.09	—
	(0.02)	
Observations	1,191	1191

Notes: All variables in logs, standard errors in parentheses. Instruments: GDP, workforce of exporter, route.

cent of the value of the good for each day spent in shipping. Further, each additional day spent in shipping lowers the probability that a country will export a commodity by 1 percent.

In this section, we estimate the degree to which time lags are a function of the frequency of liner visits to a particular port, and in turn, a function of the scale of trade moved along a route. To identify this relationship we regress shipment times, in days, on shipment distances; the volume of trade shipped by the exporter; and the volume of trade shipped by other countries along the same route. As before, trade volumes are instrumented by exporter GDP and population, and the GDP and population of other countries along the route. The results are displayed in Table 14.3.

Doubling shipment distances (Australia to the U.S. west coast is roughly twice as far as Spain to the U.S. east coast) increases shipping times by 65 percent, or about ten days. The elasticity on both bilateral and regional quantities is around –0.10. Increasing bilateral and regional quantities by one standard deviation relative to the mean reduces shipping times by 31 and 25 percent, respectively.

Freight Rates

Finally, increases in trade scale may result in many subtle adjustments in shipping technology, as well as pro-competitive effects on prices, that we cannot estimate separately and directly. We can, however, examine the cumulative effect of trade scale on shipping prices.

Our dataset includes a cross-section of importers and exporters in 1994. We examine how trade quantities at various levels affect within-commodity variation in freight rates. The identification comes from variation in the quantities at the commodity level, the country-pair level, and the importer-region level. However, if scale economies in shipping are in some sense "shared" over these levels of aggregation, we will not be able to measure them.

Denoting importers by *i*, exporters by *j*, and commodities by *k*, we write ad valorem freight rates as

$$\ln f_{ij}^{k} = a^{k} + \beta_1 \ln DIST_{ij} + \beta_2 \ln q_{ij}^{k} + \beta_3 \ln q_{ij} + \beta_4 \ln q_{iRj} + e_{ij}^{k} \tag{11}$$

Commodity-level freight rates (*f*) are a function of a commodity-specific intercept, which captures cross-commodity differences in weight, bulk, and handling requirements; the distance shipped; and three measures of (nominal) quantities shipped. We include the quantity of the individual commodity (measured at the six-digit HS level) for a country pair, the aggregate quantity of bilateral trade between the country pair (for all commodities other than k), and the (weighted) quantity of trade between the importer and exporters along j's "route" for all exporters other than j.[6]

We instrument for the bilateral quantity of trade in a category k using prices (p) and tariffs (TAR). Following gravity models, we instrument for aggregate bilateral quantities using the output and labor force of the importer and exporter.[7] Similarly, we instrument for aggregate trade along a route using the weighted sum of output and workforce of countries along j's route.

The data for this exercise cover the bilateral trade of six importers (Argentina, Brazil, Chile, Paraguay, Uruguay, and the United States) with all exporters worldwide, measured at the six-digit level of the Harmonized Classification System (5000-plus categories) in 1994. We observe shipment values V, weight (WGT), the total freight bill paid (F), and the ad valorem tariff rate (t). All included variables have true importer-exporter-commodity category variation. All data are expressed relative to commodity means, which subsumes differences in units across categories. Data on V, WGT, and F are taken from national data sources for the importers. Bilateral tariff rates are taken from extracts of the UNCTAD Trade Analysis Information System (TRAINS) database.[8] Incomes and workforce data are taken from the Summers and Heston Penn World Tables data. Summary statistics for the data are included in the appendix.

Table 14.4 Scale Economies in Transport

Dependent Variable	Instruments	Bilateral Commodity Quantity	Bilateral Aggregate Quantity	Route Aggregate Quantity	$DIST_{ij}$	Number of Observations
LogFreight	(a)	–0.32	0.21	–0.12	0.32	231,311
		(0.0089)	(0.0073)	(0.0023)	(0.0026)	
LogFreight	(b)	–0.23	0.17	–0.13	0.31	224,784
		(0.008)	(0.0066)	(0.002)	(0.0024)	

(Eq. 11) $\ln f_{ij}^{k} = a^{k} + \beta_1 \ln DIST_{ij} + \beta_2 \ln q_{ij}^{k} + \beta_3 \ln q_{ij} + \beta_4 \ln q_{iRj} + e_{ij}^{k}$

Notes: Instrument (a): importer and exporter incomes and workforce, tariffs, and regional weighted incomes; instrument (b): all instruments above, plus prices. All variables are in logs, standard errors in parentheses.

The results of this regression are contained in Table 14.4. We provide two specifications, with and without using shipment prices as instruments for quantities in the first stage. In both cases we find a negative effect of commodity-level quantities on the ad valorem freight rate, a positive effect of aggregate bilateral quantities, and a negative effect of aggregate route quantities.

The negative sign on the route quantity is the most interesting effect. A one standard deviation increase in the route quantity relative to the mean would reduce shipping costs by one-third. To put this in terms of a policy experiment, suppose regional tariffs were reduced by 10 percentage points. Using an elasticity of trade quantity with respect to price of six, this would increase regional quantities by 60 percent. As a consequence freight rates within the region would fall by around 7 percent.

The effect of a tariff reduction on an importer-exporter pair is more difficult to calculate. A tariff reduction would increase quantities for individual commodities, lowering the freight rate, but it would also increase the aggregate quantity, pulling the freight rate back up. The net effect, summing over all commodities, will be a reduction in shipping costs for two reasons. First, the negative coefficient on commodities is greater in absolute magnitude than the positive coefficient on aggregate quantities. Second, all variables here are in logs, and the sum of the log of individual shipments will exceed the log of the sum of individual shipments due to the convexity of the natural log function. We cannot calculate the precise effect without knowing all of the individual changes, but we know that it will be negative.

Implications and Conclusions

We show, theoretically and empirically, how lowering political barriers to trade can lead endogenously to a reduction in other trade frictions. In our model a monopoly shipper decides whether to adopt a low marginal cost technology as a function of the tariff and corresponding level of demand. Tariffs increase trade quantities, making it more likely that liberalizing countries face a complementary reduction in shipping costs.

We find direct evidence that increased trade scale improves technology, and in particular the use of containerized shipping. Increased trade scale also increases the frequency of shipping, lowering implicit time costs of trade. We also find that doubling trade quantities along a route reduces shipping costs by 12 percent for all countries on that route, with an additional direct reduction in costs for the bilateral pair.

This chapter focuses on a positive analysis of the joint determination of trade quantities and shipping costs, but it suggests an interesting set of normative questions. In particular, how is the standard welfare analysis of regional trade liberalization affected by the endogeneity of shipping costs?

It is well known that the welfare gains from regional liberalization depend on transportation costs. Krugman (1991) and Frankel, Stein, and Wei (1996) show that liberalizing with "natural" trading partners is more likely to be welfare enhancing because prices, inclusive of shipping, are lower for natural partners. That is, regional liberalization leads in these cases to trade creation rather than trade diversion.

This analysis supposes that trade costs are unaffected by equilibrium quantities of trade. However, if scale economies in shipping *along a particular route* are sufficiently strong, then trading partners may endogenously become natural. That is, regional liberalization boosts the quantity of bilateral trade, leading to a reduction in transportation costs.

To illustrate, consider the merits of a regional trade pact such as an FTAA. In a model in which freight rates are fixed exogenously Argentina and Brazil compete with each other for the U.S. market. Each would want the United States to lower tariffs selectively, excluding the other country from the block. In a world with endogenous freight rates there is a countervailing force. Argentina benefits from increased Brazilian trade with the United States because this trade lowers shipping costs for Argentina as well.

Next consider the merits of liberalizing regionally through an FTAA, or pursuing multilateral negotiations through the WTO. With exogenously given shipping costs the standard trade creation/diversion results suggest that an FTAA may or may not be beneficial. However, the first best solution is clearly to liberalize multilaterally.

The preference for multilateral liberalization is no longer obvious in a world with endogenous shipping costs. Suppose that multilateral liberalization leads European and South American exporters to share the U.S. market. Sharing the market might lead to a volume of trade insufficient for shippers to adopt the low marginal cost shipping technology. However, liberalizing selectively through an FTAA may generate sufficient quantities along the north-south route that the shippers are willing to pay the higher fixed costs to adopt the low marginal cost technology. A consequence can be that welfare is maximized by the concentration of trade along a single route, and differential tariffs provide an effective way to provide that concentration.

Of course, this logic can easily run the other way. Suppose that trade volumes pre-liberalization were high between U.S.-Europe and low on U.S.–South America routes. In this case, an FTAA could balance trade volumes, preventing the realization of scale gains on the north-north route.

In these cases the welfare rankings of policies will depend on a host of parameters, but the key variable is the responsiveness of shipping costs to trade quantities. We demonstrate here that the response is not negligible: political trade liberalizations can lead to a virtuous cycle of increased trade, increased investment in trade infrastructure, and further reductions in trade costs.

Appendix: Table 14.5 Summary Statistics of the Variables

		Statistic	
Variable	Unit	Mean	Standard Deviation
Ad valorem freight rate		0.12	0.16
Distance	Km	9,064	4,853
Exporter's labor force	thousands	51,168	126,750
Exporter's GDP	$ billion	1,080	1,790
Importer's labor force	thousands	58,431	56,389
Importer's GDP	$ billion	2,820	3,330
Route weighted labor force	thousands	15,079	46,982
Route weighted GDP	$ billion	379	809
Commodity level trade volume	$ thousands	2,439	73,000
Bilateral volume of trade	$ billion	7	21
Route weighted volume of trade	$ thousands	1,690	4,010

Data Appendix

Imports and Transport Cost Data

A summary of these data is given in Table 14.5.

U.S. Census Bureau, "U.S. Imports of Merchandise"
These data report extremely detailed customs information on U.S. imports from all exporting countries (approximately 160) for 1994. The data are reported at the 10-digit Harmonized System level (approximately 15,300 goods categories), which we aggregate to the 6-digit level for comparability with the other trade data. Data include the

valuation of imports, inclusive and exclusive of freight and insurance charges; shipment quantity by count and by weight; transportation mode; district of entry into the United States; and duties paid. Goods are valued FAS, or "free alongside ship," meaning that freight charges include loading and unloading expenses.

ALADI Secretariat, "Latin American Trade"
These data report imports of Argentina, Brazil, Chile, Paraguay, and Uruguay from 1994 at the 6-digit Harmonized System level (approximately 3,000 goods). Data include exporter, value of imports, weight, freight charges, and insurance charges (separately). Freight charges are based on FOB ("free on board," or exclusive of loading costs) valuation of goods. For overland transport within the ALADI countries it appears that the freight field has a zero value. This is because charges are only incurred between exit and entry ports, and these are the same for overland transport. Note, however, that this does not change the relative valuation of freight charges across export partners. All trade incurs some overland shipping from factory to exporting port and from importing port to location of consumption, and these costs are missing from all the data. One can then think of the observed values as a distribution that is simply shifted to the left relative to the true set of values.

Other Data

Distance
The usual method for measuring bilateral distance is the "great circle" straight-line distance between partner countries, which may involve polar transit or travel that intersects a continent. We improve on this in two ways. First, we use port-to-port distances constructed by forcing shipments to round continental bodies. The difference can be substantial in some cases. As an example, German goods shipped to the U.S. east coast travel in an approximately straight line, whereas goods shipped to the U.S. west coast must transit through the Panama Canal, roughly doubling the east-coast distance.

We use U.S. Census data on U.S. District of Entry, which can be used to separate imports coming into Hawaii from those entering Miami, Boston, and Los Angeles. A common complaint with census data on U.S. district of entry (for imports) or exit (for exports) is that these districts do not necessarily capture the ultimate U.S. consumer or the original U.S. producer of traded goods. This is not a concern here as we are primarily interested in the measured cost of freight in getting the goods to the entry point where customs officials stop calculating freight charges.

Tariff Data

Bilateral tariff data at the six-digit HS level are available for the six importers. While the precise year varies somewhat across countries, most of the data are from 1994. The data originally come from the TRAINS dataset, and we employ a special extract provided by Jon Haveman that painstakingly constructs bilateral tariff rates using preference indicators in these data.

Shipping Schedule

Data on ocean shipping times are derived from a master schedule of shipping for 1999 taken from www.shipguide.com. This shipping schedule describes all departures and arrivals of all commercial vessels operating worldwide in this period. From this, we construct a matrix of shipping times between all ports everywhere in the world and all U.S. entry ports. Several modifications are necessary. First, direct shipments are not available for every port-port combination (e.g., Tunis does not ship directly to Houston). In these cases, we calculate all possible combinations of indirect routings (Tunis to Rotterdam to Houston, Tunis to Rio to Houston, and so on) and take the minimum shipment time available through these routings. Second, there are generally multiple ports within each origin country. In this section, a within-country average of shipment time from these ports is employed. Because U.S. data include entry-port detail, these are combined with destination-port-specific arrival times.

References

Bougheas, Spiros, Panicos Demetriades, and Edgar Morgenroth. 1999. "Infrastructure, Transport Costs, and Trade." *Journal of International Economics* 47 (1): 169–89.

Fink, Carsten, Aaditya Mattoo, and Ileana Cristina Neagu. 2001. "Trade in International Maritime Services: How Much Does Policy Matter?" *World Bank Economic Review* 16: 81–108.

Frankel, Jeffrey, Ernest Stein, and Shang-Jin Wei. 1996. "Regional Trading Arrangements: Natural or Super-Natural?" *American Economic Review* 86 (2): 52–6.

Haveman, Jon. "The Ultimate Trade Barrier Catalog." http://www.eiit.org/Protection/extracts.html. Data retrieved in 2002.

Hummels, David. 2001. "Time as a Trade Barrier." Purdue University. Photocopy.

Jones, Ronald, and Henry Kierzkowski. 1990. "The Role of Services in Production and International Trade: A Theoretical Framework." In *The Political Economy of International Trade: Essays in Honor of Robert E. Baldwin*, edited by Ronald W. Jones and Anne O. Krueger. Oxford: Blackwell.

Krugman, Paul. 1991. "Is Bilateralism Bad?" In *International Trade and Trade Policy*, edited by Elhanan Helpman and Assaf Razin. Cambridge, MA: MIT Press.

Limao, Nuno, and Anthony Venables. 2001. "Infrastructure, Geographical Disadvantage, Transport Costs and Trade." *World Bank Economic Review* 15: 451–79.

Notes

We thank Simon Evenett, Gordon Hanson, Ed Leamer, and seminar participants at Purdue for helpful comments.

1 This difference in freight costs is 6.5 percent ad valorem. This number is robust to two methods of calculation. The first method directly compares goods imported from both countries (a fairly small set). The second method subtracts commodity-specific means, then constructs an aggregate rate as the simple mean over all shipments for each exporter.

2 Vessel itineraries are taken from www.shipguide.com.

3 Given the fairly linear geography of coastlines in North and South America it is not entirely clear whether it is feasible for a similar hub system to arise.

4 There is a literature arguing, from contestability theory, that potential entry into liner routes is sufficient to keep even single-service providers from charging monopoly markups. The theory has not been tested.

5 See Boughcas, Demetriades, and Morgenroth (1999) and Limao and Venables (2001).

6 A country m may frequently but not always occur on the same itinerary with the exporter in question. Accordingly, we weight the trade of m's exports to i by the frequency with which vessels visiting exporter j also visit exporter m. We then sum the weighted quantities over all exporters.

7 Results are qualitatively similar using endowments rather than GDP.

8 TRAINS data excerpted from Haveman in 2002.

15

What Has Happened to Wages in Mexico since NAFTA? Implications for Hemispheric Free Trade

Gordon H. Hanson

Introduction

The proposed Free Trade Agreement of the Americas (FTAA) would alter dramatically trading relationships in the Western Hemisphere. Eliminating trade barriers within the region would, among other effects, induce economies to specialize more in export production. Such specialization would enable countries in Latin America to realize gains from trade, but it is not likely that these income gains would be shared equally by all individuals in society. In Brazil, for instance, farmers growing oranges or workers producing shoes are likely to benefit more from an FTAA than are capital-intensive manufacturers. As a result, an FTAA is likely to redistribute national incomes in the region. Latin America's long history of income inequality makes the impact of an FTAA on the distribution of earnings an important issue for policy makers.

In this chapter I use Mexico as a test case for how regional free trade affects labor earnings. I examine how trade reform in Mexico, and the North American Free Trade Agreement (NAFTA) in particular, has altered the country's wage structure. Mexico is a useful case to study because it has opened itself to trade aggressively. It unilaterally liberalized foreign trade and investment policies in the 1980s and then enacted NAFTA in 1994, which further reduced trade barriers and helped lock in reform by enshrining it in a multilateral treaty. Mexico is now as closely tied to the North American economy as at any point in its history. In 2000, it sent 88.7 percent of its exports to and bought 73.1 percent of its imports from the United States. Greater openness has helped increase the share of trade in Mexico's GDP from 11.2 percent in 1980 to 32.2 percent in 2000.

There are several channels through which North American economic integration affects Mexico's labor market. One is by equalizing the price of traded goods between economies. Trade theory predicts that convergence in prices between countries creates pressure for convergence in factor prices. In Mexico, this would affect both wage levels and the relative wages of low- and high-skilled labor. A second channel through which trade reform may shock labor demand is through its impact on capital flows. Given that capital appears to complement skilled labor, capital inflows may increase the demand for skill. In Mexico, NAFTA appears to have raised capital inflows in part by raising investor confidence in the country's commitment to free trade. From 1980 to 1994, foreign direct investment (FDI) averaged 1.3 percent of Mexico's GDP, while from 1995 to 2000 it averaged 2.8 percent of GDP (Chiquiar 2001). About two-thirds of this FDI comes from the United States. In Mexico's export-assembly sector, capital inflows expand trade directly. The creation of export-assembly plants, or *maquiladoras*, by U.S. firms in Mexico has increased trade in intermediate inputs. In 2000, *maquiladoras* accounted for 47.7 percent of Mexico's exports and 35.4 percent of Mexico's imports.

In using Mexico to preview the effects of an FTAA, it is important to recognize that it differs from the rest of Latin America in some important respects. In particular, Mexico shares a land border with the United States that creates opportunities for migration abroad that other countries do not enjoy. During the 1990s, net immigration into the United States from Mexico was about 400,000 individuals per year. In the absence of migration flows, trade reform in Mexico might have generated even more trade and FDI than has occurred. Any estimate of the impact of regional free trade on Mexico, then, may understate the impact an FTAA would have on the rest of the region.

The body of this chapter has two parts. In the first I examine changes in Mexico's wage structure following reforms in the 1980s. Here I rely on a substantial body of research that examines the impact of specific policy changes on labor earnings. This work finds that lower barriers to foreign trade and investment have changed Mexico's wage structure. The evidence suggests that tariff reductions have increased relative wages for skilled workers; increased foreign investment has raised the relative demand for skilled labor; and tariff and quota reductions have altered interindustry wage differentials. Mexico's economic opening thus appears to have raised the skill premium and reduced industry rents going to labor. It also appears to have increased wages in states along the U.S. border relative to the rest of the country.

In the second part I use data from the 1990 and 2000 Mexico population census to examine changes in Mexican wages over the period during which NAFTA was implemented. During the 1990s in Mexico, the returns to skill continued to rise and regional differences in wages continued to widen. Wage gains were largest in regions most exposed to international trade, FDI, and/or opportunities for migration to the United States. After controlling for regional exposure to globalization, other regional characteristics appear to be unimportant in explaining wage changes. Overall, wage gains were largest for more-educated workers living close to the United States and smallest for less-educated workers living in the country's south. There is little evidence of convergence in wages between Mexico and the United States. I conclude the chapter by discussing the implications of these results for an FTAA.

Policy Change and Wages in Mexico: The First Reform Wave

The last two decades in Mexico have not been a quiet period. Since 1980, the country has had three currency crises, bouts of high inflation, and severe macroeconomic contractions. The reform of the country's trade and investment policies has been, in part, a response to this turmoil. Following a balance of payments crisis in 1982, the country eased restrictions on *maquiladoras*. In 1985 Mexico joined the General Agreement on Trade and Tariffs (GATT), which entailed cutting tariffs and eliminating many nontariff barriers. In 1989 Mexico eased restrictions on the rights of foreigners to own assets in the country. In 1994 NAFTA consolidated and extended these reforms and tied them to reciprocal access to the U.S. and Canadian markets. Concomitant with its economic opening, Mexico privatized state-owned enterprises, deregulated entry restrictions in many industries, and used wage and price restraints to combat inflation.

The policy shocks to Mexico's labor markets have attracted much academic attention. A large body of work examines the impact that these policy changes have had on wages in the country. In this section, I briefly survey the literature, organizing the discussion around three questions: Why have skill premia in Mexico risen? Has greater economic openness affected regional wage differences in Mexico? And, is there evidence of labor-market integration between Mexico and the United States?

Rising Skill Premia in Mexico

Relative to the United States, Mexico has abundant supplies of less-skilled labor and scarce supplies of human and physical capital. Trade and investment reforms would be likely to alter the relative demand for labor of different types, producing changes in the premia for skill. Recent research shows that Mexico has indeed experienced changes in the relative wages of skilled workers, but ones that are quite different from what many would have expected given Mexico's relative factor supplies.

Since the mid 1980s Mexico has experienced widening wage inequality associated with rising returns to skill. Cragg and Epelbaum (1996) show that between 1987 and 1993, though average real wages rose by 30 percent, the wages of urban workers with a primary education (completed grade six) fell relative to the wages of urban workers with secondary education (completed grade nine) by 15 percent and relative to the wages of urban workers with post-secondary education by 60 percent. The returns to labor-market experience also rose markedly over this time period. Skill premia continued to rise in the 1990s. Robertson (2001) finds that the annual return to schooling for urban workers rose from 0.035 in 1987, to 0.05 in 1994, and to 0.07 in 1998. Consistent with evidence that skill premia and average educational attainment among workers have increased simultaneously, Cragg and Epelbaum (1996) suggest that Mexico's rising skill premia are due mostly to increases in the relative demand for skill.

Why has the relative demand for skilled labor in Mexico risen? The literature proposes a several answers to this question. The one that has attracted the most attention is that rising skill premia are due to trade and investment liberalization. Attributing rising skill premia to trade reform may seem counterintuitive, given Mexico's presumed comparative advantage in low-skill activities (Leamer 1993). The natural expectation might be that skill premia in Mexico would fall, not rise, after liberalization.[1]

This line of reasoning, however, does not accord with the pattern of trade protection in Mexico before reform. At the time Mexico began to lower its trade barriers, labor-intensive sectors had the highest tariff barriers. Hanson and Harrison (1999) find that 1984 industry tariffs are negatively correlated with the 1984 industry ratio of white-collar to blue-collar employment and that the 1984–90 change in industry tariffs is positively correlated with this employment ratio. This suggests that trade protection was initially higher in less-skill-intensive sectors and was reduced by more in these sectors during reform. If these tariff changes had passed through to changes in goods' prices, then the logic of the Stolper-Samuelson Theorem (1941) would imply that the relative wage of skilled labor would have risen. Robertson (2001) suggests that this is exactly what happened. He finds that over the period 1987–93 the relative price of skill-intensive goods in Mexico rose and that the tariff-induced change in relative prices had the effect of raising the relative wage for white-collar labor. Interestingly, tariff reductions in Mexico due to NAFTA have been larger in more-skill-intensive sectors, suggesting that the final stage of trade reform may halt the increase in skill premia.

In related work, Feliciano (2001) finds that between 1986 and 1990 wage dispersion in Mexico rose more in tradables than in nontradables. She also finds that trade reform altered interindustry wage differentials. Industry wage premia fell more in industries with larger reductions in import-license requirements, but not in industries with larger reductions in tariffs. Consistent with these results, Revenga (1997) finds that over the period 1984–90 manufacturing plants in industries with larger reductions in tariffs and nontariff barriers had higher reductions in employment. These findings suggest that industries that enjoyed high rents before trade reform, as indicated by high average wages after controlling for observable worker characteristics, experienced relatively large reductions in wages and employment after trade reform.

Another mechanism through which trade and investment reform may have increased the demand for skilled labor in Mexico is outsourcing to the country by foreign firms. A large fraction of U.S.-Mexico trade in manufactured products is the result of U.S. firms establishing *maquiladoras* in Mexico. These plants import nearly all parts and components from the United States, assemble final goods in Mexico, and export most output back to the United States. In 1995 exports by *maquiladoras* accounted for 40.2 percent of all Mexican exports to the United States.[2] From 1980 to 1997 the *maquiladora* share of national manufacturing employment in Mexico rose from 5.6 percent to 25.1 percent. The plants are concentrated in Mexican states on the U.S. border.[3]

How has the growth of *maquiladoras* affected labor demand in Mexico? Feenstra and Hanson (1997) show in theory that if policy reform allows U.S. firms to outsource more production to Mexico, these firms will choose to move the least skill-intensive activities that they perform. By moving low-skill activities to Mexico, the average skill intensity of production would rise in both the United States and Mexico. This would raise the relative demand and earnings of high-skilled workers in both countries, contributing to a binational increase in wage inequality.

To test these predictions, Feenstra and Hanson examine whether the relative demand for skilled workers in Mexico has risen more in regions where foreign investment has been concentrated. They use regional data on *maquiladoras* to measure the spatial distribution of foreign direct investment in Mexico. Consistent with their theory, during the 1980s the relative demand for high-skilled workers was higher in regions where *maquiladoras* expanded most rapidly. *Maquiladora* growth can account for over 50 percent of the increase in the skilled labor wage share that occurred during the late 1980s. These results suggest that U.S. outsourcing to Mexico, in the form of creating *maquiladoras*, has contributed to the rise in wage inequality in the country.

Beyond the specific activity of outsourcing, FDI in general is likely to affect the level and structure of wages in Mexico. Aitken, Harrison, and Lipsey (1996) find that, controlling for plant, industry, and region characteristics, manufacturing plants that are foreign owned pay their skilled workers 21.5 percent more and their unskilled workers 3.3 percent more than plants that are domestically owned. Similar results hold for Venezuela. These results are consistent with several interpretations. Workers may be more productive in multinational firms, multinationals may attract more able workers, or multinationals may earn rents and share these rents with their workers.

Regional Wage Differences in Mexico

Mexico's proximity to the United States suggests that trade liberalization for Mexico was tantamount to economic integration with its northern neighbor. Given that northern Mexico enjoys relatively low-cost access to the U.S. market, we would expect that North American economic integration would raise the demand for labor in the region relative to the rest of the country. Hanson (1996, 1997) examines how trade reform has affected Mexico's regional economies. Following trade reform, there has been a decline in relative industrial activity in central Mexico and an expansion in northern Mexico. In 1980, five years before trade reform began, 46 percent of the Mexico's manufacturing labor force was located in the Mexico City area and 21 percent was located in states on the U.S. border (Hanson 1997). In 1993, after eights years of reform, the share of manufacturing activity in Mexico City had fallen to 29 percent and the share at the border had risen to 30 percent. By 1998, four years after NAFTA, Mexico City's employment share had fallen further to 23 percent and the border's employment share had risen to 34 percent (Chiquiar 2001).

Movements in regional relative wages also suggest North American economic integration has benefited northern Mexico disproportionately. Hanson (1996) estimates state manufacturing wages relative to national manufacturing wages as a function of distance to Mexico City (the largest market in the country prior to trade reform) and distance to the United States (the largest market for the country's goods after trade reform). Regional relative wages are negatively correlated with distance to Mexico City and with distance to the Mexico-U.S. border. Prior to trade reform, a 10 percent increase in distance from Mexico City was associated with a 1.9 percent decrease in the relative state nominal wage, and a 10 percent increase in distance from the Mexico-U.S. border was associated with a 1.3 percent decrease in the relative state nominal wage. After trade reform, the regional wage gradient shifts. The effect of distance from Mexico City on state wages weakens and the effect of distance from the United States strengthens.

In related work, Chiquiar (2001) finds that for the period 1970–85 there was convergence in per capita GDP levels across Mexican states, but that after 1985 this process broke down. For the period 1985–93, there is strong divergence in state per capita GDP levels, and for the period 1993–98 relative state GDP levels remain roughly constant. The divergence in regional growth occurs at the time of trade reform.

The experience of Mexico suggests that trade policy plays an important role in determining regional economic fortunes. While trade reform raises wages in Mexican border states, it may lower wages in regions of the country that had a privileged role under the closed economy or that have poor access to the U.S. market.

Convergence in Mexican and U.S. Wages

Have the flows of goods, capital, and people helped integrate the labor markets of Mexico and the United States? In one of the few papers to address the topic, Robertson (2000) examines whether shocks to Mexican wages are correlated with shocks to U.S. wages. Using household data from the two countries over the period 1987–97, Robertson takes mean wages by age, schooling, region of residence, and time period and constructs a panel of synthetic cohorts. He then regresses the quarterly change in regional Mexican wages for a given age-education cell on quarterly changes in U.S. wages for the same age-education cell and on the lagged difference in U.S. and Mexican wages for the cell. The first variable captures the strength of labor-market integration between the two countries and the second captures the rate of wage convergence between the two countries.

Wage changes in Mexico are positively correlated with wage changes in the United States. This suggests that there is at least partial labor-market integration between the two countries. A shock that raises U.S. wages by 10 percent would raise wages in Mexican interior cities by 1.8 percent and wages in Mexican border cities by 2.5 percent. Wage changes in Mexico are negatively correlated with the lagged U.S.-Mexico wage difference, which suggests that over time wages in the two economies tend to converge. The estimated convergence rates are very rapid, with equilibrium U.S.-Mexico wage differentials being reached within one to two quarters. This finding of rapid convergence seems at odds with rising levels of trade, investment, and migration between the two countries, which suggests that integration of U.S. and Mexican markets is incomplete and that wage convergence between the two countries would be more gradual.

Revenga and Montenegro (1998) offer a related analysis of U.S.-Mexico wage differentials. They use data on Mexican manufacturing plants and U.S. manufacturing industries for the period 1984–90 to examine the evolution of average industry wages in Mexico relative to the United States. They regress the log ratio of average wages in Mexican plants to average wages in the corresponding U.S. industry on average industry tariffs in Mexico, average industry import-license requirements in Mexico, and other controls. The analysis is performed separately for less- and more-skilled workers. The Mexico-U.S. wage is positively correlated with Mexican tariffs and import-license requirements. The estimated regression coefficients for the sample of production workers and for the sample of nonproduction workers are very similar. A 50 percent reduction in tariffs would be associated with a 3.7 percent reduction in relative Mexico-U.S. wages for less-skilled workers and a 4.3 percent reduction in relative Mexico-U.S. wages for more-skilled workers.

It is tempting to interpret these results to mean that trade liberalization in Mexico depressed wages for Mexican workers relative to their U.S. counterparts. Were this the case, one might expect the effects on more- and less-skilled workers to be asymmetric, but they are not. An alternative and more plausible interpretation is that trade barriers in Mexico allowed firms to earn rents, which they shared with workers in the form of higher wages. Trade reform would have reduced these rents, producing a positive correlation between trade protection in Mexico and relative Mexico-U.S. wages for all labor types.

Summary

Recent literature suggests that liberalizing barriers to trade and investment have contributed to changes in Mexico's wage structure.[4] There is evidence consistent with tariff reductions having increased relative wages for skilled workers, increased foreign investment having raised the relative demand for skilled labor, and tariff and quota reductions having altered interindustry wage differentials. Mexico's economic opening thus appears to have raised the demand for skill and reduced industry rents going to labor. Both changes appear to have had adverse consequences for low-skilled workers.

Several larger messages also emerge from the literature. One is that Mexico's comparative advantage in low-skill activities is not as strong as many had thought. Mexico's trade reform entailed larger tariff reductions in less-skill-intensive industries, reflecting the high levels of protection afforded these industries under import-substitution industrialization. After trade reform, less-skill-intensive industries ended up taking the hardest hit in terms of wage and employment declines. This may come as a surprise, given Mexico's presumed comparative advantage in labor-intensive activities. While Mexico may have such a comparative advantage relative to the United States, it probably does not relative to China or South Asia. Trade liberalization exposed Mexico's vulnerability in very low-end manufacturing, as producers in this segment lost out to imports. Replacing these producers were export-assembly plants in apparel, auto parts, and electronics. While Mexico may have a cost disadvantage relative to China in finished goods such as tee shirts, plastic footwear, and simple consumer electronics, it appears to have a cost advantage in assembly services for the U.S. economy. Mexican manufacturing has, in effect, reoriented itself from producing simple consumer goods to being a subcontractor for the North American economy.

A second message to emerge from the literature is that trade and FDI appear to be complements. Trade reform freed up resources in manufacturing that allowed Mexico to become more specialized in export assembly. But to make this transition, the country needed FDI. The arrival of foreign firms brought in needed capital and new technology for managing assembly operations and handling the logistics of importing intermediate inputs and exporting outputs. These assembly operations, as it turns out, are intensive in the use of skilled labor relative to other Mexican manufacturing plants. The combination of freer trade, which allowed greater specialization, and fewer restrictions on FDI, which allowed plants in Mexico to become part of North American production networks, induced in shift from low-end production for the domestic economy to the provision of input-processing services for the North American economy.

Wages and Employment in Mexico, 1990 and 2000

Previous literature has focused on how Mexico's reforms affected wages and employment in the country during the 1980s and early 1990s. There is little work on the post-NAFTA period or that evaluates the relative impact of Mexico's economic reforms on labor-market outcomes in the country. In the next two sections, I attempt to address these shortcomings. I study changes in Mexico's wage structure over the period 1990–2000. The goals of this exercise are: to examine whether changes in Mexican wages in the 1990s mirrored those in the 1980s, to assess whether there has been convergence between U.S. and Mexican wages, and to evaluate how different forms of economic openness have impacted Mexico's wage structure.

Data and Summary Statistics

The data I use for the analysis are 1 percent random samples from the 1990 and 2000 Mexico population census. Much previous research limits the analysis to the manufacturing sector and/or to workers in large cities and so gives only a partial view of how Mexico's wage structure has evolved. The census provides comprehensive data on earnings and employment in Mexico. By looking over the entire decade of the 1990s, the analysis spans both the planning and negotiation period for NAFTA and the period following its enactment. This helps account for the possibility that firms began adjusting to NAFTA before the treaty was formally approved. It also extends the time period well beyond the severe recession Mexico suffered in 1995 when real GDP fell by 6.2 percent, which was precipitated by a bungled devaluation of the peso.

Table 15.1 gives summary statistics on the sample of individuals in 1990 and 2000. To focus on potential wage earners, I include only individuals sixteen to sixty-five years old. Over time, Mexico has experienced increases in educational attainment. From 1990 to 2000, the share of working-age individuals with eight years of education or less declined from 59.3 percent to 47.5 percent for males and from 63.3 percent to 51.4 percent for females. There are marked increases in the share of individuals completing secondary school (nine years) or preparatory school (twelve years). Despite large wage differences across regions (as discussed in the last section), there is little interregional migration. The border region, which has the highest wages in the country, had its share of the national population increase by only 1.0 percent for males and 0.5 percent for females. Within regions, there has been rural-to-urban migration. The share of individuals living in cities with more than 500,000 inhabitants rose by 4.8 percent for males and 4.4 percent for females and the share of individuals living in localities with less 2,500 inhabitants fell by 4.0 percent for males and 3.2 percent for females.

Despite increases in schooling, average hourly earnings fell in the 1990s. When deflated by Mexico's consumer price index (CPI), the average hourly wage in 1990 dollars declined for males from $1.33 to $1.11 and for females from $1.24 to $1.13. Wage declines are larger when controls are added for individual characteristics. These wage movements reflect in part the effects of Mexico's economic collapse in 1995. Even with falling wages, labor-force participation rates rose modestly for males and sharply for females over the decade. By 2000, 30.9 percent of working-age women were wage earners, up from 20.7 percent in 1990.

Table 15.2 shows the distribution of employed individuals across industries in 1990 and 2000. The major change in industrial specialization over the period was a decline in employment in agriculture and mining. The sector's share of male employment fell from 28.9 percent to 20.7 percent, due in part to the reform of the land tenure system in Mexico and the breakup of rural cooperatives, or *ejidos*. Manufacturing's share of total employment remained steady over the 1990s at around 20 percent.

Table 15.1 Summary Statistics of the Variables

	Males 1990	Males 2000	Females 1990	Females 2000
Age	32.7	33.8	32.7	33.7
Literate	91.3	94.5	86.3	91.7
Highest grade of schooling completed (%)				
0	11.6	5.7	15.6	7.8
1 to 4	19.1	14.8	19.6	15.9
5 to 8	28.6	27.0	28.1	27.7
9	13.9	20.4	12.3	18.8
10 to 11	7.7	7.2	7.4	6.7
12	6.5	10.0	7.6	11.3
13 to 15	5.2	4.9	5.1	4.6
16+	7.2	9.6	4.0	6.8
Married	53.7	51.4	53.9	50.3
Region				
Border	17.6	18.6	16.8	17.3
North	10.4	10.0	10.3	10.0
Center	33.6	32.7	34.3	34.0
Capital	23.7	23.8	24.0	24.1
Yucatán	4.7	5.4	4.5	5.1
South	10.0	9.5	10.0	9.4
Size of locality				
500k+	23.9	28.7	24.3	28.7
100–500k	23.5	22.3	24.3	22.7
15–100k	12.9	13.7	13.3	13.9
2.5–15k	13.2	12.8	13.2	13.1
<2.5k	26.5	22.5	24.9	21.7
Migration				
Prior to last 5 Years	22.4	23.5	23.0	23.9
Within 5 Years	5.7	5.7	5.7	5.2
Self-employed	22.0	21.3	3.3	7.9
Wage earner	66.1	68.7	20.7	30.9
Hourly wage (US$)				
Current prices	1.33	1.80	1.24	1.82
1990 pesos		1.11		1.13
1990 dollars		1.37		1.38
N	211,133	265,797	228,964	288,228

Notes: This table shows summary statistics on a 1 percent sample of individuals 16–65 years old in the 1990 and 2000 Mexico *Censo de Poblacio y Vivienda*. Border: Baja California, Chihuahua, Coahuila, Nuevo Leon, Sonora, Tamaulipas; North: Aguascalientes, Baja California Sur, Durango, Nayarit, San Luis Potosí, Sinaloa, Zacatecas; Center: Colima, Guanajuato, Hidalgo, Jalisco, Michoacán, Morelos, Puebla, Queretaro, Tlaxcala, Veracruz; Capital: Federal District, México; South: Chiapas, Guerrero, Oaxaca; Yucatán: Campeche, Tabasco, Quintana Roo, Yucatán.

Table 15.2 Distribution of Employment across Industries

	Males 1990	Males 2000	Females 1990	Females 2000
Agriculture, Mining	28.9	20.7	3.5	4.7
Manufacturing	20.7	20.0	20.5	19.3
Trans., Comm., Elec., Water	6.6	7.7	2.2	2.3
Construction	9.1	11.8	0.9	0.8
Commerce	12.3	14.3	18.9	23.0
Public Administration	3.8	4.2	5.1	4.5
General Services	4.1	6.0	6.5	6.3
Restaurants, Hotels	2.6	3.6	6.2	7.8
Social assistance	5.1	5.1	23.1	16.8
Repair, Domestic services	6.8	6.6	13.1	14.5

Notes: This table shows the allocation of workers across industries. See Table 15.1 for details on the sample.

OLS Wage Regressions, 1990 and 2000

To summarize changes in Mexico's wage structure, I present results from OLS wage regressions. Since most regressors in the estimation are dummy variables, these results summarize the conditional mean of log wages with respect to education, region, industry, and other characteristics. This is a compact way to characterize the returns to observable characteristics at different points in time.

Tables 15.3a and 15.3b present the estimation results for males and females. The dependent variable is log average hourly earnings. The independent variables are dummy variables for 7 categories of education attainment (the excluded category is no schooling), age and age squared, a dummy variable for whether an individual is married, dummy variables for 4 categories of city/locality size (the excluded category is localities with fewer than 2,500 inhabitants), dummy variables for 5 regions (the excluded region is the South), and dummy variables for 9 industries (the excluded sector is agriculture and mining). To reduce the effects of measurement error, I drop observations with the lowest or highest 0.5 percent of wage values.[5] The sample is wage earners twenty-five to sixty-five years old. The tables report results for the full sample and excluding the self-employed. In unreported regressions I find little impact of excluding those who work less than twenty hours per week or of further restricting extreme wage values.

Table 15.3a OLS Wage Regressions, Males in 1990 and 2000

	Full Sample		Without Self-Employed	
Variable	1990	2000	1990	2000
Highest grade of schooling completed				
1 to 4	0.112	0.101	0.092	0.084
	(0.01)	(0.01)	(0.01)	(0.01)
5 to 8	0.255	0.240	0.218	0.213
	(0.01)	(0.01)	(0.01)	(0.01)
9	0.410	0.381	0.373	0.345
	(0.01)	(0.01)	(0.01)	(0.01)
10 to 11	0.553	0.557	0.516	0.516
	(0.01)	(0.02)	(0.02)	(0.02)
12	0.686	0.686	0.643	0.645
	(0.01)	(0.01)	(0.01)	(0.01)
13 to 15	0.873	1.006	0.835	0.983
	(0.02)	(0.02)	(0.02)	(0.02)
16+	1.221	1.352	1.168	1.329
	(0.01)	(0.01)	(0.01)	(0.01)
Age	0.045	0.032	0.042	0.029
	(0.00)	(0.00)	(0.00)	(0.00)
$Age^2/100$	–0.047	–0.033	–0.045	–0.031
	(0.00)	(0.00)	(0.00)	(0.00)
Married	0.095	0.115	0.090	0.112
	(0.01)	(0.01)	(0.01)	(0.01)
Size of locality				
500k+	0.293	0.308	0.238	0.286
	(0.01)	(0.01)	(0.01)	(0.01)
100–500k	0.243	0.251	0.190	0.233
	(0.01)	(0.01)	(0.01)	(0.01)
15–100k	0.235	0.162	0.159	0.151
	(0.01)	(0.01)	(0.01)	(0.01)
2.5–15k	0.164	0.110	0.110	0.10
	(0.01)	(0.01)	(0.01)	(0.01)
Border	0.375	0.460	0.260	0.418
	(0.01)	(0.01)	(0.01)	(0.01)
North	0.281	0.274	0.150	0.229
	(0.01)	(0.01)	(0.01)	(0.01)
Center	0.246	0.225	0.130	0.183
	(0.01)	(0.01)	(0.01)	(0.01)
Capital	0.216	0.215	0.114	0.189
	(0.01)	(0.01)	(0.01)	(0.01)
Yucatán	0.084	0.062	-0.028	0.065
	(0.01)	(0.01)	(0.02)	(0.01)

Continued on next page

Table 15.3a OLS Wage Regressions, Males in 1990 and 2000, continued

	Full Sample		Without Self-Employed	
Variable	1990	2000	1990	2000
Manufacturing	0.292	0.221	0.220	0.196
	(0.01)	(0.01)	(0.01)	(0.01)
Trans., Comm.,	0.328	0.209	0.237	0.172
Elec., Water,	(0.01)	(0.01)	(0.01)	(0.01)
Construction	0.372	0.263	0.277	0.213
	(0.01)	(0.01)	(0.01)	(0.01)
Commerce	0.286	0.134	0.125	0.057
	(0.01)	(0.01)	(0.01)	(0.01)
Public admin.	0.063	0.185	0.033	0.174
	(0.01)	(0.01)	(0.01)	(0.01)
General Services	0.397	0.277	0.268	0.204
	(0.01)	(0.01)	(0.02)	(0.01)
Restaurants,	0.215	0.127	0.050	0.012
Hotels	(0.02)	(0.02)	(0.02)	(0.02)
Social Assistance	0.274	0.375	0.236	0.375
	(0.01)	(0.01)	(0.01)	(0.01)
Repair,	0.305	0.153	0.144	0.066
Domestic services	(0.01)	(0.01)	(0.01)	(0.01)
N	93,999	121,873	67,409	89,778
R^2	0.306	0.418	0.295	0.449

Notes: Standard errors are in parentheses. The sample for the estimation is a 1 percent random sample of individuals 25–65 years old from the 1990 and 2000 Mexico *Censo de Población y Vivienda*. Individuals with wages in the highest or lowest 0.5 percent of wage values have been dropped (see text for details). The first two columns show results for all wage earners. The second two columns show results excluding the self-employed. Sampling weights were used in the 2000 census but not in the 1990 census. Accordingly, the 1990 regressions are unweighted while the 2000 regressions are weighted. See Table 15.1 for other details.

In Table 15.3a, several changes in earnings for males from 1990 to 2000 are apparent. First, there is a sharp increase in the returns to high levels of schooling (but not to low or moderate schooling). The returns to completing 13 to 15 years of schooling (the equivalent of some college) rose by 13.3 log points and the returns to completing 16 or more years of schooling (the equivalent of at least a college education) rose by 13.1 log points. Second, there is a decrease in returns to age. A 30-year-old man received a boost in wages for an extra year of

Table 15.3b OLS Wage Regressions, Females in 1990 and 2000

	Full Sample		Without Self-Employed	
Variable	1990	2000	1990	2000
Highest grade of schooling completed				
1 to 4	0.124	0.172	0.092	0.153
	(0.02)	(0.02)	(0.02)	(0.02)
5 to 8	0.224	0.351	0.188	0.312
	(0.02)	(0.02)	(0.02)	(0.02)
9	0.459	0.542	0.438	0.493
	(0.02)	(0.02)	(0.02)	(0.02)
10 to 11	0.592	0.762	0.575	0.726
	(0.02)	(0.02)	(0.03)	(0.03)
12	0.736	0.865	0.718	0.819
	(0.02)	(0.02)	(0.02)	(0.02)
13 to 15	0.877	1.201	0.856	1.167
	(0.02)	(0.02)	(0.02)	(0.03)
16+	1.089	1.398	1.055	1.351
	(0.02)	(0.02)	(0.02)	(0.02)
Age	0.048	0.045	0.043	0.040
	(0.00)	(0.00)	(0.00)	(0.00)
$Age^2/100$	–0.051	–0.046	–0.045	–0.039
	(0.00)	(0.00)	(0.01)	(0.00)
Married	0.121	0.093	0.108	0.101
	(0.01)	(0.01)	(0.01)	(0.01)
Size of locality				
500k+	0.268	0.319	0.184	0.279
	(0.02)	(0.02)	(0.02)	(0.02)
100–500k	0.227	0.266	0.143	0.230
	(0.02)	(0.02)	(0.02)	(0.02)
15–100k	0.144	0.175	0.052	0.140
	(0.02)	(0.02)	(0.02)	(0.02)
2.5–15k	0.123	0.131	0.039	0.115
	(0.02)	(0.02)	(0.02)	(0.02)
Border	0.277	0.416	0.235	0.347
	(0.02)	(0.02)	(0.02)	(0.02)
North	0.145	0.202	0.096	0.133
	(0.02)	(0.02)	(0.02)	(0.02)
Center	0.104	0.178	0.066	0.118
	(0.02)	(0.02)	(0.02)	(0.02)
Capital	0.179	0.249	0.145	0.199
	(0.02)	(0.02)	(0.02)	(0.02)
Yucatán	0.00	0.160	–0.026	0.102
	(0.03)	(0.02)	(0.03)	(0.02)

Continued on next page

Table 15.3b OLS Wage Regressions, Females in 1990 and 2000, continued

	Full Sample		Without Self-Employed	
Variable	1990	2000	1990	2000
Manufacturing	–0.008	0.003	–0.013	0.01
	(0.02)	(0.02)	(0.02)	(0.02)
Trans., Comm.,	0.178	0.227	0.166	0.204
Elec., Water,	(0.03)	(0.03)	(0.03)	(0.03)
Construction	0.287	0.167	0.229	0.129
	(0.05)	(0.04)	(0.05)	(0.04)
Commerce	0.007	–0.10	–0.091	-0.101
	(0.02)	(0.02)	(0.02)	(0.02)
Public Admin.	–0.052	0.171	–0.053	0.162
	(0.03)	(0.02)	(0.02)	(0.02)
General Services	0.183	0.154	0.136	0.111
	(0.03)	(0.02)	(0.03)	(0.02)
Restaurants,	0.003	–0.018	–0.111	–0.118
Hotels	(0.02)	(0.02)	(0.03)	(0.02)
Social Assistance	0.124	0.310	0.113	0.301
	(0.02)	(0.02)	(0.02)	(0.02)
Repair,	–0.174	–0.135	0.221	–0.162
Domestic services	(0.02)	(0.02)	(0.02)	(0.02)
N	26,583	47,008	21,988	37,066
R^2	0.294	0.475	0.329	0.523

Note: See Table 15.3a for details on the estimation.

age of 1.7 log points in 1990 but only 1.2 log points in 2000. Third, there are changes in regional wage differentials. Between 1990 and 2000, wages in the border region rose by 8.5 log points relative to the southern region, while wages in other regions were stable relative to the South. Fourth, there are changes in interindustry wage differentials. Wages in agriculture, the excluded sector, rose relative to all industries except public administration and social assistance. This may reflect the reform of agriculture. With the breakup of *ejidos*, only relatively high-wage workers may have remained in the sector.

Some results are sensitive to whether or not the self-employed are included in the sample. Excluding the self-employed, wages in all regions except the Yucatan rose relative to the South. The border again showed the largest increase in relative wages.

Table 15.3b shows wage regressions for females. For women, there were increases in returns to education at all levels, with the largest increases occurring at the highest schooling levels. Wages in the South fell relative to wages in all other regions, with the border having the largest wage increases. In contrast to males, females in manufacturing earn relatively low wages. The results for women should be interpreted with caution. The large increase in female labor-force participation in the 1990s suggests that the composition of females in the labor force may have changed over time. Self-selection into work may introduce bias into the estimation for women.

Summary

Wages changes in the 1990s mirrored those in the 1980s. Returns to schooling appeared to rise, the border wage premium rose, and industry wages shifted in favor of agriculture. While manufacturing employment became more concentrated in the border region, the border's share of the national population increased only slightly.

Economic Openness and Changes in Mexico's Wage Structure

In this section, I examine the role that economic openness has played in Mexico's evolving wage structure. To do so, we need to measure shocks to the economy and to define groups of workers that have similar sensitivities to these shocks. Lacking data on individuals over time, I construct a panel of synthetic cohorts. For 1990 and 2000, I calculate average hourly earnings for individuals in the sample and then take mean wages for cells broken down by sex, age, education, and region. I define cells according to four age categories in 1990 (16–25, 26–35, 36–45, and 46–55 years), seven education categories (0–4, 5–8, 9–11, 12, 13–15, and 16-plus years of schooling), and each of Mexico's 32 states. I then track wage changes for the same cohort between 1990 and 2000 (e.g., the change in wages between 26–35-year-old males with 12 years of education in a given state in 1990 and 36–45-year-old males with 12 years of education in the same state in 2000).

Wages Changes for Mexican and U.S. Cohorts

The first exercise is to compare wage changes in Mexico and the United States. Evidence using high-frequency data in Robertson (2001) suggests that Mexico-U.S. wage convergence is occurring. I revisit the issue using long-run time changes. This requires constructing a matching panel of U.S. synthetic cohorts. To do so, I use the 1990 and 2000 Current Population Survey (CPS) for merged outgoing rotation groups. These cohorts are defined for the United States as a whole for the same age and education categories as for their Mexican counterparts. One problem with the CPS is that it does not identify country of birth in 1990. U.S. cohorts thus include both immigrant and native-born workers. This is unfortunate because during the 1990s large numbers of immigrants with low education levels arrived in the United States. Immigration changes the underlying population of individuals from which the CPS sample is drawn, with the change being largest for the cohorts with the lowest education levels.

Table 15.4 summarizes changes in Mexican wages relative to changes in U.S. wages over the 1990s for the panel of synthetic cohorts. All wage changes are weighted by average cohort size in 1990 and 2000. In terms of nominal dollar values, Mexican wages rose relative to U.S. wages by 3.1 log points over the period 1990–2000. But Mexico's small relative nominal gains were swamped by higher relative inflation in Mexico. As a result, Mexico's average real CPI wage fell by 17.3 log points. For mean wages, there thus appears to be no evidence of Mexico-U.S. wage convergence.

Table 15.4 Changes in Mexico-U.S. Relative Wages, 1990–2000

	Males		Females	
	Mean	St. Dev.	Mean	St. Dev.
Change in log wages				
Nominal Mexico wages	0.291	0.205	0.474	0.258
Real Mexico wages (CPI)	–0.190	0.205	–0.006	0.258
Nominal U.S. wages	0.260	0.050	0.300	0.055
Real U.S. wages (CPI)	–0.016	0.050	0.024	0.055
Change in log Mexico/U.S. wages				
Nominal wages	0.031	0.192	0.175	0.242
Real wages (CPI)	–0.173	0.192	–0.030	0.242

Notes: This table shows changes in wages for a panel of synthetic cohorts in Mexico and the United States for two years (1990 and 2000), four 1990 age categories (16–25, 26–35, 36–45, and 46–55 years), seven education categories (0–4, 5–8, 9–11, 12, 13–15, and 16+ years of schooling), and Mexico's 32 states (U.S. cohorts are defined for the nation as a whole). Nominal Mexico and U.S. wages are in current U.S. dollars.

The results in Table 15.4 suggest that there has been substantial variation in wage change across labor-market groups in Mexico. To see this variation more clearly, Table 15.5 breaks out changes in Mexico real wages (CPI deflated) and Mexico-U.S. relative real wages (CPI deflated) for the sample of cohorts by age, education, and region. Real Mexico wages and real Mexico-U.S. wages fall least for younger cohorts. Young women are the only cohort to experience real wage gains both in absolute terms and relative to the United States. Given the data in Tables 15.3a and 15.3b, it is not surprising to see that more-educated workers have higher wage growth. Men with thirteen or more years of education have positive real wage gains, but only males with thirteen to fifteen years of education have real wage gains relative to the United States. Women with twelve or more years of education have real absolute and relative wage gains, and again those with thirteen to fifteen years of education show the strongest gains.

Turning to regions, we see that on average all regions show real absolute and relative wage declines. These declines are smallest in the border region and largest in the south and the Yucatan. In Tables 15.3a and 15.3b, more educated workers and workers in the border region were among those with the highest wages in 1990. The results in Table 15.5 suggest that young, highly educated workers living in the border region had the strongest wage growth during the 1990s. Together, these two findings suggest that there was little wage convergence across labor market groups during the 1990s. This lack of convergence is consistent with Chiquiar's (2001) results on the late 1980s and early 1990s.

Estimation Results on Mexico-U.S. Wage Convergence

To examine the contribution of economic openness to changes in Mexico's wage structure, I estimate regressions of wage changes for the panel of synthetic cohorts. The dependent variable is the 1990–2000 change in log wages by Mexican cohort. The independent variables are drawn from the following set: the 1990 log wage for the Mexican cohort; the 1990 log wage for the same age-education U.S. cohort; the 1990–2000 change in log wages for the U.S. cohort; dummies variables for age, education level, and region; and measures of regional exposure to globalization.

I begin by replicating the specification in Robertson (2000), in which the independent variables are the log difference in lagged Mexico and U.S. wages and the log change in U.S. wages. He allows regression coefficients to differ between border and interior regions in order

Table 15.5 Change in Log Real CPI Wages, 1990–2000

Real CPI Wages	Age in 1990	Males	Females	Years of Education	Males	Females	Region	Males	Females
Mexico	16–25	–0.125	0.087	4	–0.341	–0.233	Border	–0.053	0.081
Mex/U.S.		–0.113	0.020		–0.288	–0.204		–0.041	0.052
Mexico	26–35	–0.182	–0.031	5–8	–0.225	–0.037	North	–0.187	0.043
Mex/U.S.		–0.157	–0.029		–0.204	–0.055		–0.170	0.016
Mexico	36–45	–0.292	–0.150	9–11	–0.141	–0.003	Center	–0.222	–0.042
Mex/U.S.		–0.282	–0.132		–0.132	–0.050		–0.202	–0.065
Mexico	46–55	–0.373	–0.303	12	–0.083	0.043	Capital	–0.193	–0.013
Mex/U.S.		–0.311	–0.308		–0.076	0.009		–0.183	–0.040
Mexico				13–15	0.105	0.258	Yucatán	–0.273	0.023
Mex/U.S.					0.118	0.274		–0.252	–0.001
Mexico				16+	0.021	0.129	South	–0.312	–0.142
Mex/U.S.					–0.067	0.045		–0.285	–0.156

Notes: This table shows the mean change in real CPI wages for Mexico and for Mexico relative to the U.S. by age, schooling, and region of Mexico. The sample is the panel of synthetic cohorts. See Table 15.4 for details.

to capture possibly stronger links between Mexican and U.S. labor markets for Mexican regions closer to the United States. Similarly, I interact regressors with a dummy variable for border states.

Table 15.6a reports the regression results for males and Table 15.6b reports the regression results for females. In column 1 of Table 15.6a, the regressors are the 1990 difference in log Mexico and U.S. wages, the 1990–2000 change in log U.S. wages, the interactions of the wage variables with the border dummy, and region dummy variables. The coefficient on the 1990 difference in Mexico-U.S. wages indicates whether there is wage convergence between Mexico and the United States. In column 1, this coefficient is negative, small in magnitude, and imprecisely estimated. However, the interaction between this wage variable and the border dummy is negative and precisely estimated. For border states, but not for interior states, wage growth is higher for cohorts where initial Mexico wages are lower relative to U.S. wages. This is consistent with convergence between Mexico and U.S. wages in Mexican border states.

There is a strong positive correlation between wage growth in Mexico and wage growth in the United States. The precisely estimated coefficient of 1.3 indicates that Mexican wages increase more than one for one with increases in U.S. wages. This is consistent with labor markets in Mexico and the United States being integrated, through some combination of trade, investment, and migration flows. The border interaction with this variable is positive, though imprecisely estimated, showing weak evidence that Mexico-U.S. integration is stronger in border states than in interior states.

The large coefficient on U.S. wage growth is surprising and invites skepticism. One concern about the specification in column 1 is that by forcing the coefficients on 1990 Mexico wages and 1990 U.S. wages to be equal and of opposite sign we are possibly convoluting Mexico-U.S. wage convergence with convergence or divergence in wages across Mexican cohorts. To address this issue, in column 2 I add the 1990 log Mexico wage, and its interaction with the border dummy, as regressors. It is now the case that the coefficients on the difference in 1990 Mexico-U.S. wages and the border interaction with this variable are statistically insignificant. This is evidence against Mexico-U.S. wage convergence. The coefficient on 1990 Mexico wages is positive and precisely estimated and the border interaction with this variable is negative and precisely estimated. What this suggests is that during the 1990s interior regions had higher wage growth for cohorts with higher initial wages.

Table 15.6a Change in Log Wages 1990–2000 for Synthetic Cohorts, Males

$W^{90,MX}/W^{90,US}$	–0.027	–0.133	–0.015	–0.027
	(0.06)	(0.07)	(0.22)	(0.17)
$W^{00,US}/W^{90,US}$	1.276	1.202	–0.046	–0.132
	(0.18)	(0.18)	(0.34)	(0.27)
$(W^{90,MX}/W^{90,US})$*Border	–0.221	–0.067	0.05	0.008
	(0.09)	(0.10)	(0.08)	(0.09)
$(W^{00,US}/W^{90,US})$*Border	0.446	0.538	0.175	0.186
	(0.31)	(0.31)	(0.25)	(0.23)
Border	–0.256	0.033	0.391	0.099
	(0.21)	(0.23)	(0.18)	(0.19)
North	0.106	0.106	0.143	0.05
	(0.05)	(0.05)	(0.03)	(0.04)
Center	0.071	0.072	0.108	0.052
	(0.04)	(0.04)	(0.03)	(0.04)
Capital	0.105	0.098	0.122	–0.022
	(0.04)	(0.04)	(0.03)	(0.04)
Yucatán	0.006	0.005	0.003	–0.015
	(0.05)	(0.05)	(0.04)	(0.04)
$W^{90,MX}$		0.096	–0.277	–0.374
		(0.03)	(0.22)	(0.18)
$(W^{90,MX})$*border		–0.139	–0.148	–0.133
		(0.05)	(0.04)	(0.04)
Age cohort 26–35			–0.031	–0.014
			(0.06)	(0.05)
Age cohort 36–45			–0.064	–0.032
			(0.09)	(0.08)
Age cohort 46–55			–0.099	–0.069
			(0.09)	(0.08)
Grades 5–8			0.129	0.143
			(0.04)	(0.03)
Grades 9–11			0.232	0.264
			(0.05)	(0.04)
Grade 12			0.398	0.450
			(0.11)	(0.09)
Grade 13–15			0.631	0.697
			(0.13)	(0.11)
Grade 16			0.708	0.818
			(0.23)	(0.18)
State GDP growth 1993–99				0.143
				(0.14)
Mfg. share of state GDP 1993–99				0.009
				(0.16)
Agr. share of state GDP 1993–99				–0.159
				(0.32)

Continued on next page

Table 15.6a Change in Log Wages 1990–2000 for Synthetic Cohorts, Males, continued

FDI share of state GDP 1994–99				2.821
				(1.12)
State share of *maquila* employment				0.147
				(0.16)
Import share of state GDP 1993–99				1.506
				(0.75)
Km. to U.S. border				–0.014
				(0.01)
State-U.S. migration rate 1955–59				3.281
				(0.46)
N	728	728	728	728
R^2	0.239	0.254	0.595	0.667

Notes: This table shows regressions using as the dependent variable the 1990–2000 change in log wages for synthetic age-education-state cohorts of males in Mexico. Standard errors are in parentheses. All wage measures are in logs as is GDP used to calculate the 1993–99 change in the variable. All share measures are entered in levels. See Table 15.5 for more details on the age and education definitions for the cohorts.

In other words, there was wage divergence in interior regions, but not in the border region. This evidence of growing wage dispersion is not surprising, given the rising returns to skill evident in Table 15.3. Overall, evidence of Mexico-U.S. wage convergence appears to be fragile. This confirms the impression from mean relative wage changes in Table 15.4.

In column 3 of Table 15.6a I examine the sensitivity of changes in Mexico wages to changes in U.S. wages by adding dummy variables for three age categories (16–24 years of age is the excluded category) and dummy variables for five education categories (0–4 years of schooling is the excluded category) to the regression. The dummy variables for age are individually and jointly statistically insignificant. After controlling for education and U.S. cohort wage changes, there appear to be no age specific wage changes in Mexico. The dummy variables for education are positive and precisely estimated, with larger magnitudes for higher education levels that suggest rising returns to schooling.

With controls for age and education included, the coefficient on U.S. wage changes becomes small and imprecisely estimated. Since U.S. wages vary only by age and education, the only variation left in U.S. wage changes after including age and education dummies are age-specific changes in the returns to education. The results suggest that it is the commonality in overall changes in returns to education that account for the strong positive correlation between Mexico and U.S. wage changes. These results are not evidence against Mexico-U.S. labor market integration. Instead, they imply that the mechanisms that link wages in Mexico and the United States (be they trade, FDI, and/or migration) work through broad changes in the returns to education.

Estimation Results for Regional Exposure to Globalization

In column 4 of Table 15.6a, I add controls for regional exposure to globalization to the specification. To control for regional variation in business cycles, I also include the log change in state real GDP as a regressor. I include six measures of regional exposure to foreign trade and investment. The share of manufacturing in state GDP and the share of agriculture in state GDP control for variation across regions in industrial specialization in traded goods. The share of net foreign direct investment flows in state GDP controls for how attractive the state is to multinational enterprises. The state share of national *maquiladora* employment controls for the attractiveness of the state to foreign firms that specialize in export assembly operations. Some but not all FDI is in *maquiladoras*. Imports as a share of state GDP capture the exposure of the state to foreign trade (similar measures for exports are unavailable). Distance to the United States (nearest U.S. border crossing) captures physical proximity to U.S. markets.

Several estimation issues merit comment. Most globalization variables are in terms of shares averaged over the 1990s, rather than as changes in shares, to avoid introducing simultaneity into the regression. Average shares of FDI, imports, manufacturing, or agriculture in GDP capture cross-sectional differences in regional exposure to globalization. Changes in shares would capture state-specific globalization shocks that might be correlated with unobserved shocks to wages. By regressing changes in wages on average cross-sectional characteristics, I capture transitional dynamics in state wages associated with adjustment to NAFTA (and other shocks). Results are similar when shares in the initial period are used instead of average shares.

I include one measure of regional opportunities to migrate to the United States. Some background is helpful to understand this measure. A large literature documents that some Mexican states are more likely than others to send migrants to the United States and have been for many decades (e.g., Woodruff and Zenteno 2001). These states are mostly in agricultural regions in western Mexico. They are neither the poorest states in the country nor those that are closest to the United States. Most research attributes these migration patterns to longstanding regional networks that help Mexican workers find jobs in the United States. The persistence of these migration networks suggests that historical migration flows are a good indicator of current regional opportunities for migration abroad. The measure I use is the share of the 1960 state population that migrated to the United States over the period 1955–59. I obtain similar results for current migration flows.[6] Historical measures reduce concerns about endogeneity.

Column 4 of Table 15.6a reports the results. Wage changes are uncorrelated with the share of state GDP in manufacturing or in agriculture. It appears that industrial specialization (at least measured at this aggregate level) is not associated with changes in regional wage differences. Mexican regions with larger manufacturing sectors do have higher wage levels but did not enjoy higher wage growth in the 1990s.

There are strong positive correlations between wage growth and the share of FDI and between wage growth the share of imports in state GDP. It appears that states with greater exposure to multinational firms and/or greater exposure to foreign trade enjoyed higher wage growth in the 1990s. This suggests, perhaps not surprisingly, that regions with better access to global markets for goods and capital had larger increases in the demand for labor during the 1990s. The correlation between wage changes and the state share of national *maquiladora* employment is positive but statistically insignificant. What this may suggest is that, controlling for FDI inflows (and for state proximity to the United States), there is nothing special about a state having a particular concentration in export assembly operations. What matters is overall access to foreign capital.

There is a strong positive correlation between wage changes and historical state migration rates to the United States. States with better opportunities for migration abroad had higher wage growth during the 1990s. This suggests that migration abroad put upward pressure on wages in the region from which workers were drawn.

Regional exposure to globalization appears to account for a large portion of regional wage differentials. To see this clearly, compare results in columns 3 and 4 of Table 15.6a. The regression in column 3 includes controls for age, education, lagged Mexico and U.S. wages, and U.S. wage growth. In this regression coefficients on regional dummy variables are large and statistically significant. When I introduce the globalization measures in column 4 the magnitudes of these coefficients fall considerably and they become individually and jointly statistically insignificant. The regional characteristics that matter for wage in Mexico during the 1990s appear to be those related to regional exposure to foreign trade, investment, and migration.

The results for females are shown in Table 5.6b. With a few exceptions, the results for males and females are similar. For females, there remains the concern that changes in their labor-force participation may complicate analysis of their wage changes. For women, there is stronger evidence of wage convergence between Mexico and the United States (columns 1 and 2). For women, as for men, there is evidence of wage divergence in interior regions of the country, a strong positive correlation between Mexican wage growth and U.S. wage growth, and strong positive correlations between wage growth and the share of FDI in state GDP and historical state migration rates to the United States. There is no positive correlation between wage growth and the import share of GDP, as there is for men. Also in distinction from men, the globalization variables do not render regional dummy variables statistically insignificant.

For males and females, I have estimated alternative specifications to gauge the robustness of the findings. The results on the globalization variables are robust to: allowing for interactions between returns to schooling and either border dummies or distance to the United States, using as the dependent variable changes in Mexico wages minus changes in U.S. wages, and measuring U.S. wages using data on the four U.S. border states only rather than data for the U.S. as a whole.

Implications of Mexico's Experience for an FTAA

In this chapter I have surveyed recent literature on the impact of trade and investment liberalization in Mexico on wages in the country and examined recent changes in the country's wage structure. Over the last two decades, Mexico has dramatically opened its economy to the rest of the world. During this period, Mexico has experienced three significant changes in its wage structure: overall wage levels have had large temporary declines, usually following a macroeconomic contraction; wages in states on the Mexico-U.S. border have increased relative to wages in the rest of the country; and there has been a sustained increase in the returns to skill in the country, leading to an overall increase in wage inequality.

Table 15.6b Change in Log Wages 1990–2000 for Synthetic Cohorts, Females

$W^{90,MX}/W^{90,US}$	–0.452	–0.80	–0.237	–0.23
	(0.05)	(0.08)	(0.25)	(0.23)
$W^{00,US}/W^{90,US}$	1.972	2.046	0.256	0.266
	(0.24)	(0.23)	(0.30)	(0.28)
$(W^{90,MX}/W^{90,US})$*border	–0.181	0.054	0.216	0.092
	(0.10)	(0.13)	(0.11)	(0.11)
$(W^{00,US}/W^{90,US})$*border	–0.689	–0.683	–0.547	–0.62
	(0.41)	(0.40)	(0.35)	(0.32)
Border	0.234	0.669	0.90	0.611
	(0.21)	(0.24)	(0.21)	(0.21)
North	0.190	0.191	0.172	0.097
	(0.04)	(0.04)	(0.04)	(0.05)
Center	0.116	0.124	0.130	0.118
	(0.04)	(0.04)	(0.03)	(0.05)
Capital	0.198	0.199	0.211	0.119
	(0.05)	(0.04)	(0.03)	(0.06)
Yucatán	0.154	0.149	0.133	0.163
	(0.06)	(0.06)	(0.04)	(0.05)
$W^{90,MX}$		0.269	–0.471	–0.516
		(0.04)	(0.25)	(0.24)
$(W^{90,MX})$*Border		–0.167	–0.173	–0.156
		(0.07)	(0.05)	(0.05)
Age cohort 26–35			0.011	0.029
			(0.06)	(0.06)
Age cohort 36–45			0.023	0.044
			(0.08)	(0.07)
Age cohort 46–55			–0.069	–0.048
			(0.08)	(0.08)
Grades 5–8			0.209	0.211
			(0.03)	(0.03)
Grades 9–11			0.361	0.373
			(0.04)	(0.04)
Grade 12			0.570	0.590
			(0.10)	(0.10)
Grade 13–15			0.870	0.897
			(0.14)	(0.13)
Grade 16			0.893	0.925
			(0.22)	(0.21)
State GDP growth 1993–99				–0.069
				(0.19)
Mfg. share of state GDP 1993–99				–0.02
				(0.20)
Agr. share of state GDP 1993–99				0.459
				(0.40)

Continued on next page

Table 15.6b Change in Log Wages 1990–2000 for Synthetic Cohorts, Females, continued

FDI share of state GDP 1994–99				4.208
				(1.38)
State share of *maquila* employment				0.211
				(0.21)
Import share of state GDP 1993–99				–0.326
				(0.90)
Km. to U.S. border				0.011
				(0.02)
State-U.S. migration rate 1955–59				2.287
				(0.73)
N	702	702	702	702
R^2	0.311	0.375	0.624	0.649

Notes: See notes to Table 15.6a.

The breadth of Mexico's reforms complicates the task of identifying their effects on labor markets in the country. Compounding these problems are the effects of Mexico's recent macroeconomic instability. Nevertheless, a number of important lessons emerge from Mexico's experience for how economic integration with other countries, and in particular with a large, rich neighbor, impacts labor markets in a developing country. These lessons are useful for gauging how an FTAA might affect other Latin American countries.

The liberalization of barriers to foreign trade and investment appears to have contributed to an increase in the relative demand for skill in Mexico. Recent literature suggests that tariff reductions increased relative wages for skilled workers, increased foreign investment raised the relative demand for skilled labor, and tariff and quota reductions altered interindustry wage differentials. Mexico's economic opening thus appears to have raised the premium paid to skilled workers and reduced rents in industries that prior to reform paid their workers relatively high wages. Both of these outcomes have increased wage dispersion in the country.

One factor that contributed to how trade affected wages in Mexico was that, prior to trade reform, the country had relatively high tariffs on less-skill-intensive industries. These industries thus bore the brunt of adjustment to Mexico's economic opening. Similar tariff adjustments following an FTAA are unlikely to be a common occurrence in the rest of Latin America. One reason for this is that many countries have already engaged in some degree of unilateral trade liberalization. Columbia, for instance, reduced its trade barriers in the early 1990s. As in Mexico, trade reform in Columbia led to larger tariff reductions in less-skill-intensive industries (Goldberg and Pavcnik 2001). Thus, the shock of trade reform related to tariff reductions in low-skill industries may have already been delivered in many Latin American countries.

In the 1990s Mexico consolidated its economic opening by signing and enacting NAFTA. The decade saw further increases in the premium paid to workers in Mexican states on the U.S. border and in the premium paid to more-skilled workers. Following Mexico's peso crisis of 1994–95, real wage levels declined both in absolute terms and relative to the United States. Increases in the returns to education during the 1990s in Mexico were nationwide and appeared to follow closely increases in the returns to education in the United States. Partial labor-market integration between Mexico and the United States is a likely explanation for these cross-border wage comovements. Changes in regional wage differentials in Mexico appear to be explained almost entirely by regional variation in exposure to foreign markets. Wage growth has been much stronger in regions with higher levels of FDI, higher levels of exposure to foreign trade, and higher rates of migration to the United States.

Overall, the workers in Mexico who have fared the best in the country's newly globalized economy are those with relatively high skill levels living in regions with relatively good access to foreign markets. Less-skilled workers and workers in regions with relatively poor access to foreign markets have fared poorly. This aspect of Mexico's experience with globalization holds important lessons for an FTAA. Multinational firms and firms in export-intensive sectors appear to have relatively strong demand for more-skilled labor and appear to place a premium on locating in regions with relatively high-quality transportation and communication infrastructure. In Mexico, NAFTA appeared to fortify incentives for FDI. If an FTAA does the same in the rest of Latin America, it is likely to be skilled workers who benefit first, and in particular those living in larger cities or near international ports or airports. At least in the initial periods of adjustment to trade reform, the effects of greater economic openness appear to be greater dispersion in wages (with unknown effects on average wage levels). This is an unfortunate message for a region with already high levels of inequality.

A related lesson from Mexico's adjustment to NAFTA is that FDI appears to play an important role in shaping the pattern of specialization that emerges in an economy following a reduction in trade barriers. Much of Mexico's export growth has occurred in *maquiladoras*, whose expansion was made possible by a combination of lower trade barriers and relaxed restrictions on FDI in Mexico and tariff breaks on imports with U.S. content in the United States. If an FTAA does not also address restrictions on FDI in Latin America, it may not produce the same degree of regional specialization in export production that NAFTA has generated in Mexico.

References

Aitken, Brian, Ann E. Harrison, and Robert E. Lipsey. 1996. "Wages and Foreign Ownership: A Comparative Study of Mexico, Venezuela, and the United States." *Journal of International Economics* 40 (3–4): 345–71.

Bell, Linda A. 1997. "The Impact of Minimum Wages in Mexico and Columbia." *Journal of Labor Economics* 15 (3): S102–35.

Chiquiar, Daniel. 2001. "Regional Implications of Mexico's Trade Liberalization." University of California San Diego. Photocopy.

Cragg, Michael I., and Mario Epelbaum. 1996. "The Premium for Skills in LDCs: Evidence from Mexico." *Journal of Development Economics* 51 (1): 99–116.

Fairris, David H. 2002. "Unions and Wage Inequality in Mexico." *Industrial and Labor Relations Review* 56 (3) (April): 481–97.

Feenstra, Robert C., and Gordon H. Hanson. 1997. "Foreign Direct Investment and Relative Wages: Evidence from Mexico's *Maquiladoras*." *Journal of International Economics* 42 (3–4): 371–94.

Feliciano, Zadia. 1998. "Does the Minimum Wage Affect Employment in Mexico?" *Eastern Economic Journal* 24 (2): 165–80.

———. 2001. "Workers and Trade Liberalization: The Impact of Trade Reforms in Mexico on Wages and Employment." *Industrial and Labor Relations Review* 55 (1): 95–115.

Goldberg, Pinelopi K., and Nina Pavcnik. 2001. "Trade Protection and Wages: Evidence from the Colombian Trade Reforms." National Bureau of Economic Research Working Paper no. 8575, Cambridge, MA.

Hanson, Gordon H. 1996. "Localization Economies, Vertical Organization, and Trade." *American Economic Review* 86 (5): 1266–78.

———. 1997. "Increasing Returns, Trade, and the Regional Structure of Wages." *Economic Journal* 107 (440): 113–33.

Hanson, Gordon H., and Ann E. Harrison. 1999. "Trade, Technology, and Wage Inequality in Mexico." *Industrial and Labor Relations Review* 52 (2): 271–88.

Leamer, Edward E. 1993. "Wage Effects of a U.S.-Mexico Free Trade Agreement." In *The Mexico-U.S. Free Trade Agreement*, edited by P. M. Garber. Cambridge, MA: MIT Press.

Marcouiller, Douglas, Veronica Ruiz de Castilla, and Christopher Woodruff. 1997. "Formal Measures of the Informal Sector Wage Gap in Mexico, El Salvador and Peru." *Economic Development and Cultural Change* 45 (2): 367–92.

Revenga, Ana L. 1997. "Employment and Wage Effects of Trade Liberalization: The Case of Mexican Manufacturing." *Journal of Labor Economics* 15 (3): S20–43.

Revenga, Ana L., and Claudia Montenegro. 1998. "North American Integration and Factor Price Equalization: Is There Evidence of Wage Convergence between Mexico and the United States?" In *Imports, Exports, and the American Worker*, edited by Susan Collins. Washington, DC: Brookings Institution Press.

Robertson, Raymond. 2000. "Wage Shocks and North American Labor Market Integration." *American Economic Review* 90 (4): 742–64.

———. 2001. "Relative Prices and Wage Inequality: Evidence from Mexico." Macalester College. Photocopy.

Robbins, Donald. 1995. "Trade, Trade Liberalization, and Inequality in Latin America and East Asia: Synthesis of Seven Country Studies." Harvard Institute for International Development, Cambridge, MA. Photocopy.

Stolper, Wolfgang, and Paul A. Samuelson. 1941. "Protection and Real Wages." *Review of Economic Studies* 9 (1): 51–68.

Woodruff, Christopher. 1999. "Inflation Stabilization and the Vanishing Size-Wage Effect." *Industrial and Labor Relations Review* 53 (1): 103–22.

Woodruff, Christopher, and Rene M. Zenteno. 2001. "Remittances and Microenterprises in Mexico." University of California San Diego. Photocopy.

Notes

I thank Daniel Chiquiar, Antoni Estevadeordal, Bill Maloney, Pablo Sanguinetti, Alan Taylor, and participants at the "FTAA and Beyond" conferences at Harvard and Punta del Este, Uruguay, for helpful comments.

1 See Robbins (1995) for a cross-country comparison of changes in wage inequality following trade reform.

2 Most *maquiladoras* assemble one of three types of goods: apparel, electronics, or auto parts. In 1995, these three industries accounted for 80.5 percent of total exports by *maquiladoras* to the United States.

3 It is often asserted that the growth of *maquiladoras* was the result of special trade advantages afforded to goods produced by these plants on their entry into the United States. Tariffs are levied only on the value added abroad (i.e., in Mexico) and not on the value of the U.S. inputs used in the assembly of the goods. Mexican firms that use domestically produced inputs enjoy no such advantage. An alternative view is that *maquiladoras* have expanded in part because Mexico, given its relative abundance of low-wage labor, has a comparative advantage in assembly-type activities (rather than in entire industries). Since NAFTA was implemented in 1994, *maquiladoras* have lost their special trade advantages in most industries. Yet, until 2000 *maquiladoras* continued to grow faster than any other sector in the economy. This suggests that their initial trade advantages relative to other firms in Mexico cannot fully account for their growth.

4 There is also evidence that other reforms affected Mexico's labor market. During the 1980's, real minimum wages declined substantially. Bell (1997) finds that this didn't affect formal-sector employment due to low initial minimum wages and noncompliance with minimum wage laws (see Feliciano [1998] for evidence of stronger minimum-wage effects). Woodruff (1999) finds that government encouragement of wage restraints to combat inflation in the late 1980s had a larger impact on large firms than on small firms, leading to a disappearance of the employer-size wage effect. Fairris (2002) finds that during the late 1980s and early 1990s the observed increase in wage dispersion in Mexico was larger in the unionized sector (though lower in this sector to begin with), perhaps indicating a decline in union bargaining power.

5 The 1990 sample has a large number of observations with very low hourly wages. To account for what appears to be more severe measurement error in 1990, I first drop observations (3,031 in total) with wages below $0.006 dollars per hour, for which there is zero mass in the 2000 sample, and then trim the 1 percent tails.

6 As one indication of this, the correlation between the shares of the state population that migrated to the United States over the period 1995–2000 and over the period 1955–59 is 0.68.

16

Can an FTAA Suspend the Law of Gravity and Give the Americas Higher Growth and Better Income Distributions?

Bernardo S. Blum and Edward E. Leamer

Introduction

In this Chapter we explore three related ideas:

1. The *export sector* is the fundamental source of both wealth and inequality: You are what you export. Exporting manufactures has been essential for high incomes and low levels of inequality. Exporting crops and raw materials is associated with low incomes and unequal income distributions.

2. The mix of exports is determined by three fundamental factors: *resources*, *remoteness*, and *climate*. Manufacturing industries are suited to cool climates, an educated workforce, and locations close to the high-wage marketplaces of Europe and North America.

3. The *volume* of exports and the wealth formation that comes from the export sector can be impeded by inward looking, isolationist policies. Governments can affect the export mix only slightly, and mostly through policies that alter the effects of the fundamental drivers, for example, by encouraging the formation of institutions that make a country effectively closer to global marketplaces.

By focusing on these framework concepts, the Free Trade Area of the Americas (FTAA) agreement can have two effects. It can set free the fundamental determinants of exports (resources, location, and climate) and allow the participating countries to become "all they are capable of being." This is not necessarily entirely good news for Latin

America, whose abundant resources, far-away locations, and tropical climates tend to support relatively low per capita incomes and unequal income distributions. But, more optimistically, the FTAA may also bring Latin America closer to global GDP, both by supporting higher per capita GDPs in the region (thus lifting the region by its own bootstraps), and also by the creation of institutions that have the effect of making Latin America closer to the high-wage marketplaces of North America.

The first part of this chapter presents our view about the fundamental determinants of wealth and inequality. In the second part we assemble a body of evidence, much of which suggests that far-away, resource-abundant, tropical countries have great difficulties attracting manufacturing activities other than mundane and labor-intensive tasks such as sewing hems on tee shirts. Communities that attract neither the human-capital-intensive tasks in manufacturing nor the human-capital-intensive tasks in the services of the postindustrial age (e.g., digital entertainment and financial management and business consulting) are destined to have low per capita incomes and uncomfortable levels of inequality. To assemble the evidence, we have cast our data net broadly and use a comprehensive dataset including countries' trade, outputs, inequality, production resources, climate, and location. Finally, in the third section, we use the framework and the evidence to offer an opinion regarding what impacts an FTAA agreement may have on export patterns, income, and inequality in the region.

We find in the data considerable support for the argument that exports are symptoms of the process of wealth accumulation and distribution. Exporters of machinery and chemicals tend to have high per capita incomes while exporters of tropical agriculture have per capita incomes that are on average more than 80 percent lower. Moreover, because exporters of machinery and chemicals have a large fraction of their wealth invested in human capital, their incomes are generally equally distributed, while exporters of agriculture and natural resources have incomes that are quite concentrated. The data also support the idea that location, resources, and climates are key exogenous determinants of the export composition of the countries. Capital-intensive manufacturing activities, for example, are not performed in hot climates or in remote parts of the globe.

We thus offer a fundamental explanation for the economic dilemma facing the region. With respect to the possible effects of an

FTAA agreement on incomes and inequality, our analyses indicate that a substantial impact should not be expected. Even though the removal of the existing trade impediments should bring the region "closer" to the world markets, most of the countries in the region will still be too far away to be able to perform the complex tasks that are associated with high incomes and equality, and clearly an agreement would have no impact on climates.

We are certainly not the first to propose a link between physical geography and economic development. References about such a possibility date back at least to Machiavelli (1519). Gallup, Sachs, and Mellinger (1998) indicate four major areas where it has been suggested that physical geography may have a direct impact on economic productivity: transport cost, human health, agricultural productivity, and proximity and ownership of natural resources. In that publication, as well as in Sachs (2001), empirical evidence is provided to support the argument that geography indeed has direct, as well as indirect, effects on economic development. Hall and Jones (1999) and Engerman and Sokoloff (1997) propose additional ways in which physical geography may affect economic development by shaping countries' institutions. Acemoglu, Johnson, and Robinson (2001), Rodrik, Subramanian, and Trebbi (2002), and Easterly and Levine (2002) go one step further, suggesting that, once controlled for the effects through institutions, geography has no direct impact on economic development. However, McArthur and Sachs (2001) show that the results in Acemoglu et al. (2001) are not robust to increases in the sample of countries used in the analyses.

This literature misses, we suggest, the two primary mechanisms that make geography so important. First, as explained in Leamer (2001), the fixed costs of expensive capital equipment need to be covered by operating the equipment at high pace for long hours. This creates a distinct disadvantage for the tropics. Second, as explained in Leamer and Storper (2001), the exchange of complex, uncodifiable messages can only be done on a face-to-face basis among participants who are within a handshake of each other. Vast improvements in transportation and communication technologies over the last half-century, which might have rendered geography less relevant, have not done so, since these technologies have not improved the long-distance exchange of ideas and commitments. Thus the production of the ideas and the production of the new products remain tightly clustered, leaving much of manufacturing firmly "rooted" where it is—in the United States and Europe. Apparel and footwear are footloose; machinery and pharmaceuticals are not.[1]

The Process of Wealth Creation and Distribution

Exports Are the Most Important Source of Wealth and Inequality

Wealth is primarily generated by exports. This is not true universally, since so far the moon has been a recipient of very few exports. It is true for individuals in advanced developed countries, who, because of a very fine division of labor, "export" almost 100 percent of what they produce. (How much economics does an economics professor consume?) Between the earth and the individual are a very few large countries, which, like the earth overall, experience internally driven growth. A prominent example is the United States during the Internet rush from 1997 to 2000, when growth was driven internally by a mad dash for the World Wide Web. But most countries are more like individuals than the earth. Their production structures are specialized and their growth comes from efficiently expanding the activities they are good at and exporting the surplus to the rest of the world.

Compensation for various kinds of inputs varies greatly and depends on the export mix. Raw labor power and human capital are widely owned, but where human capital is poorly rewarded compared with other capital assets, ownership of the most important productive inputs tends to be concentrated. Thus, if we know what a community exports and why, we are 90 percent of the way toward understanding its per capita income and its levels of inequality.

Table 16.1 offers a classification of exports that is intended to capture our ideas about wealth and inequality. The table identifies eight different categories of exports in which communities might specialize and the kinds of capital and other assets needed to produce these items. There are five broad groups of products and services: products made with raw labor only, primary products and crops, distribution services, manufactures, and intellectual services. The inputs needed to produce these items fall into the three usual, broad categories of land, labor, and capital. Land includes the usual mineral resources and fertile cropland, but also location (closeness to sources of inputs and closeness to markets). The raw labor inputs are physical and mental exertions. Capital takes the form of equipment, skills, knowledge, experience, reputation, and human networks, the latter being critical inputs into the activities of distribution, finance, and the creation of ideas and content (e.g., Hollywood).

The last two columns in Table 16.1 indicate the level of incomes and inequality that are typically associated with communities that specialize in these activities. Inequality is determined largely by the ownership of the productive inputs. Of these assets, only the human skills that are created by training are broadly owned and only communities with heavily skill-based economies have equal incomes. The latter means manufacturing. In contrast, land, physical capital, and human ability are assets with concentrated ownership. Thus countries that export primary products, crops, ideas, and content have unequal incomes.

Wealth and Inequality in Resource-Based, Industrial, and Postindustrial Communities.

In the schema in Table 16.1, natural resources support three kinds of activities: extracting/growing, processing, and distribution. In the extracting/growing economies, capital is embodied in permanent crops (coffee plantations); cleared, irrigated, and otherwise improved land; transportation systems; and housing. These activities require very little human capital, and wealth comes from an abundance of natural resources. Income inequality is then determined by the distribution of ownership of the natural resources, which is usually highly unequal. Human capital plays a greater role at distribution centers and processing locations, which often are close to the natural resource. At these distribution locations, incomes are often higher and more equally distributed.

Global trade prior to the industrial revolution consisted largely of the exchange of handicrafts, raw materials, foodstuffs, and distribution services. With the dawn of the industrial age, the nature of global trade shifted to manufactured products, led by textiles, footwear, and apparel. While much of manufacturing capital, even at the beginning of the twentieth century, was structures, the shift in favor of equipment has been very substantial. In the investment boom of the 1990s, the ratio of investment in producer durables and software relative to structures rose to a record high of three to one.

The operation of equipment requires human capital, and most capital in the industrial communities is embodied in equipment and humans skills. Ownership of the equipment can be and often is highly

Table 16.1 Export Classifications

Export Group	Export Example	Capital Assets	Other Assets	Incomes	Inequality
Products of unskilled labor					
1 Handmade goods	Handicrafts, handmade textiles	None		Low	Low
Natural resource based					
Primary products and crops					
2 Raw materials and crops	Coffee beans, logs	Permanent crops, equipment	Land	Low	High
Distribution					
3 Distribution services	Shipping, warehousing	Distribution networks, infrastructure	Location	Moderate	Moderate
Manufacturing and food/ Resource processing					
4 Footloose manufacturing	Apparel, footwear	Equipment, skills		Medium	Low
5 Processing	Food products, lumber, paper	Equipment, skills	Closeness to inputs	Medium	Low
6 Noncodifiable manufactures	Pharmaceuticals	Equipment, knowledge	Agglomerations	High	Moderate
Intellectual services					
7 Financial services	Investment banking	Trust networks	Instincts	High	Moderate
8 Ideas and content	R&D, entertainment, marketing, design	Experience, reputation, idea networks	Ability	High	High

concentrated, as is the ownership of natural resources. Ownership of human skills, however, by its essential nature, is necessarily broad. The equipment of the industrial age, such as a forklift, requires trainable skills that depend very little on native ability. Thus on the factory floor the return on human-capital investment is high and pretty much the same for everyone.

If it does not matter much who operates a forklift, it matters greatly who types on a computer keyboard. Thus, like the industrial age, the postindustrial age has services produced with a combination of equipment (e.g., recording studios) and human capital (e.g., singing skills). While manufacturing requires trainable skills, the postindustrial activities of finance and innovation require knowledge and understanding. Unlike the industrial age, in the postindustrial age the rate of return to investments in human capital varies greatly from individual to individual. This brings with it a concentration of capital in the hands of the few and inequality levels that are reminiscent of the preindustrial age.

In the Industrial Age, Wealth Has Come Especially from Exporting Manufactures

Not all countries are equally well suited to compete in manufacturing, and some countries in the industrial age remain suppliers of raw materials and foodstuffs. These activities have not been technologically stagnant. On the contrary, both agriculture and resource extraction have experienced an increase in mechanization that closely parallels progress in manufacturing.

Mechanization of agriculture and raw-materials extraction is both similar to and different from mechanization of manufacturing activities. It is similar in the sense that it puts into the hands of workers expensive equipment that needs to be operated for long hours at high pace to cover capital costs. This creates high-effort, high-wage opportunities for workers with some formal education. It is also similar in the sense that it lowers the labor to output ratio. The difference is that agriculture and resource extraction have a fixed input—land. Mechanization lowers the worker to land ratio and thus reduces the number of jobs in agriculture. In manufacturing the number of jobs can be maintained or even increased in the face of increased mechanization provided that manufacturing can attract the needed amount of capital.

For example, the United States experienced a sharp drop in its agricultural workforce over the twentieth century but an increase in its manufacturing workforce. In 1900, 10 million agricultural workers comprised 40 percent of the workers. In 1970, only 4 million farm jobs remained, comprising only 5 percent of the workforce. Meanwhile, manufacturing jobs increased from 5 million to 20 million, rising from 20 percent of the workforce to 30 percent.

This rise in the proportion of jobs in manufacturing cannot be explained only by the absence of a fixed factor, since consumers, facing a fixed set of products, must eventually become satiated: how many horse-drawn carriages can you possibly desire? With a fixed product mix the return on capital in manufacturing would have surely fallen to a level too low to attract more investment, and jobs would have expanded instead in services. If we had today the same mix of products as existed in 1900—no automobiles, or refrigerators, no televisions, no personal computers, and so on—we surely would have a much smaller global workforce in manufacturing. But the twentieth century has experienced wondrous product innovation that has paralleled the process innovation. Thus the fundamental reason for the expansion of the global manufacturing jobs in the first seven decades of the twentieth century has been product innovation.

The difference between agriculture and manufacturing should alarm exporters of natural-resource-based products, processed or otherwise. Countries that cannot attract manufacturing activities face the very difficult problem of how to find work both for new entrants into the labor force and also for the natural-resource workers who are inevitably displaced by mechanization.

Manufacturing Is Done in Cold Climates, Close to Markets, and Separated from Agriculture

The ability of a country to attract manufacturing is determined by three features: resources, location, and climate. Manufacturing equipment functions optimally in cold climates where it can be operated without breakdowns, at a high pace, and for long hours during the day. Manufacturing seeks stable real exchange rates and an educated workforce, neither of which are offered by natural-resource-rich countries. And many manufacturing activities prefer to cluster next to like activities and close to the high-wage markets of North America, Europe, and Japan.

The Transition from a Preindustrial to an Industrial Economy is Difficult for Natural-Resource-Rich Countries

The conceptual framework that we use for thinking about these issues is a three-factor (land, labor, and capital), multigood, Heckscher-Ohlin model with variable effort levels which looks like technological differences. This framework suggests that an abundance of natural resources is helpful in the preindustrial age but can be a hindrance toward progress in the industrial age. Natural-resource-rich communities invest their scarce savings mostly in improvements in land, permanent crops, and extractive equipment, but invest very little in human capital, which has a very low return; for example, on a coffee plantation. This creates a barrier to development because, once the resource is fully developed and further wealth accumulation can come only from the expansion of manufacturing, the educational system may not be ready to prepare the workforce for jobs on the factory floor. Equipment may then seek workers in other communities that have the literacy skills and work ethics needed in the command-and-control, hierarchical organizations that lead the global competition in manufacturing.

There are some notable exceptions to the hindering effects of natural resources in the northern regions of Europe (Finland and Sweden) and North America (Canada). Yet the comparison between Latin America and these northern softwood producers may not be completely meaningful. First, softwood logs are different from such products as coffee, since wood processing can extend from sawing to the much more human- and physical-capital-intensive operations in pulp and paper. Food processing is more limited in scope and may not support extensive investment in human capital. Second, as we will argue below, manufacturing is most productive in cold weather, which is in abundant supply in Canada, Finland, and Sweden, but very scarce in Latin America. Also, these northern softwood producers may be different from Latin American countries with regard to human-capital formation, since they may have made a heavy commitment to broad human-capital accumulation for noneconomic reasons prior to the period when the private rate of return to human capital exceeded the private rate of return to physical capital. Furthermore, they sit right next to the attractive markets in Europe and North America, while Latin America is far away. That distance, among other factors, may prevent investments in Latin America from having a sure payoff. Indeed, Argentina, formerly a wealthy natural-resources exporter, had substantial measured human-capital accumulation, but nonetheless did not manage to make the transition to an industrial economy.

Climate: Equipment is More Productive in Cold Climates

The shift from the Agrarian Age to the Industrial Age came with a movement of wealth creation from the Mediterranean climates to cooler climes for two reasons. First, there is a fundamental difference in the technology of agricultural production and the technology of manufacturing. A field can be tended by many or by few, and adding a worker does not affect the productivity of others. Two lazy workers equal one productive worker, but a machine can be tended by only one worker. The output of a machine at the end of the day depends on the speed of work and the attentiveness of the worker. Because farm workers can be paid on a piece-rate system, the owner of a farm does not need to distinguish between two unproductive workers and one productive worker—in the end the land commands the same rent. But the owner of an expensive machine cannot use a piece-rate system because a lazy worker may not produce enough output to cover the cost of the machine (see Leamer 1999).

The need to spread the fixed cost of capital over a large labor input makes industrial equipment and factories seek climates in which the equipment can be operated for long hours during the day at high speeds. The problems confronting manufacturing in the tropics are many. Human effort and attentiveness are hard to maintain for extended periods of time in hot and humid climates, and machines break down more frequently. It is only with the advent of air conditioning that manufacturers started moving "south" in search of low wages, but in these hot and humid climates workers must, in effect, rent the equipment and pay both the added capital costs for the air conditioning and the marginal operating costs. This keeps a permanent gap between wages in "the North" and wages in "the South."

Location: Communication of Complex Ideas Requires Face-to-Face Meetings

Both the industrial age and the postindustrial age require workers to master complex new tasks that new equipment and new products demand. Leamer and Storper (2001) argue that this human capital is created only by close human interactions (watching the master), a communication technology which dictates the geographic concentration of innovative manufacturing. While great improvements in transportation and communication technologies have made it much cheaper to transport goods and codifiable messages, these technologies help very little in the transfer of uncodifiable knowledge. Only when products mature and become standardized can the knowledge of how to produce them be codified in words and blueprints and sent to remote locations where the products can be made successfully. The productive activities at these remote locations tend toward the mundane and the repetitive, and thus require much less human capital than the innovative activities done at the great centers of both the industrial and postindustrial ages. Without broadly owned human capital, these remote locations may have greater inequality than do the centers of the industrial age.

Location: Enforcement of Contracts Is Best Done in Close Proximity
In addition to allowing the transfer of complex messages, closeness can be important for the maintenance of guarantees. "Search goods" whose value is transparent from a single inspection can be exchanged through long-distance and faceless transactions. But "experience goods" have value that is revealed only through years of use, and it is essential for the buyer to be able to find the seller in the event that the product does not live up to its explicit or implicit guarantees.

Data Evidence

Within the limits of this chapter we cannot provide compelling evidence in support of every one of these arguments, but we can offer some significant support for many of them.

The Link between Exports, Incomes, and Inequality

Substantial evidence of the argument that "you are what you export" comes from clustering countries in terms of their export patterns and then computing how the average per capita GDPs and average Gini coefficients differ between the clusters. We find, among other things, that exporters of tropical agricultural products have lower per capita GDPs and higher Ginis.

Next we report some simple regressions that include more than one export product and also remoteness and trade dependence. Even in this horse race between competing explanations, exporting tropical agricultural products contributes to low per capita GDPs and unequal incomes. After controlling for export mix, being far away does not seem to affect per capita GDP but it does contribute to higher Ginis.

Clustering of Countries, 1987

In Table 16.2 we report two groups of countries based on their export shares, first exporters of tropical agricultural products and second exporters of (footloose) labor-intensive manufactures.[2] Exporters of tropical agriculture products rarely export other goods, especially not manufacturing. In contrast, the heterogeneity within the group of exporters of labor-intensive manufactures is the largest among any of the groups (except the mixed comparative advantage group that is precisely defined based on its heterogeneity). Interestingly there are countries in this group that also export capital-intensive manufactures or machinery, but at the same time there are tropical agriculture exporters.

Table 16.2 Two Clusters of Countries: Exports/Total Trade

	Pet.	R. Mat.	For.	Trop. Ag.	Anl.	Cer.	Lab.	Cap.	Mach.	Chem.
Tropical Agriculture Products										
MDG	0	0.03	0	0.39	0.09	0.02	0.01	0.03	0	0.01
HND	0	0	0.03	0.38	0.05	0.01	0.01	0	0	0
TZA	0.01	0	0.01	0.28	0.01	0.13	0.01	0.02	0	0
CRI	0	0	0.01	0.27	0.06	0.01	0.04	0.03	0.01	0.02
FJI	0.05	0	0.03	0.27	0.04	0.01	0.03	0.02	0.02	0
GTM	0.01	0	0.01	0.25	0.02	0.03	0.02	0.03	0	0.04
SLV	0.01	0.01	0.01	0.25	0.02	0.02	0.02	0.03	0.01	0.03
GHA	0.01	0.14	0.07	0.23	0.02	0	0.03	0	0	0
COL	0.15	0.03	0.01	0.23	0.02	0.01	0.06	0.02	0.01	0.02
ECU	0.2	0	0.01	0.17	0.12	0.01	0.01	0	0	0
LKA	0.02	0	0	0.16	0.01	0.01	0.17	0.02	0.01	0
ETH	0.01	0	0	0.15	0.07	0.01	0	0	0	0
CMR	0.06	0.02	0.04	0.13	0.01	0.02	0.01	0.01	0.03	0.01
Labor-Intensive Manufactures										
HKG	0	0.01	0.01	0.01	0.01	0.01	0.22	0.14	0.11	0.02
ISR	0	0.01	0	0.03	0.01	0.01	0.16	0.07	0.08	0.06
DOM	0	0	0	0.09	0.01	0.02	0.15	0.06	0.02	0
PRT	0.01	0	0.06	0.02	0.01	0.01	0.15	0.06	0.07	0.02
IND	0.02	0.02	0	0.05	0.03	0.03	0.15	0.1	0.03	0.02
MLT	0.01	0	0	0	0	0.01	0.14	0.06	0.1	0.01
THA	0	0.01	0.01	0.1	0.06	0.06	0.14	0.05	0.05	0.01
PHL	0.01	0.05	0.03	0.06	0.03	0.05	0.13	0.03	0.11	0.02
TUN	0.09	0.01	0	0.02	0.02	0.02	0.12	0.03	0.03	0.08
TUR	0.01	0.02	0.01	0.06	0.02	0.03	0.11	0.09	0.05	0.03
GRC	0.02	0.02	0	0.05	0.01	0.05	0.09	0.06	0.01	0.01

Table 16.3 Summary Statistics by Country Group

Country Group	Obs.	Per Capita GDP	Gini
Animal products	2	12731	36
Machinery, cap., and chem.	10	11999	32
Forestry but also machinery	4	11838	35
Mixed comp. advantage	12	6424	40
Labor-intensive manufacture	11	4851	41
Raw materials	8	3759	47
Petroleum	6	3353	40
Cereal	2	3107	54
Tropical agriculture	13	1820	46

Now that we know what they export, what are they like? Is it true that "you are what you export?" Table 16.3 reports average per capita GDPs and average Ginis for each of these groups of countries. These are sorted by per capita GDP. At the top with high per capita GDPs and low Ginis are exporters of animal products and exporters of machinery and chemicals. At the other end with low per capita GDPs and unequal incomes are the exporters of tropical agricultural products and cereals, and petroleum and raw materials. Exporting labor-intensive manufactures helps some, but not very much.

Persistence of Trade Patterns, 1980–1997

Another claim that we have made is that while natural resources are certainly not footloose, neither is much of manufacturing. This leaves countries hoping to develop by stepping up on the first wrung of the ladder of manufactures scrambling to attract the small segment of manufacturing that is footloose.

Table 16.4 reports the correlation of 1980 and 1997 export shares and net exports relative to total trade. The products are sorted from most to least persistent. At the top of the persistence chart are the natural resource dependent activities: animal products, raw materials. But exports of machinery are more persistent than exports of petroleum or tropical agricultural products. Chemical are also very persistent. The footloose products are of course: labor-intensive manufactures and what we are calling capital-intensive manufactures (meaning not much human capital). That's textiles and steel.

Table 16.4 Correlation Between 1980 and 1997 Export Patterns

Products	Exports Share	Net Exports Share
Animal products	0.91	0.91
Raw materials	0.89	0.89
Machinery	0.87	0.83
Petroleum	0.85	0.81
Tropical agriculture	0.84	0.84
Chemicals	0.82	0.75
Forestry	0.81	0.83
Cereals	0.78	0.75
Cap.	0.58	0.57
Lab.	0.32	0.37

Table 16.5 Joint Effects of Exports Patterns and Remoteness

Variable	Inequality	GDP per capita
Net exports of tropical agriculture	35.44	–11403
	(3.25)	(2.5)
Net exports of machinery	–17.95	8182
	(1.92)	(2)
Net exports of chemicals	16.21	55354
	(0.44)	(3.5)
Remoteness	0.001	–0.2
	(3.13)	(0.9)
Trade dependence	–1.53	1704
	(0.61)	(1.5)
Constant	31.1	9896
	(11.46)	(8.4)
R^2	0.48	0.6

Multiple Regressions, 1987

Table 16.5 reports multiple regressions that explain inequality and GDP per capita in terms of export mix (net exports as a share of total trade), trade dependence, and remoteness. The choice of exports comes from trimming out insignificant predictors. This leaves two important trade determinants of income and inequality levels: machinery and chemicals, and tropical agriculture. After controlling for the product mix, trade dependence does not matter and remoteness is bad for inequality but does not much affect income levels. In fact, 60 percent of the variability across countries in GDP per capita can be explained by

Table 16.6 Distance Elasticity from Gravity Equation

Variable / Year	1982	1987	1992	1997
Petroleum	–1.26	–1.13	–1.26	–1.33
	(0.07)	(0.06)	(0.06)	(0.05)
Raw materials	–0.88	–0.77	–0.96	–1.05
	(0.04)	(0.04)	(0.04)	(0.04)
Forest products	–1.08	–1.05	–1.23	–1.36
	(0.03)	(0.04)	(0.03)	(0.03)
Tropical agriculture	–0.7	–0.66	–0.82	–0.82
	(0.04)	(0.03)	(0.03)	(0.03)
Animal products	–0.73	–0.77	–0.86	–0.81
	(0.04)	(0.04)	(0.03)	(0.03)
Cereals	–0.62	–0.63	–0.79	–0.93
	(0.04)	(0.04)	(0.03)	(0.03)
Labor-intensive manufactures	–1.09	–1.05	–1.03	–1.18
	(0.01)	(0.03)	(0.03)	(0.03)
Capital-intensive manufactures	–1.06	–0.99	–1.07	–1.17
	(0.03)	(0.03)	(0.03)	(0.03)
Machinery	–1.04	–0.93	–1	–1.12
	(0.03)	(0.03)	(0.03)	(0.03)
Chemicals	–1.14	–1.18	–1.27	–1.34
	(0.03)	(0.03)	(0.03)	(0.03)

Note: Standard errors in parentheses.

trade composition alone. Inequality, as measured by Ginis, is harder to predict, but exporting tropical agricultural products seems undeniably associated with unequal incomes.

What Determines Exports? Resources, Climate, and Location

Given the stability of export patterns and the undeniable correlation between these and incomes and inequality we turn next to the empirical evidence relating exports to their underlying determinants: resources, location, and climate.

Location

The gravity model has been used often to study the choice of trade partners, but less often to study the composition of trade, although an exception is Leamer (1997). Table 16.6 reports the distance component of a gravity model applicable to each of our ten trade aggregates. This shows the distance effect on countries' bilateral trade in different products for 136 countries in 5 different years. Except for the dummy variables the equations were estimated in logs and included the GDP of the countries, a dummy for pairs of countries that speak the same language, and a dummy for pairs of countries that share a common border, in addition to the distance separating them in kilometers.

Table 16.6 has two important messages. First, distance affects different goods differently. Cereals, tropical agriculture, animal products, and raw materials are the least affected by distance while trade in forest products, petroleum, and manufacturing goods are severely hurt by distance. Even footloose, labor-intensive manufactures has a large negative distance elasticity. They are not so footloose after all.

The second message of Table 16.6 is that the distance effects do not seem to be fading away over time, as "globalization" enthusiasts and opponents suggest. For every one of the products in the sample the effects of distance have increased, if anything, between 1982 and 1997. The substantial and persistent distance effect on manufactures is evidence of one of our important points: any manufacturing that involves complex, uncodifiable tasks, including the customization of equipment and inputs, has a powerful hysteresis effect.

It seems surprising that the great rise in global trade in the last several decades has not been associated with declining distance elasticity. It might be the case, however, that although the marginal effects of distance on trade have not decreased over time the average effects have. The average distance, in kilometers, that one U.S. dollar worth of different products traveled in different years[3] confirms that goods were not traveling longer distances in 1997 than they were in 1982. Why, then, the big increase in trade compared with GDP? If the globe is not getting smaller, what is happening? The gravity model has the answer: GDP is getting more dispersed. The growth of trade across the Pacific comes from having more equal GDPs in North America and Asia.

Resources

The simple gravity model suffers from a lack of variables that measure comparative advantage. As a consequence, it is possible that too much is attributed to distance. It could be that machinery and chemicals are produced close to markets and tropical agriculture produced in remote areas just because the global distribution of endowments dictates so. Next we deal with both resources and distance at the same time.

The descriptive model that drives this two-step estimation has potential net exports as a function of resources *P*(Resources) but actual trade reduced by a gravity effect: Net Exports/Worker = Potential Trade(Resources/Worker) · Volume Effect(distance, country size). A very rough way of estimating this model is reported here. Table 16.7 reports regressions of the *absolute* value of a country's net exports divided by its labor force—a measure of trade dependence—on our measure of remoteness and on the country's GDP a measure of market size (Sombart's Law). As expected, both market size and remoteness reduce the country's trade dependence. We then use these estimated remoteness and GDP elasticities to create an adjustment factor for the net exports of the countries, scaling up the level of net exports to put all countries on an equal footing in terms of access and market size. The adjustment factor scales up net exports of distant and large countries and scales down the net exports of close and small countries. These adjusted net exports, always scaled by the country's labor force as well, are then regressed against the countries' factor endowments and distance to markets. The results are reported in Table 16.8.

Besides the expected effects of endowments in exports, long predicted by the Heckscher-Ohlin model, Table 16.8 shows that remoteness continues to hurt exports of capital-intensive manufacture, machinery, and chemicals. Even after controlling for factor endowments as sources of comparative advantage, more distant countries still are at a disadvantage in the production of those goods. The opposite happens to raw materials, tropical agriculture, and animal products: after controlling for endowments the more distant countries seem to have a comparative advantage in this case.

Climate

An important part of our view about wealth and inequality is that climate influences the activities a country may perform efficiently. It cannot be surprising that tropical agriculture requires tropical climates. That is not the point. The point is that manufacturing, especially the most capital-intensive segments, cannot efficiently be performed in hot climates.

Table 16.9 shows that the data lend strong support to this claim. A regression of the countries' exports per worker against remoteness, standardized to have mean zero and unit variance, and the percentage of the population in tropical, temperate, snow, and other climates, indicate that being in the temperate zone is indeed a strong predictor of a country's ability to export manufactures. Interestingly, even after controlling for climate, remoteness still hurts the ability of a country to export manufacturing, this being particularly true for chemicals, machinery, and capital-intensive manufactures.

Table 16.7 Trade Dependence Log Versus Distance and GDP, 1987

	Petroleum	Raw Materials	Forest Products	Tropical Agriculture	Animal Products	Cereals	Labor Int. Manuf.	Capital Int. Manuf.	Mach.	Chem.
log(distance)	−1.74**	−1.52**	−2.01**	−0.77*	−2.18**	−1.43**	−1.93**	−1.76**	−1.31**	−1.14**
log(GDP)	0.05	−0.09	−0.1	−0.19	−0.22	−0.18	−0.12	−0.23*	−0.25*	−0.17*
Constant	18.7*	18.4*	22.6**	14.2**	26.3**	19.4**	23.1**	23.8**	21.2**	17.3**
Observations	68	68	68	68	68	68	67	68	68	67
R^2	0.26	0.14	0.28	0.08	0.25	0.18	0.27	0.27	0.2	0.19

Note: Dependent variable is log(|NetExports/Labor|).
*Significant at 5%.
**Significant at 1%.

Table 16.8 Comparative Advantage

	Petroleum	Raw Materials	Forest Products	Tropical Agriculture	Animal Products	Cereals	Labor Int. Manuf.	Capital Int. Manuf.	Mach.	Chem.
Capital/labor	17360	49197	4398	1743	42674	23802	17554	–4448	–159213*	–19812
$(\text{Capital/labor})^2$	–167423	–417918	–60420	948	–425622	–220714	–597716	357008	1445048	242139
Primary edu/labor	–87	203	–129	298	–1010	–93	181	–676	1070	–201
Secondary edu/labor	–601	1133	–4	56	–702	285	1914	–1757	2566	–414
Terciary edu/labor	–1305*	–3098	469	523	3158	–685	–2683	–1066	2299	518
Cropland/labor	53	180	–24	19	–237	93	123	–163	102	31
Forest land/labor	–2.65	8.41	0.82	–2.16	–1.21	–1.63	–5.98	0.16	–2.79	–0.77
Pasture land/labor	–2.41	–26.02	0.52	–3.32	28.69	–7.36	–20.67	21.49	5.31	2.15
Energy/labor	0.23	–0.66	0.01	–0.29	–1.35	–0.45	–0.36	0.11	1.59	0.11
Remoteness	–0.01	0.19**	0	0.04**	0.24**	0.09**	0.01	–0.08*	–0.43**	–0.05**
Observations	69	69	69	69	69	69	69	69	69	69
R^2	0.22	0.28	0.05	0.29	0.47	0.35	0.08	0.17	0.44	0.32

*Significant at 5%.
**Significant at 1%.

Table 16.9 Climate Effects on Exports per Worker in Manufacturing in 1992

Climate Zone	Chemicals	Machinery	Cap.	Lab.
Tropical & subtropical	213	568	296	304
Temperate	877**	1971**	1172**	1415**
Snow	–678	669	–613	–1401*
Other	–57.97	–128.31	–100.6	–114.24
Remoteness	–314**	–701**	–347**	–233.46

*Significant at 5%.
**Significant at 1%.

The Truly Exogenous Determinants of Incomes and Inequality

The evidence presented so far states clearly that endowments, location, climate, export composition, incomes, and inequality are unequivocally linked. There is, however, a high degree of collinearity among these variables and we may find it difficult to sort out the separate effects, not to mention speak to causal directions. However, we have been able to link the countries' income and inequality measures with their exogenous determinants. It is this link that will be explored when we address the possible effects an FTAA agreement may have in the region.

Among the variables we expect to be linked to the countries' income and inequality measures we argue that the following are truly exogenous to the process of wealth creation and distribution: share of area under a given climate zone, remoteness, land endowments, and energy reserves. Table 16.10 shows how these variables affect income and inequality in the countries. These are weighted regressions with variance of the residual assumed to be equal to the labor force, thus producing regression estimates analogous to a mean with weights equal to the labor force. There is no constant in the equation because the sum of the climate shares equal one. Furthermore, for computing the t-statistics, the mean has been subtracted from dependent variable, and the t-statistics on the climate proportions test if that climate zone is unusual compared with all the others, not a test if the effect is zero. Finally, the resource variables are standardized to have mean zero and variance one, thus allowing the coefficients on the climate variables to refer to the effect of climate on a country with average endowments and to allow the coefficients on the resource variables to

Table 16.10a Weighted Regression Estimates: GDP Per Capita and Gini versus Climate in 1987

	GDP Per Capita Estimates		GINI Estimates		Climate Data				
Climate Shares	Coeff.	*t*-stat	Coefficient	*t*-stat	Total	Brazil	Arg.	US	Sweden
Snow humid	$19,082	5.6	48.77	1.33	5%	0%	0%	26%	69%
Temp. humid	$12,143	4.8	37.63	−0.34	22%	5%	26%	32%	26%
Snow dry winter	$9,590	0.4	68.65	0.95	0%	0%	0%	0%	0%
Tropical humid	$6,596	0.3	30.86	−1.15	11%	20%	0%	0%	0%
Tropical monsoon	$4,846	−0.5	46.8	1.09	3%	2%	0%	0%	0%
Temp. Medit.	$4,277	−0.8	40.96	0.3	8%	0%	0%	6%	0%
Arid steppe	$3,194	−0.6	32.99	−0.4	7%	0%	28%	18%	0%
Highland	$2,968	−0.9	72.8	2.52	8%	0%	17%	11%	0%
Tropical dry winter	$2,926	−2.8	49.54	3.11	21%	63%	0%	0%	0%
Temp. subtrop.	$1,694	−1.7	27.08	−1.51	7%	10%	12%	0%	0%
Arid desert	$1,506	−2.3	36.14	−0.47	8%	0%	16%	4%	0%
Ice tundra	−$18,807	−1.3	−134.35	−2.93	1%	0%	0%	3%	5%

Note: t-statistics on climate variables test for differences among the coefficients, not zero. The weight used is the square root of labor.

Table 16.10b Weighted Regression Estimates: GDP Per Capita, Gini versus Resources in 1987

	GDP Per Capita Estimates		GINI Estimates		Resources Data				
Resources: Stand. Dev. From Mean	Coeff.	*t*-stat	Coefficient	*t*-stat	Total	Brazil	Arg.	US	Sweden
Cropland	2898	4.8	0.48	0.24	0	0.2	1.8	–0.2	0.8
Energy	984	1.8	1.93	1.11	0	–0.3	–0.1	–0.2	0.1
Forestland	–909	–0.6	16.35	2.89	0	0.4	0	0.1	–0.2
Remoteness	–1828	–2.3	1.09	0.43	0	0.8	1.3	–1.1	–0.8
R^2	0.88		0.4						

Note: The weight used is the square root of labor.

measure the effect of a one standard-error increase. The climate variables in the table have been sorted by the climate effect on GDP per capita and the resource variables by the resource effect. The final columns of the table indicate climate shares of several countries to help make clear what these climate variables represent.

The GDP per capita regression has a successful R^2 of 0.80 and several statistically significant findings. For GDP per capita, the best climate zones are the cold and cool ones (snow humid and temperate humid), climates the United States and Sweden "enjoy," but Brazil does not. These climates are associated with per capita GDPs of US$19,000 and $12,000. These climates support GDP per capita that are statistically higher than average. In the other direction, the climates that are statistically inferior are tropical dry winter and arid desert. Brazil has the former and Argentina the latter. These climates support GDP per capita of only $2,926 and $1,506 respectively.

Abundance of cropland contributes to GDP per capita. A one standard deviation increase in cropland increases GDP per capita by $2,898. Remoteness is not beneficial: a one standard-deviation increase in remoteness reduces GDP per capita by $1,828.

The Gini regression is less successful, with an R^2 of only 0.40. But it confirms what we suspect: the climate with tropical dry winter that yields a weak GDP per capita also yields a high Gini coefficient. A highland climate is also associated with unequal incomes, while ice tundra (e.g., Canada and Norway) comes with equal incomes. While remoteness lowers per capita incomes, it does not increase inequality. Forestland is estimated to raise inequality. That variable does not distinguish hardwood from softwood forests and may be reflecting mostly the cutting of tropical hardwoods. Indeed, as can be seen in the data, it is Brazil not Sweden that has abundant forestland.

Possible Effects of an FTAA on Income and Inequality in the Americas

This section analyzes the effects that an FTAA agreement will likely have on exports, wealth, and inequality in the Americas. We first describe the region's characteristics regarding resources, climates, location, and export patterns, and then we analyze the effects the trade agreement should have on wealth and inequality.

Resources, Location, Climate, and Exports in the Americas

Out of the twenty-one North, Central, and South American countries in our sample, fourteen of them—all in Latin America—are classified either as exporters of petroleum, raw materials, cereals, or tropical agriculture products. Add to that four other countries (Brazil, Uruguay, Panama, and Barbados) that, although classified as "mixed comparative advantage," are still heavy exporters of one or more of the goods above, and the low income and high inequality levels of the region should not be a surprise. Two countries in the region break the patterns and are the only machinery, chemicals, and capital-intensive manufactures exporter—the United States and Canada. Those are also the only countries with high income levels and relatively equal societies.

Do resources, climate, and location explain the export patterns of the countries in the Americas? We now turn to that question.

Resources in the Americas

Figure 16.1 shows in a Leamer triangle the capital, labor, and land intensity of some countries in the Americas, together with other countries and regions that are meant to provide a relevant basis for comparison. In such a display device the closer a country (or region) is to one of the vertices the more abundant it is in the resource represented in that vertex. Moreover, countries on the same ray emanating from one of the vertices, for example the capital vertex, have the same

Figure 16.1 Leamer Triangle Representation of Factor Abundance

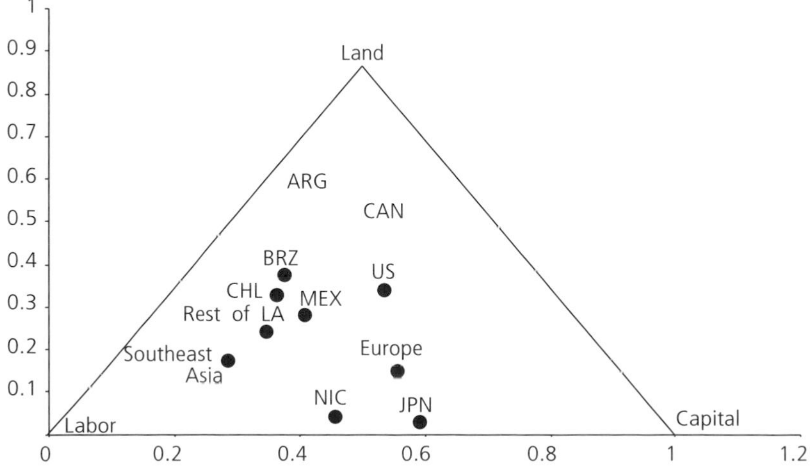

Table 16.11 Close, Intermediate, and Remotely Located Countries in the Americas

Country	Distance (Km.) 1982	Rank	Country	Distance (Km.) 1997	Rank	Gains/ Losses
Close countries						
Canada	2348	6	Canada	2574	6	0
U.S.	3691	15	U.S.	4031	19	–4
Intermediate countries						
Dominican	4674	24	Dominican	5103	28	–4
Jamaica	4719	25	Jamaica	5134	29	–4
Honduras	5411	30	Honduras	5854	31	–1
Barbados	5445	31	Barbados	5904	32	–1
El Salvador	5480	32	El Salv.	5926	33	–1
Mexico	5513	34	Mexico	5939	34	0
Guatemala	5558	35	Guatemala	6006	35	0
Venezuela	5502	33	Venezuela	6010	36	–3
Panama	5753	36	Panama	6219	37	–1
Costa Rica	5784	37	Costa Rica	6229	38	–1
Remote countries						
Colombia	6106	38	Colombia	6596	40	–2
Suriname	6223	39	Suriname	6653	41	–2
Ecuador	6612	42	Ecuador	7104	44	–2
Peru	7785	49	Peru	8250	53	–4
Brazil	7918	50	Brazil	8297	54	–4
Bolivia	7984	51	Bolivia	8400	55	–4
Uruguay	8529	55	Uruguay	8674	57	–2
Argentina	9186	59	Argentina	9529	61	–2
Chile	9344	61	Chile	9673	62	–1

relative intensity of the other two production factors—labor to land ratio in the case of the capital vertex.[4]

The message from Figure 16.1 is clear: the American continent is, by and large, land abundant. Within the region the United States and Canada are distinguished by their high capital-per-worker measures while the rest of the region is extremely capital scarce. Using attained educational levels as a proxy for the human-capital distribution in the countries, it is confirmed that the incentives to accumulate human capital, at least in the form of secondary and tertiary educations, are not present in the nonmanufacture exporting economies of Latin America.[5] On the other side the land abundant, well-located machinery exporters—Canada and the United States—are very abundant in human capital.

Location

In terms of location the American continent can be divided into three groups of countries as shown in Table 16.11. The first group is composed of Canada and the United States, countries with relative positions comparable to the closest countries in the world, the western European economies. In the second group are Mexico and the Central American countries. Those countries benefit from being close to the United States, and in relative terms they are as well positioned geographically as Hong Kong, for example. The last group is mainly composed of the South American countries. In this group even the closest countries, such as Colombia or Venezuela, are very remote. Remarkably, no country in the region became better positioned—in relative terms—in the fifteen-year period analyzed. At best, Canada, Mexico, and Guatemala kept their relative place. In other words, the region is becoming more and more remote.

In order to get a sense of the burden of distance in the Americas we looked at the share of the world's production in different products that takes place in remote areas of the globe.[6] The portion of world GDP that is generated in those remote areas provides a meaningful basis for comparison. The conclusion is that in terms of location Latin America seems too far away to be able to produce manufactures efficiently in general. Machinery, electronics, vehicles, and instruments are very rarely produced in such remote areas of the globe.

Climate

Because of its orientation (north-south) and its large extension, the American continent has every type of climate. The vast majority of its land, however, is located between the tropics and therefore is under some sort of tropical climate. Except for Canada, the United States, Uruguay, Chile, and Argentina, most of the population in the rest of the countries in the Americas lives in tropical or subtropical climates.[7]

Effects of an FTAA on the Americas

An FTAA May Pull the Region Closer

Again, an FTAA agreement might affect incomes and inequality by changing the region's effective economic location in the world. Regardless of its geographic position, one way a country can place itself in a remote area of the globe is by adopting isolationist policies. Indeed, that may be argued to be the history of most of the Latin American countries. The adoption of an FTAA agreement may pull the region effectively "closer" by eliminating trade impediments.

Table 16.12 Trade Dependence versus Distance, GDP, and Latin American Dummy, 1987

	Petroleum	Raw Materials	Forest Products	Tropical Agriculture	Animal Products	Cereals	Labor Int. Manuf.	Capital Int. Manuf.	Mach.	Chem.
Latin Amer. dummy	0.59	0.41	–0.01	0.65	0.46	0.19	–0.30	0.11	0.15	0.37
log(distance)	–1.85**	–1.60	–2.00**	–0.89*	–2.26**	–1.47*	–1.86**	–1.77**	–1.33**	–1.20**
log(GDP)	0.07	–0.08	–0.10	–0.18	–0.21	–0.18	–0.13	–0.23*	–0.25*	–0.17
Constant	19**	18**	22**	14**	26**	19**	22**	23**	21**	17**
R^2	0.28	0.15	0.28	0.11	0.26	0.18	0.27	0.27	0.20	0.2[illegible]

Note: Dependent variable is log(|NetExports/Labor|).
*Significant at 5%.
**Significant at 1%.

In order to evaluate whether such a mechanism should have a significant impact on the region we start by asking whether there is scope for an FTAA agreement to bring the region closer to markets. If the countries in the region trade considerably less than what is expected for countries of equivalent sizes and remoteness, lifting trade impediments may indeed have a large effect. If, however, they trade at the approximate level that would be expected from them the scope of the liberalizing measures should be limited.

The equations estimated in Table 16.7 can help answer this question. We reestimate these equations with a dummy for Latin American countries and the results are shown in Table 16.12. It turns out that the Latin American dummy variables are not significantly different from zero, suggesting that trade impediments have not made the region more remote than geography alone dictates.

We can use the parameters presented in Table 16.7 to calculate the typical distance from markets of a country that has a given GDP and a given absolute level of net exports. We call this measure the "trade implied remoteness" (TIR). We then compare this number to the country's actual remoteness measure in order to evaluate whether trade impediments other than remoteness actually are making the country closer or more remote than geography indicates.

The TIR variable is calculated as:

$$\log(\text{TIR}) = \left(\frac{1}{\gamma}\right) \cdot \left(\log\{\text{Abs}[\text{NetExports}(i) / \text{Lab}] - \alpha - \beta \cdot \log(\text{GDP})\}\right),$$

where the coefficients come from estimates of the equation shown in Table 16.7.[8]

This data is bad news to those who expect an FTAA agreement to have a dramatic impact through increases in market access. The countries in the Americas do not trade significantly less than what is expected for countries of their sizes and locations. This suggests that trade integration is unlikely to bring countries much closer and therefore is unlikely to have a dramatic effect on incomes and inequality in the region.

On the other side of the Pacific, Hong Kong, Korea, Malaysia, Singapore, and Japan trade significantly more than expected indicating that policy decisions placed them effectively much closer than geography dictates. Even more relevant to Latin America are the experiences of Australia and New Zealand, the most distant countries in the sample. Both these countries managed to overcome the burden of remoteness and trade in every product much more than expected.[9]

An FTAA May Push Exports toward Countries' Comparative Advantages

Another way in which an FTAA agreement can affect incomes and inequality in the region is by eliminating trade distortions and pushing countries' exports toward the goods in which they have comparative advantage. Given the region's land abundance, lack of human capital, strong predominance of tropical or subtropical climates, and geographic remoteness, we are lead to believe that manufacturing activities, and machinery and chemicals in particular, are not likely to be promoted by the adoption of the agreement. Instead tropical agriculture, natural-resource abundant activities, and possibly some labor-intensive manufacturing should be the expanding sectors after the creation of an FTAA.

Because it is machinery and chemicals that are generally associated with higher incomes and equality, whereas tropical agriculture is associated with lower incomes and inequality, the expected effects of the described compositional changes in exports are not very promising. Nevertheless, quantifying these effects is an extremely hard task.

As we did in the last section, we start here by asking whether there is scope for an FTAA agreement to affect export patterns in the region. If the exports composition of the countries in the region is significantly different from the expected composition for countries with similar climates, resources, and locations, lifting trade distortions may indeed have a large effect. If, however, export patterns conform to what is expected, the scope of the liberalizing measures should be limited.

Table 16.13 shows how countries' exogenous characteristics affect its net exports shares in machinery, chemicals, and tropical agriculture, the three sectors empirically associated with income and inequality measures. The reason to look at net exports shares instead of exports shares is that trade distortions may not promote exports but instead lead to import substitution, which would be captured by the former but not by the later variable. Once again the equations presented are weighted regressions with the variance of the residual assumed to be equal to the labor force, thus producing regression estimates analogous to a mean with weights equal to the labor force. There is no constant in the equation because the climate shares add to one. Furthermore, for

Table 16.13 Exogenous Determinants of Export Shares, 1987

Climate shares	Chemicals	Machinery	Tropical Agriculture
Latin America dummy	–128	–322	101*
Tropical humid	43	–39	163
Tropical monsoon	159	601	–33
Tropical dry winter	14	379	33
Arid steppe	183	–61	–26
Arid desert	–43	–4	–49
Temperate mediterranean	–386**	–542	69
Temperate subropical dry winter	224	973	–54
Snow dry winter	–1551*	–996	–33
Ice tundra	703	–11861**	–402
Highland	160	1228	61
Temperate humid	225**	477	–125*
Snow humid	–469*	2259**	–199
Resources: stand. dev. from mean			
Energy	0	–108	–12
Cropland	–5	–24	–2
Forestland	21	50	5
Remoteness	–129**	–251	–14
R^2	0.53	0.43	0.4

Note: Dependent variable: net exports as a share of total trade (deviations from mean).
*Significant at 5%.
**Significant at 1%.

computing the *t*-statistics, the mean has been subtracted from the dependent variable, and the *t*-values on the climate proportions test whether that climate zone is unusual compared with all the others, not a test if the effect is zero. The resource variables are standardized to have mean zero and variance one, thus allowing the coefficients on the climate variables to refer to the effect of climate on a country with average endowments and to allow the coefficients on the resource variables to measure the effect of a one-standard error increase. Finally, a dummy variable for Latin American countries is introduced to pick up disproportionate net export shares in those countries.

The results show that the trade patterns of the Latin American countries in chemicals, machinery, and tropical agriculture are not significantly distorted relative to what would be predicted for countries with the climates, locations, and resources in question. That leads us to conclude that the adoption of an FTAA agreement should not have a major impact on the regions' export patterns and therefore should not affect, at least through this channel, the countries' income and its distribution.

Conclusion

In the never-ending search for villains and heroes, there is a natural tendency to attribute to governments great power over income levels and the degree of inequality. If not them, then who is responsible for these economic conditions? And if not an FTAA, then what can lift Latin America from its unfortunate position in the economic hierarchy of nations? Our answer is, perhaps, no one. If there is a significant effect of an FTAA on incomes and inequality, it will surely take a very long time to show up.

Our data demonstrate that climate, natural resources, and location can together explain a great deal of the variability of trade, incomes, and inequality across countries. Latin America is far away, is rich in natural resources, and has a tropical climate, all of which contribute to low average incomes and great inequality. Further, after controlling for climate, natural resources, and location, Latin America is not unusual in its trade dependence, export composition, GDP per capita, or income inequality. This leaves little obvious scope for an FTAA to change the outcomes materially.

One of the clouds overhanging any plan to improve the economic health of the region is the unfortunate fact that the world is awash in countries competing to do mundane manufacturing tasks, and that route toward progress is foreclosed by overcrowding. If there is a ray of hope, it comes from the examples of Canada, Sweden, and Finland, countries rich in natural resources that nonetheless have managed to attract high-wage, complex manufacturing tasks. The successes of these countries surely depend partly on education and closeness. From these observations we can draw an essential lesson: the long-term economic health of Latin America cannot be established without much improvement in education and without great reductions of the economic, legal, and cultural distance of the region from the high-income markets in North America and Europe.

References

Acemoglu, Daron, Simon Johnson, and James A. Robinson. 2001. "The Colonial Origins of Comparative Development: An Empirical Investigation." *American Economic Review* 91 (5): 1369–1401.

———. 2002. "The Rise of Europe: Atlantic Trade, Instituional Change and Economic Growth." National Bureau of Economic Research Working Paper no. 9378, Cambridge, MA.

Blum, Bernardo. S. 2001. "Trade in Factor Services and Geography: An Account of Global Trade and its Mysteries." University of California Los Angeles. Photocopy.

Deininger, Klaus, and Lyn Squire. 1996. "A New Data Set Measuring Income Inequality." *World Bank Economic Review* 10 (3): 565–91.

Easterly, Willian, and Ross Levine. 2002. "Tropics, Germs, and Crops: How Endowments Influence Economic Development." National Bureau of Economic Research Working Paper no. 9106, Cambridge, MA.

Engerman, Stanley L., and Kenneth L. Sokoloff. 1994. "Factor Endowments, Institutions, and Differential Paths of Growth Among New World Economies: A View from Economic Historians of the United States." National Bureau of Economic Research Working Paper no. H0066, Cambridge, MA.

Feenstra, Robert C., Robert E. Lipsey, and Harry P. Bowen. 1997. "World Trade Flows, 1970–1992, with Production and Tariff Data." National Bureau of Economic Research Working Paper no. 5910, Cambridge, MA.

Fujita, M., Paul Krugman, and Anthony Venables. 1999. *The Spatial Economy: Cities, Regions, and International Trade*. Cambridge, MA: MIT Press.

Hall, Robert, and Charles I. Jones. 1999. "Why do Some Countries Produce So Much more Output per Worker than Others?" *Quarterly Journal of Economics* 114 (1): 83–116.

Hillberry, R., and David Hummels. "Explaining Home Bias in Consumption: the Role of Intermediate Input Trade." National Bureau of Economic Research Working Paper no. 9020, Cambridge, MA.

Leamer, Edward E. 1984. *Sources of International Comparative Advantage: Theory and Evidence*. Cambridge, MA: MIT Press.

———. 1987. "Paths of Development in the Three-Factor, n-Good General Equilibrium Model." *Journal of Political Economy* 95 (5): 961–99.

———. 1997. "Access to Western Markets and Eastern Effort." In *Lessons from the Economic Transition, Central and Eastern Europe in the 1990s*, edited by Salvatore Zecchini, pp. 503–26. Dordrecht: Kluwer Academic Publishers.

———. 1999. "Effort, Wages and the International Division of Labor." *Journal of Political Economy* 107 (6): 1127–63.

Leamer, Edward E., Hugo Maul, Sergio Rodriquez, and Peter Schott. 1999. "Does Natural Resource Abundance Increase Latin American Income Inequality?" *Journal of Development Economics* 59 (1): 3–42.

Leamer, Edward E., and Christopher Thornberg. 2000. "Effort and Wages: A New Look at the Inter-Industry Wage Differentials." In *The Impact of International Trade on Wages*, edited by Robert C. Feenstra, pp. 37–84. Chicago: University of Chicago Press.

Leamer, Edward E., and Michael Storper. 2001. "The Economic Geography of the Internet Age." *Journal of International Business Studies* 32 (4): 641–55.

Machiavelli, Niccolò 1519. *Discourses on Livy*. (Reprint, New York: Oxford University Press, 1987).

Overman, Henry G., Stephen Redding, and Anthony J. Venables. 2001. "The Economic Geography of Trade, Production, and Income: A Survey of Empirics." Photocopy.

Redding, Stephen, and Peter K. Schott. 2003. "Distance, Skill Deepening and Development: Will Peripheral Countries Ever Get Rich?" *Journal of Development Economics* 72 (2): 515–41.

Rodrik, Dani, Arvind Subramanian, and Francesco Trebbi. 2002. "Institutions Rule: The Primacy of Institutions over Geography and Integration in Economic Development." National Bureau of Economic Research Working Paper no. 9305, Cambridge, MA.

Sachs, Jeffrey D. 2001. "Tropical Underdevelopment." National Bureau of Economic Research Working Paper no. 8119, Cambridge, MA.

Sachs, Jeffrey D., and John W. McArthur. 2001. "Institutions and Geography: Comment on Acemoglu, Johnson, and Robinson (2000)." National Bureau of Economic Research Working Paper no. 8814, Cambridge, MA.

Strauss-Kahn, Vanessa. 2003. "Globalization and Wage Premia: Reconciling Facts and Theory." Insead Working Paper 2003/04/EPS.

Venables, Anthony J., and Nuno Limao. 2002. "Geographical Disadvantage: A Heckscher-Ohlin-VonThunen Model of International Specialization." *Journal of International Economics* 58 (2): 239–63.

Endnotes

1 Our chapter is related to but different from the so-called New Economic Geography literature summarized in Fujita, Krugman, and Venables (1999). This literature deals with how increasing returns to scale, agglomeration economies, transport costs, and product differentiation can affect the way economic activity is spatially organized, even when physical geography is undifferentiated. Even though recent developments by Strauss-Kahn (2001), Venables and Limao (2002), and Redding and

Schott (2002) incorporate some physical geography into the picture, the mechanisms we suggest are very different.

2 There are nine clusters in all. See the website at http://www.anderson.ucla.edu/acad_unit/gem/faculty/leamer/index.htm for more details.

3 Not shown but available online at http://www.anderson.ucla.edu/acad_unit/gem/faculty/leamer/index.htm.

4 For a complete description of the properties of the Leamer Triangles, as well as an application, see Leamer (1987).

5 Not shown but available online at http://www.anderson.ucla.edu/acad_unit/gem/faculty/leamer/index.htm.

6 Not shown but available online at http://www.anderson.ucla.edu/acad_unit/gem/faculty/leamer/index.htm.

7 For a table with detailed information on this issue see the web page address referred to in note 4.

8 Graphs plotting the "trade implied remoteness" measures against the countries' actual remoteness measures are available online at the web page address referred to in note 4.

9 Not shown but available online at http://www.anderson.ucla.edu/acad_unit/gem/faculty/leamer/index.htm.

17

Regional Integration and Productivity: The Experiences of Brazil and Mexico

Ernesto López-Córdova and Mauricio Mesquita Moreira

Introduction

One of the key motivations behind agreements such as a Free Trade Area of the Americas (FTAA)—a major endeavor of the so-called new regionalism—is the hope to increase productivity. Productivity growth, as known to economists ever since Adam Smith's pin factory, is not an end in itself. It is arguably the main source of economic growth and rising standards of living and, accordingly, of crucial importance to regions such as Latin America and the Caribbean, where long-term, sustainable growth has been an elusive goal. Since the 1960s, growth in the region has been trailing behind that of East Asia and in the last two decades it has fallen below the developing countries' average (Inter-American Development Bank 2001).

Growth accounting exercises suggest that Latin America has been not only slow in accumulating inputs, but also particularly bad in raising productivity. For instance, the World Bank (1991) estimates that the region's average productivity growth in the period 1967–87 was zero, whereas the averages for East Asia and developing countries as a whole were, respectively, 1.9 and 0.6 percent. The Inter-American Development Bank (IDB) (2001), in turn, estimates that productivity in Latin America has declined in the 1980s and 1990s, despite the gains obtained elsewhere, particularly in the developed world.

Against this dismal background, it seems clear that by promising productivity gains the move to regional integration has touched a raw nerve in the region. Why and how these gains are supposed to be delivered and what empirical evidence is available is the focus of this chapter. It concentrates on the two largest economies in the region, Brazil and Mexico, and on the performance of their manufacturing sectors. While these two, given the size, geography, and relative sophistication of their economies, might not serve as good points of comparison for all Latin American countries, their experiences with, respectively, MERCOSUR and NAFTA provide valuable "policy experiments" to assess the implications of regional integration for productivity.

The chapter is divided into the three following sections. The next section briefly reviews the theory behind the links between integration and productivity and the hard facts in the region. The following section takes up the case of Brazil and Mexico, presenting, first, a few stylized facts about these countries' integration strategies and ensuing manufacturing performance; and, second, an econometric exercise that tries to pin down the precise impact of integration (i.e., trade and foreign direct investment) on productivity. The final section draws relevant conclusions.

Why Regional Integration Matters for Productivity

Regional integration is, perhaps more than anything, about promoting trade and investment among countries. One can argue, then, that the nature of the costs and benefits involved is, to a great extent, the same as that of a process of unilateral, nonpreferential integration into the world economy. This is particularly true for the "channels" that might impact productivity. Yet, there are some important specificities related to the preferential nature of the integration that cannot be overlooked. For analytical purposes, though, it is worth looking first at the more general (nonpreferential) case of integration and then move on to the specifics of the regional schemes.[1] The literature usually refers to two main channels through which integration might affect productivity: trade and foreign direct investment.

The Trade Channel

The linkages between trade and productivity are seen to operate in at least three dimensions: the economy as whole, the sector, and the firm. The first dimension is the best known and the arguments can be divided into two groups according to the dynamics of their productivity effects. The comparative-advantage gains immortalized by Ricardo (resource reallocation toward the country's comparative advantages) and the scale gain (advantages of large scale production; see, e.g., Helpman and Krugman 1985) fall into the group of "level effects." They tend to produce a once-and-for-all jump in the level of productivity, but they do not provide fuel for constant improvements. The long-term impacts on productivity, or "growth effects," would come from "learning by doing" (e.g., Young 1991) and innovation gains (e.g., Grossman and Helpman 1991). Either by moving resources toward sectors in which the potential for learning is higher or by improving a country's accesses to foreign knowledge, trade would have a permanent impact on a country's ability to learn and produce knowledge and, therefore, would increase productivity.

On the lesser-known sectoral and firm dimensions of the trade-productivity nexus, four effects stand out in the literature:[2] greater availability of world class inputs, technology acquisition via import or exports, import discipline, and higher turnover.

The rationale of the first effect is that trade would boost productivity by expanding the range of intermediate inputs available and, therefore, allowing producers more flexibility in matching their input mix to the technology available (Ethier 1982). The second link is about trade increasing producers' access to foreign knowledge via, for example, imported intermediate inputs, imitation of import varieties (see, e.g., Keller 2001), and access to knowledgeable buyers (learning by exporting; see e.g., Westphal 2001). The third effect would come through import discipline, which would affect productivity in at least three ways: by reducing the slack in firm management (so-called X-efficiency), by forcing firms to increase their output and therefore improve their "scale efficiency," and by increasing the firms' incentive to innovate. Finally, the high-turnover argument suggests that "trade can promote industry productivity growth without necessarily affecting intrafirm efficiency" (Melitz 2002). This is because the simultaneous expansion of imports and exports would force the least efficient firm to contract or exit and the most efficient to expand.

Among these four effects, those related to technology acquisitions and import discipline, by acting on the firms' acquisition of knowledge and incentive to innovate, would be more likely to boost productivity growth.

The Foreign Direct Investment Channel

On the FDI channel, the literature (see, e.g., Blomström and Kokko 1998 and Markusen and Maskus 2001) points to four main effects: an entry effect, competition, knowledge spillovers, and linkage effects. All these conduits are close cousins of the trade-related channels. The first is the FDI counterpart of the turnover argument. The idea is that the entry of "world class" competitors would raise the industry average productivity. One can also draw a parallel between the pro-competitive effect and the import-discipline hypotheses. As in the case of trade, FDI is expected to improve firm management, raise scale efficiency, and provide more incentives to innovation. Knowledge spillovers and linkage effects are the channels more likely to have long-term implications for productivity growth, since they might improve the firms' ability to innovate. FDI knowledge spillovers are said to take place when local firms increase their productivity by copying the technology of affiliates of foreign firms. Given the foreign firms' strong interest in protecting their competitive edge and, therefore, minimizing technology transfer, spillovers would more likely be "vertical" (among their clients and suppliers) than "horizontal" (among their competitors) (Kugler 2000). Finally, FDI is believed to generate positive pecuniary externalities (linkages effects) to local firms by improving the local supply (quality and variety) of intermediate goods (see, e.g., Markusen and Venables 1999).

What Does Regional Integration Specifically Bring to Productivity?

The preferential character of regional integration adds some specificity to the way trade and FDI channels operate. This is particularly important for the trade-related linkages, since the implications for FDI are mainly related to the level and type of flows, and their impact on productivity is at best indirect.[3] On the trade side, there are two major issues worth considering: comparative advantage and the scale effects.

When integration is regional, the traditional comparative-advantage gains from trade are no longer assured given the possibility of trade diversion. Trade diversion reduces productivity because the importer country is not buying from the most efficient suppliers and the exporter country is moving away from its comparative advantage. The overall comparative-advantage gain of regional integration, then, is ambiguous, depending upon the balance between trade creation and diversion.

When the issue is scale, the specificities of regional integration are not so clear cut. What is readily evident is that the potential gains from scale are much higher in the context of a nonpreferential, worldwide integration, than in a regional setting. The former offers the world, the latter only a region of this world. This, though, is just one part of the story. The other part lies in the uncertainty of these scale gains. There is always the threat of increasing returns industries being dislocated by imports. These scale losses might also have long-term negative implications for productivity growth, compromising the financial viability of research and development activities and the potential for learning. One can argue, then, that regional integration for involving a smaller number of partners lowers the risk of damaging dislocations, whereas, at the same time, it boosts the scale advantages of the member countries vis-à-vis the rest of the world.[4]

What Does the Evidence in the Region Show?

Looking first at the macro, economy-wide level, the results for the 1990s—the decade when virtually all of Latin America embraced integration—are mixed. Most studies suggest that the regional average total-factor productivity (TFP) growth was negative or low, even by the region's standards (see, e.g., IDB 2001; Baier, Dwyer, Jr., and Tamura 2002; and Loyaza, Fajnzylber, and Calderón 2002). True, one could argue that these studies also show a considerable heterogeneity in the countries' TFP performances and that, despite this heterogeneity, most countries improved their performance vis-à-vis the 1980s. Yet they, at the very least, indicate that for the majority of the countries in the region, the integration-related gains, if they existed, were not strong enough to offset other negative influences on productivity such as macroeconomic volatility.

At the sectoral level—more specifically in manufacturing, the most protected sector during the import-substitution years—the picture is not so gloomy. For instance, Figure 17.1 shows that labor productivity in the region's largest countries has grown substantially during the 1990s, particularly in Argentina, Brazil, and Mexico. These three countries outperformed the United States (though not Korea) by a large margin, probably reducing the productivity gap vis-à-vis the best practice. Although impressive, this evidence has some important pitfalls. First, since labor productivity does not take into account all the inputs used in production, it gives only a partial view of what actually has happened to technology. Second, these data only cover a handful of countries in the region. Third, as with the macro evidence, it does not tell much about the causal relationship between integration, regional or otherwise, and productivity.

Studies based on firm-level data have made progress in addressing the first and the last of these problems, although the number of

Figure 17.1 Labor Productivity in Manufacturing in Selected Latin American Countries, Korea, and the United States

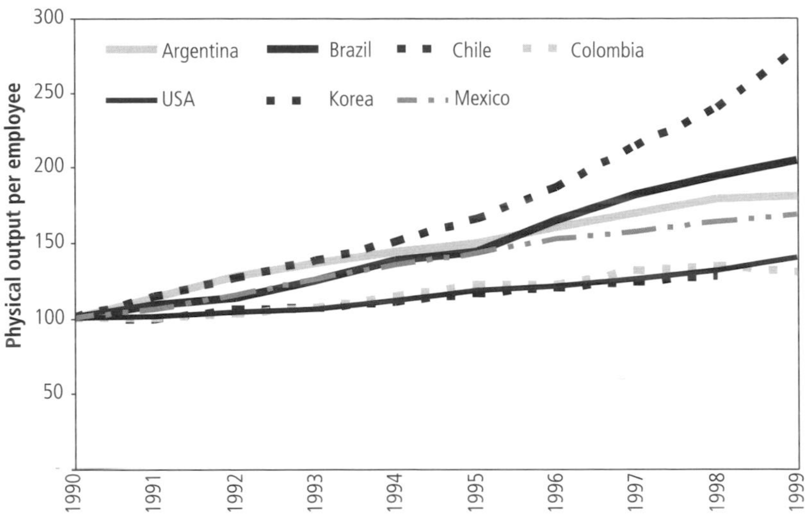

Source: Countries' statistical offices.

countries studied is still limited and some important methodological hurdles have yet to be overcome.[5] One could argue, though, that they are the best information available. For instance, studies on Mexico, Brazil, Chile, and Colombia report positive rates of TFP growth in manufacturing during the trade-liberalization period (see, respectively, Tybout and Westbrook 1995, Muendler 2002, Pavcnik 2000, and Fernandes 2001). They also find evidence of trade-productivity links, mainly through import-discipline effects. There is little evidence, though, supporting the other trade effects. The exceptions are Pavcnik (2000) on Chile, whose estimates suggest that import discipline would have been dwarfed by the turnover effect, and Muendler (2002) on Brazil, who finds evidence of relatively unimportant turnover and imported-inputs effects. It is also worth mentioning a few studies that focus on export externalities but with mixed results. Clerides, Lach, and Tybout (1998) found no evidence of learning by exporting on plant level data for Colombia (1981–91) and Mexico (1984–90), but the World Bank (2000), based on plant-level data for Mexico 1990–98, does find suggestive signs of learning by exporting.

Finally, the (scarce) evidence on the FDI channel tends to support the prevalence of vertical (interindustry) over horizontal (intraindustry) spillovers and highlight the importance of the countries' absorptive capacity.[6] For instance, Aitken and Harrison (1999) find that horizontal spillovers are negative in Venezuela (1976–89). Likewise, Kugler (2000) reports limited horizontal spillovers for Colombian manufacturing plants over 1974–1998, but finds evidence of "widespread inter-industry spillovers from FDI." Kugler's and Kokko, Tansini and Zejan's (1996) results support the relevance of the absorptive capacity, the latter focusing on Uruguayan plants (1988).

Integration and Productivity in Brazil and Mexico

Both Brazil and Mexico moved toward integration after at least half a century of import-substitution policies. For some time these policies were effective in promoting growth and in pushing their economies through a substantial structural change. Yet, by the late seventies there were clear signs that this "model" was not sustainable. For instance, productivity, after an initial period of high growth, set into a downward trend and by the early 1980s was clearly stagnated (on Brazil, see Bacha and Bonelli 2001 and Pinheiro, Gill, Serven, and Thomas 2001; on Mexico see World Bank 1998). This slowdown, compounded by macroeconomic mismanagement, eventually led to the collapse of the "old regime" amid the debt crisis of the 1980s. The countries' response to that technological and economic stagnation was integration into the world markets.

Mexico moved first and faster, and by the early 1990s had already made substantial progress. Tariffs on an MFN basis fell from 28.5 percent in 1985 (the first year of trade liberalization) to 11.4 percent in 1993, while only 192 tariff lines were subject to import licenses (in contrast to all imports being subject to them in 1982.[7] In manufacturing, tariffs fell from around 30 percent in 1985 to 15.5 in 1993, although in general it was less subject to import licensing requirements. From 1994, and as a result of NAFTA, these tariffs experienced a rapid and further decline (see Figure 17.2). Trade liberalization was accompanied by FDI deregulation, also deepened by NAFTA, which led to the removal of most sectoral restrictions and approval and performance requirements.[8]

Brazil, by contrast, took longer to open up. The removal of non-tariff barriers and a drastic drop in tariffs had to wait until 1990. The average MFN tariffs fell from 52 percent in 1987 to 9.9 percent in 1994

Figure 17.2 Average Manufacturing Tariff: Mexico, 1993–2000

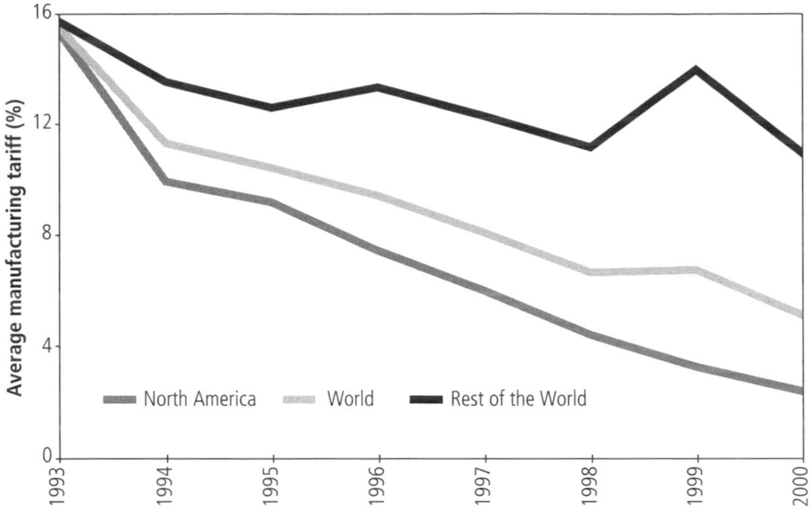

Source: López-Córdova (2002).

and edged up to 12.9 percent by 2000, reflecting Brazil's response to the 1995 Mexican crisis.[9] Tariffs on manufacturing followed a similar trend (see Figure 17.3). As in Mexico, trade liberalization was deepened by a regional trade agreement, MERCOSUR, and was associated with a broad FDI deregulation. The former brought the intraregional average tariff from 59.5 in 1987 (one year after the first Brazil-Argentina agreement) to close to zero in 2000, and the latter extended national treatment to foreign firms except for a few sectors.[10]

These policy changes had a profound impact on trade and investment flows in both countries. In Mexico, both imports and exports boomed. Total imports grew on average by 16.3 percent a year from 1985 to 2000, followed closely by exports, which reached an average growth of 14.2 percent annually. Manufacturing exports and intraregional (NAFTA) trade were the key factors behind the export take-off. The share of manufactured goods in total exports rose from 27 percent in 1985 to 83 percent in 2000, whereas NAFTA's share of total Mexican trade went from 78 to 83 percent (and the share of total exports from 80 to 91 percent) during the same period.[11] FDI also experienced a rapid growth, with average flows increasing from US$2.6 billion in 1980–88 to US$5.7 billion in 1989–93. During the initial

Figure 17.3 Average MFN and MERCOSUR Tariff: Brazil, 1987–2002

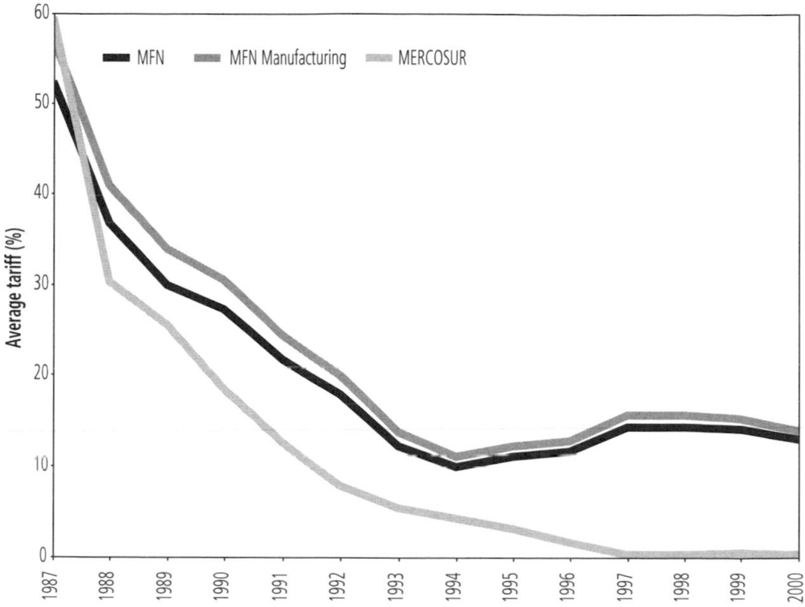

Source: For MFN, Kume, Paini, and Souza (2000) and Receita Federal. For MERCOSUR, Estevadeordal, Goto, and Zaez (2000) and Receita Federal.

NAFTA period (1994–2000), FDI flows seem to have received another boost, reaching an average of US$14.5 billion. [12]

In Brazil, the trade boom was mainly restricted to imports, which increased on average by 13.8 percent per year in the postliberalization period 1990–2000. Exports also grew but at the much more modest rate of 5.8 percent. The changes in the export composition were also modest, with manufacturing exports increasing their share of total exports from 54 to 58 percent over the same period. Exports to MERCOSUR, though, proved to be more dynamic, increasing at 16.8 percent per year, which increased the regional agreement's share of total exports from 5.6 percent in 1990 to 14 percent in 2000 (from 6 to 20 percent in the case of manufacturing exports). The share of MERCOSUR in Brazil's total trade followed a similar trend jumping from 7 to 14 percent over the same period.[13] FDI flows also responded to the new regime, but only after inflation was controlled in the second half of the 1990s.[14] Average flows, which were close to US$1.3 billion in 1980–94, climbed to US$19.3 billion in 1995–2000.

Figure 17.4 Import Penetration and Export Ratios in Manufacturing: Brazil and Mexico, 1988–2000

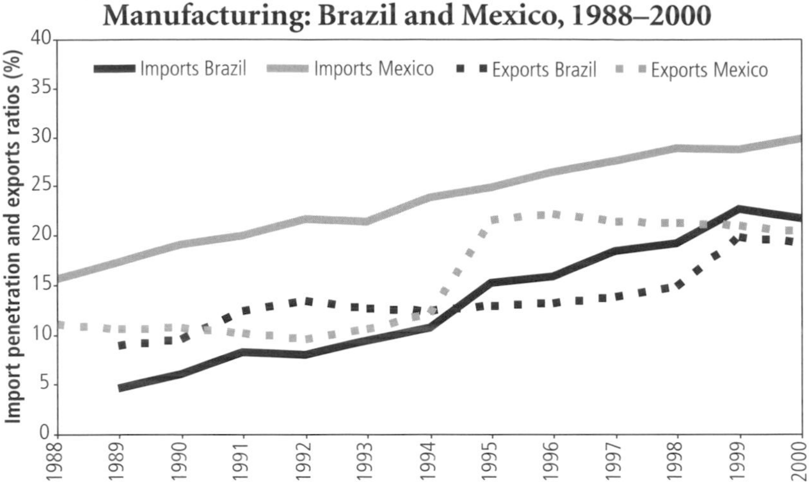

Note: Import penetration divided by domestic consumption. Export ratio is exports divided by output. Data for Mexico does not include *maquiladoras.*

Source: Author's calculations based on Instituto Brasileiro de Geografia e Estatística, Annual Industrial Survey 1989–2000, Rio de Janeiro; and Instituto Nacional de Estadistica Geografia e Informática, Manufacturing Annual Industrial Survey, 1988–2000, Aguas Calientes.

Figure 17.4 presents a good picture of what all these changes in trade flows meant for manufacturing in the two economies. There are three issues worth noting. First, the two countries were in distinctly different positions when they moved into trade liberalization. In the first year of Mexico's trade reforms, 1985, the import penetration ratio in manufacturing was 9.3 percent (Weiss 1999, not shown in the figure), whereas in Brazil in an equivalent year (1989) it was 4.9 percent. In other words, Brazil went much further down the road of import substitution. Second, import penetration increased substantially in both countries, but the "openness gap" remained considerable and in favor of Mexico. And third, export ratios (excluding Mexico's *maquiladora* exports) also showed an upward, if more volatile, trend in both countries, but the gap between them was and remained much smaller than that of import penetration, despite the differences in export performance.[15]

Productivity Performance

In light of this substantial opening of the Brazilian and Mexican economies one should expect to find a measurable impact on economic efficiency in the two countries. The importance of this impact, though, should vary on a country-by-country basis given the differences, inter alia, in macroeconomic environment, initial openness, depth and scope of the reforms, and the strategy of regional integration. Some of these issues are particularly relevant. For instance, as mentioned before, Mexico was considerably more open than Brazil when the new trade policy was put in place. One could argue, therefore, that Brazil stood to gain relatively more from opening up than Mexico, with productivity, at least in the first years of reform, growing faster in the former country than in the latter.

On the other hand, on the issue of the depth and scope of reforms, there is little doubt, judging by the level of tariffs and trade indicators, that Mexico was much more aggressive in pursuing trade-related gains than was Brazil. The option for a north-south regional integration agreement can be seen as part of this aggressiveness. By linking with the United States and Canada, given the differences in size and resources involved, Mexico got much closer to reproducing free trade at a multilateral level than did Brazil with MERCOSUR. The latter, comprising countries of limited size and similar resources, was bound to offer more limited trade-related productivity gains (or costs), at least when seen as an end in itself. So, if one believes that the gains of integration tend to outweigh its costs, a reasonable premise would be that Mexico would present a better productivity performance, or at least would reap more trade-related gains, than Brazil.

In order to ascertain such possibilities, one first needs to gauge the behavior of productivity in the two economies. To this end, the following discussion relies on micro data for the Brazilian and Mexican manufacturing sectors; the appendix provides a description of the methodology used herein.[16]

Figure 17.5 presents aggregate indices of total factor productivity (TFP) for Brazilian and Mexican manufacturing during their periods of trade liberalization. Two estimates with similar firm-level methodologies covering different periods are included for each of the two countries. For Brazil we use Muendler (2002), which covers most of the liberalization period (1986–98), and this chapter's estimates, which refers to the second half of the 1990s (1996–2000). For Mexico, we use Tybout and Westbrook (1995), which covers Mexico's nonpreferential

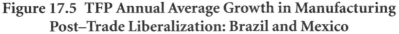

Figure 17.5 TFP Annual Average Growth in Manufacturing Post–Trade Liberalization: Brazil and Mexico

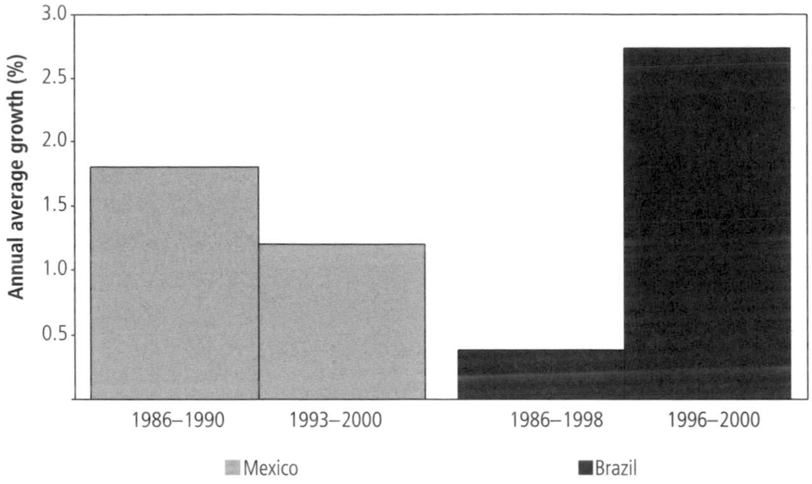

Source: Mexico, Tybout and Westbrook (1995); Brazil, Muendler (2002).

liberalization (1986–90), and this chapter's estimates, which focus on the NAFTA period (1993–2000). Keeping in mind that this comparison should be taken with a grain of salt given that the methodologies are similar but not exactly the same, the results suggest that productivity growth in Mexico was higher during the first, nonpreferential period than in the "regional" period. One possible explanation is that the policy changes were more radical in the first period and, therefore, most of the "level effects" occurred during this period. A second possibility would be that there were factors other than trade policy, such as the 1994–95 peso crisis, that might have affected the periods differently.

In the case of Brazil, the 1986–98 estimate suggests that productivity growth was positive but significantly lower than that of Mexico in both periods, which might be seen as supporting the aggressiveness argument raised above. Yet the estimates for the second half of the decade support the initial-conditions argument, showing an impressive productivity growth that outstrips that of Mexico's NAFTA period and it is close to East Asian standards of 3 percent or more of TFP growth. The fact that the most radical changes in trade policy, including MERCOSUR, took place in the first half of the decade, might imply that stagflation, which prevailed for most of the first half of the decade, would have been a major drag on Brazil's productivity, particularly on trade-related productivity gains. This also underlines the difficulty in looking at the impact of integration without controlling for other relevant factors at play.

Before moving into a more careful attempt to uncover the integration-productivity links in these two countries, it is worth looking behind these aggregate figures to get a sense of, first, how trade orientation correlates with productivity growth among manufacturing industries and, second, the relative importance of intrafirm vis-à-vis intra- and inter-industry gains.

TFP by Trade Orientation

Figures 17.6a and 17.6b, relying now just on this chapter's estimates, show that there were wide differences in productivity performance among manufacturing industries. Trade policy, to the extent that it treats industries differently, might be one of the key factors behind this variation. As a first approximation to evaluating such possibility, Figures 17.7a and 17.7b distinguish TFP performance according to industry or plant characteristics. Leaving, for the moment, plant characteristics aside, one would expect to find that, in the context of a more liberal trade regime, those industries that are more exposed to competition from imported goods or that participate more actively in foreign markets would perform better than industries in which little trade takes place.

Figures 17.7a and 17.7b offer some support to the view that trade is an important force behind productivity improvements.[17] Productivity growth among Brazilian tradable industries was clearly higher than in those little exposed to trade. The performance of industries that trade with MERCOSUR was also impressive, although not as strong as that of tradable industries as a whole. In Mexico, tradable industries were also the top performers, but with an even clearer lead over nontradable industries than in the case of Brazil.

Intrafirm versus Reallocation Gains

Another way of looking behind the aggregate figures is to decompose annual change in TFP into three effects: intrafirm gains, i.e., variations in productivity that occurred inside the firms as a result of technological and managerial innovations; intraindustry reallocation or turnover, reflecting changes in market share between low and high productivity firms within the same industry; and interindustry reallocation, measuring changes in TFP brought about by shifts in the composition of manufacturing output (e.g., the share of the car industry

Figure 17.6a Average Firm TFP Growth: Brazil, 1996–2000

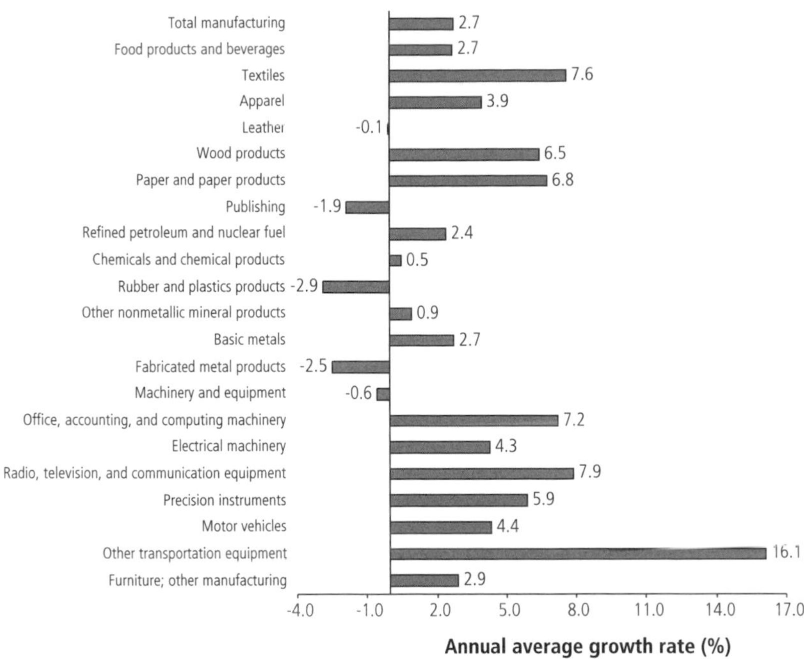

Figure 17.6b Average Firm TFP Growth: Mexico, 1993–2000

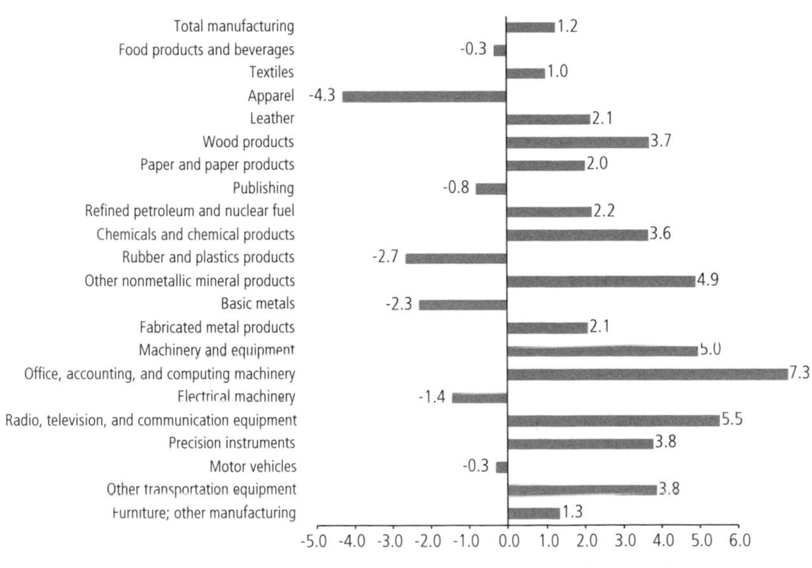

Figure 17.7a Average Firm TFP Growth, by Industry or Firm Characteristics: Brazil, 1996–2000

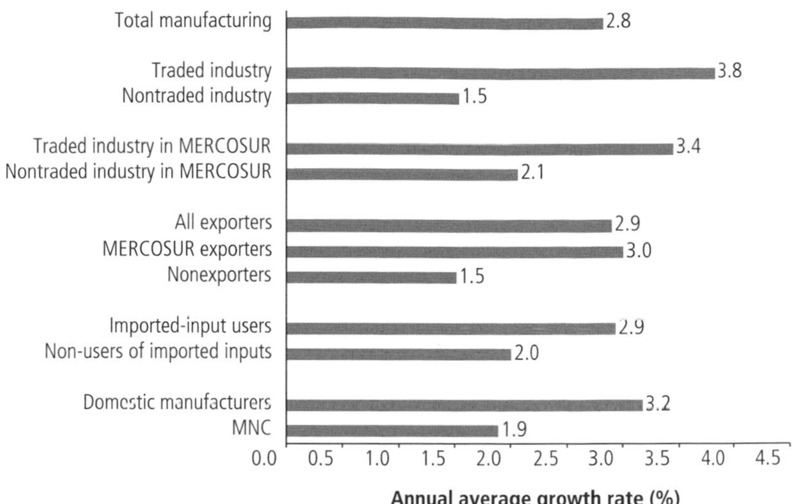

Figure 17.7b Average Firm TFP Growth, by Industry or Firm Characteristics: Mexico, 1996–2000

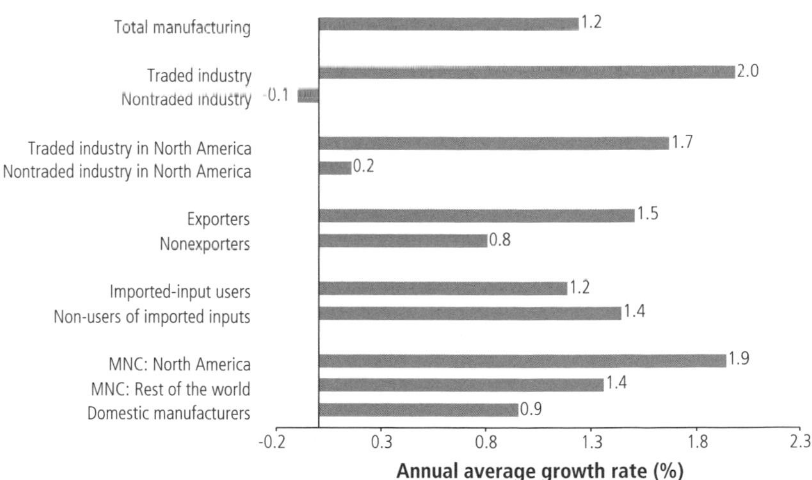

Figure 17.8a Productivity Decomposition: Brazil, 1996–2000

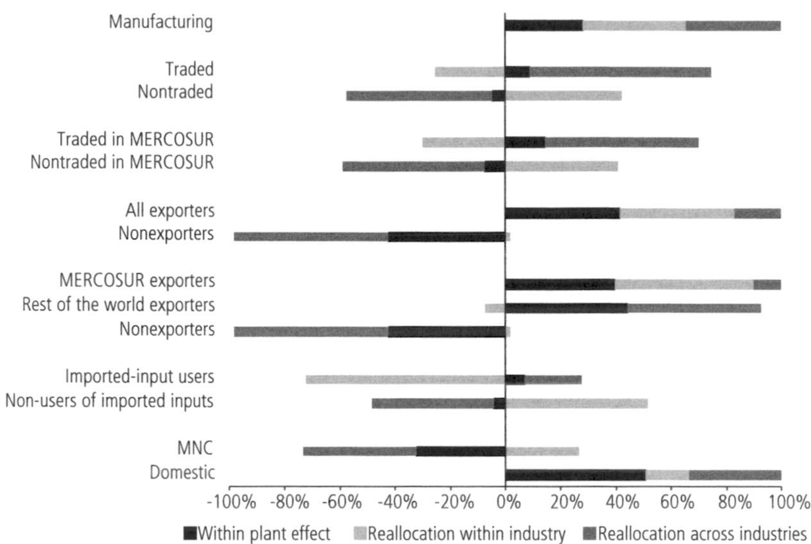

Note: See appendix for methodology.

Figure 17.8b Productivity Decomposition: Mexico, 1993–2000

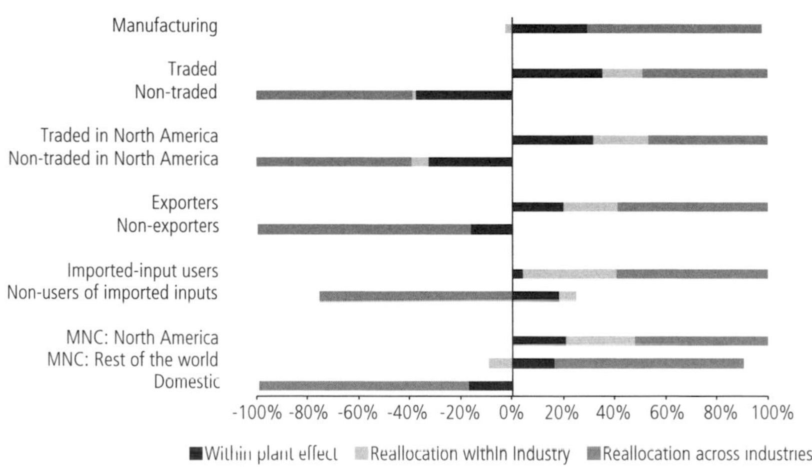

Note: See appendix for methodology.

rises whereas that of textiles falls). The details of this decomposition are in the appendix and Figure 17.8 presents the results.

What seems immediately evident in Figures 17.8a and 17.8b is that in both countries the reallocation effects, particularly across industries, were a major force behind productivity growth. Reallocation accounted for more than 70 percent of the total productivity growth in both cases, with firm-level efficiency gains accounting for the remaining 30 percent. In Brazil, reallocation from less to more productive industries "explains" around half of all reallocation gains; the remaining half is explained by intraindustry reallocations from less to more productive firms. In Mexico, output-share increases in the more productive industries account for the bulk of all reallocation gains.

When industries are grouped by trade orientation, what stands out is that in both countries traded industries accounted for almost all TFP growth and intrafirm gains. Industries with strong global trade links increased their share of manufacturing output relative to those industries with weak links and thus were responsible for all reallocation productivity gains. Moreover, firms in traded industries accounted for almost 70 percent of all firm-level efficiency gains in Brazil. Remarkably, in Mexico, all firm-level gains occurred in traded industries, as productivity among firms in nontraded industries actually declined. The previous exercise also hints at the relative importance of regional integration for both countries. Although it is difficult to disentangle regional from extraregional effects, economic integration with North America seems to have played a major role for Mexico, explaining virtually all TFP and intrafirm improvements. For Brazil, trade with other MERCOSUR partners seems to have had a positive role in reallocating resources to more efficient industries and in raising firm-level productivity performance.[18]

The previous findings are in line with those of other studies that show that turnover is an important driver of productivity performance. Moreover, even though, on the basis of this evidence alone, one cannot attribute these changes directly to trade, they clearly suggest that trade might have played a role in the replacement of low by high productivity firms. They also indicate that the dislocation of high-productivity industries—such as those that exhibit increasing returns or that are knowledge producing—might not have been significant, or, at least, not significant enough to offset comparative-advantage and scale gains.

Integration and Productivity Links

While Figures 17.7 and 17.8 are highly suggestive of positive links between trade liberalization and productivity growth, one cannot yet conclude that trade policy, or trade itself, was behind the contrasting industry performance or the intrafirm or intra- and inter-industry gains. Indeed, establishing such link proves rather challenging since a number of events affected the economies of the two countries during the same period, from the devaluation of the Mexican peso in December 1994 and the Brazilian real in 1999, to rapid U.S. productivity growth and the Asian financial crisis in the second half of the decade. In order to provide a more conclusive indication of whether trade liberalization, either regionally or otherwise, has had a positive impact on productivity, the following discussion relies on econometric evidence. This evidence seeks to isolate trade and FDI from the other forces that influence manufacturing efficiency. Some of these forces are specific to a firm, such as its age and its size, whereas others reflect industry-wide characteristics and macroeconomic conditions that are external to the firm. The latter include, inter alia, industrial output concentration either across firms or regions, exchange-rate fluctuations that affect external supply and demand, and changes in domestic consumption over the business cycle. The appendix describes the econometric approach.

Import Discipline

Tables 17.1 and 17.2 summarize the main results of the econometric exercise used for analyzing trade liberalization in Brazil and Mexico. A first finding is that heightened competition from foreign goods resulting from the elimination of import duties has had a substantial and positive impact on productive efficiency. In the case of Brazil, the results suggest that a 1 percent increase in the import ratio (the industry's imports divided by shipments) would raise the firms' level of TFP by 0.1 percent (columns 1 to 4) and its growth by 1.3 percentage points (columns 5 to 19). They also suggest that a 1 percentage point reduction in tariffs would boost productivity levels by another 0.1 percent. The impact of tariffs on growth, though, was not statistically significant, suggesting only level effects. Muendler (2002), also working on firm level data but covering a longer and earlier period (1986–98), reaches qualitatively similar conclusions. He argues that import penetration and tariff reduction explained a good deal of the increase in TFP in Brazil. A 10 percentage-point reduction in tariffs, for instance, would have increased TFP by 2.8 percent.

Table 17.1 Total Factor Productivity and Integration in Brazil: Regression Results

	Dependent Variable: Log TFP				Dependent Variable: Change in Log TFP														
Explanatory Variables	Reg 1	Reg 2	Reg 3	Reg 4	Reg 5	Reg 6	Reg 7	Reg 8	Reg 9	Reg 10	Reg 11	Reg 12	Reg 13	Reg 14	Reg 15	Reg 16	Reg 17	Reg 18	Reg 19
Competition from imports																			
Log imports/industry	0.1244	0.1242	0.1241	0.1243	1.2890	1.2191	1.2894	1.3521	1.2940	1.2913	1.2889	1.3524	1.3465	1.2943	1.2873	1.2918	1.2874	1.2894	1.2[illegible]69
Output	(0.0285)‡	(0.0287)‡	(0.0285)‡	(0.0285)‡	(0.2433)‡	(0.2333)‡	(0.2432)‡	(0.2614)‡	(0.2437)‡	(0.2443)‡	(0.2433)‡	(0.2613)‡	(0.2605)‡	(0.2436)‡	(0.2422)‡	(0.2442)‡	(0.2436)‡	(0.2432)‡	(0.2[illegible]31)‡
Brazil MFN tariffs	–0.1250	–0.1282	–0.1250	–0.1248	0.0507	0.0565	0.0507	0.0560	0.0504	0.0507	0.0507	0.0560	0.0584	0.0504	0.0515	0.0507	0.0517	0.0507	0.0[illegible]14
	(0.0389)‡	(0.0400)‡	(0.0388)‡	(0.0388)‡	(0.0448)	(0.0440)	(0.0449)	(0.0464)	(0.0449)	(0.0449)	(0.0448)	(0.0464)	(0.0461)	(0.0449)	(0.0447)	(0.0449)	(0.0449)	(0.0449)	(0.0[illegible]49)
FDI spillovers																			
Intraindustry FDI	0.3939	0.3962	0.3935	0.3918	–0.7933	0.5698	–0.7933	–0.8340	–0.7990	–0.7940	–0.7927	–0.8339	–0.8443	–0.7990	–0.8043	–0.7939	–0.7973	–0.7927	–0.7[illegible]50
	(0.1487)‡	(0.2080)*	(0.1435)‡	(0.1483)‡	(0.2003)‡	(0.3411)*	(0.2004)‡	(0.2112)‡	(0.2014)‡	(0.2006)‡	(0.2003)‡	(0.2112)‡	(0.2116)‡	(0.2015)‡	(0.2011)‡	(0.2006)‡	(0.2005)‡	(0.2003)‡	(0.2[illegible]03)‡
FDI–forward linkages	–0.0686	0.2783	–0.0679	–0.0682	–1.2510	–3.[illegible]10[illegible]	–1.2522	–1.3035	–1.2629	–1.2555	–1.2509	–1.3045	–1.2644	–1.2639	–1.2293	–1.2568	–1.2422	–1.2521	–1.[illegible]39
	(0.2721)	(0.4828)	(0.2717)	(0.2715)	(0.5408)†	(1.0440)‡	(0.5400)†	(0.5658)†	(0.5408)†	(0.5428)†	(0.5407)†	(0.5650)†	(0.5583)†	(0.5401)†	(0.5347)†	(0.5420)†	(0.5407)†	(0.5400)†	(0.[illegible]01)†
FDI–backward linkages	–0.3345	–0.2521	–0.3332	–0.3322	–1.3815	–1.6298	–1.3821	–1.4342	–1.3844	–1.3820	–1.3813	–1.4347	–1.4341	–1.3850	–1.3851	–1.3827	–1.3751	–1.3819	–1.[illegible]44
	(0.2444)	(0.3777)	(0.2450)	(0.2448)	(0.3806)‡	(0.7372)†	(0.3805)‡	(0.4000)‡	(0.3813)‡	(0.3811)‡	(0.3805)‡	(0.3999)‡	(0.4007)‡	(0.3812)‡	(0.3808)‡	(0.3810)‡	(0.3802)‡	(0.3804)‡	(0.[illegible]97)‡
Intraindustry FDI · local		0.0104				–1.5700													
firm dummy		(0.2653)				(0.4101)‡													
FDI–forward linkages		–0.3987				2.4556													
· local firm dummy		(0.4976)				(0.9835)†													
FDI–backward linkages		–0.0796				0.3977													
· local firm dummy		(0.2851)				(0.781[illegible])													
Exporting activity																			
MERCOSUR exporter											–0.0047							–0.0047	–0.0[illegible]55
											(0.0137)							(0.0137)	(0.0[illegible]57)
World exporter										0.0144						0.0144	–0.0101		
										(0.0145)						(0.0145)	(0.0690)		
MERCOSUR exporter																			0.0[illegible]35
· local firm dummy																			(0.0[illegible]71)
World exporter · local																	0.0254		
firm dummy																	(0.0705)		
Mercosur exports/sales									0.0039					0.0039	–0.0042				
									(0.0017)†					(0.0017)†	(0.0046)				
Exports/sales								0.0041				0.0041	0.0000						
								(0.0008)‡				(0.0008)‡	(0.0019)						
MERCOSUR exports/ sales · local firm dummy															0.0093				
															(0.0048)†				
World exports/sales													0.0046						

Continued on next page

Table 17.1 Total Factor Productivity and Integration in Brazil: Regression Results, continued

	Dependent Variable: Log TFP				Dependent Variable: Change in Log TFP														
Explanatory Variables	Reg 1	Reg 2	Reg 3	Reg 4	Reg 5	Reg 6	Reg 7	Reg 8	Reg 9	Reg 10	Reg 11	Reg 12	Reg 13	Reg 14	Reg 15	Reg 16	Reg 17	Reg 18	Reg 19
· local firm dummy													(0.0022)†						
Imported intermediate goods																			
Imported–input/ material costs			−0.0002	−0.0009			0.0001					0.0001	−0.0016	0.0001	−0.0015	0.0001	−0.0016	0.0001	−0.0016
			(0.0002)	(0.0005)*			(0.0004)					(0.0004)	(0.0009)*	(0.0004)	(0.0009)*	(0.0004)	(0.0009)*	(0.0004)	(0.0009)*
Imported input · local firm dummy				0.0009									0.0021		0.0020		0.0021		0.0021
				(0.0006)									(0.0010)†		(0.0010)†		(0.0010)†		(0.0010)†
Observations	47664	47664	47664	47664	36274	36274	36274	36274	36274	36274	36274	36274	36274	36274	36274	36274	36274	36274	36274
Number of id	11177	11177	11177	11177	10253	10253	10253	10253	10253	10253	10253	10253	10253	10253	10253	10253	10253	10253	10253
Ho: Sum FDI variables =0 (χ^2)	0.0022	0.0504	0.0015	0.0057	20.6111	17.9101	20.6724	19.8252	20.8239	20.5319	20.6235	19.8804	19.77	20.8814	20.82	20.5929	20.492	20.6849	20.56
Prob > χ^2	0.96	0.82	0.97	0.94	0	0	0	0	0	0	0	0	0	0	0	0	0	0	0
Ho: Sum input and ownership variables= 0 (χ^2)				0.01									1.3014		1.3141		1.387		1.3715
Prob > χ^2				0.9396									0.25		0.25		0.24		0.24
Ho: Sum export and ownership variables= 0 (χ^2)													24.39		9.14		1.07		1.37
Prob > χ^2													0		0.0025		0.3017		0.2415

Notes:

1. All regressions were estimated using fixed effects on a panel of firms.

2. All regressions include the following controls: Size, industry output (excluding the plant's own output), capacity utilization, industrial and geographic concentration indices, U.S. consumption, log of exchange rate times US PPI in the industry, and year dummies. Regressions 5 to 19 also include log TFP in year t.

3. Standard errors in parentheses.

* Significant at the 10% level.

† Significant at the 5% level.

‡ Significant at the 1% level.

Table 17.2 Total Factor Productivity and Integration in Mexico: Regression Results

	Dependent Variable: Log TFP				Dependent Variable: Change in Log TFP														
Explanatory Variables	Reg 1	Reg 2	Reg 3	Reg 4	Reg 5	Reg 6	Reg 7	Reg 8	Reg 9	Reg 10	Reg 11	Reg 12	Reg 13	Reg 14	Reg 15	Reg 16	Reg 17	Reg 18	Reg 19
Competition from imports																			
Log imports/industry output	0.5148	0.3994		0.5159	0.2398	0.1223		0.2390	0.2399	0.2506	0.2386	0.2387	0.2495	0.2372	0.2498				
	(0.0440)‡	(0.0341)‡		(0.0437)‡	(0.0537)‡	(0.0421)=		(0.0531)‡	(0.0539)‡	(0.0549)‡	(0.0536)‡	(0.0538)‡	(0.0548)‡	(0.0538)‡	(0.0546)‡				
Mexican tariff on total imports	–0.0028	–0.0033		–0.0027	–0.0040	–0.0039		–0.0039	–0.0040	–0.0049	–0.0039	–0.0039	–0.0049	–0.0039	–0.0049				
	(0.0010)‡	(0.0009)‡		(0.0010)‡	(0.0014)‡	(0.0014)=		(0.0014)‡	(0.0014)‡	(0.0013)‡	(0.0014)‡	(0.0014)‡	(0.0013)‡	(0.0014)‡	(0.0013)‡				
FDI spillovers																			
Intraindustry FDI	–0.2706		–0.1503	–0.0242	0.0209		0.0304	0.0733	0.0210	–0.0178	0.0210	0.0211	–0.0177	0.0226	–0.0188				
	(0.0480)‡		(0.0440)‡	(0.1069)	(0.0489)		(0.0441)*	(0.1024)	(0.0488)	(0.0465)	(0.0488)	(0.0488)	(0.0465)	(0.0488)	(0.0464)				
FDI–forward linkages	0.9286		0.1429	1.2100	0.4698		0.0748	0.4448	0.4698	0.4761	0.4668	0.4667	0.4736	0.4631	0.4745				
	(0.1052)‡		(0.0530)‡	(0.1912)‡	(0.1190)‡		(0.0510)	(0.1789)†	(0.1190)‡	(0.1181)‡	(0.1188)‡	(0.1188)‡	(0.1179)‡	(0.1186)‡	(0.1174)‡				
FDI–backward linkages	0.9684		1.1038	0.5621	1.2233		1.2462	1.0181	1.2232	1.1870	1.2218	1.2216	1.1849	1.2265	1.1870				
	(0.1187)‡		(0.1032)‡	(0.2917)*	(0.1166)‡		(0.1063)‡	(0.2846)‡	(0.1166)‡	(0.1114)‡	(0.1166)‡	(0.1166)‡	(0.1113)‡	(0.1165)‡	(0.1114)‡				
Intraindustry FDI • local firm dummy				–0.3051				–0.0621											
				(0.1178)‡				(0.1132)											
FDI–forward linkages • local firm dummy				–0.3057				0.0234											
				(0.1835)*				(0.1722)											
FDI–backward linkages • local firm dummy				0.4483				0.2289											
				(0.3028)				(0.2931)											
Exporting activity																			
U.S. Tariff (Mx – RofW)	–0.0351	–0.0288		–0.0351	–0.0164	–0.0069		–0.0163	–0.0164	–0.0158	–0.0162	–0.0162	–0.0156	–0.0161	–0.0156				
	(0.0037)‡	(0.0031)‡		(0.0036)‡	(0.0048)‡	(0.0041)*		(0.0047)‡	(0.0048)‡	(0.0047)‡	(0.0048)‡	(0.0048)‡	(0.0047)‡	(0.0048)‡	(0.0047)‡				
Exporter									0.0003			0.0007		–0.0079					
									(0.0047)			(0.0047)		(0.0147)					
Exports/sales										0.0129			0.0145		0.0516				
										0.0139)			(0.0139)		(0.0371)				
Exporter • local firm dummy														0.0092					
														(0.0156)					
Exports/sales • local firm dummy															–0.0427				
															(0.0403)				
Imported intermediate goods																			
Imported–input/material costs											–0.0338	–0.0339	–0.0320	–0.1014	–0.0908				
											(0.0138)†	(0.0138)†	(0.0134)†	(0.0365)‡	(0.0347)‡				
Imported input • local firm dummy														0.0786	0.0686				
														(0.0396)†	(0.0379)*				
Observations	38024	38401	38527	38024	31940	32248	32365	31940	31940	30922	31940	31940	30922	31940	30922				
Number of group (clase folio)	5935	5980	6012	5935	5779	5819	5854	5779	5779	5647	5779	5779	5647	5779	5647				

Continued on next page

Table 17.2 Total Factor Productivity and Integration in Mexico: Regression Results, continued

	Dependent Variable: Log TFP				Dependent Variable: Change in Log TFP														
Explanatory Variables	Reg 1	Reg 2	Reg 3	Reg 4	Reg 5	Reg 6	Reg 7	Reg 8	Reg 9	Reg 10	Reg 11	Reg 12	Reg 13	Reg 14	Reg 15	Reg 16	Reg 17	Reg 18	Reg 19
Ho: Sum FDI variables=0 (χ^2 of F–stat)	94.70		91.04	82.08	110.25		147.38	101.34	110.36	111.49	109.98	110.10	111.34	110.84	111.59				
Prob > F or χ^2	0.00		0.00	0.00	0.00		0.00	0.00	0.00	0.00	0.00	0.00	0.00	0.00	0.00				
Ho: Exports*domestic=0 (χ^2)														0.06	0.35				
Prob > χ^2														0.7991	0.559				
Ho: Imported inputs*domestic=0 (χ^2)															2.32	2.30			
Prob > χ^2														0.1277	0.1293				

Notes:

1. All regressions were estimated using two–stage least squares on a panel with fixed effects. Endogenous variables: Mexican and US tariffs, imports/output, industry real exchange rate. Instrumental variables: NAFTA–negotiated tariffs, predicted imports/output from gravity equation, and nominal exchange rate multiplied by US industry producer price index.
2. All regressions include the following controls: Size, industry output (excluding the plant's own output), capacity utilization, industrial and geographic concentration indices, U.S. consumption, log of exchange rate times US PPI in the industry, and year dummies. Regressions 5 to 15 also include log TFP in year t.
3. "Mexican tariff" is the ISIC (rev 3) 4–digit industry tariff on world imports, weighted by trade. "US tariff"" is the difference between effective tariffs on Mexican imports and on imports from the rest of the world in the industry. FDI variables refer to the fraction of output produced by foreign plants; linkages were calculated using Mexican input–output data as weights.
4. Standard errors in parentheses.

* Significant at the 10% level.
† Significant at the 5% level.
‡ Significant at the 1% level.
Other controls: Herfindhal geographic and industrial concentration indices, capacity utilization.

Similarly, the experience of Mexico from 1993 to 2000 confirms that tariffs negatively impact both the level and the growth rate of productivity. Since tariffs on the rest of the world also affect productivity, one should consider total Mexican duties and not simply those applied on North American goods.[19] Nonetheless, the previous discussion suggests that NAFTA has been, by far, the main factor behind tariff changes in Mexico during the 1990s. Quantitatively, as the estimates in Table 17.2 suggest, the ten-point reduction in import duties from 1993 to 2000 would account for an increase of around 3 percent in firm-level TFP (columns 1 to 4). Since firm productivity grew by around 9 percent during the period, the estimates suggest that tariff cuts during NAFTA's first seven years contributed significantly to the sector's average growth, possibly offsetting other forces that affected productivity negatively during the 1990s. In addition, the elimination of Mexican tariffs also had a positive impact on productivity growth, with a ten percentage-point reduction in import duties increasing the growth rate by roughly 4 percent (columns 5 to 15). Moreover, the elasticity of productivity with respect to the import-output ratio was 0.5, in levels, and 0.25 for the change in log TFP.

Scale and Learning by Exports

As argued earlier, global and regional integration may also be conducive to enhanced efficiency through economies of scale and learning associated with improved export opportunities in the expanded market. Both Brazil and Mexico saw the proportion of their manufacturing firms that participate in world markets increase during the 1990s, from 41 percent in 1996 to 47 percent in 2000 in Brazil, and from 30.4 to 45.7 percent in Mexico during the 1993–2000 period.[20] At the same time, the proportion of exports as a fraction of firm output in the two countries rose from 12.0 to 18.6 percent in Brazil in 1996–2000 and, in Mexico, from 16.2 percent in 1993 to 31.2 percent in 2000. In Brazil, the fraction of firms exporting to other MERCOSUR countries increased in tandem, from 29 to 35 percent. Although the data available for Mexico does not contain information on where exports went, there is some indication that the preferential margin on Mexican products entering the U.S. market that resulted from NAFTA's tariff phase-out has increased the probability that a manufacturing plant becomes an exporter.[21]

Has export activity induced higher productivity among Brazilian and Mexican manufacturers? As Figure 17.7 illustrates, exporters, regional or otherwise, in both countries seem to have experienced more rapid productivity growth than nonexporters. The following discussion considers whether such a result holds under the more rigorous econometric analysis described in the appendix. Consider first the case of NAFTA and Mexico. An increase in the preferential margin enjoyed by Mexican exporters in the U.S. market over their competitors from the rest of the world suggests that NAFTA would have created export opportunities for Mexican producers that, in turn, would have translated into more rapid productivity growth. Another possibility, though, is that the preferential access to the U.S. market would have lessened the incentives for Mexican manufacturers to improve their efficiency. The econometric results show, however, that an increase in the tariff margin in favor of Mexican goods in the U.S. market is positively associated with an increase in productivity. A one-point increase in the tariff preference granted to Mexican producers yields a 3 percent increase in productivity (see Table 17.2, columns 1 to 4).

The previous finding, though, is not confirmed by estimates of the correlation between TFP growth and export activity, measured either by export status or export propensity—the export to sales ratio (see Table 17.2, columns 9 and 10).[22] This result is in line with other studies that fail to find a causal link between exporting and productivity growth and that argues that, instead, it is high-productivity plants that make inroads in foreign markets. Recall, however, that the previous discussion regarding Figure 17.8 argued that reallocation of resources toward exporting firms is an important channel for industry-wide productivity gains. Thus, even though exporting might not have an impact on the productivity of Mexican producers, it might result in aggregate productivity gains as more efficient firms and industries expand relative to less efficient ones.

In contrast to Mexico, TFP growth among Brazilian manufacturers seems to be positively correlated to export propensity (the ratio of exports to sales), with one percentage-point increase in the ratio of exports to sales increasing annual productivity growth by 0.4 percentage points (see Table 17.1, column 8). Exports to MERCOSUR seem to provide a similar "kick" to productivity (column 9).[23] These results are qualified when an ownership dummy is interacted with export propensity. For both world and MERCOSUR exporters, the evidence suggests that it is only local firms (defined as those in which the majority of the voting rights are owned by residents) who learn by exporting, which seems consistent with the fact that foreign affiliates, by definition, have other, more direct means of tapping into the stock of international knowledge (columns 13 and 15). To check whether these results were hiding sectoral specificities, a sectoral dummy (ISIC 2 digits) was interacted with the export-propensity variable for both MERCOSUR and world exports. The results, though, did not show any sector-specific behavior worth mentioning.[24]

Imported Inputs

Another channel through which integration by Brazil and Mexico might have enhanced manufacturing efficiency is the improved availability of world-class intermediate inputs. From 1996 to 2000, the fraction of Brazilian firms using imported inputs remains fairly constant, from 36.9 to 35.9 percent, and imported inputs went from 8.5 percent of material costs to 8.9 percent. The use of imported inputs in Mexico seems to have risen more rapidly, as they went from 28.5 to 34.1 percent of all nonwage costs of production from 1993 to 1999, with the fraction of all plants using imported inputs rising from 50.9 to 55.4 percent during the eight-year span.

Is there evidence to suggest that the expanded use of imported inputs favored productivity improvements? The evidence in Figures 17.7a and 17.7b is mixed. In Brazil, users of foreign inputs saw productivity rise faster, but in Mexico the opposite happened. However, a more careful look at the data using econometric techniques does not lend any support to the argument. The use of imported inputs, measured as the ratio of imported inputs to material costs, seems to have a limited and negative impact on TFP levels and growth among Brazil's foreign affiliates. The impact on local firms, in turn, is not statistically significant (Table 17.1, columns 4 for level and columns 13–9 for growth). These results are consistent with Muendler's (2002), who argues that foreign inputs contributed minimally to Brazilian manufacturing TFP growth during the 1986–98 period.

For Mexico, imported inputs seem to have an adverse impact on productivity growth (columns 11–3). However, when we interact imported-input use (as a fraction of total costs) with a domestic-firm dummy, we see that the previous result is due solely to foreign firms (columns 14 and 15). Among domestic firms, using imported inputs does not affect firm efficiency. The latter finding, which may seem paradoxical at first sight, might reflect differences between foreign producers that use Mexico as a base for simple assembly operations of imported materials with little productivity dynamism and foreign firms that are not attracted to Mexico solely due to its relatively low wages. Unfortunately, the dataset does not allow us to delve further into this topic, since, for example, *maquiladora* plants are not in the original survey.

The FDI Channel

Beyond the trade effects analyzed so far, there is the issue of whether higher FDI inflows have had an impact on productivity in Brazil and Mexico. Figures 17.7a and 17.7b compare TFP growth differentials between domestic and foreign producers (the latter are referred to as multinational corporations, or MNCs). Whereas in Mexico productivity growth among foreign firms outpaced that among domestic producers, in Brazil domestic manufacturers' TFP grew faster. The latter result, however, is reversed once one takes into account industry and firm size productivity differences. After controlling for these characteristics, foreign firms are suggested to be 13 percent more productive than their local counterparts in Mexico, and 18 percent in Brazil. Furthermore, in Mexico, productivity among U.S.- and Canadian-owned plants grew faster than among other foreign plants. The results shown in Figures 17.8a and 17.8b tell a similar story.

The better performance of foreign producers in Mexico and Brazil suggests that their increasing presence might have had a positive impact on productivity growth. The FDI impact might have reflected the combination of entry, competitive, knowledge, and linkages effects discussed earlier. To disentangle the contribution of each one of these effects is a daunting, if not impossible, task. Yet, by using information on ownership and on the firms' cost and demand structure (see appendix), it is possible to estimate at least in part the overall impact of FDI on productivity, and to assess whether its effects were more important to the foreign firms' competitors (intraindustry effects) or to their buyers and suppliers (interindustry effects).

The results for Mexico are more in line with those of the literature of FDI spillovers. Intraindustry FDI, perhaps reflecting the affiliates attempts to protect their technology and increase market share, appears to have a negative impact on TFP levels (Table 17.2, columns 1, 3, and 4). It seems to be a level effect since there is no evidence that it affects TFP growth (columns 5 and 7–15). Backward and forward linkages, as expected, have a positive impact both in the TFP levels and growth and the net FDI effect is always positive, both for domestic and foreign firms.

For Brazil, the results are less intuitive and are on the whole at odds with the theory. The evidence points to a positive impact of intraindustry FDI on TFP (Table 17.1, columns 1–4), suggesting that the competition effect might have prevailed. The interaction with the ownership dummy, though, indicates that this might be the case only for foreign affiliates established in the same industry but not to local firms. As in Mexico, the growth effect does not seem to be relevant (columns 5–19). Rather unexpectedly, backward and forward linkages came out with a negative sign for both level and growth effects, but only the results for the impact on growth were statistically significant. Overall, the net FDI impact on TFP levels was not different from zero, and negative on TFP growth. There are a number of hypotheses behind these results. First, this might have to do with the low absorptive capacity of Brazilians firms. Yet, preliminary tests, using the ratio of blue to white collars as a proxy for absorptive capacity, do not suggest that this is the case. Moreover, the fact that industry-wide measures of demand and cost structures are being used (see appendix) to calculate the FDI linkages might be biasing the results.

Conclusions

Economic theory suggests that integration can be the handmaiden of productivity growth, through either trade or foreign investment. This potential is particularly important for a region such as Latin America, which, with a few exceptions, has a dismal record on productivity and has been struggling in recent decades to get back on a sustainable growth path. The theory also indicates that both global and regional integration can offer substantial productivity gains. The former, for involving larger markets and a larger spectrum of comparative advantages, would involve larger potential gains. The latter, though, could be seen as a strategic stepping stone to global integration by speeding up negotiations, mitigating adjustment costs, and offering safeguards against the downside risks of integration.

After more than a decade since protrade polices spread throughout the region, the empirical evidence on the relevance of these productivity-related gains is still rather sketchy. Economy-wide measures of productivity suggest, with a few exceptions, a rather gloomy scenario of low or even negative productivity growth. Yet, analysis of manufacturing, by far the sector most affected by integration in the region, suggests a different and more upbeat story, indicating, perhaps that the gains did not reach the economies' nontradable side. In any case, this type of sectoral analysis, based on more reliable plant-level data, does not cover more than a handful of countries in the region, giving little ground for generalizations.

Against this background of scarce evidence, the case study of Brazil and Mexico throws some light in the more general links between productivity and integration and on the nuances of different strategies of regional integration. On the former, the results show that productivity growth in manufacturing was positive in both countries, reversing a downward trend that prevailed until the 1980s. The two countries also coincided in three other points. First, they did not show signs of a change in the composition of output that would indicate dislocation of high productivity sectors. Second, and as a consequence, they experienced reallocation effects, which accounted for most of the productivity growth. And third, when it comes to direct evidence on trade-productivity links, import discipline emerged as the dominant effect.

The results on learning by exporting and FDI effects varied between countries. Brazil shows signs of learning by exporting, whereas in Mexico, despite higher export orientation and the export boom experienced during the 1990s, the only evidence comes from the positive impact of U.S. preferential tariffs. On FDI, foreign firms appear to have had a positive impact on their buyers and suppliers in Mexico, despite the lower local content and greater export orientation of Mexico's industry. In Brazil, the overall impact was statistically insignificant on TFP levels and negative on TFP growth, raising questions about local firms' absorptive capacity and about the measurement of the FDI linkages.

On the strategy of regional integration, Mexico's more aggressive stance with NAFTA seems to have paid off, at least as far as productivity is concerned. Tariff reductions undertaken during the agreement appear to have had a sizable positive impact on productivity growth, which added to the already substantial gains reaped during the period of nonpreferential liberalization. As the theory suggests, the differences in labor costs between NAFTA partners appears to have kept the threat of damaging dislocations in increasing returns and knowledge-intensive sectors at bay. This is an encouraging outcome for countries in the region, which are negotiating an FTAA.

On the other hand, there is not enough evidence to argue that Brazil's more cautious approach to trade, which involved MERCOSUR, was misguided. The fact that the preferential and nonpreferential liberalizations were carried out simultaneously makes it very difficult to disentangle regional and nonregional effects. What one can argue, though, without erring too much on the side of speculation, is that the lion's share of Brazil's productivity gains during this period came from the nonpreferential liberalization, given that MERCOSUR at its peak did not account for more than 17 percent of Brazil's total trade. This comes at no surprise in view of the relative size and resources of Brazil's partners in the regional agreement, a limitation that put a severe cap on the type of learning-by-exporting gains uncovered by the econometric exercise. The elasticity of the productivity gains by unit of product exported seems to be roughly the same for world and MERCOSUR (local firm) exporters, yet the latter are constrained by a very limited market.

Given the limits of MERCOSUR gains, the importance of the import-discipline effect, and the fact that productivity growth only took off in the second half of the 1990s, one feels tempted to believe that Brazil would have had a better performance if it had pursued a more aggressive approach toward integration—one that would not have excluded MERCOSUR, but that would have gone beyond it, in search of more sizable trade gains. A broad agreement such as an FTAA, negotiated in a way that balances the interest of all parties, might just provide such opportunity.

Leaving strategic and counterfactual considerations aside, the bottom line seems to be that both Brazil and Mexico reaped important productivity gains from integration. It is perhaps too early to tell how much of these gains were "level or growth effects" or whether or not the "integration shock" will produce the same sort of rapid, sustainable and long-term productivity growth seen in East Asia. It will depend very much on the long-tem effects of import discipline on the countries' rate of innovation. In any case, one could not realistically expect that integration would do the entire job. When it comes to a stable macroeconomic environment and investment in education, technological capabilities, and institutions, all key ingredients of productivity growth, both countries, not to mention the whole region, still have a considerable agenda ahead of them.

Appendix: Empirical Methodology

This appendix presents a brief description and a summary of the impact that integration in Brazil and Mexico has had on total factor productivity in the manufacturing sector.[25] The underlying analysis relies on panel data at the firm (Brazil) or plant level (Mexico), which pose a number of challenges but allow researchers to obtain better estimates of productivity.

Methodology

The analysis applies an algorithm proposed by Olley and Pakes (1996) to account for simultaneity and sample-selection issues in estimating the parameters of a Cobb-Douglas production function with skilled (L^s) and unskilled (L^u) labor, materials (M), and capital (K) inputs as regressors, and output (Y) as the dependent variable:

$$\ln Y_{ijt} = \beta_o + \beta_u \ln L^u_{ijt} + \beta_s \ln L^s_{ijt} + \beta_m \ln M_{ijt} + \beta_k \ln K_{ijt} + p_{ijt} + \varepsilon_{ijt}.$$

Here $p_{ijt} \equiv \ln P_{ijt}$ represents total factor productivity (in logs) for firm i in industry j during year t. Different production functions were estimated for eight manufacturing industries (industries thirty-one to thirty-eight in the International Standard Industrial Classification, second revision). Productivity was then defined as the unexplained residual

$$\hat{p}_{ijt} = \ln Y_{ijt} - \hat{\beta}_u \ln L^u_{ijt} - \hat{\beta}_s \ln L^s_{ijt} - \hat{\beta}_m \ln M_{ijt} - \hat{\beta}_k \ln K_{ijt}.$$

Figures 17.6 and 17.7 reflect the output-weighted, average firm-level productivity growth, excluding the lower and upper 1 percent tails of the distribution of TFP to remove outlying observations. The analysis underlying Figure 17.8 extends the productivity decomposition proposed by Griliches and Regev (1995) by further distinguishing between intra- and inter-industry reallocation of resources. Specifically, letting $p_{jt} = \Sigma_{i\in j} s^j_{it} P_{ijt}$ represent industry j's aggregate TFP (in levels) in year t, manufacturing sector-wide productivity is $P_t = \Sigma_j s^t_j P_{jt}$, where s^j_{it} represents firm i's share of industry j's output and s^j_t represents industry j's share of total manufacturing output. Then, productivity growth in the manufacturing sector is given by the expression

$$\Delta P_t = \underbrace{\Sigma_j \Sigma_{i\in j} \overline{s}_j \overline{s}^j_{it} \Delta P_{ijt}}_{\text{Within-firm TFP gains}} + \underbrace{\Sigma_j \Sigma_{i\in j} \overline{s}_j P_{ijt} \Delta s^j_{it}}_{\text{Within-industry reallocation}} + \underbrace{\Sigma_j P_j \Delta s^j_t}_{\text{Reallocation across industries}}.$$

The first term on the right reflects the contribution to TFP growth of within-firm efficiency improvements, whereas the second and third terms reflect the contribution of resource reallocation from less to more productive firms within or across industries, respectively. A bar over a variable indicates the average over t and $t+1$ for a given variable. Since performing such decomposition requires aggregating across firms in industries with different production functions, TFP estimates were normalized as in Pavcnik (2000) by subtracting the productivity level of a so-called "reference firm" in the initial year (1996 for Brazil and 1993 for Mexico). Thus, the implicit TFP growth rates in Figure 17.8 are not readily comparable to those in Figures 17.6 and 17.7. In the decomposition exercise, we follow Bernard and Jensen (2001) in classifying firms according to alternative industry typologies.

With the productivity estimates in hand, we explain a firm's efficiency as a function of trade policy variables (e.g., tariffs), foreign capital participation and FDI, exports, imported input use, as well as other controls needed to prevent omitted variable biases. Thus, one may estimate equations of the form

$$\text{Productivity}_{ijt} = \text{Trade}_{ijt}\beta_1 + \text{FDI}_{ijt}\beta_2 + \text{controls} + \varepsilon_{ijt},$$

where Trade_{ijt} and FDI_{ijt} are matrices of trade- and FDI-related variables. The dependent variable, productivity, is either ln(TFP) or the change in ln(TFP) from t to $t+1$; in the latter case, all variables on the right are measured at year t. The availability of panel data allows tracking of each plant over time and controlling for unobserved plant characteristics via fixed-effect panel techniques.

Since trade policy is potentially endogenous—for example, less productive industries may receive more protection from policymakers—one needs to find appropriate instrumental variables to obtain consistent estimates of the coefficients in vector β_1. In the Mexican case the analysis uses the NAFTA-agreed tariffs as instruments for the actual Mexican tariffs on world trade, as well as for U.S. tariffs on Mexican goods. NAFTA tariff phase out negotiations finished in August 1992. Moreover, according to NAFTA Annex 302.2, paragraph 2, the base rate for determining import duties after applying the staging category agreed upon "generally reflect the rate of duty in effect on July 1, 1991." Thus, we can safely consider that they are exogenous (that is, they are not influenced by plant-level TFP levels during the 1993–2000 period). Moreover, they are highly correlated with actual tariffs. For Brazilian tariffs, we use Mexican most-favored-nation tariffs as instruments; the two variables have 0.5 correlation coefficient and it seems unlikely that Brazilian producers adjust their efficiency levels to Mexican protection, as the two countries engage in little bilateral trade. For both countries, we instrumented import penetration (more specifically, imports divided by shipments) using a gravity-equation approach as in Frankel and Romer (1999). Last, since exporting activities and the use of imported inputs are potentially endogenous, with more productive plants engaging in exports or establishing links with world-class input suppliers, we only include this kind of variable in regressions in which the dependent variable is the change in ln(TFP). We believe this decision ameliorates our concern of biased estimates since what we capture is the impact that, for example, exporting today has on productivity growth over the coming year.

Data

The data come from annual industrial surveys in Brazil (*Pesquisa Industrial Anual*) and Mexico (*Encuesta Industrial Anual*) that contain information, respectively, on approximately 11,000 and 6,500 manufacturing firms (in Brazil) or plants (in Mexico). These data were complemented with trade, tariff, and other information from official sources in Brazil, Mexico, and the United States. The data set covers the 1996–2000 period for Brazil and 1993–2000 for Mexico.

In order to measure intra- and inter-industry spillovers from FDI, the analysis uses information on the percent of equity owned by foreigners (in 1996 for Brazil and in 1993 for Mexico). The analysis assumes that the structure of ownership remained unchanged through 2000. A firm is considered to be "foreign" if foreigners owned more than 50 percent of its equity. With this information at hand, we took the fraction of industry output produced by foreign plants in each industry as the measure for foreign capital participation. In order to account for the possibility of spillovers from industries upstream or downstream in the production process, the analysis considers average foreign capital participation in industries with backward or forward linkages based on input-output information for each country.

References

Aitken, Brian, and Ann E. Harrison. 1999. "Do Domestic Firms Benefit from Foreign Direct Investment? Evidence from Venezuela." *American Economic Review* 89: 605–18.

Bacha, Edmar, and Regis Bonelli. 2001. "Crescimento e produtividade no Brasil: O que nos diz o Registro de Longo Prazo." Seminários Dimac no. 52, Institute de Pesquisa Económica Aplicada, Rio de Janeiro.

Baier, Scott L., Gerald P. Dwyer, Jr., and Robert Tamura. 2002. "How Important Are Capital and Total Factor Productivity for Economic Growth?" Working Paper Series 2002–2, Federal Reserve Bank of Atlanta.

Bernard, Andrew, and J. Bradford Jensen. 2001. "Exporting and Productivity." National Bureau for Economic Research Working Paper no. 7135 (April), Cambridge, MA.

Blomström, Magnus, and Ari Kokko. 1998. "Multinational Corporations and Spillovers." *Journal of Economic Surveys* 12: 247–77.

Blomström, Magnus, Ari Kokko, and Mario Zejan. 2000. *Foreign Direct Investment: Firm and Host Country Strategies*. London: Macmillan.

Clerides, Sofronis, Saul Lach, and James Tybout. 1998. "Is Learning By Exporting Important? Micro Dynamics Evidence from Colombia, Mexico, and Morocco." *Quarterly Journal of Economics* 113: 903–47.

Dussel Peters, Enrique, L. M. G. Paliza, and Eduardo Loria Diaz. 2003. "Condiciones y efectos de la inversión extranjera directa y del proceso de integración regional en México durante los años noventa: Una perspectiva microeconómica. Red INTAL Series (Integration Research Centers Network), the Institute for the Integration of Latin America and the Caribbean (INTAL), Inter-American Development Bank, Buenos Aires.

Estevadeordal, Antoni, Juchini Goto, and Raul Saez. 2000. "The New Regionalism in the Americas: The Case of MERCOSUR." Departmento de Integración y Programas Regionales Working Paper no. 5, Inter-American Developing Bank, Washington, DC.

Ethier, Wilfred. 1982. "National and International Returns to Scale in the Modern Theory of International Trade." *American Economic Review* 72: 950–59.

Fernandes, Ana. 2001. "Trade Policy, Trade Volumes and Plant Level Productivity in Colombian Manufacturing Industries." Department of Economics, Yale University. Photocopy.

Frankel, Jeffrey. A., and David Romer. 1999. "Does Trade Cause Growth?" *American Economic Review* 89: 379–99.

Griliches, Zvi, and Haim Regev. 1995. "Firm Productivity in Israeli Industry 1979–1988." *Journal of Econometrics* 65: 175–203.

Grossman, Gene, and Elhanan Helpman. 1991. *Innovation and Growth in the Global Economy*. Cambridge, MA: MIT Press.

———. 1994. "Technology and Trade." National Bureau for Economic Research Working Paper no. 4926 (November), Cambridge, MA.

Helpman, Elhanan, and Paul Krugman. 1985. *Market Structure and Foreign Trade*. Cambridge, MA: MIT Press.

Inter-American Development Bank (IDB). 2001. "Competitiveness: The Business of Growth." In *Economic and Social Progress in Latin America.* Washington, DC.

Katayama, Hajime, Lu Shihua, and James Tybout. 2003. "Why Plant-Level Productivity Studies are Often Misleading, and an Alternative Approach to Inference." Pennsylvania State University. Photocopy.

Keller, Wolfang. 2001. "International Technology of Diffusion." National Bureau for Economic Research Working Paper no. 8573, Cambridge, MA.

Kokko, Ari, Ruben Tansini, and Mario C. Zejan. 1996, "Local Technological Capability and Productivity Spillovers from FDI in the Uruguayan Manufacturing Sector." *Journal of Development Studies* 32: 602–11.

Kugler, Maurice. 2000. "The Diffusion of Externalities from Foreign Direct Investment: Theory Ahead of Measurement." University of Southampton Discussion Papers.

Kume, Honório, Guida Piani, and Carlos F. Bráz de Souza. 2000. "A política brasileira de importação no período 1987–98: Descrição e avaliação." Instituto Pesquisa Económica Aplicada, Rio de Janeiro. Photocopy.

López-Córdova, Ernesto. 2001. "Las negociaciones de acceso a los mercados en los tratados de libre comercio de México con Bolivia y Costa Rica." In *Las Américas sin barreras: Negociaciones comerciales de acceso a mercados*, edited by A. Estevadeordal and C. Robert, pp. 213–47. Washington, DC: Inter-American Development Bank.

———. 2002. "NAFTA and Mexico's Manufacturing Productivity: An Empirical Investigation using Micro-Level Data." Inter-American Development Bank, Washington, DC. Photocopy.

López-Córdova, Ernesto, and Mauricio Mesquita Moreira. 2003. "Regional Integration and Productivity: The Experiences of Brazil and Mexico." Institute for the Integration of Latin America and the Caribbean, Integration Department (INTAL-ITD) Working Paper no. 14, Inter-American Developing Bank, Washington, DC.

Loayza, Norman, Pablo Fajnzylber, and César Calderón. 2002. "Economic Growth in Latin America and the Caribbean: Stylized Facts, Explanations and Forecasts." World Bank, Washington, DC. Photocopy.

Markusen, James, and Keith Maskus. 2001. "General Equilibrium Approaches to the Multinational Firm: A Review of Theory and Evidence." National Bureau for Economic Research Working Paper no. w8335 (June), Cambridge, MA.

Markusen, James, and Anthony J. Venables. 1999. "Foreign Direct Investment as a Catalyst for Industrial Development." *European Economic Review* 43: 355–56.

Melitz, Marc J. 2002. "The Impact of Trade on Intra-Industry Reallocations and Aggregate Industry Productivity." Harvard University, Department of Economics. Photocopy.

Muendler, Marc-Andreas. 2002. "Trade, Technology and Productivity: A Study of Brazilian Manufacturers, 1986–1998." University of California Berkley. Photocopy.

Olley, Steven and Ariel Pakes. 1996. "The Dynamics of Productivity in the Telecommunications Equipment Industry. *Econometrica* 64: 1263–97.

Pavcnik, Nina. 2000. "Trade Liberalization, Exit and Productivity Improvements: Evidence from Chileans Plants." Department of Economics, Dartmouth College. Photocopy.

Pinheiro, Armando Castelar, Fabio Giambiagi, and Mauricio Mesquita Moreira. 2001. "Brazil in the 1990s: A Successful Transition?" Banco Nacional de Desenvolvimento Econômico e Social Discussion Paper no. 91, Rio de Janeiro.

Pinheiro, Armando Castelar, Indermit S. Gill, Luis Servén, and Mark Roland Thomas. 2001. "Brazilian Economic Growth, 1900–2000: Lessons and Policy Implications." Paper presented at the Third Annual Conference on Global Development Network, Rio de Janeiro, Brazil.

Roberts, Mark J., and James R. Tybout, eds.1996. *Industrial Evolution in Developing Countries*. New York: Oxford University Press.

Ten Kate, Adriaan. 1992. "Trade Liberalization and Economic Stabilization in Mexico: Lessons of Experience." *World Development* 20: 659–72.

Tybout, James R. 2000. "Manufacturing Firms in Developing Countries: How Well Do They Do and Why?" *Journal of Economic Literature* 38: 11–44.

———. 2001. "Plant and Firm-Level Evidence on New Trade Theories." National Bureau for Economic Research Working Paper no. w8418 (August), Cambridge, MA.

Tybout, James R., and M. Daniel Westbrook. 1995. "Trade Liberalization and the Dimensions of Efficiency Change in Mexican Manufacturing Industries." *Journal of International Economics* 39: 53–78.

Weiss, John. 1999. "Trade Reform and Manufacturing Performance in Mexico: From Import Substitution to Dramatic Export Growth." *Journal of Latin American Studies* 31: 151–66.

Westphal, Larry. 2001. "Technologies Strategies For Economic Development in a Fast Changing Global Economy." Department of Economics, Swarthmore College. Photocopy.

World Bank. 1991. *World Development Report*. Washington, DC.

———. 1998. "Mexico: Enhancing Factor Productivity Growth." Country Economic Memorandum Report 17392-ME, Washington, DC.

———. 2000. "Mexico, Export Dynamics and Productivity: Analysis of Mexican Manufacturing in the 1990s." Report 19864-ME, Washington DC.

Young, Alwyn. 1991. "Learning by Doing and the Dynamic Effects of International Trade." *Quarterly Journal of Economics* 106: 396–406.

Notes

1 Hereafter, the term *integration* is used to refer to the general process of economic (trade and investment) integration, be it preferential or otherwise.

2 For a review of this literature see Tybout (2000, 2001).

3 See, e.g., IDB (2002, Chapter 10).

4 One could also argue that regionalism by formally guaranteeing market access among member countries, reduces the uncertainty that might restrict scale (or enlarged market) gains.

5 For a general review see Tybout (2001). The main hurdle is related to the lack of firm-level price deflators. See Katayama, Shihua, and Tybout (2003).

6 For a general review that includes studies from other regions see Blomström, Kokko, and Zejan (2000).

7 See Ten Kate (1992) and López-Córdova (2001).

8 See Dussel Peters, Paliza, and Diaz (2002) for details.

9 See Kume, Piani, and Bráz de Souza (2000) for details.

10 E.g., investment in communication services.

11 Mexico trade data is from Banco of Mexico, www.banxico.org.mx. Unless otherwise stated, figures include *maquiladora* (i.e., in-bond assembly) trade.

12 Due to methodological changes, pre- and post-NAFTA figures are not strictly comparable. See Dussel Peters, Paliza, and Diaz (2002).

13 Brazil's trade data is from Secex, http://www. mdic.gov.br.

14 For details see Pinheiro, Gimabigi, and Moreira (2001).

15 Manufacturing exports (defined as SITC 5 to 8, except for 68) grew at an average rate of 22 percent a year in Mexico and 5.4 percent a year in Brazil in 1990–2000.

16 For the case of Brazil we use firm-level data, whereas for Mexico we rely on plant-level data. The text employs the term "firm" indistinctly. The sample of Mexican plants used in this estimation does not include

maquiladora (in-bond assembly) plants. Productivity figures for Brazil come from López-Córdova and Moreira (2002) and for Mexico from López-Córdova (2002).

17 In what follows, import-competing and exporting industries are defined as those in which import penetration or the ratio of exports to output, respectively, are in the upper quartile of the manufacturing distribution. Nontraded industries are those that are neither import competing nor exporting.

18 Industries traded in MERCOSUR and NAFTA were defined as those whose import penetration and export ratio were in the fourth quartile of their distribution. Although this definition ensures that the regional markets are important for those industries, it does not eliminates the overlap with industries traded in extraregional markets. In the case of firm characteristics there is also overlapping among the regional trade categories, since MERCOSUR exporters might also be world exporters. In fact, 76 percent of MERCOSUR exporters are also world exporters.

19 Total Mexican duties are calculated as the trade-weighted average of preferential and nonpreferential rates.

20 We look at a balanced panel of firms in order to focus on the likelihood that a given firm becomes an exporter, or on a firm's share of output that is exported. Using an unbalanced panel fails to correct for sample compositional changes that might reflect a greater likelihood that exporters remain in operation. These percentages refer to the proportion of exporters in a sample of manufacturing firms in Brazil and Mexico, which is biased toward medium to large firms. The corresponding figures for all manufacturing firms would be smaller.

21 The latter stems from an econometric exercise that estimates the probability that a plant is an exporter. The preferential margin in the U.S. market on Mexican goods is positively correlated with the probability of exporting.

22 Bernard and Jensen (2001) perform such an exercise on U.S. data.

23 When export activity is measured by exporter status, rather than by export propensity, the coefficients were not significant (columns 10 and 11). This might have been related to the fact that there might be a threshold in the terms of volume and year of experience, below which there might not be any significant productivity gains.

24 These results are not shown in the table, but are available upon request.

25 The following discussion is based on work by López-Córdova and Moreira.

18

The FTAA and the Location of Foreign Direct Investment

Eduardo Levy Yeyati, Ernesto Stein, and Christian Daude

In recent decades we have seen an increase in the number and depth of regional integration agreements (RIAs) around the world. The proliferation of trade agreements has been quite widespread. The former European Economic Community has evolved into a single market (EU) and most of its members have recently adopted a common currency. Other European countries have formed free trade areas with the EU or are presently in line for accession to the European Monetary Union. Likewise, countries in Southeast Asia agreed to form the ASEAN free trade area.

The Americas have been no exception to this trend. While a number of regional integration agreements have been either created (e.g., MERCOSUR, NAFTA) or strengthened (Andean Community) in the 1990s, some countries such as Mexico and Chile have been actively forming bilateral trade agreements with countries both in their continents and in other regions. Most importantly, an FTAA, currently under negotiation, is supposed to create a free trade area from Alaska to Tierra del Fuego by the year 2005.

At the same time, the world has been experiencing a dramatic surge in flows of foreign direct investment (FDI). During the last two decades, while world trade has increased by a factor of two, flows of FDI have increased by a factor of ten. The surge in FDI involves flows toward both developed and developing countries. In fact, foreign direct investment has recently become, by a large margin, the main source of foreign financing for emerging markets, and for Latin America in particular.

In light of these developments, the role of regional integration agreements as a determinant of the location of FDI has become an increasingly relevant issue for emerging economies. While the concerns regarding the impact of RIAs on FDI for countries in Latin America may be related to a number of RIA initiatives of different types (subregional south-south agreements, agreements with the EU, etc.), the largest effects are likely to be associated with an FTAA. In this regard, there are a number of highly relevant questions, for instance: What effect will an FTAA have on FDI from the United States and Canada to Latin American countries? How will it affect FDI from the rest of the world? What are the implications for a country such as Mexico, whose preferential access to the U.S. may be diluted? Should we expect to see winners and losers, and if so, what determines whether a particular country wins or loses? To address these questions we look at the impact of regional integration on FDI and attempt to derive conclusions regarding the likely impact of an FTAA on countries in Latin America.

A difficulty in assessing the role of regional integration agreements on FDI is that there are many channels through which RIAs could potentially have an impact on the location of FDI. The impact of regional integration, for example, depends on whether or not the source country is a member of the RIA. Thus NAFTA has affected flows of FDI to Mexico from U.S. sources differently than it has affected flows to Mexico from German sources. The same is true of whether or not the host country is a member of the RIA. NAFTA has affected FDI flows from the U.S. to Mexican hosts differently than it has affected flows from the U.S. to countries in Central America, which may compete with Mexico as potential FDI sites. In addition, the impact of RIAs will likely be a function of specific characteristics of the host countries that make them relatively more or less attractive than their RIA partners as a potential location of foreign investment.

Another important consideration that will affect the impact of RIAs on the location of foreign investment is the predominant driver of FDI. For instance, a firm may invest abroad in order to serve, through sales of a foreign affiliate, a protected market that it could otherwise serve only at a high cost through trade. In this case, integration could make the market less protected and thus weaken the firm's motive for this type of FDI, which is known in the literature as "horizontal." Alternatively, the firm may invest abroad in order to exploit different countries' comparative advantages for the various stages of production of a good. After some stages the good will cross national boundaries and incur tariff costs; integration reduces such costs and so strengthens the firm's motive for "vertical" FDI.[1] Depending on the motive for foreign investment, therefore, the relaxation of trade barriers implicit in an RIA may have completely different implications for the location of FDI. For this reason, it is worthwhile to discuss in more detail the nature of horizontal and vertical FDI.

Vertical and Horizontal FDI

Models of vertical FDI typically feature a firm with a corporate facility (which may produce management services and research and development) and a production facility; the two are presumed to be geographically separable.[2] As the corporate facility and the production facility require a different mix of factors of production, firms localize each "stage" of production to take advantage of international differences in factor prices. The production facility produces for the markets in both the host country and the source country. An implication of the model is that no FDI would be observed between countries with similar factor endowments: such countries would have similar factor prices, eliminating the advantage of geographically separating firms' corporate and production stages.

Models of horizontal FDI typically feature firms with multiple production facilities producing a homogeneous good. One of these facilities is located together with the company's headquarters.[3] Each production facility supplies its domestic market. A key assumption in the horizontal model is the presence of firm-level fixed costs, arising from the necessity of one, and only one, corporate facility per firm. Firm-level fixed costs imply economies of scale that give multinational firms an advantage over domestic firms.

The volume of horizontal FDI depends on the interplay between firm-level fixed costs, plant-level fixed costs, and trade costs.[4] In the absence of trade costs there would be no reason for multinational production: firms would concentrate their production in a single facility at a single location, incurring plant-level fixed costs only there and serving other markets through trade. As trade costs increase, so does multinational production. The presence of firm-level fixed costs, coupled with high trade costs, implies that the least costly way to serve local markets is to operate local facilities as branches of a multinational firm. In this sense one can think of horizontal multinational activity as a "tariff-jumping" strategy.

As expected, the empirical implications of the horizontal model of multinational activity differ from those of the vertical model. Unlike vertical FDI, horizontal FDI is less likely to be found among countries with very different factor proportions. Dissimilar factor proportions imply dissimilar factor prices, which induce firms to produce only in the location where the factor used intensively has the lowest price, and serve the other markets through trade. In addition, horizontal FDI is discouraged by differences in country size. With a large country and a small country as potential plant locations, a firm is likely to produce only in the country with the large home market and serve the other country through trade, incurring trade costs on a small trade volume, but foregoing the cost of establishing a second plant.

The implications of the horizontal and vertical FDI models seem to suggest that direct investment flows from north to south —that is, between countries whose sizes and factor proportions differ substantially—are more likely of the vertical kind, while north-north and south-south flows are more likely to be of the horizontal kind. But the matter is not so clear cut. First, countries in the North tend to have much lower trade barriers, at least in the manufacturing sector. As discussed above, trade barriers, both natural and policy related, are a key ingredient of horizontal FDI. The general absence of high trade barriers among developed countries weakens the likelihood that north-north FDI is horizontal. If the tariffs to be jumped are small, there is little point in tariff jumping.[5]

Second, horizontal FDI can arise between northern and southern countries, even when their factor endowments are very different, as long as trade barriers are high enough. The automobile industry in Latin American countries during the period of import substitution (or even today, within the protected environment of MERCOSUR) is an example of horizontal FDI. Finally, a large portion of FDI among countries in the North may not be placed squarely within either of the two categories discussed by Markusen and Maskus (2001), but instead belong to a different class, one in which firms have multiple plants, as in the horizontal model, but produce different varieties of a final good, both for export and for domestic consumption, rather than a homogeneous good.[6] Thus, unlike the homogeneous good horizontal variety, this type of FDI does not substitute trade.

Integration and FDI: What Does the Empirical Literature Say?

Existing data on FDI does not classify it according to its vertical or horizontal nature. It is not straightforward to identify the motives for investment with any precision. To a certain extent, however, the nature of FDI flows between a pair of countries may be inferred from some characteristics of the source and host countries involved: whether the host country's economy is open or closed, whether the source and host countries are rich or poor, or whether they are similar or dissimilar in resources. Most existing studies of the impact of RIAs on FDI focus on the last two variables—the countries' levels of development and the similarity of their resource endowments. The relation of regional integration to FDI is thus examined most often by segregating the data into cases of north-north integration (between highly developed countries with resource endowments abundant in capital and skills), south-south integration (between less developed countries with endowments abundant in labor), and north-south integration (between countries of dissimilar levels of development and dissimilar endowments). In each of these cases, studies typically stress the difference between the impact on FDI between RIA partners, and that on FDI inflows from outside sources.

Among recent studies of north-north agreements, Dunning (2000) finds that, since Europe's 1985 launch of its Internal Market Program, both intra-EC and extra-EC FDI have been stimulated, particularly the latter; FDI has grown the most in knowledge-intensive activities; and the growth of FDI has been complementary to the growth of trade. Of south-south agreements, Chudnovsky and López (2001) find that FDI in MERCOSUR has been largely from extraregional sources; has taken the form primarily of mergers and acquisitions; has displaced domestic investment; and has been directed toward supplying the internal market. Of north-south agreements, Waldkirch (2001) finds that NAFTA has increased substantially FDI in Mexico, mostly from its intraregional partners Canada and the United States, and infers that the agreement's impetus to vertical integration is the likely explanation.

Blomström and Kokko (1997) take a similar approach, although they group three case studies together to work toward a more comprehensive analysis. The Canada-U.S. free trade agreement, a north-north RIA, reduced the relative importance of intraregional FDI for both countries but increased extraregional FDI to Canada. In neither case was the effect dramatic, though, a fact attributed to the lack of major changes in economic policy resulting from the agreement.[7] The south-south RIA, MERCOSUR, witnessed a substantial expansion of extraregional FDI, though macroeconomic stability is found to be a more important determinant of the inflows than the RIA. The north-south RIA, NAFTA, is found to have witnessed a dramatic increase in FDI inflows, particularly extraregional FDI to Mexico, due to a combination of broader policy reforms undertaken contemporaneously in Mexico as well as Mexico's proximity to the U.S. market and its abundance of labor.[8]

The case-studies methodology has the advantage that one can take into account the institutional detail of the countries under study when reaching conclusions about the impact of integration on FDI. At the same time, however, it illustrates the difficulty of drawing strong conclusions when so many other variables complicate the particular cases. In MERCOSUR, for example, it is hard to disentangle the effect of the RIA from that of macroeconomic stabilization, which occurred approximately at the same time. In Mexico, the effect of NAFTA is hard to distinguish from that of other changes in FDI-related policies that took place contemporaneously. Moreover, the particular circumstances of each of the cases studied make it difficult to extrapolate the findings to other potential RIAs, particularly when these do not share the same context. To what degree was FDI influenced by the unique circumstances of each set of countries and to what degree was it driven by the general characteristics of an RIA? Case studies, however well informed, cannot provide definitive answers.[9]

Another way to proceed, which provides a nice complement to the case studies, is to control for some of those circumstances within a large sample of countries, all of which are sources or hosts of FDI, and most of which are parties to RIAs. There are enough RIAs in existence, and enough bilateral FDI data, to try to sort out quantitatively the effects of an RIA from the effects of other circumstances. In a companion paper, Levy Yeyati, Stein, and Daude (2003) have studied the relationship between integration and FDI using bilateral data on FDI stocks for a large sample of countries. In the rest of this chapter we will discuss their results and use them to draw conclusions regarding the potential impact of the FTAA on the location of foreign direct investment. Before presenting the evidence, however, it is useful to discuss briefly the different channels through which RIAs may affect FDI.

Effects on FDI from Insiders

If the source and host countries become members of the same RIA, the impact on bilateral FDI is theoretically ambiguous and depends on the kind of FDI that predominates. If FDI is horizontal, with tariff jumping as its motive, the reduction in trade barriers implicit in the RIA will probably lead to a reduction in FDI, as trade and foreign investment are alternative ways to serve the domestic market. If FDI is vertical, with integration of stages of production as its motive, the RIA should increase FDI, as transactions costs to engage in vertical integration across international borders are reduced. The net effect may depend, among other things, on the size of trade barriers and the similarities in factor proportions, since these two factors affect the vertical versus horizontal composition of FDI. Note that, regardless of its impact on total FDI, an RIA will likely change the composition of FDI from horizontal to vertical.[10]

Extended Market Effect

The entrance of a country into an RIA may make it a more enticing host of FDI in activities subject to economies of scale through an extended market effect, particularly if the FDI is horizontal. MERCOSUR, for example, may have become a more attractive market for outside sources after the formation of the customs union, making it more worthwhile for foreign firms to "jump" the common external tariff instead of supplying each individual country through trade. The extension of the market due to an RIA may encourage vertical FDI as well, since it reduces the costs of locating different stages of production in different countries within the region. In fact, this effect can also be present for the case of FDI from source countries within the same RIA. Thus, whatever the motive for FDI, the extended market effect of a host country's entry into an RIA should result in more FDI for the RIA as a whole.

Yet within the RIA there may be winners and losers. Notwithstanding the increased FDI brought to the region as a whole, there may be a redistributive effect of FDI within the region. Before the RIA is launched, for instance, a multinational corporation might have horizontal FDI in each of the countries in the region. When barriers to trade within the region are eliminated, the firm may choose to concentrate production in a single country (perhaps the one that offers a more attractive overall package) and supply the rest of the countries through trade.[11]

Diversion/Dilution Effect

When a source country enters into or expands an RIA, host countries may experience investment diversion or dilution. If membership in a regional integration agreement makes each member a more attractive host of FDI—as it does in the vertical model—then the RIA will make nonmembers appear relatively less attractive. We call this effect *FDI diversion* in an analogy to Viner's (1950) classic trade diversion concept: FDI from a source to nonpartners may decline as the source enters an RIA.[12]

A similar effect may be endured by members of an RIA when the agreement is enlarged. Take, for instance, the potential effects of an FTAA on FDI flows from the United States to Mexico. To the extent that U.S. investment in Mexico is intended to exploit some locational advantages of Mexico, then as the preferential access of Mexico to the United States gets *diluted* by the FTAA, part of the FDI may be relocated to members of the larger agreement that have similar advantages.[13]

Empirical Results

In order to look at the impact of RIAs on FDI we used data on bilateral FDI stocks from the OECD *International Direct Investment Statistics Yearbook* (2000). The dataset covers FDI from twenty source countries, all of them from the OECD, to sixty host countries, from 1982 through 1999. One shortcoming of this data is that it does not cover FDI between developing countries. Yet, it is the most complete source available for bilateral FDI, which is a key ingredient in a study of the effects of integration on foreign investment.

The methodology used in Levy Yeyati, Stein, and Daude (2003) is loosely based on the gravity model, which has been employeed widely in the literature on the determinants of bilateral trade, and more recently has been used to study the determinants of FDI.[14] The traditional gravity model is modified in a number of ways by including: (1) country-pair fixed effects, to control for all the characteristics of country pairs that are invariant over time, such as distance, common border, similarity of factor proportions, as well as other variables that may be relevant for FDI location but that may be difficult to observe (including these pair fixed effects allows us to focus on the effects of changes in RIAs on the bilateral FDI within country pairs, leaving out the cross-sectional dimension); (2) year dummies to control for the spectacular increase in FDI over time; and (3) a number of variables associated to the effects of regional integration.

The first regional integration variable is *Same RIA*, a dummy variable that indicates whether the source and host countries belong to the same regional integration agreement.[15] This variable captures a combination of channels: tariff jumping, international vertical integration, and the potential effect of investment provisions on FDI. The expected impact is ambiguous. A second integration variable is *Extended Market*

Host, which captures the size of the extended market of the host country.[16] For example, for the case of Brazil in the years before MERCOSUR, *Extended Market Host* is the log of Brazil's GDP at the time; for the years after MERCOSUR, it takes the value of the log of the combined GDP of the four MERCOSUR countries. Following the previous discussion, we expect an increase in the size of the extended market to have positive effects on FDI for the RIA as a whole. Finally, a third integration variable is *Extended Market Source*, which captures the FDI diversion/dilution effects. We expect its coefficient to have a negative sign, suggesting that FDI to a host country diminishes when firms in the source country have other FTA partners in which to locate their investments.

The results of the regressions are presented in Tables 18.1 and 18.2. Column 1 in Table 18.1 presents the basic results in which the dependent variable is ln(1+FDI).[17] The coefficient for *Same RIA* is positive and highly significant, suggesting that, on average, any potential loss of FDI due to the tariff-jumping argument associated to horizontal FDI is more than offset by other effects (vertical integration and investment provisions) that operate in the opposite direction. The size of the coefficient suggests that a source country will increase FDI to a host country by around 27 percent once they become partners in a trade agreement.[18] The host and source extended-market variables are also significant, and have the expected signs, positive for host and negative for source. The coefficient for extended-market host, which can be interpreted as an elasticity, suggests that a 1 percent increase in the size of the extended market (after controlling for the host country's GDP) increases FDI from all sources by 0.10 percent.[19] Similarly, a one percent increase in the size of the extended market of the source country, after controlling for the source country's GDP, reduces FDI to all hosts by 0.05 percent. Columns 2 through 4 show that the results are robust to the inclusion of other variables that may explain FDI location, such as the stock of privatization to date (to control for the fact that most FDI linked to privatization is in nontradables), the rate of inflation (to control for macroeconomic conditions), and an index of institutional quality.[20]

An interesting exercise that provides a notion of the magnitude of these effects is to compare the impact that the creation of an FTAA would have for FDI from the United States to Mexico and Argentina, according to the basic model of column 1. Consider first the case of Argentina. Since it does not have an FTA with the United States, it would

Table 18.1 The Impact of Regional Integration on FDI
OLS Estimation: Dependent Variable ln(FDI Stock + 1)

	(1)	(2)	(3)	(4)
GDP host	0.1912	0.18	0.2326	0.2403
	(5.864)***	(5.540)***	(6.512)***	(5.567)***
GDP source	0.518	0.518	0.5152	0.4435
	(7.259)***	(7.288)***	(6.961)***	(5.473)***
Extended market host	0.1022	0.1118	0.1062	0.0534
	(5.684)***	(6.234)***	(5.663)***	(1.926)*
Extended market source	–0.0481	–0.051	–0.031	–0.0183
	(2.730)***	(2.905)***	(1.699)*	(0.767)
Same RIA	0.2393	0.2821	0.2768	0.2086
	(3.983)***	(4.703)***	(4.630)***	(2.717)***
Privatizations		0.0411	0.0351	0.0462
		(9.609)***	(8.026)***	(8.229)***
Inflation			0.0471	0.0514
			(4.013)***	(3.272)***
Institutions				0.137
				(3.522)***
Constant	–6.9546	–6.9168	–7.614	–6.2566
	(7.260)***	(7.249)***	(7.510)***	(5.607)***
Observations	12483	12483	11421	7666
Number of pairs	1083	1083	1045	994
R^2 between	0.5126	0.5072	0.5056	0.5126
F pair dummies	[61.65]***	[61.54]***	[59.95]***	[48.15]***
F year dummies	[42.12]***	[40.45]***	[37.28]***	[23.45]***

Notes: Absolute value of t-statistics in parentheses. Absolute value of F-statistics in square brackets.
*Significant at 10%.
**Significant at 5%.
***Significant at 1%.

benefit from the direct effect of sharing an FTA with the source, increasing the U.S.-originated FDI stock by 27 percent. In addition, the Argentinean economy would become more attractive to FDI because of the extension of its market from MERCOSUR to the FTAA (which, using GDP data for 1999, implies that the extended market increases by a factor of ten). This increase in the size of the extended market would lead to an increase of 26.8 percent in the stock of FDI originated in the United States (as well as other source countries).[21] On the other hand, the source extended-market effect would partially offset these increases. An FTAA, however, would only represent an increase of around

Table 18.2 The Impact of Regional Integration on FDI
Fixed Effects Estimation: Dependent Variable
ln(FDI Stock + 1)

	(1)	(2)	(3)	(4)
GDP host	0.1912	0.1992	0.1136	0.1075
	(5.864)***	(6.199)***	(3.049)***	(2.888)***
GDP source	0.518	0.514	0.4994	0.4939
	(7.250)***	(7.205)***	(6.192)***	(6.131)***
Extended market host	0.1022	0.0925	0.0918	0.0968
	(5.684)***	(5.465)***	(5.051)***	(5.321)***
Extended market source	–0.048	–0.0489	–0.0115	–0.0133
	(2.730)***	(2.772)***	(0.563)	(0.653)
Same RIA	0.2393	–0.3692	–0.0482	–0.7146
	(3.983)***	(2.370)**	(0.501)	(4.007)***
Same RIA × average openness		0.009		0.0096
		(4.235)***		(4.437)***
Same RIA × abs. diff. % labor force with secondary education			0.0113	0.0127
			(2.561)**	(2.871)***
Constant	–6.9546	–6.8741	–6.0459	–5.9588
	(7.260)***	(7.180)***	(5.533)***	(5.458)***
Observations	12483	12483	9758	9758
Number of pairs	1083	1083	828	828
R^2 between	0.5126	0.5147	0.4623	0.4623
F pair dummies	[61.65]***	[61.26]***	[57.00]***	[56.44]***
F year dummies	[42.12]***	[42.10]***	[35.88]***	[35.95]***
Total Effect of Same RIA				
MIN		*–0.197*	*0.048*	*–0.551*
MEAN		0.283	0.181	0.245
MAX		*2.876*	*0.706*	*3.687*
Average Openness				
MIN		16.97		16.97
MEAN		72.25		73.08
MAX		370.25		370.25
Abs. Diff. % Labor Force with Secondary Education				
MIN			0.03	0.03
MEAN			20.32	20.32
MAX			66.72	66.72

Notes: Absolute value of *t*-statistics in parentheses. Absolute value of *F*-statistics in square brackets.
*Significant at 10%.
**Significant at 5%.
***Significant at 1%.

16 percent in the extended market of the United States, with an associated decline in U.S. FDI of 0.71 percent due to the diversion/dilution effect.[22] Altogether, the overall effect of the creation of an FTAA would be a substantial increase of around 60 percent in the United States' direct-investment position in Argentina.[23]

The result for Mexico would be quite different. Since Mexico and the United States are already members of the same FTA, an FTAA would have no direct effect. The increase of the extended market of Mexico would be lower than that of the United States, as Mexico already had FTAs with Colombia, Venezuela, and Bolivia at the end of the sample period, yielding an extension of the host market of only 13 percent and a corresponding increase in bilateral stocks of 1.25 percent. Netting the source extended-market effect, which was calculated in the previous paragraph as –0.71 percent, we arrive at a net increase of U.S. FDI stocks in Mexico of around 0.5 percent.[24]

The numbers in this simple exercise can illustrate potential asymmetries in the impact of an FTAA for different countries—but they must be taken with a great deal of caution. The estimates that we use represent the average impact of our regional-integration variables over the whole sample. However, the impact may differ according to the characteristics of the countries in question. For example, the impact of *Same RIA* may depend on the horizontal or vertical nature of the investments, which in turn may depend on the degree of protection in the host country, or the similarity in factor proportions vis à vis the source. Other things being equal, closed economies are expected to have a larger share of horizontal FDI, which, according to the theory, should decrease with regional integration. Economies that are similar in their factor endowments are not expected to have a substantial volume of vertical FDI, suggesting that FDI between similar countries should not react much to integration.

The difference in the impact of *Same RIA* for countries of different characteristics is examined in Table 18.2. In column 2, we include an interaction term in which *Same RIA* is multiplied by the average openness in the host country throughout the sample period. The interaction term is positive and significant, suggesting that the impact of common membership in an RIA will increase with the openness of the host country. Column 3 presents the results when *Same RIA* is interacted with the absolute difference in the percentage of the labor force with secondary education between the source and host countries, averaged over the period.[25] In column 4, we include both interaction terms together. The coefficients for the interaction terms are very similar to those of the previous columns, and so is the *Same RIA* impact evaluated at the mean of openness and factor proportions. The effect of *Same RIA* on FDI as a function of different levels of openness and difference in factor proportions is presented in Figures 18.1 and 18.2. Interestingly, Figure 18.1 suggests that common membership in RIAs may lower FDI for host countries that are below a critical level of openness (imports plus exports over GDP below 50 percent). Within Latin America, countries such as Argentina, Brazil, and Colombia are well below this critical level.

Simulating the Impact of an FTAA on FDI to Its Member Countries

We have in our sample ten countries that are scheduled to launch an FTAA in 2005. These are Argentina, Brazil, Canada, Chile, Colombia, Costa Rica, Mexico, Panama, the United States, and Venezuela. In what follows, we simulate the potential impact of an FTAA in each of these countries, using the regressions presented above. In each case, we look at the effects from inside sources (the United States and Canada) as well as from the rest of the world. To do this, we first use the coefficients of our baseline regression (column 1 in Tables 18.1 and 18.2)

Figure 18.1 Difference in Openness and the Impact of Same RIA on FDI Stock

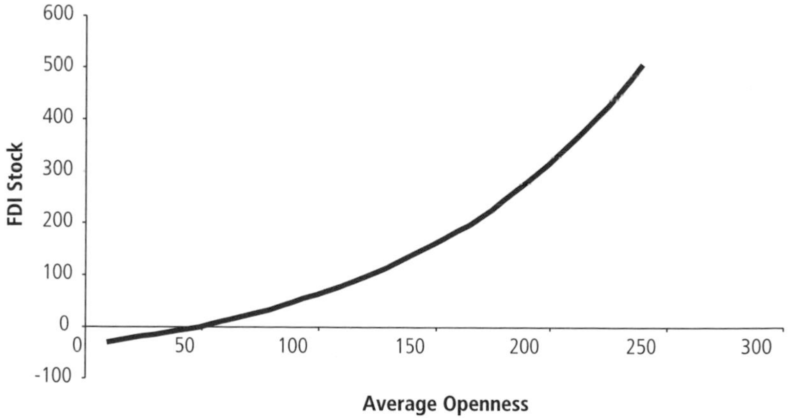

Note: The coefficients correspond to Regression 4 of Table 3, and are evaluated at the mean of skill difference.

Figure 18.2 Absolute Difference in Education Per Worker and the Impact of Same RIA on FDI Stock

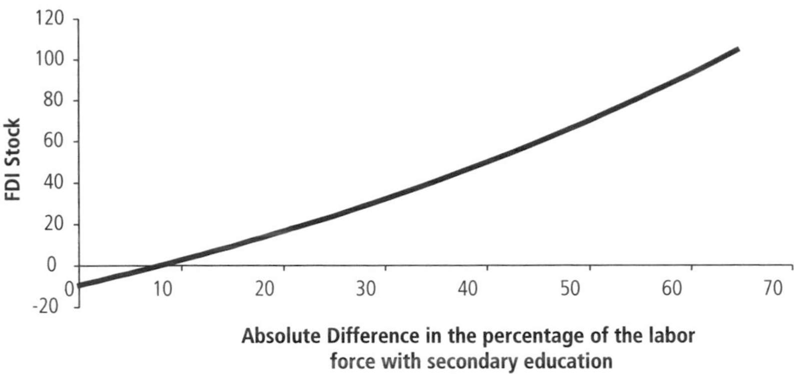

Note: The coefficients correspond to Regression 4 of Table 2, and are evaluated at the mean of Openness.

and estimate the FDI stocks that each country would have from each source country if an FTAA were implemented. That is, we compute the fitted value of the FDI stock using the coefficients estimated in the baseline regression but replacing the variables *Same FTA*, *Extended Market Source* and *Extended Market Host* with the values they would have assumed had an FTAA entered into force in 1999. Then, we aggregate these values by host country according to whether the FDI stocks come from the United States and Canada or from the rest of the world and calculate the percentage change in the stocks relative to their fitted values in the absence of an FTAA.

Table 18.3 shows the results for the ten future FTAA members represented in our sample. The first thing to notice is that impacts on FDI stocks are exactly the same for countries that belong to the same trading bloc, such as Argentina and Brazil. This is an expected result since the changes in the explanatory variables we are taking into account—*Extended Market Host*, *Extended Market Source*, and *Same FTA*—are equal for both countries. Accordingly, each of the countries in MERCOSUR would increase its stocks from the United States and Canada by approximately 60 percent and from the rest of the world almost by 26 percent. The figures for the countries of the Andean Community are larger (82 percent from insiders, and 44 percent from the rest of the world). The countries in which the estimated impact is largest are

Table 18.3 Simulating the Impact of the FTAA
Percent Change in FDI Stocks

	Baseline Regression		Regression with Openness		Regression with Openness and Skill Difference	
	From U.S. and Canada	From ROW	From U.S. and Canada	From ROW	From U.S. and Canada	From ROW
Argentina	58.93	26.05	1.87	27.44	21.70	28.88
Brazil	58.93	26.05	2.71	27.44	22.62	28.88
Canada	0.65	1.43	0.70	1.50	1.35	1.57
Chile	98.13	57.15	82.44	60.54	56.97	64.10
Colombia	81.81	44.20	34.20	46.72	11.43	49.35
Costa Rica	124.92	78.40	153.06	83.35	155.83	88.57
Mexico	0.03	0.81	0.05	0.84	0.67	0.88
Panama	136.11	87.27	161.87	92.91	206.02	98.86
U.S.	0.65	1.43	0.70	1.50	1.35	1.57
Venezuela	81.81	44.20	55.44	46.72	53.58	49.35

Panama, Costa Rica, and Chile, which have the greatest increase in their extended market size. At the other end of the spectrum are Mexico, Canada, and the United States, all cases in which the effects would be minimal.

The fact that the results are similar for countries within each bloc does not mean, however, that the distribution of the FDI gains will be equally distributed among the bloc members. It simply shows that we cannot uncover the asymmetric effects within each bloc with this model. In the second panel of Table 18.3 we repeat the exercise including the interaction between *Same RIA* and *Openness*. As we expected, more open economies would benefit more from the FTAA. Notice in particular the reduction in the impact from the United States and Canada in the case of Argentina and Brazil, which are the least open economies in the group. Remember that the extended-market effect (from all sources) in the case of Argentina in the example discussed previously was around 26.8 percent. The total impact from insiders in this model is around 2 percent, which suggests that the direct *Same RIA* effect in these cases is negative. In the third panel we add the interaction of *Same FTA* with the difference in factor proportions (corresponding to equation 4 in Table 18.2).

Naturally, the figures for the impact of an FTAA on FDI obtained in these simulations should only be taken as indicative. As it is obvious from Table 18.3, they change considerably depending on the specification used for the simulations. In spite of this, we believe that they provide a very useful first look at the potential impact of an FTAA on FDI. We suggest that this impact is statistically significant, economically important, and very unevenly distributed.

FDI Policy in Integrating Countries

The discussion throughout this chapter has implicitly equated gains in FDI with gains in general welfare. The national "winners" from RIAs are associated with those whose FDI inflows increase, and the national "losers" are those whose FDI inflows decline. However, the question of whether FDI generates positive welfare effects for host countries has been a subject of great debate. While most authors believe that FDI tends to be beneficial, there are some who believe that foreign investment is at best a mixed blessing, bringing with it a measure of harm that may outweigh the good.

The presumption that FDI is good is based on the idea that FDI may generate positive spillovers for the rest of the economy. These spillovers may flow through a variety of channels. If a foreign firm is technologically more advanced than most domestic companies, the interaction of its technicians, engineers, and managers with domestic firms may result in knowledge spillovers. Positive spillovers may also arise if the foreign firm trains workers who are eventually hired by domestic firms. Other possible sources of spillovers identified in the literature are related to the development of new inputs spurred by the demand from multinationals, which then become available to domestic producers (Rodriguez-Clare 1996), or to the example set by exporting multinationals, which may induce domestic producers to become exporters as well (see Aitken, Hanson, and Harrison 1997). Borensztein, De Gregorio, and Lee (1998) find evidence that FDI has a positive effect on growth, provided that the level of human capital in the host country is sufficiently high. Thus, in order to benefit from the advanced technology introduced by foreign firms, the host country has to have the capacity to absorb it.[26]

However, FDI may also generate negative spillovers. Domestic firms may be displaced by the foreign firm, or may find that the cost of factors of production increases as a result of the foreign investment. At the same time, foreign firms tend to import a larger share of their inputs. This may generate balance-of-payments concerns, and at the same time affect domestic suppliers of intermediate inputs, whose demand may decline when a domestic firm is sold to foreign nationals. While most of the earlier empirical literature on the subject supports the presence of positive externalities, recent work based on firm-level data has found some evidence of negative externalities instead. An example is the work of Aitken and Harrison (1999), who find, for the case of Venezuela, that growth of total-factor productivity was lower for domestic firms in sectors in which FDI was greater. These authors focus on within-industry spillovers, however. Kugler (2000) and IDB (2002) find evidence of important, positive interindustry spillovers for the cases of Colombia and Mexico, respectively.[27]

This discussion of the potential benefits and costs of FDI suggests that not all FDI carries similar benefits. In particular, FDI may be more beneficial if it targets more advanced industries (so that potential technological spillovers are larger); establishes strong forward and backward linkages with domestic firms (which may thereby absorb the spillovers); exports part of the production (relaxing balance-of-payments concerns and inducing domestic firms to follow suit); and if domestic firms have the capacity to absorb those spillovers. The key question is, what kind of policies can countries adopt in order to ensure that the resulting FDI inflows are of the beneficial kind? In addition, how does regional integration affect the desirability and effectiveness of those policies? And how can countries maximize the FDI benefits associated with agreements such as an FTAA?

Some of the policies that countries have traditionally used to try to get the most out of FDI are technology transfer and performance requirements. Domestic affiliates of foreign-owned firms may be required to train domestic workers to certain standards, to locate research and development activities in the country, to use a minimum content of local inputs, to export a certain proportion of their output, or to employ certain technologies. Yet the evidence suggests that performance requirements have been ineffective. Blomström, Kokko and Zejan (2000, ch. 13) offer strong evidence that such requirements actually reduce multinationals' employment of technology, and weaker evidence that they increase capital imports as well. In addition, some of these requirements, such as local-content or trade-balancing requirements, are either prohibited or being phased out under current WTO rules.

Whether or not performance requirements are beneficial under some circumstances, they are least likely to be so in circumstances of regional integration. RIAs tend to promote vertical FDI over horizontal;

they also tend to extend the market for horizontal FDI from individual countries to that of the RIA, thus making FDI more footloose within the region. While a horizontal multinational firm may accept performance requirements if it is necessary to serve a particular country's protected market, enlargement of the market with an RIA allows the firm to choose as its host whichever member country has the fewest requirements. A vertical multinational, with even greater ease, may simply choose another country for a particular stage of production.[28] Performance requirements, in other words, may be best suited for a state of the world that RIAs are designed deliberately to dismantle. The implication for regional integration policy is that, when it comes to an RIA's investment chapter, national treatment may work better than any alternative to help a country avoid becoming an FDI loser.[29]

If performance requirements are not helpful in attracting FDI to integrating countries, which policies would be? And, more specifically, what can countries do to become FDI winners in the regional integration game? With regard to this last question, the evidence discussed in this chapter suggests that the FDI gains of RIAs are unlikely to be distributed evenly, and that the gains may be smaller for countries that have factor endowments similar to those of the source countries and that are relatively closed to international trade.

While not much can be done to change a country's factor endowments in the short run, openness is certainly amenable to policy action. Not only would openness amplify the impact of the RIA on FDI, it will also change the composition of FDI from horizontal to vertical. Since horizontal FDI sometimes occurs as a result of distortions (high protection), while vertical FDI tends to follow comparative advantages, this shift may strengthen the benefits a country derives from multinational activities. Beyond the impact of factor endowments and openness discussed above, Levy Yeyati, Stein, and Daude (2003) show that countries that present a more attractive overall package to foreign investors are also likely to gain more FDI from the formation of RIAs. This begs the question of how to enhance the country attractiveness.

In this regard, one can think of two polar strategies. The first, which has been compared to a "beauty contest" by Oman (2000), involves improving the quality of a country's institutions, educating the labor force, and developing its infrastructure. The second entails aggressive use of fiscal and financial incentives to attract foreign investors. This simplified division entails an obviously false dichotomy, as countries tend to do a little of both, but it still provides a useful way of organizing the discussion.

One important advantage of the "beauty contest" view is that improvements in infrastructure, education, or the quality of the institutional environment will certainly benefit domestic citizens and firms, regardless of their impact on FDI. Beyond these general benefits, there is evidence to suggest that improving the quality of institutions can have a large impact on FDI (see for example, Stein and Daude 2001). In particular, these authors show that reducing excessive regulation, enforcing property rights, improving the quality of the bureaucracy, and reducing corruption are some of the most promising policies in terms of attracting foreign investors.[30]

The evidence regarding the impact of education and infrastructure on the location of FDI is weaker.[31] However, this does not mean that countries should not pursue these policies. While education may not contribute to the total amount of FDI a country receives, it may affect the benefits host countries derive from FDI through a variety of channels. First, an educated labor force may affect the type of FDI a country receives, shifting it toward more advanced industries, which may generate larger spillovers. Second, for a given type of investment, education increases the capacity of the labor force and of domestic firms to absorb spillovers. In addition, foreign firms that are attracted by an educated labor force become a strong constituency in favor of further improvements in education.[32] In contrast, foreign firms that are attracted by cheap labor will probably lobby the government to ensure the continuous availability of cheap labor, which does not sound appealing as a development strategy.

The case for aggressive competition in incentives is not as clear. To the extent that FDI produces positive spillovers, it makes sense for governments to offer incentives to potential investors in order to lure them into their territory.[33] Provided that there are economies of scale, eliminating trade barriers will induce firms to produce in just one location within a bloc and serve the extended market from this location. Competition among countries for FDI may become too intense, however. The problem is distributional in nature: if social rates of return on an investment are similar across countries, foreign firms will be able to extract most of the benefits associated with the investment. Improving the distribution of the benefits of FDI in favor of host countries may require some form of coordinated action among the region's hosts.[34] As difficult as this coordination may be for the case of south-south RIAs, it may be an even greater challenge for a north-south RIA such as an FTAA, in which the interests of source and host countries are more likely to come into conflict.

Appendix Table 18.4 Free Trade Agreements

FTA	Creation	Members
European Union (EU)	1957	Austria (since 1995), Belgium, Denmark (since 1973), Finland (since 1995), France, Germany, Greece (since 1981), Ireland (since 1973), Italy, Luxembourg, Netherlands, Portugal (since 1986), Spain (since 1986), Sweden (since 1995), United Kingdom (since 1973)
European Free Trade Association (EFTA)	1960	Austria (until 1994), Denmark (until 1972), Finland (1986–1994), Iceland (since 1970), Liechtenstein (since 1991), Norway, Portugal (until 1985), Sweden (until 1994), Switzerland, United Kingdom (until 1972)
European Economic Area (EEA)	1994	All members of the European Union, Iceland, Liechtenstein, Norway
Central European Free Trade Area (CEFTA)	1992	Czech Republic, Hungary, Poland, Slovak Republic, Slovenia (since 1995)
North American Free Trade Agreement (NAFTA)	1989	Canada, U.S., Mexico (since 1994)
Mercado Común del Sur (MERCOSUR)	1995	Argentina, Brazil, Paraguay, Uruguay
Andean Community (formerly Andean Pact)	1969	Bolivia, Colombia, Ecuador, Peru, Venezuela
Central American Common Market (CACM)	1959	Costa Rica, El Salvador, Guatemala, Honduras, Nicaragua
Group of Three	1994	Colombia, Mexico, Venezuela
Bolivia-Mexico FTA	1995	Bolivia, Mexico
Association of Southeast Asian Nations FTA (ASEAN)	1992	Brunci, Indonesia, Malaysia, Philippines, Singapore, Thailand, Vietnam (since 1995)
Australia-New Zealand Closer Economic Relations (ANZCER)	1983	Australia, New Zealand
South African Custom Union	1910	Botswana, Lesotho, Namibia (since 1990), South Africa, Swaziland

Appendix Table 18.5 Data Sources

Variable	Source
Privatizations	Chong and López-de-Silanes (2002)
Inflation	International Monetary Fund, International Financial Statistics
FDI stock	OECD (2002)
Factor endowments	Spilimbergo, Londono, and Szekely (1999)
Distance, border, common language and colonial links	The World Economic Factbook, CIA website www.cia.gov/cia/publications/factbook/index.html
GDP	World Development Indicators

References

Aitken, Brian, Gordon Hanson, and Ann E. Harrison. 1997. "Spillovers, Foreign Investment, and Export Behavior." *Journal of International Economics* 43: 103–32.

Aitken, Brian, and Ann E. Harrison. 1999. "Do Domestic Firms Benefit from Direct Foreign Investment? Evidence from Venezuela." *American Economic Review* 89: 605–18.

Baldwin, Richard E., Rikard Forslid, and Jan Haaland. 1999. "Investment Creation and Investment Diversion: Simulation Analysis of the Single Market Programme." In *Dynamic Issues in Applied Commercial Policy Analysis*, edited by R. E. Baldwin and J. F. Francois. Cambridge: Cambridge University Press.

Bhagwati, Jagdish, and Richard Brecher. 1980. "National Welfare in an Open Economy in the Presence of Foreign-Owned Factors of Production." *Journal of International Economics* 10: 103–15.

Blomström, Magnus, and Ari Kokko. 1997. "Regional Integration and Foreign Direct Investment: A Conceptual Framework and Three Cases." World Bank Policy Research Working Paper no. 1750, Washington, DC.

———. 1998. "Multinational Corporations and Spillovers." *Journal of Economic Surveys* 12: 247–77.

Blomström, Magnus, Ari Kokko, and Mario Zejan. 2000. *Foreign Direct Investment: Firm and Host Country Strategies*. New York: St. Martin's Press.

Blonigen, Bruce A., and Ronald B. Davies. 2000. "The Effects of Bilateral Tax Treaties on U.S. FDI Activity." National Bureau of Economic Research Working Paper no. 7929, Cambridge, MA.

Borensztein, Eduardo, José De Gregorio, and Jong-Wha Lee. 1998. "How Does Foreign Direct Investment Affect Economic Growth?" *Journal of International Economics* 45: 115–135.

Brainard, S. Lael. 1993. "A Simple Theory of Multinational Corporations and Trade with Trade-off Between Proximity and Concentration." National Bureau of Economic Research Working Paper no. 4269, Cambridge, MA.

Caves, Richard E. 1996. *Multinational Enterprise and Economic Analysis.* 2d ed. Cambridge: Cambridge University Press.

Chong, Alberto, and Florencio López-de-Silanes. Forthcoming. "Privatization and Labor Force Restructuring Around the World." National Bureau for Economic Research Working Paper, Cambridge, MA.

Chudnovsky, Daniel, and Andrés López. 2001. "La inversión extranjera directa en el MERCOSUR: Un análisis comparativo." In *El boom de inversión extranjera directa en el MERCOSUR*, edited by Daniel Chudnovsky. Buenos Aires: Siglo XXI.

Dunning, John H. 1993. *Multinational Enterprises and the Global Economy.* Reading, England: Addison-Wesley.

———. 2000. "The Impact of the Completion of the European Internal Market on FDI." In *Regions, Globalization, and the Knowledge-Based Economy.* Oxford: Oxford University Press.

Eaton, Jonathan, and Akiko Tamura. 1994. "Bilateralism and Regionalism in Japanese and U.S. Trade and Direct Foreign Investment Patterns." *Journal of the Japanese and International Economies* 8: 478–510.

Fernández-Arias, Eduardo, Ricardo Hausmann, and Ernesto Stein. 2001. "Courting FDI: Is Competition Bad?" Inter-American Development Bank, Research Department, Washington, DC. Photocopy.

Frankel, Jeffrey A., Ernesto Stein, and Shang-Jin Wei. 1997. "Trading Blocs and the Americas: The Natural, the Unnatural, and the Super-Natural." *Journal of Developing Economics* 47: 61–95.

Frankel, Jeffrey A., and Shang-Jin Wei. 1997. "Regionalization of World Trade and Currencies: Economics and Politics." In *The Regionalization of the World Economy*, edited by J. Frankel. Chicago: University of Chicago Press.

Graham, Edward M., and Paul Krugman. 1995. *Foreign Direct Investment in the United States.* 3d ed. Washington, DC: Institute for International Economics.

Hanson, Gordon. 2001. "Should Countries Promote Foreign Direct Investment?" G 24 Discussion Paper Series 9, United Nations Conference on Trade and Development, and Center for International Development, Harvard University.

Helpman, Elhanan. 1984. "A Simple Theory of Trade with Multinational Corporations." *Journal of Political Economy* 92: 451–71.

———. 1985. "Multinational Corporations and Trade Structure." *Review of Economic Studies* 52: 443–58.

Helpman, Elhanan, and Paul Krugman. 1985. *Market Structure and International Trade*. Cambridge, MA: MIT Press.

Inter-American Development Bank (IDB). 2002. *Beyond Borders: The New Regionalism in Latin America*. Economic and Social Progress Report, Washington, DC.

Kaufmann Daniel, Aart Kraay, and Pablo Zoido-Lobatón. 1999. "Governance Matters." World Bank Policy Research Working Paper no. 2196, Washington, DC.

Kugler, Maurice. 2000. "The Diffusion of Externalities From Foreign Direct Investment: Theory Ahead of Measurement." Discussion Paper in Economics and Econometrics, University of Southampton, November 23.

Levy Yeyati, Eduardo, Ugo Panizza, and Ernesto Stein. 2001. "The Cyclical Nature of FDI Flows." Inter-American Development Bank, Washington, DC. Photocopy.

Levy Yeyati, Eduardo, Ernesto Stein, and Christian Daude. 2003. "Regional Integration and the Location of FDI." Working Paper WP-492, Inter-American Development Bank, Washington, DC.

Markusen, James. 1984 "Multinationals, Multi-Plant Economies, and the Gains from Trade." *Journal of International Economics* 16: 205–26.

———. 1997. "Trade Versus Investment Liberalization." National Bureau of Economic Research Working Paper no. 6231, Cambridge, MA.

Markusen, James, and Keith Maskus. 2001. "General-Equilibrium Approaches to the Multinational Firm: A Review of Theory and Evidence." National Bureau of Economic Research Working Paper no. 8334, Cambridge, MA.

Markusen, James, and Anthony J. Venables. 1998. "Multinational Firms and the New Trade Theory." *Journal of International Economics* 46: 183–203.

Organization for Economic Cooperation and Development (OECD). 1996. *Detailed Benchmark Definition of Foreign Direct Investment*. 3d ed. Paris: OECD.

———. 2000. *International Direct Investment Statistics Yearbook*. Paris: OECD.

Oman, Charles. 2000. "Beauty Contests or Prisoner's Dilemma? The Perils of Competition for Foreign Direct Investment." Development Center, Organization for Economic Cooperation and Development, Paris. Photocopy.

Panizza, Ugo, Eduardo Fernández-Arias, and Ernesto Stein. 2002. "Trade Agreements, Exchange Rate Disagreements." Research Department, Inter-American Development Bank, Washington, DC. Photocopy.

Rodriguez-Clare, Andrés. 1996 "Multinationals, Linkages, and Economic Development." *American Economic Review* 86: 852–73.

Slemrod, Joel. 1990. "Tax Effects on FDI in the United States: Evidence from a Cross-Country Comparison." In *Taxation in the Global Economy*, edited by A. Razin and J. Slemrod, pp. 79–117. Chicago: University of Chicago Press.

Spilimbergo, Antonio, Juan Luis Londoño, and Miguel Szekely. 1999. "Income Distribution, Factor Endowments, and Trade Openness." *Journal of Development Economics* 59: 77–101.

Stein, Ernesto, and Christian Daude. 2001. "Institutions, Integration, and the Location of Foreign Direct Investment." In *New Horizons for Foreign Direct Investment*. Paris: Organization for Economic Cooperation and Development, Global Forum on International Investment.

Viner, Jacob. 1950. *The Customs Union Issue*. New York: Carnegie Endowment for International Peace.

Venables, Anthony J. 1998. "The Assessment: Trade and Location." *Oxford Review of Economic Policy* 14: 1–6.

Waldkirch, Andreas. 2001. "The 'New Regionalism' and Foreign Direct Investment: The Case of Mexico." Working Paper, Oregon State University. Photocopy.

Wei, Shang-Jin. 1997. "Why is Corruption So Much More Taxing Than Tax? Arbitrariness Kills." National Bureau of Economic Research Working Paper no. 6255, Cambridge, MA.

———. 2000. "How Taxing is Corruption to International Investors?" *Review of Economics and Statistics* 82: 1–11.

Notes

The authors thank Josefina Posadas for her invaluable research assistance and Stephen Meardon for his contribution to the policy discussion. We are grateful to Andres Rodriguez-Clare, Antoni Estevadeordal, Renato Flores, Jose Luis Machinea, Andrés Velasco, and seminar participants at the IDB-Harvard conference for comments and suggestions.

1 For a good discussion of the horizontal and vertical models, see Markusen and Maskus (2001).

2 Helpman (1984) and Helpman and Krugman (1985) are early, seminal models of vertical FDI.

3 For models of the horizontal variety, see Markusen (1984) and Markusen and Venables (1998), among others.

4 Trade costs include both trade barriers and other transaction costs associated with trade, such as transportation costs.

5 The importance of tariff jumping as a motive for FDI is contested. Caves (1996: 55) writes that "historical evidence strongly confirms the effect of a tariff to lure the MNE's [multinational enterprses'] production behind

the barrier," yet Markusen (1997: 2) argues that "stylized facts suggest that . . . direct investment is not caused primarily by trade-barrier avoidance."

6 Helpman (1985) has modeled multinationals that produce different varieties of a final good in different locations. Helpman called this FDI horizontal, a label criticized by Markusen and Maskus (2001).

7 Tariffs between the United States and Canada were already low at the time the agreement was signed.

8 Blomström and Kokko's study (1997) emphasizes the increase of extraregional FDI flows to Mexico, while Waldkirch's (2001) emphasizes intraregional flows to Mexico, because of changes in the data found in the time between their studies.

9 The problem is one of too many variables that may matter, but too few observations from which to make inferences.

10 An RIA can also increase bilateral FDI, regardless of its motives, if it includes investment provisions to liberalize capital flows, homogenize legal norms, and set up institutions to handle cross-border disputes.

11 One of the factors that may explain who loses and who wins in this game is country size. If there is some uncertainty regarding the future of the RIA, firms may not want to be trapped in a small country. The biggest losers could be medium-sized countries, since small countries are more likely to be supplied by trade rather than FDI with or without the RIA. If the RIA is credible, central location may be a more important factor. Beyond market size and location, countries that offer a more attractive overall package for foreign investors due to the quality of their institutions, the quality of their labor force, the development of their infrastructure, or their tax treatment of multinationals will be more likely to be winners in this redistributive game.

12 As in Viner's trade diversion, the formation of an RIA may divert FDI from the most efficient location to a partner. For example, a U.S. firm may locate in Mexico, following NAFTA, the production of an intermediate input it may have otherwise located in Costa Rica in the absence of the preferential access enjoyed by Mexico. What we call investment diversion in this chapter is the loss suffered by Costa Rica, as well as other countries, as a result of the creation of NAFTA.

13 Dilution is conceptually different from diversion: going back to the example of NAFTA and U.S. FDI to Mexico and Costa Rica, dilution in a way is the result of leveling the playing field, at least for a certain group of countries. In this case, with an FTAA, Costa Rica and Mexico will be playing under the same rules, and FDI will go to the most efficient location within the region.

14 See Eaton and Tamura (1994), Frankel and Wei (1997), Wei (1997, 2000), Blonigen and Davis (2000), Stein and Daude (2001) and Levy Yeyati,

Panizza, and Stein (2001). In its simplest formulation the gravity model presumes that bilateral trade flows (or bilateral FDI stocks) are related positively to the product of the GDPs of both economies and negatively to the distance between them. Other variables typically added are whether the countries have a common border, common language, colonial links, etc.

15 The dummy takes a value of one for the case of free trade areas, customs unions, or single markets, but not when countries share membership in preferential trade agreements in which trade barriers among members are reduced but not eliminated. The source for this variable is Frankel, Stein, and Wei (1997). See the appendix for a list of RIAs considered in this chapter.

16 It is defined as the log of the joint GDP of all the countries to which the host has tariff-free access due to common membership in an FTA (we include the host's own GDP as well).

17 The reason to add one to FDI before taking logs is to avoid losing the observations with zero FDI, which represent nearly 40 percent of the sample, and provide useful information. For a discussion of the methodological issues associated with the treatment of the observations with zero FDI, see Levy Yeyati, Stein, and Daude (2003).

18 The coefficient for *Same RIA* in the table is 0.24. Since FDI is in logs, it is necessary to transform this coefficient by computing $\exp(0.24) - 1 = 0.27$

19 While this effect appears at first sight to be small, it can actually make a big difference, as will become clear below. As an example, the formation of NAFTA increased the extended market of Mexico by a factor of eighteen.

20 The only exception is the extended market source, which loses significance in one of the regressions. See the appendix for variable definitions and sources

21 $\exp(0.1022 \cdot \ln(10.21)) - 1 = 0.268$.

22 $\exp(-0.0481 \cdot \ln(1.16)) - 1 = 0.0071$.

23 $1.27 \cdot 1.268 \cdot (1-0.0071) - 1 = 0.60$.

24 $1.2569 \cdot (1-0.0071) - 1 = 0.005$.

25 One shortcoming of this variable is that it is only available for about three quarters of the observations. Note that we do not include this variable by itself in the regressions, since it is already captured by the country-pair fixed effects.

26 For a more complete discussion of spillovers from FDI, see Blomström and Kokko (1998) and Hanson (2001).

27 Kugler (2000) argues that the lack of intraindustry spillovers may be due to the fact that foreign affiliates will appropriate as many of the benefits

as possible of their imported technology, and thus they try to prevent spillovers from leaking to their competitors. On the other hand, they may want to upgrade the technological capabilities of a supplier, which explains the existence of interindustry spillovers.

28 Coordinated adoption of performance requirements may solve the problem of location within the extended market, but it does not stop vertical FDI from seeking more convenient locations.

29 The FTAA draft, as of spring 2002, includes in its investment chapter an article on performance requirements that would proscribe them. But the text is thoroughly bracketed and includes several bracketed exceptions. The question is under negotiation. (See http://www.ftaa-alca.org/ftaadraft/eng/draft_e.asp. Last consulted May 2, 2002.)

30 These authors show that a one standard deviation improvement in an index of institutional quality developed by Kaufmann, Kray, and Zoido-Lobatón (1999) results in an increase in bilateral FDI of 130 percent.

31 See Stein and Daude (2001).

32 This is clearly the case of Intel in Costa Rica, where the enrollment in engineering schools has doubled in a matter of only a couple of years.

33 This argument holds as long as the government is considered a social planner seeking to maximize the country's welfare. A potential problem with incentive-based competition, however, is that negotiations with potential entrants are rarely transparent and open to public scrutiny, so they could lead to arbitrariness and corruption.

34 See Fernández-Arias, Hausmann, and Stein (2001). These authors show that the complete elimination of incentive-based competition is not the optimal solution for host countries and, under some circumstances, may leave them worse off than under incentive-based competition.

PART VII

FTAA and Beyond

19

Labor Standards and the FTAA

Kimberly Ann Elliott

The Miami Summit launching the Free Trade Area of the Americas process recognized that free markets and free societies work best when they work together. The core labor standards—freedom of association and the right to organize and bargain collectively, freedom from forced labor, the abolition of child labor, and freedom from discrimination—are part of the Summit-FTAA processes because they strengthen both markets and democracy. These core standards are broadly recognized as fundamental rights to which all workers are entitled, regardless of the level of development of the country or the sector in which they work. And, in an environment that promotes democracy and market-oriented economies, as the FTAA is intended to do, there is no trade-off between these principles and development; indeed, they become mutually reinforcing.

At a time when the importance of social institutions in development has been widely recognized, the real debate is over how and with what urgency to promote the core labor standards. In this debate the questions include whether *universal* means *uniform* and what that implies for development. And, of course, the central question is whether implementation and enforcement of global labor standards should be explicitly linked to trade agreements. The paper begins by making the case that global labor standards are not just politically necessary but also substantively complementary to economic integration in the hemisphere. It then summarizes the situation with respect to implementation of the core labor standards in the hemisphere. It also reviews recent developments in the treatment of labor issues in trade agreements and assesses the various options for addressing labor issues in an FTAA.

Two sets of issues should be mentioned that are not addressed in detail in this chapter. First, the implications of an FTAA for workers obviously go far beyond standards issues. Important policy issues related to the need for adjustment assistance and safety nets are addressed in two other chapter in this volume (Chapter 21 by López-Calva and Lustig, and Chapter 22 by Bustillo and Ocampo) and are mentioned only in passing here. The second issue not treated extensively is the potential use of trade sanctions to enforce labor standards in trade agreements. Elliott and Freeman (2003: Chapter 4) review the evidence on sanctions effectiveness and on the probability of protectionist capture. We concluded that trade measures could be designed that would contribute to improved compliance with labor standards in discrete situations while also guarding against protectionist abuse. We recommended a limited role for the WTO in disciplining *trade-related* violations of core labor standards but concur with those who argue that the International Labor Organization should have the principal role in promoting and enforcing international labor standards generally.

The reason for not repeating those arguments here is that the recent pattern of bilateral and regional negotiations suggests that the push to include enforceable labor standards in trade agreements has shifted from the dead-end track of nonnegotiability to a track of nominal success but practical futility. Although recent trade agreements between the United States and Jordan, Singapore, and Chile include enforceable labor standards provisions, they seem to be aimed primarily at finding procedurally elegant and politically acceptable trade-labor mechanisms that permit trade agreements to proceed. They are a useful precedent supporting the importance of labor standards but it is not yet clear whether they will give a meaningful boost to improved compliance. Moreover, obstacles in negotiating are likely to remain a bar to progress at the broader regional level.

Thus, this chapter concludes with suggestions for a way forward that uses a parallel track to negotiate labor issues but that also links progress in those negotiations more closely to the trade negotiations than usually contemplated.[1] The problem with parallel tracks is that, absent an explicit political commitment or linkage, there is nothing to guarantee that the trains on the two tracks move at similar speeds. Indeed, advocates of labor standards suspect that the practical effect will be to allow the free trade train to move ahead while the labor standards train remains stuck in the station. Addressing that concern is the key to breaking the impasse over trade and labor standards in the hemisphere and elsewhere.

Why Globalization, Development, and Labor Standards Naturally Go Together

There is relatively little controversy surrounding the importance of three of the four core standards. No one is in favor of forced labor, and discrimination on a broad range of grounds is also rejected as morally unacceptable. Moreover, gender discrimination is now widely recognized as detrimental to both economic and social development (World Bank 2001). The Miami Summit process also recognizes the particular needs and vulnerabilities of indigenous peoples throughout the hemisphere, who are often marginalized and unable to reap the benefits of globalization. The abolition of child labor is more controversial, but on pragmatic, not principled grounds—no one disagrees on the goal, just on how to get there and at what speed. There is also broad agreement that countries should move quickly to eliminate the "worst forms" of child labor, as defined in the new ILO convention (no. 182).[2]

The real heat is generated by the right to freedom of association and associated union rights and the push to link compliance with core labor standards to negotiation of the FTAA. But promoting social dialogue, including with unions, can make economic reforms more acceptable and sustainable. International enforcement of labor standards can also help to prevent races to the bottom from the bottom, particularly for relatively more progressive countries that find themselves competing with other low-wage but weak or nondemocratic countries. Attention to labor standards issues can also address concerns of the critics—in both developed and developing countries—that economic globalization today is unbalanced, disproportionately favoring capital over labor and other social groups.

Freedom of Association under Globalization

The ambivalence (or hostility) toward unions derives in part from the examples in Latin America and elsewhere of politically powerful and monopolistic trade unions that live up to the caricature of corrupt, elitist, rent-seeking entities interested mainly in protecting their insider advantages at the expense of outsiders. But of course, the same can be said of firms and politicians in countries where this is true. The appropriate response in these cases is the same for unions as for corrupt firms and politicians: expose them to competition and ensure that they are accountable to stakeholders. Globalization and democratization help to promote the "voice face" of unions, which can reduce conflicts, improve productivity, and make globalization and the reform process more inclusive (Freeman and Medoff 1984). In addition, a World Bank survey of evidence on the effects of unions shows that coordinated bargaining can help small, open economies adjust to economic shocks more quickly and at a lower cost (Aidt and Tzannatos 2002). Evidence in the study also supports the intuition that more competitive product markets constrain the market of unions, as they do of firms. But unions can still play a useful role in this environment in improving working conditions for workers, settling grievances, and providing other services, such as training or job placement assistance.

Improved "voice" mechanisms are also essential in sustaining and expanding needed reforms in the region. Currently, labor-market regulations in many Latin American countries make it difficult or expensive to hire and fire workers. Simply doing away with these regulations has proved politically difficult and, where progress has been made, it has often produced a backlash against reforms.[3] Moreover, because economic growth in the region has not responded as expected to liberalizing reforms, workers often find that flexibility for employers means increased risk for them—without the promised increases in employment or a safety net to fall back on.[4] In addition to expanding and strengthening safety nets where needed, strengthening the institutions of social dialogue are a complement to reforms to increase labor-market flexibility. In addition to giving workers a voice in the reform process, strengthened association and bargaining rights enable workers to negotiate to protect their own interests without having to resort to detailed, interventionist government regulation. In sum, labor-market reforms are likely to be more effective and less painful if they are undertaken in the context of a comprehensive "decent work" program that addresses all four of the pillars targeted by the ILO: employment, standards, social protection, and social dialogue (Somavia 1999).

In addition, the role workers play in monitoring labor standards needs to be strengthened. The primary problem in most countries is not the law but the lack of capacity to enforce it, a problem that has grown worse with the need for fiscal rectitude. Workers are on the job every day and are thus in the best position to monitor compliance with labor standards, whether incorporated in voluntary codes of conduct, collective bargaining agreements, or government regulations. Governments, employers, and multinational corporations sourcing in developing countries should think of unions as a cost-effective mechanism for responding to the pressures from civil society for more monitoring and verification of labor standards, *particularly* in developing countries where government capacity is limited.[5]

Making Standards Global

The question remains, however, whether there is any reason for *global* promotion and enforcement of labor standards. First, while there is little evidence of the feared race to the bottom from the top, a race to the bottom from the bottom is more plausible, especially in highly price-competitive and footloose sectors such as footwear and, especially, apparel. But this is not inevitable, especially where democracy and social institutions are strong, and some countries are beginning to promote good labor standards as a competitive *advantage* in attracting multinational corporations with strong brand identities and an interest in "reputation insurance." What these countries need is independent verification of their claims, as the International Labor Organization is now doing in Cambodia.

A second rationale for giving higher priority to global labor standards is that political support for the current system of global economic governance is increasingly undermined by the perception that it is unbalanced. Rules protecting trade, capital flows, and intellectual property have progressed much further and faster than rules to protect workers or the environment. If this lack of public enthusiasm in developed countries for multilateral rules and reciprocal negotiations on integration further erodes political support for the international trade system, it is developing countries that will suffer most.

Indeed, progressive, democratic developing countries might have particular interest in strengthening *international* enforcement of labor standards to resolve potential collective action problems. While there is little evidence of a race to the bottom from the top, Chau and Kanbur (2000) have developed a theoretical model showing how a race to the bottom from the bottom can develop, particularly among small countries that cannot affect their terms of trade. This should not be interpreted as meaning that higher labor standards undermine *comparative* advantage, and Chau and Kanbur note that this dynamic depends on a variety of factors and is not inevitable.[6] For example, Costa Rica, when faced with increasing competition in traditional low-wage sectors, advertised its political stability and high literacy rates to attract foreign investment in electronics and other higher valued-added sectors. In other words, Costa Rica chose to opt out of the race to the bottom and was able to do so. Cross-country studies likewise do not show that countries that have low labor standards necessarily grow faster, and most show a negative correlation between the level of labor standards and inward foreign direct investment (Rodrik 1996; Morici and Schulz 2001; Kucera 2001).

But not all countries are as stable, democratic, and relatively well educated as Costa Rica. Repression of labor standards under some circumstances can give a *competitive* advantage—or the perception of such an advantage—to a particular firm or sector. Some studies find correlations between various measures of low standards and textile and apparel exports by low-wage countries, but these results are not robust and other studies find no effect on labor costs (Rodrik 1996; Morici and Schulz 2001; Kucera 2001; and Elliott and Freeman 2003: Chapter 1 for a survey). Yet some countries and employers clearly behave as if they believe that improved compliance with labor standards, particularly freedom of association, would threaten their profit level. Bangladesh, Pakistan, Panama, and a few other countries explicitly restrict organizing or bargaining rights in export sectors or zones. Problems in practice are far more widespread, and officials from some countries concede privately that foreign investors threaten not to invest in countries in which they have to deal with unions (ILO 2002: 7).

Nevertheless, with regard to trade negotiations, former Costa Rican trade minister Jose Manuel Salazar-Xirinachs (2003: 336) argues that most developing countries are more interested in addressing the continuing imbalances they face in market access and regard debates over labor, the environment, and other new issues as diversions from this core priority. But the growing backlash in Latin America and elsewhere against "Washington consensus" reforms suggests that concerns about imbalances related to globalization are not restricted to developed countries. In order to rebuild support for trade liberalization and other market-oriented reforms, governments need to address labor and social issues as well. And developing countries also have an interest in avoiding further backlash against such agreements and against the multilateral trade system more broadly among consumers and voters in the United States, Canada, and elsewhere.

In addition to the diversion of attention argument, and despite generally positive rhetoric about the legitimacy of the core labor standards, concerns remain that the push for global standards is a misguided attempt to force inappropriate developed-country labor institutions on less-developed countries (Salazar-Xirinachs 2003: 319). On this front, useful lessons on how *not* to address labor issues in the context of trade agreements may be found in the WTO's agreement on trade-related intellectual property (TRIPs). Similar to the ILO, the World Intellectual Property Organization is a specialized UN agency with roots going back more than a century. But, like many worker organizations today, corporations producing intellectual-property-rich products regarded it as too weak to protect their interests and wanted to incorporate stronger and globally consistent rules in the World Trade Organization with trade sanctions to enforce them. The approach taken by the Uruguay Round negotiators, who opted for broadly *uniform* minimum rules on intellectual property, stands in contrast to the consensus on international labor standards, which emphasizes principles that are universally applicable but that leave broad scope for national diversity in implementation.[7] Contrary to what many assume, the legal conventions that are the basis for implementing the core standards also leave substantial room for national differences; they do not, for example, prescribe any particular set of industrial-relations institutions. Even with respect to issues such as minimum wages, which cause the most concern among developing countries, ILO conventions focus on the process, of the "wage-setting machinery," not the outcome (what the wage should be in any particular case).

Before it was even fully implemented, criticisms arose that the TRIPs agreement was inappropriate for poor countries that do not have intellectual property owners to protect and who would be forced to transfer millions of dollars annually in royalties and monopoly prices to rich-country firms. In order to come into compliance, these countries could also be forced to spend scarce resources to pass new legislation and to create the enforcement capacity needed to implement it. Spurred in particular by the AIDS crisis in Africa, the agreement is currently being renegotiated to make it more flexible and to recognize the special needs of less-developed countries. This experience would seem to underscore the need to focus more narrowly on the truly trade-related aspects of nontraditional issues and to pay more attention than in the past to the need for technical assistance and financial transfers to developing countries to help them implement increasingly complex international agreements. Thus, while TRIPs is not a good model for how to include labor standards in trade agreements, the arguments used in promoting it—fairness and ethical concerns, the weakness of the World Intellectual Property Organization and the need for an agreement with "teeth"—make it far harder to argue that labor (and environmental) standards have no role at all in trade agreements, especially when violations are *trade related.*

There are other pragmatic political-economy arguments for paying attention to labor standards in the FTAA process. Large majorities of survey respondents in the United States say that they think trade agreements should include minimum labor standards and that they would avoid buying goods if they knew they were made under bad conditions. The U.S. Congress also included labor issues as a principal negotiating objective when it passed "trade promotion authority" in August 2002, and it seems unlikely that even a majority-Republican Congress will be able to ratify an FTAA without any reference to labor standards.

Most governments in Latin America support labor standards in principle but oppose including them in trade agreements with sanctions to enforce them out of fear that they might be manipulated to restrict exports. The experience with American antidumping and countervailing duty policies certainly gives developing countries ample reason to be suspicious of potential new avenues for "contingent protection." Given the stridency of the debate, however, there is surprisingly little evidence from existing trade-labor linkages to support the fears (Elliott and Freeman 2003: Chapter 4). What the labor-friendly administration of President William Clinton negotiated in the NAFTA side agreement and in the U.S.-Jordan Free Trade Area is actually quite modest (discussed below), and no complaint submitted under the NAFTA labor agreement has gone beyond ministerial consultations. Nor was the Clinton administration more aggressive than its predecessors in using worker rights as an excuse to withdraw developing-country trade benefits under the Generalized System of Preferences. Despite all the rhetoric, the Clinton administration actually did rather little to promote trade-labor linkages in practice. This was in part because it could not convince trading partners to accept stronger links, but it was also because the administration was no more interested in blocking trade than is the current President George W. Bush (arguably less so in light of their differing approaches to steel imports).

In sum, core labor standards and globalization are complementary policies that strengthen one another and compensate for one another's weaknesses. Just as globalization can discipline the monopolistic tendencies of unions and shine a light on abuses such as forced labor, the core standards can encourage a broader distribution of the benefits of globalization than markets alone often produce. The opportunities provided by economic and political openings, combined with respect for the core standards, can encourage the development of human capital and reassure consumers and reputation-conscious foreign investors that conditions are minimally acceptable. In so doing, attention to labor-standards issues also increases public support for trade agreements.

The Current Status of Labor Standards in the Western Hemisphere

Table 19.1 compares Latin America and the Caribbean to other developing regions on readily available indicators for three of the four core standards: the incidence of child labor (the percentage of children aged ten to fourteen that are in the labor force); differences between female and male illiteracy rates (a proxy for gender discrimination); and union density. In broad terms, the results are as expected, with the relatively higher-income Latin American region having far lower overall illiteracy rates and child labor participation rates than Sub-Saharan Africa or South Asia. It is more difficult to interpret the figures on union density, since one might see higher demand for unions where conditions are bad and lower where conditions are good (political repression of unions aside).[8] But it is not surprising that the rates are lower in poorer regions with smaller formal sectors.

Not all the results track income levels so neatly, however. Despite higher per capita incomes, child labor rates are as high on average in Latin America as in the developing countries of East Asia, and the levels in some countries (Brazil, Bolivia, and the Dominican Republic) reach those of South Asia (Table 19.2). No matter how gender differences in illiteracy are measured, higher-income Latin America does better than other developing regions and, for those countries with available data, there are fewer large outliers than for child labor. Despite higher income levels, the Middle East and North Africa do relatively poorly on the discrimination measures and, by one calculation, East Asia has the worst record on gender literacy differences. There is less comparable cross-country data available on freedom of association indicators and forced labor. Overall, however, these measures support the argument that labor standards rise with incomes, but clearly not in linear fashion.

Going beyond these broad regional trends, it is possible to identify the most common or most serious labor-rights problems in the region using the various reports from the International Labor Organization

Table 19.1 Latin America in Comparative Perspective, 2000

	Percentage of Children 10–14 in the Labor Force	Adult Illiteracy Rate (%)	Differences in Female and Male Illiteracy Rates		Union Membership as a % of the Non-Ag. Labor Force	GNI per Capita (US$, Atlas Method)
			Ratio	Difference (% points)		
Latin America & Caribbean	8.2	11.6	1.2	1.8	15.9	3,560
Middle East & North Africa	4.4	35.2	1.9	21.1	20.7[b]	2,000
East Asia & Pacific[a]	8.2	14.5	2.6	13.1	10.1[c]	900
Sub-Saharan Africa	29.0	38.5	1.6	16.5	13.8	470
South Asia	15.0	45.2	1.7	23.4	5.1	450

Source: World Bank World Development Indicators database.

[a]Excludes developed countries, South Korea, and Taiwan.

[b]Egypt, Jordan, and Morocco only; most of the undemocratic oil-exporting regimes restrict or ban unions.

[c]Excludes China's misleading 55 percent; includes Indonesia, Malaysia, Philippines, and Thailand.

Table 19.2 Labor Outcomes, Economic, and Political Indicators, 1995

			Union Membership (Select Years 1992–95)					
	Percentage of Children 10–14 in the Labor Force	Female-Male Illiteracy Rates (% points)	% of Non-Ag. Labor Force	% of Formal Sector Wage Earners	Formal Sector as % of Total Non-Ag. Employment	Population (thousands)	GDP Per Capita US$	Freedom House Rank[b]
Average	6.2	2.7	15.9	35.3	51.9	22,228	4,285	5.4
Antigua/Barbuda	n.a.	n.a.	n.a.	53.8[a]	n.a.	65	6,930	4.5
Argentina	4.5	0.1	25.4	65.6	50.7	34,768	8,030	5.5
Bahamas	0.0	−1.3	n.a.	n.a.	n.a.	278	11,830	6.5
Barbados	0.0	n.a.	n.a.	n.a.	n.a.	264	6,590	7.0
Belize	2.4	n.a.	n.a.	n.a.	n.a.	217	2,650	7.0
Bolivia	14.4	14.7	16.4	59.7	n.a.	7,414	870	5.5
Brazil	16.1	0.5	32.1	66.0	53.5	159,346	3,690	5.0
Canada	0.0	n.a.	31.0	37.4[a]	n.a.	29,615	19,460	7.0
Chile	0.0	0.5	15.9	33.0	61.2	14,210	3,880	6.0
Colombia	6.6	0.3	7.0	17.0	44.4	38,542	1,880	4.0
Costa Rica	5.5	−0.1	13.1	27.3	56.7	3,374	2,570	6.5
Dominica	n.a.	n.a.	n.a.	n.a.	n.a.	73	2,900	7.0
Dominican Republic	16.1	0.7	17.3	n.a.	n.a.	7,823	1,430	5.0
Ecuador	5.4	4.2	9.8	22.4	36.3	11,460	1,400	5.5
El Salvador	15.1	6.2	7.2	10.7	n.a.	5,669	1,570	5.0
Grenada	n.a.	n.a.	n.a.	n.a.	n.a.	95	2,830	6.5
Guatemala	16.2	15.4	4.4	7.7	n.a.	9,976	1,400	4.0
Guyana	0.0	1.5	25.2	n.a.	n.a.	830	620	2.0
Haiti	25.3	5.2	n.a.	n.a.	n.a.	7,168	300	1.5

Continued on next page

Table 19.2 Labor Outcomes, Economic, and Political Indicators, 1995, continued

	Percentage of Children 10–14 in the Labor Force	Female-Male Illiteracy Rates (% points)	Union Membership (Select Years 1992–95)		Formal Sector as % of Total Non-Ag. Employment	Population (thousands)	GDP Per Capita US$	Freedom House Rank[b]
			% of Non-Ag. Labor Force	% of Formal Sector Wage Earners				
Honduras	8.5	1.2	4.5	20.8	42.9	5,654	670	5.0
Jamaica	0.1	–8.5	n.a.	n.a.	n.a.	2,522	1,570	5.5
Mexico	6.7	4.6	31.0	72.9	56.8	91,145	3,800	4.0
Nicaragua	14.0	0.1	23.4	48.2	n.a.	4,426	360	4.0
Panama	3.5	1.3	14.2	29.0	62.9	2,631	2,950	5.5
Paraguay	7.9	3.1	9.3	50.1	n.a.	4,828	1,740	4.5
Peru	2.5	10.8	7.5	18.3	44.9	23,532	2,320	3.5
St. Kitts & Nevis	n.a.	n.a.	n.a.	n.a.	n.a.	41	5,500	6.5
St. Lucia	n.a.	n.a.	n.a.	n.a.	n.a.	156	3,400	6.5
St. Vincent & Grenadines	n.a.	n.a.	n.a.	n.a.	n.a.	111	2,320	6.5
Suriname	0.5	n.a.	n.a.	n.a.	n.a.	409	880	5.0
Trinidad & Tobago	0.0	1.9	n.a.	n.a.	n.a.	1,287	3,780	6.5
United States	0.0	n.a.	12.7	14.2[a]	n.a.	262,761	27,410	7.0
Uruguay	2.1	-0.8	11.6	20.2	56.7	3,218	5,120	6.5
Venezuela	0.9	1.2	14.9	32.6	55.5	21,844	3,040	5.0

Sources: World Bank World Development Indicators database; ILO 1997; Freedom House, Freedom in the World database.

[a]All wage and salary earners.

[b]The Freedom House rank has been recalculated so that 1 indicates unfree and 7 indicates free.

supervisory system.[9] Potential problems in consistency should be noted here as well, however. As a result of the 1998 Declaration on Fundamental Principles and Rights at Work, all ILO members are required to report routinely on their laws and practices with respect to the four core standards. But only the reports of those countries that have ratified the associated conventions are subjected to systematic scrutiny and comment by the ILO's Committee of Experts on the Application of Conventions and Recommendations (CEACR). When the CEACR identifies serious problems, the politically more prominent Conference Committee on the Application of Conventions and Recommendations (CCACR) may review them and invite the country's government delegate to respond in public session. Similarly, allegations of violations under Articles 24 and 26 of the ILO Constitution can generally only be lodged against countries that have ratified the relevant convention. The exception to these procedures is freedom of association, which is regarded as so fundamental that complaints may be brought against any member, regardless of whether they have ratified convention 87 or 98, and these will be referred to the specialized Committee on Freedom of Association.[10]

Table 19.3 summarizes some of the data available from the searchable ILO database on standards (ILOLEX). On average, Western hemisphere nations have ratified 44 of the ILO's 180 some-odd conventions and 7 of the 8 "core" conventions.[11] The countries that have ratified fewer conventions tend to be the smaller island nations of the Caribbean and, most notably, the United States. Only tiny St. Kitts and Nevis, with a population of 41,000, has ratified fewer conventions overall than the United States, but even that country has ratified 7 of the 8 core conventions. The United States, by contrast, has ratified only Conventions 105, on the abolition of forced labor, and 182, on the worst forms of child labor. The Clinton administration submitted Convention 111, on nondiscrimination, to the Senate Foreign Relations Committee for ratification but no vote had been held as of the end of 2003. Unless several additional ratifications occur, it seems unlikely that the United States will alter its position of seeking only the enforcement of national laws, not international standards, when it tries to include labor issues in trade agreements (see below).

Of the two conventions that the United States has accepted, Convention 105 on forced labor has been ratified by all thirty-four FTAA countries, and Convention 182 on the worst forms of child labor likely will be within a few years. As of fall 2002, Convention 182 had thirty

Table 19.3 Evidence on the Formal Implementation of Core Labor Standards

	ILO Conventions Ratified (Fall 2002)	Core Conventions Ratified (Fall 2002)	Observations on Core Conventions by CCACR[a] (1990–2001)	Number of Freedom of Association Complaints (1990–2001)
Average	44	7	3	10
Antigua/Barbuda	27	7	0	0
Argentina	71	8	1	33
Bahamas	33	8	0	2
Barbados	39	8	0	1
Belize	42	8	0	1
Bolivia	46	6	4	2
Brazil	89	7	12	11
Canada	30	5	1	33
Chile	59	8	1	10
Colombia	59	7	13	25
Costa Rica	50	8	4	16
Dominica	23	8	0	0
Dominican Republic	35	8	5	5
Ecuador	59	8	5	14
El Salvador	25	6	1	11
Grenada	28	5	0	0
Guatemala	72	8	8	21
Guyana	46	8	0	0
Haiti	23	6	1	5
Honduras	22	8	2	5
Jamaica	26	6	1	0
Mexico	78	6	1	9
Nicaragua	59	8	0	12
Panama	74	8	7	9
Paraguay	36	7	3	13
Peru	69	8	9	37
St. Kitts & Nevis	8	7	b	b
St. Lucia	28	7	1	0
St.Vincent & Grenadines	21	7	0	b
Suriname	28	4	0	0
Trinidad & Tobago	16	6	0	0
United States	14	2	0	3
Uruguay	103	8	0	8
Venezuela	53	7	6	26

Source: International Labor Organization, ILOLEX database.

[a]Numbers refer to comments on core conventions only. Individual observations by the ILO Conference Committee are reserved for the more serious or long-standing problems identified by the Committee of Experts on the Application of Conventions and Recommendations.

[b]Indicates conventions ratified in 1998–2001 and no reports yet reviewed.

ratifications in the region and was gaining new adherents at a rapid pace globally. Indeed, it may be the first ILO convention to achieve universal ratification. On forced labor, only the United States, Bolivia, and Canada have not also ratified number 29, while number 138, setting a minimum age for employment, is the least ratified of the eight, regionally and globally. Among those not ratifying 138 that have ratified 182 are Canada, Mexico, Paraguay, St. Kitts and Nevis, St. Lucia, Saint Vincent and the Grenadines, and the United States. Only Haiti and Suriname have ratified neither. On nondiscrimination, only the United States and Suriname have ratified neither number 100, on equal remuneration, nor number 111 on nondiscrimination in employment. Finally, only the United States and El Salvador have ratified neither Convention 87 on freedom of association nor number 98 on the right to organize and bargain collectively; beyond that, only Brazil has not ratified Convention 87 and Canada and Mexico have not ratified number 98.

As a first step in assessing compliance, it is obvious that the ILO supervisory system has generated far more cases on forced labor and freedom of association issues than on child labor and discrimination. This does not necessarily mean that there are fewer problems in these areas. But, recognizing that child labor is usually the product of poverty and that no country has clean hands when it comes to discrimination, CEACR comments on the applications of these conventions are generally promotional in nature, reminding countries what their obligations are under the conventions and asking for information on implementation. The ILO has also substantially beefed up its technical assistance programs for child labor, especially to promote compliance with convention 182 on the worst forms, which include forced labor and illicit activities such as prostitution, pornography, and drug trafficking. At least with respect to countries in the Western hemisphere, child labor and discrimination are rarely brought before the CCAR, which focuses attention on the more serious problems identified by the CEACR each year, and these areas are also rarely the subject of Article 24 complaints.

Indeed, in twelve years from 1990 through 2001, there was not a single complaint against a Western hemisphere country alleging violations of the minimum age for child labor, again for reasons of efficacy and not because no violations occurred. As found in most studies, however, available data shows that child labor in the region is broadly correlated with poverty, with the highest labor participation rates by children between ten and fourteen occurring in Haiti, Nicaragua, Guatemala, El Salvador, and Bolivia, but also in the Dominican Republic and Brazil. Interestingly, however, and suggesting that there is scope for policy measures other than just economic growth to address the problem, simple correlation coefficients show a closer (negative) relationship between child labor and democracy (as measured by the Freedom House rankings) than between child labor and per capita income.

Discrimination, which is rooted in history, culture, and institutions, is also generally treated by the ILO as an area in which promotional measures are preferred. CEACR observations and "direct requests" typically relate to the need for additional information, especially statistical data on relative levels of employment and wages of women and men, as well as plans the government has to achieve the goals of the conventions. The most common requests from the experts in the 1990s related to clarification as to whether national laws on equal remuneration are consistent with the goal of "equal wages for work of equal *value*" rather than the lesser standard of equal pay for equal work. Several countries were also asked to provide information on vocational training for women as a means of achieving the goals of nondiscrimination in employment and remuneration. In a few cases, explicit discrimination in labor laws or collective bargaining contracts have been identified by the CEACR and, usually, rectified.

Both the most frequent and the most serious allegations in the hemisphere relate to freedom of association and forced labor. From 1990 through 2001, there were 314 Article 24 complaints against Western Hemisphere countries; of those, 312 related to alleged violations of freedom of association and the other 2 to forced labor (in Brazil and Guatemala). These cases can be made on relatively technical grounds and the numbers reflect complaints, not confirmation of any ILO body of a violation. Individual observations by the Conference Committee, however, are reserved for relatively more serious and substantiated problems and over the same period, there were eighty-six of these regarding countries in the Americas and the Caribbean, 93 percent relating to either freedom of association or forced labor, mostly the former. Of the thirty-four FTAA countries, fourteen were not the subject of an individual observation and most others were the subject of just a few. Six countries were the subject of more than five observations, with only Brazil and Colombia reaching double digits.

Colombia, because of the many murders of union organizers and members during its civil conflict, is the only Latin American country in recent years to be the subject of an Article 26 investigation, a procedure reserved for the gravest violations. This case fits the pattern of the most serious allegations, which typically involve situations of conflict and political repression and weak or nonexistent democracy. In the 1970s, when the human rights situation deteriorated in a number of Latin American countries, Argentina, Bolivia, Chile, and Uruguay were all the subject of Article 26 investigations, usually involving conventions 87 and 98. In recent years, in addition to Colombia, the most serious problems with freedom of association have been in Venezuela and Guatemala. Peru has actually been the most frequent target of freedom of association complaints over the past decade or so, mostly issues related to anti-union discrimination and restrictions on collective bargaining or the right to strike, but without the levels of violence seen in Colombia. Table 19.3 also shows large numbers of freedom of association complaints against Argentina and Canada, democratic countries where unions are relatively strong. In Canada, the primary role of the provinces in regulating labor markets also boosts the number of cases filed.

Beyond the most serious allegations of violence against and political repression of union organizers, common complaints include the failure of governments to punish antiunion discrimination by employers, including dismissals, and restrictions on the right to strike. Also common are complaints about administrative impediments to establishing and organizing unions that workers freely choose (regulations on the proportion or absolute number of workers required to register a union, restrictions on the nationality of officers, and preferential treatment of employer-established worker associations (i.e., "company unions"). Among the most common complaints and sources of comment by the CEACR are restrictions on the right of public employees to organize, bargain collectively, and strike (for example, by defining "essential services" too broadly).

With respect to forced labor, the most serious but least common allegations involve debt bondage, deceptive recruiting practices, and other forms of coerced labor, mainly among indigenous peoples, in plantation agriculture, forestry, and mining, in Brazil, Paraguay, and Peru.[12] There are also problems with forced child labor in domestic service in Haiti, and, earlier in the 1990s, forced labor by (often illegal) Haitians on Dominican Republic sugar plantations. More frequently in this area, CEACR reports ask for clarification or technical corrections to laws that countries claim are not enforced, for example, restrictions on leaving public service, particularly the military and police, and maritime services. A number of CEACR observations relate to prison labor—under what conditions the work occurs, including whether it is for private profit, and for what offenses (for example, to punish political dissent or unauthorized strikes). Beyond the core standards, the most common complaints relate to health and safety issues, which are probably among the most common globally, and to respect for the rights of indigenous peoples, which may be a bigger problem in the Western Hemisphere than elsewhere.

To sum up, in terms of ratification of the core conventions in the region, it is close enough to universal to suggest that the U.S. position of asking countries to agree to enforce their own laws would approximate a commitment to international standards for most of the region. Ironically, it is the United States that is the clear outlier on ratification, if not on compliance with the broad principles embodied in the standards. Unlike some other countries that view convention ratification as a statement of an aspiration to comply, the United States will not ratify a convention until it determines that its law is consistent. At this stage, the government seems unwilling to change U.S. labor laws in ways that would allow it to ratify additional conventions, except possibly for 111 on nondiscrimination. Convention 29 on forced labor is a problem because of the trend toward prison privatization and private-sector employment of prison labor for commercial production. Although a variety of alleged inconsistencies between U.S. law and practice and the provisions of conventions 87 and 98 on association rights have been alleged, among the most important are sectoral exclusions from collective bargaining rights, particularly in the public sector, and various restriction on the right to strike, including a legal provision allowing employers to hire permanent strike worker replacements, which the ILO has concluded undermines the right to strike.[13] U.S. practice is probably in broad compliance with number 100 on equal remuneration, but the refusal by Congress to enact comparable-worth pay legislation would make it politically difficult to ratify this convention. With respect to Convention 138 setting a minimum age for child labor, U.S. practice is again broadly in compliance, but the diversity of state laws in this area, combined with the relatively technical nature of this convention, make it difficult to bring U.S. law into compliance. The paucity of U.S. ratifications leads to charges of hypocrisy and effectively rules out any language in an FTAA agreement that would condition membership on compliance with *international* labor standards.

In terms of compliance with the core standards, there are problems that could rise up to haunt governments and employers in the region if they are not addressed more vigorously and systematically. A comparison of the top ten exports of each FTAA country with the sectors cited in ILO supervisory documents shows that most countries in the hemisphere are potentially vulnerable to a worker-rights scandal that could hit key exports (Table 19.4).[14] In particular, the allegations of forced and child labor in plantation agriculture and other natural-resource sectors and of repression of freedom of association in export-processing zones are serious and could become more visible with increased integration. The pressure on Ecuador in late 2002 to address labor problems on its banana plantations as a condition of gaining eligibility for expanded U.S. trade preferences is one example. In addition, the AFL-CIO has already announced that it will focus closely on labor standards compliance during free trade area negotiations between the United States and Central America (Costa Rica, El Salvador, Guatemala, Honduras, and Nicaragua) in 2003–04.

Recent Precedents for Linking Labor Standards and Trade

In fall 2001, the U.S. Congress approved the U.S.-Jordan Free Trade Agreement with enforceable labor (and environmental) standards in the main body of the agreement. In August 2002, it passed "trade promotion authority" that incorporates labor issues as negotiating objectives and endorses "equivalent" dispute-settlement procedures and remedies. In spring 2003, President George W. Bush and U.S. Trade Representative Robert Zoellick, respectively, signed bilateral trade agreements with Chile and Singapore. These agreements reportedly have labor standards in the main text, subject to the same dispute-settlement procedures as commercial disputes, but with fines rather than trade measures as the principal enforcement mechanism. While the Bush administration is not suggesting that the same mechanisms are necessarily appropriate in all other trade negotiations, they were used as the basis for negotiations with Central America and they clearly make it more difficult for negotiators to completely de-link trade and labor issues in future negotiations.

Two key questions typically arise in discussions over how to address labor issues during trade negotiations (if they are addressed at all). First, should labor issues be addressed in the main body of an agreement text, in a supplementary or "side" agreement, or in parallel negotiations de-linked from trade negotiations? Second, should trade

Table 19.4 Labor Standards Violations Investigated in Key Export Sectors, 1996–2000

Country	Type of ILO Supervision Involved[a]	Export Sector Involved[b]
Argentina	FOA case	Petroleum
Bolivia	CC observation on FOA	Agriculture
	FOA case	Mining
Brazil	CC observation on forced labor	Agriculture
	FOA cases	Automotive vehicles and parts, citrus
Chile	FOA case	Agriculture
Colombia	CC observations and FOA cases	Horticultural and agricultural products, bananas, petroleum
	FOA cases	Cement, glass, and ceramics; textiles and apparel; coffee
Costa Rica	CC observations and FOA cases	Agriculture, bananas
	CC observation on FOA	EPZs
Ecuador	CC observation and FOA case	Petroleum
	CC observation on FOA	EPZs
	FOA case	Bananas
El Salvador	FOA cases	Coffee, EPZs—apparel
Guatemala	CC observation and FOA cases	Bananas, coffee, agriculture generally, EPZs
	FOA cases	Sugar, steel, textiles
Haiti	FOA case	Apparel
Honduras	FOA case	EPZs—apparel
Mexico	FOA case	Petroleum
Nicaragua	FOA cases	Bananas, EPZs—apparel
Panama	CC observation on FOA	EPZs
Paraguay	FOA case	Meat
Peru	CC observations on forced labor, FOA and FOA cases	Gold mining, other mining and metals
	CC observation on forced labor	Agriculture
	FOA cases	Textiles, petroleum
Uruguay	FOA case	Dairy
Venezuela	CC observations and FOA cases	Petroleum and products

Sources: International Labor Organization, ILOLEX database; UNCTAD/WTO International Trade Center, trade database.

[a]Only Conference Committee (CC) observations, freedom of association (FOA) cases, and Article 24 and 26 complaints are included. Countries not listed have not come under these types of scrutiny.

[b]Only the top ten export sectors, based on the average value in 1996–2000 for each country, are included.

measures be available to enforce labor standards, as they are in other commercial disputes? Existing agreements answer these questions in a variety of ways (see Table 19.5). The only common element is that each agreement requires only that the parties to it enforce their own national labor laws, with no requirement that those laws be consistent with the core labor standards as defined by the ILO. This is an unfortunate feature of these agreements because it undercuts the international consensus that has been reached on the core standards and it could discourage improvements in local law. But, as noted, this situation is unlikely to change as long as the United States has ratified so few ILO core conventions.

The North American Free Agreement on Labor Cooperation (NAALC) and Canada-Chile and Canada-Costa Rica free trade agreements all have side agreements on labor issues with their own institutional structures and dispute-settlement resolution mechanisms. The labor provisions in the Canada-Costa Rica FTA authorize ministerial consultations on labor issues but include no enforcement mechanism. The other two agreements provide for ministerial consultations on a list of eleven labor standards, including all the core standards, but authorize monetary fines as a last resort only for child labor and technical standards relating to wages and health and safety conditions. In the case of a bilateral dispute between the United States and Mexico, bilateral tariff concessions can be withdrawn to the extent necessary to collect the value of the fine, but this provision is not regarded as authorizing trade sanctions. Under these agreements, disputes will be referred for dispute settlement only if there is a "persistent pattern" of failures to enforce relevant labor laws and if the violations are in trade-related sectors.[15]

The U.S.-Jordan FTA, completed in late 2000 and approved in fall 2001, includes a section on labor in the main text that is subject to the same dispute-settlement procedures as the rest of the agreement. The principal risks in this model, however, arise from the vague language of the dispute-settlement procedures, not from the language on labor standards. At the end of the day, if consultations, a dispute-settlement panel, and the joint committee created to implement the agreement do not result in resolution of a dispute, the complaining party is authorized "to take *any* appropriate and commensurate measure" (emphasis added). But the labor standards text is so weak it seems unlikely that any dispute would get that far. Most paragraphs in this section require only that the parties "strive to ensure" that domestic laws are consistent with "internationally recognized labor rights," and that they

Table 19.5 Approaches to Linking Trade and Labor Standards

Approach	Pros	Cons
Social clause in trade agreements authorizing trade measures:		
• Against *any* violation of labor standards		Not appropriate since most labor violations are in non-traded sectors and trade experts are not competent to resolve labor standards disputes
• Against trade-related violations of labor standards	Intellectual consistency	A political nonstarter for the foreseeable future
U.S.-Jordan FTA: labor standards in main text	Treats trade-related labor standards violations equally with other potential distortions of trade and investment flows	Labor language so weak as to exert little upward pressure on labor standards Vague dispute-settlement provisions risk abuse by leaving too much discretion to individual governments
NAALC: side agreement on labor	Provides mechanism for problems to be investigated and discussed, enforcement with fines possible for technical labor issues and child labor	Creates tiers for labor standards that are inconsistent with international consensus on core labor standards Provisions requiring only enforcement of national laws provide disincentive to raise standards
Canada-Chile FTA: side agreement on labor	Similar to above	Same as above Relies on local judiciary to enforce, which could be problematic in less-developed countries
USTR proposal for Chile and Singapore bilateral agreements, as reported by press: labor standards in main text	Provides for "equivalent," though not identical, dispute settlement procedures Does not distinguish among the core labor standards	Not clear how the fines would be collected or how they would be used and, therefore, whether they would be likely to contribute to improved working conditions

do not "waive or otherwise derogate from . . . such laws as an encouragement for trade." The only "shall" in the labor text refers to the obligation of the parties not to "fail to effectively enforce its laws" on a sustained basis in a way that affects trade. But other paragraphs in that section preserve the discretion of governments to adopt, modify, and enforce labor laws and regulations so that a party will be in compliance with its labor obligations under the agreement if "a course of action or inaction [in enforcing labor laws] reflects a reasonable exercise of such discretion, or results from a bona fide decision regarding the allocation of resources" (section 4(b) of Article 6 of the agreement). It is certainly conceivable that a protectionist American president could abuse this language, but there is no evidence from U.S. implementation of worker conditionality in the Generalized System of Preferences or the side agreement to NAFTA to suggest that is remotely likely.[16]

During the congressional debate over trade promotion authority, then Senate Finance Committee Chair Max Baucus (D-MT) insisted that all future trade agreements should meet the "Jordan standard" of having enforceable labor standards in the main text. Since passage of the Trade Act of 2002, Baucus and other Democrats have continued to assert that this is the interpretation of the labor provisions that U.S. Trade Representative Robert Zoellick should follow. Senator Charles Grassley (R-IA), who took over as chair of the Finance Committee in the Congress in January 2003, is equally adamant that this is a misinterpretation of congressional intent.

The only thing that seems reasonably clear in late 2003 is that it will be difficult for U.S. trade negotiators to ignore labor issues entirely. In the section of the 2002 Trade Act providing trade promotion authority, references to worker rights and labor standards appear as an "overall" and a "principal" trade negotiating objective, as well as one of several other priorities that the president should promote "in order to address and maintain" U.S. competitiveness. The key section, 2102(b)(11), essentially copies the language from the U.S.-Jordan agreement in defining principal U.S. negotiating objectives with respect to labor (and the environment), emphasizing the legitimacy of discretion in setting and enforcing one's own laws.

In an amendment that muddies the enforceability question, however, Senator Phil Gramm (R-TX), a leading linkage opponent, convinced his House colleagues to insert additional language barring retaliation "based on the exercise of these rights [to discretion in enforcement] or the right to establish domestic labor standards."

Gramm's intent has been variously reported as an attempt to take sanctions off the table for enforcing labor and environmental standards or an attempt to prevent the use of a trade agreement to change U.S. labor laws. Moreover, the interpretation of this provision is further complicated by the next negotiating objective on the list, which requires U.S. negotiators to "seek provisions" that treat all the "principal negotiating objectives equally with respect to" the availability of "equivalent dispute settlement-procedures and remedies."

In its first attempt to interpret this potentially conflicting language, the USTR office devised a clever and creative compromise for the bilateral FTA negotiations with Chile and Singapore. The labor provisions in these agreements are similar and are based on a combination of the NAALC and the Jordan FTA. Like the NAALC, the new text follows the practice of basing labor-related obligations on the effective enforcement of each country's own laws in trade-related sectors. It also, like the NAALC, authorizes monetary fines in the case of unresolved disputes over covered labor issues, allows the suspension of tariff concessions if necessary to *collect* the fine (explicitly *not* a sanction), and caps the fine at a given level (US$). Like the Jordan agreement, however, labor obligations are included in the main text of the agreements, violations are subject to the same dispute settlement procedures as commercial disputes, and, unlike NAALC, there is no distinction among applicable labor standards and the fines would continue to accrue annually if the problem remains unresolved. In commercial disputes, the country in violation of the agreement could choose to pay a fine, but traditional trade retaliation would also remain an option. USTR officials argue that, while not "mirror images," the mechanisms for enforcement of labor and commercial disputes would be equally effective and would, therefore, meet the congressional standard of equivalence.

Where's the Beef?

It is almost certainly no coincidence that the U.S. agreements explicitly linking trade and labor issues that have been reached or proposed so far (with the exception of Mexico) are with relatively small trading partners with little negotiating leverage and relatively good labor standards. The agreements with Jordan, Singapore, and Chile set a precedent in terms of bilateral FTAs and they provide an opening to discuss labor issues with trading partners. But it is not clear that they will be used as examples of how labor standards can be improved under globalization.

Moreover, larger trading partners and developing-country blocs are less susceptible to U.S. pressure and are unlikely to be as accommodating, so that even less is likely to be achieved on labor issues in the FTAA or WTO negotiations than in these bilateral agreements.

Workers, labor rights supporters, and other activists nevertheless try to link the issues they care about to issues, like trade, that corporations and governments care strongly about because that is the only way they can get a hearing. Labor activists are also right to be suspicious of parallel tracks because the support for them to date has been mostly rhetorical. USTR Zoellick recently proposed increasing the funding for trade capacity building by a third overall with US$140 million allocated just for the Western Hemisphere.[17] This is nearly twice the US$86 million requested for the Department of Labor's Bureau of International Labor Affairs for Fiscal Year 2003, which funds the entire U.S. budget for technical assistance on labor. Moreover, this figure is a substantial cut from the peak of US$150 million under the Clinton administration.[18]

Nevertheless, the push to increase technical assistance and use it more productively is at least consistent with how the Bush administration and most developing-country governments around the world say they want to approach labor-standards issues. This more positive attitude is in stark contrast with the consistent opposition to the use of trade sanctions to enforce labor standards. This suggests there may be more scope for progress in holding the Bush administration to its promises to create a separate "tool box" for labor standards than in continuing to try to block the international trade agenda by insisting on an enforceable linkage to labor issues. This is particularly true now that the Doha round of multilateral trade negotiations has been launched and President Bush has trade promotion authority from Congress. A change in strategy of this kind should also be more appealing to workers and governments in the rest of the hemisphere that are concerned about the potential for protectionist abuse of trade sanctions to enforce labor-standards clauses. It would thereby facilitate a broadening of the coalition in favor of doing something serious to promote higher labor standards and better compliance throughout the region.

The first focus of efforts to make the parallel track for labor issues credible should be to pressure donor countries and the multilateral development agencies to put money on the table. Equally important, NGOs, unions, and other elements of civil society need to continue to play an oversight role and to agitate as necessary to ensure that the money is used effectively. The "plan of action" agreed to at the twelfth conference of inter-American labor ministers in Ottawa in October 2001 has one brief paragraph calling on member states to "devote the necessary and available" economic resources needed to implement the plan. But the plan of action primarily calls for more working groups, more studies, and more technical workshops to build on the working groups, studies, and workshops conducted under the plan of action adopted at the eleventh conference of ministers held three years earlier. And, finally, a meaningful parallel track for labor should harness the energies of all the relevant actors—not just the governments and international organizations, but civil society and the private sector as well.

The obvious starting point for designing a real plan of action, following what environmentalists have suggested, is to prepare systematic "national assessments" to help governments—and workers and other citizens—to understand and prepare for the labor-market adjustments that will be required by the FTAA. The Hemispheric Cooperation Program approved at the Quito Ministerial in October 2002 calls on countries seeking assistance to "develop national or regional strategies" identifying areas in which their capacity to participate in the FTAA is inadequate, including in the area of "adjusting to integration." This could be a hook for addressing technical assistance needs in the labor area as well. But it would be useful, first, to have a baseline picture of the application of the core labor standards across the region, perhaps prepared by the ILO regional office, against which requests for technical assistance could be compared. In addition, since the implications for workers of hemispheric integration go well beyond standards issues, it would also be useful to have some external oversight, perhaps by ECLAC, of governments' own assessments of the likely sectoral and regional effects in order to ensure that adequate provision is being made for safety net and other adjustment programs. Apparently some of this is being done on an ad hoc basis, but a more systematic effort is needed to identify and prepare for the potentially large adjustments that will be required.

Second, while recognizing that the worst labor abuses are typically not in export sectors, the ILO and human rights groups have identified problems with child labor and forced labor in commercial agriculture and mining in some countries and with freedom of association and discrimination in the garment and other manufacturing sectors, especially in export-processing zones. Programs to address labor violations in those sectors could have several benefits. They could be designed to build capacity in ways that would be generally applicable, they might generate other spillovers as examples of best practice in labor relations, and they would help to broaden public support for an FTAA.

In addition to getting money on the table and meaningful action plans in place, the labor track needs to involve all the relevant actors. In improving labor standards compliance, for example in export-processing zones, civil society and the private sector can play important roles. With increasing global integration, consumers in northern countries are increasingly aware of and concerned about the conditions under which products they consume are made. In turn, most major retailers and importing firms in certain industries (especially clothing, footwear, and a few food products) are now aware that their brand reputations are at risk if their goods are exposed as being produced under abusive conditions. As a result, a number of multi-stakeholder initiatives and social auditing firms—some for profit, some nonprofit—have emerged to fill the demand for monitoring of codes of conduct.[19]

As of mid-2002, however, only 6 of 127 facilities certified by Social Accountability International (SAI) were in Latin America, all in Brazil. There were only four (of eleven) auditors accredited by the Fair Labor Association (FLA) operating in the Western hemisphere, mostly in Mexico and the United States. The volume of monitoring activities in Central America and the Caribbean should increase as the FLA, which focuses on the garment and footwear sectors, gets fully up and running. Other manufacturing sectors could be encouraged to seek certification under SAI's SA 8000 code, which is not sector specific. But, while Dole Foods is an SAI member and both SAI and the UK-based Ethical Trade Initiative are doing pilot projects on how to monitor code compliance by agricultural facilities, none of the code-of-conduct initiatives adequately deal with this sector.

While these kinds of initiatives are expanding as a result of market forces, the public sector could also encourage the process. The Organization of American States or ECLAC could sponsor workshops in areas with concentrations of export-processing zones or labor-intensive agricultural operations to inform them about the major monitoring initiatives and how social auditing works. The Inter-American Development Bank could also stimulate the market for monitors by requiring social audits on projects that it funds where labor violations are a potential problem. In the interim, while private-sector monitoring capacity is being built, the ILO, at the request of concerned governments, might supplement local inspection resources as it is currently doing in Cambodia (Elliott and Freeman 2003: Chapter 6). But if the ILO is asked to do more, its financial and operational capacity will also have to be strengthened.

In sum, the way forward in the FTAA process involves taking steps to ensure, not just that the labor and trade tracks are parallel, but that the trains on them run at roughly similar speeds. For that to happen, workers and labor activists need to keep the pressure on, but they need to shift their attention from sanctions to enforce standards in trade agreements to pressuring governments to adopt concrete, real plans of action for raising labor standards and to provide the financial resources to implement them.

References

Aidt, Toke, and Zafiris Tzannatos. 2002. *Unions and Collective Bargaining: Economic Effects in a Global Environment.* Washington, DC: World Bank.

Audley, John, and Edward Sherwin. 2002. "Politics and Parallel Negotiations: Environment and Trade in the Western Hemisphere." Carnegie Endowment Working Papers no. 25 (April), Carnegie Endowment for International Peace, Washington, DC.

Carnegie Endowment for International Peace. 2001. "Breaking the Labor-Trade Deadlock." Carnegie Endowment Working Paper no. 17 (February). Trade Policy Group of the Inter-American Dialogue and the Economic Reform Project of the Carnegie Endowment for International Peace, Washington, DC.

Chau, Nancy C., and Ravi Kanbur. 2000. "The Race to the Bottom, From the Bottom." Cornell University, Department of Applied Economics and Management. Photocopy.

Compa, Lance. 2000. *Unfair Advantage: Workers' Freedom of Association in the United States Under International Human Rights Standards.* Washington, DC: Human Rights Watch.

Elliott, Kimberly Ann, and Richard B. Freeman. 2003. *Can Labor Standards Improve Under Globalization?* Washington, DC: Institute for International Economics.

Freedom House. Freedom in the World Country Ratings. http://www.freedomhouse.org/ratings/index.htm.

Freeman, Richard B., and James Medoff. 1984. *What Do Unions Do?* New York: Basic Books.

Hufbauer, Gary Clyde, Jeffrey J. Schott, Diana Orejas, and Ben Goodrich. 2002. *North American Labor Under NAFTA*. Washington, DC: Institute for International Economics. http://www.iie.com.

International Labor Office, International Labor Organization. 1997. *World Labour Report: Industrial Relations, Democracy and Social Stability.* Geneva.

———. 2002. "Employment and Social Policy in Respect of Export Processing Zones (EPZs)." Governing Body Document no. GB.285/ESP/5, Geneva.

International Labor Organization. Database of International Labor Standards (ILO ILOLEX). http://www.ilo.org/ilolex/english/index.htm.

Kucera, David. 2001. "The Effects of Core Worker Rights on Labour Costs and Foreign Direct Investment: Evaluating the Conventional Wisdom." Decent Work Research Program, International Institute for Labor Studies Discussion Paper DP/130/2001, International Labor Organization, Geneva.

Morici, Peter, and Evan Schulz. 2001. *Labor Standards in the Global Trading System.* Washington, DC: Economic Strategy Institute.

Navia, Patricio, and Andrés Velasco. 2003. "The Politics of Second Generation Reforms in Latin America." In *After the Washington Consensus: Restarting Growth and Reform in Latin America*, edited by John Williamson and Pedro Pablo Kuczynski. Washington, DC: Institute for International Economics.

Potter, Edward E. 1984. *Freedom of Association, the Right to Organize and Collective Bargaining: The Impact on U.S. Law and Practice of Ratification of ILO Conventions No. 87 & 98.* Washington, DC: Labor Policy Association, Inc.

Rodrik, Dani. 1996. "Labor Standards in International Trade: Do They Matter and What Do We Do About Them?" In *Emerging Agenda for Global Trade: High Stakes for Developing Countries*, edited by Robert Z. Lawrence, Dani Rodrik, and John Whalley. Washington, DC: Overseas Development Council.

Saavedra, Jaime. 2003. "Labor Markets in Latin America." In *After the Washington Consensus: Restarting Growth and Reform in Latin America,* edited by John Williamson and Pedro Pablo Kuczynski. Washington, DC: Institute for International Economics.

Salazar-Xirinachs, José Manuel, and Jorge Mario Martínez-Piva. 2003. "Trade, Labour Standards and Global Governance: A Perspective from the Americas." In *International Economic Governance and Non-Economic Concerns: New Challenges for the International Legal Order,* edited by Stefan Griller. New York: Springer Verlag.

Somavia, Juan. 1999. *Decent Work.* Report of the Director-General to the International Labor Conference (June), International Labor Office, International Labor Organization, Geneva.

United Nations Conference on Trade and Development and World Trade Organization International Trade Centre. International Trade Statistics. http://www.intracen.org/tradstat/welcome.htm.

World Bank. 2001. *Engendering Development.* Washington, DC.

———. 2003. World Bank World Development Indicators. http://www.worldbank.org/data/wdi2003/index.htm.

Notes

I would like to thank Jose Manuel Salazar-Xirinachs for his thoughtful and challenging comments on the chapter, as well as the participants in two project seminars, at Harvard University in May 2002 and Punta del Este, Uruguay, in December 2002. I would also like to thank Alica Robinson for her help in compiling information on labor standards and exports in the region. Finally, the views expressed herein are mine and do not necessarily reflect the views of the Institute's Board of Directors, Advisory Committee, or other staff.

1 For a similar proposal addressing environmental issues in the FTAA negotiations, see Audley and Sherwin (2002); for an alternative proposal suggesting de-linking trade and labor negotiations, see Carnegie (2001).

2 These include forced labor; recruitment of child soldiers; illicit activities such as drug trafficking, prostitution, and pornography; and "other hazardous" work to be defined by each country adhering to the convention.

3 Navia and Velasco (2003: Figure 3) note that labor market reforms have barely begun in most of the region; see also Saavedra in the same volume.

4 See Saavedra (2003) for analysis of the labor market trends in Latin America during the recent period of structural reforms, as well as recommendations for changes in policy; also see chapters 21 and 22 in this volume.

5 Saavedra (2003) also makes recommendations for reforming the collective bargaining process.

6 For example, the key assumption underlying the Chau and Kanbur model is that higher standards must raise costs and adversely affect exports. But, in practice, unions might raise productivity enough to offset the wage premium union members usually receive. Whether discrimination promotes or undermines exports depends on whether it occurs in the traded or nontraded sector.

7 The TRIPs agreement provides for some flexibility in implementation—longer phase-ins for developing countries and limited opt-outs in the form of compulsory licenses in emergencies—but the basic rules are the same for all WTO members, despite widely differing circumstances.

8 The figure for the Middle East and North Africa should be taken with a large grain of salt as it is based on only three countries and would be much lower if data were available for the oil-exporting states of the Middle East.

9 A broad picture of the application of the core labor standards around the world may also be found in the "global reports" submitted by the director general each year to the International Labor Conference. Initial reports on freedom of association, forced labor, child labor, and discrimination were released in 2000, 2001, 2002, and 2003, respectively, and are available on the ILO website.

10 The ILO supervisory system is discussed in detail in the FAQs section of the International Labor Standards page on the ILO website (http://www.ilo.org).

11 The conventions in order of adoption are: 29 on forced labor; 87 on freedom of association; 98 on the right to organize and bargain collectively; 100 on equal remuneration for men and women for work of equal value; 105 on the abolition of forced labor; 111 on nondiscrimination in employment; 138 setting a minimum age for child labor; and 182 calling for immediate action against the "worst forms" of child labor.

12 These problems are also rooted in discrimination but the complaints are usually addressed under the forced-labor conventions.

13 As it is wont to do, the Committee on Freedom of Association used far more circumspect language, concluding that the use of permanent strike replacement workers "entails a risk of derogation from the right to strike which may affect the free exercise of trade union rights." See Potter (1984) for an employers' group perspective on the changes to U.S. law that would be required by ratification of conventions 87 and 98 and the Human Rights Watch report (Compa 2000) on how U.S. law and practice fails to protect workers.

14 Most FTAA countries have been the target of Committee of Experts observations on laws or practices that are inconsistent with international core standards, but only the more serious cases are included in Table 19.4.

15 See Hufbauer et al. (2002) for a more detailed description and assessment of the NAFTA side agreement.

16 See Elliott and Freeman (2003: Chapter 4) on the GSP program and Hufbauer et al. (2002) on the NAFTA side agreement.

17 *Inside U.S. Trade,* November 8, 2002: 23.

18 Although every Bush budget has proposed cuts in funding for international labor affairs, Congress has thus far maintained spending at roughly the levels of the last years of the Clinton administration. For fiscal year 2004, the administration requested only US$12 million for this account, not enough even to cover current operating costs.

19 For more on the monitoring initiatives and the "market for standards," see Elliott and Freeman (2003: chapters 2 and 3).

20

The Environmental Dimension of Economic Integration: The FTAA and Beyond

Daniel C. Esty

Introduction

From the streets of Seattle to the *stradas* of Genoa, international economic meetings have been disrupted by protests and even rioting in opposition to trade liberalization and economic integration. One element of this antiglobalization backlash centers on a fear that freer trade will undermine efforts to protect the environment. Finding ways to respond to this concern and to build environmental sensitivity into the efforts to promote hemispheric integration is thus a key challenge facing the Free Trade Area of the Americas (FTAA) negotiators.

This chapter explores the trade-environment conflict in the context of efforts to promote Western hemispheric economic integration. It maps the sources of "trade and environment" tensions and spells out the logic of managing the trade-environment interface overtly and carefully. The chapter also reviews options—both procedural and substantive—for integrating environmental protection and trade liberalization through an FTAA.

Rising Trade and Environment Tensions

Not very long ago, there seemed to be little connection between trade and environmental policy making. The General Agreement on Tariffs and Trade (GATT) of 1947 did not mention the word *environment*, and the phrase *sustainable development* had not yet even been coined. Today, however, trade and environmental policy making seem to be deeply interconnected—and often in considerable tension.

Inescapable Linkages

The 1991 GATT "tuna-dolphin case" highlighted the possibility that environmental rules and standards might be challenged in the context of trade obligations and agreements (Housman and Zaelke 1992). The GATT panel decision, judging America's embargo against Mexican tuna imports to be inconsistent with the international trade obligations of the United States, precipitated a battle over trade and the environment that has not yet ended (Esty 1994a; Runge 1994). The tuna-dolphin decision convinced many in the environmental community that efforts to promote freer trade represented a significant threat to existing programs of environmental protection.

While the trade community initially argued that efforts to promote freer trade need not be inconsistent with efforts to protect the environment (Jackson 1992; Repetto 1993), a series of disputes that unfolded during the 1990s—beef hormones, reformulated gasoline, shrimp-turtle, and so on—convinced many environmentalists that there was a fundamental tension. New conflicts have recently emerged over biotechnology, genetically modified organisms, and climate change (Sampson 2000). Because public health standards, food safety requirements, emissions limits, waste management and disposal rules, packaging and recycling regulations, and labeling policies all have the potential to disrupt trade flows, there is no end in sight to trade and environment disputes. Conversely, market-access commitments and other trade disciplines designed to reduce nontariff trade barriers can constrain environmental protection efforts. Many observers, in both the trade and environmental communities, have thus become convinced that the tensions between these two policy realms must be managed more systematically.

Beyond this descriptive reality, the trade-environment link requires attention as a normative matter. Simply put, absent control of transboundary pollution spillovers and careful management of shared natural resources, the economic efficiency of international commerce cannot be guaranteed (Esty 2001). Without coordination to address the "collective action" problem, open-access resources such as the atmosphere and ocean fisheries will be over exploited, potentially resulting in a "tragedy of the commons" (Olson 1965). Similarly, the failure to internalize pollution externalities results in distorted competition, reduced gains from trade, lower social welfare, and unnecessary ecological degradation.

The political economy of trade liberalization creates further pressure at the trade-environment interface. Experience suggests that efforts to promote freer trade will not succeed absent some focus on environmental concerns. NAFTA won ratification by the U.S. Congress in part because of the significant efforts that were made to address environmental issues (Esty 1994b; Audley 1997). Recent attempts to authorize fast-track negotiating authority have failed, in part because they lacked serious attention to environmental issues. Indeed, a number of studies have suggested that the political coalition in the United States that supports trade liberalization is narrow and fragile (Schott 2001; Aranson 2001). Legislative success in advancing trade liberalization requires the votes of pro-trade, pro-environment representatives and senators (Esty 1998a; Destler and Balint 1999). And as Steve Charnovitz (1998) has demonstrated, issue linkage has long been part of the political economy of trade policy making.

Thus, the reality of trade-environment conflicts, the logic of trade and economic theory, and the demands of trade politics all argue for a careful focus on making economic integration and trade liberalization proceed in a fashion that accommodates environmental goals and programs. Given the degree of interlinkage, the choice ultimately is not *whether* to address trade and environment issues but *how* to address them. Governments can negotiate rules and design procedures that work to make trade and environmental policies mutually reinforcing in an overt, systematic, and transparent fashion or they can handle the issues that arise in an unstructured, crisis-driven, ad hoc manner.

Environmental Concerns about Freer Trade

The Effects of Economic Growth

From an environmental perspective, there are a number of concerns that arise from the prospect of trade and investment liberalization. First, many environmental advocates worry about the very fact that trade is designed to promote economic growth, which they see as leading to increased pollution and the unsustainable consumption of natural resources. Most environmentalists today reject this "limits to growth" philosophy in favor of a *sustainable development* paradigm, which recognizes that economic growth can be environmentally positive. But even those who understand the potential for environmental gains from freer trade worry that, in practice, the results will not be positive.

As a matter of theory, the effect of expanded trade and economic growth on the environment can be separated into three distinct effects (Grossman and Krueger 1995; Esty 2001). "Scale" effects represent the rise in pollution and resource use due to expanded economic activity and greater consumption. But this negative impact may be offset by "technique" effects that arise from the tendency toward the use of cleaner production processes as wealth increases and as trade expands access to cutting-edge technologies and environmental best practices. Similarly, a "wealth" or "composition" effect may shift consumer preferences toward cleaner goods as income rises.

As an empirical matter, it appears that in the early stages of economic development the negative environmental impacts of the scale effect may outweigh the positive contributions of the technique and composition effects.[1] At least with regard to some pollution control challenges, there appears to be an environmental Kuznet's curve. This inverted-U shape relationship suggests that environmental conditions may deteriorate in the early stages of industrialization and then improve as nations hit middle-income levels. A number of studies have found that the critical turning point is a GDP per capita of approximately US$5,000–8,000 (Grossman and Krueger 1995; Shafik and Bandyopadhyay 1992; Seldon and Song 1994). Others have found a somewhat higher "tipping point" (Antweiler, Copeland, and Taylor 1998; Harbough, Levinson, and Wilson 2000). Thus, it appears that, at least over time, the technique and composition effects overwhelm the scale effects, making it likely that increased trade, resulting in higher incomes, will translate into reduced pollution harms.

But this principle does not apply to all environmental problems. As Dua and Esty (1997: 74) argue, when environmental issues are spread spatially or temporally, the incentives for governments to address them may become too weak to induce action. Thus, while local air pollution may get better with added wealth, there is no empirical evidence that greenhouse gas emissions go down with increased income.

The Effects of Trade Agreements

Another set of concerns focuses on the impact of the trade-liberalization process. Environmental advocates fear that the market-access commitments negotiated as part of a trade agreement will constrain domestic regulatory authority. Although fear mongering about lost "sovereignty" can be overdone (Perot 1993; Wallach and Sforza 1999), it is true that trade agreements seek to limit nontariff barriers through various "disciplines" that limit regulatory flexibility. The hope is that trade rules will be constructed in a careful fashion that permits legitimate environmental protection efforts to go forward while screening out purported "environmental" programs, which are actually protectionism in a green guise.

Unfortunately, GATT jurisprudence in this regard has not historically been very sophisticated in its interpretation of Article XX, which lays out the exceptions that are permitted under the usual rules of nondiscrimination (Charnovitz 1992). In balancing trade principles against environmental prerogatives, GATT dispute-settlement panels have traditionally looked to whether the environmental policy was "necessary" (Article XX(b)). This standard sounds reasonable except that, historically, *necessity* was determined by examining whether the chosen policy instrument was the "least trade restrictive" available.[2] This standard proved nearly impossible to meet, even for quite legitimate environmental policies and programs (Esty 1994a).

In other cases, specific market disciplines have been poorly crafted. Most notoriously, NAFTA's Investment Chapter has an "expropriation" provision that is so loosely drafted that several legitimate exercises of environmental regulation have been challenged as "tantamount to expropriation" (Mann and Araya 2002).

Competitiveness Impacts

Perhaps the most persistent fear about the negative effects of trade liberalization centers on the risk that jurisdictions with high environmental standards will come under pressure to weaken their pollution controls in order to maintain the competitiveness of their industries in an integrated marketplace in which some competitors will be located in environmentally less demanding jurisdictions. There is, however, little evidence of broad-based industrial migration to "pollution havens" (Gallagher 2002; Neumayer 2001). Thus, in its most stark form, the fear of a "race toward the bottom" seems overdrawn. Only a few cases have been identified in which a jurisdiction actually lowered its environmental standards or relaxed enforcement to attract investment, factories, or jobs (van Beers and van den Bergh 1997). But economic theory predicts that tougher environmental standards will affect industrial location, at least in polluting industries (Baumol and Oates 1988; Copeland and Taylor 1995). The risk appears to emerge less in the form of competitiveness harms and more in the form of "regulatory chill" in the environmental policy making domain (Esty 1996). In the United States, for example, the debate surrounding the Clean Air Act of 1990 was replete with industry claims that higher standards would be a disadvantage in a global marketplace. Likewise, the Clinton Administration's attempt to raise energy taxes collapsed in the face of competitiveness concerns.

In the academic literature, a debate has raged in recent years over the theoretical foundations for a race to the bottom. Some observers have argued that regulatory competition is healthy. They see little reason to fear that competitiveness pressures will translate into lower environmental standards (Revesz 1992, 2001; Bhagwati and Hudec 1996). Others worry that strategic behavior in standard setting could lead to a regulatory dynamic that results in suboptimal standards (Esty 1996; Esty and Geradin 2001a; Engel and Ackerman 2001). The prevailing argument appears to be: "it depends." Regulatory competition seems likely to yield social-welfare benefits when the market in "locational rights" functions in a fashion that resembles perfect competition. However, where market failures intrude, the prospects for welfare losses from this competitive dynamic emerge. Esty and Geradin (2001b: xxv) identify a number of other variables that also affect the likelihood that divergent environmental standards, and the competitiveness pressures they create, will unleash a welfare-reducing strategic response:

- the scope of uninternalized externalities;
- the information base of the particular "market" and whether it provides a sufficient foundation for competition or is incomplete in ways that undermine competitive practices;
- the capacity of citizens and companies to obtain and to understand information that is relevant to their choices and options;
- the underlying mobility of both companies and people;
- the existence of regulatory economics of scale;
- the geographic heterogeneity of the issue at hand;
- the degree of public-choice distortion that affects decision making; and
- the existence of Prisoners' Dilemma-driven strategic behavior in standard setting and how close to perfect competition the market in locational rights seems to be.

With little empirical evidence to draw on, there remains an important question in the economic-integration context about whether harmonization of standards (and what sort of harmonization) will be welfare enhancing (Bhagwati and Hudec 1996; Esty and Geradin 1997).

Process Concerns

Another trade-environment tension centers on a lack of transparency in the trade policy making process. Traditionally, trade negotiations take place in secret on the theory that governments find it easier to commit to true liberalization outside of the scrutiny of rent-seeking special interests who will fight any effort to eliminate the protectionism from which they benefit. But this closed-door approach to decisionmaking has resulted in a deep suspicion that the trade policy making process is dominated by those with "insider" access, particularly in multinational corporations. In any case, in the post-Seattle world, the trade regime can no longer operate below the public radar. Trade policy making is now a very high profile part of the international affairs agenda, making a more transparent decisionmaking process a necessity.

Similarly, the future legitimacy of the trade regime depends on a more transparent dispute-resolution process to interpret and refine trade rules (Esty 2002). The current practice of conducting the business of dispute-settlement panels behind closed doors gives rise to an appearance of "secret tribunals," which are considered unacceptable by almost any modern standard of judicial appropriateness.

Beyond transparency, there is a growing sense that the trade policy process would benefit from a more inclusive structure of decisionmaking. Charnovitz (2002), Esty (1998b), and others have argued that the outcomes generated by the trade policy making process would be more robust if nongovernmental organizations were allowed to present their perspectives on the issues at hand, both in negotiations and in dispute settlement cases. In effect, these outside interests, including business entities as well as environmental groups, serve as "competitors" to government officials, forcing them to make more careful and well-considered decisions (Esty and Geradin 2001a).

Environmental Effects on Trade

As distressed as the environmental community has been about the current practices of the trade regime, trade policy makers are increasingly exasperated by the degree of burden they perceive the trade regime to be under from the environmental quarter. As noted earlier, a wide array of environmental standards can be manipulated into hidden trade barriers. Even when protectionist motives are not present, poorly crafted environmental standards can easily become nontariff barriers to trade. The failure of the environmental policy making world to take seriously the need to adopt standards and regulatory programs that do not have adverse trade effects has become a major bone of contention.

The trade community is perhaps even more concerned about the use of trade measures as a strategy for advancing environmental goals. In particular, they fear the use of trade penalties for enforcing the commitments made under multilateral environmental agreements. They see, for example, the use of trade sanctions to promote the phase-out of ozone-layer-damaging CFCs under the Montreal Protocol to be a serious strain on freer trade. Worry that trade benefits will be withdrawn if a country does not meet a certain environmental standard is a widespread concern in the trade world, particularly among developing-country officials. The Mexicans, most notably, remain very distressed about the provisions in the NAFTA Environmental Side Agreement that provide for trade sanctions if a country is found to have failed to uphold its own environmental standards (Araya 2002). As a result, until recently, Mexico led the charge to block any environmental negotiations in the FTAA process.

A number of trade officials worry that the environmental agenda is being advanced by those with protectionist intentions. They fear that calls for dialogue on trade-environment issues might result in stringent, global-scale environmental standards that developing countries would have trouble meeting. Specifically, they see the push for stronger environmental protection as a threat to the comparative advantage of developing countries that arises from the decision to have less demanding environmental requirements.

More broadly, a significant number of free traders see environmental advocates as stalking horses for protectionist interests. The sight of environmentalists marching in the streets of Seattle arm-in-arm with avowed protectionists convinced many in the trade community that environmentalists are really protectionists. But while the tactical partnership of some environmental groups with protectionist interests has been misguided, a sweeping conclusion that all environmentalists are protectionist—or that the logic of an environmental dimension to trade agreements is not sound—cannot be sustained.

Trade and Environment in an FTAA

How trade and the environment issues will play out in the context of a Free Trade Area of the Americas is not yet certain. On the one hand, at the launch of the FTAA process at the 1994 Summit of the Americas in Miami, a commitment was made to advance "social well-being and economic prosperity in ways that are fully cognizant of our impact on the environment."[3] The presidents and prime ministers who gathered in Miami further pledged to create partnerships for sustainable energy use, biodiversity, and pollution prevention. This package might be viewed as a commitment to address the environment systematically in the context of Western Hemisphere economic integration (Audley and Sherwin 2002). Just two years later, at the 1996 Santa Cruz Summit of the Americas in Bolivia, the thirty-four governments present committed themselves to a sustainable-development agenda (Segger et al. 2002). Most recently, the final declaration issued at the April 2001 Quebec City Summit of the Americas identified the environment as an element of what was necessary for "creating prosperity" in the Western Hemisphere. And the declaration from the 2002 Quito Ministerial Meeting reiterated this pledge.

At the same time, the trade negotiators charged with executing the FTAA have expressly declined to create an environmental negotiating group. Indeed, it was agreed in 1994 that the environment would *not* be a topic for negotiations (Deere and Esty 2002). This posture represents a dramatic step back from the significant role that environment played in the NAFTA negotiations (Johnson and Beaulieu 1996). At that time, environmental negotiators were part of a number of the NAFTA working groups. Environmental provisions were written into a number of articles of NAFTA itself, and the "parallel track" environmental negotiations resulted in broad-based agreement on environmental cooperation and other elements aimed at protecting ecological resources in the context of deeper North American trade relations (Esty 1994b). This backtracking reflects, in part, the bitterness of Mexican trade negotiators about how they feel they were treated in the closing rounds of the NAFTA negotiations (Araya 2002).

More generally, the hesitation on the part of nearly all of the Latin American countries[4] to even sit down at the table to discuss environmental issues reflects a deep-seated suspicion about U.S. motivations in general and the pressures likely to be exerted by the North American environmental community in particular. Many Latin American trade officials see the specter of northern environmental standards being imposed on them, depriving their industries of comparative advantage and resulting in a loss of the potential gains from trade.

This "just say no" attitude toward trade and environment issues in the context of the FTAA process seems unlikely to be sustained. A number of counter-pressures have emerged, including: the decision to take environment issues up in the next WTO round of negotiations, the emerging NAFTA "trade and environment" results, the trade-environment provisions being built into other regional trade pacts, and the evolving WTO trade and environment case law (Araya and Esty 2002). Whether the parties set up an environmental working group or agree to address environmental issues within one or more of the existing negotiating groups does not matter a great deal. That there is a recognition that some environmental issues need to be addressed within the FTAA and that others should be discussed on a parallel track focused on promoting environmental cooperation is what is crucial.

The Doha Declaration

Despite the hesitancy of developing countries, and largely as a result of pressure from the European Union (where the ecological, economic, and political logic of a carefully managed trade-environment relationship is now broadly accepted), the work program spelled out at the World Trade Organization Ministerial Meeting in Doha for the next round of multilateral negotiations includes a number of environmental provisions. The ministers agreed, in particular, to launch negotiations aimed at exploring the relationship between WTO rules and trade obligations set out in multilateral environmental agreements. The WTO members also instructed their Committee on Trade and the Environment (CTE) to address the potential effect of environmental measures on market access, especially for developing countries. The parties further agreed to try to identify strategies for eliminating fisheries subsidies that are both trade distorting and environmentally harmful. Commitments were also made to address ecolabels and to support capacity building for developing countries so they can potentially better address trade and environment issues. Finally, the countries gathered in Qatar established the CTE as a forum for identifying and debating potential environmental aspects of the negotiations to be carried forward under the Doha Declaration.

This negotiating mandate, while not as broad as the European Union (or the environmental community) would have liked, affirms the existence of inescapable trade-environment linkages. It highlights a number of priority issues for consideration and makes it overwhelmingly likely that there will be a significant environmental component to whatever agreement emerges from the Doha Round of multilateral negotiations. The fact that governments will be negotiating in the WTO context on a range of trade and environment questions makes it difficult for the FTAA negotiators to continue to dodge the same issues. Indeed, as I discuss below, it may well be that some countries will find it easier to take these issues up first in the context of the FTAA and then try to transfer the results to the WTO.

NAFTA Experience

Those countries wishing to address trade and environment issues in the FTAA—the United States, Canada, and Chile—will undoubtedly stress the success of the integration of environmental considerations into NAFTA as a way of demonstrating that environmental negotiations need not end badly. In fact, a number of recent studies have suggested that the environmental dimensions of the NAFTA are working quite well (Deere and Esty 2002; Hufbauer et al. 2001). The provisions written into the agreement to ensure that environmental considerations are taken seriously have not generated the trade frictions that some feared they might. Specifically, the Chapter 7 provisions dealing with sanitary and phytosanitary measures and Chapter 9 standards-related measures have guaranteed the NAFTA parties the opportunity to set their own levels of protection based on their own judgments about environmental risk so long as those standards are based on science. In addition, the Chapter 104 provision, ensuring that the trade obligations created under NAFTA would not take precedence over international environmental agreements including the Montreal Protocol, the Basel Convention, and CITES, has generated no disputes.

The cooperation promoted by the Environmental Side Agreement has also generated solid results. Although the North American Commission for Environmental Cooperation (NACEC) has not achieved all that some had hoped for, it has proven itself to be a useful mechanism for ensuring that environmental issues that arise in the context of closer trade relations do not get ignored. The commission has also demonstrated its value as a forum for engaging environmental groups, other NGOs, and civil society more broadly in an ongoing conversation about what environmental issues matter and how the three countries of North America might best address them. While each of these NAFTA parties has, at times, found itself on the receiving end of NACEC criticisms,[5] no one has suggested that the scrutiny was unjustified.

Ironically, the one dimension of NAFTA that has generated considerable friction is the Chapter 11 set of market disciplines aimed at protecting foreign investment. The investment chapter's poorly drafted provisions relating to compensation for expropriation-like governmental activities has generated a great deal of controversy. Similarly, the article in the NAFTA Environmental Side Agreement that calls for trade sanctions if a country fails to uphold its environmental standards has not provided the promised "teeth" for the agreement but rather has generated a great deal of antagonism on the Mexican side.

Although the logic of folding environmental considerations into NAFTA was particularly strong given the long borders shared between the parties, a similar argument supports some degree of environmental cooperation in the context of an FTAA. The Americas constitute a continuous geographic entity with a series of linked ecosystems. A number of species migrate across many countries through the hemisphere. As a result of both the ecological interdependence and the environmental dimensions of deeper economic interdependence, the argument for some kind of environmental agreement to be negotiated alongside the FTAA is strong.

Several recent studies (Segger et al. 2002; Deere and Esty 2002; Audley and Sherwin 2002) examine the experience of NAFTA closely and conclude that a carefully constructed and narrowly tailored set of environmental provisions within the FTAA itself and a broader degree of environmental cooperation activities to be worked out on a parallel track make sense. These analyses call for the rectification of some of the errors of NAFTA. Specifically, each of the studies rejects the use of trade sanctions as provided in the NAFTA Environmental Side Agreement in favor of a system that spotlights deficiencies and seeks to generate assistance for those who are underperforming. Several seek a refined investment chapter that does not repeat the poorly crafted expropriation language of NAFTA.

Other Regional Trade Agreements

Further pressure for an environmental dimension of an FTAA might be created by the presence of environmental components in several other regional free trade efforts. The bilateral Chile-Canada Free Trade Agreement expressly reinforces aspects of NAFTA that are perceived to be working and refines those that are not. As a result, the Chile-Canada Accord stresses a cooperative approach to environmental compliance, rejects the use of trade sanctions for environmental deficiencies, and offers an interesting model of a looser institutional structure in support of ongoing trade and environment discussions between countries that are not physically coterminous and thus not under the same degree of pressure that existed in NAFTA.

The Canada–Costa Rica Bilateral Trade Agreement also has an important environmental dimension with a special focus on access to environmental information and capacity building to promote stronger national environmental policy (Segger et al. 2002). The MERCOSUR countries have also committed to a significant degree of environmental cooperation in the context of their free trade area.[6]

Evolving WTO Jurisprudence

There are a number of aspects of recent WTO dispute-settlement panel decisions that have softened the edges of the trade-environment clash (Wofford 2000). Most notably, the Appellate Body Decision in the recent shrimp-turtle case makes it clear that countries can take actions to protect endangered species so long as these efforts are consistent with the "head note" of Article XX of GATT. This decision appropriately focuses on whether environmental measures are disguised barriers to trade rather than whether they are aimed at regulating products or production processes and methods (PPMs).

The move beyond the product-PPM distinction is particularly important. Indeed, under conditions of ecological interdependence, the traditional distinction cannot be maintained. *How* things are produced is often as important as *what* is produced. For example, a country that sought to block imports of semiconductors produced using CFCs in violation of the Montreal Protocol should be seen as acting within its rights, not only because of the existence of a multilateral environmental agreement but also because it was acting to discipline an environmentally harmful production practice with transboundary impacts. The FTAA negotiators may find it hard to resist the chance to fold these new principles into their own agreement so as to ensure that it represents cutting-edge thinking about how best to manage the trade and environment relationship.

FTAA Integration Opportunities

An FTAA represents an opportunity to advance both the theory and that practice of how best to integrate the goals of trade liberalization and environmental protection. The negotiators have an opportunity both to sharpen the process by which difficult issues are worked out and to refine the substantive rules that govern the trade-environment interface.

Procedural Advances

The FTAA process is an opportunity to carry out trade negotiations in a new and more transparent way. The old logic that better deals will be cut under conditions of secrecy no longer applies. Trade policy making has become very high profile. While some aspects of negotiation will continue to need to be done behind closed doors, a much greater commitment to public understanding of the issues and process should be the new norm. The best approach to getting out from under the grips of special interests now lies in a strategy of full debate and disclosure of all lobbying, including the identification of all nongovernmental interests and their attempts to influence the outcome of the negotiating process (Esty 1998b). The argument for transparency applies both to efforts by business interests to carve out special conditions of market preference and to environmental groups whose proposals might be advanced in collusion with protectionist interests.

The logic for a more open trade policy-making process that engages not just the business community but also nongovernmental organizations broadly centers on the suggestion that greater transparency and a fuller debate around the difficult issues will generate an outcome that is more authoritative and legitimate (Esty 2001; Keohane and Nye 2001). Legitimacy increasingly turns on the issue of whether the process by which the outcome was delivered is seen as fair and open (whether due process was accorded to all those that wish to be involved) and whether it generates robust answers to difficult questions that are a product of an analytically rigorous give-and-take process.

Another procedural advance that could be taken up in the FTAA context is a commitment to environmental assessments of the potential agreement at both national and hemispheric scales. The United States has already agreed to do such an assessment.[7] It would be useful if other countries agreed to do their own environmental reviews and if there were an agreement on a common methodology for analyzing the critical issues raised by closer trade relations across the hemisphere.[8]

As noted above, a number of proposals have now been advanced for a parallel agreement on environmental cooperation, perhaps tracking the model established in the recent Chile-Canada Free Trade Agreement. A clear commitment to negotiate *within* the context of the trade agreement itself on those issues that are tightly linked to market disciplines and on other aspects of the trade relationship would make sense. In addition, a *parallel* negotiation on dimensions of environmental cooperation and institutional support for technology exchange, capacity building, policy coordinates, and other collaborative aspects would also be a step in a positive direction.

Substantive Issues

As noted above, the FTAA process is an opportunity to make progress on a series of issues that remain unresolved at the trade-environment interface. First, the FTAA negotiators could, tracking some of the provisions of NAFTA, commit themselves to a modernized dispute-settlement process that would include open hearings, opportunities for interested nongovernmental parties to submit amicus briefs, and the publication of decisions. Moving the dispute-settlement process toward a more quasi-judicial approach and away from the traditional model of an extended negotiation would help to reinforce the broader effort to construct a trade regime that is rules based rather than focused on tit-for-tat tariff exchanges.

Second, FTAA negotiators might also find language to recognize that multilateral environmental agreements should not be trumped by trade rules. To the contrary, trade obligations should be interpreted in a fashion that reinforces the goals of broadly supported environmental accords. The language from NAFTA in this regard might be repeated and refined, perhaps providing a foundation for a multilateral agreement on such a provision in the context of the post-Doha WTO negotiations.[9]

While the language on multilateral environmental agreements from NAFTA provides a good starting point for an FTAA, the investment language adopted by the United States, Canada, and Mexico must be carefully recrafted to ensure that the mistakes of NAFTA are not repeated. Again, an opportunity exists to define an appropriate set of disciplines to protect foreign investment that do not interfere with legitimate environmental protection. Such language would be useful both at the WTO and as a guide to efforts to revise NAFTA.

Ecolabels represent a third issue that has been a source of trade-environment tension. On the one hand, labels are a much less trade-disruptive environmental policy tool than many of the alternatives, such as import bans. Thus, in the spirit of promoting freer trade, it would make sense to provide incentives for the use of ecolabels. On the other hand, there is a risk that ecolabels could be misleading or protectionist. Thus, there is good reason to try to establish appropriate disciplines on the use of ecolabels that would acknowledge their value but ensure that they do not distort trade. A properly constructed set of regulations would ensure basic standards are met, such as truthfulness, accuracy, and relevance. At the same time, the use of ecolabels should be affirmed as generally acceptable even to the extent that the labels address issues that are related to production processes and methods.

Fifth, and more generally, the FTAA negotiators would do well to incorporate the recent WTO jurisprudence on PPMs into the proposed hemispheric trade accord. The language used in the WTO Appellate Body Decision in the shrimp-turtle case provides a very good starting point in this regard (Wofford 2000). Incorporating this language into an FTAA would go some distance toward modernizing the basic structure of trade rules and getting past the existing product-PPM tangle.

Sixth, FTAA negotiators can advance a win-win agenda that promotes both trade liberalization and environmental protection with commitment to zero tariffs on environmental goods and services. Such a commitment would ensure the maximum degree of technology transfer in support of pollution control and other environmental goals.

Finally, phasing out subsidies that are both environmentally harmful and trade disruptive would be appropriate. Particular focus might be given to energy, agriculture, water, fisheries, and timber subsidies. In each case, there would be substantial environmental benefits from eliminating the subsidies, and the distortion of trade that they represent could be reduced. In each of these cases two other "wins" are simultaneously achieved. Governments benefit when they do not have to bear the budget burden of paying the subsidies, and developing countries likely gain from lower subsidies—particularly from a reduction in agricultural support—which act as a barrier to entry into the U.S. market.

Conclusion

The link between trade and environmental policies is inescapable in theory and in practice. A failure to address this relationship in the context of the FTAA negotiations invites an endless series of trade and environment disputes. A carefully constructed trade-environment agenda for the FTAA would, in contrast, reduce the tensions in this domain and promote a fuller and more effective system of economic integration and trade liberalization. Just as markets need regulation to function efficiently, some effort is required to define the terms of engagement for international commerce with regard to environmental regulations. Transboundary environmental externalities must be internalized to avoid pervasive market failures. Absent such a structure, in the context of hemispheric trade, allocative efficiency will not be achieved and the full benefits of an FTAA will not be reached.

Not only does a carefully constructed trade and environment agenda with an FTAA promise to reduce trade disputes and promote economic efficiency, it might also be seen as essential to the political process of winning support for deeper hemispheric economic integration. In the United States, Canada, and a growing number of other countries, large segments of the public are beginning to insist that trade policy be pursued with an eye to a set of values and issues beyond economic growth and gains in GDP. In many countries of the Americas, the public would like trade liberalization that is attentive to environmental protection, poverty alleviation, and the promotion of human rights. An FTAA that folds sensitivity to these other issues into its fabric is much more likely to generate popular support. Integration built on this broader political foundation is also likely to be more durable than a narrow trade and investment liberalization strategy.

Ultimately, managing interdependence is not just a matter of economics but also contains an important ecological dimension. To maximize social welfare, trade liberalization must be pursued with this broader vision in mind. The FTAA process is an opportunity to build on past efforts to make trade policy and environmental policy mutually reinforcing. Western hemisphere integration also provides an opportunity to break new ground in this regard, providing a model for other free trade agreements.

References

Antweiler, Werner, Brian R. Copeland, and M. Scott Taylor. 1998. "Is Free Trade Good for the Environment?" National Bureau of Economic Research Working Paper no. W6707 (August), Cambridge, MA.

Aranson, Susan. 2001. *Redefining the Terms of Trade Policymaking.* Washington, DC: National Policy Association.

Araya, Monica. 2002. "Trade and Environment Lessons from NAFTA for the FTAA." In *Greening the Americas: NAFTA's Lessons for Hemispheric Trade,* edited by Carolyn Deere and Daniel C. Esty. Cambridge, MA: MIT Press.

Araya, Monica, and Daniel C. Esty. 2002. "Bridging the Trade-Environment Divide in the FTAA." Paper presented at the Inter-American Dialogue Conference "Bridging the Divide: Toward a Consensus on Free Trade in the Americas," Nov. 22–23, Washington, DC.

Audley, John. 1997. *Green Politics and Global Trade: NAFTA and the Future of Environmental Politics.* Washington, DC: Georgetown University Press.

Audley, John, and Edward Sherwin. 2002. *Politics and Parallel Negotiations: Environment and Trade in the Western Hemisphere.* Carnegie Endowment for International Peace Working Paper no. 25, Washington, DC.

Baumol, William J., and Wallace E. Oates. 1988. *The Theory of Environmental Policy.* 2d ed. Cambridge: Cambridge University Press.

Bhagwati, Jagdish, and Robert Hudec. 1996. *Fair Trade and Harmonization: Prerequisites for Free Trade?* Cambridge, MA: MIT Press.

Charnovitz, Steve. 1992. "GATT and the Environment: Examining the Issues." *International Environmental Affairs* 4: 203–33.

———. 1998. "Linking Topics in Treaties." *University of Pennsylvania Journal of International Economic Law* 19: 329–45.

———. 2002. "WTO Cosmopolitics." *New York University Journal of International Law and Politics* 34: 299–354.

Copeland, Brian R., and M. Scott Taylor. 1995. "Trade and Transboundary Pollution." *American Economic Review* 85 (4): 716–37.

Deere, Carolyn, and Daniel C. Esty. 2002. "Trade and Environment in the Americas: Lessons from the North American Free Trade Agreement." In *Greening the Americas: NAFTA's Lessons for Hemispheric Trade,* edited by Carolyn Deere and Daniel C. Esty. Cambridge, MA: MIT Press.

Destler, I. M., and Peter J. Balint. 1999. *The New Politics of American Trade: Labor and the Environment.* Washington, DC: Institute for International Economics.

Dua, André, and Daniel C. Esty. 1997. *Sustaining the Asia Pacific Miracle: Environmental Protection and Economic Integration.* Washington, DC: Institute for International Economics.

Engel, Kirsten, and Susan Rose-Ackerman. 2001. "Environmental Federalism in the United States: The Risks of Devolution." In *Regulatory Competition and Economic Integration: Comparative Perspectives*, edited by Daniel C. Esty and Damien Geradin. Oxford: Oxford University Press.

Esty, Daniel C. 1994a. *Greening the GATT: Trade, Environment and the Future.* Washington, DC: Institute for International Economics.

———. 1994b. "Making Trade and Environmental Policies Work Together: Lessons from NAFTA." *Aussenwirschaft* 49: 59–79.

———. 1996. "Revitalizing Environmental Federalism." *Michigan Law Review* 95 (3): 570–653.

———. 1998a. "Environmentalists and Trade Policy-Making." In *Constituent Interests and U.S. Trade Policies*, edited by Alan W. Deardorff and Robert M. Stern. Ann Arbor: University of Michigan Press.

———. 1998b. "Non-Governmental Organizations at the World Trade Organization: Cooperation, Competition, or Exclusion." *Journal of International Economic Law* 1 (1): 123–47.

———. 2001. "Bridging the Trade-Environment Divide." *Journal of Economic Perspectives* 15 (3): 113–130.

———. 2002. "The World Trade Organization's Legitimacy Crisis." *World Trade Review* 1 (1): 7–22.

Esty, Daniel C., and Damien Geradin. 1997. "Environmental Protection and International Competitiveness: A Conceptual Framework." *Journal of World Trade* 32 (3): 5–46.

———. 2001a. "Regulatory Competition." In *Regulatory Competition and Economic Integration: Comparative Perspectives*, edited by Daniel C. Esty and Damien Geradin. Oxford: Oxford University Press.

———. 2001b. "Introduction." In *Regulatory Competition and Economic Integration: Comparative Perspectives*, edited by Daniel C. Esty and Damien Geradin. Oxford: Oxford University Press.

Gallagher, Kevin P. 2002. "Economic Integration, Environment and Development: Lessons from Mexico." Ph.D. dissertation in progress, Tufts University.

Grossman, Gene M., and Alan B. Krueger. 1995. "Economic Growth and the Environment." *Quarterly Journal of Economics* 110 (2): 353–77.

Harbaugh, William, Arik Levinson, and David Wilson. 2000. "Re-examining the Empirical Evidence for an Environmental Kuznets Curve." National Bureau of Economic Research Working Paper no. 7711 (May), Cambridge, MA.

Housman, Robert and Durwood Zaelke. 1992. "The Collision of the Environment and Trade: The GATT Tuna/Dolphin Decision." *Environmental Law Reporter* 22: 10268.

Hufbauer, Gary et al. 2001. *NAFTA and the Environment.* Washington, DC: Institute for International Economics.

Jackson, John H. 1992. "World Trade Rules and Environmental Policies: Congruence or Conflict?" *Washington Lee Law Review.* 49 (Fall): 1227.

Johnson, Pierre, and Andre Beaulieu. 1996. *The Environment and NAFTA: Understanding and Implementing the New Continental Law.* Washington, DC: Island Press.

Keohane, Robert, and Joseph Nye. 2001. "The Club Model of Multilateral Cooperation and Problems of Democratic Legitimacy." In *Efficiency, Equity and Legitimacy: The Multilateral Trading System at the Millennium,* edited by Roger Porter. Washington, DC: Brookings.

Lomborg, Bjorn. 2001. *The Skeptical Environmentalist.* Cambridge: Cambridge University Press.

Mann, Howard, and Monica Araya. 2002. "An Investment Regime for the Americas: Challenges and Opportunities for Environmental Sustainability." In *Greening the Americas: NAFTA's Lessons for Hemispheric Trade,* edited by Carolyn L. Deere and Daniel C. Esty. Cambridge, MA: MIT Press.

Neumayer, Eric. 2001. *Greening Trade and Investment.* London: Earthscan.

Olson, Mancur. 1965. *The Logic of Collective Action: Public Goods and the Theory of Groups.* Cambridge, MA: Harvard University Press.

Perot, Ross. 1993. *Save Your Job, Save Our Country: Why NAFTA Must Be Stopped Now!* New York: Hyperion.

Repetto, Robert. 1993. "A Note on Complimentarities Between Trade and Environmental Policies." In *The Greening of World Trade,* 78 (EPA 100-R-93–002). Washington, DC: Environmental Protection Agency.

Revesz, Richard. 1992. "Rehabilitating Interstate Competition: Rethinking the 'Race-to-the-Bottom' Rationale for Federal Environmental Regulation." *New York University Law Review* 67: 1210–54.

———. 2001. "Federalism and Regulation: Some Generalizations." In *Regulatory Competition and Economic Integration: Comparative Perspectives,* edited by Daniel C. Esty and Damien Geradin. Oxford: Oxford University Press.

Runge, C. Ford. 1994. *Freer Trade, Protected Environment: Balancing Trade Liberalization and Environmental Interests.* New York: Council on Foreign Relations.

Sampson, Gary P. 2000. *Trade, Environment and the WTO: The Post-Seattle Agenda.* Washington, DC: Johns Hopkins University Press.

Schott, Jeffrey. 2001. *Prospects for Free Trade in the Americas.* Washington, DC: Institute for International Economics.

Segger, Marie-Claire Cordonier, Maria Leichner, Nicola Borregaard, and Ana Karina González. 2002. "A New Mechanism for Hemispheric Cooperation on Environmental Sustainability and Trade?" Draft paper for consultation in the Thirteenth Forum of LAC Environment Ministers and the WSSD LAC Regional Preparatory Committee Meeting, Rio de Janiero, Oct. 23, 2001.

Seldon, Thomas M., and Daqing Song. 1994. "Environmental Quality and Development: Is There a Kuznets Curve for Air Pollution Emissions?" *Journal of Environmental Economics and Management* 27 (2): 147–52.

Shafik, Nemat, and Sushenjit Bandyopadhyay. 1992. "Economic Growth and Environmental Quality: Time Series and Cross-Country Evidence." World Bank, Washington, DC. Photocopy.

van Beers, Cees, and Jeroen C. J. M. van den Bergh. 1997. "An Empirical Multi-Country Analysis of the Impact of Environmental Regulations on Trade Flows." *Kyklos* 50: 1–25.

Wallach, Lori, and Michelle Sforza. 1999. *Whose Trade Organization: Corporate Globalization and the Erosion of Democracy*. Washington, DC: Public Citizen.

Wofford, Carrie. 2000. "A Greener Future at the WTO: The Refinement of WTO Jurisprudence on Environmental Exceptions to the GATT." *Harvard Environmental Law Review* 24 (2): 563–92.

Notes

The author thanks participants in the Inter-American Development Bank/INTAL/Harvard University "FTAA and Beyond" conferences for thoughts and guidance, with special appreciation to José Manuel Salazar-Xirinachs and Dani Rodrik for detailed comments. Thanks as well to Monica Araya and Kelly Levin for research assistance.

1 From a broader perspective, even when the negative environmental "scale effects" are big, industrialization and economic growth might still generate net social benefits such as health, education, or other factors that affect welfare (Lomborg 2001).

2 There is an emerging GATT jurisprudence that is making this standard easier to meet and, more generally, showing greater deference to environmental considerations (Wofford 2000; Charnovitz 2002).

3 The full text of the Miami Declaration can be found at http://www.ftaa-aka.org

4 Chile stands as the major exception.

5 Most notably, the NACEC annoyed Mexico when it investigated whether the building of a new pier in Cozumel was done in compliance with Mexican law.

6 See *Acuerdo Marco Sobre Medio Ambiente del MERCOSUR*, approved text from the Twentieth Reunion del Consejo Mercado Comun, 22 June, 2001, Asunción, MERCOSUR/CMC/DEC.no2/01.

7 The U.S. Review will be undertaken pursuant to Executive Order 13141. See 65 Fed. eg. 75, 763 (Dec. 4, 2000). See also http://www.ustr.gov /regions/whemishpere/envir.

8 This process could become part of the National Action Plans for Trade-Related Capacity Building that FTAA countries agreed to undertake in Quito in 2002.

9 Alternatively, the Doha Round may develop language that guides the FTAA process.

21

Social Protection and Inclusive Trade: Strengthening the Sources of Convergence within FTAA

Luis Felipe López-Calva and Nora Lustig

Introduction

What is the purpose of a Free Trade Area of the Americas (FTAA)? More generally, what has been the purpose of the resurgence of regional integration in the Americas? According to the 2002 Report of the Inter-American Development Bank "Beyond Borders: the New Regionalism in Latin America," there are four main reasons behind the so-called new regionalism:

> One is to reinforce market opening undertaken at the unilateral and multilateral levels. The formation of a regional market is also meant to create a more controlled and stable environment for firms to gain export experience. . . . (T)he scale economics, attraction of foreign direct investment and competition generated by a credible regional market are meant over time to dynamically raise productivity and develop international competitiveness. Regional integration also is being used as a geopolitical tool to fortify bargaining positions and promote cooperation.

An FTAA brings the largest prize: the possibility to have access to the largest market of the world with the consequential enhancement of the effects described above. What most governments in Latin America and the Caribbean hope for is that an FTAA will result in higher growth rates for their economies.

If an FTAA is to bring with it better living standards for large portions of the people in the region, why is it that nearly 10 million voters in Brazil have expressed their opposition in an unofficial referendum organized by more than 60 organizations in September 2002?[1] There are several explanations. Some argue that people are against an FTAA because of ignorance and ideological manipulations by a left that has replaced its quest for the socialist revolution with an antiglobalization movement. This explanation does not lead us very far: there may be valid reasons for the fears expressed by many grassroots organizations and unskilled or semiskilled workers in Latin America. For example, there is a fundamental mistrust toward the United States and its willingness to open the markets that are important for the rest of the countries in the region. Second, the fears of losing one's job or having one's skills become obsolete are valid concerns as well, particularly in the light of the very few safety nets and retraining programs in existence in Latin America.

Also, there is very little faith that the large gaps between poor and rich countries, and poor and rich regions within and between countries, will shrink as a result of fostering greater economic integration with the United States if only market forces are at play. In the background is the idea that in order to accelerate "convergence" there will have to be explicit transfers from the richer countries and regions to the poorer ones to close the infrastructure and education gaps. Otherwise, regions lagging behind today will be even farther behind the more prosperous areas in the future.

To what extent is this view correct? In order to answer this question we have looked at the experience of the European Union. To what extent has convergence taken place among the richer and poorer countries and regions? What has been the role of the various regional funds in reducing the gap? To answer these questions we use state-of-the-art convergence analysis to examine the impact of the large investments in the Puebla-Panama Plan designed to close the gap in per capita income among the countries included in that project. We analyze this case study to see if there is any empirical evidence in support of the claim that such region-wide initiatives would actually accelerate the reduction of inequities between countries and regions under an FTAA.

The main findings of this chapter are:

1. The evidence for Europe tends to favor the convergence hypothesis. There are, however, regional differences, and some countries have converged at a slower rate.

2. In terms of intracountry convergence, cohesion funds have played a significant role, especially in those countries where the inflow of funds has been accompanied by stronger regional development policies. Italy, as an example, is a case of nonconvergence because of the lack of such policies. On the other hand, Spain is an example where regional policies complemented the cohesion funds.
3. Taking the Puebla-Panama Plan (PPP)[2] region as an example, we observe that the southern part of Mexico has been lagging behind the rest of the country and has "converged" relatively more with Central American countries than with the northern part of Mexico. In order to help the PPP region converge and better integrate to world markets, specific policies are desirable.
4. If we decompose the convergence rate among the PPP countries and states, infrastructure and education explain most of the observed trends. Thus, investing in those two factors could strengthen the position of the region relative to the U.S. and the rest of Mexico.

The methodology used in our PPP analysis consists first of standard convergence regressions. Second, we use decomposition of the speed of convergence (following De la Fuente 2000) to understand the determinants of the convergence process in the region. The latter is called in the literature "convergence accounting."

Before turning to our empirical studies, the next section of analyzes the theoretical links between integration and convergence.

Regional Integration and Convergence: Theoretical Links

The question we address is whether an FTAA that contains schemes similar to the European cohesion funds and the Puebla-Panama Plan investment program can accelerate regional convergence in the Americas. To do so, we must first understand the theoretical links, if any exist, between integration, productivity enhancement, and convergence.

The typical convergence regression takes the simple form

$$\frac{y_{i,t} - y_{i,t-\tau}}{\tau} = \alpha - \beta y_{i,t-\tau} + u_{it}$$

where i is the index for the specific region, t is the time period, y_{it} is per capita income, τ is the observation interval, β is the rate of convergence, and u_{it} is an error term (Barro and Sala-i-Martin 1990, 1991). The convergence coefficient β is the key variable to look at in order to understand the rate at which y_{it} approaches its steady state level. The so-called β-convergence consists of poorer countries growing faster than the richer ones. The type of model presented above allows for the steady levels of income to differ across countries, depending on country-specific characteristics, defining what is called conditional β-convergence. In this case, the latter is the interesting concept, as we want to analyze how the per capita income of a particular economy is converging toward the average level of the region to which it belongs (Barro and Sala-i-Martin 2001). As discussed below, Barro and Sala-i-Martin found evidence of absolute convergence within Europe. A different, though related, view is that of the so-called σ-convergence, which refers to the decline over time in the cross-sectional dispersion of per capita incomes.

Theoretically, from the neoclassical growth model, the rate of convergence depends on the productivity of capital and the willingness to save. Thus, factors affecting the productivity of capital will affect the speed of convergence, and that brings about the link with regional integration.

The links between regional integration and productivity, and thus on convergence, exist in three main avenues: the trade channel, the FDI channel, and the infrastructure channel. López-Córdova and Mesquita (2002) have discussed these different links. The trade channel has a main component in the reallocation of resources to respond to static comparative advantages, representing an important "level effect" for productivity growth. There are, however, other components related to trade, such as the availability of world-class inputs, acquisition of new technologies through exchange of goods, the discipline introduced by competition via imports, and the higher turnover induced by changing market conditions. Among those, Helpman and Krugman (1989) have emphasized the importance of competition-induced managerial changes, which reduce X-inefficiency, improve scale efficiency, and introduce stronger incentives to innovate.

It is well-known that FDI flows are an important factor in trade liberalization strategies. Rules of origin are typically based on FDI incentives. This brings about the second channel—changes induced through FDI. Among the latter are three main components: stronger competition, knowledge spillovers, and backward-forward linkages. Rodríguez-Clare (1996) has shown the relevance of linkages and productivity and quality enhancements induced by the competitive pressure on suppliers, and evidence shows that type of effects in recent Latin American history (Larraín et al. 2000).

Finally, regional integration can have an important effect on infrastructure requirements and may induce higher levels of investment, which in turn can coordinate expectations and move the economy to a higher investment equilibrium, following a "big push" type of process (Murphy et al. 1989). Trade liberalization in this context also has a commitment effect, in which the government signals a switch in policy whose reversibility is costly (Esquivel and Tornell 1998).

All the above-mentioned effects have an impact on productivity and the rate of convergence, though their relative importance is difficult to disentangle. An attempt to separate the specific effect of infrastructure is shown below, following a "convergence-accounting" methodology proposed by De La Fuente (2000, 2001). Such decomposition will shed light on the potential effect of the PPP on regional convergence. The next section reviews whether the theoretical links discussed above have been supported by the evidence in the European integration experience, and the role that cohesion funds have played in that process.

The European Union, Cohesion Funds, and Convergence

Structural and cohesion funds are among the most important policy instruments used by the European Union (EU) to promote regional development. They comprise about a third of the total EU budget and are spent on a wide range of programs that primarily aim to develop infrastructure, restructure industry, or enhance education. Studies have looked into the question of how effective these funds have been in promoting economic growth and reducing welfare differences in the EU, and their main findings can be summarized as follows:

1. In general, there is strong evidence to support the convergence hypothesis, though a number of studies have found slower convergence rates.
2. The role of cohesion funds in fostering convergence is significant as long as such funds do not weaken local regional development policies. Also, convergence seems to have been faster during the 1980s and early 1990s, but has slowed considerably since.
3. The allocation of cohesion funds in Europe has been relatively progressive, though such progressivity could be strengthened.

We now turn to the discussion of this evidence. Figure 21.1 demonstrates the argument that "cohesion policy fulfills a necessary condition for its effectiveness: poor regions tend to receive more support

Figure 21.1 Structural and Cohesion Funds and GDP Per Capita in Europe (1994–99)

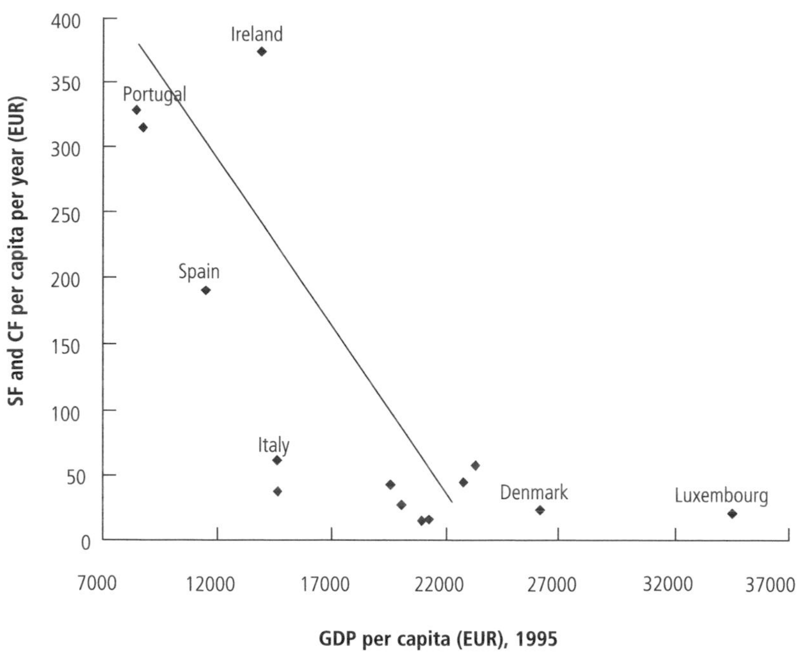

than rich regions" (Ederveen et al. 2002). However, each member state receives some support, independent of its level of development. Martin (1998b) argues that redistribution is less strong than is often believed; if those projects that are likely to contribute most to the stock of public capital are considered (called "investment in the productive sector") then the spread of cohesion support is less progressive. According to Martin, redistribution is weakened further if one takes the regional policy of nations into account. In particular, he stresses the fact that some states tend to be relatively more active in their regional development policies, and that plays a fundamental role. There seems to be a clear interaction between receipts of cohesion aid and local development policies.

Have the Countries in the EU Converged?

The European Commission showed enthusiasm with "the surprisingly rapid rhythm of convergence in an historical or international prospect over the period 1986–96" (European Commission 2000). Others suggest that convergence has been weak (Boldrin and Canova 2001) or even has come to an end (Fagerberg and Verspagen 1996) just after the early 1980s. A general overview, however, shows stronger support for the convergence hypothesis.

Ederveen et al. (2002) review a large number of studies and find strong evidence for regional convergence, even within countries. The estimated yearly speed of convergence is significant and ranges from 1.4 percent in Spain to 5.2 percent in the Netherlands. Austria, Finland, Greece, and Portugal also lie within this range. In Belgium and the United Kingdom, the convergence hypothesis weakens. Italy is the exception—divergence is the rule for regions in Italy, as illustrated by the bad performance of the relatively poor southern part of Italy, the so-called Mezzogiorne. All that notwithstanding, the rate of convergence across countries is quite low, about 2 percent per year.

That is not the generalized view, however. For example, Cappelen et al. (2001) argue that "within countries there is on average no convergence." The European Commission (2000) suggests that convergence at the level of member states is accompanied by a widening of regional disparities in countries experiencing high growth. Fayolle and Lecuyer (2000) also hold the latter view.

What Is the Role of Cohesion Funds in the Convergence Process?

Even for those who accept the view of convergence within and between countries in Europe, crucial questions remain: What is the contribution of cohesion policy to this process of convergence? Is convergence a process that works via the market, as suggested by neoclassical theory? Or is it realized through or strengthened by the transfer of funds?

People in favor of cohesion policies state that cohesion support may compensate for alternative economic processes that bring about convergence. Others believe that such funds may stop local processes that would otherwise bring a faster convergence. In particular, Boldrin and Canova (2001) point out that cohesion support might induce laborers to remain in poor regions from which they would otherwise have migrated, moving toward richer regions. Since labor mobility is a powerful means to achieve wage equalization, cohesion support slows down convergence. The most radical opponents of cohesion policy do not hesitate to state that it can be seen as a policy that subsidizes unemployment.

Why are views so different? In large part because there are a number of factors involved in explaining the difference between the potential and the actual impact of cohesion policies on growth rates. The effects can be divided as follows:

1. For several reasons, a large portion of cohesion support flows to relatively rich regions, as have been pointed out in different studies (De la Fuente 2003)

2. There may be crowding out of national regional aid and policy by European cohesion funds. This means that the receipt of funds may induce local governments to reduce local efforts of regional development policy. Even though the European Commission imposes cofunding requirements, the analysis suggests that the crowding-out effect remains important (Everdeen et al. 2002).

3. There may be rent-seeking and moral-hazard effects. Regional and national authorities may deliberately use funds for relatively less-productive projects. This has been analyzed mainly through case studies.

4. Finally, cohesion policy may replace endogenous convergence mechanisms. For instance, as discussed above, cohesion support may reduce the mobility of labor.

Thus, cohesion funds are not effective if local development efforts are missing. The effect of cohesion policies on growth depends on the relative importance of the above-mentioned effects. The outcome then becomes an empirical question. The actual effects have been analyzed through simulation, case studies, and econometric evaluation. Let us look at the evidence.

De la Fuente and Vives (1995) estimate a growth model that includes public and human capital. They conclude that infrastructure and education largely determine the location of mobile production factors. De la Fuente and Vives use their estimates to simulate the effect of cohesion support on growth, simulations that show that public investments in infrastructure and education may indeed help to reduce regional disparities in income and growth of GDP per capita. The same paper, however, argues that the effect is weakened by an apparent regressivity in the allocation of funds.

Ederveen et al. (2002) find that cohesion support fosters economic growth of lagging member states, conditional on the openness of the economy. It is suggested that openness disciplines governments, which may stimulate more productive investment of cohesion support. At the margin, they also find evidence of crowding out. In their attempt to show a thorough review of the evidence, the paper summarizes other studies by transforming their results into a single, comparable statistic called the "impact elasticity." They proceed to analyze the evidence based on such an indicator, which they define as:

$$\frac{d\hat{y}}{\left(\frac{CS}{GDP}\right)}$$

where $d\hat{y}$ represents the increase of the annual growth rate of GDP per capita that is attributable to cohesion policy, *CS* the amount of cohesion support, and *GDP* the gross domestic product of the respective region, group of regions, member state, or group of member states. The statistic can be read as measuring "additional growth per unit of cohesion funds." Results are shown in Table 21.1.

As the table shows there is no consensus about the impact of cohesion policy on convergence. Researchers have found different effects, from a small negative impact of cohesion policy on economic growth rates to high positive effects. The evidence seems to be inclined, however, to a generally positive effect. Indeed, those who show a negative effect have either small effects in magnitude or lower statistical significance.

One of the main conclusions is that the positive effect of cohesion funds is theoretically feasible and requires two preconditions to be realized: first, funds should be allocated as progressively as possible; and second, domestic regional development policies must accompany the effort in a consistent manner.

Convergence in the Americas: The Case of the Puebla-Panama Plan

The Puebla-Panama Plan (PPP) is an initiative aimed at improving fundamentally the conditions to attract investment, reduce transport costs, and foster economic growth in the region. It was originally suggested by President Vicente Fox of Mexico and has received general support from Central American governments and international organizations. The plan, which was launched in 2001 with the goal of

Table 21.1 Growth Elasticity of Cohesion Support

	Greece	Ireland	Portugal	Spain	Other
Model simulations					
Lolos and Zonzilos (1994)	0.33[a]				
Goybet and Bertoldi (1994)					0.30[b]
Bradley (1995)		0.03			
Lolos, Suwa-Eisenmann, and Zonzilos (1995)	0.01				
Bradley, Herce and Modesto (1995)		0.18	0.11	0.3	
Christodoulakis and Kalvytis (1998a)	0.15				
Christodoulakis and Kalvytis (1998b)	0.12				
Christodoulakis and Kalvytis (2000)	0.15				
Hallet (2000)					0.10
European Commission (1999d)[c]	0.15	0.24	0.24		
European Commission (1999d)[d]	0.24	0.43	0.28	0.27	
European Commission (1999d)[e]	0.29	0.29	0.34	0.45	
European Commission (1999d)[f]	0.09	0.14	0.09	0.09	
European Commission (1999d)[g]	0.03	0.14	0.06	0.09	
Pereira (1999)	0.15	0.06	0.10	0.13	
Pereira and Gaspar (1999)			0.20		
Mean elasticity model simulations	0.18				
Econometric analysis					
Fagerberg and Verspagen (1996)					–0.23
Fagerberg and Verspagen (1996)					–0.42
Cappelen et al. (2001)					0.21
Cappelen et al. (2001)[h]					0.25
Cappelen et al. (2001)					–0.03
Garcia-Solanes and Maria-Dolores (2001)					0.20
Garcia-Solanes and Maria-Dolores (2001)					0.04
Garcia-Mila and McGuire (2001)				0.07	
Ederveen et al. (2002)					–0.35
Ederveen et al. (2002)[i]					0.02
Ederveen et al. (2002)[j]					0.70
Mean elasticities member states	0.16	0.19	0.18	0.20	0.07
Mean elasticity overall: 0.15					

Source: Ederveen et al. 2002.

[a]Average of lower bound 0.25 and upper bound 0.40; [b]Includes only objective 1 support; [c]Pereira; [d]Beutel 89–93; [e]Beutel 94–99; [f]QUEST II, 89–93; [g]QUEST II, 94–99; [h]Including the time slope dummy; [i]With country specific dummies; [j]With region specific dummies.

promoting economic and social development and regional integration, includes an initiative to create a Mesoamerican network of highways. The network, which is largely based on existing roads, comprises two main corridors on the Atlantic and the Pacific and a series of complementary routes. Initially, US$1.8 billion were made available from a variety of sources, including national budgets, multilateral loans, and bilateral grants. The institutions involved are IDB, the World Bank, the Central American Bank for Economic Integration, the Andean Development Corporation, the Economic Commission for Latin America, the Japan Bank for International Cooperation, the Japanese International Cooperation Agency, and the United States Agency for International Development. The logic behind it is that a reduction of transport costs, the development of infrastructure, and the linkage of the region to world markets will fundamentally improve competitiveness and jump-start a sustained growth process. The plan has also included initiatives for cooperation in health and education programs, as well as prevention of natural disasters.[3]

What is its conceptual logic? Dávila, Kessel, and Levy (2002) show the potential gains from such a strategy by using an extended Krugman-Venables framework with three regions. The simple fact of connecting the low labor cost region to the world market may induce large amounts of investment and foster growth. Within the FTAA strategy, the PPP can be seen as a policy experiment with which to analyze the potential benefits of cohesion funds similar to those of Europe to prompt a faster convergence process in the region.

In 2002 the PPP fund made available US$800 to be devoted to infrastructure, including roads, railroads, ports, and electronic networks. Moreover, the PPP has included local initiatives to assist vulnerable groups, such as community centers and shelters in indigenous communities, centers for the development of traditional medicine, and innovative educational pilot programs.

A similar strategy proposed in South America is the initiative for the Integration of the Regional Infrastructure in South America (IIRSA). IIRSA was launched at a summit in Brazil in September 2000 by nations of South America with the support of the IDB, the Andean Development Corporation, and the Financial Fund for the Development of the River Plate Basin. The goal is to improve integration infrastructure to foster productivity and competitiveness in three areas: energy, transportation, and telecommunications. IIRSA is a multinational, multisectoral, and multidisciplinary initiative for setting up coordination mechanisms between governments, multilateral financial institutions, and the private sector. As stated in its objectives, IIRSA also has a regional political and strategic vision based on the development of a hub strategy encompassing—for the first time—the twelve countries of South America.

The PPP initiative is more ambitious, in principle, and tries to deal with issues of infrastructure, but also education and regional development in general. Theoretically, a program like PPP should have an important impact on productivity in the region and may induce a faster convergence. Looking at the relative magnitude of such effects is the theme of this section.

Taking data for the countries involved in the PPP strategy, we can analyze the trends in terms of overall convergence and its determinants. First, looking at the standard deviation of log per capita income—the so-called sigma (σ) convergence—the trend shows a fast convergence process between 1970 and 1980, which then came to a halt during the following two decades (see Figure 21.2). At least the process seems to have weakened severely. Not surprisingly, that trend is correlated with a sharp reduction in public investment in infrastructure due to the debt crisis of the 1980s. We should remember that

Figure 21.2 Mexico and Central America σ-convergence (1970–1998)

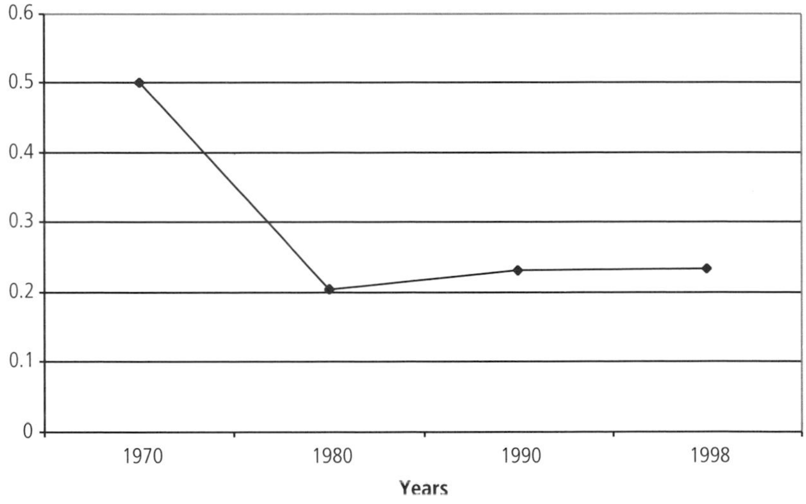

Source: Author's calcuations

during the mid 1980s Mexico started aggressive trade liberalization and structural reform policies, which were strengthened during the 1990s. The integration process, however, has been slower, especially with respect to Latin American countries. It was not until June 2000, for example, that the trade agreement between Mexico and Central America was completed and formalized.

The data presented in Tables 21.2, 21.3, and 21.4, support three main results. First, there is a process of convergence occurring within the region, though Central America and southern Mexico are lagging behind compared to the rest of Mexico, which is catching up with the United States. Second, productivity patterns are not optimistic for growth potential in the Central American region. Third, there is convergence of southern Mexico with Central America.

A simple absolute-convergence regression confirms the third result (Table 21.2). The absolute-convergence coefficient is negative and significant for the whole period and even larger for the period 1970–80, but falls and becomes insignificant for subsequent decades.[4] Data restrictions do not allow us to run a detailed conditional convergence regression. It is possible, however, to analyze the effect of an important variable for our analysis—infrastructure—the results of which are presented in Table 21.3. Infrastructure development is highly uneven in the region (see also the appendix).

Table 21.4 shows the results of the determinants of growth in the region by adding time dummies and an infrastructure indicator that is commonly used in the literature—telephone density. The effect of infrastructure on growth is statistically significant and economically relevant. The same exercise was carried out with a normalized index of paved roads and the effect holds. This effect, of course, is estimated after controlling also for a human capital index—average years of schooling in the country.

Table 21.2 Absolute Convergence

Period	β	Regression
1970–2000	–0.563* (0.106)	Prob >F = 0.000; R^2 = 0.576
1970–1980	–0.720* (0.132)	Prob >F = 0.003; R^2 = 0.827
1980–1990	–0.107 (0.114)	Prob >F = 0.394; R^2 = 0.225
1990–2000	–0.001 (0.056)	Prob >F = 0.998; R^2 = 0.200

Note: Standard errors in parenthesis.
*Significant at 99 percent confidence level.

Table 21.3 Transportation Infrastructure

	Roads			Railways			Air		
	Total Road Network km	Paved Roads %	Goods Hauled Million Ton-km	Passenger-km per US$Million of PPP GDP	Goods Transported Ton-km per US$ Million of PPP GDP	Diesel Locomotive Available %	Aircraft Departures Thousands	Passengers Carried Thousands	Air freight Million Ton-km
Country	1995–99[a]	1995–99[a]	1995–99[a]	1995–99[a]	1995–99[a]	1995–99[a]	1999	1999	1999
Costa Rica	35,876	22.0	3,070	—	—	50	32	1,055	85
El Salvador	10,029	19.8	—	—	—	—	32	1,624	44
Guatemala	14,118	34.5	—	—	—	—	7	506	3
Honduras	13,603	20.4	—	—	—	—	—	—	—
Mexico	318,952	34.3	179,085	2,578	61,435	68	310	19,263	309
Nicaragua	18,000	10.1	—	—	—	—	1	59	1
Panama	11,400	34.6	—	—	—	—	21	933	15
United States	6,348,227	58.8	1,534,430	1,020	350,942	—	8,512	634,365	27,317

Source: World Bank, 2001

[a]Data are for the latest year available in the period shown and national air carriers.

Table 21.4 Effect of Infrastructure on Growth

Variable	Without Time Dummies	Including Time Dummies
β	–0.7009** (0.1135)	–0.6905** (0.0989)
Telephone Density	2.773* (1.218)	4.090** (1.205)
Regression	Prob>F = 0.000; R^2 = 0.652	Prob>F = 0.000; R^2 = 0.759

Note: Standard errors in parenthesis.
*Significant at 95 percent confidence level.
**Significant at 99 percent confidence level.

The development of infrastructure in Central America recovered during the 1990s after a long period of depreciation. López-Calva (2001) shows the evolution of different infrastructure indicators in the region and the obstacle they have represented for competitiveness. Only in Nicaragua, as an example, 73 percent of the total roads were declared to be in bad condition in 1996.

There is a vast literature on the effect of infrastructure on productivity and growth.[5] This effect of infrastructure on growth, however, is still isolated from the speed of convergence in a ceteris paribus fashion. The detailed econometric work of Castañeda et al. (2000) shows the relevance of electricity and roads to Mexican manufacturing growth, with a differential effect by sectors. We would like to know, however, what the effect of infrastructure is on the *speed* of convergence. The next section is devoted to analyzing this issue.

Convergence Accounting

De la Fuente (2003) suggests a way to decompose the sources of convergence into different components. Income per capita in country i is decomposed into

$$ypc_i = ypj_i + e_i = (p_i + sub_i + q_i) + (wwap_i + lfpr_i + erlf_i)$$

where ypj_i is income per job, e_i stands for jobs per capita, p_i is output price level, sub_i is the level of operating subsidies, and q_i is real output per job. The variables $wwap_i$, $lfpr_i$, and $erlf_i$ stand for the weight of the working-age population, the labor force participation rate, and the number of jobs per active worker, respectively. All variables are measured as log differences with respect to the geometric regional mean. The productivity factor, q_i, is in turn decomposed as

$$q_i = a_i + \theta_k k_i + \theta_{\text{inf}} \text{inf}_i + \theta_h h_i$$

where a_i is total factor productivity, k_i and inf_i are physical capital and infrastructure per job in the country, and h_i is the level of human capital. Each component of ypc_i in t contributes to ypc growth,

$$\Delta ypc_{it} = \sum_k \Delta z_{kit},$$

where each component´s growth during a period of length s is calculated as

$$\Delta z_{it} = \frac{z_{i,t+s} - z_{i,t}}{s}.$$

In this way, we get to

$$\Delta z_{kit} = -\beta_k ypc_{it}$$

for the kth component. Each of those corresponds to "the rate of (unconditional) beta convergence that would have been observed in a hypothetical world in which the relative income of each country changed only due to one of the factors under consideration, with all the economies displaying average behavior in terms of other variables." The summation of all the partial betas must add up to the value of β in the convergence regression (running Δypc_{it} on ypc_{it}). It is important to notice that, in this framework, the employment component of income per capita depends fundamentally on labor force participation and unemployment rates, whereas the productivity component relies on stocks of productive factors such as physical capital, human capital, and infrastructure. Compared to Europe and the Untied States, Latin America has a very different pattern of participation and unemployment rates due to its labor-market regulation and the nonexistence of unemployment insurance.

Aggregate Trends

Let us look first at the aggregate trends in terms of productivity and income per capita growth. As shown above, the rate of convergence within Mexico becomes insignificant after the 1980s, a period that corresponds to a higher integration of Mexico with the rest of the world, specially the United States. What could explain the reversion of the convergence pattern?

Even though Mexico has a more favorable growth pattern than the rest of the region, previous work has shown the breakdown of that convergence pattern also within Mexico. The southern and southeastern regions have lagged behind the rest of the country. Indeed, as

Figure 21.3 GDP Per Capita Growth

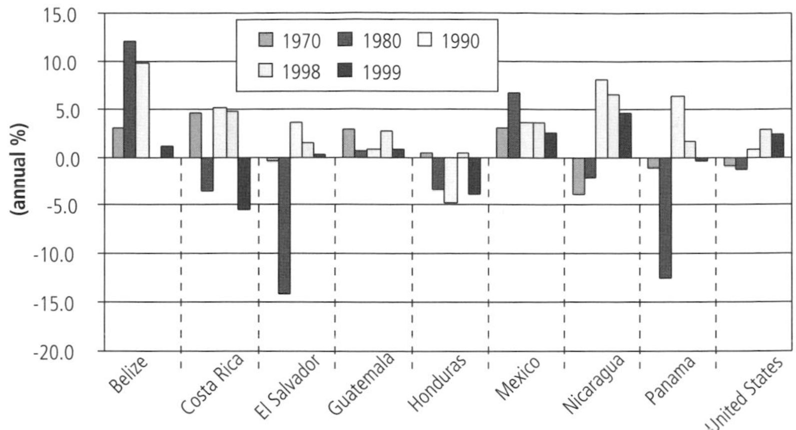

Source: Authors' calculations based on official statistics.

shown in Figures 21.3 and 21.4, the income level of the southern Mexican states is not far above that of Central American countries.

The southern Mexican states have diverged from their northern counterparts and gotten closer, on average, to Central American levels. Figures 21.5 and 21.6 show the divergence in productivity that has taken place across Mexican states during the period of liberalization in both manufacturing and service sectors.

Decomposition

We now carry out a convergence regression using only the Mexican states and Central American countries included in the PPP initiative. We run the following model:

$$\frac{y_{i,t} - y_{i,t-\tau}}{\tau} = \alpha - \beta y_{i,t-\tau} + \gamma D_{i,t} + u_{it}$$

where the standard regression is only modified to include a dummy variable, D=1 for all Mexican states and D=0 for the Central American countries. This means that we run the regression excluding all the Mexican states that are not in the PPP initiative and considering those included as individual entities, together with the countries in the PPP region. Interestingly, the results (Table 21.5) show that there is still convergence for the last two decades. The southern Mexican states have not been able to catch up with the rest of Mexico and have followed a convergent pattern with the Central American countries. This

Figure 21.4 GDP Per Capita, Puebla-Panama Plan

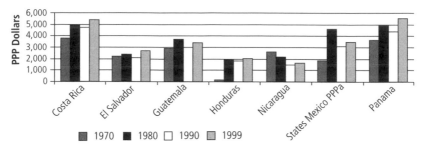

PPP Dollars
6,000
5,000
4,000
3,000
2,000
1,000
0
Costa Rica
El Salvador
Guatemala
Honduras
Nicaragua
States Mexico PPPa
Panama
1970 1980 1990 1999

Source: Authors' calculations based on official statistics.

means that the whole PPP region needs a specific policy to be able to reverse the divergent pattern from those markets that are well integrated to the world economy.

Not only has the convergence pattern remained stable during the last two decades, but the speed seems to have increased. Data constraints do not allow us to carry out the convergence accounting

Figure 21.5 Sigma (σ)-Convergence in Productivity Among the Mexican States (Industrial Sector)

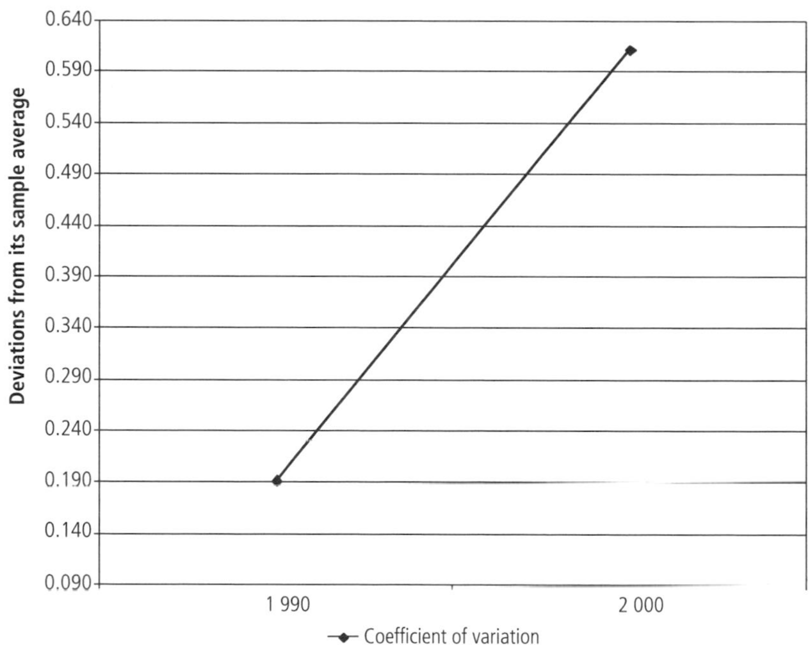

Source: Authors' calculations based on official statistics.

Table 21.5 Absolute Convergence: PPP States and Central America

Period	β	Regression
1980–1990	–0.285* (0.114)	Prob >F = 0.003; R^2= 0.342
1990–2000	–0.324* (0.156)	Prob >F = 0.010; R^2 = 0.305

Note: Standard errors in parenthesis.
*Significant at 95 percent confidence level.

Source: Authors' calculations based on official statistics.

exercise at a more disaggregated level, but the results open an interesting discussion. Regarding the sources of convergence or nonconvergence in the region, we see that the structure of the labor force is characterized by an increase in the participation rate of female workers, and thus an increase in the overall participation rate. The highest rates of participation of women occur in Costa Rica and Mexico (Table 21.6). The process has been accompanied by a higher level of

Figure 21.6 Sigma (σ)-Convergence in Productivity among the Mexican States (Services)

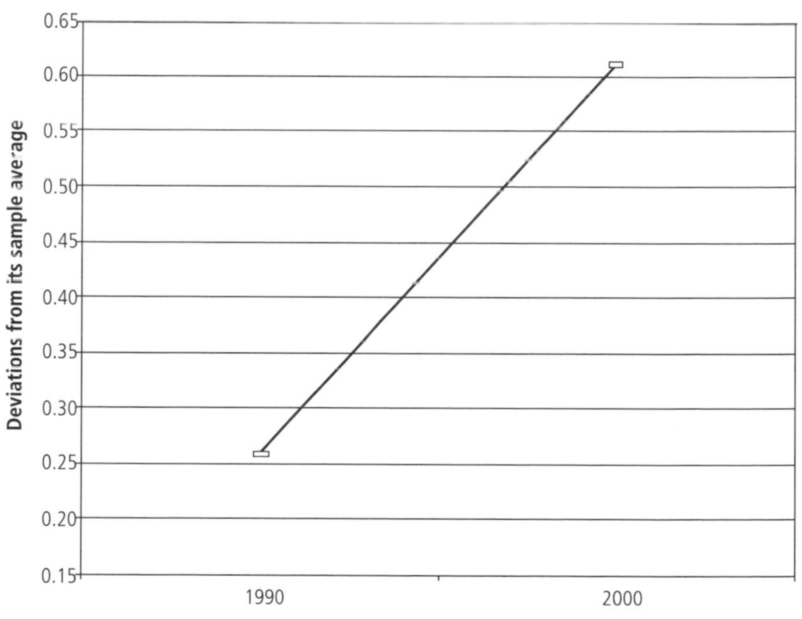

Source: Authors' calculations based on official statistics.

Table 21.6 Structure of the Labor Force

	1970		1980		1990		1999	
Countries	F %	M %	F %	M %	F %	M %	F %	M %
Belize	19.4	80.6	20.9	79.1	20.7	79.3	23.9	76.1
Costa Rica	18.1	81.9	20.8	79.2	28.1	71.9	30.8	69.2
El Salvador	20.6	79.4	26.5	73.5	31.6	68.4	36.0	64.0
Guatemala	18.8	81.2	22.4	77.6	23.4	76.6	28.4	71.6
Honduras	22.3	77.7	25.2	74.8	27.7	72.3	31.4	68.6
México	19.1	80.9	26.9	73.1	30.0	70.0	32.9	67.1
Nicaragua	23.1	76.9	27.6	72.4	31.7	68.3	35.5	64.5
Panamá	25.2	74.8	29.9	70.1	32.4	67.6	35.0	65.0

Source: World Development Indicators, 2001
F = female; M = male

open unemployment during the 1980s and 1990s, but especially by a higher level of "informalization" of the economy.

In terms of productivity, measured by GDP per worker, Honduras, Guatemala, and El Salvador show a poor performance in the period for which data is available. Mexico, Costa Rica, Panama, and Nicaragua show a more stable or even increasing pattern (Figure 21.7). Here, again, other studies have shown that the trend is strongly positive in Mexico for specific sectors, especially those that are charac-

Figure 21.7 GDP Per Worker in Mexico and Central America

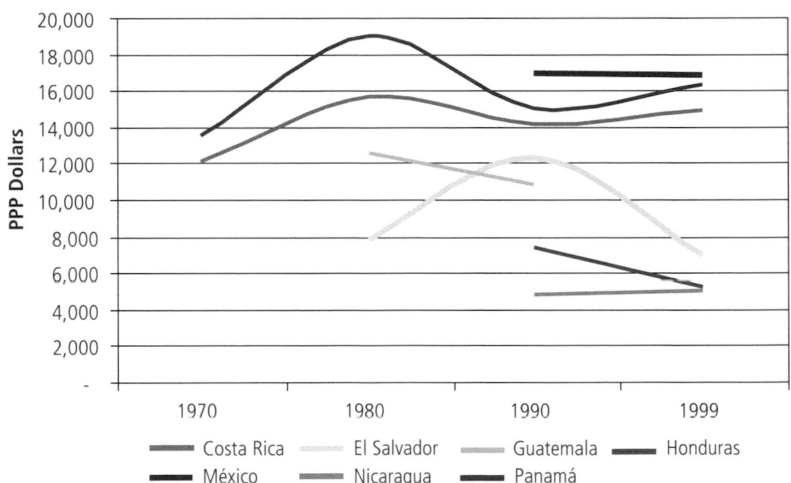

Source: Authors' calculations based on official statistics.

Figure 21.8 Decomposition of the Speed of Convergence (Divergence)

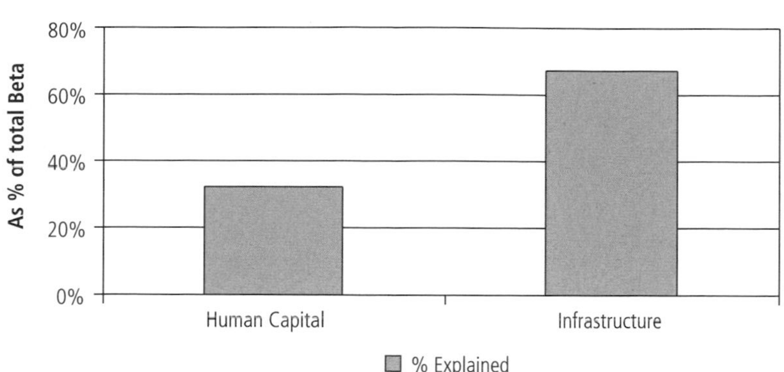

teristic of the northern regions. The trend is smoothed by the inclusion of lower productivity regions.

Once the decomposition is carried out, we can see the relative importance of the factors in explaining the convergence pattern. Figure 21.8 shows the results when infrastructure and human capital are taken as the explanatory factors of the speed of convergence in the region. Clearly, infrastructure plays a more important role. We can interpret such a variable as an indicator of connectivity of the region to world markets.

Thus, regional efforts to catch up with the rest of the world should emphasize the elements of infrastructure and human capital. The results in Figure 21.8 imply that 70 percent of the convergence pattern is explained by infrastructure and 30 percent by human capital (measured by educational levels). This makes a case in favor of cohesion funds in the region, which can be framed into the FTAA negotiations. Such negotiations, once conceptually justified, can specifically discuss the need for grants versus loans, local cofunding requirements, targeting, financing, and rules of progressivity in the allocation of such funds.

Conclusions

This chapter has analyzed the potential effect of compensatory funds to help poor countries converge to higher growth rates during the process of integration. We have used the Puebla-Panama Plan as an example of specific funds devoted to increasing competitiveness by targeting resources on the region's competitive weakness. The evidence suggests that there is room for increasing the speed of convergence in the southern part of Mexico and the Central American region by investing in infrastructure projects that link them to world markets. That could potentially result in higher standards of living in the region.

If we decompose the convergence rate among the PPP countries and states, infrastructure and education explain most of the observed trends. Thus, investing in those two factors could additionally strengthen the position of the region relative to the United States and the rest of Mexico.

It must be said that this type of funding can be targeted not only to infrastructure or physical capital projects, but also to the development of social protection and poverty alleviation schemes. They represent a policy tool that must be considered during the negotiation of the FTAA if the initiative is really aimed at promoting inclusive trade, instead of widening the development gaps in the Americas.

Appendix

Table 21.7 Air Transport, Passengers Carried (thousands)

	1970	1980	1990	1999
Belize	—	—	—	—
Costa Rica	256	431	467	1,055
El Salvador	138	265	525	1,624
Guatemala	113	119	156	506
Honduras	296	508	610	—
Mexico	2,967	12,890	14,341	19,263
Nicaragua	107	115	130	59
Panama	307	355	266	933

Source: World Development Indicators, 2001.

Table 21.8 Air Transport, Freight (million tons per km)

	1970	1980	1990	1999
Belize	—	—	—	—
Costa Rica	9	22	39	85
El Salvador	11	17	5	44
Guatemala	6	6	9	3
Honduras	4	4	4	—
Mexico	37	132	143	309
Nicaragua	1	1	4	1
Panama	4	3	3	15

Source: World Development Indicators, 2001.

Table 21.9 Electric Power Consumption (kwh per capita)

	1980	1990	1999
Belize	—	—	—
Costa Rica	860	1,111	1444.3
El Salvador	274	358	465.4
Guatemala	240	226	293.8
Honduras	215	369	479.7
Mexico	846	1,204	1565.2
Nicaragua	303	284	369.2
Panama	828	883	1147.9

Source: World Development Indicators, 2001.

Table 21.10 Mobile Phones (per 1,000 people)

	1970	1980	1990	1999
Belize	—	26.50	91.60	156.0
Costa Rica	23.10	68.90	101.00	204.0
El Salvador	7.90	15.20	24.10	76.0
Guatemala	7.20	11.90	21.20	55.0
Honduras	—	8.10	17.20	44.2
Mexico	17.00	40.20	64.80	112.0
Nicaragua	8.20	11.00	12.60	30.4
Panama	—	64.90	92.70	164.0

Source: World Development Indicators, 2001.

Table 21.11 Average Cost of Local Telephone Call (US$ per three minutes)

	1990	1999
Belize	—	0.07
Costa Rica	0.06	0.02
El Salvador	—	0.06
Guatemala	0.04	0.09
Honduras	0.01	0.06
Mexico	0.1	0.14
Nicaragua	7.14	0.09
Panama	0	—

Source: World Development Indicators, 2001.

Table 21.12 Telephone Mainlines per Employee

	1980	1990	1999
Belize	22	44	91
Costa Rica	59	86	178
El Salvador	—	17	50
Guatemala	23	39	130
Honduras	11	20	72
Mexico	98	107	130
Nicaragua	9	13	65
Panama	41	57	106

Source: World Development Indicators, 2001.

References

Barro, R. and Sala-i-Martin, X. 1990. "Economic Growth and convergence across the United States." Working paper no. 3419, NBER. Cambridge. MA.

Barro, R. and Sala-i-Martin, X. 1991. "Convergence." Journal of Political Economy, 100, No.2 (abril):223–51.

Barro, R. and Sala-i-Martin, X. 1991. "Convergence across States and Regions." Brookings Papers on Economic Activity, v.1:107–82.

Basile, R., S. de Nardis, and A. Girardi. 2002. "Regional Inequalities and Cohesion Policies in the European Union." Istituto di Studi e Analisi Economica, Rome.

Boldrin, M., and F. Canova. 2001. "Inequality and Convergence in Europe's Regions: Reconsidering European Regional Policies." *Economic Policy: A European Forum* 0 (32): 205–45.

Bradley, J., J. A. Herce, and L. Modesto. 1995. The Macroeconomic Effects of the CSF 1994–99 in the EU Periphery: An Analysis Based on the HERMIN Model." *Economic Modeling* 12 (3): 323–33.

Bradley, J., K. Whelan, and J. Wright. 1995. "HERMIN Ireland." *Economic Modeling* 12 (3): 249–74.

Cappelen, A., F. Castellaci, J. Fagerberg, and B. Verspagen. 2001. The Impact of Regional Support on Growth and Convergence in the European Union." Paper presented at the European meeting on Applied Evolutionary Economics, Vienna.

Castañeda, A., P. Cotler, and O. Gutiérrez. 2000. "The Impact of Infrastructure on Mexican Manufacturing Growth." *Economia Mexicana* 9 (2): 143–64.

Christodoulakis, N. M., and S. C. Kalvytis. 1998a. "The Second CSF (Delors' II Package) for Greece and Its Impact on the Greek Economy: An

Ex-Ante Assessment Using a Macroeconometric Model." *Economics of Planning* 31 (1): 57–79.

———. 1998b. "A Four-Sector Macroeconometric Model for Greece and the Evaluation of the Community Support Framework 1994–1999." *Economic Modeling* 15 (4): 575–620.

———. 2000. "The Effects of the Second Community Support Framework 1994–99 on the Greek Economy." *Journal of Policy Modeling* 22 (5): 611–24.

Dávila, E., G. Kessel, and S. Levy. 2002. "El sur rambién existe: Un ensayo sobre el desarrollo regional de México." *Economía Mexicana*, Nueva época 11 (2): 205–60.

De la Fuente, A. 2000. "Convergence across Countries and Regions: Theory and Empirics." *EIB Papers/BEI Cahiers* 5 (2): 25–46.

———. 2002. "On the Sources of Convergence: A Close look at the Spanish Regions." *European Economic Review* 46 (3): 569–99.

———. 2003. "Regional Convergence in Spain 1965–1995." In *Economic Convergence and Divergence in Europe: Growth and Regional Development in an Enlarged European Union*, edited by Gertrude Tumpel-Gugerell and Peter Mooslechner, pp. 72–85. Cheltenham, UK: Edward Elgar.

De la Fuente, A., and X. Vives. 1995. "Infrastructure and Education as Instruments of Regional Policy: Evidence from Spain." *Economic Policy* 20: 11–40.

Ederveen, S., J. Gorter, R. de Mooij, and R. Nahuis. 2002. "Funds and Games: The Economics of European Cohesion Policy." CPB Netherlands Bureau for Economic Policy Analysis, Den Haag

Esquivel, G., and M. Messmacher. 2002a. "Economic Integration and Sub-National Development: The Mexican Experience with NAFTA." World Bank, Washington, DC. Photocopy.

———. 2002b. "Sources of Regional (non) Convergence in Mexico." World Bank, Washington, DC. Photocopy.

Esquivel, G., D. Lederman, M. Messmacher, and R. Villoro. 2002. "Why NAFTA Did Not Reach the South." World Bank, Washington, DC. Photocopy.

Esquivel, G., and Tornell, A. 1998. "The Political Economy of Mexico's Entry to NAFTA." National Bureau of Economic Research Working Paper no. 5322. Cambridge, Mass.

European Commission. 1999. "Sixth Periodic Report on the Social and Economic Situation and Development of the Regions of the European Union." Office for official publications of the European Communities, Luxembourg.

European Commission. 2000. "Real Convergence and Catching-Up in the EU." Chapter 5 in *European Economy* 71: 185–221.

Fagerberg, J., and B. Verspagen. 1996. "Heading for Divergence? Regional Growth in Europe Reconsidered." *Journal of Common Market Studies* 34 (3): 431–48.

Fayolle, J., and A. Lecuyer. 2000. "A croissance regionale, appartenance nationale et fonds structurels europeens: Un bilan d'etape." *Revue de L'OFCE* 0 (73): 165–96.

Garcia-Mila, T., and T. J. McGuire. 2001. "Do Interregional Transfers Improve the Economic Performance of Poor Regions? The Case of Spain." *International Tax and Public Finance* 8: 281–95.

García-Solanes, J., and R. María-Dolores. 2001. The Impact of Structural Funds on Economic Convergence in European Countries and Regions. Photocopy.

Goybet, P. H., and M. Bertoldi. 1994. "The Efficiency of the Structural Funds." In *Improving Economic and Social Cohesion in the European Community*, edited by J. Mortensen, pp. 229–40. New York: St. Martin's Press.

Hallet, M. 2000. "Regional Specialisation and Concentration in the EU." Economic Paper 141. European Commission.

Helpman, E., and P. Krugman. 1989. "Trade Policy and Market Structure." Cambridge, Mass.: MIT Press.

Inter-American Development Bank. 2002. "Beyond Borders: The New Regionalism in Latin America." Economic and Social Progress in Latin America: 2002 Report. Washington, DC.

Larraín, F., L.F. López-Calva, and A. Rodríguez-Claire. 2000. "Intel: A Case Study of Foreign Direct Investment in Central America." Center for International Development, Harvard University, Cambridge, Mass. Photocopy.

Lolos, S., A. Suwa-Eisenmann, and N. Zonzilos. 1995. "Evaluating the CSF with an Extended Computable General Equilibrium Model: The Case of Greece (1988–1995)." *Journal of Policy Modeling* 17: 177–97.

Lolos, S., and N. Zonzilos. 1994. "The Impact of European Structural Funds on the Development of the Greek Economy: A Comparison of Two Models." *Economic and Financial Modeling* 1 (2) (Summer): 87–104.

López-Calva, L. F. 2001. "Infrastructure Services: Moving Goods, People, and Ideas Effectively." In *Economic Development in Central America*, edited by F. Larraín. Cambridge, MA: Harvard University Press.

López-Córdova, E., and M. Mesquita. 2003. "Regional Integration and Productivity: The Experiences of Brazil and Mexico." Inter-American

Development Bank, Integration and Regional Programs Department, INTAL-ITD-STA Working Paper 14. Cambridge, Mass.

Martin, R. 1998a. "Regional Incentive Spending for European Regions." *Regional Studies* 32 (6): 527–36.

———. 1998b. *Regional Policy in the European Union*. Centre for European Policy Studies, Brussels.

———. 1999a. Regional Convergence in the EU: Determinants for Catching-Up or Staying Behind." *Jahrbuch für Regionalwissenschaft/Review of Regional Research* 19 (2): 157–81.

———. 1999b. *The Regional Dimension in European Public Policy: Convergence or Divergence?* New York: St. Martin's Press.

Pereira, A. M. 1999. "International Public Transfers and Convergence in the European Union." *Public Finance Review* 27 (2): 194–219.

Murphy, K. M., Andrei Shleifer, and Robert W. Vishny. 1989. "Industrialization and the Big Push." *Journal of Political Economy* 97 (5): 1003–26.

Murphy, K. M. 1989. "Building Blocks of Market Clearing Business Cycle Models." National Bureau of Economic Research Working Paper no. 3004. Cambridge, Mass.

Murphy, K. M. "Increasing Returns, Durables and Economic Fluctuations." National Bureau of Economic Research Working Paper no. 3014. Cambridge, Mass.

Pereira, A. M., and V. Gaspar. 1999. "An Intertemporal Analysis of Development Policies in the EU." *Journal of Policy Modeling* 21 (7): 799–822.

Pereira, A. M. 1999. "International Public Transfers and Convergence in the European Union." *Public Finance Review* 27 (2): 194–219.

Rodriguez-Claire, A. 1996. "Multinationals, Linkages, and Economic Development." *American Economic Review* 86 (4): 852–73.

Sala-i-Martin, X. 1996. "Regional Cohesion: Evidence and Theories of Regional Growth and Convergence." *European Economic Review* 40: 1325–52.

World Bank. 2001. *World Development Indicators*. Washington, DC.

Notes

The authors would like to thank Gerardo Esquivel and participants at the INTAL-IADB meeting on FTAA at Harvard (DRCLAS) and Punta del Este, Uruguay, for useful comments and suggestions. Miguel Reyes and Mario Torres provided able research assistance.

1 Approximately 98 percent of the 10.1 million people who responded to a survey conducted September 1–7, 2002, in 3,894 municipalities throughout Brazil gave a resounding "no" to the question: "Should the

Brazilian government sign the FTAA treaty?" *Inter Press Service*, Rio de Janeiro, September 18, 2002.

2 The initiative includes seven countries (Guatemala, Belize, El Salvador, Nicaragua, Costa Rica, Honduras, and Panama) and the southeastern region of Mexico.

3 For a detailed description of objectives and programs, see http://www.iadb.org/ppp

4 The regression was also run excluding Nicaragua, which shows some data problems for the period, and the result maintains.

5 López-Calva (2001) contains a summary of the literature.

22

Asymmetries and Cooperation in the FTAA

Inés Bustillo and José Antonio Ocampo

In 1994 Latin American and Caribbean countries (except Cuba) embarked with Canada and the United States on the construction of the Free Trade Area of the Americas (FTAA). The FTAA would be the largest free trade area in the world with a combined population of 800 million and a gross domestic product (GDP) of about US$11 trillion. It is, indeed, an ambitious project and a formidable challenge given the wide asymmetries in size and economic development of the participating countries.

A confluence of different factors—including developments in global markets, country-specific conditions, and economic policies—will have a bearing on the extent to which countries will benefit from hemispheric trade liberalization. This chapter argues that the way asymmetries are addressed will have an effect on the capacity of countries, particularly the smaller and less developed, to benefit from expanded trade opportunities. In particular, it claims that it will be important for development that member countries preserve margins of flexibility in FTAA disciplines to adopt active productive development policies to improve competitiveness and to manage their capital accounts. Furthermore, it argues that convergence of development levels among the countries of the hemisphere may require new, ambitious initiatives, particularly the design of cohesion/integration funds and increased labor mobility. Alongside the FTAA agreement, hemispheric cooperation on these topics will effectively help strike a balance among countries with wide disparities in size and level of development.

The first section looks at the FTAA in the context of current trade policies and agreements. The second analyzes the treatment of asymmetries in trade agreements and suggests that the current practice of dealing with asymmetries might impose serious constraints on developing countries. Section three addresses the importance of preserving autonomy to foster productive development and manage capital flows. The fourth section examines prospects for income convergence and highlights the experience of Puerto Rico in the postwar period. The final section suggests areas in which cooperation could be broadened.

The Context for an FTAA

In an effort to meet the challenges posed by globalization, Latin American and Caribbean countries have been opening up their trade regimes and seeking to redefine their linkages with the global economy at least since the mid-1980s. The steps taken to open up to trade were swift and extensive. Alongside unilateral liberalization, integration processes were encouraged and a large set of free trade agreements was signed. The ECLAC characterized this trade policy mix as "open regionalism" (ECLAC, 1994).[1]

Close ties were also sought with countries outside the region, mainly with the United States, Canada, and the European Union.[2] The first of these agreements, the North American Free Trade Agreement (NAFTA), was the first reciprocal agreement between developing and developed countries. Mexico, which previously was a beneficiary of the Generalized System of Preferences (GSP) of the United States and Canada, entered into an agreement characterized by obligations similar to those of the developed countries. Many of the agreements after NAFTA have, to some extent, followed a similar model in terms of structure, scope, and treatment of asymmetries.

NAFTA marked a turning point in economic relations between Latin American and Caribbean countries and the United States and set a precedent for the negotiations toward a hemispheric-wide free trade area. In 1994, two years after NAFTA was signed, the process to construct an FTAA was launched in the context of the Summit of the Americas, a broader social and political process among thirty-four countries in the Western Hemisphere.

Improved market access, with the U.S. market as the main attraction, is one of the potential gains from hemispheric trade liberalization. The relative importance of the U.S. market in terms of each country's foreign trade activity varies widely throughout the region. However, even in countries where trade with the United States is relatively less important, this market may constitute an important destination for some manufactures, and improved access would provide an opportunity for export diversification. On the other hand, in agriculture, elimination of barriers to market access and export subsidies, together with reduced domestic support, are expected to provide gains for participating countries.[3]

For countries that are beneficiaries of U.S. unilateral preferences, participation in an FTAA means reducing uncertainty—an insurance against discretion in the granting of preferences.[4] The cost of this insurance is, obviously, reduced protection and policy autonomy. Irrespective of securing market access, remaining outside a hemispheric-wide free trade area does not appear to be a viable alternative, particularly for the smaller economies, if access to the largest market in the hemisphere is to be preserved. This is especially the case for countries in the Caribbean Basin who lost market share and investment when Mexico gained access to the U.S. market through NAFTA. Moreover, countries desiring to benefit from existing preferential schemes must comply with eligibility criteria in order to participate in FTAA negotiations.

Beyond the traditional incentives of securing access and expanding exports, an FTAA could help countries attract foreign investment. This could be particularly important for smaller economies willing to participate more actively in international outsourcing. Moreover, an FTAA represents an opportunity to discipline the use of contingent protection measures, such as antidumping and countervailing duties, that create unjustified barriers. The application of the trade remedies has affected important exports from the region—steel from Brazil and Argentina, flowers from Colombia, grapes and salmon from Chile, and crude oil and steel from Venezuela, among others (see Table 22.1).

From Special and Differential Treatment to a "Level Playing Field"

The scope of the FTAA agenda is broad, reflecting the consensus to negotiate a wide and diverse range of issues seeking to expand and deepen reciprocal commitments into new areas beyond the reduction of tariff and other border barriers. It includes the traditional market-access disciplines for trade in goods as well as new issues such as services and intellectual property, including areas (competition policy and investment) that have not been the subject of multilateral negotiations in the WTO. It also seeks to improve WTO rules and disciplines wherever possible and appropriate.

Moreover, the FTAA is set to constitute a single undertaking of mutual rights and obligations. It will be a reciprocal agreement such that all countries, regardless of size and level of development, will ultimately have to assume the full set of obligations. Similarly, in the Canada-Chile, Mexico-European Union, and Mexico-EFTA free trade agreements, among others, trade relations are governed by reciprocity. Differences in size and level of development, which as shown in Table 22.2 are several times larger than those characteristic of the European Union, are expected to be addressed through technical cooperation programs and longer periods for compliance with obligations, among other possible alternatives.

As in NAFTA, treatment of asymmetries will be a result of the negotiation process. The transitional measures included in NAFTA, which allow for differential treatment, were indeed the result of the negotiating process and not an a priori concession granted to Mexico on account of its level of development. NAFTA, as well as other recent trade agreements between developed and developing countries, have tended to address asymmetries through specific, transitory, and negotiated provisions, rather than through exemptions to general rules and disciplines, allowing in particular more flexibility and time for the implementation of commitments. In the Canada-Costa Rica agreement, for example, asymmetries were reflected in differences in tariff elimination schedules and in more flexibility in the enforcement of rules of origin for a few products. Technical cooperation programs were also provided in the area of trade facilitation and of technical barriers to trade.

The current approach for dealing with asymmetries is a result of a shift in thinking on development and trade policies. Furthermore, the emphasis on transitional time frames and on the provision of technical assistance has tended to narrow down alternatives, relative to the range of methods used in other negotiation processes.[5] Until about the mid-1980s the prevailing belief was that the dynamics of development were different in developing countries. In particular, patterns of economic specialization—the high level of dependence on commodities with low income elasticity of demand—and the associated balance of payments vulnerabilities were viewed as obstacles to income convergence.[6] Overcoming asymmetries required both changes in the international economic order as well as efforts at promoting industrialization through import substitution and export promotion. In the multilateral trading system these changes translated into demands for preferential access by developing countries to developed countries' markets, flexibility in the application of disciplines, and, more broadly,

Table 22.1 Antidumping Investigations Initiated by the United States (1980–2001)

	Antidumping Investigations Initiated			Antidumping Orders Issued			Percent Restrictive*		
Country	1980–89	1990–2001	Total	1980–89	1990–2001	Total	1980–89	1990–2001	Total
All Countries	383	527	910	174	225	399	45	43	44
Latin America & the Caribbean	59	82	141	22	26	48	37	32	34
Argentina	6	11	17	3	5	8	50	45	47
Brazil	24	22	46	10	10	20	42	45	43
Chile	2	5	7	2	2	4	100	40	57
Colombia	4	1	5	1	0	1	25	0	20
Costa Rica	1	4	5	0	0	0	0	0	0
Ecuador	1	1	2	1	0	1	100	0	50
El Salvador	1	0	1	0	0	0	0	0	0
Mexico	8	23	31	2	7	9	25	30	29
Peru	1	0	1	0	0	0	0	0	0
Trinidad & Tobago	1	3	4	1	0	1	100	0	25
Venezuela	10	12	22	2	2	4	20	17	18

Source: ECLAC based on U.S. Dept of Commerce, International Trade Administration, July 2002.

* Percent restrictive refers to the percentage of AD orders issued with respect to total AD investigations initiated.

nonreciprocal trade relations between developed and developing countries. The asymmetrical treatment of developing countries was applied through exemptions to general rules and disciplines in a form that would allow for the protection of markets and subsidies to industries in order to strengthen and diversify the industrial base. Policy discretion included the right to maintain trade barriers to deal with balance of payment problems and to protect infant industries using industrial and trade policy measures that otherwise would be inconsistent with multilateral obligations (Gibbs 1998). At the same time, more favorable and nonreciprocal access to markets in developed countries was granted through GSP and other preferential schemes determined unilaterally by developed countries.[7]

Table 22.2 Disparities in Levels of Development and Size

	1960	1980	1999
A. GDP per capita (constant 1995 US$)			
Coefficient of variation			
European Union (EU)	0.46	0.36	0.37
EU and candidates	0.52	0.65	0.78
FTAA	1.16	1.16	1.26
Highest/lowest			
EU	5.95	3.70	4.28
EU and candidates	10.76	20.55	41.49
FTAA	25.90	34.60	83.20
B. GDP per capita, PPP (current international $)			
Coefficient of variation			
European Union (EU)		0.22	0.26
EU and candidates		0.38	0.49
FTAA		0.79	0.85
Highest/lowest			
EU		1.95	2.77
EU and candidates		4.54	8.43
FTAA		9.02	21.80
C. Population, total			
Coefficient of variation			
European Union (EU)	1.09	1.07	1.07
EU and candidates	1.19	1.16	1.18
FTAA	2.81	2.55	2.42
Highest/lowest			
EU	230.78	214.59	190.05
EU and candidates	230.78	214.59	190.05
FTAA	3,542.55	5,117.57	6,806.00

Source: World Bank, World Development Indicators (2001).

Since the mid-1980s the emphasis on unilateral liberalization has led to a reconsideration of the approach for addressing asymmetries and of the usefulness of differential treatment as it had been conceived. The thinking changed from a focus on preferential access and differential provisions to an emphasis on the difficulties faced by developing countries in the implementation of WTO commitments. An alternative paradigm emerged whereby the basic objective of trade relations was to provide a "level playing field" for the efficient operation of free-market forces.

The practice of leveling the playing field has led to the adoption of common obligations (rules and disciplines). The Canada-U.S. Free Trade Agreement (CUSFTA), for instance, has been interpreted as a series of concessions made by Canada, the smaller partner, in exchange for assurances against future trade policy by the larger partner (McLaren 1997). Whalley (1996) suggests a similar conclusion regarding Mexico in the negotiations leading to NAFTA. Mexico's objective of strengthening domestic policy reform via importing common rules and disciplines would explain the one-sidedness of the concessions.

The adoption of common FTAA rules and disciplines is not in itself undesirable, as the experience of Mexico would suggest (López Cordova 2001). However, significant tradeoffs may emerge. As we will see in the following section, conflicts may result from further liberalization of investment and, particularly, from the lack of adequate instruments to manage capital-account volatility. As the experience of the region in the 1990s suggests, the flexibility to impose restrictions on capital flows to facilitate the adoption of countercyclical macroeconomic policies may be necessary to reduce the vulnerability of the countries to cyclical swings in external financing. A level-playing-field approach imposing similar obligations would generate, in this case, a false equality. Thus, the greater macroeconomic vulnerability of the countries of the region to external shocks underscores the need to strike a balance between these competing interests in the FTAA negotiations.

The practice of leveling the playing field may also worsen asymmetries. If agreed rules eliminate the autonomy to adopt active production-development strategies, they would weaken the linkages between export and GDP growth and may lead countries to specialize in sectors of reduced dynamism in world trade. This would be the case if constraints were imposed on policies that foster innovation technological development and strengthen the export base. Also, intellectual-property disciplines, such as provisions related to patent protection, could increase the costs of foreign technologies, inhibit development of new technologies, and slow down both national learning processes and the narrowing of the technological gap with the more advanced economies.[8] In contrast to patenting trends in developed economies and in the newly industrialized countries in Southeast Asia, the number of patents applied for by nonresidents in Latin America is growing much faster than those requested by residents. This trend is related to the use of patents by foreign corporations, which in some cases could hinder the development of local production and technological capabilities (Aboites and Cimoli 2001).

Thus, unless asymmetries are properly accounted for, common rules may end up limiting the promotion of new comparative advantages that, as will be argued below, are of vital importance to the countries of Latin America and the Caribbean in order to strengthen the relationship between exports and economic growth.

Autonomy to Foster Productive Development and Manage Volatility

The outcome of the reallocation of production and consumption patterns that hemispheric trade liberalization is expected to bring about will depend on the final nature of the agreement—the depth and scope of its disciplines—but also on a confluence of other factors. Among the latter, the capacity of countries to promote competitiveness and to manage capital account volatility will have an effect on the extent to which they will benefit from hemispheric trade liberalization.

In the case of the smaller economies of the region, size and vulnerability pose additional constraints. Recent developments in both trade and growth theories suggest that trade among asymmetric countries may also lead to an increase in income gaps, as technological advantages may be cumulative (Ros 2000; ECLAC 2000, Ch.11).[9]

Export and Production Linkages

Despite overall advances in some countries, opening up the economy is not a sufficient condition for improving the region's growth performance.[10] During the 1990s Latin America and the Caribbean had one of the world's highest rates for merchandise trade in terms of both volume and value. The average annual increase in merchandise exports amounted to 8.4 percent in volume—a rate surpassed only by China and a few of the Asian economies. However, the dynamism of exports was not reflected in behavior of the economy; the region's strong export performance had weak returns in terms of economic growth (see Figure 22.1). The average annual rate of economic growth of the region since 1990, 2.6 percent, was less than one-third of the growth in real exports.

This outcome can be read, first of all, as the net result of the opposing effects on aggregate demand of export growth and a sharp increase in the import coefficient, associated with a reduction in levels of protection, the tendency toward a revaluation of the exchange rate, and the high import content of inputs in many of the robust export industries, especially in the manufacturing sector (Moreno-Brid 2002). On the other hand, static comparative advantages led the economies to specialize in sectors of reduced dynamism in world trade. In structural terms, although import penetration did contribute to the modernization of production and to new exports based on the increased incorporation of imported inputs, it also weakened the linkages between exports and overall economic activity.

The region's share of international trade rose from 4.5 percent to 5.5 percent during the decade, most of it concentrated in Mexico. Overall, though, this increase was to a large extent the result of competitiveness gains in slow-growth products rather than of gains in more dynamic trade flows. Thus, an assessment of the region's export specialization during the last decade, measured in terms of the relative weight of high-demand products in the export basket, reveals that its quality was quite poor (Table 22.3).

Three patterns of specialization have prevailed. In Mexico and some countries of Central American and the Caribbean, export specialization can be characterized by integration into vertical flows of trade in manufactures mainly centered in the United States market. This pattern of specialization allowed these countries to benefit from some dynamic manufacturing markets—and, curiously, more so in the case of the Central American markets than Mexico, as Table 22.3 indicates—but at the cost of reduced domestic linkages, given the high import content of such manufactures (*maquila* in the extreme case).

A second pattern, which prevailed in South America, is specialization in horizontal production and marketing networks, mainly of raw materials and natural resource–based manufactures. This pattern allowed more domestic linkages (including technological developments), but generally led countries to specialize in goods that are losing share in world trade; the latter feature was particularly problematic in the case of the Andean countries (see Table 22.3). Interestingly, intraregional trade was a major element in South American trade during the 1990–97 expansion, providing a large content in manufactures with domestic linkages, but such flows were significantly affected by the broad-based slowdown that affected the region since the Asian crisis.

Finally, countries in the Caribbean and Panama reveal a third pattern of a high predominance of export of services, for the most part tourism but also financial and transportation services. The most important of all, tourism, is a dynamic component of world trade, but also has been characterized by high import contents, particularly in the smaller economies.

The export performance of Latin America and the Caribbean in the 1990s thus suggests that strong export-GDP growth linkages and improved competitiveness, particularly in dynamic segments of world trade, are not automatic outcomes of greater openness. This implies that unless countries engage in a coherent effort to stimulate the linkages between export sectors and domestic economic activities, thus increasing the value added (i.e., GDP) of exports, as well as to encourage dynamic, knowledge-based comparative advantages, export-GDP linkages will be weak and exports will tend to be concentrated in products for which demand is less dynamic and more vulnerable in world trade.

Figure 22.1 Exports and GDP

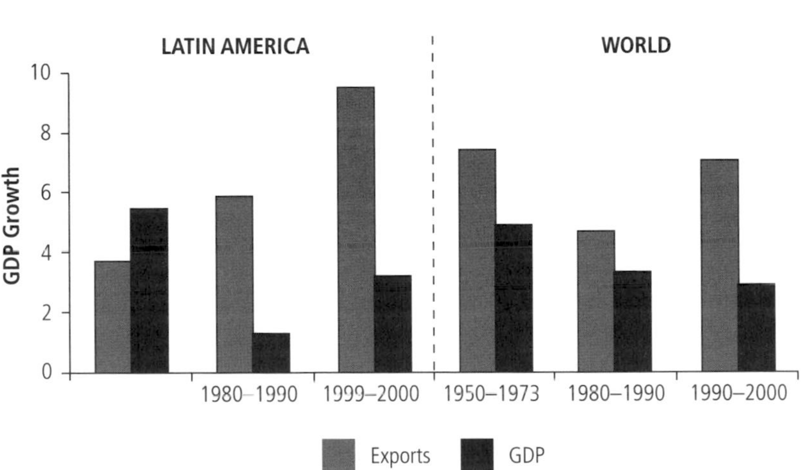

In this regard, valuable lessons can also be drawn from the experience of the East Asian economies. Recent research has noted that an important part of the success of the East Asian countries' integration into global trade flows rested on discretion to use a variety of policy measures and incentives targeted at specific sectors and industries that were successful in building competitive export supply capacities. Strategic integration was not only confined to trade but also included policies that promoted technology transfer.[11] One important lesson from the East Asian experience is that while a deliberate and active approach to integration through a measured and properly sequenced set of policies towards trade and investment cannot guarantee economic success, success without it seems to be the exception rather than the rule.

For Latin American and Caribbean countries, active participation in a hemispheric market requires speeding the rate of innovation, including the transfer of technology, development of new production sectors, and support of learning processes. This entails devising strategies to promote new firms and activities, restructure sectors that are not competitive, and support small and medium-sized enterprise to help strengthen the ties between exports and productive sectors and thus participate in new trade flows on a competitive basis. Building competitive export supply capacities demands creating linkages between activities that are successful in international markets and the rest of the production system. A stronger export orientation, particularly based

Table 22.3 Latin America and the Caribbean: Changes in Market Shares and Relative Specialization Index for High-Demand Products

	Market Share (%)				Relative Specialization Index for High-Growth Products[a]		
	1990	1993	1996	1999	1990–93	1993–96	1996–99
Mexico	1.292	1.446	1.911	2.441	0.515	0.844	0.679
MERCOSUR	1.552	1.528	1.545	1.499	0.645	0.828	0.655
Andean Community	0.888	0.822	0.913	0.822	0.298	0.622	0.369
CACM	0.190	0.230	0.274	0.350	1.550	0.975	1.323
CARICOM	0.182	0.163	0.145	0.131	0.787	0.711	0.348

Source: ECLAC, on the basis of data obtained from the Competitive Analysis of Nations Program (2002 version).

[a]Ratio of exports of high-growth products to exports of low-growth products.

on the promotion of exports that are knowledge intensive or involve a high level of value added, is crucial for export capacity to translate into greater economic growth.

Although WTO disciplines (and the FTAA seeks to be WTO-plus) have reduced the scope for using the more generalized policy interventions of the East Asian approach, a strategy of this type will require flexibility in the way countries commit to common FTAA obligations. In particular, it is necessary to preserve margins of autonomy in an FTAA for adopting open-economy oriented policies to improve competitiveness. This includes intellectual property schemes that promote the transfer of technology, the use of incentives to support the diversification of the export supply, and mechanisms to increase the national content of exports.

External Vulnerability

Policy autonomy is essential as well in the use of instruments to manage external shocks. In this regard, exchange-rate policy should not be subject to restrictions—though macroeconomic convergence schemes in subregional agreements should be allowed—and autonomy should also be maintained to use capital account restrictions for macroeconomic purposes, particularly to reduce capita-account volatility.

A competitive real exchange rate and real macroeconomic stability are essential for hemispheric trade liberalization to be successful and contribute to an efficient allocation of resources. To stimulate the production of tradables, a favorable and stable real effective exchange rate must be maintained—that is, an exchange rate that fluctuates on the basis of long-term factors and is not overly correlated with short-term capital movements.

Developments in the 1990s underscore the difficulties that Latin American countries found in maintaining a competitive exchange rate consistent with their commitment to trade liberalization in a situation marked by sizeable and volatile capital flows. The vulnerability of the region to cyclical swings in external financing thus proved to be a particularly serious constraint to sustainable trade flows.

As Figure 22.2 shows, the growth pattern of Latin America and the Caribbean during the 1900s was very unstable and highly dependent on external flows. Variations in capital flows were the main factor behind the pronounced business cycles. Severe slowdowns or outright recession followed brief periods of economic growth. External credit booms facilitated rapid growth in 1991–94 and 1996–97, and a recovery in

2000, but these periods were followed by deep adjustments in 1995, 1998–99 and 2001–02. The result was unstable and mediocre regional growth averaging 2.6 percent between 1990 and 2002.

Countries' reliance on highly volatile financing flows, in particular short-term credit lines and portfolio flows, was a key element behind vulnerability to fluctuations in external financing. The impact of sharp swings in international financing was accentuated by a procyclical pattern of macroeconomic management. Upsurges in capital inflows were accompanied by excessive domestic credit, liquidity expansion, and appreciation of the exchange rate that led to deterioration in the current account of the balance of payments. When external capital inflows were reversed, liquidity contracted, and a fear of depreciation accelerated the loss of reserves and led to a severe adjustment in the current account. Booms in external financing, which occurred against a backdrop of financial liberalization and weak prudential regulation and supervision, ended up in domestic financial crises.

Dealing with the destabilizing effects of the boom-and-bust cycles in volatile capital flows requires a comprehensive strategy for growth with stability. In this regard, macroeconomic stability should be viewed in a broad sense that includes, in addition to the control of the fiscal deficit and reduction of inflation, real goals in terms of economic growth and its stability. As ECLAC has proposed, such a strategy should be founded upon action in three areas: strengthening the international financial system's ability to prevent and manage crises and countries' capabilities for designing preventive macroeconomic policies; speeding the pace of export development and improvements in the region's access to international financial markets; and increasing national saving and promoting domestic financial development so that available resources can be increased and adequately channeled into investment (ECLAC 2002b).

Within the above parameters, it is essential to design policies that protect from crises and that are consistent with the realities of developing countries. In this vein, capital account regulations are important complementary tools of well-designed macroeconomic policies, providing additional degrees of freedom to avoid excessive borrowing and help to avoid as well an unsustainable appreciation of the exchange rate. The capital-account regulation mechanisms adopted by Chile and Colombia in the 1990s represent successful experiences in managing foreign-account surges through unremunerated reserve requirements on capital inflows.[12]

Figure 22.2 Latin America and the Caribbean: Procyclical Movements in Economic Activity and Net Resource Transfer

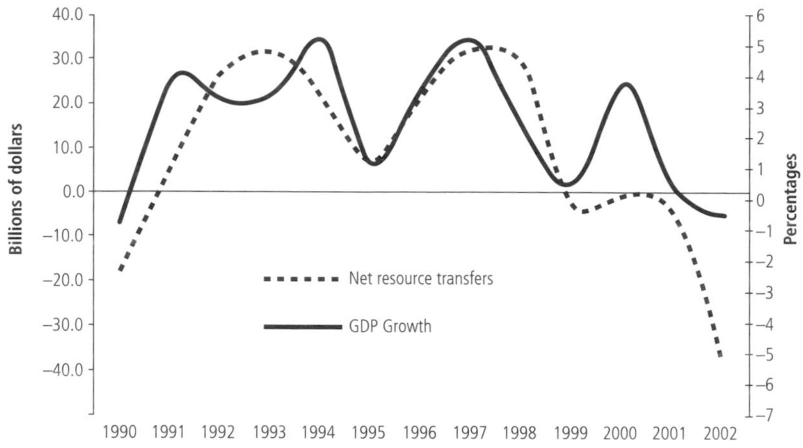

Billions of dollars
40.0
30.0
20.0
10.0
0.0
−10.0
−20.0
−30.0
−40.0
Percentages
6
5
4
3
2
1
0
−1
−2
−3
−4
−5
−6
−7
Net resource transfers
GDP Growth
1990 1991 1992 1993 1994 1995 1996 1997 1998 1999 2000 2001 2002

Source: ECLAC.

Therefore, preserving autonomy within an FTAA in the use of tools for the prudential management of capital flows is essential to confront the impacts of destabilizing crises and disruptions of trade flows.

Size and Vulnerability

The smaller economies of the region face additional constraints. Smallness has disadvantages:[13] it inhibits economies of scale and scope, leading to higher production costs and unfavorable competitive positions. These disadvantages affect both the public and the private sectors. For instance, the cost of public services per capita is usually higher in smaller economies than in larger ones since most public goods and infrastructure services are characterized by their indivisibility. Activities in the private sector face similar difficulties since economies of scale and externalities cannot be achieved adequately due to the small size of the domestic market.

Though higher direct unit costs affect the tradable sector, they are especially critical in nontradable sectors. In the production of tradables, foreign markets offer the opportunity to exploit economies of scale and scope, though at the cost of further specializing in a narrow range of sectors and products, thus increasing vulnerability (see below). However, scale economies are critical in nontradable sectors, for which the market is, by definition, domestic. To the extent that nontradable goods and services are inputs for the production in tradable sectors (including activities such as domestic financing and marketing services), the absence of economies of scale in the production of the former will spill over into the competitiveness of the latter (ECLAC 2000).

In addition to these constraints, smaller economies are more vulnerable than larger economies in the sense that they are more prone to external shocks and risks as a result of geographic (country size and its location), demographic, and economic factors. Exports from smaller countries tend to be highly concentrated in a narrow range of products and markets, and thus more exposed to external shocks in prices and quantities and more likely to suffer from higher terms-of-trade volatility than larger countries. This in turn increases any costs of adjustment associated with trade liberalization. At the same time, their macroeconomic policy autonomy is more limited, in particular the ability to change relative prices through exchange-rate policy and to smooth out business cycles through an autonomous interest-rate policy.

Moreover, the greater fiscal dependence on foreign trade of several of the region's smaller economies compounds the burdens of adjustment associated with the loss of income from FTAA tariff reductions. In some countries (Bahamas, Dominica, Grenada, St. Kitts and Nevis, and St. Lucia), international trade taxes account for more than 50 percent of government revenue (Escaith and Inoue 2001). In addition, the lost revenue will potentially be more problematic for those countries that, in addition to being dependent on trade taxes, face a relatively large fiscal deficit, as shown in Table 22.4.

There appears to be broad agreement on the constraints on the ability of the smaller economies of the region to benefit from the process of hemispheric liberalization and from technical cooperation and capacity building (Seventh FTAA Trade Ministerial, Quito, Ecuador, November 2002). However, more longer-term advantages in terms of room of maneuver to adopt strategies to improve competitiveness are required. Moreover, as the next section will highlight, free trade, even with special provisions, may be insufficient to promote convergence.

Trade Liberalization and Convergence

Will an FTAA, which involves large asymmetries in terms of size and levels of development of member countries, be a force for between-country income convergence among its members? Empirical work on trade liberalization and income convergence give ambiguous answers to this question. While some studies suggest that trade liberalization plays a key role or even that it may be sufficient for income convergence, others emphasize the role played by nontrade factors. The convergence study by Barro and Sala-i-Martin (1991) would suggest that among regions that are open to each other the poorer grow faster than average. The authors find that, in the case of states of the United States and regions of Europe, poorer regions converged to richer ones at a pace of about 2 percent between 1960 and 1985. They maintain that convergence does indeed occur, though at a slow pace. In turn, Ben-David (1993, 1996) finds that the removal of trade barriers among the main European Economic Community countries was followed by significant income convergence. Convergence, while far from being a worldwide phenomenon, seems to prevail among countries that trade extensively with one another.

Rodríguez and Rodrik (2001) and Slaughter (2001) have challenged the empirical evidence for convergence on several grounds, including issues related to the measurement of openness and the time period of analysis, and have thus questioned the empirical results that trade liberalization necessarily leads to faster convergence. Even if convergence occurs, many factors other than trade—including common laws and institutions, labor mobility, and income transfers—are potentially at play.

In the Western Hemisphere this challenge is best illustrated by the case of Puerto Rico. Indeed, Puerto Rico's development experience in the postwar period serves to illustrate the links between trade openness and income convergence, but also the effects of other factors that accompanied trade liberalization, particularly industrial incentives, transfer payments, and labor mobility (see tables 22.5 and 22.6).

Puerto Rico's development strategy Operation Bootstrap, initiated in the 1940s, yielded robust growth by attracting U.S. investment and transforming Puerto Rico's agricultural base into an economy led by manufacturing and services. In the 1950s and 1960s the average annual growth of Puerto Rico's real GDP per capita was 5.3 percent and 6.4 percent, respectively. The gap between income per person in the United States and Puerto Rico declined rapidly, from a factor of nearly 6 in 1950, to 4 in 1960, and to 2.7 in 1970 (Dietz 2001). After 1970 the relative gap between incomes in the two economies failed to converge any further. In the 1990s the income gap started to close again, although at a very slow pace, declining to a factor of two in 2001.

Table 22.4 Latin America and the Caribbean: Fiscal Balance and Dependency on Trade Taxes (1995–1999 averages)*

Dependency on Trade Revenues	Surplus or Small Deficit	Moderate Deficit	Large Deficit
Low	Trinidad & Tobago	El Salvador Mexico	Bolivia Brazil Costa Rica Uruguay
Moderate	Chile	Argentina Barbados Guatemala Panama Paraguay Peru	Ecuador Guyana
High	Dominican Republic	Netherlands St. Kitts & Nevis St. Lucia St. Vincent & the Grenadines Venezuela	Antigua & Barbuda Bahamas Belize Colombia Dominica Grenada Haiti Honduras Nicaragua Jamaica

Source: Escaith and Inouse (2001).
**Notes:* Deficit levels are strictly for comparison purposes and do not necessarily imply fiscal fragility. These were determined by the average deficits during the period between 1995 and 1999. Countries at the upper end of the sample had average deficits of over 2 percent of GDP (and/or have had volatile changes in their deficits). A middle group had deficits of between 1 and 2 percent of GDP, and another group had surpluses of less than 1 percent.

The main ingredient of Puerto Rico's Bootstrap strategy was the attraction of U.S. capital for investment purposes in industries oriented toward exports to the U.S. market within a virtually tax-free environment. Labor mobility, with unrestricted out-migration to the United States and a large positive inflow of transfer payments from the United States were two key factors that supported this strategy.

The package of incentives included industrial tax exemptions and other incentives under both Puerto Rican and U.S. laws. From the beginning of Operation Bootstrap up to the Industrial Incentive Act of 1978, Puerto Rico offered full tax exemption from local taxes and other fees and provided a variety of subsidies on rent and labor costs. In addition to these incentives, exemption from U.S. corporate income taxes was granted to firms (qualifying U.S. "possessions corporations") operating in Puerto Rico. Under Section 936 of the U.S. Internal Revenue Code (Section 931 until 1976), U.S. corporations obtained tax credits against federal taxes attributable to the income earned from business operations and certain financial investments in Puerto Rico. Section 936 stimulated investment, for the most part mainland capital for export.

Puerto Rico's industrial incentives and Section 936 shaped the manufacturing sector, which grew and shifted from labor to capital-intensive manufacturing industries. The "936 corporations," as they were called, came to dominate Puerto Rico's manufacturing sector, whose share of total output increased from 22 percent in 1950 to 39 percent in 1990, with Puerto Rico ranking above all fifty states of the mainland in manufacturing's share of gross domestic product. Manufacturing was the leading force in Puerto Rico's growth of trade, particularly exports of chemical products such as drugs and pharmaceuticals.[14]

On the other hand, Figures 22.3 and 22.4 illustrate the important countercyclical role played by federal transfers in Puerto Rico's economy, in particular since the 1970s, following the slowdown in economic growth in Puerto Rico that left the income gap between the United States and Puerto Rico unchanged from 1970 to 1990. Federal transfers—which have represented since the mid-1970s close to 10 percent of Puerto Rico's GDP—are strongly correlated with the business cycle.[15] As shown in Figure 22.3, there is a strong positive correlation between federal transfers and unemployment, thus indicating the countercyclical nature of federal transfers.

Moreover, the net flow of official transfers compensated for the low saving rates in the period, helping to maintain the level of consumption when income and employment levels fell. Federal transfers have been much higher than domestic savings as a percentage of GDP since 1974 (see Figure 22.4). For the period as a whole (1960–2001), domestic savings as a share of GDP amounted to 3.7 percent while net transfers to individuals amounted to more than 10 percent.

Furthermore, the high level of sustained inflows of external capital was fundamental to finance Puerto Rico's investment rate during the period, given the low level of domestic savings. The inflows of external capital averaged almost 16 percent of GDP in the period, which helps to explain the investment rate of almost 21 percent (see Table 22.7).

Table 22.5 Puerto Rico: Real GDP Per Capita

	Average Annual Growth
1950–60	5.3
1960–70	6.4
1970–80	2.6
1980–90	2.6
1990–2000	3.3
1950–2000	4.0

Source: ECLAC on the basis of Puerto Rico National Accounts and Baumol and Wolf (1995).

Table 22.6 Puerto Rico: Exports

	Percentage of GDP
1950	33.7
1960	37.2
1970	34.8
1980	56.8
1990	67.5
2000	65.7

Source: Puerto Rico Planning Board.

During the 1960–2001 period, federal transfers showed a strong negative correlation with the rate of investment as a share of GDP and a strong positive correlation with the unemployment level as a share of the labor force. The correlation between the investment ratio and the unemployment rate was also strong and negative. Federal transfers were thus strongly correlated with the business cycle, assuming a fundamental countercyclical role.

In addition to the effect of transfers on the economy, the massive migration of Puerto Ricans to the United States also played a mitigating role. Puerto Rico's industrial sector was not capable of absorbing labor at the desired level, resulting in a high unemployment rate in the postwar period.[16] Since the 1950s unemployment has exceeded 10 percent of the labor force. The unemployment rate reached its lowest level in 1970 (10.3 percent of the labor force) and its highest level in 1983 (23.5 percent of the labor force). The unemployment rate decreased in the 1990s, but still remained above the 1970 minimum.

It is hard to imagine how Puerto Rico's high level of unemployment in the postwar period would have been sustainable in the absence of unrestricted out-migration and the significant level of federal transfers. Net emigration reached almost one million persons in the period 1950–90, declining from a peak of 42,200 per year in the 1950s, to 15,700 in the 1960s, and 9,200 in the 1970s. Net emigration increased to an average of 27,600 per year in the 1980s, however (see Table 22.8). According to Puerto Rico's Planning Board, net emigration reached a total of 62,169 persons in the 1990–2000 period, almost 2 percent of Puerto Rico's total population in the year 2000.

The role played by tax incentives, transfer payments, and unrestricted migration to the mainland in fostering economic growth has been subject of debate in the economic literature on Puerto Rico.[17] For instance, Baumol and Wolff (1996) suggest that annual growth in GDP per capita in Puerto Rico during the 1950–90 period would have been impressive (3.8 percent) even without these advantages, only about 10 percent less than the actual rate. However, their results also show that, although the effects of these special advantages were very

Figure 22.3 Puerto Rico:
Net Transfers from the Federal Government and Unemployment

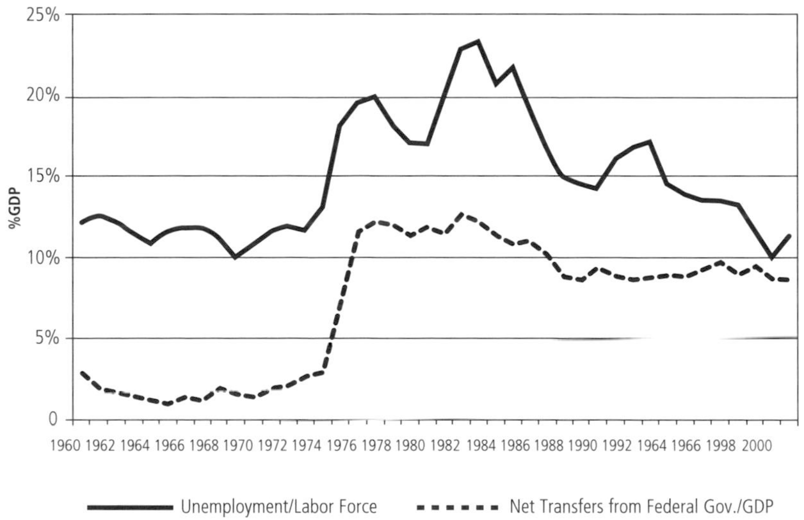

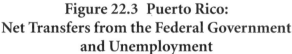

Source: ECLAC on the basis of data from Puerto Rico's Planning Board.

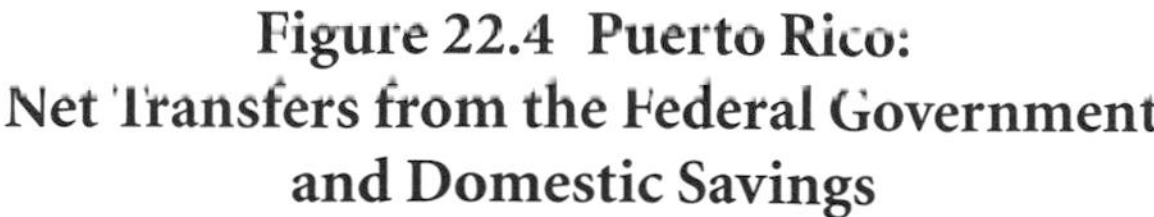

**Figure 22.4 Puerto Rico:
Net Transfers from the Federal Government
and Domestic Savings**

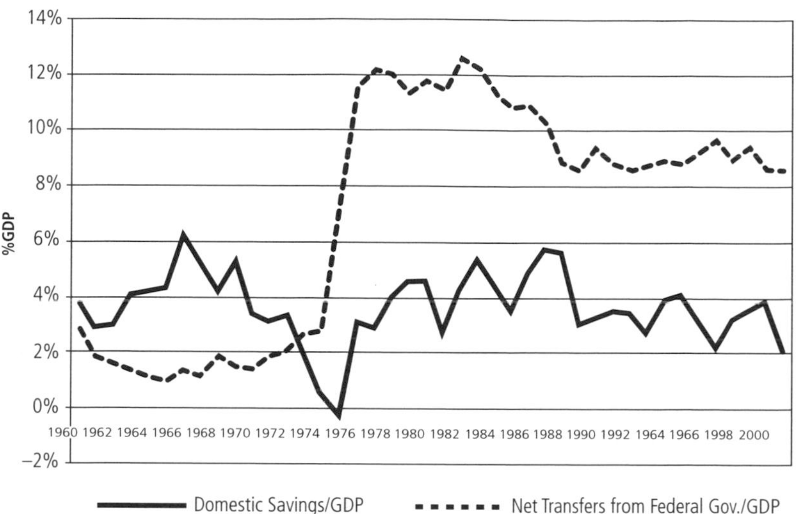

Source: ECLAC on the basis of data from Puerto Rico's Planning Board.

small in the 1950s and 1960s, they became important to Puerto Rico's growth during the 1970s and 1980s.

Baumol and Wolff also suggest that federal transfer payments during the 1970s, which came to represent more than 20 percent of Puerto Rican personal incomes (between 1975 and 2001, transfers to individuals averaged 15 percent of GDP, compared to an average of only 5 percent from 1960 to 1975), may have added a full percentage point to the growth in GDP per capita. In the 1980s federal transfers added almost half a percentage point to GDP per capita growth.

Furthermore, these authors estimated that emigration added another quarter of a percentage point to GDP per capita growth during the 1980s. Other authors point to a stronger effect. Notwithstanding the controversy over the extent of the effect of migration, it is clear that the unemployment rate would have been even higher without migration, which served as a safety valve, supported incomes, and allowed per capita income to increase more rapidly.

Table 22.7 Puerto Rico: Matrix of Correlations (1960–2001)

	Total Gross Domestic Investment/GDP	Net Inflow of External Capital, Adjusted/GDP	Domestic Savings/GDP	Net Transfers to Individuals/GDP	Net Transfers from Federal Government/GDP	Unemployment/Labor Force
Average share of GDP, 1960–2001	20.67%	15.66%	3.66%	10.28%[a]	7.12%	14.87%
Total gross domestic investment/GDP	1					
Net inflow of external capital, adjusted/GDP	0.39	1				
Domestic savings/GDP	–.12	–.22	1			
Net transfers to individuals/GDP	–.88	–.22	0	1		
Net transfers from federal government/GDP	–.92	–.29	0.05	0.99	1	
Unemployment/labor force	–.76	0.01	0.05	0.8	0.78	1

Source: ECLAC, on the basis of data from Puerto Rico's Junta de Planificación.

[a]This share, given the availability of information, corresponds to the period 1963–2001.

Table 22.8 Puerto Rico: Net Emigration

Period	Net Emigration Annual Average (1,000s)
1950–60	42.2
1960–70	15.7
1970–80	9.2
1980–90	27.6
1990–2000	23.7

Source: Baumol and Wolff (1996).

Toward Increased Cooperation

The gains that many countries could obtain from an FTAA will depend on the availability of adequate technical assistance. The need to strengthen the capacity of countries to implement FTAA disciplines and participate fully in the agreement has already been acknowledged in the Hemispheric Cooperation Program (HCP) launched by the ministers responsible for trade in Quito on November 1, 2002. The HCP envisages the provision of technical cooperation to address the institutional constraints that can be an impediment to meeting the obligations assumed under the agreement.

The HCP also recognizes that overcoming the challenges associated with trade liberalization in an FTAA involves more than technical assistance to implement common disciplines. The HCP envisages, inter alia, cooperation for "adjusting to integration." This would include strengthening productive capacity, fostering competitiveness, encouraging the development of innovation, and technology transfer. If successfully developed and implemented, the HCP can make an important contribution to addressing many of the constraints of the smaller and less developed economies.

However, for an FTAA to contribute to income convergence in the hemisphere, it must meet several additional requirements. As we have indicated, the way asymmetries are dealt with in the FTAA will be a crucial determinant of the capacity of developing country partners of the agreement—particularly the smaller ones—to benefit from an expanded hemispheric market. The gains that many countries could obtain will depend on their success in transforming productive structures and strengthening the export-GDP growth linkages. This involves policies to stimulate and diversify exports and to speed up innovation and technological development. Progress in this area will depend on adapting the practice of leveling the playing field to the realities of countries in the hemisphere, thus preserving flexibility in FTAA obligations to adopt active production development policies to improve competitiveness.

In addition, gains will depend on curbing the vulnerability of the economies to capital flows. This, in turn, means that there must be sufficient autonomy to adopt countercyclical macroeconomic policies, including capital-account regulations. Again, regulation of capital flows gives additional room to moderate cyclical upswings and avoids unsustainable appreciation of the exchange rate, thus serving as a complementary tool of sound macroeconomic policies. Through its effects on the real exchange rate and its stability, it may also serve a sustainable transformation of productive structures in the face of deeper trade liberalization.

Ultimately, free trade, even with special provisions that take asymmetries into account, may be insufficient as a force for between-country income convergence. Two fundamental complements are cohesion/integration funds and increased labor mobility. Funds can play a key role in accelerating convergence of income levels within the hemisphere. As the experience of Puerto Rico illustrates, such transfers can play a crucial role in alleviating economic and social adjustment costs in the more disadvantaged areas, and can also provide a useful countercyclical device.

The European Union is obviously the case in which this principle has been applied most forcefully. It is indeed symptomatic of the political philosophy underlying European integration that deepening economic integration during the final decade of the twentieth century was accompanied by the increased use of explicit cohesion policy (Marín 1999). What is more, this policy was extended to the Central and Eastern European countries that are candidates for joining the EU. The possibility of creating a cohesion or integration fund to provide the necessary backing for hemispheric agreement was put forward by the number of heads of state at the Summit of the Americas held in Quebec in April 2001,[18] and therefore warrants special attention.

Labor migration can also be a major force for a more equitable distribution of FTAA gains. Along with liberalization of trade and investment, inclusion of labor mobility in the hemispheric agenda could have an equalizing force. As Rodrik (1997) has shown, the lack of labor mobility relative to that of capital skews the distribution of income against the less mobile factor, particularly the abundant low skilled labor in the developing economies. Thus, the key for labor mobility as an equalizing force is to include not only skilled workers but also less-skilled workers.[19] Winters (2002) has estimated that movements of workers for limited periods of time from developing to industrial countries could produce gains that exceed the full liberalization of trade in goods.[20] These results suggest that global gains from unskilled labor mobility exceed those from skilled labor mobility.

Labor mobility is no doubt a controversial subject. Economic theory indicates that an inflow of low-skilled workers from developing countries would put downward pressure on wages of those in industrial countries. This is supported by empirical evidence, which indicates that the inflow of unskilled workers to the United States has contributed to a decline in the relative earnings of unskilled workers, thus exacerbating the skill bias of technological change (Borjas, Freeman, and Katz 1997).

It has been suggested that a mitigating factor is that demographic trends in the United States (and in other industrial countries as well) could lead to rising relative wages for unskilled labor. As a consequence, there would be a high potential for increased flows of unskilled workers in an environment of stable relative wages (World Bank 2002). Moreover, immigrant workers can play a crucial role in meeting a country's growing need for labor. As recent research suggests, the economy of the United States in the 1990s was overwhelmingly dependent on immigrant workers for its employment growth (Sum, Fogg, and Harrington 2002).

On the other hand, a selective migration policy that favors skilled labor mobility increases income gaps in source countries. It also drains their human capital, generally a scarce factor of production, and may thus become an additional determinant of income divergence. Furthermore, skilled labor may end up being employed in jobs requiring lesser skills in the recipient countries due to other disadvantages it faces (language disadvantages, lack of knowledge of recipient labor markets, inadequate educational accreditation agreements, and so on). This consideration implies that, from the point of view of source countries, a more balanced migration policy in recipient countries or even a bias in favor of unskilled labor is certainly preferable.

Greater collaborative action on this highly sensitive economic and political issue could take place within the Summit of the Americas process, which provides the broader framework for an FTAA. Already the summit offers opportunities for greater collaborative action and its agenda includes explicit commitments on migration, human rights, and equity, and calls for the strengthening of cooperation among the countries to address these issues.

References

Aboites, Jaime, and Mario Cimoli. 2001. "Intellectual Property Rights and National Innovation Systems: Some Lesson from the Mexican Experience." Paper presented at the Danish Research Unit for Industrial Dynamics–Nelson and Winter Conference, Aalborg, Denmark (June).

Akyuz, Yilmaz, Ha-Joon Chang, and Richard Kozul-Wright. 1998. "New Perspectives on East Asian Development." *Journal of Development Studies* 34 (6): 4–35.

Amsden, Alice. 2001. *The Rise of "The Rest": Challenges to the West from Late Industrializing Countries.* New York: Oxford University Press.

Barro, Robert, and Xavier Sala-i-Martin. 1991. "Convergence across States and Regions." Brookings Institution Papers on Economic Activity 1: 107–182, Washington, DC.

Baumol, William, and Edward Wolff. 1996. "Catching up in the Postwar Period: Puerto Rico as the Fifth Tiger." *World Development* 24: 869–85.

Ben-David, Dan.1993. "Equalizing Exchange: Trade Liberalization and Income Convergence." *Quarterly Journal of Economics* 108: 653–79.

———. 1996. "Trade and Convergence Among Countries." *Journal of International Economics* 40: 279–98.

Borjas, George J., Richard B. Freeman, and Lawrence F. Katz. 1997. "How Much Do Immigration and Trade Affect Labor Market Outcomes?" Brookings Institution Papers on Economic Activity 1: 1–90, Washington, DC.

Chang, Ha-Joon. 2001. "Infant Industry Promotion in Historical Perspective: A Rope to Hang Oneself or a Ladder to Climb With?" Paper presented at the conference Development Theory at the Threshold of the Twenty-First Century, Economic Commission for Latin American and the Caribbean, Santiago, Chile, August.

Dietz, James L. 2001. "Puerto Rico: The Three-Legged Economy, Integration and Trade, Journal, Institute for the Integration of Latin America and the Caribbean." *Integration and Trade* 5 (15) (September–December): 247–73.

Economic Commission for Latin America and the Caribbean (ECLAC). 1991, 1993, and 1995. *Economic Survey of Puerto Rico*. Washington, DC.

———. 1994. *Open Regionalism in Latin America and the Caribbean: Economic Integration as a Contribution to Changing Production Patterns with Social Equity*. Santiago, Chile: United Nations.

———. 2000. *Equity, Development and Citizenship*. Santiago, Chile: United Nations.

———. 2002a. *Globalization and Development*. Santiago, Chile: ECLAC Books.

———. 2002b. *Growth with Stability: Financing for Development in the New International Context*. Santiago, Chile: ECLAC Books.

Escaith, Hubert, and Keiji Inoue. 2001. "Small Economies' Tariffs and Subsidies Policies in the Face of Trade Liberalization in the Americas." *Integration and Trade* 5 (14) (May–August): 3–28.

French-Davis, Ricardo, and Heriberto Tapia. 2001. "Three Varieties of Capital Surge Management in Chile." In *Financial Crises in Successful Emerging Economies*, edited by R. French-Davis. Washington, DC: ECLAC Books and Brookings Institution.

Gibbs, Murray. 1998. "Special and Differential Treatment in the Context of Globalization." United Nations Conference on Trade and Development, Geneva. Photocopy.

Hausmann, Ricardo.1995. "En camino hacia una mayor integración con el Norte." In *Crecimiento economico: Teoría, instituciones y experiencia internacional*, edited by Mónica Aparicio and William Easterly. Bogotá: Banco de la República and the World Bank.

López-Córdova, Ernesto. 2001. "NAFTA and The Mexican Economy: Analytical Issues and Lessons for the FTAA." Occasional Paper no. 9, Institute for the Integration of Latin America and the Caribbean and the Inter-American Development Bank, Washington, DC.

Marín, Manuel. 1999. "Integración y cohesión: La experiencia europea." Paper prepared for the Sixth Montevideo Circle Meeting, Santo Domingo, Dominican Republic (November).

McLaren, John.1997. "Size, Sunk Costs, and Judge Bowker's Objection to Free Trade." *American Economic Review* 87: 400–20.

Monteagudo, Josefina, and Masakazu Watanuki. 2002. "Evaluating Agricultural Reform Under the FTAA and MERCOSUR-EU FTA for Latin America: A Quantitative CGE Assessment." Inter-American Development Bank, Washington, DC (October). Photocopy.

Moreno-Brid, Juan Carlos. 2002. "Por qué fue tan bajo el crecimiento económico de América Latina en los noventa? Una interpretación estructuralista." Mexico City. Photocopy.

Nogués, Julio J. 1993. "Social Costs and Benefits of Introducing Patent Protection for Pharmaceutical Drugs in Developing Countries." *Developing Economies* 31 (1): 24–53.

Ocampo, José Antonio. 2001. "Raúl Prebisch and the Development Agenda at the Dawn of the Twenty-First Century." *CEPAL Review* (75): 25–40.

———. 2002. "Small Economies in the Phase of Globalization." Third William G. Demas Memorial Lecture.

———. 2003. "Capital Account and Counter-Cyclical Prudential Regulations in Developing Countries." In *Capital Flows to Emerging Markets since the Asian Crisis*, edited by R. Ffrench-Davis and S. Griffith-Jones. Santiago and Helsinki: Economic Commission for Latin America and the Caribbean and World Institute for Development Economics Research.

Ocampo, José Antonio, and Camilo Tovar. 1998. "Capital Flows, Savings and Investment in Colombia, 1990–96." In *Capital Flows and Investment Performance: Lessons from Latin America*, edited by Ricardo French-Davis and Helmut Reisen. Paris and Santiago: Economic Commission for Latin America and the Caribbean–OECD Development Centre.

———. 1999. "Price-Based Capital Account Regulations: The Colombian Experience." Financiamiento del Desarrollo Series no. 87 (LC/L.1262-P) (October). Economic Commission for Latin American and the Caribbean, Santiago, Chile.

Primo Braga, Carlos, Carsten Fink, and Claudia Paz Sepúlveda. 2000. "Intellectual Property Rights and Economic Development." World Bank Discussion Paper no. 412, Washington, DC.

Puerto Rico Planning Board. 1999–2000. "Economic Report to the Governor." Commonwealth of Puerto Rico, Office of the Governor, San Juan.

Rodríguez, Francisco, and Dani Rodrik. 2001. "Trade Policy and Economic Growth: A Skeptic's Guide to the Cross-National Evidence." In *National Bureau of Economic Research Macroeconomics*, edited by Ben S. Bernanke and Kenneth Rogoff. Cambridge, MA: MIT Press.

Rodrik, Dani.1997. *Has Globalization Gone Too Far?* Washington, DC: Institute for International Economics, Washington, DC.

———. 2001. "The Global Governance of Trade as if Development Really Mattered." Report prepared for the United Nations Development Programme (UNDP), Trade and Sustainable Human Development Project, Geneva. Photocopy.

Ros, Jaime. 2000. *Development Theory and The Economics of Growth*. Michigan: University of Michigan Press.

Santiago, Carlos E. 1992. *Labor in the Puerto Rican Economy*. New York: Praeger Publishers.

Slaughter, Matthew J. 2001. "Trade Liberalization and Per Capita Income Convergence: A Difference-in-Differences Analysis." *Journal of International Economics* 55: 203–28.

Sum, Andrew, Neeta Fogg, and Paul Harrington. 2002. "Immigrant Workers and the Great American Job Machine: The Contributions of New Foreign Immigration to National and Regional Labor Force Growth in the

1990s." Paper prepared for the National Business Roundtable, Northeastern University, Washington, DC, November.

United Nations Conference on Trade and Development (UNCTAD). 1994. "The Outcome of the Uruguay Round: An Initial Assessment." Supporting Papers to the Trade and Development Report.

———. 1999. "Special and Differential Treatment in the Millennium Round." *World Economy* 22, (8): 1095–117.

Whalley, John. 1996. "Why do Countries Seek Regional Trade Agreements?" National Bureau of Economic Research Working Paper Series no. 5552, Cambridge, MA.

Winters, L. Alan. 2002. "Doha and the World Poverty Targets." Paper presented at the Annual Bank Conference on Developments Economics, World Bank, Washington, DC, April.

World Bank. 2002. "Globalization, Growth, and Poverty." World Bank Policy Research Report, Washington, DC.

Notes

The authors wish to thank participants in the IDB/INTAL-Harvard University Forum, and particularly Jorge Chami Batista for comments, as well as Rex García for assistance in the preparation of the manuscript.

1 The rebirth of integration in the region, marked by the creation of the Southern Common Market (MERCOSUR) in 1991, was accompanied by a proliferation of bilateral free trade agreements and by new impetus in the region's older subregional agreements, the Central American Common Market (CACM), the Andean Community (CAN), and the Caribbean Community and Common Market (CARICOM).

2 The shift in United States' trade policy from multilateralism to a multilevel approach, which took place in 1985 when President Reagan instructed trade negotiators to explore regional and bilateral agreements, was key to the reemergence of regional initiatives worldwide.

3 See, for example, Monteagudo and Watanaki (2002).

4 U.S. unilateral preference schemes include the Caribbean Basin Economic Recovery Act of 1983, the Andean Trade Preference Act of 1991, and, more recently, the Caribbean Basin Trade Partnership Act of 2000.

5 Differential treatment within trade arrangements to address asymmetries in levels of development and size has traditionally included five types of provisions: time-limited derogations from obligations and longer periods for implementing obligations; more favorable thresholds for undertaking certain commitments; flexibility in obligations and procedures; other commitments and best-endeavor clauses; and technical assistance and advice. See UNCTAD (1994).

6 See, for instance, Ocampo (2001) and Whalley (1999).

7 The latter include those schemes mentioned in note 3, as well as the Lomé (now Cotonou) Convention, among others.

8 See Primo Braga, Fink, and Sepúlveda (2000). Moreover, as in the experience of Argentina with TRIPS implementation, while there is no guarantee that benefits will be secured, the costs can be quite high. Nogués (1993) estimated that the transfer from Argentine consumers to foreign producers would be about US$425 million per year (17 percent of the value of patented pharmaceuticals sold in Argentina in 1999).

9 By contrast, neoclassical trade theory postulates that when a small country liberalizes trade with a large one the gains flow disproportionately to the former since the small country will undergo relatively larger changes in its price structure and obtain greater gains on account of the reallocation of production and consumption.

10 This section draws from ECLAC (2002a).

11 See Amsden (2001); Akyüz, Chang, and Kozul-Wright (1998); and Chang (2001).

12 For an analysis of capital-surge management in Chile and Colombia, see French-Davis and Tapia (2001); Ocampo (2003); and Ocampo and Tovar (1998, 1999).

13 On the other hand, smallness is also associated with advantages, for example, that of greater social cohesion. Ocampo (2002) explores the advantages and disadvantages of size, focusing on the Caribbean economies.

14 By the 1990s Puerto Rico provided 50 percent of U.S. pharmaceutical imports and close to 25 percent of the worldwide demand for drug products.

15 See Hausmann (1995), who pointed to the strong correlation of net federal transfers with the business cycle from 1960 to 1993.

16 For an analysis of Puerto Rico's insufficient creation of employment see Santiago (1992). A wage policy more adapted to Puerto Rico's factor endowments and a larger proportion of local capital in manufacturing investment might have produced a somewhat more balanced economy in Puerto Rico, capable of absorbing a bigger share of the labor force.

17 On this controversy, see Baumol and Wolff (1996) and Dietz (2001). A major issue in the debate is the sustainability of Puerto Rico's development strategy.

18 The president of Mexico made particular reference in Quebec to a cohesion fund, and a number of prime ministers from the Caribbean drew attention to the importance of integration funds. The government of Ecuador, which coordinated the negotiations until November 2002, later proposed that a fund be established to promote competitiveness.

19 In NAFTA, the movement of natural persons is limited to business personnel.

20 The effects of increasing temporary workers' permits in industrial countries by 3 percent of their current skilled and unskilled forces would produce economic benefits exceeding US$150 billion per year, compared with those of US$66 billion for complete goods-trade liberalization, shared between developed and developing countries.

23

The FTAA's Impact on Democratic Governance

Mark Barenberg and Peter Evans

The FTAA's consequences for governance in the hemisphere are likely to be at least as significant as its effects on the flow of goods and capital. Yet, policy analysts focus on projected changes in such economic flows, largely ignoring the potentially profound effects on governance. This chapter seeks to redress the balance. It outlines some of the likely features of the FTAA's governance provisions and assesses their implications for democratic governance, the rule of law, and state capacities to promote equitable economic development in the hemisphere.

Introduction

Governance institutions are the rules, practices, and organizations that enable societies to deliberate about what goals are desirable, make choices about the set of norms and administrative apparatuses that will best realize those goals, implement those choices, adjudicate disputes regarding implementation, and engage in reflexive evaluation, experimentation, and transformation of the institutions. As economic historians such as Douglass North (1981; 1986; 1990) have shown, differences in the quality of these institutions provide the best historical explanations for differential rates of economic growth. There is also consensus in the Western hemisphere that governance institutions must be democratic.[1] Most would agree that the long-run requirements of economic prosperity include some desirable conceptions of democratic governance, the rule of law, and adequate state capacity.[2]

An FTAA will provide the beginnings of "constitutive ground rules" for hemispheric governance, whether intended or unintended.[3] Therefore, three of the most important questions that must be asked of an FTAA are: Will it make the governance institutions of the hemisphere more or less democratic? Will it promote a desirable conception of the rule of law? And will it strengthen state capacities to promote equitable economic development?

The next section of this chapter examines the threshold question: What are the new governance arrangements that the proposed FTAA will likely put in place? Based on the text and negotiating history of the prospective FTAA, we find that current NAFTA institutions, especially those generated by Chapter 11 on investor rights, are likely to form the core of FTAA governance. Political contention over the extension of Chapter 11 to the hemisphere is indicated both by recent U.S. congressional debates and by open disagreement within the hemispheric business community.[4] Contributing to this debate is one of the principal practical aims of this chapter.

The third section then outlines the chief substantive and procedural features of NAFTA's Chapter 11 and explains why the implications of that provision for large-scale governance must be taken seriously, even at this early stage of regional integration.[5] The core of our analysis is presented in the fourth section, which shows that Chapter 11 institutions suffer severe deficits in democracy, the rule of law, and administrative effectiveness. Notwithstanding these deficits, Chapter 11 tribunals have installed at the regional level several fundamental principles of the pre–New Deal regulatory state in the United States, even though democratic contests at the domestic level have recently rejected precisely that restoration of the *laissez-faire* "constitution in exile." The NAFTA model similarly imposes sanctions against constitutive, democratic regulatory practices in Mexico and Canada and, if extended to the hemisphere, would override analogous norms in Argentina, Brazil, and other countries.

Opening debate about regional institutions that might have positive consequences for democratic governance, the rule of law, and state capacity is an equally important objective of this chapter. The fifth section begins that task. In search of such positive models, we turn to the labor side agreement of NAFTA. In spite of its drastic shortcomings, the side agreement in principle encourages improvements in, rather than supplanting, domestic social rights. We offer broad principles for strengthening the weak machinery of the side agreement and for generating robust, institutionalized multiparty input into its formally democratic component.

Based on our analysis of the operation of the governance provisions embodied in NAFTA, we conclude that the prospective FTAA will likely have a negative effect on democracy, the rule of law, and state capacities in the hemisphere—unless prospective FTAA governance institutions, *and the crucial process of negotiating those institutions*, are deeply revised.

What Governance Provisions are Likely to be Included in the FTAA?

The content of the FTAA's governance provisions will not be known until the treaty is fully drafted and made public. By then it will likely be too late to subject them to real deliberation and debate. We must therefore look to the currently available evidence of the eventual governance provisions.

In the most recent draft of the FTAA, which was made public after the November 2002 Quito ministerial meeting, the key governance provisions remain in brackets, indicating that they have not yet been finalized. Within those brackets, the existing text of NAFTA Chapter 11 is replicated, together with potential incremental revisions that, even if adopted, would not alter the basic structure of the Chapter 11 model.

While the character of the negotiating process does not necessarily predict the content of the outcome, the history of that process is also consistent with the replication of the NAFTA model.[6] Over the eight years since the thirty-four governments participating in the first Summit of the Americas agreed to negotiate a hemispheric trade treaty in December of 1994 there have been eight ministerial meetings. The composition of the U.S. negotiating team reflects that of other countries: seventeen of the twenty-one negotiators come from the office of the USTR itself.[7] The composition is very similar to the teams that negotiated NAFTA—appointed officials with strictly economic portfolios. There is no participation by elected representatives or appointed officials whose mandate encompasses broad issues of democratic governance.

From the beginning of the FTAA process there were strenuous requests by a variety of civil society groups to gain access to the negotiating process. All were rejected.[8] Requests merely to see the bracketed draft text of the agreement were denied until after the tumultuous demonstrations in Quebec in the spring of 2001. The Committee of Government Representatives on the Participation of Civil Society was finally created in 1998, three years after ministerial meetings commenced. The Committee's process, however, consisted essentially of a suggestion box and was widely perceived as a "slap in the face" to civil society organizations (CSOs).[9] More recent efforts to increase the role of civil society, such as the first regional forum on the FTAA held in Merida in July 2002, appear to be grudging acknowledgements of a public relations problem rather than real efforts to engage civil society groups.[10] To be sure, the Quito ministerial meeting did see the first face to face meeting of ministers and representatives of CSOs, but it was a symbolic confrontation rather than a substantive discussion.

There is one notable exception to the exclusionary character of the FTAA negotiating process. The Business Forum of the Americas met for the first time in July 1995, immediately following the first Trade Ministerial Meeting. The forum met prior to each ministerial meeting, including the most recent one in Quito, at the same locale as, and with ample access to, the official negotiators. Prior to its first meeting, President Clinton's deputy commerce undersecretary publicly stated, "We expect the business people to get together on a sector-by-sector basis and come up with directions for the government in terms of what needs to be done in terms of free trade and immigration."[11] While it is difficult to quantify the Business Forum's influence on the ministerial meetings, the forum's post-ministerial effusions suggest that the mutual expectations of negotiators and lobbyists were not disappointed.[12]

The negotiating history, then, gives little reason to expect that FTAA governance provisions will deviate substantially from the NAFTA model in the absence of a significant political reconfiguration. Those provisions may, however, more tightly align with the proposals of the transnational business lobby represented by the Business Forum of the Americas. This calls for analysis of the way the NAFTA model has begun to reshape regional and domestic institutions of governance.[13]

The NAFTA (and Prospective FTAA) Model of Governance

Many features of the NAFTA architecture affect the processes and substance of governance. This section describes only NAFTA's investment and labor provisions. These two sets of provisions, however, have particularly salient impact on governance, and not surprisingly are among the most politically controversial features of NAFTA. More important for the purposes of our inquiry, NAFTA's investment and labor provisions embody divergent models of regional and domestic governance. These models are analyzed in parts 4 and 5 of this chapter.

NAFTA's Investment Provisions

Chapter 11 of NAFTA sets forth substantive and procedural protections for foreign investment. These include the most comprehensive disciplines afforded foreign investors in any multilateral investment agreement (Brand and Zamora 1990; Dolzer and Stevens 1995).[14]

The Substantive Protections Afforded Foreign Investors

Part A of Chapter 11 enumerates the substantive disciplines imposed on NAFTA signatory states. Investors are entitled to compensation for governmental measures that: accord foreign investors less favorable treatment than domestic investors (under the "national treatment standard" of Article 1102); accord foreign investors of one state less favorable treatment than foreign investors of other states (under the "most-favored-nation standard" of Article 1103); fail to afford investors minimum standards of "fair and equitable treatment and full protection and security" as defined by international law (under the "minimum international standards" of Article 1105); impose certain enumerated performance requirements on foreign investments (under Article 1106); or expropriate the investment whether "directly or indirectly" or by any measure "tantamount to expropriation" (under Article 1110).[15]

NAFTA arbitrators' interpretations of these broad investor protections are discussed below. Investors have brought Chapter 11 cases demanding government compensation for such government regulations as: the California governor's phase-out of the gasoline additive MTBE; a Mississippi trial court's verdict in commercial litigation; a Mexican state governor's designation of an ecological zone; the Canadian Pest Management Authority's ban on the hazardous pesticide lindane; British Columbia's regulation of fresh-water exports; and the Canadian minister of the environment's regulation of PCB wastes in order to conform with the Basel Convention, a multilateral treaty on the movement of hazardous wastes.

To date, investors have filed more than thirty claims under NAFTA Chapter 11, and arbitrators have rendered opinions in approximately one-third of those cases. Such a relatively small number of claims and opinions cannot give definitive guidance about the domestic regulations that might ultimately be subject to successful NAFTA challenges. Nonetheless, the cases point to the key questions that NAFTA tribunals will likely address and the range of substantive decisions they will likely render.[16]

The small number of Chapter 11 cases does not fully capture the practical impact of that provision. As a historical matter, large-scale transformations in domestic governance have at times been inaugurated by similarly small numbers of landmark cases. One important example—the so-called Lochner Era of *laissez-faire* governance in the United States—bears a close resemblance to the emerging architecture of governance reflected in the Chapter 11 cases. This resemblance is discussed below.

The high-profile claims brought under Chapter 11 have also triggered (and legitimated) copycat claims under similar provisions among the more than 1800 bilateral investment treaties now in force.[17] In addition, investors now routinely threaten to file Chapter 11 claims to apply lobbying pressure against North American governments promulgating or enforcing regulations (Mann 2002: 28). Strategic uses of Chapter 11 played significant roles in campaigns that successfully turned back major regulatory initiatives, such as Canada's proposed regulation of cigarette packaging and of the gasoline additive MMT. According to North American legislators and administrators, the possibility that investors will bring Chapter 11 claims against the public fisc has a chilling effect on new social and economic regulation, even in the absence of actual or threatened claims.

Procedures for Investor-State Claims

Rights under international law are generally held by states and enforceable by states; claims under international law are therefore typically "state to state." NAFTA's investment provisions are a departure from that norm. Section B of Chapter 11 creates an investor-state dispute mechanism (ISDM). Through that mechanism, a private investor of one signatory state may submit to arbitration a claim that another state has violated its substantive obligations under section A. A successful claimant receives monetary compensation.

Investors may bring their NAFTA claims under one of three arbitral regimes affiliated with the World Bank or the United Nations.[18] Each of the three systems has its own broad arbitration procedures, which were originally developed for resolution of commercial disputes between private enterprises. Within those broad procedures, each NAFTA tribunal is free to devise its own rules of procedure and evidence.

NAFTA establishes neither a standing body of independent judges nor a system of appellate review.[19] Each ISDM tribunal is an ad hoc body composed of three arbitrators, one selected by each of the two disputing parties and the third confirmed by agreement among the parties (Article 1123). Since a majority of two arbitrators suffices to make an authoritative award, it is possible that a ruling will be reached exclusively by arbitrators that the private investor has selected or confirmed. Arbitrators are not bound to follow the precedents of earlier NAFTA decisions (Article 1136(1)). The arbitrators are typically international lawyers and are paid by the disputing parties. Their fees and expenses may total millions of dollars.

None of the three arbitration systems allows public access to oral hearings. The decision of whether to disclose documents containing substantive evidence and legal argument is left to the discretion of each tribunal and the parties to the cases. Based on the text of NAFTA and of the three arbitral systems, therefore, there is no assurance that the public will learn of all NAFTA proceedings or obtain full documentation.[20]

NAFTA's Labor Side Agreement

NAFTA itself includes no provisions on labor rights. However, the United States insisted on negotiation of a side agreement on labor—the North American Agreement on Labor Cooperation (NAALC)—in an effort to ensure congressional approval of NAFTA. For purposes of this chapter, the following features of the NAALC are noteworthy.

First, the NAALC requires each signatory state to effectively enforce its domestic labor laws and to strive to improve those laws, but imposes no supranational labor rights. Second, the NAALC permits private parties, such as worker representatives, to request that the NAALC Commission initiate inquiries about whether a signatory state has failed to effectively enforce its domestic labor laws. The three-member NAALC Commission is composed of the ministers of labor of each signatory state.

Third, the commission has discretion to decide whether the inquiry will move through the three remedial phases provided by the NAALC. The three phases are: *consultation* among the three ministers of labor; a *report* by a committee of experts; and *arbitration* by tribunalists chosen by NAFTA states. Private parties have no venue to seek an order requiring consultation, expert reporting, or arbitration of any NAALC dispute.

Fourth, the NAALC provides that disputes over a state's effective enforcement of rights of association and collective bargaining may not proceed beyond the consultative phase, regardless of whether the commissioners wish to exercise their discretion to do so. Disputes over employment discrimination, forced labor, and immigrant worker rights may not proceed beyond an expert committee. Only disputes over child labor, minimum wages, and occupational safety and health may proceed to arbitration. To date, the NAALC Commission has not exercised its discretion to move any inquiry beyond the consultative phase. That is, there has been no expert report or arbitration under the NAALC.

There are manifest asymmetries between the protections afforded to investors in Chapter 11 and those afforded to workers in the NAALC. The implications for governance are explored below.

Implications of Chapter 11 for Democratic Governance, Administrative Capacity, and the Rule of Law

In their interpretations of the substantive disciplines of Chapter 11, NAFTA arbitrators have announced rules that override constitutive institutions of governance in the United States, Canada, and Mexico and would, if extended geographically, override analogous regimes in other countries in the hemisphere. We use the term "constitutive institutions" to denote fundamental frameworks for economic and social regulation, whether entrenched in constitutional law, statutory regimes, or informal practice. Constitutive domestic institutions are typically forged in periods of intense public debate and popular political mobilization. The scope, content, and normative implications of the new Chapter 11 rules are described in the following points.

The Scope of Chapter 11 Disciplines

It is true that Chapter 11 is merely one of the several textual provisions through which NAFTA attempts to restructure markets and affect substantive law making by signatory states. But the rulings of NAFTA arbitrators have given great sweep to Chapter 11. Indeed, two of the most prominent Chapter 11 rulings would impose the substantive disciplines of Chapter 11 on all significant social and economic regulations by domestic governments and allow private parties to enforce those disciplines against government regulations affecting not only property rights but also flows of trade, effectively extending Chapter 11's jurisdiction to all the core provisions of NAFTA.

In one case, a U.S. lumber company, Pope & Talbot, claimed that the Canadian government expropriated its investment in Canada by unfairly allocating quotas among companies exporting softwood into the U.S. market. (Canada imposed and allocated the export quotas in order to conform to the U.S.-Canada Softwood Lumber Agreement.) The NAFTA tribunal agreed with the company's argument that its "market share" and its "access to the U.S. market" are property interests protected against expropriation by Article 1110.[21]

The definition of "investment" established by the Pope & Talbot case expands the general reach of Chapter 11 protections in the two fundamental ways set forth above. Under familiar legal doctrine, the category of governmental measures that affect cross-border market share or market access may include almost all intrastate economic and social regulation.[22] Hence, this definition of investment extends Chapter 11 disciplines to almost all domestic regulations.

The Pope & Talbot definition of investment also brings almost all claims related to NAFTA's core trade protections within the ambit of investors' power to bring private claims against states under the Chapter 11 machinery. Recall that once an interest in the cross-border flow of goods is recognized as a Chapter 11 interest, that interest is protected not only against expropriation under Article 1110 but also against discriminatory and unfair treatment in the same way that such flows are protected by the core rules of free trade—protected, that is, by the national treatment standard (by virtue of Article 1102), by the most-favored-nation standard (Article 1103), and by international minimum standards (Article 1105). After the Pope & Talbot case, private investors can challenge any intrastate regulation on the ground that it affects cross-border trade in a way that violates one of these standards.

A second prominent case reinforces Pope & Talbot's drastic expansion of the scope of Chapter 11 governance. In the S. D. Meyers case, the claimant was a U.S. corporation that processes hazardous PCBs in the United States. S. D. Meyers challenged Canada's ban on the export of PCB waste from Canada to the United States. Canada's minister of the environment imposed the ban for the stated purposes of protecting public health and the environment and complying with the multilateral Basel Convention on the transboundary movement of hazardous wastes. The Chapter 11 tribunal interpreted the national treatment standard of Article 1102 to impose the most stringent legal test on Canada's regulation of PCB waste—the so-called "necessity test," discussed in the next section. The tribunal based this interpretation, in part, on unspecified "language" and "case law" arising out of the "WTO family of agreements" and on general principles of "open trade."[23] The tribunal also ruled that S. D. Meyers was an "investor" within the meaning of Chapter 11, although the U.S. company's only economic interest was its access to cross-border flows of PCBs from Canada.[24] As in Pope & Talbot, then, the tribunal incorporated the most stringent rules of trade law into the protections of Chapter 11, authorized private parties to enforce those rules based on the parties' interest not in property rights but in cross-border trade, and thereby extended Chapter 11's private enforcement to almost all social and economic regulations.

The Content of Chapter 11 Disciplines

Constraints on Economic and Social Regulation under the National Treatment Standard

Some prominent critics of Chapter 11 maintain that the national treatment standard is the most defensible of its provisions, not least because its interpretation is relatively uncontested. The NAFTA cases suggest, to the contrary, that the national treatment standard is subject to elastic interpretation that may impose rigorous tests on domestic regulation—tests that override long-established deference to social regulation under domestic law throughout the hemisphere.[25]

NAFTA tribunals have ruled that governments may regulate only in ways that are "necessary" to achieve "legitimate" government purposes through regulatory measures that are "least restrictive" of cross-border commerce and investment. For example, the S. D. Meyers tribunal required that Canada's minister of the environment choose the means of regulating hazardous waste that is least restrictive of the property and commercial rights protected by NAFTA investment provisions and by unspecified concepts of "open trade."

In order to apply the "necessity test" in a rigorous fashion, an arbitral tribunal faces three tasks: defining precisely the environmental or social objectives that are *legitimately* pursued by a domestic government,[26] detailing the *alternative imaginable policy instruments* that technically advance those objectives, and determining which of the instruments achieves the multidimensional objectives with the least intrusion on the equally multidimensional interests of investors and of "open trade."[27]

In adopting the stringent "necessity test," the NAFTA arbitrators foreclose an alternative standard—familiar throughout the hemisphere—known as the "rationality test." Since the constitutional revolution of the New Deal, the U.S. Supreme Court upholds a regulatory measure so long as it is a rational means to serve any legitimate public purpose.[28] In broad outlines, the current U.S. ground rules are similar to those in many other regimes in the Western hemisphere, including Mexico, Argentina, Brazil, and Chile.[29] The post–New Deal courts explicitly have declined to enter into the more probing inquiry of whether there are alternative means of fulfilling important government objectives that may have less impact on rights of property and contract than the regulatory measures chosen by legislatures or administrators.

The rationality test embodies two pillars of modern regulatory states. First, determinations made by the elected branches about the relative importance of policy goals and the relative effectiveness of regulatory instruments to serve those goals are not supplanted by the subsequent value determinations and factual assessments of unelected arbiters. Second, constitutional ground rules do not subordinate social and personal rights to property rights and unregulated markets. The substantive balance between social rights and property rights is not constitutionally foreclosed but is instead left to the play of "ordinary" democratic politics.[30]

Chapter 11 tribunals have rejected this foundation of contemporary governance and imposed the stricter, pre–New Deal standard of review of social and economic regulation—in the name, explicitly, of free commerce and investment.

Constricted Discretion of Regulatory Bodies under Minimum International Standards

Chapter 11 arbitrators have required that governments compensate investors when regulatory bodies exercise "excessive" discretion even when those bodies have not acted arbitrarily and have been empowered by the highest sovereign authorities to exercise such discretion. NAFTA tribunals thereby have overruled the domestic resolution of intense political contests over the discretionary authority of regulatory bodies in the modern state.

In the Metalclad case, for example, a Mexican municipal government denied the U.S.-based Metalclad Corporation a permit to develop and operate a hazardous-waste landfill, and a Mexican state governor declared that the landfill was located in an area designated for ecological protection. The Mexican government submitted its sovereign opinion that the local governments had acted within their constitutional jurisdiction. Although Chapter 11 imposes no requirement that arbitrators have any knowledge of the domestic law of the NAFTA states, the Metalclad arbitrators substituted their own view of Mexican constitutionalism.[31] The Metalclad tribunal found that the Mexican government violated minimum international standards, under Article 1105, by failing to provide sufficient predictability and certainty to Metalclad. The tribunal found, in effect, that Chapter 11 requires the Mexican federal government to constrain the regulatory discretion of state and local authorities, even though the Mexican government opposed such constraints.[32]

In the countries under consideration, the division of labor between legislators and administrative regulators is a central question of national and subnational governance.[33] The issue is fought at the level of both constitutional and ordinary politics. At the level of ordinary politics, the issue of administrative capacity arises in innumerable national, state, and provincial contests over legislation and executive decrees that define the authority of regulatory agencies overall, the structure and authority of particular agencies, and the governance mechanisms for supervising and disciplining the agencies. These matters constitute the politics of "administrative law," which, although little known beyond political elites and the legal profession, is critical to the governance of the modern regulatory state.

At the level of constitutional politics, a crucial aspect of the New Deal transformation in governance was the U.S. Supreme Court's abandonment of the so-called nondelegation doctrine. That doctrine curtailed the regulatory state by prohibiting Congress from authorizing administrative agencies to exercise broad, as opposed to tightly constrained, discretion in making and implementing regulatory rules.[34] Mexican constitutional jurisprudence also rejects the nondelegation doctrine. It is precisely this doctrine that has reemerged in NAFTA tribunals' requirement that governments compensate investors when regulatory bodies exercise excessively broad discretion even when acting pursuant to sovereign authorization.

Expansive Compensation of Investors for Regulatory Expropriations

Chapter 11 tribunals have pronounced new doctrines that give investors greater protections than those afforded by domestic laws on regulatory expropriations. The tribunals have enlarged the definition of property protected against expropriation and diminished the degree of regulation necessary to require compensation of affected property holders.

In the Metalclad case, for example, the NAFTA tribunal ruled that the Mexican government's failure to compensate Metalclad constituted an indirect expropriation, which it defined in broad terms: "[E]xpropriation under NAFTA includes . . . covert or incidental interference with the use of property which has the effect of depriving the owner, in whole or in significant part, of the use of reasonably-to-be-expected economic benefit of a property."[35]

When this test is combined with the definition of "investment" pronounced in the Pope & Talbot case, a government must compensate a private enterprise on the mere demonstration that some government measure has *partially* deprived the enterprise of some *expected* gain in *imports, exports*, or *market share*. These protections for property exceed those provided by the United States Supreme Court. Recent, highly visible domestic legislative initiatives sought but failed to gain the expanded property rights now installed by Chapter 11 arbitrators.[36]

The potential effect of NAFTA's expanded doctrine of regulatory expropriation is not limited to compensation for discrete regulatory decisions. The logic of the doctrine applies to entire regulatory programs now taken for granted in welfare states. Leading theorists of the expanded doctrine insist that it would, for example, require compensation to all employers who must conform to the rights of worker association codified in domestic statutes, such as legislation that prohibits employers from firing workers who wish to organize a labor union (Epstein 1985). Only the political pragmatism of the lawyers serving as Chapter 11 arbitrators limits such radical implementation of the doctrine of regulatory expropriation. Their formal mandate does not.[37]

Chapter 11's Reshaping of the Process of Governance

Reshaping the Rule of Law and Administrative Capacities

There is no single understanding of the rule of law or its virtues. One understanding, embodying the virtues of predictability and fairness, is simple uniformity and transparency in the application of rules to similar factual settings (Hart 1961). A second is comprehensiveness, in the sense that gaps in existing rules are predictably filled by new rules based on more general principles and policies that are discernable in existing rules (Dworkin 1977). A third is adaptivity or experimentalism—the notion that rules will evolve over time through coherent, well-considered adaptation of rules to social problems or through experimental innovation in the rule structure. This third conception embodies the ideals not only of common law judges but of flexible, well-trained administrative bodies with jurisdiction over entire subject matters of social regulation—ideals which blur into the virtues of a legislative rule-*making*, as distinguished from a judicial rule-*applying*, body (Dorf and Sabel 1998).[38]

The Chapter 11 dispute mechanism is ill suited to implement any of these understandings of the rule of law and administrative capacity. In addition to the more obvious failures of transparency and due process, NAFTA tribunals are not required to follow the precedent of earlier tribunals. If the tribunals were drawn from a standing tribunal, then one might expect that tribunals would de facto rely on the reasoning of earlier tribunals. NAFTA tribunals, however, are composed by the parties' ad hoc selection of arbitrators. Further, the tribunal members are generally private-sector lawyers drawn from many countries. They are untrained and unsocialized in the ways of professional judges or in any one, consistent jurisprudential tradition outside of international law. They need not be trained in economic, environmental, labor, health, or other fields of social regulation, although, as described above, they claim the authority to make sensitive decisions about which means of regulation are most effective at achieving regulatory ends with least restriction on investment and market processes.

In light of this ad hoc procedural framework, economic and social actors cannot expect uniform application of rules protecting investors and markets and of constraints on economic, social, and environmental regulation. Actors also cannot expect comprehensive application of rules. Gaps in the structure of rules about investment, market processes, and various fields of regulation are unlikely to be filled by new rules based on a coherent body of economic or social principles that inhere in existing rules.

The failure of the ISDM to satisfy rule-of-law virtues is ironic. NAFTA's Chapter 11 tribunals are intended, among other things, to provide foreign investors with an adjudicatory mechanism that is superior to Mexico's weak judiciary. The ISDM allows North American investors to circumvent domestic courts, whether robust or fragile, and protect their interests through procedures that do not instantiate the rule of law. As a regional model of dispute resolution, then, the ISDM may diminish rather than enhance the quality of justice.

The deficiencies of the ISDM framework are even more severe, measured by the standards of administrative capacity, especially adaptability and experimentalism. The NAFTA Chapter 11 tribunals exercise authority to review and, in a real sense, supplant the functioning of administrative agencies and legislatures. Individual NAFTA tribunals lack the continuity, expertise, comprehensive purview of subject matter, and political accountability to carry out those functions effectively and legitimately.

Crucially, the tribunals are empowered to render decisions in the discredited command-and-control or "policing" style of regulation. That is, the arbitrators' brute monetary penalty against state activity is not embedded in a network of dialogue and learning among actors who must bear the consequences at the regional, national, and subnational levels. The tribunals' nontransparent proceedings and ad hoc decisions mark a closure of regulatory discussion rather than promotion of an ongoing process of regulatory capacity building for wider strategies of economic development and fair distribution of its fruits.

Reshaping Federalism

To the extent that participatory democracy is a value that is realized in the authority of subnational government, it is diminished in the NAFTA model of governance. All three NAFTA signatory states are federal states, as are Brazil, Argentina, and other potential FTAA members. The degree of centralization in domestic administrative bodies is, of course, a significant question of governance even in states that are not formally federalist. At least four features of the NAFTA model encourage centralization or otherwise unthinkingly reshape the contours of domestic federalism.

First, the NAFTA tribunals' application of the national treatment standard has diminished the capacity of subnational governments to regulate for the public welfare. In the S. D. Myers case, for example, the tribunal ruled that Canada violated the national treatment standard by implementing a regulation, based largely on the regulation's disproportionate *effect* on cross-border commerce. This test is much more strict than analogous United States domestic law that defines the national "common market" among the fifty states. Under the commerce clause of the U.S. constitution, a state is permitted to impose regulations that disproportionately affect interstate commerce, so long as the benefit to intrastate welfare outweighs the burden on commerce.[39]

Second, NAFTA is, of course, an interstate treaty. The authority to negotiate such treaties is vested in national governments and is explicitly excluded from state and provincial governments as a constitutional matter. To the extent that such treaty making imposes new constitutive ground rules, as illustrated above, it is a mode of large-scale reconstruction of regulatory frameworks that tends to diminish the role of popular mobilization and of the nonfederal bodies that are formally vested with authority to participate in such reconstruction.[40]

Third, national governments fashion laws and enforce policies to ensure domestic conformance with the constitutive transformations imposed by the NAFTA Chapter 11 regime. This marks a practical upward shift in the balance of actual lawmaking and administration about important political matters. Central governments must ensure conformance with the new protections for property holders and the new constraints on environmental, health, and labor regulation imposed by Chapter 11. To the extent that state, provincial, or local governments have implemented such regulatory programs, decentralized social and democratic rule making is corroded.

Fourth, and perhaps most important, each domestic regime attempts to fine-tune the multifaceted values underpinning the allocation of lawmaking authority among vertically divided levels of government.[41] NAFTA tribunals, comprised largely of private lawyers selected by and assessing the claims of private investors, are not well-suited to respect and elaborate the constitutive balance of federalist values fashioned by national and subnational governing bodies.[42]

Reshaping Multilateral Governance

NAFTA's pattern of privileging investment and trade rights over social and environmental interests is replicated at the level of regional and multilateral governance. Chapter 11's rights and remedies for broadly defined investments are robust enough to constitute international "hard law." That is, Chapter 11 affords investors several explicit supranational entitlements that exceed substantive domestic rights; provides investors with arbitral forums empowered to render authoritative judgments and to impose monetary awards; and empowers domestic courts to use their sovereign coercive power to enforce the awards after minimal substantive review.

The full effect of this multilateral regime of "hard law" for investors can be understood only against the backdrop of multilateral regimes of "soft law" in the areas of social, environmental, and human rights, such as the various multilateral environmental agreements, the U.N. Covenants on Human Rights and Social Rights, and the NAFTA labor side agreement.

The point is not merely that investor interests are afforded "better" rights, tribunals, and sanctions. In addition, investor regimes of hard law *interact* with the social regimes of soft law in a way that diminishes the latter. When Chapter 11 obligations conflict with environmental, labor, and human-rights obligations in soft-law instruments, signatory states' implementation of those instruments may be strictly constrained. One illustration, discussed above, is NAFTA's limitation of Canada's capacity to implement the Basel Convention on hazardous materials. Another is NAFTA's potential constraint on the NAALC, the labor side accord to NAFTA itself. We have seen that an expanded doctrine of regulatory takings may curtail domestic protection of labor rights, including the core right of worker association. It is therefore not true that NAFTA—including the NAALC's multilateral requirement that each country enforce existing domestic labor rights—leaves regional labor standards unchanged by multilateral rules. It may instead affirmatively diminish labor standards.

Hence, Chapter 11 rules and tribunals may undermine the long post–New Deal effort to promote social and environmental values through multilateral international law.

The Normative Significance of Chapter 11's Effect on Governance

The upshot of the preceding points is that Chapter 11 institutions suffer deficits in democratic legitimacy, rule of law, and administrative competence. Unelected, ad hoc arbitrators chosen *by* private investors to rule on the claims *of* private investors have been delegated the authority to preempt constitutive democratic frameworks for social and economic regulation at the national and subnational levels.

Interpreting the national treatment standard, Chapter 11 tribunals claim the authority to judge whether domestic regulation serves a legitimate purpose and whether there are alternative policy instruments that serve those purposes with lesser restriction of exceptionally broad concepts of secure property and open trade. Nothing in the NAFTA regime, however, ensures that the private lawyers who serve as Chapter 11 arbitrators have the economic or other technical proficiency to formulate such alternative policy instruments, to analyze the capacity of those instruments to achieve environmental or other social goals, or to assess their consequences for trade and investment.[43] The S. D. Meyers tribunal, for example, failed to engage in environmental or economic analysis. It simply asserted that Canada's democratically authorized environmental measures were not as well-suited to meet legitimate environmental goals as other (unspecified) measures. Chapter 11 arbitrators also patently lack the democratic accountability and legitimacy to inquire whether the government's social and environmental goals constitute legitimate public purposes. As already described, they are chosen and paid by private investors, hold hearings in closed session, make their own procedural rules, and do not release substantive evidentiary and legal documents to the public.

Interpreting minimum international standards, NAFTA arbitrators have restored the nondelegation doctrine of the pre–New Deal *laissez-faire* state, overriding profound democratic choices to delegate regulatory discretion to administrative agencies and subnational governments. Interpreting Chapter 11's expropriation provisions, NAFTA arbitrators have reversed the longstanding policy that the "polluter pays for externalities" and substituted the notion that "the public pays the polluter." This revision of domestic policies is mirrored at the multilateral level: Chapter 11's hard-law protections of property and trade eclipse soft-law protections of the environment and social rights embodied in multilateral instruments that are another hallmark of post–New Deal governance.

In sum, Chapter 11 has restored several crucial ground rules and policies of the pre–New Deal economic constitution, contradicting domestic settlements achieved after decades of sustained popular and elite political struggles.[44] There is no evidence that the three North American legislatures understood that they were delegating to ad hoc tribunals of private lawyers the authority to radically revise constitutive domestic governance in these ways.

Proponents of NAFTA—and its extension throughout the hemisphere—might object that this account is not of great normative interest since, to take the example of the United States, the president and the Congress duly negotiated and approved NAFTA and will presumably do the same respecting an FTAA. This objection would be misplaced, however, on at least three major grounds.

First, as a matter of U.S. constitutional law, international treaties can neither circumvent the structures of lawmaking codified in the constitution nor override constitutionally protected individual rights.[45] In negotiating and ratifying free trade agreements, the president and Congress follow a procedure known as the "congressional-executive agreement"—a procedure that patently fails to fulfill the requirements for amending the Constitution. Hence, NAFTA arbitrators' incursions on constitutional doctrines such as equal protection, federalism, and nondelegation are not necessarily legitimated by the fact that the president and Congress formally installed such arbitral power.

There is a second, broader point to be made. Substantive law-making can be divided into constitutive rule making, on the one hand, and the ordinary politics of legislative and executive rule making within the framework of constitutive ground rules on the other (cf. Ackerman 1991). Constitutive rules codify the settlement of arduous popular and elite mobilization over political fundamentals. These rules can be embodied either in the actual constitution—as occurred in the aftermaths of the U.S. revolution and civil war—or in statutory regimes that entrench basic patterns of interaction among civil society and the various branches of government—as in the New Deal.[46] Once such a vigilant period of "higher" rule making has given way to "ordinary" interest-group politics, the burden should not be casually shifted to those who seek to defend constitutive regulatory regimes against political end runs that fail to satisfy robust conceptions of democratic and transparent politics.

Hence, even if the rules of trade agreements were installed pursuant to formal legal requirements, the *normative* analysis of the process of treaty formation would not end there. We cannot presume that the political processes of the United States or other governments satisfy strong or even merely adequate standards of democratic governance simply because formal procedures have been followed.

Indeed, Chapter 11 itself assumes that NAFTA's signatory states, left to their own devices, may be incapable of assuring fair and effective governance in certain cross-border affairs by virtue of weak judiciaries or, more important, interest-group politics that may favor certain domestic business interests over other groups, foreign and domestic. There is no guarantee that, in the process of tying their own hands through interstate agreement, the NAFTA states rose above this fundamental flaw in democratic governance. To the contrary, as discussed above, U.S. corporate and financial elites have played an undemocratically disproportionate and nontransparent role in the crafting and ongoing defense of the prospective FTAA's exceptionally broad investor protections.

Finally, and perhaps most importantly, even if a trade agreement were negotiated through *processes* that were formally lawful and robustly democratic, the substantive *institutions* created or reshaped thereby—at the regional and domestic levels—are not immune from evaluation from the standpoints of democracy, rule of law, administrative capacity, economic efficiency, or other norms. To the contrary, the institutional consequences of NAFTA provide a rare social experiment that permits evaluation and proposals for reform prior to any extension of similar institutions throughout the hemisphere.

Could an FTAA Make Governance in the Hemisphere More Democratic?

There are, broadly speaking, four strategies for reform of the Chapter 11 regime as part of either a new NAFTA for the North American countries or a proposed FTAA for the hemisphere. These four strategies might be called "retrenchment," "juridification," "administrative capacity building," and "democratization."

The retrenchment strategy would simply eliminate Chapter 11—or would at most retain Chapter 11's national-treatment standard as the single protection for foreign investors, protecting them against discrimination relative to domestic investors.[47] This strategy rests on the view that Chapter 11's hard regime of expansive property rights not only curtails democratic domestic regulation but *inevitably* eclipses the soft multilateral instruments that ostensibly protect social rights and the environment. With no prospect in sight of "hardening" the latter instruments, the only solution is to retrench hard-law international protection for investor rights.

The juridification strategy aims to correct the rule-of-law and legitimacy deficiencies of the ISDM rather than eliminating it. This strategy would establish a standing tribunal, bound by *stare decisis,* to adjudicate Chapter 11 claims. The members of the tribunal would be chosen by and accountable to the sovereign states, not private investors. They would be well trained in the regulatory programs that, under Chapter 11's disciplines, must be accommodated with investor rights. The establishment of an appellate body to review the decisions of tribunals could strengthen the integrity and acceptability of ISDM decisions. Due-process values would be entrenched through requirements of transparency, rules of evidence, and procedures akin to other adjudicatory bodies. Signatory states could be empowered to screen investor claims when initially filed and reject those that conflict with policy objectives.

The tribunal's scope of action might even exceed case-by-case adjudication, extending to administrative rule making in order to coherently harmonize entire regulatory and investment programs and to reap the benefits of expertise, adaptability, and experimentation that come with administrative capabilities. In that event, the second strategy, juridification, would shift to the third strategy of building administrative capacity.[48] Both the second and third strategies could be combined with a fine-tuning of Chapter 11's substantive rules to redress the most egregious imbalances between investor and social rights.

The fourth strategy, democratization, starts by recognizing that decisions balancing the rights of investors and the rights of other stakeholders in social governance, including the public, are fundamentally political or value laden in nature. It is true that the third strategy—developing administrative capacity at the regional level—may be premised on this same recognition. The creation of a regional administrative body, however, is a technocratic solution to a political problem. Democratization promises legitimacy in decision making that the other three strategies, if implemented alone, cannot provide. Democratization is not incompatible with the fortification of regional administrative and judicial capacity but, to the contrary, may ensure its legitimacy and effectiveness.

But is there a plausible path of democratization at the regional level? And if there is such a path, could it strengthen rather than weaken democratic governance at the national and subnational levels? If the regional actors have the political will to implement multitiered democratic governance, there is in fact no shortage of institutional models. It is true that the architecture of regional democracy can only emerge from inclusive and sustained political debate or, indeed, from some novel form of regional "constitutional convention."[49] A blueprint cannot be handed down by hegemonic states and certainly not by academic drafters. But, drawing on working models, one can speculate about the broad contours of regional, multitiered democracy if only to establish, as a first step, that the design project is worth a second step. Many federal nation-states, as well as regional institutions such as the EU, grew by establishing federal regulatory structures that overarch the continuing, democratic governance of constituent states. The design features of these institutions provide a store of possibilities for North America and the Western hemisphere. More compelling, perhaps, is the fact that NAFTA itself contains some seeds of regional multitiered democracy.

The NAALC, in spite of its drastic shortcomings, is one source of architectural elements. First, in the NAALC, the signatory states commit themselves to improve their performance across a large set of social rights—rights of organizing, collective bargaining, the right to strike, antidiscrimination, the rights of immigrant workers, occupational safety and health, and so on. Although these rights are very broadly defined, they are in fact more specific than the four abstract "core labor rights" that most proponents of international labor rights wish to see inserted in multilateral agreements.

The breadth of these categories of rights is compensated by a second feature of the NAALC. Recall that the primary obligation imposed by the NAALC on signatory states is the duty to enforce existing labor rights under domestic law. This core obligation has drawn much criticism for the obvious reason that it creates no new supranational labor rights and therefore appears to add no new substantive duties to the states' preexisting labor law.

In fact, however, the NAALC's requirement that states "effectively enforce" their domestic labor law is a potentially powerful international standard. NAFTA's three signatory states have quite strong substantive rules of labor and employment in their existing codes and case law. However, at least two of the NAFTA states, the United States and Mexico, are notoriously lax in enforcing their existing laws. Significant strengthening of labor-rights enforcement in the United States and Mexico would very likely yield dramatic improvements in actual labor conditions—including substantial increases in new union organizing by workers exercising their rights of association (Barenberg 1994; Weiler 1983).

If effective enforcement offers a potentially powerful regional standard, effective enforcement *of existing law* is a standard with unexpected advantages as well. Notions such as core labor rights or other broad categories of rights are so abstract that they provide little real traction on behalf of social standards in the widely varying local contexts in which those rights are to be given specific content, especially within regional arrangements that encompass labor-relations systems and labor markets that differ markedly from one another.

The problem of deducing specific, applicable rules from abstract statements of rights or policies bedevils all systems of law and administration. For our purposes, workers' right of association offers one of innumerable illustrations. There is general agreement that this right is intended to encompass workers' capacity to organize unions. But the rules of union organizing and membership vary greatly across political and legal systems, and are equally greatly contested. Do such specific rules as those permitting closed shops, prehire agreements, or company provision of space and time for union activity violate or instead conform to workers' abstract right of association? If the answer to this question varies with local labor-relations context, does invocation of the phrase right of association help answer this finely textured inquiry?

In this light, the NAALC's dual requirement—that states commit themselves, first, to improve rights definition within broad categories of social rights and, second, to improve enforcement of domestic law within those categories—may not contain the worst of both worlds, as its detractors have insisted, but the best, at least as a seed of regional democracy. Domestic law provides a baseline of specific rules that are generally well adapted to national and subnational patterns of labor relations. Such a baseline is absent from supranational incantations of abstractions such as right of association.

At the same time, the signatory states' commitment to define rights more robustly has advantages similar to those embodied in the states' commitment more effectively to enforce domestic law. Both requirements lend themselves to supranational supervision and coordination that potentially "ratchet up" substantive rules and enforcement mechanisms from an insufficient, but locally well-defined, baseline.[50] In the process, regional oversight may strengthen rather than supplant local democratic capacities by building national and subnational *administrative capacities* to define and enforce well-specified social rights. At best, regional institutions may act as coordinating bodies that provide material and symbolic incentives for domestic governments to achieve improvements in defining and enforcing social rights in a race to the top with similarly situated governments across the hemisphere.

What, then, accounts for the negligible benefits that the NAALC has yielded? The answer lies, precisely, in its failure to provide robust juridical and administrative means of implementing its principles and standards on the one hand, and the weakness of its democratic architecture on the other. That is, the NAALC's procedural mechanisms, not its substantive standards, are the root of its deficiencies. Unlike the ISDM, the NAALC provides no judicial or administrative mechanism with the capacity to ensure remediation in the broad sense, just discussed, of improved local capacities to define and enforce social rights.

At the same time, the NAALC, unlike the ISDM, has a formally democratic component, its commission. This body has wide discretion to articulate and coordinate regional responses to a signatory state's failure to improve the definition and enforcement of its own labor rights. The commission, however, lacks the political will and democratic capacity that would make it equal to the task. It is comprised of the three NAFTA states' respective ministers of labor, who head weak ministries that are not empowered to launch meaningful initiatives based on effective deliberation among their civil-society constituents.

The commission would gain greater democratic legitimacy and political will if its deliberations included not only government representatives but also worker organizations and employer federations from the constituent states. To overcome the antidemocratic exclusivity and political gridlock of a tripartite organization such as the International Labor Organization, however, the ISDM Commission's deliberations should be multipartite. The commission might include representatives of the informal sector—a large and growing labor market not only in poor countries but in rich ones as well. It might also include representatives of other significant labor-market stakeholders in a globalized economy, such as small businesses, domestic and transnational migrants, agrarian workers, and women workers.[51]

Deliberation by an inclusive regional body could promote the virtuous circle, described above, through which regional and local bodies together give specific content to abstract social rights. Facing regional requirements of transparency and disclosure, local representatives of governments and civil society would be obligated to justify and defend their performance in defining and enforcing social rights. Through regional deliberations over one another's performance, local actors would learn from their counterparts throughout the hemisphere. On the basis of such democratic deliberations about relative local performance, region-wide administrative bodies could implement the incentives, described above, for improved definition and enforcement of rights by national and subnational actors (Barenberg 1994; Dorf and Sabel 1998).[52]

This architecture, together with the convening of democratic fora for designing it, might weaken political resistance to establishing regional social rights. Low-wage states presently resist the creation of supranational social rights even though they and their working populations would, in theory, benefit from social standards that prevent a race to the bottom that disproportionately benefits rich-country investors over other regional stakeholders. Much of the current resistance flows from weaker states who, quite rightly, believe that the United States will unduly and unfairly influence the definition and enforcement of social rights to serve its own economic or geopolitical interests. One response to this resistance is retrenchment of regional bodies. Another is greater regional democratization and inclusion.

Conclusion

Both the current draft and the negotiating history of the FTAA point to the distinct possibility that the governance institutions of the future FTAA will follow the model of NAFTA's principal governance mechanism, Chapter 11. Analysis of that mechanism yields a pessimistic assessment of the FTAA's implications for governance—unless the proposed FTAA were revised to incorporate new institutions for building regional democracy, the rule of law, and administrative capacity.

NAFTA arbitrators impose sanctions against economic, social, and environmental regulations enacted by democratically constituted bodies. In so doing, NAFTA tribunals invoke a *substantive* conception of political ordering that elevates rights of investment and trade over social and environmental interests—by imposing "necessity tests" on social regulation, by constraining the delegation of authority to regulatory bodies, by expanding the doctrine of regulatory expropriation, and by constricting federalist values of local democracy and experimentation. The substantive rules of the NAFTA model embody to an astonishing degree the "restorationist" program of conservative jurists and politicians in the United States. That program aims to bring back the pre–New Deal framework of governance in which common-law rights of property and contract are strictly protected against regulation in the name of public welfare. Domestic political and juridical campaigns have recently failed to restore the pre–New Deal "constitution in exile." It has found a home instead in the regional architecture of Chapter 11.

At the same time, NAFTA's *procedural* framework installs a denatured judicial form of regional governance. NAFTA tribunals lack the due-process and rule-of-law virtues of full judicial process. They lack the democratic legitimacy of legislatures. They lack administrative agencies' expert, continuous, and publicly transparent oversight of comprehensive fields of social regulation. And they lack the capacity for regional coordination of local efforts to enhance experimentation, participation, and self-evaluation in solving social problems. And yet,

NAFTA authorizes them to supplant the authority of domestic legislators, administrators, courts, and popular political initiatives.[53]

Perversely, then, the Chapter 11 model weakens democratic governance, the rule of law, and administrative capacity concurrently and mutually at regional, national, and subnational levels of governance.

This need not be so. There are imaginable and practical forms of multitiered regional institutions through which central and decentralized bodies reciprocally enhance one another's capacity to define democratically and effectively implement social rights and policy. We have offered some speculative thoughts about how NAFTA's labor side agreement, woefully inadequate though it now may be, could be fortified to turn NAFTA's vicious circle of governance into a virtuous one.[54]

Such speculative ideas, however, are at best a small contribution to deliberations that must occur among governments, labor movements, environmental organizations, and other groups in civil society if regional governance is to be democratic and practically embraced throughout the hemisphere. For that reason, *redesign of the FTAA negotiating process* itself is a first priority for strengthening democracy in regional governance. If the current negotiating process proceeds without such redesign, the prospective FTAA will likely undermine democratic governance in the hemisphere.

References

Ackerman, Bruce. 1991. *We the People: Foundations*. Cambridge, MA: Harvard University Press.

Barenberg, Mark. 1994. "Democracy and Domination in the Law of Workplace Cooperation: From Bureaucratic to Flexible Production." *Columbia Law Review* 9: 753–983.

Brand, Ronald, and Stephen Zamora, eds. 1990. *Basic Documents of International Economic Law*. Washington, DC: Commerce Clearing House.

Dolzer, Rudolf, and Margaret Stevens. 1995. *Bilateral Investment Treaties*. London: Kluwer.

Dorf, Michael C., and Charles F. Sabel. 1998. "A Constitution of Democratic Experimentalism." *Columbia Law Review* 98: 267–473.

Dworkin, Ronald. 1977. *Taking Rights Seriously*. Cambridge, MA: Harvard University Press.

Epstein, Richard A. 1985. *Takings: Private Property and the Power of Eminent Domain*. Cambridge, MA: Harvard University Press.

Hart, H. L. A. 1961. *The Concept of Law*. Oxford: Clarendon Press.

Korzeniewicz, Roberto Patrick, and William C. Smith. 2001. "Protest and Collaboration: Transnational Civil Society Networks and the Politics of Summitry and Free Trade in the Americas." North-South Agenda Paper no. 51, University of Miami.

Mann, Howard. 2002. *Private Rights, Public Problems.* Winnipeg: International Institute for Sustainable Development.

North, Douglass. 1981. *Structure and Change in Economic History*. New York: Norton.

———. 1986. "The New Institutional Economics." *Journal of Institutional and Theoretical Economics* 142: 230–37.

———. 1990. *Institutions, Institutional Change, and Economic Performance.* Cambridge: Cambridge University Press.

Pogge, Thomas. 1997. "Creating Supra-National Institutions Democratically: Reflections on the European Union's Democratic Deficits." *Journal of Political Philosophy* 5 (20) (June): 163–82.

Rodrik, Dani. 1999. "Institutions for High-Quality Growth: What Are They and How to Acquire Them." Paper presented at the International Monetary Fund Conference on Second-Generation Reforms, November 8–9, Washington, DC.

Sabel, Charles F., Dara O'Rourke, and Archon Fung. 2000. "Ratcheting Labour Standards: How Open Competition Can Save Ethical Sourcing." In *Visions of Ethical Sourcing*, edited by R. Thamotheram. London: Prentice Hall.

Tribe, Lawrence H. 2000. *American Constitutional Law.* 3d ed. New York: Foundation Press.

Weiler, Paul. 1983. "Promises to Keep: Securing Workers' Rights to Self-Organization under the NLRA." *Harvard Law Review* 96: 1769–827.

Notes

1 At least in the minimal sense of combining basic civil liberties, including freedom of association, with selection of political leaders based on one-person, one-vote elections, and the transparent, rule-bound resolution of disputes. At various points in this chapter we propose more robust conceptions of democratic governance.

2 See, for example, Rodrik (1999), who argues that it may be "helpful to think of participatory political institutions as meta-institutions that elicit and aggregate local knowledge and thereby help build better institutions." Even those skeptical of the existence of a systematic connection between democratic institutions and higher levels of economic growth would agree that there is no evidence that undemocratic institutions contribute in a predictable, systematic way to higher rates of growth.

Since all of the states participating in the FTAA negotiations place a high intrinsic value on democratic institutions per se, evidence for a superior contribution of undemocratic institutions to growth would have to be overwhelming and incontrovertible before even considering the abandonment of democracy as the primary criterion for judging institutions; even then it is unlikely that most citizens of the hemisphere would knowingly agree to give up their democratic rights.

3 We use the term "constitutive ground rules" to apply not only to formal constitutions, but also to statutory regimes and informal practices that constitute fundamental ground rules of social and economic regulation. Therefore, we need not inquire whether NAFTA ground rules meet the "existence conditions" of a constitution in the traditional, juridical sense.

4 Chapter 11 cannot be taken as a "red herring" or a "mistake" that is therefore unlikely to be included in an FTAA. To the contrary, the NAFTA negotiators who formulated Chapter 11 have made abundantly clear that the provisions reflected their intentions and should, in their view, be central to future treaties. The failure of consensus occurred at the Seventh Business Forum of the Americas VII in Quito. See http://www.abfecaudor2002.com.

5 This chapter puts aside the highly indeterminate question of whether free investment and trade will indirectly and in the long run yield more democratic and effective governance. We focus instead on the actual institutions directly created by NAFTA and their immediate effects on governance—a much less speculative endeavor. The Chapter 11 institutions are the only significant new governance mechanisms to enforce NAFTA obligations. Although Chapter 11 is only one of the major textual provisions of the NAFTA economic constitution, NAFTA arbitrators have ruled that the fundamental principles of the sweeping *trade* provisions of NAFTA and the World Trade Organization are incorporated in NAFTA's already broad *investment* provisions. Hence, NAFTA's trade principles, as well as its investment provisions, are currently enforceable by private investors under Chapter 11.

6 Expectation that FTAA provisions will mimic those of NAFTA is further reinforced by the fact that the text of the Chile and Canada Free Trade Agreement (CCFTA), signed in December 1996, mirrored the NAFTA text, following Chile's apparent goal of accession to NAFTA.

7 See http://www.ustr.gov/regions/whemisphere/sub.pdf for a complete listing. The USTR team is complemented by a lawyer from the Department of Justice working on competition policy, two representatives of the commerce department, and a lone representative from the State Department in charge of the Participation of Civil Society (see discussion below).

8 The exclusion of civil-society groups from the FTAA process stands in interesting contrast to the relatively systematic efforts to engage civil-society organizations in at least the first two Summits of the Americas (see Korzeniewicz and Smith 2001: 4–10).

9 Korzeniewicz and Smith (2001: 10) summarize the results of this effort as follows: "the fact that the FTAA's civil society committee's final report contained none of the substantive recommendations put forward by the CSOs [Civil Society Organizations] was seen by both 'insiders' and 'outsiders' as a slap in the face."

10 For example, the tribunalists on the "transparency and civil society panel" (one of three at the Merida meeting) were a Canadian foreign service officer on sabbatical at a Canadian foundation, the special counsel of the U.S. Humane Society (which is concerned with animal rights), and the president of FICOMEXT (socially conscious business graduates and students). In short, these are hardly the CSOs that have been demanding dialog for the past eight years.

11 Associated Press, June 28 1995, Business News, AM cycle, by Sandy Shore, AP Business Writer.

12 See http://www.abfecuador2002.com. In anticipation of the seventh ministerial meeting to be held in Quito in November 2002, the Americas Business Forum–Ecuador's website promised that "[b]usinessmen, who will meet in Quito for the Seventh Business Forum of the Americas on October 30 and 31 and November 1 of this year will have the great opportunity to analyze the draft agreement and make any necessary recommendation and proposal aimed at better defining the base document." http://www.abfecuador2002.com/abf/ingles/in_presentacionenglish.htm.

13 The United States recently concluded bilateral trade agreements with Chile and Singapore, respectively. To date, the texts of those agreements have not been made public, official summaries indicate that the investor-state procedure remains intact, although the public is granted access to hearings and documents. Equally important, several expansive substantive protections for investors—apart from NAFTA's anti-expropriation provisions, which are slightly revised by the bilateral agreements—would be largely unchanged. As explained in the fourth section of this chapter, the former protections pose a greater threat to democratic governance, social rights, state institutional capacity, and rule of law than do the expropriation rules, even though the latter have been the lightning rod for political contention until now.

14 There are in force more than 1800 bilateral investment treaties. The key provisions of Chapter 11 formed the core of the negotiating text of the OECD's ultimately abandoned Multilateral Agreement on Investment.

15 Article 1110 affords protection against expropriation not only of "property" (the interest traditionally protected under the international and domestic law of expropriation) but more broadly of "investments," defined as any enterprise, securities or other entitlement to share in an enterprise's income or profit, loans, real estate, or other tangible or intangible property. See NAFTA Article 1139.

16 Both investors and governments have closely followed and debated the meaning of the few NAFTA cases on the assumption that those cases do, in fact, provide important interpretive guidance for assessing the outcome of future claims and the permissibility of future regulatory measures.

17 Interviews with U.S., Canadian, and Mexican governmental officials, New York City (April 26 and 27, 2002). The precise number of such claims is unknown, in light of the nonpublic nature of bilateral investment treaty proceedings, similar to the lack of transparency in NAFTA proceedings discussed below.

18 The three systems are: the International Center for the Settlement of Investment Disputes (ICSID); the Additional Facility Rules of ICSID; and the Arbitration Rules of the United Nations Center for International Trade Law (UNCITRAL).

19 If a losing party refuses to comply with an arbitral award, the investor may seek enforcement in the domestic courts sitting in the location of the arbitration. However, the rules of the three arbitral bodies—and the pertinent rules of domestic law—sharply limit the scope of judicial review of arbitral awards. Domestic courts may overturn the awards if the tribunal was improperly constituted or acted arbitrarily, but may not generally second-guess the arbitrators' factual findings or substantive interpretations of Chapter 11. There is, therefore, nothing akin to full appellate review of NAFTA arbitrators.

20 Members of the public have therefore compiled documentation of NAFTA cases by private search and request for disclosure. On July 31, 2001, the three signatory states issued an Interpretive Statement, committing themselves to disclose the documents of Chapter 11 cases unless disclosure is prevented by the "the relevant arbitral rules, as applied." The latter qualification may nullify the stated commitment to disclosure in light of the fact that NAFTA tribunals are entitled to regulate disclosure in applying the relevant arbitral rules.

21 The tribunal found that, in this case, Canada's allocation of export quotas had not caused a "substantial deprivation" of that property interest and was therefore not a compensable expropriation.

22 The rulings of the United States Supreme Court indicate that almost any intra-state economic and social regulation affects the flow of commerce across state lines. See *Wickard v. Filburn,* 317 U.S. 111 (1942); *Katzenbach*

v. McClung, 379 U.S. 294 (1961). A fortiori, such regulation affects market supply and demand within state borders.

23 *S. D. Meyers, Inc. v. Government of Canada*, Partial Award in a NAFTA Arbitration under the UNCITRAL Arbitration Awards (November 13, 2000), Para. 221.

24 The S. D. Myers tribunal was not as explicit as the Pope & Talbot tribunal in defining investment interests to include interests in imports or exports. Formally, the S. D. Meyers arbitrators relied on the fact that the company bought its PCB waste from a Canadian waste broker that it owned. But the tribunal explicitly declined to find that Meyers Canada (the buyer and seller of PCBs) was a joint venture, an affiliate, or a debtor of the actual claimant, a U.S.-based corporation. Formally, the arbitrators relied on the fact that Meyers Canada and S. D. Meyers were owned by common parties. (This fact is generally insufficient under domestic or international law to attribute Meyers Canada's corporate rights and responsibilities to S. D. Meyers—that is, to "pierce the corporate veil" of Meyers Canada. The tribunal simply asserted that that fact is sufficient, "in light of [NAFTA] objectives," to establish unity between the companies.) Since the Canadian regulation did not in any way discriminate against Meyers Canada—which could buy and even process waste equally with other Canadian waste brokers and processors—the only possible discrimination by Canada was against S. D. Meyers, and the only interest of S. D. Meyers affected by the Canadian regulation was its interest in importing PCB waste.

25 Recall that the national treatment principle requires that governments not "discriminate" against foreign investors. NAFTA tribunals must therefore determine when one regulated actor (the foreign investor) is sufficiently similarly situated to require equal treatment with another, differently regulated or nonregulated actor (the domestic investor). In so doing, as demonstrated by the S. D. Meyers tribunal, NAFTA arbitrators must effectively decide the more general question whether a challenged regulation is based on criteria that fairly determine whether one party should be subject to particular regulations and another not, *regardless of whether the parties are domestic or foreign*. The NAFTA tribunal, that is, effectively reviews the validity of decisions made by legislators and administrators that particular categories of economic actors should be subject to particular regulations while actors outside that category should not. Hence, the claim by a *foreign* investor is the *occasion* for arbitral review, but the arbitrators' strict scrutiny and potential penalty against the state turns on their decision about whether the law is discriminatory in its application to *any* party.

26 Independent of the "least restrictive alternative" test, NAFTA Article 1110 requires the tribunal to decide whether regulatory measures serve legitimate "public purposes."

27 This analysis requires that the NAFTA arbitrators decide several additional thorny issues, such as: Must the government choose a regulatory instrument that has lesser impact on investors and "open trade" even if the instrument imposes greater administrative costs on the government? If the government's environmental objectives are multidimensional, what weight should be assigned to each of the multiple objectives in order to devise a metric by which to measure the adequacy of the alternative policy instruments in achieving the objectives?

28 This "rational basis" test has prevailed since the U.S. Supreme Court's "constitutional revolution" of the 1930s, upholding New Deal regulatory programs against challenges based on *laissez-faire* principles (*United States v. Carolene Products*, 304 U.S. 144 [1938]). This is the test for determining whether regulatory measures comply with constitutional requirements of equal protection and substantive due process. Regulatory measures, of course, must also comply with other substantive constitutional strictures, such as the rights of free speech and privacy.

29 Even in the more deeply integrated European Union, the European Court of Justice has refused to apply the stringent constraints on domestic regulation imposed by NAFTA arbitrators. The court does not make the substantive judgment regarding whether domestic regulation is "necessary" and "least restrictive." It instead asks only whether domestic regulators have reasonably engaged in that inquiry.

30 In the famous pronouncement of Justice Holmes, the constitution does not codify Darwinian economics (*Lochner v. New York*, 198 U.S. 45 [1905] [Holmes, J., dissenting]).

31 The Chapter 11 tribunal ruled that the Mexican municipality and state had no legitimate basis for their land-use and environmental determinations against Metalclad and that Metalclad was entitled to rely on earlier permits granted by the Mexican federal and state authorities.

32 The tribunal ordered the Mexican government to pay over 16 million dollars to Metalclad. In a suit to enforce the NAFTA tribunal's award, the Supreme Court of British Columbia upheld an award of approximately 16 million dollars against the Mexican government, but on different grounds than those relied on by the NAFTA tribunal.

33 Under domestic law, national legislatures delegate rule-making authority to administrative agencies, which are typically authorized to make regulatory rules, with the full force of law, within their substantive field. There are numerous rationales for such delegation: the agencies have the time, expertise, and capacities for supervision of social activity; the agencies are capable of implementing decentralized experimentation; or, less virtuously, elected officials wish to avoid difficult tradeoffs and so pass the decisions on to less visible bureaucrats.

34 *Schechter Poultry v. United States*, 295 U.S. 495 (1935).

35 *Metalclad Corp v. United Mexican States*, Case No. ARB(AF)/97/1, Award (Aug. 30, 2000), ICSID Rev. – FOREIGN INV. L.J. 168, 195 (2001).

36 For example, the House of Representatives in the 104th Congress enacted a "takings compensation" provision, but the Senate declined to act on the measure.

37 In recent legislation reauthorizing the president to engage in trade negotiations, the U.S. Congress stated that the president should instead ensure that new trade agreements provide investors with protections that are "comparable" to those available under U.S. legal "principles and practices." But this directive to the president is precatory and elastic, not mandatory and specific; faces stiff resistance from corporate lobbyists; and has yet to be concretely codified in proposed FTAA drafts.

38 Common-law judges, on a case-by-case basis, adapt the law to social problems and may overrule decisions that are unviable, failed "experiments." Because common-law judges are constrained to apply traditional judicial instruments to the case before them, however, they lack the capacity of administrators to adapt and experiment with rules systemically across broad fields using a variety of tools.

39 *Pike v. Bruce Church. Co.*, 379 U.S. 137. Even if the burden on interstate commerce outweighs the intrastate benefit, Congress may affirmatively authorize the state to enact the regulation in question.

40 See U.S. Constitution Article V.

41 These values may include maximizing local participation; ensuring that citizens whose interests are vitally affected by particular decisions are represented in decision-making bodies; encouraging local experimentation, innovation, and accountability; ensuring that decision makers effectively draw on local knowledge; ensuring that decision makers have incentives to internalize territorial externalities; and so on.

42 Not surprisingly, NAFTA's reworking of domestic federalism—as well as its substantive constraints on subnational social and environmental regulation—has generated a political backlash by state, provincial, and local governments, including campaigns in the United States by local lawmakers and citizens advocating retrenchment of NAFTA Chapter 11 rule making and arbitration. In the United States, opposition to Chapter 11 has been voiced by the National Conference of State Legislatures, the National League of Cities, the U.S. Conference of Mayors, and the National Association of State Attorneys General.

43 The brief hearing in the S. D. Meyers case, and the tribunal's decision, focused more on the business history of the company and on selected aspects of the political process that preceded Canada's regulation of PCBs,

and rather less on the substantive environmental and economic consequences of the regulation. In domestic courts or expert administrative bodies in the U.S. and elsewhere, an assessment of the impact of an environmental decision of such magnitude, and of alternative means of regulation, typically requires many days if not weeks of expert economic and environmental testimony, documentation, and analysis.

44 It is true that, while the *courts* in the U.S. may not strictly scrutinize federal or state regulation, it is constitutionally permissible for *Congress* to impose such scrutiny upon itself and the states. Nonetheless, it is highly doubtful that Congress may constitutionally *delegate* the power to strictly scrutinize federal and state regulation to bodies such as ad hoc NAFTA tribunals made up of three private lawyers chosen by private investors. In any event, wholly apart from its constitutional defects, such delegation does not satisfy norms of democracy, rule of law, and effective governance, for reasons discussed below.

45 *Boos v. Barry*, 485 U.S. 312, 324 (1988); *Reid v. Covert*, 354 U.S. 1, 16 (1947); Tribe (2000: vol. 1, 643, 647–8).

46 In Ackerman's theory, "higher law making"—including the seismic regulatory transformations of the New Deal—by definition generates actual constitutional amendments, written or unwritten. For our purposes, it suffices to say that periods of higher lawmaking through popular and elite mobilization generate new "constitutive" frameworks, whether constitutional or statutory in form. Our ultimate point is that undemocratic, nontransparent, and administratively incompetent organs such as NAFTA arbitral tribunals should not be delegated authority to override such fundamental regulatory regimes. Such delegation violates a variety of well-accepted norms—norms of democracy, rule of law, and effective problem solving, among others.

47 This view fails to consider the elasticity of the national treatment standard. As discussed in section four of this chapter, Chapter 11 tribunals have constrained domestic regulation by a "necessity test" generated by expansive readings of that standard.

48 Note that some regulatory agencies have developed comprehensive regulatory rules by means of case-by-case decision rather than legislative-style rule making. One example in the United States is the National Labor Relations Board. However, the regime of "common-law" rules created by the NLRB's adjudicatory approach is notably incoherent. Rule-making, alongside adjudication, may afford greater administrative strength and flexibility. Alternatively, some combination of local experimentation in the common-law tradition and centralized coordination and articulation of norms may promote effective problem solving together with sheer administrative strength and adaptability.

49 For a political philosopher's argument that regional democratic institutions are best designed by something like inclusive democratic "constitutional conventions" at the regional level—and that the current democracy deficit in the European Union stems from a failure to follow this design procedure—see Pogge (1997).

50 The metaphor of "ratcheting" labor standards has been used before in reference to efforts by private monitoring organizations to improve continuously corporate codes and practices (Sabel, O'Rourke, and Fung 2000). We use the term to refer instead to enhancement of national and subnational labor laws defined and implemented by sovereign public bodies (Barenberg 1994).

51 Women workers and workers newly recruited from agrarian villages make up most of the export-processing workforces, are an increasing segment of affluent labor markets, and have distinct interests centered on work-and-family or work-and-village issues.

52 We want to reemphasize that precise design questions such as this—that is, the proper membership of a multipartite body authorized to promote social rights—cannot be answered by academic blueprint, but should emerge from regional fora or constitutional assemblies with the legitimacy to forge at least rough consensus over questions of democratic inclusiveness.

53 Ironically, the procedures of NAFTA tribunals fail to meet minimal standards of the rule of law, even though they are empowered to decide whether domestic courts and administrators meet such standards. Indeed, NAFTA arbitrators have taken upon themselves the power to reject sovereign legal authorities' interpretation of fundamental domestic rules. See section four of this chapter. NAFTA, then, provides investors a route to bypass domestic courts and the rigors of due process to obtain rulings that impose sanctions against constitutive law.

54 See section five of this chapter.

INDEX

(Please note that organizations and entities are referenced under both their full names and their acronyms.)

C